BPF Performance Tools

BPF Performance Tools

Linux System and Application Observability

Brendan Gregg

Addison-Wesley

BPF Performance Tools

For information about buying this title in bulk quantities, or for special sales opportunities (which may include electronic versions; custom cover designs; and content particular to your business, training goals, marketing focus, or branding interests), please contact our corporate sales department at corpsales@pearson.com or (800) 382-3419.

For government sales inquiries, please contact governmentsales@pearsoned.com.

For questions about sales outside the U.S., please contact intlcs@pearson.com.

Visit us on the Web: informit.com/aw

Library of Congress Control Number: 2019951981

ISBN-13: 978-0-13-655482-0

ISBN-10: 0-13-655482-2

Printed by Ashford Colour Press Ltd

Editor-in-Chief
Mark L. Taub

Series Editor
Brian Kernighan

Executive Editor
Greg Doench

Managing Editor
Sandra Schroeder

Senior Project Editor
Lori Lyons

Production Manager
Aswini Kumar/
CodeMantra

Indexer
Ken Johnson

Proofreader
Abigail Manheim

Cover Designer
Chuti Prasertsith

Compositor
CodeMantra

Contents at a Glance

Contents

Foreword

Programmers sometimes say that they "cook a patch" rather than "implement a patch". I've been fascinated with programming since my school years. To produce good code the programmer needs to pick the best "ingredients". While different programming languages offer various building blocks, "ingredients", when it comes to Linux kernel programming, there is nothing but the kernel itself.

In 2012 I had to add a set of kernel features, but the "ingredients" I needed did not then exist. I could have started writing building blocks inside the kernel. They would be ready to use years later. Instead, I decided to create a "universal ingredient" that when in the hands of a skilled programmer could be both a layer 2 networking bridge and a layer 3 networking router inside the kernel.

I had some important requirements: The "universal ingredient" had to be safe to consume, no matter the programming skills. A malicious or inexperienced developer should not be able to prepare a virus out of it. The "universal ingredient" shouldn't allow it.

There was something already in the Linux kernel which had similar properties called BPF (Berkeley Packet Filter): A minimal instruction set that can be used to filter packets before they are seen by an application such as tcpdump. I borrowed that name for my "ingredient" and called it eBPF, where 'e' stands for 'extended'.

Several years later the distinction between eBPF and classic BPF has vanished. My "universal ingredient" has taken over under the name BPF. Well-known corporations have built large systems out of it to provide services to billions of people like you and me. Its foundational principle of safety by design allows many "cooks" to become world-renowned "chefs".

The first BPF chef was Brendan Gregg. He saw that in addition to its uses in networking and security BPF could be used for performance analysis, introspection, and observability. Making such tools and interpreting their measurements requires practice and knowledge though.

I hope this book will become your favorite "cookbook" where you can learn from master chef how to use BPF in your Linux kitchen.

—Alexei Starovoitov
Seattle, Washington
August, 2019

Preface

"extended BPF use cases: ...crazy stuff."

— *Alexei Starovoitov, creator of the new BPF, February 2015 [1]*

In July 2014, Alexei Starovoitov visited the Netflix offices in Los Gatos, California, to discuss a fascinating new technology that he was developing: extended Berkeley Packet Filter (abbreviated eBPF or just BPF). BPF was an obscure technology for improving packet filter performance, and Alexei had a vision of extending it far beyond packets. Alexei had been working with another network engineer, Daniel Borkmann, to turn BPF into a general-purpose virtual machine, capable of running advanced networking and other programs. It was an incredible idea. A use case that interested me was performance analysis tools, and I saw how this BPF could provide the programmatic capabilities I needed. We made an agreement: If Alexei made it connect to more than just packets, I'd develop the performance tools to use it.

BPF can now attach to any event source, and it has become the hot new technology in systems engineering, with many active contributors. To date, I have developed and published more than 70 BPF performance analysis tools which are in use worldwide and are included by default on servers at Netflix, Facebook, and other companies. For this book, I've developed many more, and I've also included tools from other contributors. It's my privilege to share this work here in *BPF Performance Tools* to give you practical tools that you can use for performance analysis, troubleshooting, and more.

As a performance engineer, I am obsessed with using performance tools in a quest to leave no stone unturned. Blind spots in systems are where performance bottlenecks and software bugs hide. My prior work used the DTrace technology, and included my 2011 Prentice Hall book *DTrace: Dynamic Tracing in Oracle Solaris, Mac OS X, and FreeBSD*, where I shared the DTrace tools I had developed for those operating systems. It's exciting to now be able to share similar tools for Linux—tools that can do and see even more.

Why Do You Need BPF Performance Tools?

BPF performance tools can help you get the most out of your systems and applications, by helping you improve performance, reduce costs, and solve software issues. They can analyze much further than traditional tools, and allow you to pose arbitrary questions of the system and get answers immediately, in production environments.

About This Book

This book is about BPF tools as used primarily for observability and performance analysis, but these tools have other uses as well: software troubleshooting, security analysis, and more. The hardest part about learning BPF is not how to write the code: you can learn any of the interfaces in a day or so. The hard part is knowing what to do with it: What should you trace out of the many thousands of available events? This book helps to answer that question by giving you the necessary background for performance analysis and then analyzing many different software and hardware targets using BPF performance tools, with example output from Netflix production servers.

BPF observability is a superpower, but only because it is extending our visibility into systems and applications—not duplicating it. For you to wield BPF efficiently, you need to understand when to use traditional performance analysis tools, including iostat(1) and perf(1), and when to use BPF tools. The traditional tools, also summarized in this book, may solve performance problems outright, and when they do not, they provide useful context and clues for further analysis with BPF.

Many of this book's chapters include learning objectives to guide you to the most important take-aways. The material in this book is also used for an internal Netflix training class on BPF analysis, and some chapters include optional exercises.[1]

Many of the BPF tools in this book are from the BCC and bpftrace repositories, which are part of the Linux Foundation IO Visor project. These are open source and available for free, not only from the repository websites but also packaged for various Linux distributions. I have also written many new bpftrace tools for this book, and I include their source code here.

These tools were not created to arbitrarily demonstrate various BPF capabilities. They were created to do battle in production environments. These are the tools I've needed for solving production issues beyond the abilities of the current analysis toolset.

For the tools written in bpftrace, the source code has been included in the book. If you wish to modify or develop new bpftrace tools, you can learn the bpftrace language from Chapter 5, and you can also learn by example from the many source code listings here. This source code helps explain what each tool is doing and the events they instrument: It is like including pseudocode that you can run.

The BCC and bpftrace front ends are reaching maturity, but it is possible that future changes will cause some of the source code included in this book to stop working and require updates. If a tool originates in BCC or bpftrace, check those repositories for updated versions. If a tool originated in this book, check this book's website: http://www.brendangregg.com/bpf-performance-tools-book.html. What matters most is not that a tool works, but that you *know* about the tool and want it to work. The hardest part with BPF tracing is knowing what to do with it; even broken tools are a source of useful ideas.

New Tools

To provide you with a comprehensive set of analysis tools that double as code examples, more than 80 new tools were developed for this book. Many of them are pictured in Figure P-1. In this diagram, preexisting tools appear in black text, and the new tools created for this book appear in red or gray (depending on the version of the book you're reading). Both preexisting and new tools are covered in this book, though many later diagrams do not use the red/gray/black color scheme to differentiate them.

---

1 There are also *mode switches*: Linux syscalls that do not block may only (depending on the processor) need to switch modes between user- and kernel-mode.

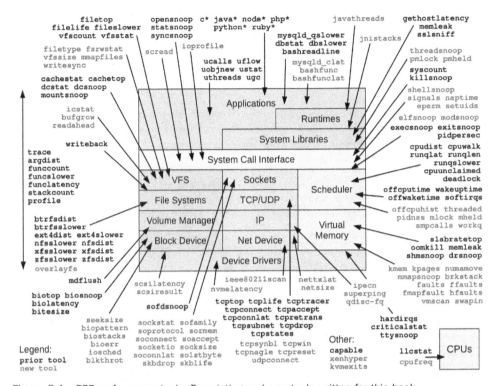

Figure P-1   BPF performance tools: Preexisting and new tools written for this book

About GUIs

Some of the BCC tools have already become sources of metrics for GUIs—providing time series data for line graphs, stack traces for flame graphs, or per-second histograms for heat maps. I expect that more people will use these BPF tools via GUIs than will use the tools directly. Regardless of how you end up using them, they can provide a wealth of information. This book explains their metrics, how to interpret them, and how to create new tools yourself.

About Linux Versions

Throughout this book, many Linux technologies are introduced, often with the kernel version number and year they appeared. I've sometimes named the developers of the technology as well so that you can recognize supporting materials written by the original authors.

Extended BPF was added to Linux in parts. The first part was added in Linux 3.18 in 2014, and more has been added throughout the Linux 4.x and 5.x series since then. To have sufficient capabilities available to run the BPF tools in this book, Linux 4.9 or higher is recommended. The examples in this book are taken from Linux 4.9 to 5.3 kernels.

Work has begun to bring extended BPF to other kernels, and a future edition of this book may cover more than just Linux.

What This Book Does Not Cover

BPF is a large topic, and there are many use cases outside BPF performance tools that are not covered in this book. These include BPF for software-defined networking, firewalls, container security, and device drivers.

This book focuses on using bpftrace and BCC tools, as well as on developing new bpftrace tools, but it does not cover developing new BCC tools. The BCC source listings are usually too long to include, but some examples have been provided as optional content in Appendix C. There are also examples of tool development using C programming in Appendix D and BPF instructions in Appendix E, which may also be useful for those wishing to gain a deeper understanding of how BPF tools work.

This book does not specialize in the performance of one language or application. Other books do that, and they also cover language debugging and analysis tools. You are likely to use some of these other tools alongside BPF tools to solve problems, and you will find that the different toolsets can be complementary, each providing different clues. Basic systems analysis tools from Linux are included here, so that you can find easy wins without having to reinvent any wheels before moving to BPF tools that can help you see further.

This book includes a brief summary of the background and strategy for each analysis target. These topics are explained in more detail in my earlier Prentice Hall book, *Systems Performance: Enterprise and the Cloud* [Gregg 13b].

How This Book Is Structured

There are three parts to this book. The first part, Chapters 1 to 5, covers the background needed for BPF tracing: performance analysis, kernel tracing technologies, and the two core BPF tracing front ends: BCC and bpftrace.

The second part spans Chapters 6 to 16 and covers BPF tracing targets: CPUs, memory, file systems, disk I/O, networking, security, languages, applications, the kernel, containers, and hypervisors. While you could study these chapters in order, the book is designed to support skipping to a chapter of particular interest to you. These chapters all follow a similar format: background discussion, analysis strategy suggestions, and then specific BPF tools. Functional diagrams are included to guide you through complex topics and help you build mental maps of what you are instrumenting.

The last part, spanning Chapters 17 and 18, covers some additional topics: other BPF tools, and tips, tricks, and common problems.

The appendixes provide bpftrace one-liners and a bpftrace cheat sheet, introductions for BCC tool development, C BPF tool development including via perf(1) (the Linux tool), and a BPF instructions summary.

This book uses numerous terms and abbreviations. Where possible, they are explained. See the Glossary for a full reference.

For further sources of information, see the Supplemental Material and References section at the end of this Preface, as well as the Bibliography at the end of the book.

Intended Audience

This book is designed to be useful to a wide range of people. No coding is necessary to use the BPF tools in this book: You can use it as a cookbook of prewritten tools that are ready for you to run. If you do wish to write code, all the included code and Chapter 5 will help you learn to quickly write your own tools.

A background in performance analysis is also not necessary; each chapter summarizes the necessary background details.

Specific audiences for this book include:

- **Systems administrators, site reliability engineers, database administrators, performance engineers, and support staff** responsible for production systems can use this book as a resource for diagnosing performance issues, understanding resource usage, and troubleshooting problems.

- **Application developers** can use these tools to analyze their own code and instrument their code along with system events. For example, disk I/O events can be examined along with the application code that triggered them. This provides a more complete view of behavior, beyond application-specific tools that have no direct visibility into kernel events.

- **Security engineers** can learn how to monitor all events to find suspicious behavior and create whitelists of normal activity (see Chapter 11).

- **Performance monitoring developers** can use this book to get ideas about adding new observability to their products.

- **Kernel developers** can learn how to write bpftrace one-liners for debugging their own code.

- **Students** studying operating systems and applications can use BPF instrumentation to analyze the running system in new and custom ways. Instead of learning about abstract kernel technologies on paper, students can trace them and see how they operate live.

So that this book can focus on the application of BPF tools, it assumes a minimum knowledge level for the topics covered—including basic networking (such as what an IPv4 address is) and command line usage.

Source Code Copyright

This book contains the source code to many BPF tools. Each tool has a footnote to explain its origin: whether it comes from BCC, bpftrace, or was written for this book. For any tool from BCC or bpftrace, see its full source in the respective repository for applicable copyright notices.

The following is the copyright notice for the new tools I developed for this book. This notice is included in the full source of these tools released in the book repository, and this notice should not be removed when sharing or porting these tools:

```
/*
 * Copyright 2019 Brendan Gregg.
 * Licensed under the Apache License, Version 2.0 (the "License").
 * This was originally created for the BPF Performance Tools book
 * published by Addison Wesley. ISBN-13: 9780136554820
 * When copying or porting, include this comment.
 */
```

It is expected that some of these tools will be included in commercial products to provide advanced observability, as has been the case with my earlier tools. If a tool originated from this book, please provide attribution in the production documentation for this book, the BPF technology, and me.

Figure Attributions

Figures 17-02 to 17-09: Vector screenshots, © 2016 Netflix, Inc.

Figure 17-10: grafana-pcp-live screenshot, Copyright 2019 © Grafana Labs

Figures 17-11 to 17-14: Grafana screenshots, Copyright 2019 © Grafana Labs

Supplemental Material and References

Readers are encouraged to visit the website for this book:

http://www.brendangregg.com/bpf-performance-tools-book.html

All the tools contained in the book, as well as book errata and reader feedback, can be downloaded from this site.

Many of the tools discussed in this book are also in source code repositories where they are maintained and enhanced. Refer to these repositories for the latest versions of these tools:

https://github.com/iovisor/bcc

https://github.com/iovisor/bpftrace

These repositories also contain detailed reference guides and tutorials, which I created and the BPF community maintains and updates.

Conventions Used in This Book

This book discusses different types of technology, and the way it presents material provides more context.

For tool output, bold text indicates the command that was executed or, in some cases, highlights something of interest. A hash prompt (#) signifies that the command or tool has been run as the root user (administrator). For example:

```
# id
uid=0(root) gid=0(root) groups=0(root)
```

A dollar prompt ($) signifies running the command or tool as a non-root user:

```
$ id
uid=1000(bgregg) gid=1000(bgregg) groups=1000(bgregg),4(adm),27(sudo)
```

Some prompts include a directory name prefix to show the working directory:

```
bpftrace/tools$ ./biolatency.bt
```

Italic is used to highlight new terms, and is sometimes used to show placeholder text.

Most of the tools in this book require root access or equivalent privileges to run, shown by the repeated use of hash prompts. If you are not root, one way to execute tools as root is to prefix them with sudo for the sudo(8) command (super-user do).

Some commands are executed in single quotation marks to prevent unnecessary (albeit unlikely) shell expansions. It is a good habit to form. For example:

```
# funccount 'vfs_*'
```

A Linux command name or system call is followed by the man page chapter enclosed in parentheses—for example, the ls(1) command, the read(2) system call, and the funccount(8) system administration command. Empty parentheses signify function calls from a programming language—for example, the vfs_read() kernel function. When commands with arguments are included in paragraphs, they use a monospace font.

Command output that is truncated includes an ellipsis in square brackets ([...]). A single line containing ^C indicates that Ctrl-C was typed to terminate the program.

Bibliography references for websites are numbered: e.g., [123].

Acknowledgments

Many people have worked on building all the components necessary for the BPF tracing tools to work today. Their contributions may seem obscure: solving incomprehensible problems in a kernel tracing framework, compiler toolchain, instruction verifier, or other complex component. Such work is often not understood and goes unsung. But the end result of their labors is the BPF tools you're about to run. Many of which were written by me, which might give the unfair impression that I wrote them single-handedly, but I'm really building upon many different technologies and the work of so many others. I'd like to acknowledge and thank them for their work, as well as thank others who also contributed to this book.

Technologies and their authors include:

- **eBPF:** Thanks to Alexei Starovoitov (Facebook; formerly PLUMgrid) and Daniel Borkmann (Isovalent; formerly Cisco, Red Hat) for creating the technology, leading development, maintaining the BPF kernel code, and pursuing their vision for eBPF. Thanks to all the other eBPF contributors, in particular David S. Miller (Red Hat) for supporting and improving the technology. At the time of writing, there is a BPF community of 249 different contributors to BPF kernel code with a total of 3,224 commits since 2014. After Daniel and Alexei, the current top contributors based on commit counts are: Jakub Kicinski (Netronome), Yonghong Song (Facebook), Martin KaFai Lau (Facebook), John Fastabend (Isovalent; formerly Intel), Quentin Monnet (Netronome), Jesper Dangaard Brouer (Red Hat), Andrey Ignatov (Facebook), and Stanislav Fomichev (Google).

- **BCC:** Thanks to Brenden Blanco (VMware; formerly PLUMgrid) for creating and developing BCC. Major contributors include Sasha Goldshtein (Google; formerly SELA), Yonghong Song (Facebook; formerly PLUMgrid), Teng Qin (Facebook), Paul Chaignon (Orange), Vicent Martí (github), Mark Drayton (Facebook), Allan McAleavy (Sky), and Gary Ching-Pang Lin (SUSE).

- **bpftrace:** Thanks to Alastair Robertson (Yellowbrick Data; formerly G-Research, Cisco) for creating bpftrace and insisting on quality code and extensive tests. Thanks to all other bpftrace contributors so far, especially Matheus Marchini (Netflix; formerly Shtima), Willian Gasper (Shtima), Dale Hamel (Shopify), Augusto Mecking Caringi (Red Hat), and Dan Xu (Facebook).

- **ply:** Thanks to Tobias Waldekranz for developing the first high-level tracer built upon BPF.

- **LLVM:** Thanks to Alexei Starovoitov, Chandler Carruth (Google), Yonghong Song, and others, for their work on the BPF backend for LLVM, which BCC and bpftrace is built upon.

- **kprobes:** Thanks to all those that designed, developed, and worked on kernel dynamic instrumentation for Linux, which is used extensively throughout this book. They include Richard Moore (IBM), Suparna Bhattacharya (IBM), Vamsi Krishna Sangavarapu (IBM), Prasanna S. Panchamukhi (IBM), Ananth N Mavinakayanahalli (IBM), James Keniston (IBM), Naveen N Rao (IBM), Hien Nguyen (IBM), Masami Hiramatsu (Linaro; formerly Hitachi), Rusty Lynch (Intel), Anil Keshavamurthy (Intel), Rusty Russell, Will Cohen (Red Hat), and David S. Miller (Red Hat).

- **uprobes:** Thanks to Srikar Dronamraju (IBM), Jim Keniston, and Oleg Nesterov (Red Hat) for developing user-level dynamic instrumentation for Linux, and Peter Zijlstra for technical review.

- **tracepoints:** Thanks to Mathieu Desnoyers (EfficiOS) for his contributions to Linux tracing. In particular, Mathieu developed and drove static tracepoints to be accepted in the kernel, making it possible to build stable tracing tools and applications.

- **perf:** Thanks to Arnaldo Carvalho de Melo (Red Hat) for his work on the perf(1) utility, which added kernel capabilities that BPF tools make use of.

- **Ftrace:** Thanks to Steven Rostedt (VMware; formerly Red Hat) for Ftrace and his other contributions to tracing. Ftrace has aided BPF tracing development, as where possible I've cross-checked tool output with equivalents in Ftrace. Tom Zanussi (Intel) has recently been contributing with Ftrace hist triggers.

- **(Classic) BPF:** Thanks to Van Jacobson and Steve McCanne.

- **Dynamic instrumentation:** Thanks to professor Barton Miller (University of Wisconsin Madison) and his then-student Jeffrey Hollingsworth for founding the field of dynamic instrumentation in 1992 [Hollingsworth 94], which has been the killer feature driving the adoption of DTrace, SystemTap, BCC, bpftrace, and other dynamic tracers. Most of the tools in this book are based on dynamic instrumentation (those that use kprobes and uprobes).

- **LTT:** Thanks to Karim Yaghmour and Michel R. Dagenais for developing the first Linux tracer, LTT in 1999. Also thanks to Karim for his unrelenting push for tracing in the Linux community, building support for later tracers.

- **Dprobes:** Thanks to Richard J. Moore and his team at IBM for developing the first dynamic instrumentation technology for Linux, DProbes, in 2000, which led to the kprobes technology we used today.

- **SystemTap:** While SystemTap is not used in this book, the work by Frank Ch. Eigler (Red Hat) and others on SystemTap has greatly improved the field of Linux tracing. They were often first to push Linux tracing into new areas, and encounter bugs with kernel tracing technologies.

- **ktap:** Thanks to Jovi Zhangwei for ktap, a high-level tracer that helped build support in Linux for VM-based tracers.

- Also thanks to the Sun Microsystems engineers Bryan Cantrill, Mike Shapiro, and Adam Leventhal, for their outstanding work in developing the first widely-used dynamic instrumentation technology: DTrace, launched in 2005. Thanks to Sun marketing, evangelists, sales, and many others inside and outside of Sun, for helping make DTrace known worldwide, helping drive demand for similar tracers in Linux.

Thanks to the many others not listed here who have also contributed to these technologies over the years.

Apart from creating these technologies, many of the same people have helped with this book: Daniel Borkmann provided amazing technical feedback and suggestions for several chapters, and Alexei Starovoitov also provided critical feedback and advice for the eBPF kernel content (as well as writing the Foreword). Alastair Robertson provided input on the bpftrace chapter, and Yonghong Song provided feedback for the BTF content while he was developing BTF.

We are fortunate to have had many people provide technical feedback and contributions for this book, most of whom have had an active role in the development of BPF-related technologies.

Thanks to: Matheus Marchini (Netflix), Paul Chaignon (Orange), Dale Hamel (Shopify), Amer Ather (Netflix), Martin Spier (Netflix), Brian W. Kernighan (Google), Joel Fernandes (Google), Jesper Brouer (Red Hat), Greg Dunn (AWS), Julia Evans (Stripe), Toke Høiland-Jørgensen (Red Hat), Stanislav Kozina (Red Hat), Jiri Olsa (Red Hat), Jens Axboe (Facebook), Jon Haslam (Facebook), Andrii Nakryiko (Facebook), Sargun Dhillon (Netflix), Alex Maestretti (Netflix), Joseph Lynch (Netflix), Richard Elling (Viking Enterprise Solutions), Bruce Curtis (Netflix), and Javier Honduvilla Coto (Facebook). Many sections have been rewritten, added, and improved thanks to all their help. I also had some help on a couple of sections from Mathieu Desnoyers (EfficiOS) and Masami Hiramatsu (Linaro). Claire Black also provided a final check and feedback for many chapters.

My colleague Jason Koch wrote much of the Other Tools chapter, and provided feedback on almost every chapter in the book (hand-annotated on a printed copy about two inches thick.)

The Linux kernel is complicated and ever-changing, and I appreciate the stellar work by Jonathan Corbet and Jake Edge of lwn.net for summarizing so many deep topics. Many of their articles are referenced in the Bibliography.

Completing this book has also required adding many features and fixing issues with the BCC and bpftrace front-ends. Myself and others have written thousands of lines of code to make the tools in this book possible. A special thanks to Matheus Marchini, Willian Gasper, Dale Hamel, Dan Xu, and Augusto Caringi for timely fixes.

Thanks to my current and former Netflix managers, Ed Hunter and Coburn Watson, for their support of my BPF work while at Netflix. Also thanks to my colleagues on the OS team, Scott Emmons, Brian Moyles, and Gabrielle Munoz, for helping to get BCC and bpftrace installed on production servers at Netflix, from which I was able to fetch many example screenshots.

Thanks to Deirdré Straughan (AWS), now my wife, for her professional technical editing and suggestions, and general support of yet another book. My writing has greatly improved thanks to her help over the years. And thanks to my son Mitchell for support and sacrifices while I was busy with the book.

This book is inspired by the DTrace book written by myself and Jim Mauro. Jim's hard work to make the DTrace book a success, and our endless discussions on book structure and tool presentation, have contributed to the quality of this book. Jim has also made many direct contributions to this book. Thanks, Jim, for everything.

And a special thanks to Senior Editor Greg Doench at Pearson for his help and enthusiasm for this project.

Working on this book has been an enormous privilege, providing me the opportunity to showcase BPF observability. Of the 156 tools in this book, I developed 135 of them, including 89 new tools for this book (there are over 100 new tools, counting variants, although it was never my intent to hit that milestone!). Creating these new tools required research, configuration of application environments and client workloads, experimentation, and testing. It has been exhausting at times, but it is satisfying to complete, knowing that these tools will be valuable to so many.

—*Brendan Gregg*
San Jose, California (formerly Sydney, Australia)
November 2019

About the Author

Brendan Gregg, Netflix senior performance engineer, is a major contributor to BPF (eBPF) who has helped develop and maintain both main BPF front-ends, pioneered BPF's use for observability, and created dozens of BPF-based performance analysis tools. His books include the best-seller *Systems Performance: Enterprise and the Cloud.*

Chapter 1

Introduction

This chapter introduces some key terminology, summarizes technologies, and demonstrates some BPF performance tools. These technologies will be explained in more detail in the following chapters.

1.1 What Are BPF and eBPF?

BPF stands for Berkeley Packet Filter, an obscure technology first developed in 1992 that improved the performance of packet capture tools [McCanne 92]. In 2013, Alexei Starovoitov proposed a major rewrite of BPF [2], which was further developed by Alexei and Daniel Borkmann and included in the Linux kernel in 2014 [3]. This turned BPF into a general-purpose execution engine that can be used for a variety of things, including the creation of advanced performance analysis tools.

BPF can be difficult to explain precisely because it can do so much. It provides a way to run mini programs on a wide variety of kernel and application events. If you are familiar with JavaScript, you may see some similarities: JavaScript allows a website to run mini programs on browser events such as mouse clicks, enabling a wide variety of web-based applications. BPF allows the kernel to run mini programs on system and application events, such as disk I/O, thereby enabling new system technologies. It makes the kernel fully programmable, empowering users (including non-kernel developers) to customize and control their systems in order to solve real-world problems.

BPF is a flexible and efficient technology composed of an instruction set, storage objects, and helper functions. It can be considered a virtual machine due to its virtual instruction set specification. These instructions are executed by a Linux kernel BPF runtime, which includes an interpreter and a JIT compiler for turning BPF instructions into native instructions for execution. BPF instructions must first pass through a verifier that checks for safety, ensuring that the BPF program will not crash or corrupt the kernel (it doesn't, however, prevent the end user from writing illogical programs that may execute but not make sense). The components of BPF are explained in detail in Chapter 2.

So far, the three main uses of BPF are networking, observability, and security. This book focuses on observability (tracing).

Extended BPF is often abbreviated as eBPF, but the official abbreviation is still BPF, without the "e," so throughout this book I use BPF to refer to extended BPF. The kernel contains only one execution engine, BPF (extended BPF), which runs both extended BPF and "classic" BPF programs.[1]

1.2   What Are Tracing, Snooping, Sampling, Profiling, and Observability?

These are all terms used to classify analysis techniques and tools.

Tracing is event-based recording—the type of instrumentation that these BPF tools use. You may have already used some special-purpose tracing tools. Linux strace(1), for example, records and prints system call events. There are many tools that do not trace events, but instead measure events using fixed statistical counters and then print summaries; Linux top(1) is an example. A hallmark of a tracer is its ability to record raw events and event metadata. Such data can be voluminous, and it may need to be post-processed into summaries. Programmatic tracers, which BPF makes possible, can run small programs on the events to do custom on-the-fly statistical summaries or other actions, to avoid costly post-processing.

While strace(1) has "trace" in its name, not all tracers do. tcpdump(8), for example, is another specialized tracer for network packets. (Perhaps it should have been named tcptrace?) The Solaris operating system had its own version of tcpdump called snoop(1M)[2], so named because it was used to snoop network packets. I was first to develop and publish many tracing tools, and did so on Solaris, where I (perhaps regrettably) used the "snooping" terminology for my earlier tools. This is why we now have execsnoop(8), opensnoop(8), biosnoop(8), etc. Snooping, event dumping, and tracing usually refer to the same thing. These tools are covered in later chapters.

Apart from tool names, the term *tracing* is also used, especially by kernel developers, to describe BPF when used for observability.

Sampling tools take a subset of measurements to paint a coarse picture of the target; this is also known as creating a profile or profiling. There is a BPF tool called profile(8) that takes timer-based samples of running code. For example, it can sample every 10 milliseconds, or, put differently, it can take 100 samples per second (on every CPU). An advantage of samplers is that their performance overhead can be lower than that of tracers, since they only measure one out of a much larger set of events. A disadvantage is that sampling provides only a rough picture and can miss events.

Observability refers to understanding a system through observation, and classifies the tools that accomplish this. These tools includes tracing tools, sampling tools, and tools based on fixed counters. It does not include benchmark tools, which modify the state of the system by performing a workload experiment. The BPF tools in this book are observability tools, and they use BPF for programmatic tracing.

---

1 Classic BPF programs (which refers to the original BPF [McCanne 92]) are automatically migrated to the extended BPF engine by the kernel for execution. Classic BPF is also not being developed further.

2 For Solaris, section 1M of the man pages is for maintenance and administration commands (section 8 on Linux).

1.3 What Are BCC, bpftrace, and IO Visor?

It is extremely tedious to code BPF instructions directly, so front ends have been developed that provide higher-level languages; the main ones for tracing are BCC and bpftrace.

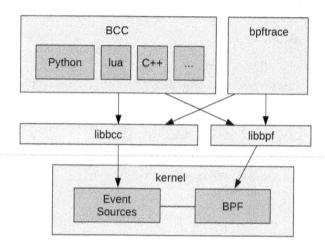

Figure 1-1   BCC, bpftrace, and BPF

BCC (BPF Compiler Collection) was the first higher-level tracing framework developed for BPF. It provides a C programming environment for writing kernel BPF code and other languages for the user-level interface: Python, Lua, and C++. It is also the origin of the libbcc and current libbpf libraries,[3] which provide functions for instrumenting events with BPF programs. The BCC repository also contains more than 70 BPF tools for performance analysis and troubleshooting. You can install BCC on your system and then run the tools provided, without needing to write any BCC code yourself. This book will give you a tour of many of these tools.

bpftrace is a newer front end that provides a special-purpose, high-level language for developing BPF tools. bpftrace code is so concise that tool source code is usually included in this book, to show what the tool is instrumenting and how it is processed. bpftrace is built upon the libbcc and libbpf libraries.

BCC and bpftrace are pictured in Figure 1-1. They are complementary: Whereas bpftrace is ideal for powerful one-liners and custom short scripts, BCC is better suited for complex scripts and daemons, and can make use of other libraries. For example, many of the Python BCC tools use the Python argparse library to provide complex and fine control of tool command line arguments.

Another BPF front end, called ply, is in development [5]; it is designed to be lightweight and require minimal dependencies, which makes it a good fit for embedded Linux environments. If ply is better suited to your environment than bpftrace, you will nonetheless find this book

---

3 The first libbpf was developed by Wang Nan for use with perf [4]. libbpf is now part of the kernel source.

useful as a guide for what you can analyze with BPF. Dozens of the bpftrace tools in this book can be executed using ply after switching to ply's syntax. (A future version of ply may support the bpftrace syntax directly.) This book focuses on bpftrace because it has had more development and has all the features needed to analyze all targets.

BCC and bpftrace do not live in the kernel code base but in a Linux Foundation project on github called **IO Visor**. Their repositories are:

> https://github.com/iovisor/bcc

> https://github.com/iovisor/bpftrace

Throughout this book I use the term *BPF tracing* to refer to both BCC and bpftrace tools.

1.4   A First Look at BCC: Quick Wins

Let's cut to the chase and look at some tool output for some quick wins. The following tool traces new processes and prints a one-line summary for each one as it begins. This particular tool, execsnoop(8) from BCC, works by tracing the execve(2) system call, which is an exec(2) variant (hence its name). Installation of BCC tools is covered in Chapter 4, and later chapters will introduce these tools in more detail.

```
# execsnoop
PCOMM            PID    PPID   RET ARGS
run              12983  4469     0 ./run
bash             12983  4469     0 /bin/bash
svstat           12985  12984    0 /command/svstat /service/httpd
perl             12986  12984    0 /usr/bin/perl -e $1=<>;$1=~/(\d+) sec/;print $1||0
ps               12988  12987    0 /bin/ps --ppid 1 -o pid,cmd,args
grep             12989  12987    0 /bin/grep org.apache.catalina
sed              12990  12987    0 /bin/sed s/^ *//;
cut              12991  12987    0 /usr/bin/cut -d  -f 1
xargs            12992  12987    0 /usr/bin/xargs
echo             12993  12992    0 /bin/echo
mkdir            12994  12983    0 /bin/mkdir -v -p /data/tomcat
mkdir            12995  12983    0 /bin/mkdir -v -p /apps/tomcat/webapps
^C
#
```

The output reveals which processes were executed while tracing: processes that may be so short-lived that they are invisible to other tools. There are many lines of output, showing standard Unix utilities: ps(1), grep(1), sed(1), cut(1), etc. What you can't see just from looking at this output on

```
# execsnoop -t
TIME(s)  PCOMM        PID    PPID   RET ARGS
0.437    run          15524  4469    0 ./run
0.438    bash         15524  4469    0 /bin/bash
0.440    svstat       15526  15525   0 /command/svstat /service/httpd
0.440    perl         15527  15525   0 /usr/bin/perl -e $l=<>;$l=~/(\d+) sec/;prin...
0.442    ps           15529  15528   0 /bin/ps --ppid 1 -o pid,cmd,args
[...]
0.487    catalina.sh  15524  4469    0 /apps/tomcat/bin/catalina.sh start
0.488    dirname      15549  15524   0 /usr/bin/dirname /apps/tomcat/bin/catalina.sh
1.459    run          15550  4469    0 ./run
1.459    bash         15550  4469    0 /bin/bash
1.462    svstat       15552  15551   0 /command/svstat /service/nflx-httpd
1.462    perl         15553  15551   0 /usr/bin/perl -e $l=<>;$l=~/(\d+) sec/;prin...
[...]
```

I've truncated the output (as indicated by the [...]), but the timestamp column shows a new clue: The time between new processes jumps by one second, and this pattern repeats. By browsing the output, I could see that 30 new processes were launched every second, followed by a one-second pause between these batches of 30 processes.

The output shown here is taken from a real-world issue at Netflix that I debugged using execsnoop(8). This was occurring on a server used for micro-benchmarking, but the benchmark results showed too much variance to be trusted. I ran execsnoop(8) when the system was supposed to be idle, and discovered that it wasn't! Every second these processes were launched, and they were perturbing our benchmarks. The cause turned out to be a misconfigured service that was attempting to launch every second, failing, and starting again. Once the service was deactivated, these processes stopped (as confirmed using execsnoop(8)), and then the benchmark numbers became consistent.

The output from execsnoop(8) aids a performance analysis methodology called *workload characterization*, which is supported by many other BPF tools in this book. This methodology is simple: Define what workload is being applied. Understanding the workload is often sufficient for solving problems, and avoids needing to dig deeper into latencies or to do drill-down analysis. In this case, it was the process workload applied to the system. Chapter 3 introduces this and other methodologies.

Try running execsnoop(8) on your systems and leave it running for an hour. What do you find?

execsnoop(8) prints per-event data, but other tools use BPF to calculate efficient summaries. Another tool you can use for quick wins is biolatency(8), which summarizes block device I/O (disk I/O) as a latency histogram.

The following is output from running biolatency(8) on a production database that is sensitive to high latency as it has a service level agreement to deliver requests within a certain number of milliseconds.

```
# biolatency -m
Tracing block device I/O... Hit Ctrl-C to end.
^C
     msecs              : count    distribution
         0 -> 1         : 16335    |****************************************|
         2 -> 3         : 2272     |*****                                   |
         4 -> 7         : 3603     |********                                |
         8 -> 15        : 4328     |**********                              |
        16 -> 31        : 3379     |********                                |
        32 -> 63        : 5815     |**************                          |
        64 -> 127       : 0        |                                        |
       128 -> 255       : 0        |                                        |
       256 -> 511       : 0        |                                        |
       512 -> 1023      : 11       |                                        |
```

While the biolatency(8) tool is running, block I/O events are instrumented and their latencies are calculated and summarized by BPF. When the tool stops running (when the user presses Ctrl-C), the summary is printed. I used the –m option here to print the summary in milliseconds.

There are interesting details in this output, which shows a bi-modal distribution as well as latency outliers. The largest mode (as visualized by the ASCII distribution) is for the 0- to 1-millisecond range, with 16,355 I/O in that range while tracing. This is fast, and likely due to on-disk cache hits as well as flash memory devices. The second mode stretches to the 32- to 63-millisecond range, which is much slower than expected from these storage devices and suggests queuing. More BPF tools can be used to drill deeper to confirm. Finally, for the 512- to 1023-millisecond range, there were 11 I/O. These very slow I/O are termed *latency outliers*. Now that we know they exist, they can be examined in more detail with other BPF tools. For the database team, these are the priority to study and solve: If the database is blocked on these I/O, the database will exceed its latency target.

1.5 BPF Tracing Visibility

BPF tracing gives you visibility across the full software stack and allows new tools and instrumentation to be created on demand. You can use BPF tracing in production immediately, without needing to reboot the system or restart applications in any special mode. It can feel like having X-ray vision: When you need to examine some deep kernel component, device, or application library, you can see into it in a way that no one ever has before—live and in production.

To illustrate, Figure 1-2 shows a generic system software stack that I've annotated with BPF-based performance tools for observing different components. These tools are from BCC, bpftrace, and this book. Many of them will be explained in later chapters.

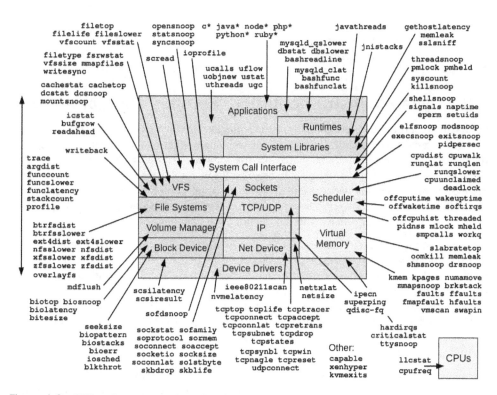

Figure 1-2   BPF performance tools and their visibility

Consider the different tools you would use to examine components such as the kernel CPU scheduler, virtual memory, file systems, and so on. By simply browsing this diagram, you might discover former blindspots that you can observe with BPF tools.

The traditional tools used to examine these components are summarized in Table 1-1, along with whether BPF tracing can observe these components.

Table 1-1   **Traditional Analysis Tools**

Components	Traditional Analysis Tools	BPF Tracing
Applications with language runtimes: Java, Node.js, Ruby, PHP	Runtime debuggers	Yes, with runtime support
Applications using compiled code: C, C++, Golang	System debuggers	Yes
System libraries: /lib/*	ltrace(1)	Yes
System call interface	strace(1), perf(1)	Yes
Kernel: Scheduler, file systems, TCP, IP, etc	Ftrace, perf(1) for sampling	Yes, in more detail
Hardware: CPU internals, devices	perf, sar, /proc counters	Yes, direct or indirect[4]

4 BPF may not be able to directly instrument the firmware on a device, but it may be able to indirectly infer behavior based on tracing of kernel driver events or PMCs.

Traditional tools can provide useful starting points for analysis, which you can explore in more depth with BPF tracing tools. Chapter 3 summarizes basic performance analysis with system tools, which can be your starting point.

1.6 Dynamic Instrumentation: kprobes and uprobes

BPF tracing supports multiple sources of events to provide visibility of the entire software stack. One that deserves special mention is dynamic instrumentation (also called dynamic tracing)—the ability to insert instrumentation points into live software, in production. Dynamic instrumentation costs zero overhead when not in use, as software runs unmodified. It is often used by BPF tools to instrument the start and end of kernel and application functions, from the many tens of thousands of functions that are typically found running in a software stack. This provides visibility so deep and comprehensive that it can feel like a superpower.

Dynamic instrumentation was first created in the 1990s [Hollingsworth 94], based on a technique used by debuggers to insert breakpoints at arbitrary instruction addresses. With dynamic instrumentation, the target software records information and then automatically continues execution rather than passing control to an interactive debugger. Dynamic tracing tools (e.g., kerninst [Tamches 99]) were developed, and included tracing languages, but these tools remained obscure and little used. In part because they involved considerable risk: Dynamic tracing requires modification of instructions in an address space, live, and any error could lead to immediate corruption and process or kernel crashes.

Dynamic instrumentation was first developed for Linux in 2000 as DProbes by a team at IBM, but the patch set was rejected.[5] Dynamic instrumentation for kernel functions (kprobes) was finally added to Linux in 2004, originating from DProbes, although it was still not well known and was still difficult to use.

Everything changed in 2005, when Sun Microsystems launched its own version of dynamic tracing, DTrace, with its easy-to-use D language, and included it in the Solaris 10 operating system. Solaris was known and trusted for production stability, and including DTrace as a default package install helped prove that dynamic tracing could be made safe for use in production. It was a turning point for the technology. I published many articles showing real-world use cases with DTrace and developed and published many DTrace tools. Sun marketing also promoted the technology, as did Sun sales; it was thought to be a compelling competitive feature. Sun Educational Services included DTrace in the standard Solaris courses and taught dedicated DTrace courses. All of these efforts caused dynamic instrumentation to move from an obscure technology to a well-known and in-demand feature.

Linux added dynamic instrumentation for user-level functions in 2012, in the form of uprobes. BPF tracing tools use both kprobes and uprobes for dynamic instrumentation of the full software stack.

---

5 The reasons for Linux rejecting DProbes are discussed as the first case study in *On submitting kernel patches* by Andi Kleen, which is referenced in the Linux source in Documentation/process/submitting-patches.rst [6].

To show how dynamic tracing is used, Table 1-2 provides examples of bpftrace probe specifiers that use kprobes and uprobes. (bpftrace is covered in Chapter 5.)

Table 1-2   **bpftrace kprobe and uprobe Examples**

Probe	Description
kprobe:vfs_read	Instrument the beginning of the kernel vfs_read() function
kretprobe:vfs_read	Instrument the returns[6] of the kernel vfs_read() function
uprobe:/bin/bash:readline	Instrument the beginning of the readline() function in /bin/bash
uretprobe:/bin/bash:readline	Instrument the returns of the readline() function in /bin/bash

1.7   Static Instrumentation: Tracepoints and USDT

There is a downside to dynamic instrumentation: It instruments functions that can be renamed or removed from one software version to the next. This is referred to as an *interface stability issue*. After upgrading the kernel or application software, you may suddenly find that your BPF tool no longer works properly. Perhaps it prints an error about being unable to find functions to instrument, or maybe it prints no output at all. Another issue is that compilers may inline functions as a compiler optimization, making them unavailable for instrumentation via kprobes or uprobes.[7]

One solution to both the stability and inlining problem is to switch to static instrumentation, where stable event names are coded into the software and maintained by the developers. BPF tracing supports tracepoints for kernel static instrumentation, and user-level statically defined tracing (USDT) for user-level static instrumentation. The downside of static instrumentation is that these instrumentation points become a maintenance burden for the developers, so if any exist, they are usually limited in number.

These details are only important if you intend to develop your own BPF tools. If so, a recommended strategy is to try using static tracing first (using tracepoints and USDT) and then switch to dynamic tracing (using kprobes and uprobes) when static tracing is unavailable.

Table 1-3 provides examples of bpftrace probe specifiers for static instrumentation using tracepoints and USDT. The open(2) tracepoint mentioned in this table is used in Section 1.8.

Table 1-3   **bpftrace Tracepoint and USDT Examples**

Probe	Description
tracepoint:syscalls:sys_enter_open	Instrument the open(2) syscall
usdt:/usr/sbin/mysqld:mysql:query__start	Instrument the query__start probe from /usr/sbin/mysqld

---

6 A function has one beginning but can have multiple ends: It can call return from different places. Return probes instrument all the return points. (See Chapter 2 for an explanation of how this works.)

7 A workaround is function offset tracing, but as an interface it is even less stable than function entry tracing.

1.8 A First Look at bpftrace: Tracing open()

Let's start by using bpftrace to trace the open(2) system call (syscall). There is a tracepoint for it (syscalls:sys_enter_open[8]), and I'll write a short bpftrace program at the command line: a one-liner.

You aren't expected to understand the code in the following one-liner yet; the bpftrace language and install instructions are covered in Chapter 5. But you may be able to guess what the program does without knowing the language as it is quite intuitive (an intuitive language is a sign of good design). For now, just focus on the tool output.

```
# bpftrace -e 'tracepoint:syscalls:sys_enter_open { printf("%s %s\n", comm,
    str(args->filename)); }'
Attaching 1 probe...
slack /run/user/1000/gdm/Xauthority
slack /run/user/1000/gdm/Xauthority
slack /run/user/1000/gdm/Xauthority
slack /run/user/1000/gdm/Xauthority
^C
#
```

The output shows the process name and the filename passed to the open(2) syscall: bpftrace is tracing system-wide, so any application using open(2) will be seen. Each line of output summarizes one syscall, and this is an example of a tool that produces per-event output. BPF tracing can be used for more than just production server analysis. For example, I'm running it on my laptop as I write this book, and it's showing files that a Slack chat application is opening.

The BPF program was defined within the single forward quotes, and it was compiled and run as soon as I pressed Enter to run the bpftrace command. bpftrace also activated the open(2) tracepoint. When I pressed Ctrl-C to stop the command, the open(2) tracepoint was deactivated, and my small BPF program was removed. This is how on-demand instrumentation by BPF tracing tools work: They are only activated and running for the lifetime of the command, which can be as short as seconds.

The output generated was slower than I was expecting: I think I'm missing some open(2) syscall events. The kernel supports a few variants of open, and I traced only one of them. I can use bpftrace to list all the open tracepoints by using -l and a wildcard:

```
# bpftrace -l 'tracepoint:syscalls:sys_enter_open*'
tracepoint:syscalls:sys_enter_open_by_handle_at
tracepoint:syscalls:sys_enter_open
tracepoint:syscalls:sys_enter_openat
```

---

8 These syscall tracepoints require the Linux CONFIG_FTRACE_SYSCALLS build option to be enabled.

Ah, I think the openat(2) variant is used more often nowadays. I'll confirm with another bpftrace one-liner:

```
# bpftrace -e 'tracepoint:syscalls:sys_enter_open* { @[probe] = count(); }'
Attaching 3 probes...
^C

@[tracepoint:syscalls:sys_enter_open]: 5
@[tracepoint:syscalls:sys_enter_openat]: 308
```

Again, the code in this one-liner will be explained in Chapter 5. For now, it's only important to understand the output. It is now showing a count of these tracepoints rather than a line per event. This confirms that the openat(2) syscall is called more often—308 times while tracing—whereas the open(2) syscall was called only five times. This summary is calculated efficiently in the kernel by the BPF program.

I can add the second tracepoint to my one-liner to trace both open(2) and openat(2) at the same time. However, the one-liner will start getting a little long and unwieldy at the command line, and at that point, it would be better to save it to a script (an executable file), so that it can be more easily edited using a text editor. This has already been done for you: bpftrace ships with opensnoop.bt, which traces both the start and end of each syscall, and prints the output as columns:

```
# opensnoop.bt
Attaching 3 probes...
Tracing open syscalls... Hit Ctrl-C to end.
PID    COMM           FD ERR PATH
2440   snmp-pass       4   0 /proc/cpuinfo
2440   snmp-pass       4   0 /proc/stat
25706  ls              3   0 /etc/ld.so.cache
25706  ls              3   0 /lib/x86_64-linux-gnu/libselinux.so.1
25706  ls              3   0 /lib/x86_64-linux-gnu/libc.so.6
25706  ls              3   0 /lib/x86_64-linux-gnu/libpcre.so.3
25706  ls              3   0 /lib/x86_64-linux-gnu/libdl.so.2
25706  ls              3   0 /lib/x86_64-linux-gnu/libpthread.so.0
25706  ls              3   0 /proc/filesystems
25706  ls              3   0 /usr/lib/locale/locale-archive
25706  ls              3   0 .
1744   snmpd           8   0 /proc/net/dev
1744   snmpd          -1   2 /sys/class/net/lo/device/vendor
2440   snmp-pass       4   0 /proc/cpuinfo
^C
#
```

The columns are process ID (PID), process command name (COMM), file descriptor (FD), error code (ERR), and the path of the file that the syscall attempted to open (PATH). The opensnoop.bt tool can be used to troubleshoot failing software, which may be attempting to open files from the wrong path, as well as to determine where config and log files are kept, based on their accesses. It can also identify some performance issues, such as files being opened too quickly, or the wrong locations being checked too frequently. It is a tool with many uses.

bpftrace ships with more than 20 such ready-to-run tools, and BCC ships with more than 70. In addition to helping you solve problems directly, these tools provide source code that shows how various targets can be traced. Sometimes there are gotchas, as we saw with tracing the open(2) syscall, and their source code may show solutions to these.

1.9   Back to BCC: Tracing open()

Now let's look at the BCC version of opensnoop(8):

```
# opensnoop
PID     COMM              FD ERR PATH
2262    DNS Res~er #657   22   0 /etc/hosts
2262    DNS Res~er #654   178  0 /etc/hosts
29588   device poll        4   0 /dev/bus/usb
29588   device poll        6   0 /dev/bus/usb/004
29588   device poll        7   0 /dev/bus/usb/004/001
29588   device poll        6   0 /dev/bus/usb/003
^C
#
```

The output here looks very similar to the output of the earlier one-liner—at least it has the same columns. But this opensnoop(8) output has something that the bpftrace version does not: It can be invoked with different command line options:

```
# opensnoop -h
usage: opensnoop [-h] [-T] [-x] [-p PID] [-t TID] [-d DURATION] [-n NAME]
                 [-e] [-f FLAG_FILTER]

Trace open() syscalls

optional arguments:
  -h, --help            show this help message and exit
  -T, --timestamp       include timestamp on output
  -x, --failed          only show failed opens
  -p PID, --pid PID     trace this PID only
  -t TID, --tid TID     trace this TID only
  -d DURATION, --duration DURATION
                        total duration of trace in seconds
```

```
  -n NAME, --name NAME  only print process names containing this name
  -e, --extended_fields
                        show extended fields
  -f FLAG_FILTER, --flag_filter FLAG_FILTER
                        filter on flags argument (e.g., O_WRONLY)


examples:
    ./opensnoop              # trace all open() syscalls
    ./opensnoop -T           # include timestamps
    ./opensnoop -x           # only show failed opens
    ./opensnoop -p 181       # only trace PID 181
    ./opensnoop -t 123       # only trace TID 123
    ./opensnoop -d 10        # trace for 10 seconds only
    ./opensnoop -n main      # only print process names containing "main"
    ./opensnoop -e           # show extended fields
    ./opensnoop -f O_WRONLY -f O_RDWR  # only print calls for writing
```

While bpftrace tools are typically simple and do one thing, BCC tools are typically complex and support a variety of modes of operation. While you could modify the bpftrace tool to only show failed opens, the BCC version already supports that as an option (-x):

```
# opensnoop -x
PID     COMM              FD ERR PATH
991     irqbalance        -1   2 /proc/irq/133/smp_affinity
991     irqbalance        -1   2 /proc/irq/141/smp_affinity
991     irqbalance        -1   2 /proc/irq/131/smp_affinity
991     irqbalance        -1   2 /proc/irq/138/smp_affinity
991     irqbalance        -1   2 /proc/irq/18/smp_affinity
20543   systemd-resolve   -1   2 /run/systemd/netif/links/5
20543   systemd-resolve   -1   2 /run/systemd/netif/links/5
20543   systemd-resolve   -1   2 /run/systemd/netif/links/5
[...]
```

This output shows repeated failures. Such patterns may point to inefficiencies or misconfigurations that can be fixed.

BCC tools often have several such options for changing their behavior, making them more versatile than bpftrace tools. This makes them a good starting point: hopefully they can solve your needs without you needing to write any BPF code. If, however, they do lack the visibility you need, you can then switch to bpftrace and create custom tools, as it is an easier language to develop.

A bpftrace tool can later be converted to a more complex BCC tool that supports a variety of options, like opensnoop(8) shown previously. BCC tools can also support using different events: using tracepoints when available, and switching to kprobes when not. But be aware that BCC programming is far more complex and is beyond the scope of this book, which focuses on bpftrace programming. Appendix C provides a crash course in BCC tool development.

1.10 Summary

BPF tracing tools can be used for performance analysis and troubleshooting, and there are two main projects that provide them: BCC and bpftrace. This chapter introduced extended BPF, BCC, bpftrace, and the dynamic and static instrumentation that they use.

The next chapter dives into these technologies in much more detail. If you are in a hurry to solve issues, you might want to skip Chapter 2 for now and move on to Chapter 3 or a later chapter that covers the topic of interest. These later chapters make heavy use of terms, many of which are explained in Chapter 2, but they are also summarized in the Glossary.

Chapter 2

Technology Background

Chapter 1 introduced various technologies used by BPF performance tools. This chapter explains them in more detail: their histories, interfaces, internals, and use with BPF.

This is the most technically deep chapter in the book, and for the sake of brevity, it assumes some knowledge of kernel internals and instruction-level programming.[1]

The learning objectives are not to memorize every page in this chapter, but for you to:

- Know the origins of BPF, and the role of extended BPF today
- Understand frame pointer stack walking and other techniques
- Understand how to read flame graphs
- Understand the use of kprobes and uprobes, and be familiar with their stability caveats
- Understand the role of tracepoints, USDT probes, and dynamic USDT
- Be aware of PMCs and their use with BPF tracing tools
- Be aware of future developments: BTF, other BPF stack walkers

Understanding this chapter will improve your comprehension of later content in this book, but you may prefer to skim through this chapter now and return to it for more detail as needed. Chapter 3 will get you started on using BPF tools to find performance wins.

2.1 BPF Illustrated

Figure 2-1 shows many of the technologies in this chapter and their relationships to each other.

---

1 To learn necessary kernel internals, refer to any guide that covers syscalls, kernel and user mode, tasks/threads, virtual memory, and VFS, such as [Gregg 13b].

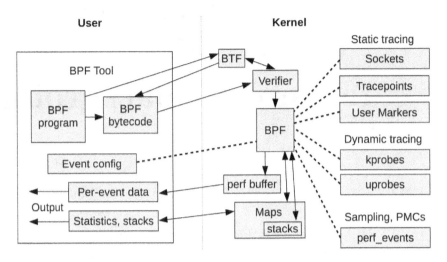

Figure 2-1   BPF tracing technologies

2.2 BPF

BPF was originally developed for the BSD operating system, and is described in the 1992 paper "The BSD Packet Filter: A New Architecture for User-level Packet Capture" [McCanne 92]. This paper was presented at the 1993 USENIX Winter conference in San Diego, alongside "Measurement, Analysis, and Improvement of UDP/IP Throughput for the DECstation 5000" [7]. DECstations are long gone, but BPF has survived as the industry standard solution for packet filtering.

BPF works in an interesting way: A filter expression is defined by the end user using an instruction set for a BPF virtual machine (sometimes called the BPF bytecode) and then passed to the kernel for execution by an interpreter. This allows filtering to occur in the kernel level without costly copies of each packet going to the user-level processes, improving the performance of packet filtering, as used by tcpdump(8). It also provides safety, as filters from user space can be verified as being safe before execution. Given that early packet filtering had to occur in kernel space, safety was a hard requirement. Figure 2-2 shows how this works.

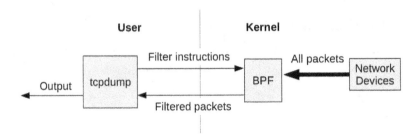

Figure 2-2   tcpdump and BPF

You can use the -d option to tcpdump(8) to print out the BPF instructions it is using for the filter expression. For example:

```
# tcpdump -d host 127.0.0.1 and port 80
(000) ldh      [12]
(001) jeq      #0x800          jt 2       jf 18
(002) ld       [26]
(003) jeq      #0x7f000001     jt 6       jf 4
(004) ld       [30]
(005) jeq      #0x7f000001     jt 6       jf 18
(006) ldb      [23]
(007) jeq      #0x84           jt 10      jf 8
(008) jeq      #0x6            jt 10      jf 9
(009) jeq      #0x11           jt 10      jf 18
(010) ldh      [20]
(011) jset     #0x1fff         jt 18      jf 12
(012) ldxb     4*([14]&0xf)
(013) ldh      [x + 14]
(014) jeq      #0x50           jt 17      jf 15
(015) ldh      [x + 16]
(016) jeq      #0x50           jt 17      jf 18
(017) ret      #262144
(018) ret      #0
```

The original BPF, now referred to as "classic BPF," was a limited virtual machine. It had two registers, a scratch memory store consisting of 16 memory slots, and a program counter. These were all operating with a 32-bit register size.[2] Classic BPF arrived in Linux in 1997, for the 2.1.75 kernel [8].

Since the addition of BPF to the Linux kernel, there have been some important improvements. Eric Dumazet added a BPF just-in-time (JIT) compiler in Linux 3.0, released in July 2011 [9], improving performance over the interpreter. In 2012, Will Drewry added BPF filters for seccomp (secure computing) syscall policies [10]; this was the first use of BPF outside of networking, and it showed the potential for BPF to be used as a generic execution engine.

2.3 Extended BPF (eBPF)

Extended BPF was created by Alexei Starovoitov while he worked at PLUMgrid, as the company was investigating new ways to create software-defined networking solutions. This would be the first major update to BPF in 20 years, and one that would extend BPF to become a general-purpose virtual machine.[3] While it was still a proposal, Daniel Borkmann, a kernel engineer at Red Hat,

---

2 For classic BPF on a 64-bit kernel, addresses are 64-bit, but the registers only ever see 32-bit data, and the loads are hidden behind some external kernel helper functions.

3 While BPF is often called a virtual machine, that only describes its specification. Its implementation in Linux (its runtime) has an interpreter and a JIT-to-native code compiler. The term *virtual machine* may imply that there is another machine layer on top of the processor, but there isn't. With JIT compiled code, instructions run directly on the processor just like any other native kernel code. Note that after the Spectre vulnerability, some distributions unconditionally enable the JIT for x86, which removes the interpreter entirely (as it gets compiled out).

helped rework it for inclusion in the kernel and as a replacement for the existing BPF.[4] This extended BPF was successfully included and has since had contributions from many other developers (see the Acknowledgments).

Extended BPF added more registers, switched from 32-bit to 64-bit words, created flexible BPF "map" storage, and allowed calls to some restricted kernel functions.[5] It was also designed to be JITed with a one-to-one mapping to native instructions and registers, allowing prior native instruction optimization techniques to be reused for BPF. The BPF verifier was also updated to handle these extensions and reject any unsafe code.

Table 2-1 shows the differences between classic BPF and extended BPF.

Table 2-1 **Classic BPF Versus Extended BPF**

Factor	Classic BPF	Extended BPF
Register count	2: A, X	10: R0–R9, plus R10 as a read-only frame pointer
Register width	32-bit	64-bit
Storage	16 memory slots: M[0–15]	512 bytes of stack space, plus infinite "map" storage
Restricted kernel calls	Very limited, JIT specific	Yes, via the bpf_call instruction
Event targets	Packets, seccomp-BPF	Packets, kernel functions, user functions, tracepoints, user markers, PMCs

Alexei's original proposal was a patchset in September 2013 titled "extended BPF" [2]. By December 2013, Alexei was already proposing its use for tracing filters [11]. After discussion and development with Daniel, the patches began to merge in the Linux kernel by March 2014 [3][12].[6] The JIT components were merged for the Linux 3.15 release in June 2014, and the bpf(2) syscall for controlling BPF was merged for the Linux 3.18 release in December 2014 [13]. Later additions in the Linux 4.x series added BPF support for kprobes, uprobes, tracepoints, and perf_events.

In the earliest patchsets, the technology was abbreviated as eBPF, but Alexei later switched to calling it just BPF.[7] All BPF development on the net-dev mailing list [14] now refers to it as just BPF.

---

4 Alexei and Daniel have since changed companies. They are also currently the kernel "maintainers" for BPF: a role where they provide leadership, review patches, and decide what gets included.

5 Without needing to overload instructions, a workaround used with classic BPF that was complicated as every JIT needed to be changed to handle it.

6 Early on, it was also called "internal BPF," before it was exposed via the bpf(2) syscall. Since BPF was a networking technology, these patches were sent to and accepted by the networking maintainer David S. Miller. Today, BPF has grown into a larger kernel community of its own, and all BPF-related patches are merged into their own bpf and bpf-next kernel trees. Tradition is steady that BPF tree pull requests are still accepted by David S. Miller.

7 I also suggested to Alexei that we come up with a different and better name. But naming is hard, and we're engineers, so we're stuck with "it's eBPF but really just BPF, which stands for Berkeley Packet Filter although today it has little to do with Berkeley, packets, or filtering." Thus, BPF should be regarded now as a technology name rather than as an acronym.

The architecture of the Linux BPF runtime is illustrated in Figure 2-3, which shows how BPF instructions pass the BPF verifier to be executed by a BPF virtual machine. The BPF virtual machine implementation has both an interpreter and a JIT compiler: the JIT compiler generates native instructions for direct execution. The verifier rejects unsafe operations, including unbounded loops: BPF programs must finish in a bounded time.

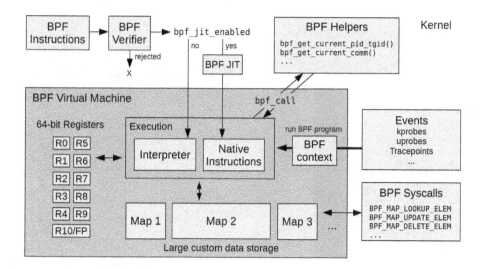

Figure 2-3 BPF runtime internals

BPF can make use of helpers for fetching kernel state, and BPF maps for storage. The BPF program is executed on events, which include kprobes, uprobes, and tracepoints.

The next sections discuss why performance tools need BPF, extended BPF programming, viewing BPF instructions, the BPF API, BPF limitations, and BTF. These sections provide a basis for understanding how BPF works when using bpftrace and BCC. In addition, Appendix D covers BPF programming in C directly, and Appendix E covers BPF instructions.

2.3.1 Why Performance Tools Need BPF

Performance tools use extended BPF in part for its programmability. BPF programs can execute custom latency calculations and statistical summaries. Those features alone would make for an interesting tool, and there are plenty of other tracing tools that have those features. What makes BPF different is that it is also efficient and production safe, and it is built into the Linux kernel. With BPF, you can run these tools in production environments without needing to add any new kernel components.

Let's look at some output and a diagram to see how performance tools use BPF. This example comes from an early BPF tool I published called bitehist, which shows the size of disk I/O as a histogram [15]:

```
# bitehist
Tracing block device I/O... Interval 5 secs. Ctrl-C to end.

    kbytes         : count    distribution
     0 -> 1        : 3        |                                       |
     2 -> 3        : 0        |                                       |
     4 -> 7        : 3395     |************************************** |
     8 -> 15       : 1        |                                       |
    16 -> 31       : 2        |                                       |
    32 -> 63       : 738      |*******                                |
    64 -> 127      : 3        |                                       |
   128 -> 255      : 1        |                                       |
```

Figure 2-4 shows how BPF improves the efficiency of this tool.

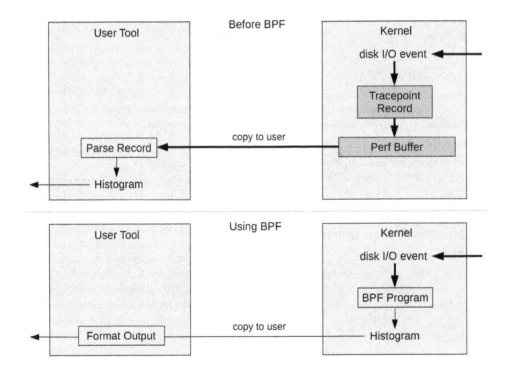

Figure 2-4   Generating histograms before and after using BPF

The key change is that the histogram can be generated in kernel context, which greatly reduces the amount of data copied to user space. This efficiency gain is so great that it can allow tools to run in production that would otherwise be too costly. In detail:

Prior to BPF, the full steps to produce this histogram summary were[8]:

1. In the kernel: enable instrumentation for disk I/O events.

2. In the kernel, for each event: write a record to the perf buffer. If tracepoints are used (as is preferred), the record contains several fields of metadata about the disk I/O.

3. In user space: periodically copy the buffer of all events to user space.

4. In user space: step over each event, parsing the event metadata for the bytes field. Other fields are ignored.

5. In user space: generate a histogram summary of the bytes field.

Steps 2 to 4 have high performance overhead for high-I/O systems. Imagine transferring 10,000 disk I/O trace records to a user-space program to parse and summarize—every second.

With BPF, the steps for the bitesize program are:

1. In the kernel: enable instrumentation for disk I/O events and attach a custom BPF program, defined by bitesize.

2. In the kernel, for each event: run the BPF program. It fetches the bytes field alone and saves it into a custom BPF map histogram.

3. In user space: read the BPF map histogram once and print it out.

This method avoids the cost of copying events to user space and reprocessing them. It also avoids copying metadata fields that are not used. The only data copied to user space is shown in the previous output: the "count" column, which is an array of numbers.

2.3.2   BPF Versus Kernel Modules

Another way to understand the benefits of BPF for observability is to compare it to kernel modules. kprobes and tracepoints have been available for many years, and they can be used from loadable kernel modules directly. The benefits of using BPF over kernel modules for tracing purposes are:

- BPF programs are checked via a verifier; kernel modules may introduce bugs (kernel panics) or security vulnerabilities.

- BPF provides rich data structures via maps.

---

8 These are the best steps available, but they don't show the only method. You could install an out-of-tree tracer, like SystemTap, but, depending on your kernel and distribution, that could be a rocky experience. You could also modify the kernel code, or develop a custom kprobe module, but both of these methods involve challenges and carry their own risks. I developed my own workaround that I called the "hacktogram," which involved creating multiple perf(1) stat counters with range filters for each row in the histogram [16]. It was horrible.

- BPF programs can be compiled once and then run anywhere, as the BPF instruction set, map, helpers, and infrastructure are a stable ABI. (However, this is not possible with some BPF tracing programs that introduce unstable components, such as kprobes that instrument kernel structures; see Section 2.3.10 for work on a solution.)

- BPF programs do not require kernel build artifacts to be compiled.

- BPF programming is easier to learn than the kernel engineering required to develop kernel modules, making it accessible to more people.

Note that there are additional benefits when BPF is used for networking, including the ability to replace BPF programs atomically. A kernel module would need to first unload out of the kernel entirely and then reload the new version into the kernel, which could cause service disruptions.

A benefit of kernel modules is that other kernel functions and facilities can be used, without the restriction to BPF helper calls only. However, this brings the additional risk of introducing bugs if arbitrary kernel functions are misused.

2.3.3   Writing BPF Programs

BPF can be programmed via one of the many front ends available. The main ones for tracing are, from lowest- to highest-level language:

- LLVM

- BCC

- bpftrace

The LLVM compiler supports BPF as a compilation target. BPF programs can be written using a higher-level language that LLVM supports, such as C (via Clang) or LLVM Intermediate Representation (IR), and then compiled into BPF. LLVM includes an optimizer, which improves the efficiency and size of the BPF instructions it emits.

While developing BPF in LLVM IR is an improvement, switching to BCC or bpftrace is even better. BCC allows BPF programs to be written in C, and bpftrace provides its own higher-level language. Internally, they are using LLVM IR and an LLVM library to compile to BPF.

The performance tools in this book are programmed in BCC and bpftrace. Programming in BPF instructions directly, or LLVM IR, is the domain of developers who work on BCC and bpftrace internals and is beyond the scope of this book. It is unnecessary for those of us using and developing BPF performance tools.[9] If you wish to become a BPF instruction developer or are curious, here are some resources for additional reading:

Appendix E provides a brief summary of BPF instructions and macros.

- BPF instructions are documented in the Linux source tree, Documentation/networking/filter.txt [17].

---

9 Having spent 15 years using DTrace, I cannot remember a time when anyone needed to write D Intermediate Format (DIF) programs directly (the DTrace equivalent of BPF instructions).

- LLVM IR is documented in the online LLVM reference; start with the llvm::IRBuilderBase Class Reference [18].

- See the Cilium BPF and XDP Reference Guide [19].

While most of us will never program BPF instructions directly, many of us will view them at times, such as when tools encounter issues. The next two sections show examples, using bpftool(8) and then bpftrace.

2.3.4 Viewing BPF Instructions: bpftool

bpftool(8) was added in Linux 4.15 for viewing and manipulating BPF objects, including programs and maps. It is in the Linux source under tools/bpf/bpftool. This section summarizes how to use bpftool(8) to find loaded BPF programs and print their instructions.

bpftool

The default output of bpftool(8) shows the object types that it operates on. From Linux 5.2:

```
# bpftool
Usage: bpftool [OPTIONS] OBJECT { COMMAND | help }
       bpftool batch file FILE
       bpftool version


       OBJECT := { prog | map | cgroup | perf | net | feature | btf }
       OPTIONS := { {-j|--json} [{-p|--pretty}] | {-f|--bpffs} |
                    {-m|--mapcompat} | {-n|--nomount} }
```

There is a separate help page for each object. For example, for programs:

```
# bpftool prog help
Usage: bpftool prog { show | list } [PROG]
       bpftool prog dump xlated PROG [{ file FILE | opcodes | visual | linum }]
       bpftool prog dump jited  PROG [{ file FILE | opcodes | linum }]
       bpftool prog pin   PROG FILE
       bpftool prog { load | loadall } OBJ  PATH \
                       [type TYPE] [dev NAME] \
                       [map { idx IDX | name NAME } MAP]\
                       [pinmaps MAP_DIR]
       bpftool prog attach PROG ATTACH_TYPE [MAP]
       bpftool prog detach PROG ATTACH_TYPE [MAP]
       bpftool prog tracelog
       bpftool prog help
```

```
      MAP := { id MAP_ID | pinned FILE }
      PROG := { id PROG_ID | pinned FILE | tag PROG_TAG }
      TYPE := { socket | kprobe | kretprobe | classifier | action |q
[...]
```

The `perf` and `prog` subcommands can be used to find and print tracing programs. bpftool(8) capabilities not covered here include attaching programs, reading and writing to maps, operating on cgroups, and listing BPF features.

bpftool perf

The `perf` subcommand shows BPF programs attached via perf_event_open(), which is the norm for BCC and bpftrace programs on Linux 4.17 and later. For example:

```
# bpftool perf
pid 1765   fd 6: prog_id 26   kprobe   func blk_account_io_start   offset 0
pid 1765   fd 8: prog_id 27   kprobe   func blk_account_io_done   offset 0
pid 1765   fd 11: prog_id 28   kprobe   func sched_fork   offset 0
pid 1765   fd 15: prog_id 29   kprobe   func ttwu_do_wakeup   offset 0
pid 1765   fd 17: prog_id 30   kprobe   func wake_up_new_task   offset 0
pid 1765   fd 19: prog_id 31   kprobe   func finish_task_switch   offset 0
pid 1765   fd 26: prog_id 33   tracepoint   inet_sock_set_state
pid 21993   fd 6: prog_id 232   uprobe   filename /proc/self/exe   offset 1781927
pid 21993   fd 8: prog_id 233   uprobe   filename /proc/self/exe   offset 1781920
pid 21993   fd 15: prog_id 234   kprobe   func blk_account_io_done   offset 0
pid 21993   fd 17: prog_id 235   kprobe   func blk_account_io_start   offset 0
pid 25440   fd 8: prog_id 262   kprobe   func blk_mq_start_request   offset 0
pid 25440   fd 10: prog_id 263   kprobe   func blk_account_io_done   offset 0
```

This output shows three different PIDs with various BPF programs:

- PID 1765 is a Vector BPF PMDA agent for instance analysis. (See Chapter 17 for more details.)

- PID 21993 is the bpftrace version of biolatency(8). It shows two uprobes, which are the BEGIN and END probes from the bpftrace program, and two kprobes for instrumenting the start and end of block I/O. (See Chapter 9 for the source to this program.)

- PID 25440 is the BCC version of biolatency(8), which currently instruments a different start function for the block I/O.

The offset field shows the offset of the instrumentation from the instrumented object. For bpftrace, offset 1781920 matches the BEGIN_trigger function in the bpftrace binary, and offset 1781927 matches the END_trigger function (as can be verified by using `readelf -s bpftrace`).

The prog_id is the BPF program ID, which can be printed using the following subcommands.

bpftool prog show

The `prog show` subcommand lists all programs (not just those that are perf_event_open() based):

```
# bpftool prog show
[...]
232: kprobe  name END  tag b7cc714c79700b37  gpl
        loaded_at 2019-06-18T21:29:26+0000  uid 0
        xlated 168B  jited 138B  memlock 4096B  map_ids 130
233: kprobe  name BEGIN  tag 7de8b38ee40a4762  gpl
        loaded_at 2019-06-18T21:29:26+0000  uid 0
        xlated 120B  jited 112B  memlock 4096B  map_ids 130
234: kprobe  name blk_account_io_  tag d89dcf82fc3e48d8  gpl
        loaded_at 2019-06-18T21:29:26+0000  uid 0
        xlated 848B  jited 540B  memlock 4096B  map_ids 128,129
235: kprobe  name blk_account_io_  tag 499ff93d9cff0eb2  gpl
        loaded_at 2019-06-18T21:29:26+0000  uid 0
        xlated 176B  jited 139B  memlock 4096B  map_ids 128
[...]
258: cgroup_skb  tag 7be49e3934a125ba  gpl
        loaded_at 2019-06-18T21:31:27+0000  uid 0
        xlated 296B  jited 229B  memlock 4096B  map_ids 153,154
259: cgroup_skb  tag 2a142ef67aaad174  gpl
        loaded_at 2019-06-18T21:31:27+0000  uid 0
        xlated 296B  jited 229B  memlock 4096B  map_ids 153,154
262: kprobe  name trace_req_start  tag 1dfc28ba8b3dd597  gpl
        loaded_at 2019-06-18T21:37:51+0000  uid 0
        xlated 112B  jited 109B  memlock 4096B  map_ids 158
        btf_id 5
263: kprobe  name trace_req_done  tag d9bc05b87ea5498c  gpl
        loaded_at 2019-06-18T21:37:51+0000  uid 0
        xlated 912B  jited 567B  memlock 4096B  map_ids 158,157
        btf_id 5
```

This output shows the bpftrace program IDs (232 to 235) and the BCC program IDs (262 and 263), as well as other BPF programs that are loaded. Note that the BCC kprobe programs have BPF Type Format (BTF) information, shown by the presence of btf_id in this output. BTF is explained in more detail in Section 2.3.9. For now, it is sufficient to understand that BTF is a BPF version of debuginfo.

bpftool prog dump xlated

Each BPF program can be printed ("dumped") via its ID. The xlated mode prints the BPF instructions translated to assembly. Here is program 234, the bpftrace block I/O done program[10]:

```
# bpftool prog dump xlated id 234
   0: (bf) r6 = r1
   1: (07) r6 += 112
   2: (bf) r1 = r10
   3: (07) r1 += -8
   4: (b7) r2 = 8
   5: (bf) r3 = r6
   6: (85) call bpf_probe_read#-51584
   7: (79) r1 = *(u64 *)(r10 -8)
   8: (7b) *(u64 *)(r10 -16) = r1
   9: (18) r1 = map[id:128]
  11: (bf) r2 = r10
  12: (07) r2 += -16
  13: (85) call __htab_map_lookup_elem#93808
  14: (15) if r0 == 0x0 goto pc+1
  15: (07) r0 += 56
  16: (55) if r0 != 0x0 goto pc+2
[...]
```

The output shows one of the restricted kernel helper calls that BPF can use: bpf_probe_read(). (More helper calls are listed in Table 2-2.)

Now compare the preceding output to the output for the BCC block I/O done program, ID 263, which has been compiled with BTF[11]:

```
# bpftool prog dump xlated id 263
int trace_req_done(struct pt_regs * ctx):
; struct request *req = ctx->di;
   0: (79) r1 = *(u64 *)(r1 +112)
; struct request *req = ctx->di;
   1: (7b) *(u64 *)(r10 -8) = r1
; tsp = bpf_map_lookup_elem((void *)bpf_pseudo_fd(1, -1), &req);
   2: (18) r1 = map[id:158]
   4: (bf) r2 = r10
;
```

---

10 This may not match what the user loaded into the kernel, as the BPF verifier has the freedom to rewrite some instructions for optimization (e.g., inlining map lookups) or for security reasons (e.g., Spectre).

11 This required LLVM 9.0, which includes BTF by default.

```
    5: (07) r2 += -8
; tsp = bpf_map_lookup_elem((void *)bpf_pseudo_fd(1, -1), &req);
    6: (85) call __htab_map_lookup_elem#93808
    7: (15) if r0 == 0x0 goto pc+1
    8: (07) r0 += 56
    9: (bf) r6 = r0
; if (tsp == 0) {
   10: (15) if r6 == 0x0 goto pc+101
; delta = bpf_ktime_get_ns() - *tsp;
   11: (85) call bpf_ktime_get_ns#88176
; delta = bpf_ktime_get_ns() - *tsp;
   12: (79) r1 = *(u64 *)(r6 +0)
[...]
```

This output now includes source information (highlighted in bold) from BTF. Note that it is a different program (different instructions and calls).

A `linum` modifier includes source file and line number information, also from BTF, if available (highlighted in bold):

```
# bpftool prog dump xlated id 263 linum
int trace_req_done(struct pt_regs * ctx):
; struct request *req = ctx->di; [file:/virtual/main.c line_num:42 line_col:29]
   0: (79) r1 = *(u64 *)(r1 +112)
; struct request *req = ctx->di; [file:/virtual/main.c line_num:42 line_col:18]
   1: (7b) *(u64 *)(r10 -8) = r1
; tsp = bpf_map_lookup_elem((void *)bpf_pseudo_fd(1, -1), &req);
[file:/virtual/main.c line_num:46 line_col:39]
   2: (18) r1 = map[id:158]
   4: (bf) r2 = r10
[...]
```

In this case, the line number information refers to the virtual files BCC creates when running programs.

An `opcodes` modifier includes the BPF instruction opcodes (highlighted in bold):

```
# bpftool prog dump xlated id 263 opcodes
int trace_req_done(struct pt_regs * ctx):
; struct request *req = ctx->di;
   0: (79) r1 = *(u64 *)(r1 +112)
       79 11 70 00 00 00 00 00
; struct request *req = ctx->di;
   1: (7b) *(u64 *)(r10 -8) = r1
       7b 1a f8 ff 00 00 00 00
; tsp = bpf_map_lookup_elem((void *)bpf_pseudo_fd(1, -1), &req);
```

```
2: (18) r1 = map[id:158]
    18 11 00 00 9e 00 00 00 00 00 00 00 00 00 00 00
4: (bf) r2 = r10
    bf a2 00 00 00 00 00 00
[...]
```

The BPF instruction opcodes are explained in Appendix E.

There is also a `visual` modifier, which emits control flow graph information in DOT format, for visualization by external software. For example, using GraphViz and its dot(1) directed graph tool [20]:

```
# bpftool prog dump xlated id 263 visual > biolatency_done.dot
$ dot -Tpng -Elen=2.5 biolatency_done.dot -o biolatency_done.png
```

The PNG file can then be viewed to see instruction flow. GraphViz provides different layout tools: I typically use dot(1), neato(1), fdp(1), and sfdp(1) for graphing DOT data. These tools allow various customizations (such as edge length: `-Elen`). Figure 2-5 shows the result of using osage(1) from GraphViz to visualize this BPF program.

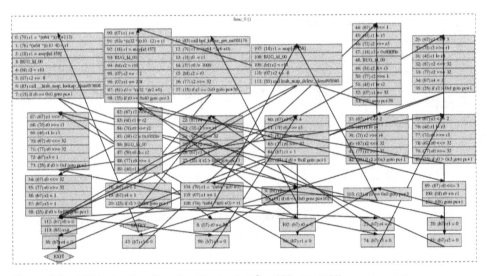

Figure 2-5   BPF instruction flow visualized using GraphViz osage(1)

It is a complex program! Other GraphViz tools spread out the code blocks to prevent the bird's nest of arrows but produce much larger files. If you need to read BPF instructions like this, you should experiment with the different tools to find the one that works best.

bpftool prog dump jited

The prog dump jited subcommand shows the machine code for the processor that is executed. This section shows x86_64; however, BPF has JITs for all major architectures supported by the Linux kernel. For the BCC block I/O done program:

```
# bpftool prog dump jited id 263
int trace_req_done(struct pt_regs * ctx):
0xffffffffc082dc6f:
; struct request *req = ctx->di;
   0:   push    %rbp
   1:   mov     %rsp,%rbp
   4:   sub     $0x38,%rsp
   b:   sub     $0x28,%rbp
   f:   mov     %rbx,0x0(%rbp)
  13:   mov     %r13,0x8(%rbp)
  17:   mov     %r14,0x10(%rbp)
  1b:   mov     %r15,0x18(%rbp)
  1f:   xor     %eax,%eax
  21:   mov     %rax,0x20(%rbp)
  25:   mov     0x70(%rdi),%rdi
; struct request *req = ctx->di;
  29:   mov     %rdi,-0x8(%rbp)
; tsp = bpf_map_lookup_elem((void *)bpf_pseudo_fd(1, -1), &req);
  2d:   movabs  $0xffff96e680ab0000,%rdi
  37:   mov     %rbp,%rsi
  3a:   add     $0xfffffffffffffff8,%rsi
; tsp = bpf_map_lookup_elem((void *)bpf_pseudo_fd(1, -1), &req);
  3e:   callq   0xffffffffc39a49c1
[...]
```

As shown earlier, the presence of BTF for this program allows bpftool(8) to include the source lines; otherwise, they would not be present.

bpftool btf

bpftool(8) can also dump BTF IDs. For example, BTF ID 5 is for the BCC block I/O done program:

```
# bpftool btf dump id 5
[1] PTR '(anon)' type_id=0
[2] TYPEDEF 'u64' type_id=3
[3] TYPEDEF '__u64' type_id=4
[4] INT 'long long unsigned int' size=8 bits_offset=0 nr_bits=64 encoding=(none)
[5] FUNC_PROTO '(anon)' ret_type_id=2 vlen=4
        'pkt' type_id=1
        'off' type_id=2
```

```
            'bofs' type_id=2
            'bsz' type_id=2
[6] FUNC 'bpf_dext_pkt' type_id=5
[7] FUNC_PROTO '(anon)' ret_type_id=0 vlen=5
            'pkt' type_id=1
            'off' type_id=2
            'bofs' type_id=2
            'bsz' type_id=2
            'val' type_id=2
[8] FUNC 'bpf_dins_pkt' type_id=7
[9] TYPEDEF 'uintptr_t' type_id=10
[10] INT 'long unsigned int' size=8 bits_offset=0 nr_bits=64 encoding=(none)
[...]
[347] STRUCT 'task_struct' size=9152 vlen=204
            'thread_info' type_id=348 bits_offset=0
            'state' type_id=349 bits_offset=128
            'stack' type_id=1 bits_offset=192
            'usage' type_id=350 bits_offset=256
            'flags' type_id=28 bits_offset=288
[...]
```

This output shows that BTF includes type and struct information.

2.3.5 Viewing BPF Instructions: bpftrace

While tcpdump(8) can emit BPF instructions with –d, bpftrace can do so with –v[12]:

```
# bpftrace -v biolatency.bt
Attaching 4 probes...

Program ID: 677

Bytecode:
0: (bf) r6 = r1
1: (b7) r1 = 29810
2: (6b) *(u16 *)(r10 -4) = r1
3: (b7) r1 = 1635021632
4: (63) *(u32 *)(r10 -8) = r1
5: (b7) r1 = 20002
6: (7b) *(u64 *)(r10 -16) = r1
7: (b7) r1 = 0
8: (73) *(u8 *)(r10 -2) = r1
9: (18) r7 = 0xffff96e697298800
11: (85) call bpf_get_smp_processor_id#8
```

---

12 I just realized I should have made it –d for consistency.

```
12: (bf) r4 = r10
13: (07) r4 += -16
14: (bf) r1 = r6
15: (bf) r2 = r7
16: (bf) r3 = r0
17: (b7) r5 = 15
18: (85) call bpf_perf_event_output#25
19: (b7) r0 = 0
20: (95) exit
[...]
```

This output will also be printed if there is a bpftrace internal error. If you develop bpftrace internals, you may find it easy to run afoul of the BPF verifier, and have a program rejected by the kernel. At that point, these instructions will be printed out, and you will need to study them to determine the cause and develop the fix.

Most people will never encounter a bpftrace or BCC internal error and never see BPF instructions. If you do encounter such an issue, please file a ticket with the bpftrace or BCC projects, or consider contributing a fix yourself.

2.3.6 BPF API

To provide a better understanding of BPF capabilities, the following sections summarize selected parts of the extended BPF API, from include/uapi/linux/bpf.h in Linux 4.20.

BPF Helper Functions

A BPF program cannot call arbitrary kernel functions. To accomplish certain tasks with this limitation, "helper" functions that BPF can call have been provided. Selected functions are shown in Table 2-2.

Table 2-2 **Selected BPF Helper Functions**

BPF Helper Function	Description
bpf_map_lookup_elem(map, key)	Finds a key in a map and returns its value (pointer).
bpf_map_update_elem(map, key, value, flags)	Updates the value of the entry selected by key.
bpf_map_delete_elem(map, key)	Deletes the entry selected by key from the map.
bpf_probe_read(dst, size, src)	Safely reads size bytes from address src and stores in dst.
bpf_ktime_get_ns()	Returns the time since boot, in nanoseconds.
bpf_trace_printk(fmt, fmt_size, ...)	A debugging helper that writes to TraceFS trace{_pipe}.
bpf_get_current_pid_tgid()	Returns a u64 containing the current TGID (what user space calls the PID) in the upper bits and the current PID (what user space calls the kernel thread ID) in the lower bits.
bpf_get_current_comm(buf, buf_size)	Copies the task name to the buffer.
bpf_perf_event_output(ctx, map, data, size)	Writes data to the perf_event ring buffers; this is used for per-event output.

BPF Helper Function	Description
bpf_get_stackid(ctx, map, flags)	Fetches a user or kernel stack trace and returns an identifier.
bpf_get_current_task()	Returns the current task struct. This contains many details about the running process and links to other structs containing system state. Note that these are all considered an unstable API.
bpf_probe_read_str(dst, size, ptr)	Copies a NULL terminated string from an unsafe pointer to the destination, limited by size (including the NULL byte).
bpf_perf_event_read_value(map, flags, buf, size)	Reads a perf_event counter and stores it in the buf. This is a way to read PMCs during a BPF program.
bpf_get_current_cgroup_id()	Returns the current cgroup ID.
bpf_spin_lock(lock), bpf_spin_unlock(lock)	Concurrency control for network programs.

Some of these helper functions are shown in the earlier bpftool(8) `xlated` output, and `bpftrace -v` output.

The term *current* in these descriptions refers to the currently running thread—the thread that is currently on-CPU.

Note that the include/uapi/linux/bpf.h file often provides detailed documentation for these helpers. Here is an excerpt from bpf_get_stackid():

```
* int bpf_get_stackid(struct pt_reg *ctx, struct bpf_map *map, u64 flags)
*       Description
*               Walk a user or a kernel stack and return its id. To achieve
*               this, the helper needs *ctx*, which is a pointer to the context
*               on which the tracing program is executed, and a pointer to a
*               *map* of type **BPF_MAP_TYPE_STACK_TRACE**.
*
*               The last argument, *flags*, holds the number of stack frames to
*               skip (from 0 to 255), masked with
*               **BPF_F_SKIP_FIELD_MASK**. The next bits can be used to set
*               a combination of the following flags:
*
*               **BPF_F_USER_STACK**
*                       Collect a user space stack instead of a kernel stack.
*               **BPF_F_FAST_STACK_CMP**
*                       Compare stacks by hash only.
*               **BPF_F_REUSE_STACKID**
*                       If two different stacks hash into the same *stackid*,
*                       discard the old one.
*
```

```
*                  The stack id retrieved is a 32 bit long integer handle which
*                  can be further combined with other data (including other stack
*                  ids) and used as a key into maps. This can be useful for
*                  generating a variety of graphs (such as flame graphs or off-cpu
*                  graphs).
[...]
```

These files can be browsed online from any site that hosts the Linux source, for example: https://github.com/torvalds/linux/blob/master/include/uapi/linux/bpf.h.

There are many more helper functions available, mostly for software-defined networking. The current version of Linux (5.2) has 98 helper functions.

bpf_probe_read()

bpf_probe_read() is a particularly important helper. Memory access in BPF is restricted to BPF registers and the stack (and BPF maps via helpers). Arbitrary memory (such as other kernel memory outside of BPF) must be read via bpf_probe_read(), which performs safety checks and disables page faults to ensure that the reads do not cause faults from probe context (which could cause kernel problems).

Apart from reading kernel memory, this helper is also used to read user-space memory into kernel space. How this works depends on the architecture: On x86_64, the user and kernel address ranges do not overlap, so the mode can be determined by the address. This is not the case for other architectures, such as SPARC [21], and for BPF to support these other architectures it is anticipated that additional helpers will be required, such as bpf_probe_read_kernel() and bpf_probe_read_user().[13]

BPF Syscall Commands

Table 2-3 shows selected BPF actions that user space can invoke.

Table 2-3   **Selected BPF syscall Commands**

bpf_cmd	Description
BPF_MAP_CREATE	Creates a BPF map: a flexible storage object that can be used as a key/value hash table (associative array).
BPF_MAP_LOOKUP_ELEM	Looks up an element via a key.
BPF_MAP_UPDATE_ELEM	Updates an element, given a key.
BPF_MAP_DELETE_ELEM	Deletes an element, given a key.
BPF_MAP_GET_NEXT_KEY	Iterates over all keys in a map.
BPF_PROG_LOAD	Verifies and loads a BPF program.
BPF_PROG_ATTACH	Attaches a BPF program to an event.
BPF_PROG_DETACH	Detaches a BPF program from an event.
BPF_OBJ_PIN	Creates a BPF object instance in /sys/fs/bpf.

---

13 This need was raised by David S. Miller at LSFMM 2019.

These actions are passed as the first argument to the bpf(2) syscall. You can see them in action by using strace(1). For example, inspecting the bpf(2) syscalls made when running the BCC execsnoop(8) tool:

```
# strace -ebpf execsnoop
bpf(BPF_MAP_CREATE, {map_type=BPF_MAP_TYPE_PERF_EVENT_ARRAY, key_size=4,
value_size=4, max_entries=8, map_flags=0, inner_map_fd=0, ...}, 72) = 3
bpf(BPF_PROG_LOAD, {prog_type=BPF_PROG_TYPE_KPROBE, insn_cnt=513,
insns=0x7f31c0a89000, license="GPL", log_level=0, log_size=0, log_buf=0,
kern_version=266002, prog_flags=0, ...}, 72) = 4
bpf(BPF_PROG_LOAD, {prog_type=BPF_PROG_TYPE_KPROBE, insn_cnt=60,
insns=0x7f31c0a8b7d0, license="GPL", log_level=0, log_size=0, log_buf=0,
kern_version=266002, prog_flags=0, ...}, 72) = 6
PCOMM             PID    PPID   RET ARGS
bpf(BPF_MAP_UPDATE_ELEM, {map_fd=3, key=0x7f31ba81e880, value=0x7f31ba81e910,
flags=BPF_ANY}, 72) = 0
bpf(BPF_MAP_UPDATE_ELEM, {map_fd=3, key=0x7f31ba81e910, value=0x7f31ba81e880,
flags=BPF_ANY}, 72) = 0
[...]
```

Actions are highlighted in bold in this output. Note that I normally avoid using strace(1) as its current ptrace() implementation can greatly slow the target process—by over 100-fold [22]. I used it here because it already has translation mappings for the bpf(2) syscall, turning numbers into readable strings (e.g., "BPF_PROG_LOAD").

BPF Program Types

Different BPF program types specify the type of events that the BPF program attaches to, and the arguments for the events. The main program types used for BPF tracing programs are shown in Table 2-4.

Table 2-4   **BPF Tracing Program Types**

bpf_prog_type	Description
BPF_PROG_TYPE_KPROBE	For kprobes and uprobes
BPF_PROG_TYPE_TRACEPOINT	For tracepoints
BPF_PROG_TYPE_PERF_EVENT	For perf_events, including PMCs
BPF_PROG_TYPE_RAW_TRACEPOINT	For tracepoints, without argument processing

The earlier strace(1) output included two BPF_PROG_LOAD calls of type BPF_PROG_TYPE_KPROBE, as that version of execsnoop(8) is using a kprobe and a kretprobe for instrumenting the beginning and end of execve().

There are more program types in bpf.h for networking and other purposes, including those shown in Table 2-5.

Table 2-5 **Selected Other BPF Program Types**

bpf_prog_type	Description
BPF_PROG_TYPE_SOCKET_FILTER	For attaching to sockets, the original BPF use case
BPF_PROG_TYPE_SCHED_CLS	For traffic control classification
BPF_PROG_TYPE_XDP	For eXpress Data Path programs
BPF_PROG_TYPE_CGROUP_SKB	For cgroup packet (skb) filters

BPF Map Types

BPF map types, some of which are listed in Table 2-6, define different types of maps.

Table 2-6 **Selected BPF Map Types**

bpf_map_type	Description
BPF_MAP_TYPE_HASH	A hash-table map: key/value pairs
BPF_MAP_TYPE_ARRAY	An array of elements
BPF_MAP_TYPE_PERF_EVENT_ARRAY	An interface to the perf_event ring buffers for emitting trace records to user space
BPF_MAP_TYPE_PERCPU_HASH	A faster hash table maintained on a per-CPU basis
BPF_MAP_TYPE_PERCPU_ARRAY	A faster array maintained on a per-CPU basis
BPF_MAP_TYPE_STACK_TRACE	Storage for stack traces, indexed by stack IDs
BPF_MAP_TYPE_STACK	Storage for stack traces

The earlier strace(1) output included a BPF_MAP_CREATE of type BPF_MAP_TYPE_PERF_EVENT_ ARRAY, which was used by execsnoop(8) for passing events to user space for printing.

There are many more map types in bpf.h for special purposes.

2.3.7 BPF Concurrency Controls

BPF lacked concurrency controls until Linux 5.1, when spin lock helpers were added. (However, they are not yet available for use in tracing programs.) With tracing, parallel threads can look up and update BPF map fields in parallel, causing corruption where one thread overwrites the update from another. This is also known as the "lost update" problem where concurrent reads and writes overlap, causing lost updates. The tracing front ends, BCC and bpftrace, use the per-CPU hash and array map types where possible to avoid this corruption. They create instances for each logical CPU to use, preventing parallel threads from updating a shared location. A map that counts events, for example, can be updated as a per-CPU map, and then the per-CPU values can be combined when needed for the total count.

As a specific example, this bpftrace one-liner uses a per-CPU hash for counting:

```
# strace -febpf bpftrace -e 'k:vfs_read { @ = count(); }'
bpf(BPF_MAP_CREATE, {map_type=BPF_MAP_TYPE_PERCPU_HASH, key_size=8, value_size=8,
max_entries=128, map_flags=0, inner_map_fd=0}, 72) = 3
[...]
```

And this bpftrace one-liner uses a normal hash for counting:

```
# strace -febpf bpftrace -e 'k:vfs_read { @++; }'
bpf(BPF_MAP_CREATE, {map_type=BPF_MAP_TYPE_HASH, key_size=8, value_size=8,
max_entries=128, map_flags=0, inner_map_fd=0}, 72) = 3
[...]
```

Using them both at the same time on an eight-CPU system, and tracing a function that is frequent and may run in parallel:

```
# bpftrace -e 'k:vfs_read { @cpuhash = count(); @hash++; }'
Attaching 1 probe...
^C

@cpuhash: 1061370
@hash: 1061269
```

A comparison of the counts reveals that the normal hash undercounted events by 0.01%.

Apart from per-CPU maps, there are also other mechanisms for concurrency controls, including an exclusive add instruction (BPF_XADD), a map in map that can update entire maps atomically, and BPF spin locks. Regular hash and LRU map updates via bpf_map_update_elem() are atomic as well and free from data races due to concurrent writes. Spin locks, which were added in Linux 5.1, are controlled by the bpf_spin_lock() and bpf_spin_unlock() helpers [23].

2.3.8   BPF sysfs Interface

In Linux 4.4, BPF introduced commands to expose BPF programs and maps via a virtual file system, conventionally mounted on /sys/fs/bpf. This capability, termed "pinning," has a number of uses. It allows the creation of BPF programs that are persistent (much like daemons) and continue running after the process that loaded them has exited. It also provides another way for user-level programs to interact with a running BPF program: They can read from and write to BPF maps.

Pinning has not been used by the BPF observability tools in this book, which are modeled after standard Unix utilities that start and stop. However, any of these tools could be converted to one that is pinned, if needed. This is more commonly used for networking programs (e.g., the Cilium software [24]).

As an example of pinning, the Android operating system makes use of pinning to automatically load and pin BPF programs found under /system/etc/bpf [25]. Android library functions are provided to interact with these pinned programs.

2.3.9 BPF Type Format (BTF)

One of the recurring issues described in this book is the lack of information about the source code that is instrumented, making it difficult to write BPF tools. As will be mentioned many times, an ideal solution to these problems is BTF, introduced here.

BTF (BPF Type Format) is a metadata format that encodes debugging information for describing BPF programs, BPF maps, and much more. The name BTF was chosen as it initially described data types; however, it was later extended to include function info for defined subroutines, line info for source/line information, and global variable information.

BTF debug info can be embedded in the vmlinux binary or generated together with BPF programs with native Clang compilation or LLVM JIT, so that the BPF program can be inspected more easily with loaders (e.g., libbpf) and tools (e.g., bpftool(8)). Inspection and tracing tools, including bpftool(8) and perf(1), can retrieve such info to provide source annotated BPF programs, or pretty print map key/values based on their C structure instead of a raw hex dump. The previous examples of bpftool(8) dumping an LLVM-9 compiled BCC program demonstrate this.

Apart from describing BPF programs, BTF is becoming a general-purpose format for describing all kernel data structures. In some ways, it is becoming a lightweight alternative to kernel debuginfo for use by BPF, and a more complete and reliable alternative to kernel headers.

BPF tracing tools often require kernel headers to be installed (usually via a linux-headers package) so that various C structs can be navigated. These headers do not contain definitions for all the structs in the kernel, making it difficult to develop some BPF observability tools: missing structs need to be defined in the BPF tool source as a workaround. There have also been issues with complex headers not being processed correctly; bpftrace may switch to aborting in these cases rather than continuing with potentially incorrect struct offsets. BTF can solve this problem by providing reliable definitions for all structs. (An earlier `bpftool btf` output shows how task_struct can be included.) In the future, a shipped Linux kernel vmlinux binary that contains BTF will be self-describing.

BTF is still in development at the time of writing this book. In order to support a compile-once-run-everywhere initiative, more information is to be added to BTF. For the latest on BTF, see Documentation/bpf/btf.rst in the kernel source [26].

2.3.10 BPF CO-RE

The BPF Compile Once - Run Everywhere (CO-RE) project aims to allow BPF programs to be compiled to BPF bytecode once, saved, and then distributed and executed on other systems. This will avoid the need to have BPF compilers installed everywhere (LLVM and Clang), which can be challenging for space-constrained embedded Linux. It will also avoid the runtime CPU and memory costs of running a compiler whenever a BPF observability tool is executed.

The CO-RE project, and developer Andrii Nakryiko, are working through challenges such as coping with different kernel struct offsets on different systems, which require field offsets in BPF bytecode to be rewritten as needed. Another challenge is missing struct members, which requires field access to be conditional based on the kernel version, kernel configuration, and/or user-provided runtime flags. The CO-RE project will make use of BTF information, and is still in development at the time of writing this book.

2.3.11 BPF Limitations

BPF programs cannot call arbitrary kernel functions; they are limited to the BPF helper functions listed in the API. More may be added in future kernel versions as needs arise. BPF programs also impose limits on loops: It would be unsafe to allow BPF programs to insert infinite loops on arbitrary kprobes, as those threads may be holding critical locks that block the rest of the system. Workarounds involve unrolling loops, and adding helper functions for common uses that need loops. Linux 5.3 included support for bounded loops in BPF, which have a verifiable upper runtime limit.[14]

The BPF stack size is limited to MAX_BPF_STACK, set to 512. This limit is sometimes encountered when writing BPF observability tools, especially when storing multiple string buffers on the stack: a single char[256] buffer consumes half this stack. There are no plans to increase this limit. The solution is to instead use BPF map storage, which is effectively infinite. Work has begun to switch bpftrace strings to use map storage instead of stack storage.

The number of instructions in a BPF program was initially limited to 4096. Long BPF programs sometimes encounter this limit (they would encounter it much sooner without LLVM compiler optimizations, which reduce the instruction count.) Linux 5.2 greatly increased the limit such that it should no longer be an issue.[15] The aim of the BPF verifier is to accept any safe program, and the limits should not get in the way.

2.3.12 BPF Additional Reading

More sources for understanding extended BPF:

- Documentation/networking/filter.txt in the kernel source [17]
- Documentation/bpf/bpf_design_QA.txt in the kernel source [29]
- The bpf(2) man page [30]
- The bpf-helpers(7) man page [31]
- "BPF: the universal in-kernel virtual machine" by Jonathan Corbet [32]
- "BPF Internals—II" by Suchakra Sharma [33]
- "BPF and XDP Reference Guide" by Cilium [19]

Additional examples of BPF programs are provided in Chapter 4 and in Appendixes C, D, and E.

---

14 You may begin wondering if BPF will become Turing complete. The BPF instruction set itself allows for the creation of a Turing complete automata, but given the safety restrictions the verifier puts in place, the BPF programs are not Turing complete anymore (e.g., due to the halting problem).

15 The limit was changed to one million instructions (BPF_COMPLEXITY_LIMIT_INSNS) [27]. The 4096 limit (BPF_MAXINSNS) still remains for unprivileged BPF programs [28].

2.4   Stack Trace Walking

Stack traces are an invaluable tool for understanding the code path that led to an event, as well as profiling kernel and user code to observe where execution time is spent. BPF provides special map types for recording stack traces and can fetch them using frame pointer–based or ORC-based stack walks. BPF may support other stack walking techniques in the future.

2.4.1   Frame Pointer–Based Stacks

The frame pointer technique follows a convention where the head of a linked list of stack frames can always be found in a register (RBP on x86_64) and where the return address is stored at a known offset (+8) from the stored RBP [Hubicka 13]. This means that any debugger or tracer that interrupts the program can read RBP and then easily fetch the stack trace by walking the RBP linked list and fetching the addresses at the known offset. This is shown in Figure 2-6.

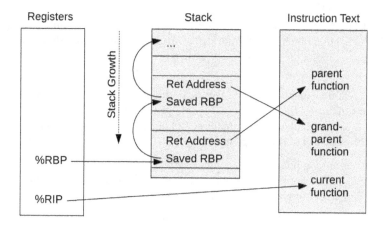

Figure 2-6   Frame pointer–based stack walking (x86_64)

The AMD64 ABI notes that the use of RBP as a frame pointer register is conventional, and can be avoided to save function prologue and epilogue instructions, and to make RBP available as a general-purpose register.

The gcc compiler currently defaults to omitting the frame pointer and using RBP as a general-purpose register, which breaks frame pointer-based stack walking. This default can be reverted using the `-fno-omit-frame-pointer` option. Three details from the patch that introduced frame pointer omission as the default explain why it was done [34]:

- The patch was introduced for i386, which has four general-purpose registers. Freeing RBP increases the usable registers from four to five, leading to significant performance wins. For x86_64, however, there are already 16 usable registers, making this change much less worthwhile. [35].

- It was assumed that stack walking was a solved problem, thanks to gdb(1) support of other techniques. This does not account for tracer stack walking, which runs in limited context with interrupts disabled.

- The need to compete on benchmarks with Intel's icc compiler.

On x86_64 today, most software is compiled with gcc's defaults, breaking frame pointer stack traces. Last time I studied the performance gain from frame pointer omission in our production environment, it was usually less than one percent, and it was often so close to zero that it was difficult to measure. Many microservices at Netflix are running with the frame pointer reenabled, as the performance wins found by CPU profiling outweigh the tiny loss of performance.

Using frame pointers is not the only way to walk a stack; other methods include debuginfo, LBR, and ORC.

2.4.2 debuginfo

Additional debugging information is often available for software as debuginfo packages, which contain ELF debuginfo files in the DWARF format. These include sections that debuggers such as gdb(1) can use to walk the stack trace, even when no frame pointer register is in use. The ELF sections are .eh_frame and .debug_frame.

Debuginfo files also include sections containing source and line number information, resulting in files that dwarf (ahem) the original binary that is debugged. An example in Chapter 12 shows libjvm.so at 17 Mbytes, and its debuginfo file at 222 Mbytes. In some environments, debuginfo files are not installed due to their large size.

BPF does not currently support this technique of stack walking: It is processor intensive and requires reading ELF sections that may not be faulted in. This makes it challenging to implement in the limited interrupt-disabled BPF context.

Note that the BPF front ends BCC and bpftrace do support debuginfo files for symbol resolution.

2.4.3 Last Branch Record (LBR)

Last branch record is an Intel processor feature to record branches in a hardware buffer, including function call branches. This technique has no overhead and can be used to reconstruct a stack trace. However, it is limited in depth depending on the processor, and may only support recording 4 to 32 branches. Stack traces for production software, especially Java, can exceed 32 frames.

LBR is not currently supported by BPF, but it may be in the future. A limited stack trace is better than no stack trace!

2.4.4 ORC

A new debug information format that has been devised for stack traces, Oops Rewind Capability (ORC), is less processor intensive than DWARF [36]. ORC uses .orc_unwind and .orc_unwind_ip ELF sections, and it has so far been implemented for the Linux kernel. On register-limited architectures, it may be desirable to compile the kernel without the frame pointer and use ORC for stack traces instead.

ORC stack unwinding is available in the kernel via the perf_callchain_kernel() function, which BPF calls. This means BPF also supports ORC stack traces. ORC stacks have not yet been developed for user space.

2.4.5 Symbols

Stack traces are currently recorded in the kernel as an array of addresses that are later translated to symbols (such as function names) by a user-level program. There can be situations where symbol mappings have changed between collection and translation, resulting in invalid or missing translations. This is discussed in Section 12.3.4 in Chapter 12. Possible future work includes adding support for symbol translation in the kernel, so that the kernel can collect and translate a stack trace immediately.

2.4.6 More Reading

Stack traces and frame pointers are discussed further in Chapter 12 for C and Java, and Chapter 18 provides a general summary.

2.5 Flame Graphs

Flame graphs are frequently used in later chapters of this book, so this section summarizes how to use and read them.

Flame graphs are visualizations of stack traces that I invented when working on a MySQL performance issue and while trying to compare two CPU profiles that were thousands of pages of text [Gregg 16].[16] Apart from CPU profiles, they can also be used to visualize recorded stack traces from any profiler or tracer. Later in this book I show them applied to BPF tracing of off-CPU events, page faults, and more. This section explains the visualization.

2.5.1 Stack Trace

A stack trace, also called a stack back trace or a call trace, is a series of functions that show the flow of code. For example, if func_a() called func_b(), which called func_c(), the stack trace at that point may be written as:

```
func_c
func_b
func_a
```

The bottom of the stack (func_a) is the origin, and the lines above it show the code flow. Put differently, the top of the stack (func_c) is the current function, and moving downwards shows its ancestry: parent, then grandparent, and so on.

2.5.2 Profiling Stack Traces

Timed sampling of stack traces can collect thousands of stacks that can be tens or hundreds of lines long each. To make this volume of data easier to study, the Linux perf(1) profiler summarizes

---

16 Inspiration for the general layout, SVG output, and JavaScript interactivity came from Neelakanth Nadgir's function_call_graph.rb time-ordered visualization for callstacks, which itself was inspired by Roch Bourbonnais's CallStackAnalyzer and Jan Boerhout's vftrace.

stack samples as a call tree, and shows percentages for each path. The BCC profile(8) tool summarizes stack traces in a different way, showing a count for each unique stack trace. Real-world examples of both perf(1) and profile(8) are provided in Chapter 6. With both tools, pathological issues can be identified quickly for situations when a lone stack is on-CPU for the bulk of the time. However, for many other issues, including small performance regressions, finding the culprit can involve studying hundreds of pages of profiler output. Flame graphs were created to solve this problem.

To understand flame graphs, consider this synthetic example of CPU profiler output, showing a frequency count of stack traces:

```
func_e
func_d
func_b
func_a
1

func_b
func_a
2

func_c
func_b
func_a
7
```

This output shows a stack trace followed by a count, for a total of 10 samples. The code path in func_a() -> func_b() -> func_c(), for example, was sampled seven times. That code path shows func_c() running on CPU. The func_a() -> func_b() code path, with func_b() running on CPU, was sampled twice. And a code path that ends with func_e() running on CPU was sampled once.

2.5.3 Flame Graph

Figure 2-7 shows a flame graph representation of the previous profile.

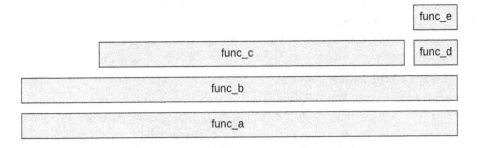

Figure 2-7   A Flame Graph

This flame graph has the following properties:

- Each box represents a function in the stack (a "stack frame").

- The y-axis shows stack depth (the number of frames on the stack), ordered from root at the bottom to leaf at the top. Looking from the bottom up, you can understand the code flow; from the top down, you can determine the function ancestry.

- The x-axis spans the sample population. It's important to note that it does *not* show the passage of time from left to right, as most graphs do. The left-to-right ordering is instead an alphabetical sort of frames to maximize frame merging. With the y-axis ordering of frames, this means that the graph origin is the bottom left (as with most graphs) and represents 0,a. The length across the x-axis does have meaning: The width of the box reflects its presence in the profile. Functions with wide boxes are more present in the profile than those with narrow boxes.

The flame graph is really an adjacency diagram with an inverted icicle layout [Bostock 10], applied to visualize the hierarchy of a collection of stack traces.

The most frequent stack in Figure 2-7 is seen in the profile as the widest "tower" in the middle, from func_a() to func_c(). Since this is a flame graph showing CPU samples, we can describe the top edge as the functions that were running on-CPU, as highlighted in Figure 2-8.

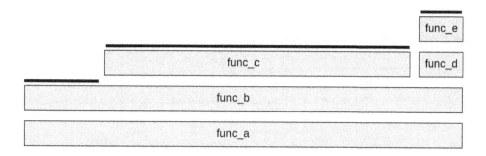

Figure 2-8   CPU Flame Graph of on-CPU Functions

Figure 2-8 shows that func_c() was directly on-CPU for 70% of the time, func_b() was on-CPU for 20% of the time, and func_e() was on-CPU for 10% of the time. The other functions, func_a() and func_d(), were never sampled on-CPU directly.

To read a flame graph, look for the widest towers and understand them first.

For large profiles of thousands of samples, there may be code paths that were sampled only a few times, and are printed in such a narrow tower that there is no room to include the function name. This turns out to be a benefit: Your attention is naturally drawn to the wider towers that have legible function names, and looking at them helps you understand the bulk of the profile first.

2.5.4 Flame Graph Features

My original flame graph implementation supports the features described in the following sections [37].

Color Palettes

The frames can be colored based on different schemes. The default is to use random warm colors for each frame, which helps visually distinguish adjacent towers. Over the years I've added more color schemes. I've found the following to be most useful to flame graph end users:

- **Hue:** The hue indicates the code type.[17] For example, red can indicate native user-level code, orange for native kernel-level code, yellow for C++, green for interpreted functions, aqua for inlined functions, and so on depending on the languages you use. Magenta is used to highlight search matches. Some developers have customized flame graphs to always highlight their own code in a certain hue, so that it stands out.

- **Saturation:** Saturation is hashed from the function name. It provides some color variance that helps differentiate adjacent towers, while preserving the same colors for function names to more easily compare multiple flame graphs.

- **Background color:** The background color provides a visual reminder of the flame graph type. For example, you might use yellow for CPU flame graphs, blue for off-CPU or I/O flame graphs, and green for memory flame graphs.

Another useful color scheme is one used for IPC (instructions per cycle) flame graphs, where an additional dimension, IPC, is visualized by coloring each frame using a gradient from blue to white to red.

Mouse-Overs

The original flame graph software creates SVG files with embedded JavaScript that can be loaded in a browser for interactive features. One such feature is that on mouse-over of frames, an information line is revealed, showing the percentage occurrence of that frame in the profile.

Zoom

Frames can be clicked for a horizontal zoom.[18] This allows narrow frames to be inspected, zooming in to show their function names.

Search

A search button, or Ctrl-F, allows a search term to be entered, and then frames matching that search term are highlighted in magenta. A cumulative percentage is also shown to indicate how often a stack trace containing that search term was present. This makes it trivial to calculate how much of the profile was in particular code areas. For example, you can search for "tcp_" to show how much was in the kernel TCP code.

2.5.5 Variations

A more interactive version of flame graphs is under development at Netflix, using d3 [38].[19] It is open source and used in the Netflix FlameScope software [39].

---

17 This was suggested to me by my colleague Amer Ather. My first version was a five-minute regex hack.

18 Adrien Mahieux developed the horizontal zoom feature for flame graphs.

19 d3 flame graphs was created by my colleague Martin Spier.

Some flame graph implementations flip the y-axis order by default, creating an "icicle graph" with the root at the top. This inversion ensures that the root and its immediate functions are still visible for flame graphs that are taller than the screen height and when displaying from the flame graph top to begin with. My original flame graph software supports this inversion with `--inverted`. My own preference is to reserve this icicle layout for leaf-to-root merging, another flame graph variant that merges from the leaves first and roots last. This is useful for merging a common on-CPU function first and then seeing its ancestry, for example: spin locks.

Flame charts appear similar to flame graphs and were inspired by flame graphs [Tikhonovsky 13], but the x-axis is ordered based on the passage of time rather than the alphabet. Flame charts are popular in web browser analysis tools for the inspection of JavaScript, as they are suited for understanding time-based patterns in single-threaded applications. Some profiling tools support both flame graphs and flame charts.

Differential flame graphs show the differences between two profiles.[20]

2.6 Event Sources

The different event sources and examples of events that can be instrumented are illustrated in Figure 2-9. This figure also shows the Linux kernel versions that BPF supported attaching to these events.

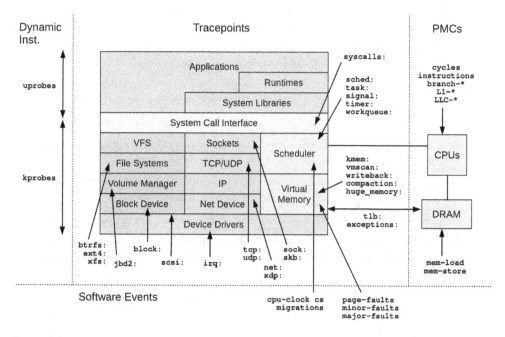

Figure 2-9   BPF event support

These event sources are explained in the following sections.

----

20 Cor-Paul Bezemer researched differential flame graphs and developed the first solution [Bezemer 15].

2.7   kprobes

kprobes provide kernel dynamic instrumentation, and were developed by a team at IBM based on their DProbes tracer in 2000. However, DProbes did not get merged into the Linux kernel, while kprobes did. kprobes arrived in Linux 2.6.9, which was released in 2004.

kprobes can create instrumentation events for any kernel function, and it can instrument instructions within functions. It can do this live, in production environments, without needing to either reboot the system or run the kernel in any special mode. This is an amazing capability: It means we can instrument any of the tens of thousands of kernel functions in Linux to create new custom metrics as needed.

The kprobes technology also has an interface called kretprobes for instrumenting when functions return, and their return values. When kprobes and kretprobes instrument the same function, timestamps can be recorded to calculate the duration of a function, which can be an important metric for performance analysis.

2.7.1   How kprobes Work

The sequence for instrumenting a kernel instruction with kprobes is [40]:

A. If it is a kprobe:

   1. Bytes from the target address are copied and saved by kprobes (enough bytes to span their replacement with a breakpoint instruction).

   2. The target address is replaced with a breakpoint instruction: int3 on x86_64.
       (If kprobe optimization is possible, the instruction is jmp.)

   3. When instruction flow hits this breakpoint, the breakpoint handler checks whether the breakpoint was installed by kprobes, and, if it was, executes a kprobe handler.

   4. The original instructions are then executed, and instruction flow resumes.

   5. When the kprobe is no longer needed, the original bytes are copied back to the target address, and the instructions are restored to their original state.

B. If it is a kprobe for an address that Ftrace already instruments (usually function entries), an Ftrace-based kprobe optimization may be possible, where [Hiramatsu 14]:

   1. An Ftrace kprobe handler is registered as an Ftrace operation for the traced function.

   2. The function executes its built-in call in the function prologue (__fentry__ with gcc 4.6+ and x86), which calls in to Ftrace. Ftrace calls the kprobe handler, and then returns to executing the function.

   3. When the kprobe is no longer needed, the Ftrace-kprobe handler is removed from Ftrace.

C. If it is a kretprobe:

   1. A kprobe is created for the entry to the function.

   2. When the function entry kprobe is hit, the return address is saved and then replaced with a substitute ("trampoline") function: kretprobe_trampoline().

3. When the function finally calls return (e.g., the ret instruction), the CPU passes control to the trampoline function, which executes the kretprobe handler.

4. The kretprobe handler finishes by returning to the saved return address.

5. When the kretprobe is no longer needed, the kprobe is removed.

The kprobe handlers may run with preemption disabled or interrupts disabled, depending on the architecture and other factors.

Modifying kernel instruction text live may sound incredibly risky, but it has been designed to be safe. This design includes a blacklist of functions that kprobe will not instrument, which include kprobes itself, to avoid a recursive trap condition.[21] kprobes also make use of safe techniques for inserting breakpoints: the x86 native int3 instruction, or stop_machine() when the jmp instruction is used to ensure that other cores do not execute instructions as they are being modified. The biggest risk in practice is instrumenting a kernel function that is extremely frequent: if that happens, the small overhead added to each invocation can add up, slowing down the system while the function is instrumented.

kprobes does not work on some ARM 64-bit systems where modifications to the kernel text section are not allowed for security reasons.

2.7.2 kprobes Interfaces

The original kprobes technology was used by writing a kernel module that defined pre- and post-handlers written in C and registering them with a kprobe API call: register_kprobe(). You could then load your kernel module and emit custom information via system messages with calls to printk(). You needed to call unregister_kprobe() when you were done.

I have not seen anyone use this interface directly, other than in the 2010 article "Kernel instrumentation using kprobes" from Phrack, a security ezine, written by a researcher using the handle ElfMaster[22] [41]. That may not be a failure of kprobes, since it was built to be used from Dprobes in the first place. Nowadays, there are three interfaces for using kprobes:

- kprobe API: register_kprobe() etc.
- Ftrace-based, via /sys/kernel/debug/tracing/kprobe_events: where kprobes can be enabled and disabled by writing configuration strings to this file
- perf_event_open(): as used by the perf(1) tool, and more recently by BPF tracing, as support was added in the Linux 4.17 kernel (perf_kprobe pmu)

The biggest use of kprobes has been via front-end tracers, including perf(1), SystemTap, and the BPF tracers BCC and bpftrace.

The original kprobes implementation also had a variant called jprobes, an interface designed for tracing kernel function entry. Over time, we have come to understand that kprobes can meet all requirements, and the jprobes interface was unnecessary. It was removed from Linux in 2018 by Masami Hiramatsu, a kprobe maintainer.

---

21 You can exclude kernel functions from tracing by listing them with the NOKPROBE_SYMBOL() macro.

22 In an unplanned coincidence, three days after writing this sentence I met ElfMaster, and he taught me many details about ELF analysis. These include how ELF tables are stripped, which I summarize in Chapter 4.

2.7.3 BPF and kprobes

kprobes provides kernel dynamic instrumentation for BCC and bpftrace, and it is used by numerous tools. The interfaces are:

- **BCC:** attach_kprobe() and attach_kretprobe()
- **bpftrace:** kprobe and kretprobe probe types

The kprobe interface in BCC supports instrumenting the beginning of a function and a function plus instruction offset, whereas bpftrace currently supports instrumenting the beginning of a function only. The kretprobe interface for both tracers instruments the return of the function.

As an example from BCC, the vfsstat(8) tool instruments key calls to the virtual file system (VFS) interface, and prints per-second summaries:

```
# vfsstat
TIME          READ/s  WRITE/s CREATE/s  OPEN/s  FSYNC/s
07:48:16:        736     4209        0      24        0
07:48:17:        386     3141        0      14        0
07:48:18:        308     3394        0      34        0
07:48:19:        196     3293        0      13        0
07:48:20:       1030     4314        0      17        0
07:48:21:        316     3317        0      98        0
[...]
```

The probes traced can be seen in the source to vfsstat:

```
# grep attach_ vfsstat.py
b.attach_kprobe(event="vfs_read", fn_name="do_read")
b.attach_kprobe(event="vfs_write", fn_name="do_write")
b.attach_kprobe(event="vfs_fsync", fn_name="do_fsync")
b.attach_kprobe(event="vfs_open", fn_name="do_open")
b.attach_kprobe(event="vfs_create", fn_name="do_create")
```

These are attach_kprobe() functions. The kernel functions can be seen after the "event=" assignment.

As an example from bpftrace, this one-liner counts the invocations of all the VFS functions, by matching "vfs_*":

```
# bpftrace -e 'kprobe:vfs_* { @[probe] = count() }'
Attaching 54 probes...
^C

@[kprobe:vfs_unlink]: 2
@[kprobe:vfs_rename]: 2
@[kprobe:vfs_readlink]: 2
@[kprobe:vfs_statx]: 88
```

```
@[kprobe:vfs_statx_fd]: 91
@[kprobe:vfs_getattr_nosec]: 247
@[kprobe:vfs_getattr]: 248
@[kprobe:vfs_open]: 320
@[kprobe:vfs_writev]: 441
@[kprobe:vfs_write]: 4977
@[kprobe:vfs_read]: 5581
```

This output shows that while tracing, the vfs_unlink() function was called twice, and the vfs_read() function was called 5581 times.

The ability to pull call counts from any kernel function is a useful capability, and can be used for workload characterization of kernel subsystems.[23]

2.7.4   kprobes Additional Reading

More sources for understanding kprobes:

- Documentation/kprobes.txt in the Linux kernel source [42]
- "An Introduction to kprobes" by Sudhanshu Goswami [40]
- "Kernel Debugging with kprobes" by Prasanna Panchamukhi [43]

2.8   uprobes

uprobes provides user-level dynamic instrumentation. Work began many years earlier, with a utrace interface similar to the kprobes interface. This eventually became the uprobes technology that was merged in the Linux 3.5 kernel, released in July 2012 [44].

uprobes are similar to kprobes, but for user-space processes. uprobes can instrument user-level function entries as well as instruction offsets, and uretprobes can instrument the return of functions.

uprobes are also file based: When a function in an executable file is traced, all processes using that file are instrumented, including those that start in the future. This allows library calls to be traced system-wide.

2.8.1   How uprobes Work

uprobes is similar to kprobes in its approach: A fast breakpoint is inserted at the target instruction, and it passes execution to a uprobe handler. When the uprobe is no longer needed, the target instructions are returned to their original state. With uretprobes, the function entry is instrumented with a uprobe, and the return address is hijacked with a trampoline function, as with kprobes.

---

23 At the time of writing, I still tend to use Ftrace for this particular task, since it is quicker to initialize and tear down instrumentation. See my funccount(8) tool from my Ftrace perf-tools repository. As of this writing, there is work under way to improve the speed of BPF kprobe initialization and teardown by batching operations. I hope it will be available by the time you are reading this.

You can see this in action by using a debugger. For example, disassembling the readline() function from the bash(1) shell:

```
# gdb -p 31817
[...]
(gdb) disas readline
Dump of assembler code for function readline:
   0x000055f7fa995610 <+0>:   cmpl   $0xffffffff,0x2656f9(%rip) # 0x55f7fabfad10
<rl_pending_input>
   0x000055f7fa995617 <+7>:   push   %rbx
   0x000055f7fa995618 <+8>:   je     0x55f7fa99568f <readline+127>
   0x000055f7fa99561a <+10>:  callq  0x55f7fa994350 <rl_set_prompt>
   0x000055f7fa99561f <+15>:  callq  0x55f7fa995300 <rl_initialize>
   0x000055f7fa995624 <+20>:  mov    0x261c8d(%rip),%rax       # 0x55f7fabf72b8
<rl_prep_term_function>
   0x000055f7fa99562b <+27>:  test   %rax,%rax
[...]
```

And now while it is instrumented using uprobes (or uretprobes):

```
# gdb -p 31817
[...]
(gdb) disas readline
Dump of assembler code for function readline:
   0x000055f7fa995610 <+0>:   int3
   0x000055f7fa995611 <+1>:   cmp    $0x2656f9,%eax
   0x000055f7fa995616 <+6>:   callq  *0x74(%rbx)
   0x000055f7fa995619 <+9>:   jne    0x55f7fa995603 <rl_initialize+771>
   0x000055f7fa99561b <+11>:  xor    %ebp,%ebp
   0x000055f7fa99561d <+13>:  (bad)
   0x000055f7fa99561e <+14>:  (bad)
   0x000055f7fa99561f <+15>:  callq  0x55f7fa995300 <rl_initialize>
   0x000055f7fa995624 <+20>:  mov    0x261c8d(%rip),%rax       # 0x55f7fabf72b8
<rl_prep_term_function>
[...]
```

Note that the first instruction has become the int3 breakpoint (x86_64).

To instrument the readline() function, I used a bpftrace one-liner:

```
# bpftrace -e 'uprobe:/bin/bash:readline { @ = count() }'
Attaching 1 probe...
^C

@: 4
```

This counts the invocations of readline() in all running and future bash shells invoked while tracing, and prints the count and exits on Ctrl-C. When bpftrace stops running, the uprobe is removed, and the original instructions are restored.

2.8.2 Uprobes Interfaces

There are two interfaces for uprobes:

- Ftrace-based, via /sys/kernel/debug/tracing/uprobe_events: where uprobes can be enabled and disabled by writing configuration strings to this file
- perf_event_open(): as used by the perf(1) tool and, more recently, by BPF tracing, as support was added in the Linux 4.17 kernel (with the perf_uprobe pmu)

There is also a register_uprobe_event() kernel function, similar to register_kprobe(), but it is not exposed as an API.

2.8.3 BPF and uprobes

uprobes provides user-level dynamic instrumentation for BCC and bpftrace, and is used by numerous tools. The interfaces are:

- **BCC:** attach_uprobe() and attach_uretprobe()
- **bpftrace:** uprobe and uretprobe probe types

The uprobes interface in BCC supports instrumenting the beginning of a function or an arbitrary address, whereas bpftrace currently supports instrumenting the beginning of a function only. The uretprobes interface for both tracers instruments the return of the function.

As an example from BCC, the gethostlatency(8) tool instruments host resolution calls (DNS) via the resolver library calls getaddrinfo(3), gethostbyname(3), and so on:

```
# gethostlatency
TIME       PID    COMM              LATms  HOST
01:42:15   19488  curl              15.90  www.brendangregg.com
01:42:37   19476  curl              17.40  www.netflix.com
01:42:40   19481  curl              19.38  www.netflix.com
01:42:46   10111  DNS Res~er #659   28.70  www.google.com
```

The probes traced can be seen in the source to gethostlatency:

```
# grep attach_ gethostlatency.py
b.attach_uprobe(name="c", sym="getaddrinfo", fn_name="do_entry", pid=args.pid)
b.attach_uprobe(name="c", sym="gethostbyname", fn_name="do_entry",
b.attach_uprobe(name="c", sym="gethostbyname2", fn_name="do_entry",
b.attach_uretprobe(name="c", sym="getaddrinfo", fn_name="do_return",
b.attach_uretprobe(name="c", sym="gethostbyname", fn_name="do_return",
b.attach_uretprobe(name="c", sym="gethostbyname2", fn_name="do_return",
```

These are attach_uprobe() and attach_uretprobe() calls. The user-level functions can be seen after the "sym=" assignment.

As an example from bpftrace, these one-liners list and then count the invocations of all the gethost functions from the libc system library:

```
# bpftrace -l 'uprobe:/lib/x86_64-linux-gnu/libc.so.6:gethost*'
uprobe:/lib/x86_64-linux-gnu/libc.so.6:gethostbyname
uprobe:/lib/x86_64-linux-gnu/libc.so.6:gethostbyname2
uprobe:/lib/x86_64-linux-gnu/libc.so.6:gethostname
uprobe:/lib/x86_64-linux-gnu/libc.so.6:gethostid
[...]
# bpftrace -e 'uprobe:/lib/x86_64-linux-gnu/libc.so.6:gethost* { @[probe] =
count(); }'
Attaching 10 probes...
^C

@[uprobe:/lib/x86_64-linux-gnu/libc.so.6:gethostname]: 2
```

This output shows that the gethostname() function was called twice during tracing.

2.8.4   uprobes Overhead and Future Work

uprobes can attach to events that fire millions of times per second, such as the user-level alloca-tion routines: malloc() and free(). Even though BPF is performance optimized, multiplying a tiny amount of overhead by millions of times per second adds up. In some cases, malloc() and free() tracing, which should be go-to use cases for BPF, can slow the target application tenfold (10x) or more. This prohibits its use in these cases; such slowdowns are acceptable only when trouble-shooting in a test environment, or in an already-broken production environment. Chapter 18 includes a section on the frequency of operations to help you work around this limitation. You need to be aware of which events are frequent to avoid tracing them if possible, and to look for slower events that you can trace instead to solve the same issue.

There may be a large improvement for user-space tracing in the future—perhaps even by the time you read this. Instead of continuing to use the current uprobes approach, which traps into the kernel, a shared-library solution is being discussed, which would provide BPF tracing of user space without the kernel mode switch. This approach has been in use by LTTng-UST for years, with performance measured at 10x to 100x faster [45].

2.8.5   uprobes Additional Reading

For more information, see Documentation/trace/uprobetracer.txt in the Linux kernel source [46].

2.9 Tracepoints

Tracepoints are used for kernel static instrumentation. They involve tracing calls that developers have inserted into the kernel code at logical places; those calls are then compiled into the kernel binary. Developed by Mathieu Desnoyers in 2007, tracepoints were originally called Kernel Markers, and they were made available in the Linux 2.6.32 release in 2009. Table 2-7 compares kprobes and tracepoints.

Table 2-7   kprobes to Tracepoints Comparison

Detail	kprobes	Tracepoints
Type	Dynamic	Static
Rough number of events	50,000+	100+
Kernel maintenance	None	Required
Disabled overhead	None	Tiny (NOPs and metadata)
Stable API	No	Yes

Tracepoints are a burden for kernel developers to maintain, and tracepoints are far more limited in scope than kprobes. The advantage is that tracepoints provide a stable API[24]: Tools written to use tracepoints should continue working across newer kernel versions, whereas those written using kprobes may break if the traced function is renamed or changed.

You should always try to use tracepoints first, if available and sufficient, and turn to kprobes only as a backup.

The format of tracepoints is *subsystem:eventname* (for example, kmem:kmalloc) [47]. Tracers refer to the first component using different terms: as a system, subsystem, class, or provider.

2.9.1 Adding Tracepoint Instrumentation

As an example of a tracepoint, this section explains how sched:sched_process_exec is added to the kernel.

There are header files for tracepoints in include/trace/events. This is from sched.h:

```
#define TRACE_SYSTEM sched
[...]
/*
 * Tracepoint for exec:
 */
TRACE_EVENT(sched_process_exec,
```

---

24 I'd call it "best-effort stable." It is rare, but I have seen tracepoints change.

```
        TP_PROTO(struct task_struct *p, pid_t old_pid,
                struct linux_binprm *bprm),

        TP_ARGS(p, old_pid, bprm),

        TP_STRUCT__entry(
                __string(   filename,      bprm->filename)
                __field(       pid_t,         pid           )
                __field(       pid_t,         old_pid       )
        ),

        TP_fast_assign(
                __assign_str(filename, bprm->filename);
                __entry->pid          = p->pid;
                __entry->old_pid     = old_pid;
        ),

        TP_printk("filename=%s pid=%d old_pid=%d", __get_str(filename),
                __entry->pid, __entry->old_pid)
);
```

This code defines the trace system as sched and the tracepoint name as sched_process_exec. The lines that follow define metadata, including a "format string" in TP_printk()—a helpful summary that is included when tracepoints are recorded with the perf(1) tool.

The previous information is also available at runtime via the Ftrace framework in /sys, via format files for each tracepoint. For example:

```
# cat /sys/kernel/debug/tracing/events/sched/sched_process_exec/format
name: sched_process_exec
ID: 298
format:
        field:unsigned short common_type;    offset:0;    size:2; signed:0;
        field:unsigned char common_flags;    offset:2;    size:1; signed:0;
        field:unsigned char common_preempt_count;    offset:3; size:1; signed:0;
        field:int common_pid;  offset:4;     size:4;      signed:1;

        field:__data_loc char[] filename;    offset:8;    size:4; signed:1;
        field:pid_t pid;             offset:12;   size:4;       signed:1;
        field:pid_t old_pid;         offset:16;   size:4;       signed:1;

print fmt: "filename=%s pid=%d old_pid=%d", __get_str(filename), REC->pid,
REC->old_pid
```

This format file is processed by tracers to understand the metadata associated with a tracepoint.

The following tracepoint is called from the kernel source in fs/exec.c, via trace_sched_process_exec():

```
static int exec_binprm(struct linux_binprm *bprm)
{
        pid_t old_pid, old_vpid;
        int ret;

        /* Need to fetch pid before load_binary changes it */
        old_pid = current->pid;
        rcu_read_lock();
        old_vpid = task_pid_nr_ns(current, task_active_pid_ns(current->parent));
        rcu_read_unlock();

        ret = search_binary_handler(bprm);
        if (ret >= 0) {
                audit_bprm(bprm);
                trace_sched_process_exec(current, old_pid, bprm);
                ptrace_event(PTRACE_EVENT_EXEC, old_vpid);
                proc_exec_connector(current);
        }
[...]
```

The trace_sched_process_exec() function marks the location of the tracepoint.

2.9.2 How Tracepoints Work

It is important that the not-enabled overhead of tracepoints be as tiny as possible, to avoid paying a performance tax for something that is not in use. Mathieu Desnoyers accomplished this by using a technique called "static jump patching."[25] It works like this, provided that a necessary compiler feature is available (asm goto):

1. At kernel compile time, an instruction is added at the tracepoint location that does nothing. The actual instruction used depends on the architecture: For x86_64, it is a 5-byte no-operation (nop) instruction. This size is used so that it can be later replaced with a 5-byte jump (jmp) instruction.

2. A tracepoint handler (trampoline) is also added to the end of the function, which iterates over an array of registered tracepoint probe callbacks. This increases the instruction text size a little (as a trampoline, it is a small routine, so execution jumps in and then immediately bounces out), which may have a small impact on the instruction cache.

---

25 Earlier versions used load immediate instructions, where the operand could be patched between 0 and 1 to control flow to a tracepoint [Desnoyers 09a][Desnoyers 09b]; however, this was not upstreamed, in favor of jump patching.

3. At runtime, when a tracer enables the tracepoint (it may already be in use by other running tracers):

   a. The array of tracepoint callbacks is modified to add a new callback for the tracer, synchronized through RCU.

   b. If the tracepoint was previously disabled, the nop location is rewritten to a jump to the tracepoint trampoline.

4. When a tracer disables the tracepoint:

   a. The array of tracepoint callbacks is modified to remove the callback, synchronized through RCU.

   b. If the last callback is removed, the static jump is rewritten back to a nop.

This minimizes the overhead of the not-enabled tracepoint such that it should be negligible.

If asm goto is not available, a fallback technique is used: Instead of patching a nop with a jmp, a conditional branch is used, based on a variable read from memory.

2.9.3   Tracepoint Interfaces

There are two interfaces for tracepoints:

- Ftrace-based, via /sys/kernel/debug/tracing/events: which has subdirectories for each tracepoint system, and files for each tracepoint itself (tracepoints can be enabled and disabled by writing to these files.)

- perf_event_open(): as used by the perf(1) tool and, more recently, by BPF tracing (via the perf_tracepoint pmu).

2.9.4   Tracepoints and BPF

Tracepoints provide kernel static instrumentation for BCC and bpftrace. The interfaces are:

- **BCC:** TRACEPOINT_PROBE()

- **bpftrace:** The tracepoint probe type

BPF supported tracepoints in Linux 4.7, but I developed many BCC tools prior to that support and had to use kprobes instead. This means that there are fewer tracepoint examples in BCC than I would like, due simply to the order in which support was developed.

An interesting example of BCC and tracepoints is the tcplife(8) tool. It prints one-line summaries of TCP sessions with various details (and is covered in more detail in Chapter 10):

```
# tcplife
PID    COMM       LADDR         LPORT RADDR         RPORT TX_KB RX_KB MS
22597  recordProg 127.0.0.1     46644 127.0.0.1     28527     0     0 0.23
3277   redis-serv 127.0.0.1     28527 127.0.0.1     46644     0     0 0.28
22598  curl       100.66.3.172  61620 52.205.89.26  80        0     1 91.79
```

```
22604 curl      100.66.3.172   44400 52.204.43.121   80      0   1 121.38
22624 recordProg 127.0.0.1     46648 127.0.0.1       28527   0   0 0.22
[...]
```

I wrote this tool before a suitable tracepoint existed in the Linux kernel, so I used a kprobe on the tcp_set_state() kernel function. A suitable tracepoint was added in Linux 4.16: sock:inet_sock_set_state. I modified the tool to support both so that it would run on both older and newer kernels. The tool defines two programs—one for tracepoints and one for kprobes—and then chooses which to run with the following test:

```
if (BPF.tracepoint_exists("sock", "inet_sock_set_state")):
    bpf_text += bpf_text_tracepoint
else:
    bpf_text += bpf_text_kprobe
```

As an example of bpftrace and tracepoints, the following one-liner instruments the sched:sched_process_exec tracepoint shown earlier:

```
# bpftrace -e 'tracepoint:sched:sched_process_exec { printf("exec by %s\n", comm); }'
Attaching 1 probe...
exec by ls
exec by date
exec by sleep
^C
```

This bpftrace one-liner prints out the process names that called exec().

2.9.5 BPF Raw Tracepoints

Alexei Starovoitov developed a new interface for tracepoints called BPF_RAW_TRACEPOINT, which was added to Linux 4.17 in 2018. It avoids the cost of creating the stable tracepoint arguments, which may not be needed, and exposes the raw arguments to the tracepoint. In a way, this is like accessing tracepoints as though they were kprobes: You end up with an unstable API, but you get access to more fields, and don't pay the usual tracepoint performance taxes. It is also a little more stable than using kprobes, since the tracepoint probe names are stable, and only the arguments are not.

Alexei showed that the performance with BPF_RAW_TRACEPOINT was better than with both kprobes and standard tracepoints, with results from a stress test [48]:

```
samples/bpf/test_overhead performance on 1 cpu:

tracepoint    base   kprobe+bpf tracepoint+bpf raw_tracepoint+bpf
task_rename   1.1M   769K       947K           1.0M
urandom_read  789K   697K       750K           755K
```

This may be especially interesting for technologies that instrument tracepoints 24x7, to minimize the overhead of enabled tracepoints.

2.9.6 Additional Reading

For more information, see Documentation/trace/tracepoints.rst in the kernel source, by Mathieu Desnoyers [47].

2.10 USDT

User-level statically defined tracing (USDT) provides a user-space version of tracepoints. USDT has been implemented for BCC by Sasha Goldshtein, and for bpftrace by myself and Matheus Marchini.

There are numerous tracing or logging technologies for user-level software, and many applications come with their own custom event loggers that can be enabled when needed. What makes USDT different is that it relies on an external system tracer to activate. The USDT points in an application can't be used, and they do nothing, without an external tracer.

USDT was made popular by the DTrace utility from Sun Microsystems, and it is now available in many applications.[26] Linux has developed a way to make use of USDT, which came from the SystemTap tracer. The BCC and bpftrace tracing tools make use of this work, and both can instrument USDT events.

One leftover from DTrace is still evident: Many applications do not compile USDT probes by default but require a configuration option such as `--enable-dtrace-probes` or `--with-dtrace`.

2.10.1 Adding USDT Instrumentation

USDT probes can be added to an application either using the headers and tools from the systemtap-sdt-dev package, or with custom headers. These probes define macros that can be placed at logical locations in your code to create USDT instrumentation points. The BCC project contains a USDT code example under examples/usdt_sample, which can be compiled using systemtap-sdt-dev headers or headers from Facebook's Folly[27] C++ library [11]. In the next section, I step through an example of using Folly.

Folly

The steps to add USDT instrumentation using Folly are:

1. Add the header file to the target source code:

   ```
   #include "folly/tracing/StaticTracepoint.h"
   ```

---

26 In some small part, this occurred through my own efforts: I promoted USDT, added USDT probes to Firefox for JavaScript inspection and other applications, and supported development efforts for other USDT providers.
27 Folly is a loose acronym of Facebook Open Source Library.

2. Add USDT probes to the target locations, of the format:

```
FOLLY_SDT(provider, name, arg1, arg2, ...)
```

The "provider" groups the probes, the "name" is the name of the probe, and then optional arguments are listed. The BCC USDT example contains:

```
FOLLY_SDT(usdt_sample_lib1, operation_start, operationId,
request.input().c_str());
```

This defines the probe as usdt_sample_lib1:operation_start, with the two arguments provided. The USDT example also contains an operation_end probe.

3. Build the software. You can check that the USDT probe exists by using readelf(1):

```
$ readelf -n usdt_sample_lib1/libusdt_sample_lib1.so
[...]
Displaying notes found in: .note.stapsdt
  Owner                 Data size  Description
  stapsdt               0x00000047 NT_STAPSDT (SystemTap probe descriptors)
    Provider: usdt_sample_lib1
    Name: operation_end
    Location: 0x000000000000fdd2, Base: 0x0000000000000000, Semaphore:
0x0000000000000000
    Arguments: -8@%rbx -8@%rax
  stapsdt               0x0000004f NT_STAPSDT (SystemTap probe descriptors)
    Provider: usdt_sample_lib1
    Name: operation_start
    Location: 0x000000000000febe, Base: 0x0000000000000000, Semaphore:
0x0000000000000000
    Arguments: -8@-104(%rbp) -8@%rax
```

The -n option to readelf(1) prints the notes section, which should show information about the compiled USDT probes.

4. Optional: Sometimes the arguments you'd like to add to a probe are not readily available at the probe location, and must be constructed using CPU-expensive function calls. To avoid making these calls all the time when the probe is not in use, you can add a probe semaphore to the source file outside of the function:

```
FOLLY_SDT_DEFINE_SEMAPHORE(provider, name)
```

Then the probe point can become:

```
if (FOLLY_SDT_IS_ENABLED(provider, name)) {
    ... expensive argument processing ...
    FOLLY_SDT_WITH_SEMAPHORE(provider, name, arg1, arg2, ...);
}
```

Now the expensive argument processing occurs only when the probe is in use (enabled). The semaphore address will be visible in readelf(1), and tracing tools can set it when the probe is used.

This does complicate tracing tools a little: When semaphore-protected probes are in use, these tracing tools typically need to have a PID specified so that they set the semaphore for that PID.

2.10.2 How USDT Works

When applications are compiled, a no-operation (nop) instruction is placed at the address of the USDT probe. This address is then dynamically changed by the kernel to a breakpoint when instrumented, using uprobes.

As with uprobes, I can illustrate USDT in action, although it's a little more work. The location of the probe from the previous readelf(1) output was 0x6a2. This is the offset from the binary segment, so you must first learn where that begins. This can vary thanks to position independent executables (PIE), which make more effective use of address space layout randomization (ASLR):

```
# gdb -p 4777
[...]
(gdb) info proc mappings
process 4777
Mapped address spaces:

       Start Addr         End Addr    Size   Offset objfile
    0x55a75372a000   0x55a75372b000   0x1000      0x0 /home/bgregg/Lang/c/tick
    0x55a75392a000   0x55a75392b000   0x1000      0x0 /home/bgregg/Lang/c/tick
    0x55a75392b000   0x55a75392c000   0x1000   0x1000 /home/bgregg/Lang/c/tick
[...]
```

The start address is 0x55a75372a000. Printing out the instruction at that address plus the offset of the probe, 0x6a2:

```
(gdb) disas 0x55a75372a000 + 0x6a2
[...]
   0x000055a75372a695 <+11>: mov     %rsi,-0x20(%rbp)
   0x000055a75372a699 <+15>: movl    $0x0,-0x4(%rbp)
   0x000055a75372a6a0 <+22>: jmp     0x55a75372a6c7 <main+61>
   0x000055a75372a6a2 <+24>: nop
   0x000055a75372a6a3 <+25>: mov     -0x4(%rbp),%eax
   0x000055a75372a6a6 <+28>: mov     %eax,%esi
   0x000055a75372a6a8 <+30>: lea     0xb5(%rip),%rdi      # 0x55a75372a764
[...]
```

And now with the USDT probe enabled:

```
(gdb) disas 0x55a75372a000 + 0x6a2
[...]
   0x000055a75372a695 <+11>: mov     %rsi,-0x20(%rbp)
   0x000055a75372a699 <+15>: movl    $0x0,-0x4(%rbp)
   0x000055a75372a6a0 <+22>: jmp     0x55a75372a6c7 <main+61>
   0x000055a75372a6a2 <+24>: int3
```

```
    0x000055a75372a6a3 <+25>: mov    -0x4(%rbp),%eax
    0x000055a75372a6a6 <+28>: mov    %eax,%esi
    0x000055a75372a6a8 <+30>: lea    0xb5(%rip),%rdi        # 0x55a75372a764
[...]
```

The nop instruction has changed to int3 (x86_64 breakpoint). When this breakpoint is hit, the kernel executes the attached BPF program with the arguments for the USDT probe. The nop instruction is restored when the USDT probe is deactivated.

2.10.3   BPF and USDT

USDT provides user-level static instrumentation for BCC and bpftrace. The interfaces are:

- **BCC**: USDT().enable_probe()
- **bpftrace**: The usdt probe type

For example, instrumenting the loop probe from the previous example:

```
# bpftrace -e 'usdt:/tmp/tick:loop { printf("got: %d\n", arg0); }'
Attaching 1 probe...
got: 0
got: 1
got: 2
got: 3
got: 4
^C
```

This bpftrace one-liner also printed out the integer argument passed to the probe.

2.10.4   USDT Additional Reading

More sources for understanding USDT:

- "Hacking Linux USDT with Ftrace" by Brendan Gregg [49]
- "USDT Probe Support in BPF/BCC" by Sasha Goldshtein [50]
- "USDT Tracing Report" by Dale Hamel [51]

2.11   Dynamic USDT

The USDT probes described previously are added to source code and compiled into the resulting binary, leaving nops at the instrumentation points and metadata in the ELF notes section. However, some languages, such as Java with the JVM, are interpreted or compiled on the fly. Dynamic USDT can be used to add instrumentation points in the Java code.

Note that the JVM already contains many USDT probes in its C++ code—for GC events, class loading, and other high-level activities. These USDT probes are instrumenting the function of the JVM. But USDT probes cannot be added to Java code that is compiled on the fly. USDT expects a pre-compiled ELF file with a notes section containing probe descriptions, and that doesn't exist for JIT-compiled Java code.

Dynamic USDT solves this by:

- Pre-compiling a shared library with the desired USDT probes embedded in functions. This shared library can be in C or C++, and it has an ELF notes section for the USDT probes. It can be instrumented like any other USDT probe.

- Loading the shared library when required with dlopen(3).

- Adding shared library calls from the target language. These can be implemented with an API that suits the language, hiding the underlying shared library call.

This has been implemented for Node.js and Python by Matheus Marchini in a library called libstapsdt,[28] which provides a way to define and call USDT probes in those languages. Support for other languages can usually be added by wrapping this library, as has been done by Dale Hamel for Ruby, using Ruby's C-extension support [54].

For example, in Node.js JavaScript:

```
const USDT = require("usdt");
const provider = new USDT.USDTProvider("nodeProvider");
const probe1 = provider.addProbe("requestStart","char *");
provider.enable();

[...]
probe1.fire(function() { return [currentRequestString]; });
[...]
```

The probe1.fire() call executes its anonymous function only if the probe was instrumented externally. Within this function, arguments can be processed (if necessary) before being passed to the probe, without concern about the non-enabled CPU cost of such argument processing since it is skipped if the probe was not in use.

libstapsdt automatically creates a shared library containing the USDT probes and ELF notes section at runtime, and it maps that section into the running program's address space.

---

28 For libstapsdt, see [52][53]. A new library called libusdt is being written for this purpose, and it might change the following code example. Check for future releases of libusdt.

2.12   PMCs

Performance monitoring counters (*PMCs*) are also known by other names, such as performance instrumentation counters (PICs), CPU performance counters (CPCs), and performance monitoring unit events (PMU events). These terms all refer to the same thing: programmable hardware counters on the processor.

While there are many PMCs, Intel has selected seven PMCs as an "architectural set" that provides a high-level overview of some core functions [Intel 16]. The presence of these architectural set PMCs can be checked using the CPUID instruction. Table 2-8 shows this set, which serves as an example of useful PMCs.

Table 2-8 **Intel Architectural PMCs**

Event Name	UMask	Event Select	Example Event Mask Mnemonic
UnHalted Core Cycles	00H	3CH	CPU_CLK_UNHALTED.THREAD_P
Instruction Retired	00H	C0H	INST_RETIRED.ANY_P
UnHalted Reference Cycles	01H	3CH	CPU_CLK_THREAD_UNHALTED.REF_XCLK
LLC References	4FH	2EH	LONGEST_LAT_CACHE.REFERENCE
LLC Misses	41H	2EH	LONGEST_LAT_CACHE.MISS
Branch Instruction Retired	00H	C4H	BR_INST_RETIRED.ALL_BRANCHES
Branch Misses Retired	00H	C5H	BR_MISP_RETIRED.ALL_BRANCHES

PMCs are a vital resource for performance analysis. Only through PMCs can you measure the efficiency of CPU instructions; the hit ratios of CPU caches; memory, interconnect, and device bus utilization; stall cycles; and so on. Using these measurements to analyze performance can lead to various small performance optimizations.

PMCs are also a strange resource. While there are hundreds of PMCs available, only a fixed number of registers (perhaps as few as six) are available in the CPUs to measure them at the same time. You need to choose which PMCs you'd like to measure on those six registers, or cycle through different PMC sets as a way of sampling them. (Linux perf(1) supports this cycling automatically.) Other software counters do not suffer from these constraints.

2.12.1   PMC Modes

PMCs can be used in one of two modes:

- **Counting:** In this mode, PMCs keep track of the rate of events. The kernel can read the count whenever desired, such as for fetching per-second metrics. The overhead of this mode is practically zero.

- **Overflow Sampling:** In this mode, the PMCs can send interrupts to the kernel for the events they are monitoring, so that the kernel can collect extra state. The events monitored can occur millions or billions of times per second; sending an interrupt for each one would grind the system to a near halt. The solution is to take a sample of events by using a programmable counter that signals the kernel when the counter overflows (e.g., once every 10,000 LLC cache miss or once every 1 million stall cycles).

The sampling mode is most interesting for BPF tracing since it generates events that you can instrument with custom BPF programs. Both BCC and bpftrace support PMC events.

2.12.2 PEBS

Overflow sampling may not record the correct instruction pointer that triggered an event due to interrupt latency (often called "skid") or out-of-order instruction execution. For CPU cycle profiling, such skid may not be a problem, and some profilers deliberately introduce jitter to avoid lockstep sampling (or use an offset sampling rate, such as 99 Hertz). But for measuring other events, such as LLC misses, the sampled instruction pointer needs to be accurate.

Intel has developed a solution called *precise event-based sampling* (PEBS). PEBS uses hardware buffers to record the correct instruction pointer at the time of the PMC event. The Linux perf_events framework supports using PEBS.

2.12.3 Cloud Computing

Many cloud computing environments have not yet provided PMC access to their guests. It is technically possible to enable it; for example, the Xen hypervisor has the vpmu command line option, which allows different sets of PMCs to be exposed to guests [55].[29] Amazon has enabled many PMCs for its Nitro hypervisor guests.

2.13 perf_events

The perf_events facility is used by the perf(1) command for sampling and tracing, and it was added to Linux 2.6.21 in 2009. Importantly, perf(1) and its perf_events facility have received a lot of attention and development over the years, and BPF tracers can make calls to perf_events to use its features. BCC and bpftrace first used perf_events for its ring buffer, and then for PMC instrumentation, and now for all event instrumentation via perf_event_open().

While BPF tracing tools make use of perf(1)'s internals, an interface for BPF has been developed and added to perf(1) as well, making perf(1) another BPF tracer. Unlike with BCC and bpftrace, the source code to perf(1) is in the Linux tree, so perf(1) is the only BPF front-end tracer that is built into Linux.

---

29 I wrote the Xen code that allows different PMC modes: ipc for instructions-per-cycle PMCs only, and arch for the Intel architectural set. My code was just a firewall on the existing vpmu support in Xen.

perf(1) BPF is still under development and is difficult to use. Covering it is beyond the scope of these chapters, which focus on BCC and bpftrace tools. An example of perf BPF is included in Appendix D.

2.14 Summary

BPF performance tools make use of many technologies, including extended BPF, kernel and user dynamic instrumentation (kprobes and uprobes), kernel and user static tracing (tracepoints and user markers), and perf_events. BPF can also fetch stack traces by using frame pointer–based walks or ORC for kernel stacks, and these can be visualized as flame graphs. These technologies are covered in this chapter, including references for further reading.

Chapter 3

Performance Analysis

The tools in this book can be used for performance analysis, troubleshooting, security analysis, and more. To help you understand how to apply them, this chapter provides a crash course in performance analysis.

Learning objectives:

- Understand the goals and activities of performance analysis
- Perform workload characterization
- Perform the USE method
- Perform drill-down analysis
- Understand checklist methodologies
- Find quick performance wins using traditional tools and the 60-second Linux checklist
- Find quick performance wins using the BCC/BPF tool checklist

This chapter begins by describing the goals and activities of performance analysis, and then it summarizes methodologies followed by traditional (non-BPF) tools that can be tried first. These traditional tools will help you find quick performance wins outright or provide clues and context for later BPF-based analysis. A checklist of BPF tools is included at the end of the chapter, and many more BPF tools are included in later chapters.

3.1 Overview

Before diving in to performance analysis, it can help to think about what your goals are and the different activities that can help you accomplish them.

3.1.1   Goals

In general, the goals of performance analysis are to improve end-user performance and to reduce operating cost. It helps to state a performance goal in terms of something measurable; such a measurement can show when the performance goal has been met, or to quantify the shortfall. Measurements include:

- **Latency:** How long to accomplish a request or operation, typically measured in milliseconds
- **Rate:** An operation or request rate per second
- **Throughput:** Typically data movement in bits or bytes per second
- **Utilization:** How busy a resource is over time as a percentage
- **Cost:** The price/performance ratio

End-user performance can be quantified as the time an application takes to respond to user requests, and the goal is to make this time shorter. This time spent waiting is often termed *latency*. It can be improved by analyzing request time and breaking it down into components: the time running on CPU and what code is running; the time waiting for resources such as disks, networking, and locks; the time waiting for a turn by the CPU scheduler; and so on. It is possible to write a BPF tool to directly trace application request time plus latency from many different components at once. Such a tool would be application specific and could incur significant overhead in tracing many different events simultaneously. In practice, smaller specific tools are often used to study time and latency from specific components. This book includes many such smaller and specific tools.

Reducing operating cost can involve observing how software and hardware resources are used and looking for optimizations, with the goal of reducing your company's cloud or datacenter spend. This can involve a different type of analysis, such as summarizing or logging how components are used rather than the time or latency of their response. Many tools in this book support this goal as well.

Bear these goals in mind when doing performance analysis. With BPF tools, it is far too easy to generate lots of numbers, and then spend hours trying to understand a metric that turns out to be unimportant. As a performance engineer, I've been sent screenshots of tool output by developers worried about an apparently bad metric. My first question is often "Do you have a known performance issue?" Their answer is often "No, we just thought this output looked...interesting." It may well be interesting, but I first need to determine the goal: are we trying to reduce request latency, or operating costs? The goal sets the context for further analysis.

3.1.2   Activities

BPF performance tools can be used for more than just analyzing a given issue. Consider the following list of performance activities [Gregg 13b] and how BPF performance tools can be of use for each of them:

	Performance Activity	BPF Performance Tools
1	Performance characterization of prototype software or hardware	To measure latency histograms under different workloads
2	Performance analysis of development code, pre-integration	To solve performance bottlenecks and find general performance improvements
3	Perform non-regression testing of software builds, pre- or post-release	To record code usage and latency from different sources, enabling faster resolution of regressions
4	Benchmarking/benchmarketing for software releases	To study performance to find opportunities to improve benchmark numbers
5	Proof-of-concept testing in the target environment	To generate latency histograms to ensure that performance meets request latency service level agreements
6	Monitoring of running production software	To create tools that can run 24x7 to expose new metrics that would otherwise be blind spots
7	Performance analysis of issues	To solve a given performance issue with tools and custom instrumentation, as needed

It may be obvious that many of the tools in this book are suitable for studying given performance issues, but also consider how they can improve monitoring, non-regression testing, and other activities.

3.1.3 Mulitple Performance Issues

When using the tools described in this book, be prepared to find multiple performance issues. The problem becomes identifying which issue matters the most: It's usually the one that is most affecting request latency or cost. If you aren't expecting to find multiple performance issues, try to find the bug tracker for your application, database, file system, or software component, and search for the word "performance." There are often multiple outstanding performance issues, as well as some not yet listed in the tracker. It's all about finding what matters the most.

Any given issue may also have multiple causes. Many times when you fix one cause, others become apparent. Or, when you fix one cause, another component then becomes the bottleneck.

3.2 Performance Methodologies

With so many performance tools and capabilities available (e.g., kprobes, uprobes, tracepoints, USDT, PMCs; see Chapter 2) it can be difficult to know what to do with all the data they provide. For many years, I've been studying, creating, and documenting performance methodologies. A *methodology* is a process you can follow that provides a starting point, steps, and an ending point. My prior book, *Systems Performance*, documents dozens of performance methodologies [Gregg 13b]. I'll summarize a few of them here that you can follow with BPF tools.

3.2.1 Workload Characterization

The aim of workload characterization is to understand the applied workload. You do not need to analyze the resulting performance, such as the latency suffered. The biggest performance wins I've found have been ones of "eliminating unnecessary work." Such wins can be found by studying what the workload is composed of.

Suggested steps for performing workload characterization:

1. Who is causing the load (e.g., PID, process name, UID, IP address)?

2. Why is the load called (code path, stack trace, flame graph)?

3. What is the load (IOPS, throughput, type)?

4. How is the load changing over time (per-interval summaries)?

Many of the tools in this book can help you answer these questions. For example, vfsstat(8):

```
# vfsstat
TIME        READ/s  WRITE/s CREATE/s   OPEN/s  FSYNC/s
18:35:32:      231       12        4       98        0
18:35:33:      274       13        4      106        0
18:35:34:      586       86        4      251        0
18:35:35:      241       15        4       99        0
18:35:36:      232       10        4       98        0
[...]
```

This shows details of the workload applied at the virtual file system (VFS) level and answers step 3 by providing the types and operation rates, and step 4 by providing the per-interval summary over time.

As a simple example of step 1, I'll switch to bpftrace and a one-liner (output truncated):

```
# bpftrace -e 'kprobe:vfs_read { @[comm] = count(); }'
Attaching 1 probe...
^C

@[rtkit-daemon]: 1
[...]
@[gnome-shell]: 207
@[Chrome_IOThread]: 222
@[chrome]: 225
@[InputThread]: 302
@[gdbus]: 819
@[Web Content]: 1725
```

This shows that processes named "Web Content" performed 1725 vfs_read()s while I was tracing.

More examples of tools for working through these steps can be found throughout this book, including the flame graphs in later chapters, which can be used for step 2.

If the target of your analysis does not already have a tool available, you can create your own workload characterization tools to answer these questions.

3.2.2   Drill-Down Analysis

Drill-down analysis involves examining a metric, and then finding ways to decompose it into its components, and then decomposing the largest component into its own components, and so on until a root cause or causes has been found.

An analogy may help explain this. Imagine that you discover you have an unusually large credit card bill. To analyze it, you log in to your bank and look at the transactions. There, you discover one large charge to an online bookstore. You then log in to that bookstore to see which books led to that amount and discover that you accidentally purchased 1000 copies of this very book (thank you!). This is drill-down analysis: finding a clue and then drilling deeper, led by further clues, until the problem is solved.

Suggested steps for drill-down analysis:

1. Start examining the highest level.

2. Examine next-level details.

3. Pick the most interesting breakdown or clue.

4. If the problem is unsolved, go back to step 2.

Drill-down analysis can involve custom tooling, which is better suited to bpftrace than to BCC.

One type of drill-down analysis involves decomposing latency into its contributing components. Imagine this analysis sequence:

1. Request latency is 100 ms (milliseconds).

2. This is 10 ms running on CPU, and 90 ms blocked off CPU.

3. The off-CPU time is 89 ms blocked on the file system.

4. The file system is spending 3 ms blocked on locks, and 86 ms blocked on storage devices.

Your conclusion here may be that the storage devices are the problem—and that is one answer. But drill-down analysis can also be used to sharpen context. Consider this alternate sequence:

1. An application is spending 89 ms blocked on the file system.

2. The file system is spending 78 ms blocked on file system writes, and 11 ms blocked on reads.

3. The file system writes are spending 77 ms blocked on access timestamp updates.

Your conclusion now is that file system access timestamps are the source of the latency, and they could be disabled (it is a mount option). This is a better outcome than concluding that faster disks were necessary.

3.2.3 USE Method

I developed the USE methodology for resource analysis [Gregg 13c].

For every resource, check:

1. Utilization

2. Saturation

3. Errors

Your first task is to find or draw a diagram of the software and hardware resources. You can then iterate over them, seeking these three metrics. Figure 3-1 shows examples of hardware targets for a generic system, including the components and buses that can be examined.

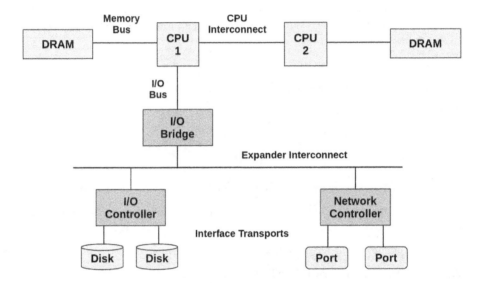

Figure 3-1   Hardware targets for USE method analysis

Consider your current monitoring tools and their ability to show utilization, saturation, and errors for every item in Figure 3-1. How many blind spots do you currently have?

An advantage of this methodology is that it begins with the questions that matter, rather than beginning with answers in the form of metrics and trying to work backward to find out why they matter. It also reveals blind spots: It begins with the questions you want answered, whether or not there is a convenient tool to measure them.

3.2.4 Checklists

A performance analysis checklist can list tools and metrics to run and check. They can focus on the low-hanging fruit: identifying a dozen or so common issues with analysis instructions for everyone to follow. These are well suited for execution by a wide variety of staff at your company, and can allow you to scale your skills.

The following sections introduce two checklists: one using traditional (non-BPF) tools suitable for a quick analysis (the first 60 seconds) and the other a list of BCC tools to try early on.

3.3 Linux 60-Second Analysis

This checklist can be used for any performance issue and reflects what I typically execute in the first 60 seconds after logging into a poorly performing Linux system. This was published by myself and the Netflix performance engineering team [56]:

The tools to run are:

1. uptime
2. dmesg | tail
3. vmstat 1
4. mpstat -P ALL 1
5. pidstat 1
6. iostat -xz 1
7. free -m
8. sar -n DEV 1
9. sar -n TCP,ETCP 1
10. top

The following sections explain each of these tools. It might seem out of place to discuss non-BPF tools in a BPF book, but not to do so would miss out on an important resource that is already available. These commands may enable you to solve some performance issues outright. If not, they may reveal clues about where the performance problems are, directing your use of follow-up BPF tools to find the real issue.

3.3.1 uptime

```
$ uptime
03:16:59 up 17 days,  4:18,  1 user,  load average: 2.74, 2.54, 2.58
```

This is a quick way to view the load averages, which indicate the number of tasks (processes) wanting to run. On Linux systems, these numbers include processes wanting to run on the CPUs, as well as processes blocked in uninterruptible I/O (usually disk I/O). This gives a high-level idea of resource load (or demand), which can then be further explored using other tools.

The three numbers are exponentially damped moving sum averages with a 1-minute, 5-minute, and 15-minute constant. The three numbers give you some idea of how load is changing over time. In the example above, the load averages show a small recent increase.

Load averages can be worth checking when first responding to an issue to see if the issue is still present. In fault-tolerant environments, a server experiencing a performance issue may be automatically removed from service by the time you can log in to take a look. A high 15-minute load average coupled with a low 1-minute load average can be a sign that you logged in too late to catch the issue.

3.3.2   dmesg | tail

```
$ dmesg | tail
[1880957.563150] perl invoked oom-killer: gfp_mask=0x280da, order=0, oom_score_adj=0
[...]
[1880957.563400] Out of memory: Kill process 18694 (perl) score 246 or sacrifice child
[1880957.563408] Killed process 18694 (perl) total-vm:1972392kB, anon-rss:1953348kB,
file-rss:0kB
[2320864.954447] TCP: Possible SYN flooding on port 7001. Dropping request.  Check
SNMP counters.
```

This shows the past 10 system messages, if any. Look for errors that can cause performance issues. The example above includes the out-of-memory killer and TCP dropping a request. The TCP message even points you to the next area for analysis: SNMP counters.

3.3.3   vmstat 1

```
$ vmstat 1
procs ---------memory---------- ---swap-- -----io---- -system-- ------cpu-----
 r  b swpd   free   buff  cache   si   so    bi    bo   in   cs us sy id wa st
34  0    0 200889792 73708 591828    0    0     0     5    6   10 96  1  3  0  0
32  0    0 200889920 73708 591860    0    0     0   592 13284 4282 98  1  1  0  0
32  0    0 200890112 73708 591860    0    0     0     0 9501 2154 99  1  0  0  0
[...]
```

This is the virtual memory statistics tool that originated in BSD, which also shows other system metrics. When invoked with the argument 1, it prints 1-second summaries; be aware that the first line of numbers is the summary *since boot* (with the exception of the memory counters).

Columns to check:

- **r:** The number of processes running on CPU and waiting for a turn. This provides a better signal than load averages for determining CPU saturation, as it does not include I/O. To interpret: an "r" value greater than the CPU count indicates saturation.

- **free:** Free memory, in Kbytes. If there are too many digits to count, you probably have enough free memory. The free -m command, included in Section 3.3.7 better explains the state of free memory.

- **si and so:** Swap-ins and swap-outs. If these are non-zero, you're out of memory. These are only in use if swap devices are configured.

- **us, sy, id, wa, and st:** These are breakdowns of CPU time, on average, across all CPUs. They are user time, system time (kernel), idle, wait I/O, and stolen time (by other guests, or, with Xen, the guest's own isolated driver domain).

The example shows that CPU time is mostly in user mode. This should direct your next steps to analyze the running user-level code using profilers.

3.3.4 mpstat -P ALL 1

```
$ mpstat -P ALL 1
[...]
03:16:41 AM  CPU    %usr   %nice  %sys %iowait  %irq  %soft %steal %guest %gnice  %idle
03:16:42 AM  all   14.27   0.00  0.75    0.44  0.00   0.00   0.06   0.00   0.00  84.48
03:16:42 AM    0  100.00   0.00  0.00    0.00  0.00   0.00   0.00   0.00   0.00   0.00
03:16:42 AM    1    0.00   0.00  0.00    0.00  0.00   0.00   0.00   0.00   0.00 100.00
03:16:42 AM    2    8.08   0.00  0.00    0.00  0.00   0.00   0.00   0.00   0.00  91.92
03:16:42 AM    3   10.00   0.00  1.00    0.00  0.00   0.00   1.00   0.00   0.00  88.00
03:16:42 AM    4    1.01   0.00  0.00    0.00  0.00   0.00   0.00   0.00   0.00  98.99
03:16:42 AM    5    5.10   0.00  0.00    0.00  0.00   0.00   0.00   0.00   0.00  94.90
03:16:42 AM    6   11.00   0.00  0.00    0.00  0.00   0.00   0.00   0.00   0.00  89.00
03:16:42 AM    7   10.00   0.00  0.00    0.00  0.00   0.00   0.00   0.00   0.00  90.00
[...]
```

This command prints per-CPU time broken down into states. The output reveals a problem: CPU 0 has hit 100% user time, evidence of a single-thread bottleneck.

Also look out for high %iowait time, which can be explored with disk I/O tools, and high %sys time, which can be explored with syscall and kernel tracing, as well as CPU profiling.

3.3.5 pidstat 1

```
$ pidstat 1
Linux 4.13.0-19-generic (...)       08/04/2018     _x86_64_    (16 CPU)

03:20:47 AM   UID       PID    %usr %system  %guest    %CPU   CPU  Command
03:20:48 AM     0      1307    0.00    0.98    0.00    0.98     8  irqbalance
03:20:48 AM    33     12178    4.90    0.00    0.00    4.90     4  java
03:20:48 AM    33     12569  476.47   24.51    0.00  500.98     0  java
03:20:48 AM     0    130249    0.98    0.98    0.00    1.96     1  pidstat

03:20:48 AM   UID       PID    %usr %system  %guest    %CPU   CPU  Command
03:20:49 AM    33     12178    4.00    0.00    0.00    4.00     4  java
03:20:49 AM    33     12569  331.00   21.00    0.00  352.00     0  java
03:20:49 AM     0    129906    1.00    0.00    0.00    1.00     8  sshd
03:20:49 AM     0    130249    1.00    1.00    0.00    2.00     1  pidstat
```

```
03:20:49 AM   UID       PID   %usr %system  %guest     %CPU  CPU  Command
03:20:50 AM    33     12178   4.00    0.00    0.00     4.00    4  java
03:20:50 AM   113     12356   1.00    0.00    0.00     1.00   11  snmp-pass
03:20:50 AM    33     12569 210.00   13.00    0.00   223.00    0  java
03:20:50 AM     0    130249   1.00    0.00    0.00     1.00    1  pidstat
[...]
```

pidstat(1) shows CPU usage per process. top(1) is a popular tool for this purpose; however, pidstat(1) provides rolling output by default so that variation over time can be seen. This output shows that a Java process is consuming a variable amount of CPU each second; these percentages are summed across all CPUs,[1] so 500% is equivalent to five CPUs at 100%.

3.3.6   iostat -xz 1

```
$ iostat -xz 1
Linux 4.13.0-19-generic (...)        08/04/2018    _x86_64_      (16 CPU)
[...]
avg-cpu:  %user   %nice %system %iowait  %steal   %idle
          22.90    0.00    0.82    0.63    0.06   75.59

Device:         rrqm/s   wrqm/s    r/s     w/s    rkB/s   wkB/s avgrq-sz avgqu-sz
await r_await w_await  svctm  %util
nvme0n1           0.00  1167.00   0.00 1220.00    0.00 151293.00   248.02     2.10
1.72     0.00    1.72   0.21  26.00
nvme1n1           0.00  1164.00   0.00 1219.00    0.00 151384.00   248.37     0.90
0.74     0.00    0.74   0.19  23.60
md0               0.00     0.00   0.00 4770.00    0.00 303113.00   127.09     0.00
0.00     0.00    0.00   0.00   0.00
[...]
```

This tool shows storage device I/O metrics. The output columns for each disk device have line-wrapped here, making it difficult to read.

Columns to check:

- **r/s, w/s, rkB/s, and wkB/s:** These are the delivered reads, writes, read Kbytes, and write Kbytes per second to the device. Use these for workload characterization. A performance problem may simply be due to an excessive load having been applied.

- **await:** The average time for the I/O in milliseconds. This is the time that the application suffers, as it includes both time queued and time being serviced. Larger-than-expected average times can be an indicator of device saturation or device problems.

---

1 Note that a recent change to pidstat(1) capped percentages to 100% [36]. This led to output that was invalid for multi-threaded applications exceeding 100%. The change was eventually reverted, but be aware in case you encounter the changed version of pidstat(1).

- **avgqu-sz:** The average number of requests issued to the device. Values greater than one can be evidence of saturation (although devices, especially virtual devices that front multiple back-end disks, typically operate on requests in parallel.)

- **%util:** Device utilization. This is really a busy percentage, showing the time each second that the device was doing work. It does not show utilization in a capacity planning sense, as devices can operate on requests in parallel.[2] Values greater than 60% typically lead to poor performance (which should be seen in the await column), although it depends on the device. Values close to 100% usually indicate saturation.

The output shows a write workload of ~300 Mbytes/sec to the md0 virtual device, which looks like it is backed by both of the nvme0 devices.

3.3.7   free -m

```
$ free -m
              total        used        free      shared  buff/cache   available
Mem:         122872       39158        3107        1166       80607       81214
Swap:             0           0           0
```

This shows available memory in Mbytes. Check that the available value is not near zero; it shows how much real memory is available in the system, including in the buffer and page caches.[3] Having some memory in the cache improves file system performance.

3.3.8   sar -n DEV 1

```
$ sar -n DEV 1
Linux 4.13.0-19-generic (...)        08/04/2018    _x86_64_      (16 CPU)

03:38:28 AM     IFACE    rxpck/s    txpck/s     rxkB/s     txkB/s    rxcmp/s    txcmp/s   rxmcst/s    %ifutil
03:38:29 AM      eth0    7770.00    4444.00   10720.12    5574.74       0.00       0.00      0.00       0.00
03:38:29 AM        lo      24.00      24.00      19.63      19.63       0.00       0.00      0.00       0.00
```

---

2 This leads to the confusing situation where a device at 100% utilization as reported by iostat(1) may be able to accept a higher workload. It is just reporting that something was busy 100% of the time, but it was not 100% utilized: it could have accepted more work. The %util reported by iostat(1) is especially misleading for volumes backed by a pool of multiple disks, which have an increased ability to run work in parallel.

3 The output of free(1) has changed recently. It used to show buffers and cache as separate columns, and it left the available column as an exercise for the end user to calculate. I like the newer version better. The separate buffers and cached columns can be shown by using −w for wide mode.

```
03:38:29 AM    IFACE    rxpck/s   txpck/s    rxkB/s    txkB/s   rxcmp/s   txcmp/s
rxmcst/s    %ifutil
03:38:30 AM     eth0   5579.00   2175.00   7829.20   2626.93      0.00      0.00
0.00      0.00
03:38:30 AM       lo     33.00     33.00      1.79      1.79      0.00      0.00
0.00      0.00
[...]
```

The sar(1) tool has many modes for different groups of metrics. Here I'm using it to look at network device metrics. Check interface throughput rxkB/s and txkB/s to see if any limit may have been reached.

3.3.9   sar -n TCP,ETCP 1

```
# sar -n TCP,ETCP 1
Linux 4.13.0-19-generic (...)        08/04/2019       _x86_64_       (16 CPU)

03:41:01 AM   active/s passive/s    iseg/s    oseg/s
03:41:02 AM      1.00      1.00    348.00   1626.00

03:41:01 AM   atmptf/s  estres/s retrans/s isegerr/s   orsts/s
03:41:02 AM      0.00      0.00      1.00      0.00      0.00

03:41:02 AM   active/s passive/s    iseg/s    oseg/s
03:41:03 AM      0.00      0.00    521.00   2660.00

03:41:02 AM   atmptf/s  estres/s retrans/s isegerr/s   orsts/s
03:41:03 AM      0.00      0.00      0.00      0.00      0.00
[...]
```

Now we're using sar(1) to look at TCP metrics and TCP errors. Columns to check:

- **active/s**: Number of locally initiated TCP connections per second (e.g., via connect())
- **passive/s**: Number of remotely initiated TCP connections per second (e.g., via accept())
- **retrans/s**: Number of TCP retransmits per second

Active and passive connection counts are useful for workload characterization. Retransmits are a sign of a network or remote host issue.

3.3.10   top

```
top - 03:44:14 up 17 days,  4:46,  1 user,  load average: 2.32, 2.20, 2.21
Tasks: 474 total,   1 running, 473 sleeping,   0 stopped,   0 zombie
%Cpu(s): 29.7 us,  0.4 sy,  0.0 ni, 69.7 id,  0.1 wa,  0.0 hi,  0.0 si,  0.0 st
```

```
KiB Mem : 12582137+total,   3159704 free, 40109716 used, 82551960 buff/cache
KiB Swap:        0 total,         0 free,        0 used. 83151728 avail Mem

    PID USER       PR  NI    VIRT    RES    SHR S  %CPU %MEM     TIME+ COMMAND
  12569 www        20   0  2.495t 0.051t 0.018t S 484.7 43.3 13276:02 java
  12178 www        20   0 12.214g 3.107g  16540 S   4.9  2.6   553:41 java
 125312 root       20   0       0      0      0 S   1.0  0.0   0:13.20 kworker/u256:0

 128697 root       20   0       0      0      0 S   0.3  0.0   0:02.10 kworker/10:2
[...]
```

At this point you'll have already seen many of these metrics with prior tools, but it can be useful to double-check by finishing with the top(1) utility and browsing the system and process summaries.

With luck, this 60-second analysis will have helped you unearth a clue or two about the performance of your system. You can use these clues to jump to some related BPF tools for further analysis.

3.4 BCC Tool Checklist

This checklist is part of the BCC repository under docs/tutorial.md and was written by me [30]. It provides a generic checklist of BCC tools to work through:

1. `execsnoop`

2. `opensnoop`

3. `ext4slower` (or `btrfs*`, `xfs*`, `zfs*`)

4. `biolatency`

5. `biosnoop`

6. `cachestat`

7. `tcpconnect`

8. `tcpaccept`

9. `tcpretrans`

10. `runqlat`

11. `profile`

These tools expose more information for new processes, opened files, file system latency, disk I/O latency, file system cache performance, TCP connections and retransmits, scheduler latency, and CPU usage. They are covered in more detail in later chapters.

3.4.1   execsnoop

```
# execsnoop
PCOMM           PID     RET ARGS
supervise       9660     0 ./run
supervise       9661     0 ./run
mkdir           9662     0 /bin/mkdir -p ./main
run             9663     0 ./run
[...]
```

execsnoop(8) shows new process execution by printing one line of output for every execve(2) syscall. Check for short-lived processes, as these can consume CPU resources, but may not show up in most monitoring tools that periodically take snapshots of which processes are running. execsnoop(8) is covered in detail in Chapter 6.

3.4.2   opensnoop

```
# opensnoop
PID     COMM            FD ERR PATH
1565    redis-server     5   0 /proc/1565/stat
1603    snmpd            9   0 /proc/net/dev
1603    snmpd           11   0 /proc/net/if_inet6
1603    snmpd           -1   2 /sys/class/net/eth0/device/vendor
1603    snmpd           11   0 /proc/sys/net/ipv4/neigh/eth0/retrans_time_ms
1603    snmpd           11   0 /proc/sys/net/ipv6/neigh/eth0/retrans_time_ms
1603    snmpd           11   0 /proc/sys/net/ipv6/conf/eth0/forwarding
[...]
```

opensnoop(8) prints one line of output for each open(2) syscall (and its variants), including details of the path that was opened and whether it was successful (the "ERR" error column). Opened files can tell you a lot about how applications work: identifying their data files, config files, and log files. Sometimes applications can misbehave and perform poorly when they are constantly attempting to read files that do not exist. opensnoop(8) is covered in more detail in Chapter 8.

3.4.3   ext4slower

```
# ext4slower
Tracing ext4 operations slower than 10 ms
TIME     COMM           PID     T BYTES  OFF_KB   LAT(ms) FILENAME
06:35:01 cron           16464   R 1249   0          16.05 common-auth
06:35:01 cron           16463   R 1249   0          16.04 common-auth
06:35:01 cron           16465   R 1249   0          16.03 common-auth
06:35:01 cron           16465   R 4096   0          10.62 login.defs
06:35:01 cron           16464   R 4096   0          10.61 login.defs
[...]
```

ext4slower(8) traces common operations from the ext4 file system (reads, writes, opens, and syncs) and prints those that exceed a time threshold. This can identify or exonerate one type of performance issue: an application waiting on slow individual disk I/O via the file system. There are variants of ext4slower(8) for other file systems, including btrfsslower(8), xfsslower(8), and zfsslower(8). See Chapter 8 for more details.

3.4.4 biolatency

```
# biolatency -m
Tracing block device I/O... Hit Ctrl-C to end.
^C
     msecs               : count    distribution
       0 -> 1            : 16335    |****************************************|
       2 -> 3            : 2272     |*****                                   |
       4 -> 7            : 3603     |********                                |
       8 -> 15           : 4328     |**********                              |
      16 -> 31           : 3379     |********                                |
      32 -> 63           : 5815     |**************                          |
      64 -> 127          : 0        |                                        |
     128 -> 255          : 0        |                                        |
     256 -> 511          : 0        |                                        |
     512 -> 1023         : 1        |                                        |
```

biolatency(8) traces disk I/O latency (that is, the time from device issue to completion) and shows this as a histogram. This better explains disk I/O performance than the averages shown by iostat(1). Multiple modes can be examined. Modes are values that are more frequent than others in a distribution, and this example shows a multi-modal distribution with one mode between 0 and 1 milliseconds, and another mode centered around the 8- to 15-millisecond range.[4] Outliers are also visible: this screenshot shows a single outlier in the 512- to 1023-millisecond range. biolatency(8) is covered in more detail in Chapter 9.

3.4.5 biosnoop

```
# biosnoop
TIME(s)         COMM        PID    DISK   T  SECTOR    BYTES  LAT(ms)
0.000004001     supervise   1950   xvda1  W  13092560  4096     0.74
0.000178002     supervise   1950   xvda1  W  13092432  4096     0.61
0.001469001     supervise   1956   xvda1  W  13092440  4096     1.24
0.001588002     supervise   1956   xvda1  W  13115128  4096     1.09
1.022346001     supervise   1950   xvda1  W  13115272  4096     0.98
[...]
```

---

4 It looks a little skewed because of the log-2 distribution: buckets span progressively larger ranges. If I needed to understand this better, I would either modify biolatency(8) to use a higher-resolution linear histogram instead, or use the biosnoop(8) tool to log disk I/O and then import that log into spreadsheet software for custom histograms.

biosnoop(8) prints a line of output for each disk I/O, with details including latency. This allows you to examine disk I/O in more detail, and look for time-ordered patterns (e.g., reads queueing behind writes). biosnoop(8) is covered in more detail in Chapter 9.

3.4.6   cachestat

```
# cachestat
   HITS   MISSES  DIRTIES HITRATIO   BUFFERS_MB  CACHED_MB
  53401    2755    20953   95.09%          14        90223
  49599    4098    21460   92.37%          14        90230
  16601    2689    61329   86.06%          14        90381
  15197    2477    58028   85.99%          14        90522
[...]
```

cachestat(8) prints a one-line summary every second (or every custom interval) showing statistics from the file system cache. Use this to identify a low cache hit ratio and a high rate of misses. This may give you a lead for performance tuning. cachestat(8) is covered in more detail in Chapter 8.

3.4.7   tcpconnect

```
# tcpconnect
PID      COMM      IP SADDR            DADDR             DPORT
1479     telnet    4  127.0.0.1        127.0.0.1         23
1469     curl      4  10.201.219.236   54.245.105.25     80
1469     curl      4  10.201.219.236   54.67.101.145     80
1991     telnet    6  ::1              ::1               23
2015     ssh       6  fe80::2000:bff:fe82:3ac fe80::2000:bff:fe82:3ac 22
[...]
```

tcpconnect(8) prints one line of output for every active TCP connection (e.g., via connect()), with details including source and destination addresses. Look for unexpected connections that may point to inefficiencies in application configuration or an intruder. tcpconnect(8) is covered in more detail in Chapter 10.

3.4.8   tcpaccept

```
# tcpaccept
PID      COMM      IP RADDR            LADDR             LPORT
907      sshd      4  192.168.56.1     192.168.56.102    22
907      sshd      4  127.0.0.1        127.0.0.1         22
5389     perl      6  1234:ab12:2040:5020:2299:0:5:0 1234:ab12:2040:5020:2299:0:5:0 7001
[...]
```

tcpaccept(8) is a companion tool to tcpconnect(8). It prints one line of output for every passive TCP connection (e.g., via accept()), with details including source and destination addresses. tcpaccept(8) is covered in more detail in Chapter 10.

3.4.9 tcpretrans

```
# tcpretrans
TIME      PID    IP LADDR:LPORT          T> RADDR:RPORT         STATE
01:55:05 0      4  10.153.223.157:22    R> 69.53.245.40:34619  ESTABLISHED
01:55:05 0      4  10.153.223.157:22    R> 69.53.245.40:34619  ESTABLISHED
01:55:17 0      4  10.153.223.157:22    R> 69.53.245.40:22957  ESTABLISHED
[...]
```

tcpretrans(8) prints one line of output for every TCP retransmit packet, with details including source and destination addresses, and the kernel state of the TCP connection. TCP retransmissions cause latency and throughput issues. For retransmissions where the TCP session state is ESTABLISHED, look for problems with external networks. For the SYN_SENT state, this may point to target kernel CPU saturation and kernel packet drops as well. tcpretrans(8) is covered in more detail in Chapter 10.

3.4.10 runqlat

```
# runqlat
Tracing run queue latency... Hit Ctrl-C to end.
^C
     usecs               : count     distribution
         0 -> 1          : 233       |***********                             |
         2 -> 3          : 742       |************************************    |
         4 -> 7          : 203       |**********                              |
         8 -> 15         : 173       |********                                |
        16 -> 31         : 24        |*                                       |
        32 -> 63         : 0         |                                        |
        64 -> 127        : 30        |*                                       |
       128 -> 255        : 6         |                                        |
       256 -> 511        : 3         |                                        |
       512 -> 1023       : 5         |                                        |
      1024 -> 2047       : 27        |*                                       |
      2048 -> 4095       : 30        |*                                       |
      4096 -> 8191       : 20        |                                        |
      8192 -> 16383      : 29        |*                                       |
     16384 -> 32767      : 809       |****************************************|
     32768 -> 65535      : 64        |***                                     |
```

runqlat(8) times how long threads were waiting for their turn on CPU and prints this time as a histogram. Longer-than-expected waits for CPU access can be identified using this tool, which threads can suffer due to CPU saturation, misconfigurations, or scheduler issues. runqlat(8) is covered in more detail in Chapter 6.

3.4.11   profile

```
# profile
Sampling at 49 Hertz of all threads by user + kernel stack... Hit Ctrl-C to end.
^C
[...]

    copy_user_enhanced_fast_string
    copy_user_enhanced_fast_string
    _copy_from_iter_full
    tcp_sendmsg_locked
    tcp_sendmsg
    inet_sendmsg
    sock_sendmsg
    sock_write_iter
    new_sync_write
    __vfs_write
    vfs_write
    SyS_write
    do_syscall_64
    entry_SYSCALL_64_after_hwframe
    [unknown]
    [unknown]
    -                iperf (24092)
        58
```

profile(8) is a CPU profiler, a tool you can use to understand which code paths are consuming CPU resources. It takes samples of stack traces at timed intervals and prints a summary of unique stack traces and a count of their occurrence. This output has been truncated and only shows one stack trace, with an occurrence count of 58 times. profile(8) is covered in more detail in Chapter 6.

3.5   Summary

Performance analysis is about improving end-user performance and reducing operating costs. There are many tools and metrics to help you analyze performance; in fact, there are so many that choosing the right ones to use in a given situation can be overwhelming. Performance methodologies can guide you through these choices, showing you where to start, steps for analysis, and where to end.

This chapter summarizes performance analysis methodologies: workload characterization, latency analysis, the USE method, and checklists. A Linux performance analysis in 60 seconds checklist was then included and explained, which can be your starting point for any performance issue. It may help you solve issues outright, or at least yield clues about where the performance issue is and direct further analysis with BPF tools. In addition, this chapter includes a BPF checklist of BCC tools, which are explained in more detail in later chapters.

Chapter 4

BCC

The BPF Compiler Collection (BCC; sometimes written as lowercase bcc after the project and package names) is an open source project that contains a compiler framework and libraries for building BPF software. It is the main front-end project for BPF, supported by the BPF developers, and is usually where the latest kernel tracing BPF additions are first used. BCC also contains more than 70 ready-to-run BPF performance analysis and troubleshooting tools, many of which are covered in this book.

BCC was created by Brenden Blanco in April 2015. Encouraged by Alexei Starovoitov, I joined the project in 2015 and became a major contributor of performance tools, documentation, and testing. There are now numerous contributors, and BCC is a default server install at companies including Netflix and Facebook.

Learning objectives:

- Gain knowledge of BCC features and components, including tools and documentation
- Understand the benefits of single-purpose vs multi-purpose tools
- Learn how to use the funccount(8) multi-tool for event counting
- Learn how to use the stackcount(8) multi-tool for discovering code paths
- Learn how to use the trace(8) multi-tool for per-event custom printing
- Learn how to use the argdist(8) multi-tool for distribution summaries
- (optional) Get exposure to BCC internals
- Be aware of BCC debugging techniques

This chapter introduces BCC and its features; shows how to install it; provides an overview of its tools, tool types, and documentation; and ends with a tour of BCC internals and debugging. If you wish to develop your own new tools, be sure to study both this chapter and Chapter 5 (bpftrace), and you will be able to choose the front end that best suits your needs. Appendix C summarizes BCC tool development using examples.

4.1   BCC Components

The high-level directory structure of BCC is shown in Figure 4-1.

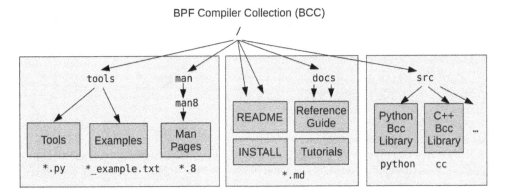

Figure 4-1   BCC structure

BCC contains documentation for the tools, man pages, and examples files, as well as a tutorial for using BCC tools and a tutorial and reference guide for BCC tool development. It provides interfaces for developing BCC tools in Python, C++, and lua (not pictured); more interfaces may be added in the future.

The repository is:

https://github.com/iovisor/bcc

In the BCC repository, the Python tools have a .py extension, but this extension is usually removed when BCC is installed via a software package. The final location of the BCC tools and man pages depends on the package you use, as different Linux distributions have packaged it differently. Tools may be installed either in /usr/share/bcc/tools, /sbin, or /snap/bin, and the tools themselves may have a prefix or suffix to show that they are from the BCC collection. These differences are described in Section 4.3.

4.2   BCC Features

BCC is an open source project created and maintained by engineers from various companies. It is not a commercial product. If it were, there would be a marketing department creating advertisements, boasting of its many features.

Feature lists (if accurate) can help you learn the capabilities of a new technology. During BPF and BCC development, I created lists of desired capabilities [57]. As these features now exist, these have become delivered feature lists and are organized into kernel- and user-level features. They are described in the following sections.

4.2.1 Kernel-Level Features

BCC can use a number of kernel-level features, such as BPF, kprobes, uprobes, and so on. The following list includes some implementation details in parentheses:

- Dynamic instrumentation, kernel-level (BPF support for kprobes)
- Dynamic instrumentation, user-level (BPF support for uprobes)
- Static tracing, kernel-level (BPF support for tracepoints)
- Timed sampling events (BPF with perf_event_open())
- PMC events (BPF with perf_event_open())
- Filtering (via BPF programs)
- Debug output (bpf_trace_printk())
- Per-event output (bpf_perf_event_output())
- Basic variables (global and per-thread variables, via BPF maps)
- Associative arrays (via BPF maps)
- Frequency counting (via BPF maps)
- Histograms (power-of-two, linear, and custom, via BPF maps)
- Timestamps and time deltas (bpf_ktime_get_ns() and BPF programs)
- Stack traces, kernel (BPF stackmap)
- Stack traces, user (BPF stackmap)
- Overwrite ring buffers (perf_event_attr.write_backward)
- Low-overhead instrumentation (BPF JIT, BPF map summaries)
- Production safe (BPF verifier)

See Chapter 2 for background on these kernel-level features.

4.2.2 BCC User-Level Features

The BCC user-level front end and BCC repository provide the following user-level features:

- Static tracing, user-level (SystemTap-style USDT probes via uprobes)
- Debug output (Python with BPF.trace_pipe() and BPF.trace_fields())
- Per-event output (BPF_PERF_OUTPUT macro and BPF.open_perf_buffer())
- Interval output (BPF.get_table() and table.clear())
- Histogram printing (table.print_log2_hist())
- C struct navigation, kernel-level (BCC rewriter maps to bpf_probe_read())
- Symbol resolution, kernel-level (ksym() and ksymaddr())

- Symbol resolution, user-level (usymaddr())

- Debuginfo symbol resolution support

- BPF tracepoint support (via TRACEPOINT_PROBE)

- BPF stack trace support (BPF_STACK_TRACE)

- Various other helper macros and functions

- Examples (under /examples)

- Many tools (under /tools)

- Tutorials (/docs/tutorial*.md)

- Reference guide (/docs/reference_guide.md)

4.3 BCC Installation

BCC packages are available for many Linux distributions, including Ubuntu, RHEL, Fedora, and Amazon Linux, making installation trivial. If desired, you can also build BCC from source. For the latest install and build instructions, check INSTALL.md in the BCC repository [58].

4.3.1 Kernel Requirements

The major kernel BPF components that BCC tools use were added between the Linux 4.1 and 4.9 releases, but improvements have been added in later releases, so the newer your kernel, the better. It is therefore recommended that you use a Linux 4.9 kernel (released in December 2016) or later.

Some kernel configuration options also need to be enabled: CONFIG_BPF=y, CONFIG_BPF_SYSCALL=y, CONFIG_BPF_EVENTS=y, CONFIG_BPF_JIT=y, and CONFIG_HAVE_EBPF_JIT=y. These options are now enabled by default in many distributions, so you typically do not need to change them.

4.3.2 Ubuntu

BCC has been packaged in the Ubuntu multiverse repository, with the package name bpfcc-tools. Install it using the following command:

```
sudo apt-get install bpfcc-tools linux-headers-$(uname -r)
```

This will place the tools in /sbin with a "-bpfcc" suffix:

```
# ls /sbin/*-bpfcc
/usr/sbin/argdist-bpfcc
/usr/sbin/bashreadline-bpfcc
/usr/sbin/biolatency-bpfcc
/usr/sbin/biosnoop-bpfcc
/usr/sbin/biotop-bpfcc
```

```
/usr/sbin/bitesize-bpfcc
[...]
```

 # opensnoop-bpfcc

```
PID    COMM              FD ERR PATH
29588  device poll        4   0 /dev/bus/usb
[...]
```

You can also fetch the latest stable and signed packages from the iovisor repository:

```
sudo apt-key adv --keyserver keyserver.ubuntu.com --recv-keys 4052245BD4284CDD
echo "deb https://repo.iovisor.org/apt/$(lsb_release -cs) $(lsb_release -cs) main"|\
  sudo tee /etc/apt/sources.list.d/iovisor.list
sudo apt-get update
sudo apt-get install bcc-tools libbcc-examples linux-headers-$(uname -r)
```

The tools are installed in /usr/share/bcc/tools.

Finally, BCC is also available as an Ubuntu snap:

```
sudo snap install bcc
```

The tools are installed in /snap/bin (which may already be in your $PATH) and available with a "bcc." prefix (e.g., bcc.opensnoop).

4.3.3   RHEL

BCC is included in the official yum repository for Red Hat Enterprise Linux 7.6 and can be installed using:

```
sudo yum install bcc-tools
```

The tools are installed in /usr/share/bcc/tools.

4.3.4   Other Distributions

The INSTALL.md also includes install instructions for Fedora, Arch, Gentoo, and openSUSE, as well as instructions for source code builds.

4.4   BCC Tools

Figure 4-2 shows major system components and many of the BCC tools available to observe them.[1]

---

1 I created this figure for the BCC repository, where you can find the latest version (see [60]). I expect to update it again after book publication, after porting some of the most important new bpftrace tools from this book to BCC.

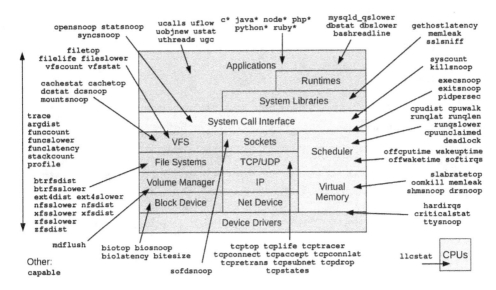

Figure 4-2   BCC performance tools

4.4.1   Highlighted Tools

Table 4-1 lists a selection of tools that are covered in detail in later chapters, organized by topic.

Table 4-1   Selected BCC Tools by Topic and Chapter

Topic	Highlighted Tools	Chapter
Debugging / multi-purpose	trace, argdist, funccount, stackcount, opensnoop	4
CPUs	execsnoop, runqlat, runqlen, cpudist, profile, offcputime, syscount, softirq, hardirq	6
Memory	memleak	7
File systems	opensnoop, filelife, vfsstatt, fileslower, cachestat, writeback, dcstat, xfsslower, xfsdist, ext4dist	8
Disk I/O	biolatency, biosnoop, biotop, bitesize	9
Networking	tcpconnect, tcpaccept, tcplife, tcpretrans	10
Security	capable	11
Languages	javastat, javacalls, javathreads, javaflow, javagc	12
Applications	mysqld_qslower, signals, killsnoop	13
Kernel	wakeuptime, offwaketime	14

Note that these chapters also contain many additional bpftrace tools not listed in Table 4-1.

After this chapter and Chapter 5, you may jump to later chapters as needed, using this book as a reference guide.

4.4.2 Tool Characteristics

The BCC tools all share these characteristics:

- They solve real observability issues, built out of necessity.

- They are designed to be run in production environments, by the root user.

- There is a man page for every tool (under man/man8).

- There is an examples file for every tool, containing example output and explanations of the output (under tools/*_example.txt).

- Many tools accept options and arguments, and most will print a USAGE message if you use the -h option.

- The tool source code begins with a block comment introduction.

- The tool source code follows a consistent style (checked using the pep8 tool).

To maintain consistency, new tool additions are reviewed by the BCC maintainers, and authors are directed to follow the BCC CONTRIBUTING_SCRIPTS.md guide [59].

The BCC tools are also designed to look and feel like other tools on the system, including vmstat(1) and iostat(1). As with vmstat(1) and top(1), it is helpful to have some understanding of how the BCC tools work, especially for estimating tool overhead. This book explains how these tools work and often describes expected overhead; the internals of BCC and kernel technologies in use are covered in this chapter and Chapter 2.

Although BCC supports different language front ends, the primary languages used by the BCC tools are Python for the user-level components and C for kernel-level BPF. These Python/C tools get the most attention and maintenance from the BCC developers, and are therefore covered in this book.

One of the suggestions in the contributors' guide is "Write the tool to solve the problem and no more." This encourages the development of single-purpose tools rather than multi-purpose tools, where possible.

4.4.3 Single-Purpose Tools

The philosophy of Unix was to do one thing and do it well. One expression of this was the creation of smaller, high-quality tools that could be connected together using pipes to accomplish more complex tasks. This led to a multitude of small, single-purpose tools that are still in use today, such as grep(1), cut(1), and sed(1).

BCC contains many similar single-purpose tools, including opensnoop(8), execsnoop(8), and biolatency(8). opensnoop(8) is a good example. Consider how the options and output are customized for the one task of tracing open(2) family syscalls:

```
# opensnoop -h
usage: opensnoop [-h] [-T] [-U] [-x] [-p PID] [-t TID] [-u UID]
                 [-d DURATION] [-n NAME] [-e] [-f FLAG_FILTER]


Trace open() syscalls

optional arguments:
  -h, --help            show this help message and exit
  -T, --timestamp       include timestamp on output
  -U, --print-uid       print UID column
  -x, --failed          only show failed opens
  -p PID, --pid PID     trace this PID only
  -t TID, --tid TID     trace this TID only
  -u UID, --uid UID     trace this UID only
  -d DURATION, --duration DURATION
                        total duration of trace in seconds
  -n NAME, --name NAME  only print process names containing this name
  -e, --extended_fields
                        show extended fields
  -f FLAG_FILTER, --flag_filter FLAG_FILTER
                        filter on flags argument (e.g., O_WRONLY)

examples:
    ./opensnoop           # trace all open() syscalls
    ./opensnoop -T        # include timestamps
    ./opensnoop -U        # include UID
    ./opensnoop -x        # only show failed opens
    ./opensnoop -p 181    # only trace PID 181
    ./opensnoop -t 123    # only trace TID 123
    ./opensnoop -u 1000   # only trace UID 1000
    ./opensnoop -d 10     # trace for 10 seconds only
    ./opensnoop -n main   # only print process names containing "main"
    ./opensnoop -e        # show extended fields
    ./opensnoop -f O_WRONLY -f O_RDWR # only print calls for writing
```

```
# opensnoop
PID    COMM            FD ERR PATH
29588  device poll      4   0 /dev/bus/usb
29588  device poll      6   0 /dev/bus/usb/004
[...]
```

For BPF tools, the benefits of this style are:

- **Easy for beginners to learn:** The default output is usually sufficient. This means that beginners can use these tools immediately without making any decisions about command line usage, or knowing what events to instrument. For example, opensnoop(8) produces useful and concise output just by running `opensnoop`. No knowledge of kprobes or tracepoints to instrument opens is needed.

- **Easy to maintain:** For the tool developer, the amount of code to be maintained should be smaller and require less testing. Multi-purpose tools may instrument a variety of workloads in a variety of different ways, so a small change to the tool may require hours of testing with different workloads, to confirm that nothing has regressed. For the end user, this means that the single-purpose tools are more likely to work when you want them to.

- **Code examples:** Each small tool provides a concise code example that is also practical. Many people who learn BCC tool development will begin with these single-purpose tools and customize and extend them as needed.

- **Custom arguments and output:** The tool arguments, positional parameters, and output do not need to accommodate other tasks and can be customized for the one single purpose. This can improve usability and readability.

For people new to BCC, the single-purpose tools are a good place to start, before moving to more complex multi-purpose tools.

4.4.4 Multi-Purpose Tools

BCC contains multi-purpose tools that can be used for a variety of different tasks. They are harder to learn than the single-purpose tools, but they are also more powerful. If you only use the multi-purpose tools occasionally, you might not need to learn them in depth; you can instead collect some one-liners to execute when needed.

The advantages of multi-purpose tools are:

- **Greater visibility:** Instead of analyzing a single task or target, you can look at various components at once.

- **Reduces code duplication:** You can avoid having multiple tools with similar code.

The most powerful multi-tools in BCC are funccount(8), stackcount(8), trace(8), and argdist(8), which are covered in the following sections. These multi-tools often let you decide which events to trace. However, to take advantage of this flexibility, you need to know which kprobes, uprobes, and other events to use—and how to use them. Later chapters on specific topics return to the single-purpose tools.

Table 4-2 lists the multi-purpose tools that are summarized in this chapter.

Table 4-2   **Multi-purpose Tools Covered in This Chapter**

Tool	Source	Target	Description
funccount	BCC	Software	Counts events including function calls
stackcount	BCC	Software	Counts stack traces that led to events
trace	BCC	Software	Prints custom per-event details
argdist	BCC	Software	Summarizes event argument distributions

See the BCC repository for full and updated lists of tool options and capabilities. A selection of the most important capabilities are summarized here.

4.5   funccount

funccount(8)[2] counts events, especially function calls, and can answer questions such as:

- Is this kernel- or user-level function being called?
- What is the rate of this function call, per second?

For efficiency, funccount(8) maintains the event count in kernel context by using a BPF map, and it only reports the total to user space. While this greatly reduces the overhead of funccount(8) compared to dump and post-process tools, high-frequency events can still cause significant overhead because of their frequency. For example, memory allocations (malloc(), free()) can occur millions of times per second, and using funccount(8) to trace them can cost CPU overhead exceeding 30%. See Chapter 18 for more on typical frequencies and overhead.

The following sections demonstrate funccount(8) and explain its the syntax and capabilities.

4.5.1   funccount Examples

1. Is the tcp_drop() kernel function ever called?

```
# funccount tcp_drop
Tracing 1 functions for "tcp_drop"... Hit Ctrl-C to end.
^C
FUNC                              COUNT
tcp_drop                              3
Detaching...
```

---

2 Origin: I developed the first version on 12-Jul-2014 using Ftrace to count kernel function calls and a BCC version of this on 9-Sep-2015. Sasha Goldshtein added other event types to the BCC version on 18-Oct-2016: user function calls (uprobes), tracepoints, and USDT.

Answer: yes. This invocation simply traces the tcp_drop() kernel function until Ctrl-C is typed. While tracing, it was called three times.

2. What is the most frequent kernel VFS function?

```
# funccount 'vfs_*'
Tracing 55 functions for "vfs_*"... Hit Ctrl-C to end.
^C
FUNC                           COUNT
vfs_rename                         1
vfs_readlink                       2
vfs_lock_file                      2
vfs_statfs                         3
vfs_fsync_range                    3
vfs_unlink                         5
vfs_statx                        189
vfs_statx_fd                     229
vfs_open                         345
vfs_getattr_nosec                353
vfs_getattr                      353
vfs_writev                      1776
vfs_read                        5533
vfs_write                       6938
Detaching...
```

This command uses a shell-like wildcard to match all kernel functions beginning with "vfs_". The most frequent kernel function while tracing was vfs_write(), with 6938 calls.

3. What is the rate of the user-level pthread_mutex_lock() function per second?

```
# funccount -i 1 c:pthread_mutex_lock
Tracing 1 functions for "c:pthread_mutex_lock"... Hit Ctrl-C to end.

FUNC                           COUNT
pthread_mutex_lock              1849

FUNC                           COUNT
pthread_mutex_lock              1761

FUNC                           COUNT
pthread_mutex_lock              2057

FUNC                           COUNT
pthread_mutex_lock              2261
[...]
```

The rate is variable, but it appears to be around 2000 calls per second. This is instrumenting a function from the libc library, and it is doing so system-wide: the output shows the rate across all processes.

4. What is the most frequent string function call from libc, system-wide?

```
# funccount 'c:str*'
Tracing 59 functions for "c:str*"... Hit Ctrl-C to end.
^C
FUNC                            COUNT
strndup                             3
strerror_r                          5
strerror                            5
strtof32x_l                       350
strtoul                           587
strtoll                           724
strtok_r                         2839
strdup                           5788
Detaching...
```

While tracing, it was strdup() with 5788 calls.

5. What is the most frequent syscall?

```
# funccount 't:syscalls:sys_enter_*'
Tracing 316 functions for "t:syscalls:sys_enter_*"... Hit Ctrl-C to end.
^C
FUNC                            COUNT
syscalls:sys_enter_creat            1
[...]
syscalls:sys_enter_read          6582
syscalls:sys_enter_write         7442
syscalls:sys_enter_mprotect      7460
syscalls:sys_enter_gettid        7589
syscalls:sys_enter_ioctl        10984
syscalls:sys_enter_poll         14980
syscalls:sys_enter_recvmsg      27113
syscalls:sys_enter_futex        42929
Detaching...
```

This could be answered using different event sources. In this case, I used tracepoints from the syscalls system and simply matched all the syscall entry tracepoints ("sys_enter_*"). The most frequent syscall while tracing was futex(), with a count of 42,929 calls.

4.5.2 funccount Syntax

The arguments to funccount(8) are options to change behavior and a string to describe the events to instrument:

```
funccount [options] eventname
```

The syntax for eventname is:

- **name** or **p:name**: Instrument the kernel function called *name()*

- **lib:name** or **p:lib:name**: Instrument the user-level function called *name()* in the library *lib*

- **path:name**: Instrument the user-level function called *name()* in the file at *path*

- **t:system:name**: Instrument the tracepoint called *system:name*

- **u:lib:name**: Instrument the USDT probe in library *lib* called *name*

- *****: A wildcard to match any string (globbing). The -r option allows regular expressions to be used instead.

This syntax is somewhat inspired by Ftrace. funccount(8) uses kprobes and uprobes when instrumenting kernel- and user-level functions.

4.5.3 funccount One-Liners

Count VFS kernel calls:

```
funccount 'vfs_*'
```

Count TCP kernel calls:

```
funccount 'tcp_*'
```

Count TCP send calls per second:

```
funccount -i 1 'tcp_send*'
```

Show the rate of block I/O events per second:

```
funccount -i 1 't:block:*'
```

Show the rate of new processes per second:

```
funccount -i 1 t:sched:sched_process_fork
```

Show the rate of libc getaddrinfo() (name resolution) per second:

```
funccount -i 1 c:getaddrinfo
```

Count all "os.*" calls in libgo:

```
funccount 'go:os.*'
```

4.5.4 funccount Usage

There is more to funccount(8) than shown so far, as summarized by the usage message:

```
# funccount -h
usage: funccount [-h] [-p PID] [-i INTERVAL] [-d DURATION] [-T] [-r] [-D]
                 pattern


Count functions, tracepoints, and USDT probes


positional arguments:
  pattern               search expression for events


optional arguments:
  -h, --help            show this help message and exit
  -p PID, --pid PID     trace this PID only
  -i INTERVAL, --interval INTERVAL
                        summary interval, seconds
  -d DURATION, --duration DURATION
                        total duration of trace, seconds
  -T, --timestamp       include timestamp on output
  -r, --regexp          use regular expressions. Default is "*" wildcards
                        only.
  -D, --debug           print BPF program before starting (for debugging
                        purposes)


examples:
    ./funccount 'vfs_*'          # count kernel fns starting with "vfs"
    ./funccount -r '^vfs.*'      # same as above, using regular expressions
    ./funccount -Ti 5 'vfs_*'    # output every 5 seconds, with timestamps
    ./funccount -d 10 'vfs_*'    # trace for 10 seconds only
    ./funccount -p 185 'vfs_*'   # count vfs calls for PID 181 only
[...]
```

The interval option (-i) allows funccount one-liners to become, in a way, mini performance tools, showing the rate of custom events per second. Custom metrics can then be created from the thousands of events available and filtered, if desired, to a target process ID using -p.

4.6 stackcount

stackcount(8)[3] counts the stack traces that led to an event. As with funccount(8), an event may be a kernel- or user-level function, tracepoint, or USDT probe. stackcount(8) can answer these questions:

- Why is this event called? What is the code path?
- What are all the different code paths that call this event, and what are their frequencies?

For efficiency, stackcount(8) performs this summary entirely in kernel context, using a special BPF map for stack traces. User space reads stack IDs and counts and then fetches the stack traces from the BPF map for symbol translation and printing out. As with funccount(8), the overhead depends on the rate of the event that is instrumented, and it should be sightly higher as stackcount(8) does more work for each event: walking and recording the stack trace.

4.6.1 stackcount Example

I noticed using funccount(8) that on an idle system, I seemed to have a high rate of ktime_get() kernel function calls—more than 8000 per second. These calls fetch the time, but why does my idle system need to fetch the time so frequently?

This example uses stackcount(8) to identify the code paths that led to ktime_get():

```
# stackcount ktime_get
Tracing 1 functions for "ktime_get"... Hit Ctrl-C to end.
^C
[...]

  ktime_get
  nvme_queue_rq
  __blk_mq_try_issue_directly
  blk_mq_try_issue_directly
  blk_mq_make_request
  generic_make_request
  dmcrypt_write
  kthread
  ret_from_fork
    52

[...]
```

---

3 Origin: I developed it on 12-Jan-2016 for kprobes only, and Sasha Goldshtein added other event types on 09-Jul-2016: uprobes and tracepoints. Previously, I frequently used kprobe -s from my Ftrace perf-tools to print per-event stacks, but the output was often too verbose and I wanted in-kernel frequency counts instead, which led to stackcount(8). I also asked Tom Zanussi for stack counts using Ftrace hist triggers, and he did add it.

```
ktime_get
tick_nohz_idle_enter
do_idle
cpu_startup_entry
start_secondary
secondary_startup_64
   1077


Detaching...
```

The output was hundreds of pages long and contained more than 1000 stack traces. Only two have been included here. Each stack trace is printed with one line per function and then the occurrence count. For example, the first stack trace shows the code path through dmcrypt_write(), blk_mq_make_request(), and nvme_queue_rq(). I would guess (without having read the code) that it is storing an I/O start time for later use with prioritization. That path from ktime_get() occurred 52 times while tracing. The most frequent stack that called ktime_get() was from the CPU idle path.

The -P option includes the process name and PID with the stack trace:

```
# stackcount -P ktime_get
[...]

ktime_get
 tick_nohz_idle_enter
 do_idle
 cpu_startup_entry
 start_secondary
 secondary_startup_64
   swapper/2 [0]
   207
```

This shows that PID 0 with process name "swapper/2" was calling ktime_get() via do_idle(), further confirming that this is the idle thread. This -P option produces more output, as stack traces that were previously grouped are now split between each separate PID.

4.6.2 stackcount Flame Graphs

Sometimes you will find only one or a few stack traces printed for an event, which can easily be browsed in the stackcount(8) output. For cases like the example with ktime_get(), where the output is hundreds of pages long, flame graphs can be used to visualize the output. (Flame graphs are introduced in Chapter 2.) The original flame graph software [37] inputs stacks in folded format, with one line per stack trace, frames (function names) delimited by semicolons, and a space and a count at the end. stackcount(8) can generate this format with -f.

The following example traces ktime_get() for 10 seconds (-D 10), with per-process stacks (-P), and generates a flame graph:

```
# stackcount -f -P -D 10 ktime_get > out.stackcount01.txt
$ wc out.stackcount01.txt
  1586   3425 387661 out.stackcount01.txt
$ git clone http://github.com/brendangregg/FlameGraph
$ cd FlameGraph
$ ./flamegraph.pl --hash --bgcolors=grey < ../out.stackcount01.txt \
    > out.stackcount01.svg
```

The wc(1) tool was used here to show that there were 1586 lines of output—representing this many unique stack and process name combinations. Figure 4-3 shows a screenshot of the resulting SVG file.

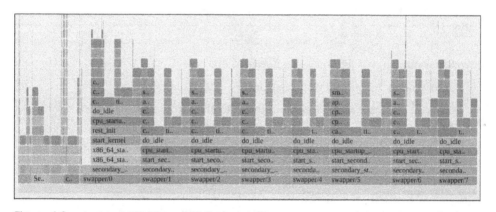

Figure 4-3   stackcount(8) ktime_get() flame graph

The flame graph shows that most of the ktime_get() calls were from the eight idle threads—one for each CPU on this system, as shown by the similar towers. Other sources are visible as the narrow towers on the far left.

4.6.3   stackcount Broken Stack Traces

Stack traces, and the many problems with getting them to work in practice, are discussed in Chapters 2, 12, and 18. Broken stack walking and missing symbols are commonplace.

As an example, the earlier stack trace shows tick_nohz_idle_enter() calling ktime_get(). However, this doesn't appear in the source code. What does appear is a call to tick_nohz_start_idle(), which has the source (kernel/time/tick-sched.c):

```
static void tick_nohz_start_idle(struct tick_sched *ts)
{
        ts->idle_entrytime = ktime_get();
        ts->idle_active = 1;
        sched_clock_idle_sleep_event();
}
```

This is the kind of small function that compilers like to inline, which in this case results in a stack where the parent function calls ktime_get() directly. The tick_nohz_start_idle symbol is not in /proc/kallsyms (for this system), further suggesting that it has been inlined.

4.6.4   stackcount Syntax

The arguments to stackcount(8) define the event to instrument:

```
stackcount [options] eventname
```

The syntax for eventname is the same as for funccount(8):

- **name** or **p:name**: Instrument the kernel function called *name*()
- **lib:name** or **p:lib:name**: Instrument the user-level function called *name*() in the library *lib*
- **path:name**: Instrument the user-level function called *name*() in the file at *path*
- **t:system:name**: Instrument the tracepoint called *system:name*
- **u:lib:name**: Instrument the USDT probe in library *lib* called *name*
- *****: A wildcard to match any string (globbing). The -r option allows regexps.

4.6.5   stackcount One-Liners

Count stack traces that created block I/O:

```
stackcount t:block:block_rq_insert
```

Count stack traces that led to sending IP packets:

```
stackcount ip_output
```

Count stack traces that led to sending IP packets, with the responsible PID:

```
stackcount -P ip_output
```

Count stack traces that led to the thread blocking and moving off-CPU:

```
stackcount t:sched:sched_switch
```

Count stack traces that led to the read() syscall:

```
stackcount t:syscalls:sys_enter_read
```

4.6.6   stackcount Usage

There is more to stackcount(8) than shown so far, as summarized by the usage message:

```
# stackcount -h
usage: stackcount [-h] [-p PID] [-i INTERVAL] [-D DURATION] [-T] [-r] [-s]
                  [-P] [-K] [-U] [-v] [-d] [-f] [--debug]
                  pattern


Count events and their stack traces


positional arguments:
  pattern               search expression for events


optional arguments:
  -h, --help            show this help message and exit
  -p PID, --pid PID     trace this PID only
  -i INTERVAL, --interval INTERVAL
                        summary interval, seconds
  -D DURATION, --duration DURATION
                        total duration of trace, seconds
  -T, --timestamp       include timestamp on output
  -r, --regexp          use regular expressions. Default is "*" wildcards
                        only.
  -s, --offset          show address offsets
  -P, --perpid          display stacks separately for each process
  -K, --kernel-stacks-only
                        kernel stack only
  -U, --user-stacks-only
                        user stack only
  -v, --verbose         show raw addresses
  -d, --delimited       insert delimiter between kernel/user stacks
  -f, --folded          output folded format
  --debug               print BPF program before starting (for debugging
                        purposes)
```

```
examples:
    ./stackcount submit_bio       # count kernel stack traces for submit_bio
    ./stackcount -d ip_output     # include a user/kernel stack delimiter
    ./stackcount -s ip_output     # show symbol offsets
    ./stackcount -sv ip_output    # show offsets and raw addresses (verbose)
    ./stackcount 'tcp_send*'      # count stacks for funcs matching tcp_send*
    ./stackcount -r '^tcp_send.*' # same as above, using regular expressions
    ./stackcount -Ti 5 ip_output  # output every 5 seconds, with timestamps
    ./stackcount -p 185 ip_output # count ip_output stacks for PID 185 only
[...]
```

A planned addition is an option to limit the stack depth recorded.

4.7 trace

trace(8)[4] is a BCC multi-tool for per-event tracing from many different sources: kprobes, uprobes, tracepoints, and USDT probes.

It can answer questions such as:

- What are the arguments when a kernel- or user-level function is called?
- What is the return value of this function? Is it failing?
- How is this function called? What is the user- or kernel-level stack trace?

As it prints a line of output per event, trace(8) is suited for events that are called infrequently. Very frequent events, such as network packets, context switches, and memory allocations, can occur millions of times per second, and trace(8) would produce so much output that it would cost significant overhead to instrument. One way to reduce the overhead is to use a filter expression to print only events of interest. Frequently occurring events are usually better suited for analysis with other tools that do in-kernel summaries, such as funccount(8), stackcount(8), and argdist(8). argdist(8) is covered in the next section.

4.7.1 trace Example

The following example shows file opens by tracing the do_sys_open() kernel function and is a trace(8) version of opensnoop(8):

```
# trace 'do_sys_open "%s", arg2'
PID     TID     COMM          FUNC                  -
29588   29591   device poll   do_sys_open   /dev/bus/usb
29588   29591   device poll   do_sys_open   /dev/bus/usb/004
[...]
```

---

4 Origin: This tool was developed by Sasha Goldshtein and included in BCC on 22-Feb-2016.

arg2 is the second argument to do_sys_open(), and is the filename opened and has the type char *. The final column, labeled "-", is the custom format string provided to trace(8).

4.7.2 trace Syntax

The arguments to trace(8) are options to change behavior and one or more probes:

```
trace [options] probe [probe ...]
```

The syntax for probe is:

```
eventname(signature) (boolean filter) "format string", arguments
```

The eventname signature is optional, and it is needed only in some cases (see Section 4.7.4). The filter is also optional, and allows Boolean operators: ==, <, >, and !=. The format string with arguments is also optional. Without it, trace(8) still prints a line of metadata per event; however, there is no custom field.

The syntax for eventname is similar to the eventname syntax for funccount(8), with the addition of return probes:

- **name** or **p:name**: Instrument the kernel function called *name*()
- **r::name**: Instrument the return of the kernel function called *name*()
- **lib:name** or **p:lib:name**: Instrument the user-level function called name() in the library lib
- **r:lib:name**: Instrument the return of the user-level function *name*() in the library *lib*
- **path:name**: Instrument the user-level function called *name*() found in the file at *path*
- **r:path:name**: Instrument the return of the user-level function *name*() found in the file at *path*
- **t:system:name**: Instrument the tracepoint called *system:name*
- **u:lib:name**: Instrument the USDT probe in library *lib* called *name*
- *****: A wildcard to match any string (globbing). The -r option allows regular expressions to be used instead.

The format string is based on printf(), and supports:

- **%u**: unsigned int
- **%d**: int
- **%lu**: unsigned long
- **%ld**: long
- **%llu**: unsigned long long
- **%lld**: long long

- **%hu**: unsigned short

- **%hd**: short

- **%x**: unsigned int, hexadecimal

- **%lx**: unsigned long, hexadecimal

- **%llx**: unsigned long long, hexadecimal

- **%c**: character

- **%K**: kernel symbol string

- **%U**: user-level symbol string

- **%s**: string

The overall syntax resembles programming in other languages. Consider this trace(8) one-liner:

```
trace 'c:open (arg2 == 42) "%s %d", arg1, arg2'
```

Here is the equivalent program in a more C-like language (for illustration only; trace(8) will not execute this):

```
trace 'c:open { if (arg2 == 42) { printf("%s %d\n", arg1, arg2); } }'
```

The ability to custom print arguments for an event is used frequently in ad hoc tracing analysis, so trace(8) is a go-to tool.

4.7.3   trace One-Liners

Many one-liners are listed in the usage message. Here is a selection with additional one-liners.

Trace the kernel do_sys_open() function with the filename:

```
trace 'do_sys_open "%s", arg2'
```

Trace the return of the kernel do_sys_open() function and print the return value:

```
trace 'r::do_sys_open "ret: %d", retval'
```

Trace do_nanosleep() with mode and user-level stacks:

```
trace -U 'do_nanosleep "mode: %d", arg2'
```

Trace authentication requests via the pam library:

```
trace 'pam:pam_start "%s: %s", arg1, arg2'
```

4.7.4 trace Structs

BCC uses the system headers as well as the kernel headers package to understand some structs. For example, consider this one-liner, which traces do_nanosleep() with the task address:

```
trace 'do_nanosleep(struct hrtimer_sleeper *t) "task: %x", t->task'
```

Fortunately, the hrtimer_sleeper struct is in the kernel headers package (include/linux/hrtimer.h), and therefore it is automatically read by BCC.

For structs not in the kernel headers package, their header files can be included manually. For example, this one-liner traces udpv6_sendmsg() only when the destination port is 53 (DNS; written as 13568 in big endian order):

```
trace -I 'net/sock.h' 'udpv6_sendmsg(struct sock *sk) (sk->sk_dport == 13568)'
```

The net/sock.h file is needed to understand struct sock, so it is included with -I. This only works when the full kernel source is available on the system.

A new technology that is in development should obviate the need for installing the kernel source—BPF Type Format (BTF), which will embed struct information in compiled binaries (see Chapter 2).

4.7.5 trace Debugging File Descriptor Leaks

Here is a much more complex example. I developed this while debugging a real-world issue of a file leak on a Netflix production instance. The goal was to get more information on socket file descriptors that were not being freed. The stack trace on allocation (via sock_alloc()) would provide such information; however, I needed a way to differentiate between allocations that were freed (via sock_release()) and those that were not. The problem is illustrated in Figure 4-4.

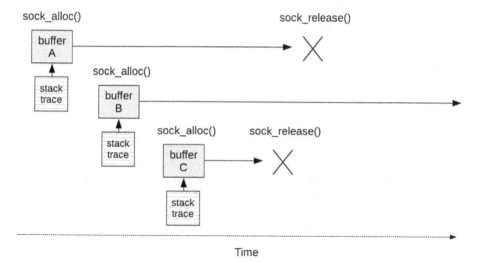

Figure 4-4   Socket file descriptor leaks

It is straightforward to trace sock_alloc() and print the stack trace, but this would produce stack traces for buffers A, B, and C. In this case, only buffer B—the one that wasn't freed (while tracing)—is of interest.

I was able to use a one-liner to solve this problem, although it required post-processing. Here is the one-liner and some output:

```
# trace -tKU 'r::sock_alloc "open %llx", retval' '__sock_release "close %llx", arg1'
TIME      PID    TID    COMM           FUNC              -
1.093199 4182   7101   nf.dependency.M sock_alloc        open ffff9c76526dac00
         kretprobe_trampoline+0x0 [kernel]
         sys_socket+0x55 [kernel]
         do_syscall_64+0x73 [kernel]
         entry_SYSCALL_64_after_hwframe+0x3d [kernel]
         __socket+0x7 [libc-2.27.so]
         Ljava/net/PlainSocketImpl;::socketCreate+0xc7 [perf-4182.map]
         Ljava/net/Socket;::setSoTimeout+0x2dc [perf-4182.map]
         Lorg/apache/http/impl/conn/DefaultClientConnectionOperator;::openConnectio...
         Lorg/apache/http/impl/client/DefaultRequestDirector;::tryConnect+0x60c [pe...
         Lorg/apache/http/impl/client/DefaultRequestDirector;::execute+0x1674 [perf...
[...]


[...]


6.010530 4182    6797   nf.dependency.M __sock_release    close ffff9c76526dac00
         __sock_release+0x1 [kernel]
         __fput+0xea [kernel]
         ____fput+0xe [kernel]
         task_work_run+0x9d [kernel]
         exit_to_usermode_loop+0xc0 [kernel]
         do_syscall_64+0x121 [kernel]
         entry_SYSCALL_64_after_hwframe+0x3d [kernel]
         dup2+0x7 [libc-2.27.so]
         Ljava/net/PlainSocketImpl;::socketClose0+0xc7 [perf-4182.map]
         Ljava/net/Socket;::close+0x308 [perf-4182.map]
         Lorg/apache/http/impl/conn/DefaultClientConnection;::close+0x2d4 [perf-418...
[...]
```

This instruments the return of the sock_alloc() kernel function and prints the return value, the address of the socket, and the stack trace (using the -K and -U options). It also traces the entry to the __sock_release() kernel function with its second argument: this shows the addresses of sockets that were closed. The -t option prints timestamps for these events.

I've truncated this output (the output and Java stacks were very long) to show just one alloc and release pair for socket address 0xffff9c76526dac00 (highlighted in bold). I was able to post-process this output to find file descriptors that were opened but not closed (i.e., no matching close event for the address) and then used the allocation stack trace to identify the code paths responsible for the file descriptor leak (not shown here).

This issue could also be solved with a dedicated BCC tool similar to memleak(8), covered in Chapter 7, which saves stack traces in a BPF map and then deletes them during free events so that the map can later be printed to show long-term survivors.

4.7.6   trace Usage

There's much more to trace(8) than shown so far, as summarized by the usage message:

```
# trace -h
usage: trace.py [-h] [-b BUFFER_PAGES] [-p PID] [-L TID] [-v] [-Z STRING_SIZE]
                [-S] [-M MAX_EVENTS] [-t] [-T] [-C] [-B] [-K] [-U] [-a]
                [-I header]
                probe [probe ...]

Attach to functions and print trace messages.

positional arguments:
  probe                 probe specifier (see examples)

optional arguments:
  -h, --help            show this help message and exit
  -b BUFFER_PAGES, --buffer-pages BUFFER_PAGES
                        number of pages to use for perf_events ring buffer
                        (default: 64)
  -p PID, --pid PID     id of the process to trace (optional)
  -L TID, --tid TID     id of the thread to trace (optional)
  -v, --verbose         print resulting BPF program code before executing
  -Z STRING_SIZE, --string-size STRING_SIZE
                        maximum size to read from strings
  -S, --include-self    do not filter trace's own pid from the trace
  -M MAX_EVENTS, --max-events MAX_EVENTS
                        number of events to print before quitting
  -t, --timestamp       print timestamp column (offset from trace start)
  -T, --time            print time column
  -C, --print_cpu       print CPU id
  -B, --bin_cmp         allow to use STRCMP with binary values
  -K, --kernel-stack    output kernel stack trace
```

```
-U, --user-stack        output user stack trace
-a, --address           print virtual address in stacks
-I header, --include header
                        additional header files to include in the BPF program


EXAMPLES:

trace do_sys_open
        Trace the open syscall and print a default trace message when entered
trace 'do_sys_open "%s", arg2'
        Trace the open syscall and print the filename being opened
trace 'sys_read (arg3 > 20000) "read %d bytes", arg3'
        Trace the read syscall and print a message for reads >20000 bytes
trace 'r::do_sys_open "%llx", retval'
        Trace the return from the open syscall and print the return value
trace 'c:open (arg2 == 42) "%s %d", arg1, arg2'
        Trace the open() call from libc only if the flags (arg2) argument is 42
[...]
```

As this is a mini programming language that you may use only occasionally, the examples at the end of the usage message are invaluable reminders.

While trace(8) is extremely useful, it is not a fully-fledged language. For a complete language, see Chapter 5 on bpftrace.

4.8   argdist

argdist(8)[5] is a multi-tool that summarizes arguments. Here is another real-world example from Netflix: A Hadoop server was suffering a TCP performance issue, and we had tracked it down to zero-sized window advertisements. I used an argdist(8) one-liner to summarize the window size in production. Here is some output from the issue:

```
# argdist -H 'r::__tcp_select_window():int:$retval'
[21:50:03]
     $retval            : count    distribution
         0 -> 1         : 6100     |****************************************|
         2 -> 3         : 0        |                                        |
         4 -> 7         : 0        |                                        |
         8 -> 15        : 0        |                                        |
        16 -> 31        : 0        |                                        |
```

---

5 Origin: This tool was developed by Sasha Goldshtein and included in BCC on 12-Feb-2016.

```
      32 -> 63        : 0        |                                        |
      64 -> 127       : 0        |                                        |
     128 -> 255       : 0        |                                        |
     256 -> 511       : 0        |                                        |
     512 -> 1023      : 0        |                                        |
    1024 -> 2047      : 0        |                                        |
    2048 -> 4095      : 0        |                                        |
    4096 -> 8191      : 0        |                                        |
    8192 -> 16383     : 24       |                                        |
   16384 -> 32767     : 3535     |************************                |
   32768 -> 65535     : 1752     |************                            |
   65536 -> 131071    : 2774     |*******************                     |
  131072 -> 262143    : 1001     |******                                  |
  262144 -> 524287    : 464      |***                                     |
  524288 -> 1048575   : 3        |                                        |
 1048576 -> 2097151   : 9        |                                        |
 2097152 -> 4194303   : 10       |                                        |
 4194304 -> 8388607   : 2        |                                        |
[21:50:04]
[...]
```

This instruments the return of the __tcp_select_window() kernel function and summarizes the return value as a power-of-2 histogram (-H). By default, argdist(8) prints this summary once per second. The histogram shows the zero-sized window issue in the "0 -> 1" line: for the above interval, a count of 6100. We were able to use this tool to confirm whether the issue was still present while we made changes to the system to rectify it.

4.8.1 argdist Syntax

The arguments to argdist(8) set the type of summary, the events to instrument, and the data to summarize:

```
argdist {-C|-H} [options] probe
```

argdist(8) requires either -C or -H:

- **-C**: Frequency count
- **-H**: Power-of-two histogram

The syntax for probe is:

```
eventname(signature)[:type[,type...]:expr[,expr...][:filter]][#label]
```

eventname and **signature** have almost the same syntax as the trace(8) command, with the exception that the kernel function name shortcut is not available. Instead, the kernel vfs_read() function is traced via "p::vfs_read", and is no longer "vfs_read". The signature is usually required. If it is left blank, empty parentheses ("()") are required.

type shows the value type that will be summarized: u32 for unsigned 32-bit integers, u64 for unsigned 64-bit integers, and so on. Many types are supported, including "char *" for strings.

expr is an expression to summarize. It may be an argument from the function or a tracepoint argument. There are also special variables that can only be used in return probes:

- **$retval**: The return value of the function
- **$latency**: The time from the entry to the return, in nanoseconds
- **$entry (param)**: The value of *param* during the entry probe

filter is an optional Boolean expression to filter events added to the summary. Boolean operators supported include ==, !=, <, and >.

label is an optional setting to add label text to the output so that it can be self-documenting.

4.8.2 argdist One-Liners

Many one-liners are listed in the usage message. Here is a selection with additional one-liners.

Print a histogram of results (sizes) returned by the kernel function vfs_read():

```
argdist.py -H 'r::vfs_read()'
```

Print a histogram of results (sizes) returned by the user-level libc read() for PID 1005:

```
argdist -p 1005 -H 'r:c:read()'
```

Count syscalls by syscall ID, using the raw_syscalls:sys_enter tracepoint:

```
argdist.py -C 't:raw_syscalls:sys_enter():int:args->id'
```

Count tcp_sendmsg() size:

```
argdist -C 'p::tcp_sendmsg(struct sock *sk, struct msghdr *msg, size_t size):u32:size'
```

Summarize tcp_sendmsg() size as a power-of-two histogram:

```
argdist -H 'p::tcp_sendmsg(struct sock *sk, struct msghdr *msg, size_t size):u32:size'
```

Count the libc write() call for PID 181 by file descriptor:

```
argdist -p 181 -C 'p:c:write(int fd):int:fd'
```

Print frequency of reads by process where the latency was >0.1ms:

```
argdist -C 'r::__vfs_read():u32:$PID:$latency > 100000
```

4.8.3 argdist Usage

There is more to argdist(8) than shown so far, as summarized by the usage message:

```
# argdist.py -h
usage: argdist.py [-h] [-p PID] [-z STRING_SIZE] [-i INTERVAL] [-d DURATION]
                  [-n COUNT] [-v] [-c] [-T TOP] [-H specifier] [-C specifier]
                  [-I header]

Trace a function and display a summary of its parameter values.

optional arguments:
  -h, --help            show this help message and exit
  -p PID, --pid PID     id of the process to trace (optional)
  -z STRING_SIZE, --string-size STRING_SIZE
                        maximum string size to read from char* arguments
  -i INTERVAL, --interval INTERVAL
                        output interval, in seconds (default 1 second)
  -d DURATION, --duration DURATION
                        total duration of trace, in seconds
  -n COUNT, --number COUNT
                        number of outputs
  -v, --verbose         print resulting BPF program code before executing
  -c, --cumulative      do not clear histograms and freq counts at each
                        interval
  -T TOP, --top TOP     number of top results to show (not applicable to
                        histograms)
  -H specifier, --histogram specifier
                        probe specifier to capture histogram of (see examples
                        below)
  -C specifier, --count specifier
                        probe specifier to capture count of (see examples
                        below)
  -I header, --include header
                        additional header files to include in the BPF program
                        as either full path, or relative to relative to
                        current working directory, or relative to default
                        kernel header search path

Probe specifier syntax:
        {p,r,t,u}:{[library],category}:function(signature)
[:type[,type...]:expr[,expr...][:filter]][#label]
```

Where:

```
        p,r,t,u    -- probe at function entry, function exit, kernel
                      tracepoint, or USDT probe
                      in exit probes: can use $retval, $entry(param), $latency
        library    -- the library that contains the function
                      (leave empty for kernel functions)
        category   -- the category of the kernel tracepoint (e.g. net, sched)
        function   -- the function name to trace (or tracepoint name)
        signature  -- the function's parameters, as in the C header
        type       -- the type of the expression to collect (supports multiple)
        expr       -- the expression to collect (supports multiple)
        filter     -- the filter that is applied to collected values
        label      -- the label for this probe in the resulting output
```

EXAMPLES:

```
argdist -H 'p::__kmalloc(u64 size):u64:size'
        Print a histogram of allocation sizes passed to kmalloc

argdist -p 1005 -C 'p:c:malloc(size_t size):size_t:size:size==16'
        Print a frequency count of how many times process 1005 called malloc
        with an allocation size of 16 bytes

argdist -C 'r:c:gets():char*:(char*)$retval#snooped strings'
        Snoop on all strings returned by gets()

argdist -H 'r::__kmalloc(size_t size):u64:$latency/$entry(size)#ns per byte'
        Print a histogram of nanoseconds per byte from kmalloc allocations

argdist -C 'p::__kmalloc(size_t sz, gfp_t flags):size_t:sz:flags&GFP_ATOMIC'
        Print frequency count of kmalloc allocation sizes that have GFP_ATOMIC
[...]
```

argdist(8) allows you to create many powerful one-liners. For distribution summaries that are beyond its capabilities, see Chapter 5.

4.9 Tool Documentation

Every BCC tool has a man page and an examples file. The BCC /examples directory has some code samples that behave like tools, but these are not documented outside of their own code. Tools that you find in the /tools directory or that are installed elsewhere on your system when using a distribution package should be documented.

The following section discusses tool documentation with opensnoop(8) as an example.

4.9.1 Man Page: opensnoop

If your tools are installed via a package, you may find that the man opensnoop command works. If you are looking at the repository, the nroff(1) command can be used to format the man pages (which are in ROFF format).

The structure of the man pages is based on those of other Linux utilities. Over the years I have refined my approach to man page content, with attention to certain details.[6] The following man page includes my explanations and advice:

```
bcc$ nroff -man man/man8/opensnoop.8
```

```
opensnoop(8)              System Manager's Manual              opensnoop(8)



NAME
        opensnoop - Trace open() syscalls. Uses Linux eBPF/bcc.

SYNOPSIS
        opensnoop.py [-h] [-T] [-U] [-x] [-p PID] [-t TID] [-u UID]
                     [-d DURATION] [-n NAME] [-e] [-f FLAG_FILTER]

DESCRIPTION
        opensnoop  traces  the  open()  syscall,  showing  which  processes are
        attempting to open which files. This can be useful for determining  the
        location  of  config and log files, or for troubleshooting applications
        that are failing, especially on startup.

        This works by tracing the  kernel  sys_open()  function  using  dynamic
        tracing, and will need updating to match any changes to this function.

        This  makes  use  of a Linux 4.5 feature (bpf_perf_event_output()); for
        kernels older than 4.5, see the version under tools/old, which uses  an
        older mechanism.

        Since this uses BPF, only the root user can use this tool.
[...]
```

This man page is in Section 8 because it is a system administration command that requires root privileges, as I state at the end of the DESCRIPTION section. In the future, extended BPF may become available to non-root users, just as the perf(1) command is. If that happens, these man pages will be moved to Section 1.

---

6 I've written and published more than 200 man pages for the performance tools I've developed.

The NAME includes a one-sentence description of the tool. It states that it is for Linux and uses eBPF/BCC (because I've developed multiple versions of these tools for different operating systems and tracers).

The SYNOPSIS summarizes the command line usage.

The DESCRIPTION summarizes what the tool does and why it is useful. It is essential to describe why the tool is useful, in simple terms—in other words, to tell what real-world problems it solves (which may not be obvious to everyone). Providing this information helps ensure that the tool is useful enough to publish. Sometimes I've struggled to write this section, making me realize that the particular tool has a use case too narrow for the tool to be worth publishing.

The DESCRIPTION section should also point out major caveats. It is better to warn users of an issue than to let them discover it the hard way. This example includes a standard warning about dynamic tracing stability and required kernel versions.

Continuing:

```
REQUIREMENTS
        CONFIG_BPF and bcc.


OPTIONS
        -h      Print usage message.


        -T      Include a timestamp column.
[...]
```

The REQUIREMENTS section lists anything special, and an OPTIONS section lists every command line option:

```
EXAMPLES
        Trace all open() syscalls:
                # opensnoop


        Trace all open() syscalls, for 10 seconds only:
                # opensnoop -d 10


[...]
```

EXAMPLES explain the tool and its various capabilities by showing how it can be executed in different ways. This may be the most useful section of the man page.

```
FIELDS
        TIME(s)
                Time of the call, in seconds.


        UID     User ID
```

```
       PID     Process ID

       TID     Thread ID

       COMM    Process name

       FD      File descriptor (if success), or -1 (if failed)

       ERR     Error number (see the system's errno.h)
[...]
```

FIELDS explains every field that the tool can output. If a field has units, it should be included in the man page. This example spells out that "TIME(s)" is in seconds.

```
OVERHEAD
       This traces the kernel open function and prints output for each  event.
       As  the  rate  of  this is generally expected to be low (< 1000/s), the
       overhead is also expected to be negligible. If you have an  application
       that  is calling a high rate of open()s, then test and understand over-
       head before use.
```

The OVERHEAD section is the place to set expectations. If a user is aware of high overhead, they can plan for it and still use the tool successfully. In this example, the overhead is expected to be low.

```
SOURCE
       This is from bcc.

            https://github.com/iovisor/bcc

       Also look in the bcc distribution for a  companion  _examples.txt  file
       containing example usage, output, and commentary for this tool.

OS
       Linux

STABILITY
       Unstable - in development.

AUTHOR
       Brendan Gregg

SEE ALSO
       funccount(1)
```

The final sections show that this tool is from BCC, and other metadata, and they also include pointers to other reading: the examples file, and related tools in SEE ALSO.

If a tool has been ported from another tracer or is based on other work, it is desirable to document that in the man page. There are many ports of BCC tools to the bpftrace repository, and the man pages in bpftrace state this in their SOURCE sections.

4.9.2 Examples File: opensnoop

Looking at output examples can be the best way to explain tools as their output may be intuitive: a sign of good tool design. Every tool in BCC has a dedicated text file of examples.

The first sentence of an examples file gives the tool name and version. Output examples are included, from basic to more advanced:

```
bcc$ more tools/opensnoop_example.txt
Demonstrations of opensnoop, the Linux eBPF/bcc version.


opensnoop traces the open() syscall system-wide, and prints various details.
Example output:

# ./opensnoop
PID    COMM      FD ERR PATH
17326  <...>      7   0 /sys/kernel/debug/tracing/trace_pipe
1576   snmpd      9   0 /proc/net/dev
1576   snmpd     11   0 /proc/net/if_inet6
1576   snmpd     11   0 /proc/sys/net/ipv4/neigh/eth0/retrans_time_ms
[...]

While tracing, the snmpd process opened various /proc files (reading metrics),
and a "run" process read various libraries and config files (looks like it
was starting up: a new process).

opensnoop can be useful for discovering configuration and log files, if used
during application startup.


The -p option can be used to filter on a PID, which is filtered in-kernel. Here
I've used it with -T to print timestamps:
```

```
./opensnoop -Tp 1956
TIME(s)          PID    COMM             FD  ERR  PATH
0.000000000      1956   supervise        9    0   supervise/status.new
0.000289999      1956   supervise        9    0   supervise/status.new
1.023068000      1956   supervise        9    0   supervise/status.new
1.023381997      1956   supervise        9    0   supervise/status.new
2.046030000      1956   supervise        9    0   supervise/status.new
2.046363000      1956   supervise        9    0   supervise/status.new
3.068203997      1956   supervise        9    0   supervise/status.new
3.068544999      1956   supervise        9    0   supervise/status.new

This shows the supervise process is opening the status.new file twice every
second.
[...]
```

The tool output is explained in the examples file, especially in the first example.

At the end of an examples file is a copy of the usage message. It might seem redundant, but it can be useful for browsing online. Examples files do not typically show every option in use, so ending with the usage message shows what else the tool can do.

4.10 Developing BCC Tools

Since most readers may prefer to program in the higher-level bpftrace language, this book focuses on bpftrace for tool development and uses BCC as a source of prewritten tools. BCC tool development is covered in Appendix C, as optional material.

Why develop tools in BCC, given the availability of bpftrace? BCC is suited for building complex tools with various command line arguments and options, and with fully customized output and actions. For example, a BCC tool can use networking libraries to send event data to a message server or database. In comparison, bpftrace is well suited for one-liners or short tools that accept no arguments or a single argument, and print text output only.

BCC also allows a lower level of control for BPF programs written in C, and for user-level components written in Python or one of the other supported languages. This comes at the cost of some complexity: BCC tools can take 10 times as long to develop as bpftrace tools, and they can include 10 times as many lines of code.

Whether you code in BCC or bpftrace, it's usually possible to port the core functionality from one to the other—once you've decided what that functionality should be. You might also use bpftrace as a prototyping and proof-of-concept language before developing tools fully in BCC.

For BCC tool development resources, tips, and examples with source code explained, see Appendix C.

The following sections cover BCC internals and debugging. If you are running but not developing BCC tools, there may nevertheless be times when you need to debug a broken tool and need to understand some BCC internals to help you do that.

4.11   BCC Internals

BCC consists of:

- C++ front-end API for composing kernel-level BPF programs, including:
  - A preprocessor for converting memory dereferences to bpf_probe_read() calls (and, in future kernels, variants of bpf_probe_read())
- C++ back-end drivers for:
  - Compiling the BPF program via Clang/LLVM
  - Loading the BPF program in the kernel
  - Attaching BPF programs to events
  - Reads/writes with BPF maps
- Language front-end APIs for composing BPF tools: Python, C++, and lua

This is pictured in Figure 4-5.

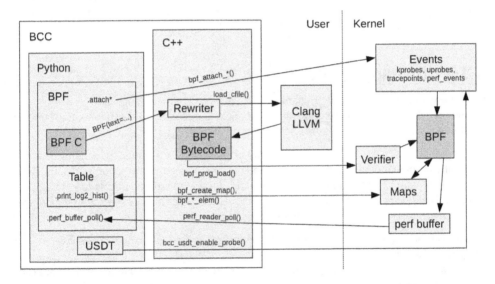

Figure 4-5   BCC internals

The BPF, Table, and USDT Python objects pictured in Figure 4-5 are wrappers to their implementation in libbcc and libbcc_bpf.

The Table object interacts with BPF maps. These tables have become BPF items of the BPF object (using Python "magic methods," like __getitem__), such that the following lines are equivalent:

```
counts = b.get_table("counts")
counts = b["counts"]
```

USDT is a separate object in Python, as its behavior is different from kprobes, uprobes, and tracepoints. It must be attached to a process ID or path during initialization because, unlike other event types, some USDT probes require semaphores to be set in the process image to activate them. These semaphores can be used by the application to determine whether the USDT probe is currently in use and whether to prepare its arguments, or if that can be skipped as a performance optimization.

The C++ components are compiled as libbcc_bpf and libbcc, which are used by other software (e.g., bpftrace). libbcc_bpf is from the Linux kernel source under tools/lib/bpf (and it originated from BCC).

The steps that BCC takes to load a BPF program and instrument events are:

1. The Python BPF object is created, and a BPF C program is passed to it.

2. The BCC rewriter pre-processes the BPF C program, replacing dereferences with bpf_probe_read() calls.

3. Clang compiles the BPF C program into LLVM IR.

4. BCC codegen adds additional LLVM IR, as needed.

5. LLVM compiles the IR into BPF bytecode.

6. Maps, if used, are created.

7. The bytecode is sent to the kernel and checked by the BPF verifier.

8. Events are enabled, and BPF programs are attached to the events.

9. The BCC program reads instrumented data either via maps or the perf_event buffer.

The next section sheds more light on these internals.

4.12 BCC Debugging

There are various ways to debug and troubleshoot BCC tools other than inserting printf() statements. This section summarizes print statements, BCC debug modes, bpflist, and resetting events. If you are reading this section because you are troubleshooting an issue, also check Chapter 18, which covers common issues such as missing events, missing stacks, and missing symbols.

Figure 4-6 shows the flow of program compilation and the various debugging tools that can be used for inspection along the way.

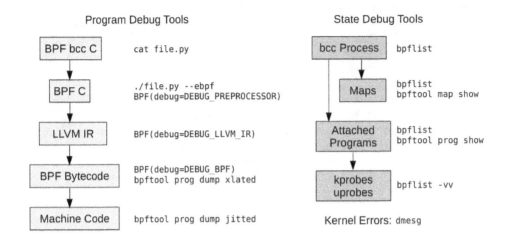

Figure 4-6   BCC debugging

These tools are explained in the following sections.

4.12.1   printf() Debugging

Debugging with printf() can feel like a hack compared to using more sophisticated debugging tools, but it can be effective and fast. printf() statements can be added not only to the Python code for debugging but also to the BPF code. There is a special helper function for this: bpf_trace_printk(). It emits output to a special Ftrace buffer, which can be read via cat(1) of the /sys/kernel/debug/tracing/trace_pipe files.

As an example, imagine that you have an issue with the biolatency(8) tool where it's compiling and running, but the output seems amiss. You could insert a printf() statement to confirm that probes are firing and that the variables used have the values they should have. Here is an example of an addition to biolatency.py, highlighted in bold:

```
[...]
// time block I/O
int trace_req_start(struct pt_regs *ctx, struct request *req)
{
    u64 ts = bpf_ktime_get_ns();
    start.update(&req, &ts);
    bpf_trace_printk("BDG req=%llx ts=%lld\\n", req, ts);
    return 0;
}
[...]
```

The "BDG" here is just my initials, added to clearly identify the output as being from my own debug session.

The tool can now be run:

```
# ./biolatency.py
Tracing block device I/O... Hit Ctrl-C to end.
```

and in another terminal session, the Ftrace trace_pipe file can be read with cat(1):

```
# cat /sys/kernel/debug/tracing/trace_pipe
[...]
    kworker/4:1H-409    [004] .... 2542952.834645: 0x00000001: BDG
req=ffff8934c90a1a00 ts=2543018287130107
    dmcrypt_write-354    [004] .... 2542952.836083: 0x00000001: BDG
req=ffff8934c7df3600 ts=2543018288564980
    dmcrypt_write-354    [004] .... 2542952.836093: 0x00000001: BDG
req=ffff8934c7df3800 ts=2543018288578569
    kworker/4:1H-409    [004] .... 2542952.836260: 0x00000001: BDG
req=ffff8934c90a1a00 ts=2543018288744416
    kworker/4:1H-409    [004] .... 2542952.837447: 0x00000001: BDG
req=ffff8934c7df3800 ts=2543018289932052
    dmcrypt_write-354    [004] .... 2542953.611762: 0x00000001: BDG
req=ffff8934c7df3800 ts=2543019064251153
    kworker/u16:4-5415   [005] d... 2542954.163671: 0x00000001: BDG
req=ffff8931622fa000 ts=2543019616168785
```

The output has various default fields that Ftrace adds, followed by our custom bpf_trace_printk() message at the end (which has line-wrapped).

If you cat(1) the trace file instead of trace_pipe, headers will be printed:

```
# cat /sys/kernel/debug/tracing/trace
# tracer: nop
#
#                               _-----=> irqs-off
#                              / _----=> need-resched
#                             | / _---=> hardirq/softirq
#                             || / _--=> preempt-depth
#                             ||| /     delay
#           TASK-PID   CPU#   ||||    TIMESTAMP  FUNCTION
#              | |       |    ||||       |          |
   kworker/u16:1-31496 [000] d... 2543476.300415: 0x00000001: BDG
req=ffff89345af53c00 ts=2543541760130509
   kworker/u16:4-5415  [000] d... 2543478.316378: 0x00000001: BDG
req=ffff89345af54c00 ts=2543543776117611
[...]
```

The differences between these files are:

- **trace:** Prints header; doesn't block.
- **trace_pipe:** Blocks for more messages and clears messages as it reads them.

This Ftrace buffer (viewed via trace and trace_pipe) is used by other Ftrace tools, so your debug messages may get mixed up with other messages. It works well enough for debugging and, if needed, you can filter the messages to see only those of interest (e.g., for this example, you could use: `grep BDG /sys/.../trace`).

With bpftool(8), covered in Chapter 2, you can print the Ftrace buffer by using: `bpftool prog tracelog`.

4.12.2 BCC Debug Output

Some tools, such as funccount(8) `-D`, already provide options for printing debug output. Check the tool USAGE message (with `-h` or `--help`) to see if a tool has this option. Many tools have an undocumented `--ebpf` option, which prints the final BPF program that the tool has generated.[7] For example:

```
# opensnoop --ebpf

#include <uapi/linux/ptrace.h>
#include <uapi/linux/limits.h>
#include <linux/sched.h>

struct val_t {
    u64 id;
    char comm[TASK_COMM_LEN];
    const char *fname;
};

struct data_t {
    u64 id;
    u64 ts;
    u32 uid;
    int ret;
    char comm[TASK_COMM_LEN];
    char fname[NAME_MAX];
};

BPF_HASH(infotmp, u64, struct val_t);
```

---

7 The –ebpf option was added to support a BCC PCP PMDA (see Chapter 17), and since it was not really intended for end-user use, it is not documented in the usage message to avoid clutter.

```
BPF_PERF_OUTPUT(events);

int trace_entry(struct pt_regs *ctx, int dfd, const char __user *filename, int flags)
{
    struct val_t val = {};
    u64 id = bpf_get_current_pid_tgid();
    u32 pid = id >> 32; // PID is higher part
    u32 tid = id;       // Cast and get the lower part
    u32 uid = bpf_get_current_uid_gid();
[...]
```

This may be useful in cases where the BPF program is rejected by the kernel: You can print it out and check for issues.

4.12.3 BCC Debug Flag

BCC provides a debugging capability that is available for all tools: adding the debug flag to the BPF object initializer in the program. For example, in opensnoop.py, there is the line:

```
b = BPF(text=bpf_text)
```

This can be changed to include a debug setting:

```
b = BPF(text=bpf_text, debug=0x2)
```

This prints BPF instructions when the program is run:

```
# opensnoop
0:  (79) r7 = *(u64 *)(r1 +104)
1:  (b7) r1 = 0
2:  (7b) *(u64 *)(r10 -8) = r1
3:  (7b) *(u64 *)(r10 -16) = r1
4:  (7b) *(u64 *)(r10 -24) = r1
5:  (7b) *(u64 *)(r10 -32) = r1
6:  (85) call bpf_get_current_pid_tgid#14
7:  (bf) r6 = r0
8:  (7b) *(u64 *)(r10 -40) = r6
9:  (85) call bpf_get_current_uid_gid#15
10: (bf) r1 = r10
11: (07) r1 += -24
12: (b7) r2 = 16
13: (85) call bpf_get_current_comm#16
14: (67) r0 <<= 32
[...]
```

The BPF debugging options are single-bit flags that can be combined. They are listed in src/cc/bpf_module.h and shown here:

Bit	Name	Debug
0x1	DEBUG_LLVM_IR	Prints a compiled LLVM intermediate representation
0x2	DEBUG_BPF	Prints BPF bytecode and registers state on branches
0x4	DEBUG_PREPROCESSOR	Prints a pre-processor result (similar to --ebpf)
0x8	DEBUG_SOURCE	Prints ASM instructions embedded with source
0x10	DEBUG_BPF_REGISTER_STATE	Prints the register state on all instructions
0x20	DEBUG_BTF	Prints BTF debugging (BTF errors are otherwise ignored)

debug=0x1f prints everything, which can be dozens of pages of output.

4.12.4   bpflist

The bpflist(8) tool in BCC lists tools that have running BPF programs along with some details. For example:

```
# bpflist
PID    COMM        TYPE    COUNT
30231  opensnoop   prog    2
30231  opensnoop   map     2
```

This shows that the opensnoop(8) tool is running with PID 30231 and is using two BPF programs and two maps. This makes sense: opensnoop(8) instruments two events with a BPF program for each, and has a map for information between probes and a map for emitting data to user space.

A -v (verbose) mode counts kprobes and uprobes, and -vv (very verbose) counts and lists kprobes and uprobes. For example:

```
# bpflist -vv
open kprobes:
p:kprobes/p_do_sys_open_bcc_31364 do_sys_open
r:kprobes/r_do_sys_open_bcc_31364 do_sys_open

open uprobes:

PID    COMM        TYPE    COUNT
1      systemd     prog    6
1      systemd     map     6
31364  opensnoop   map     2
31364  opensnoop   kprobe  2
31364  opensnoop   prog    2
```

This shows two BPF programs running: systemd (PID 1) and opensnoop (PID 31364). The -vv mode also lists open kprobes and uprobes. Note that the PID consumer, 31364, is encoded in the kprobe names.

4.12.5 bpftool

bpftool is from the Linux source tree, and can show running programs, list BPF instructions, interact with maps, and more. It is covered in Chapter 2.

4.12.6 dmesg

Sometimes a kernel error from BPF or its event sources appears in the system log and can be viewed using dmesg(1). For example:

```
# dmesg
[...]
[8470906.869945] trace_kprobe: Could not insert probe at vfs_rread+0: -2
```

This is an error about attempting to create a kprobe for the vfs_rread() kernel function; it is a typo as vfs_rread() does not exist.

4.12.7 Resetting Events

Developing software typically involves a cycle of writing new code and then fixing bugs. When introducing bugs in BCC tools or libraries, you may cause BCC to crash after tracing has been enabled. This can leave kernel event sources in an enabled state with no process to consume their events, costing some needless overhead.

This was an issue with the older Ftrace-based interfaces in /sys, which BCC originally used for instrumenting all event sources with the exception of perf_events (PMCs). perf_events used perf_event_open(), which is file-descriptor based. A benefit with perf_event_open() is that a crashing process triggers kernel cleanup of its file descriptors, which then triggers cleanup of its enabled event sources. In Linux 4.17 and later, BCC has switched to the perf_event_open() interface for all event sources, so leftover kernel enablings should become a thing of the past.

If you are on an older kernel, you can use a tool in BCC called reset-trace.sh, which cleans up the Ftrace kernel state, removing all enabled tracing events. Only use this tool if you know there are no tracing consumers still running on the system (not just BCC, but any tracer), as it will prematurely terminate their event sources.

Here is some output from my BCC development server:

```
# reset-trace.sh -v
Reseting tracing state...

Checking /sys/kernel/debug/tracing/kprobe_events
Needed to reset /sys/kernel/debug/tracing/kprobe_events
```

```
kprobe_events, before (line enumerated):
   1 r:kprobes/r_d_lookup_1_bcc_22344 d_lookup
   2 p:kprobes/p_d_lookup_1_bcc_22344 d_lookup
   3 p:kprobes/p_lookup_fast_1_bcc_22344 lookup_fast
   4 p:kprobes/p_sys_execve_1_bcc_12659 sys_execve
[...]
kprobe_events, after (line enumerated):

Checking /sys/kernel/debug/tracing/uprobe_events
Needed to reset /sys/kernel/debug/tracing/uprobe_events
uprobe_events, before (line enumerated):
   1 p:uprobes/p__proc_self_exe_174476_1_bcc_22344 /proc/self/exe:0x0000000000174476
   2 p:uprobes/p__bin_bash_ad610_1_bcc_12827 /bin/bash:0x00000000000ad610
   3 r:uprobes/r__bin_bash_ad610_1_bcc_12833 /bin/bash:0x00000000000ad610
   4 p:uprobes/p__bin_bash_8b860_1_bcc_23181 /bin/bash:0x000000000008b860
[...]
uprobe_events, after (line enumerated):

Checking /sys/kernel/debug/tracing/trace
Checking /sys/kernel/debug/tracing/current_tracer
Checking /sys/kernel/debug/tracing/set_ftrace_filter
Checking /sys/kernel/debug/tracing/set_graph_function
Checking /sys/kernel/debug/tracing/set_ftrace_pid
Checking /sys/kernel/debug/tracing/events/enable
Checking /sys/kernel/debug/tracing/tracing_thresh
Checking /sys/kernel/debug/tracing/tracing_on

Done.
```

In this verbose mode of operation (-v), all the steps reset-trace.sh is performing are printed. The blank lines in the output, after resetting kprobe_events and uprobe_events, show that the reset was successful.

4.13 Summary

The BCC project provides more than 70 BPF performance tools, many of which support customizations via command line options and all are provided with documentation: man pages and examples files. Most are single-purpose tools, each focusing on observing one activity well. Some are multi-purpose tools; I covered four of them in this chapter: funccount(8) for counting events, stackcount(8) for counting the stack traces that led to events, trace(8) for printing custom per-event output, and argdist(8) for summarizing event arguments as counts or histograms. This chapter also covers BCC debugging tools. Appendix C provides examples of how to develop new BCC tools.

Chapter 5

bpftrace

bpftrace is an open source tracer built on BPF and BCC. Like BCC, bpftrace ships with many performance tools and supporting documentation. However, it also provides a high-level programming language that allows you to create powerful one-liners and short tools. For example, summarizing the vfs_read() return value (bytes or error value) as a histogram using bpftrace one-liner:

```
# bpftrace -e 'kretprobe:vfs_read { @bytes = hist(retval); }'
Attaching 1 probe...
^C

@bytes:
(..., 0)            223 |@@@@@@@@@@@@@                                        |
[0]                 110 |@@@@@@'                                             |
[1]                 581 |@@@@@@@@@@@@@@@@@@@@@@@@@@@@@@@@@@@@                  |
[2, 4)               23 |@                                                   |
[4, 8)                9 |                                                    |
[8, 16)             844 |@@@@@@@@@@@@@@@@@@@@@@@@@@@@@@@@@@@@@@@@@@@@@@@@@@@@@@|
[16, 32)             44 |@@                                                  |
[32, 64)             67 |@@@@                                                |
[64, 128)            50 |@@@                                                 |
[128, 256)           24 |@                                                   |
[256, 512)            1 |                                                    |
```

bpftrace was created by Alastair Robertson in December 2016 as a spare-time project. Because it looked well designed and was a good fit with the existing BCC/LLVM/BPF toolchain, I joined the project and became a major contributor of code, performance tools, and documentation. We've now been joined by many others, and we finished adding the first set of major features during 2018.

This chapter introduces bpftrace and its features, provides an overview of its tools and documentation, explains the bpftrace programming language, and ends with a tour of bpftrace debugging and internals.

Learning objectives:

- Gain knowledge of bpftrace features and how they compare to other tools

- Learn where to find tools and documentation, and how to execute tools

- Learn how to read the bpftrace source code included in later chapters

- Develop new one-liners and tools in the bpftrace programming language

- (optional) Get exposure to bpftrace internals

If you want to immediately start learning bpftrace programming, you can jump to Section 5.7 and then later return here to finish learning about bpftrace.

bpftrace is ideal for ad hoc instrumentation with custom one-liners and short scripts, whereas BCC is ideal for complex tools and daemons.

5.1   bpftrace Components

The high-level directory structure of bpftrace is shown in Figure 5-1.

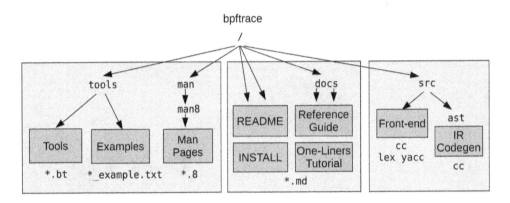

Figure 5-1   bpftrace structure

bpftrace contains documentation for the tools, man pages, and examples files, as well as a bpftrace programming tutorial (the one-liners tutorial) and a reference guide for the programming language. The included bpftrace tools have the extension .bt.

The front end uses lex and yacc to parse the bpftrace programming language, and Clang for parsing structures. The back end compiles bpftrace programs into LLVM intermediate representation, which is then compiled to BPF by LLVM libraries. See Section 5.16 for details.

5.2   bpftrace Features

Feature lists can help you learn the capabilities of a new technology. I created desired feature lists for bpftrace to guide development, and these are now delivered features and are listed in this section. In Chapter 4, I grouped the BCC feature lists by kernel- and user-level features, since those are different APIs. With bpftrace, there is only one API: bpftrace programming. These bpftrace features have instead been grouped by event sources, actions, and general features.

5.2.1   bpftrace Event Sources

These event sources use kernel-level technologies that were introduced in Chapter 2. The bpftrace interface (the probe type) is shown in parentheses:

- Dynamic instrumentation, kernel-level (`kprobe`)
- Dynamic instrumentation, user-level (`uprobe`)
- Static tracing, kernel-level (`tracepoint`, `software`)
- Static tracing, user-level (`usdt`, via libbcc)
- Timed sampling events (`profile`)
- Interval events (`interval`)
- PMC events (`hardware`)
- Synthetic events (`BEGIN`, `END`)

These probe types are explained in more detail in Section 5.9. More event sources are planned in the future and may exist by the time you read this; they include sockets and skb events, raw tracepoints, memory breakpoints, and custom PMCs.

5.2.2   bpftrace Actions

These are actions that can be performed when an event fires. The following is a selection of key actions; the full list is in the bpftrace Reference Guide:

- Filtering (predicates)
- Per-event output (`printf()`)
- Basic variables (*global*, *$local*, and *per[tid]*)
- Built-in variables (`pid`, `tid`, `comm`, `nsecs`, ...)
- Associative arrays (*key[value]*)
- Frequency counting (`count()` or `++`)
- Statistics (`min()`, `max()`, `sum()`, `avg()`, `stats()`)

- Histograms (`hist()`, `lhist()`)
- Timestamps and time deltas (`nsecs`, and hash storage)
- Stack traces, kernel (`kstack`)
- Stack traces, user (`ustack`)
- Symbol resolution, kernel-level (`ksym()`, `kaddr()`)
- Symbol resolution, user-level (`usym()`, `uaddr()`)
- C struct navigation (`->`)
- Array access (`[]`)
- Shell commands (`system()`)
- Printing files (`cat()`)
- Positional parameters (`$1`, `$2`, ...)

Actions are explained in more detail in Section 5.7. More actions may be added where there are strong use cases, but it is desirable to keep the language as small as possible to make it easier to learn.

5.2.3   bpftrace General Features

The following are general bpftrace features and components of the repository:

- Low-overhead instrumentation (BPF JIT, and maps)
- Production safe (BPF verifier)
- Many tools (under /tools)
- Tutorial (/docs/tutorial_one_liners.md)
- Reference guide (/docs/reference_guide.md)

5.2.4   bpftrace Compared to Other Observability Tools

Comparing bpftrace to other tracers that can also instrument all event types:

- **perf(1)**: bpftrace provides a higher-level language that is concise, whereas the perf(1) scripting language is verbose. perf(1) supports efficient event dumping in a binary format via perf record and in-memory summary modes such as perf top. bpftrace supports efficient in-kernel summaries, such as custom histograms, whereas perf(1)'s built-in in-kernel summaries are limited to counts (perf stat). perf(1)'s capabilities can be extended by running BPF programs, although not in a high-level language like bpftrace; see Appendix D for a perf(1) BPF example.

- **Ftrace**: bpftrace provides a higher-level language that resembles C and awk, whereas the Ftrace custom instrumentation, including hist-triggers, has a special syntax of its own. Ftrace has fewer dependencies, making it suited for tiny Linux environments. Ftrace also has instrumentation modes such as function counts that have so far been performance optimized more than the event sources used by bpftrace. (My Ftrace funccount(8) currently has faster start and stop times and lower runtime overhead than a bpftrace equivalent.)

- **SystemTap:** Both bpftrace and SystemTap provide higher-level languages. bpftrace is based on built-in Linux technologies, whereas SystemTap adds its own kernel modules, which have proven unreliable on systems other than RHEL. Work has begun for SystemTap to support a BPF back end, as bpftrace does, which should make it reliable on these other systems. SystemTap currently has more helper functionality in its libraries (tapsets) for instrumenting different targets.

- **LTTng:** LTTng has optimized event dumping and provides tools for analyzing event dumps. This takes a different approach to performance analysis than bpftrace, which is designed for ad hoc real-time analysis.

- **Application tools:** Application- and runtime-specific tools are limited to user-level visibility. bpftrace can also instrument kernel and hardware events, allowing it to identify the source of issues beyond the reach of those tools. An advantage of those tools is that they are usually tailored for the target application or runtime. A MySQL database profiler already understands how to instrument queries, and a JVM profiler already can instrument garbage collection. In bpftrace, you need to code such functionality yourself.

It is not necessary to use bpftrace in isolation. The goal is to solve problems, not to use bpftrace exclusively, and sometimes it is fastest to use a combination of these tools.

5.3 bpftrace Installation

bpftrace should be installable via a package for your Linux distribution, but at the time of writing, these packages have only begun to appear; the first bpftrace packages are a snap from Canonical[1] and a Debian package[2] that will also be available for Ubuntu 19.04. You can also build bpftrace from source. Check INSTALL.md in the bpftrace repository for the latest package and build instructions [63].

5.3.1 Kernel Requirements

It is recommended that you use a Linux 4.9 kernel (released in December 2016) or newer. The major BPF components that bpftrace uses were added between the 4.1 and 4.9 releases. Improvements have been added in later releases, so the newer your kernel, the better. The BCC documentation includes a list of BPF features by Linux kernel version, which helps explain why later kernels are better (see [64]).

Some kernel configuration options also need to be enabled. These options are now enabled by default in many distributions, so you typically do not need to change them. They are: CONFIG_BPF=y, CONFIG_BPF_SYSCALL=y, CONFIG_BPF_JIT=y, CONFIG_HAVE_EBPF_JIT=y, CONFIG_BPF_EVENTS=y.

---

1 Thanks to Colin Ian King [61].

2 Thanks to Vincent Bernat [62].

5.3.2   Ubuntu

Once the bpftrace package is available for your Ubuntu distribution, installation should be:

```
sudo apt-get update
sudo apt-get install bpftrace
```

bpftrace can also be built and installed from source:

```
sudo apt-get update
sudo apt-get install bison cmake flex g++ git libelf-dev zlib1g-dev libfl-dev \
  systemtap-sdt-dev llvm-7-dev llvm-7-runtime libclang-7-dev clang-7
git clone https://github.com/iovisor/bpftrace
mkdir bpftrace/build; cd bpftrace/build
cmake -DCMAKE_BUILD_TYPE=Release ..
make
make install
```

5.3.3   Fedora

Once bpftrace has been packaged, installation should be:

```
sudo dnf install -y bpftrace
```

bpftrace can also be built from source:

```
sudo dnf install -y bison flex cmake make git gcc-c++ elfutils-libelf-devel \
  zlib-devel llvm-devel clang-devel bcc-devel
git clone https://github.com/iovisor/bpftrace
cd bpftrace
mkdir build; cd build; cmake -DCMAKE_BUILD_TYPE=DEBUG ..
make
```

5.3.4   Post-Build Steps

To confirm that the build was successful, you can run the test suite and a one-liner as an experiment:

```
sudo ./tests/bpftrace_test
sudo ./src/bpftrace -e 'kprobe:do_nanosleep { printf("sleep by %s\n", comm); }'
```

Run sudo make install to install the bpftrace binary as /usr/local/bin/bpftrace and the tools in /usr/local/share/bpftrace/tools. You can change the install location by using a cmake(1) option, where -DCMAKE_INSTALL_PREFIX=/usr/local is the default.

5.3.5   Other Distributions

Check for an available bpftrace package, as well as the bpftrace INSTALL.md instructions.

5.4   bpftrace Tools

Figure 5-2 shows major system components, as well as tools from the bpftrace repository and this book that can observe them.

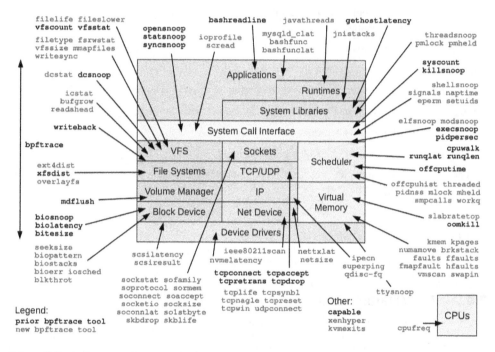

Figure 5-2   bpftrace performance tools

The current tools in the bpftrace repository are colored black, and the new bpftrace tools from this book are colored differently (red or gray, depending on your version of this book). Some variations are not included here (e.g., the qdisc variants from Chapter 10).

5.4.1 Highlighted Tools

Table 5-1 lists a selection of tools organized by topic. These tools are covered in detail in later chapters.

Table 5-1   Selected bpftrace Tools, by Topic and Chapter

Topic	Highlighted Tools	Chapter(s)
CPU	execsnoop.bt, runqlat.bt, runqlen.bt, cpuwalk.bt, offcputime.bt	6
Memory	oomkill.bt, failts.bt, vmscan.bt, swapin.bt	7
File systems	vfsstat.bt, filelife.bt, xfsdist.bt	8
Storage I/O	biosnoop.bt, biolatency.bt, bitesize.bt, biostacks.bt, scsilatency.bt, nvmelatency.bt	9
Networking	tcpaccept.bt, tcpconnect.bt, tcpdrop.bt, tcpretrans.bt, gethostlatency.bt	10
Security	ttysnoop.bt, elfsnoop.bt, setuids.bt	11
Languages	jnistacks.bt, javacalls.bt	12
Applications	threadsnoop.bt, pmheld.bt, naptime.bt, mysqld_qslower.bt	13
Kernel	mlock.bt, mheld.bt, kmem,bt, kpages.bt, workq.bt	14
Containers	pidnss.bt, blkthrot.bt	15
Hypervisors	xenhyper.bt, cpustolen.bt, kvmexits.bt	16
Debugging / multi-purpose	execsnoop.bt, threadsnoop.bt, opensnoop.bt, killsnoop.bt, signals.bt	6, 8, 13

Note that this book also describes BCC tools that are not listed in Table 5-1.

After reading this chapter, you can jump to later chapters and use this book as a reference guide.

5.4.2 Tool Characteristics

The bpftrace tools have a number of characteristics in common:

- They solve real-world observability issues.
- They are designed to be run in production environments, as the root user.
- There is a man page for every tool (under man/man8).
- There is an examples file for every tool, containing output and discussion (under tools/*_examples.txt).
- The tool source code begins with a block comment introduction.
- The tools are as simple as possible, and short. (More complex tools are deferred to BCC.)

5.4.3   Tool Execution

Bundled tools are executable and can be run immediately as the root user:

```
bpftrace/tools$ ls -lh opensnoop.bt
-rwxr-xr-x 1 bgregg bgregg 1.1K Nov 13 10:56 opensnoop.bt*

bpftrace/tools$ ./opensnoop.bt
ERROR: bpftrace currently only supports running as the root user.

bpftrace/tools$ sudo ./opensnoop.bt
Attaching 5 probes...
Tracing open syscalls... Hit Ctrl-C to end.
PID    COMM             FD ERR PATH
25612  bpftrace         23   0 /dev/null
1458   Xorg            118   0 /proc/18416/cmdline
[...]
```

These tools can be placed with other system administration tools in an sbin diectory, such as /usr/local/sbin.

5.5   bpftrace One-Liners

This section provides a selection of one-liners that are useful both in themselves and to demonstrate the various bpftrace capabilities. The next section explains the programming language, and later chapters introduce more one-liners for specific targets. Note that many of these one-liners summarize data in (kernel) memory and do not print a summary until terminated with Ctrl-C.

Show who is executing what:

```
bpftrace -e 'tracepoint:syscalls:sys_enter_execve { printf("%s -> %s\n", comm,
    str(args->filename)); }'
```

Show new processes with arguments:

```
bpftrace -e 'tracepoint:syscalls:sys_enter_execve { join(args->argv); }'
```

Show files opened using openat() by process:

```
bpftrace -e 'tracepoint:syscalls:sys_enter_openat { printf("%s %s\n", comm,
    str(args->filename)); }'
```

Count syscalls by program:

```
bpftrace -e 'tracepoint:raw_syscalls:sys_enter { @[comm] = count(); }'
```

Count syscallst by syscall probe name:

```
bpftrace -e 'tracepoint:syscalls:sys_enter_* { @[probe] = count(); }'
```

Count syscalls by process:

```
bpftrace -e 'tracepoint:raw_syscalls:sys_enter { @[pid, comm] = count(); }'
```

Show the total read bytes by process:

```
bpftrace -e 'tracepoint:syscalls:sys_exit_read /args->ret/ { @[comm] =
    sum(args->ret); }'
```

Show the read size distribution by process:

```
bpftrace -e 'tracepoint:syscalls:sys_exit_read { @[comm] = hist(args->ret); }'
```

Show the trace disk I/O size by process:

```
bpftrace -e 'tracepoint:block:block_rq_issue { printf("%d %s %d\n", pid, comm,
    args->bytes); }'
```

Count pages paged in by process:

```
bpftrace -e 'software:major-faults:1 { @[comm] = count(); }'
```

Count page faults by process:

```
bpftrace -e 'software:faults:1 { @[comm] = count(); }'
```

Profile user-level stacks at 49 Hertz for PID 189:

```
bpftrace -e 'profile:hz:49 /pid == 189/ { @[ustack] = count(); }'
```

5.6 bpftrace Documentation

Each bpftrace tool has an accompanying man page and examples file, just as the tools also do in the BCC project. Chapter 4 discusses the format and intent of these files.

To help people learn to develop new one-liners and tools, I created the "bpftrace One-Liner Tutorial" [65], and the "bpftrace Reference Guide" [66]. These can be found in the /docs directory in the repository.

5.7 bpftrace Programming

This section provides a short guide to using bpftrace and programming in the bpftrace language. The format of this section was inspired by the original paper for awk [Aho 78], which covered that language in six pages. The bpftrace language itself is inspired by both awk and C, and by tracers including DTrace and SystemTap.

The following is an example of bpftrace programming: It measures the time in the vfs_read() kernel function and prints the time, in microseconds, as a histogram. This summary section explains the components of this tool.

```
#!/usr/local/bin/bpftrace

// this program times vfs_read()

kprobe:vfs_read
{
        @start[tid] = nsecs;
}

kretprobe:vfs_read
/@start[tid]/
{
        $duration_us = (nsecs - @start[tid]) / 1000;
        @us = hist($duration_us);
        delete(@start[tid]);
}
```

The five sections after this summary cover bpftrace programming in more detail. Those sections are: probes, tests, operators, variables, functions, and map types.

5.7.1 Usage

The command:

```
bpftrace -e program
```

will execute the program, instrumenting any events it defines. The program will run until Ctrl-C, or until it explicitly calls exit(). A bpftrace program run as a -e argument is termed a *one-liner*. Alternatively, the program can be saved to a file and executed using:

```
bpftrace file.bt
```

The .bt extension is not necessary, but helps for later identification. By placing an interpreter line at the top of the file[3]:

```
#!/usr/local/bin/bpftrace
```

---

3 Some people prefer using #!/usr/bin/env bpftrace so that bpftrace can be found from the $PATH. However, env(1) comes with various problems, so its usage for the BCC repository was reverted. The bpftrace repository currently uses env(1), but that may be reverted for similar reasons.

The file can be made executable (`chmod a+x file.bt`) and run like any other program:

```
./file.bt
```

bpftrace must be executed by the root user (superuser).[4] For some environments, the root shell may be used to execute the program directly, whereas other environments may have a preference for running privileged commands via sudo(1):

```
sudo ./file.bt
```

5.7.2 Program Structure

A bpftrace program is a series of probes with associated actions:

```
probes { actions }
probes { actions }
...
```

When the probes fire, the associated action is executed. An optional filter expression can be included before the action:

```
probes /filter/ { actions }
```

The action only fires if the filter expression is true. This resembles the awk(1) program structure:

```
/pattern/ { actions }
```

awk(1) programming is also similar to bpftrace programming: Multiple action blocks can be defined, and they may execute in any order: triggered when their pattern, or probe + filter expression, is true.

5.7.3 Comments

For bpftrace program files, single-line comments can be added with a "//" prefix:

```
// this is a comment
```

These comments will not be executed. Multi-line comments use the same format as those in C:

```
/*
 * This is a
 * multi-line comment.
 */
```

This syntax can also be used for partial-line comments (e.g., `/* comment */`).

---

4 bpftrace checks for UID 0; a future update may check for specific privileges.

5.7.4 Probe Format

A probe begins with a probe type name and then a hierarchy of colon-delimited identifiers:

```
type:identifier1[:identifier2[...]]
```

The hierarchy is defined by the probe type. Consider these two examples:

```
kprobe:vfs_read
uprobe:/bin/bash:readline
```

The kprobe probe type instruments kernel function calls, and only needs one identifier: the kernel function name. The uprobe probe type instruments user-level function calls, and needs both the path to the binary and the function name.

Multiple probes can be specified with comma separators to execute the same actions. For example:

```
probe1,probe2,... { actions }
```

There are two special probe types that require no additional identifiers: BEGIN and END fire for the beginning and the end of the bpftrace program (just like awk(1)).

To learn more about the probe types and their usage, see Section 5.9.

5.7.5 Probe Wildcards

Some probe types accept wildcards. The probe:

```
kprobe:vfs_*
```

will instrument all kprobes (kernel functions) that begin with "vfs_".

Instrumenting too many probes may cost unnecessary performance overhead. To avoid hitting this by accident, bpftrace has a tunable maximum number of probes it will enable, set via the BPFTRACE_MAX_PROBES environment variable (it currently defaults to 512[5]).

You can test your wildcards before using them by running `bpftrace -l`:

```
# bpftrace -l 'kprobe:vfs_*'
kprobe:vfs_fallocate
kprobe:vfs_truncate
kprobe:vfs_open
kprobe:vfs_setpos
kprobe:vfs_llseek
```

---

5 Currently, having more than 512 probes makes bpftrace slow to start up and shut down, as it instruments them one by one. There is future kernel work planned to batch probe instrumentation. At that point, this limit may be greatly increased or even removed.

```
[...]
bpftrace -l 'kprobe:vfs_*' | wc -l
56
```

This matched 56 probes. The probe name is in quotes to prevent unintended shell expansion.

5.7.6   Filters

Filters are Boolean expressions that gate whether an action is executed. The filter

```
/pid == 123/
```

will execute the action only if the pid built-in (process ID) is equal to 123.

If a test is not specified:

```
/pid/
```

the filter will check that the contents are non-zero (/pid/ is the same as /pid != 0/). Filters can be combined with Boolean operators, such as logical AND (&&). For example:

```
/pid > 100 && pid < 1000/
```

This requires that both expressions evaluate to "true."

5.7.7   Actions

An action can be a single statement or multiple statements separated by semicolons:

```
{ action one; action two; action three }
```

The final statement may also have a semicolon appended. The statements are written in the bpftrace language, which is similar to the C language, and can manipulate variables and execute bpftrace function calls. For example, the action

```
{ $x = 42; printf("$x is %d", $x); }
```

sets a variable, $x, to 42, and then prints it using printf(). Sections 5.7.9 and 5.7.11 summarize other available function calls.

5.7.8   Hello, World!

You should now understand the following basic program, which prints "Hello, World!" when bpftrace begins running:

```
# bpftrace -e 'BEGIN { printf("Hello, World!\n"); }'
Attaching 1 probe...
Hello, World!
^C
```

As a file, it could be formatted as:

```
#!/usr/local/bin/bpftrace

BEGIN
{
        printf("Hello, World!\n");
}
```

Spanning multiple lines with an indented action block is not necessary, but it improves readability.

5.7.9   Functions

In addition to printf() for printing formatted output, other built-in functions include:

- **exit()**: Exits bpftrace
- **str(char *)**: Returns a string from a pointer
- **system(format[, arguments ...])**: Runs a command at the shell

The following action:

```
printf("got: %llx %s\n", $x, str($x)); exit();
```

will print the $x variable as a hex integer, and then treat it as a NULL-terminated character array pointer (char *) and print it as a string, and then exit.

5.7.10   Variables

There are three variable types: built-ins, scratch, and maps.

Built-in variables are pre-defined and provided by bpftrace, and are usually read-only sources of information. They include pid for the process id, comm for the process name, nsecs for a timestamp in nanoseconds, and curtask for the address of the current thread's task_struct.

Scratch variables can be used for temporary calculations and have the prefix "$". Their name and type is set on their first assignment. The statements:

```
$x = 1;
$y = "hello";
$z = (struct task_struct *)curtask;
```

declare $x as an integer, $y as a string, and $z as a pointer to a struct task_struct. These variables can only be used in the action block in which they were assigned. If variables are referenced without an assignment, bpftrace errors (which can help you catch typos).

Map variables use the BPF map storage object and have the prefix "@". They can be used for global storage, passing data between actions. The program

```
probe1 { @a = 1; }
probe2 { $x = @a; }
```

Assigns 1 to @a when probe1 fires, then assigns @a to $x when probe2 fires. If probe1 fired first and then probe2, $x would be set to 1; otherwise 0 (uninitialized).

A key can be provided with one or more elements, using maps as a hash table (an associative array). The statement:

```
@start[tid] = nsecs;
```

is frequently used: the nsecs built-in is assigned to a map named @start and keyed on tid, the current thread ID. This allows threads to store custom timestamps that won't be overwritten by other threads.

```
@path[pid, $fd] = str(arg0);
```

is an example of a multi-key map, one using both the pid builtin and the $fd variable as keys.

5.7.11 Map Functions

Maps can be assigned to special functions. These functions store and print data in custom ways. The assignment

```
@x = count();
```

counts events, and when printed will print the count. This uses a per-CPU map, and @x becomes a special object of type count. The following statement also counts events:

```
@x++;
```

However, this uses a global CPU map, instead of a per-CPU map, to provide @x as an integer. This global integer type is sometimes necessary for some programs that require an integer and not a count, but bear in mind that there may be a small error margin due to concurrent updates (see Section 2.3.7 in Chapter 2).

The assignment

```
@y = sum($x);
```

sums the $x variable, and when printed will print the total. The assignment

```
@z = hist($x);
```

stores $x in a power-of-two histogram, and when printed will print bucket counts and an ASCII histogram.

Some map functions operate directly on a map. For example:

```
print(@x);
```

will print the @x map. This is not used often because, for convenience, all maps are automatically printed when bpftrace terminates.

Some map functions operate on a map key. For example:

```
delete(@start[tid]);
```

deletes the key-value pair from the @start map where the key is tid.

5.7.12   Timing vfs_read()

You have now learned the syntax needed to understand a more involved and practical example. This program, vfsread.bt, times the vfs_read kernel function and prints out a histogram of its duration in microseconds (us):

```
#!/usr/local/bin/bpftrace

// this program times vfs_read()

kprobe:vfs_read
{
        @start[tid] = nsecs;
}

kretprobe:vfs_read
/@start[tid]/
{
        $duration_us = (nsecs - @start[tid]) / 1000;
        @us = hist($duration_us);
        delete(@start[tid]);
}
```

This times the duration of the vfs_read() kernel function by instrumenting its start using a kprobe and storing a timestamp in a @start hash keyed on thread ID, and then instrumenting its end by using a kretprobe and calculating the delta as: now - start. A filter is used to ensure that the start time was recorded; otherwise, the delta calculation becomes bogus: now - 0.

Sample output:

```
# bpftrace vfsread.bt
Attaching 2 probes...
^C
```

```
@us:
[0]                       23 |@                                                          |
[1]                      138 |@@@@@@@@@                                                  |
[2, 4)                   538 |@@@@@@@@@@@@@@@@@@@@@@@@@@@@@@@@@@@@@@@@                     |
[4, 8)                   744 |@@@@@@@@@@@@@@@@@@@@@@@@@@@@@@@@@@@@@@@@@@@@@@@@@@@@@@@@@@@@@@|
[8, 16)                  641 |@@@@@@@@@@@@@@@@@@@@@@@@@@@@@@@@@@@@@@@@@@@@@@@@@@@@@         |
[16, 32)                 122 |@@@@@@@@@                                                  |
[32, 64)                  13 |                                                           |
[64, 128)                 17 |@                                                          |
[128, 256)                 2 |                                                           |
[256, 512)                 0 |                                                           |
[512, 1K)                  1 |                                                           |
```

The program ran until Ctrl-C was entered, then it printed this output and terminated. This histogram map was named "us" as a way to include units with the output, since the map name is printed out. By giving maps meaningful names like "bytes" and "latency_ns" you can annotate the output and make it self-explanatory.

This script can be customized as needed. Consider changing the hist() assignment line to:

```
@us[pid, comm] = hist($duration_us);
```

That stores one histogram per process ID and process name pair. The output becomes:

```
# bpftrace vfsread.bt
Attaching 2 probes...
^C

@us[1847, gdbus]:
[1]                        2 |@@@@@@@@@@                                                 |
[2, 4)                    10 |@@@@@@@@@@@@@@@@@@@@@@@@@@@@@@@@@@@@@@@@@@@@@@@@@@@@@@@@@@@@@@|
[4, 8)                    10 |@@@@@@@@@@@@@@@@@@@@@@@@@@@@@@@@@@@@@@@@@@@@@@@@@@@@@@@@@@@@@@|

@us[1630, ibus-daemon]:
[2, 4)                     9 |@@@@@@@@@@@@@@@@@@@@@@@@@@@@@@                               |
[4, 8)                    17 |@@@@@@@@@@@@@@@@@@@@@@@@@@@@@@@@@@@@@@@@@@@@@@@@@@@@@@@@@@@@@@|

@us[29588, device poll]:
[1]                       13 |@@@@@@@@@@@@@@@@@@@@@@@@@@@@@@@@@@@@@@@@@@@@@@@@             |
[2, 4)                    15 |@@@@@@@@@@@@@@@@@@@@@@@@@@@@@@@@@@@@@@@@@@@@@@@@@@@@@@@@@@@@@@|
[4, 8)                     4 |@@@@@@@@@@@@@@                                             |
[8, 16)                    4 |@@@@@@@@@@@@@@                                             |
[...]
```

This illustrates one of the most useful capabilities of bpftrace. With traditional system tools, like iostat(1) and vmstat(1), the output is fixed and cannot be easily customized. But with bpftrace, the metrics you see can be further broken down into parts and enhanced with metrics from other probes until you have the answers you need.

5.8 bpftrace Usage

With no arguments (or -h), the bpftrace USAGE message is printed, which summarizes important options and environment variables and lists some example one-liners:

```
# bpftrace
USAGE:
    bpftrace [options] filename
    bpftrace [options] -e 'program'

OPTIONS:
    -B MODE        output buffering mode ('line', 'full', or 'none')
    -d             debug info dry run
    -o file        redirect program output to file
    -dd            verbose debug info dry run
    -e 'program'   execute this program
    -h, --help     show this help message
    -I DIR         add the directory to the include search path
    --include FILE add an #include file before preprocessing
    -l [search]    list probes
    -p PID         enable USDT probes on PID
    -c 'CMD'       run CMD and enable USDT probes on resulting process
    --unsafe       allow unsafe builtin functions
    -v             verbose messages
    -V, --version  bpftrace version

ENVIRONMENT:
    BPFTRACE_STRLEN            [default: 64] bytes on BPF stack per str()
    BPFTRACE_NO_CPP_DEMANGLE   [default: 0] disable C++ symbol demangling
    BPFTRACE_MAP_KEYS_MAX      [default: 4096] max keys in a map
    BPFTRACE_CAT_BYTES_MAX     [default: 10k] maximum bytes read by cat builtin
    BPFTRACE_MAX_PROBES        [default: 512] max number of probes

EXAMPLES:
bpftrace -l '*sleep*'
    list probes containing "sleep"
bpftrace -e 'kprobe:do_nanosleep { printf("PID %d sleeping...\n", pid); }'
    trace processes calling sleep
bpftrace -e 'tracepoint:raw_syscalls:sys_enter { @[comm] = count(); }'
    count syscalls by process name
```

This output is from bpftrace version v0.9-232-g60e6, 15-Jun-2019. As more features are added this USAGE message may become unwieldy, and a short and a long version may be added. Check the output for your current version to see if this is the case.

5.9   bpftrace Probe Types

Table 5-2 lists available probe types. Many of these also have a shortcut alias, which help create shorter one-liners.

Table 5-2   bpftrace Probe Types

Type	Shortcut	Description
tracepoint	t	Kernel static instrumentation points
usdt	U	User-level statically defined tracing
kprobe	k	Kernel dynamic function instrumentation
kretprobe	kr	Kernel dynamic function return instrumentation
uprobe	u	User-level dynamic function instrumentation
uretprobe	ur	User-level dynamic function return instrumentation
software	s	Kernel software-based events
hardware	h	Hardware counter-based instrumentation
profile	p	Timed sampling across all CPUs
interval	i	Timed reporting (from one CPU)
BEGIN		Start of bpftrace
END		End of bpftrace

These probe types are interfaces to existing kernel technologies. Chapter 2 explains how these technologies work: kprobes, uprobes, tracepoints, USDT, and PMCs (used by the hardware probe type).

Some probes may fire frequently, such as for scheduler events, memory allocations, and network packets. To reduce overhead, try to solve your problems by using less-frequent events wherever possible. See Chapter 18 for a discussion on minimizing overhead that applies to both BCC and bpftrace development.

The following sections summarize bpftrace probe usage.

5.9.1   tracepoint

The tracepoint probe type instruments tracepoints: kernel static instrumentation points. Format:

```
tracepoint:tracepoint_name
```

The tracepoint_name is the full name of the tracepoint, including the colon, which separates the tracepoint into its own hierarchy of class and event name. For example, the tracepoint net:netif_rx can be instrumented in bpftrace with the probe tracepoint:net:netif_rx.

Tracepoints usually provide arguments: these are fields of information that can be accessed in bpftrace via the args built-in. For example, net:netif_rx has a field called len for the packet length that can accessed using args->len.

If you're new to bpftrace and tracing, system call tracepoints are good targets to instrument. They provide broad coverage of kernel resource usage and have a well-documented API: the syscall man pages. For example, the tracepoints:

```
syscalls:sys_enter_read
syscalls:sys_exit_read
```

instrument the start and end of the read(2) system call. The man page has its signature:

```
ssize_t read(int fd, void *buf, size_t count);
```

For the sys_enter_read tracepoint, its arguments should be available as args->fd, args->buf, and args->count. This can be checked using the -l (list) and -v (verbose) modes of bpftrace:

```
# bpftrace -lv tracepoint:syscalls:sys_enter_read
tracepoint:syscalls:sys_enter_read
    int __syscall_nr;
    unsigned int fd;
    char * buf;
    size_t count;
```

The man page also describes what these arguments are and the return value of the read(2) syscall, which can be instrumented using the sys_exit_read tracepoint. This tracepoint has an additional argument not found in the man page, __syscall_nr, for the syscall number.

As an interesting tracepoint example, I will trace the enter and exit of the clone(2) syscall, which creates new processes (similar to fork(2)). For these events, I will print the current process name and PID using bpftrace built-in variables. For the exit, I will also print the return value using a tracepoint argument:

```
# bpftrace -e 'tracepoint:syscalls:sys_enter_clone {
    printf("-> clone() by %s PID %d\n", comm, pid); }
  tracepoint:syscalls:sys_exit_clone {
    printf("<- clone() return %d, %s PID %d\n", args->ret, comm, pid); }'
Attaching 2 probes...
-> clone() by bash PID 2582
<- clone() return 27804, bash PID 2582
<- clone() return 0, bash PID 27804
```

This syscall is unusual in that it has one entry and two exits! While tracing, I ran ls(1) in a bash(1) terminal. The parent process (PID 2582) can be seen to enter clone(2), and then there are two returns: one for the parent that returns the child PID (27804), and one for the child that returns zero (success). When the child begins, it is still "bash" as it has not yet executed an exec(2) family syscall to become "ls". That can be traced as well:

```
# bpftrace -e 't:syscalls:sys_*_execve { printf("%s %s PID %d\n", probe, comm,
    pid); }'
Attaching 2 probes...
tracepoint:syscalls:sys_enter_execve bash PID 28181
tracepoint:syscalls:sys_exit_execve ls PID 28181
```

This output shows PID 28181 enter the execve(2) syscall as "bash", and then exiting as "ls".

5.9.2   usdt

This probe type instruments user-level static instrumentation points. Format:

```
usdt:binary_path:probe_name
usdt:library_path:probe_name
usdt:binary_path:probe_namespace:probe_name
usdt:library_path:probe_namespace:probe_name
```

usdt can instrument executable binaries or shared libraries by providing the full path. The probe_name is the USDT probe name from the binary. For example, a probe named query__start in MySQL server may be accessible (depending on the installed path) as usdt:/usr/local/sbin/mysqld:query__start.

When a probe namespace is not specified, it defaults to the same name as the binary or library. There are many probes for which it differs, and the namespace must be included. One example is the "hotspot" namespace probes from libjvm (the JVM library). For example (full library path truncated):

```
usdt:/.../libjvm.so:hotspot:method__entry
```

Any arguments to the USDT probe are available as members of the args built-in.

The available probes in a binary can be listed using -l, for example:

```
# bpftrace -l 'usdt:/usr/local/cpython/python'
usdt:/usr/local/cpython/python:line
usdt:/usr/local/cpython/python:function__entry
usdt:/usr/local/cpython/python:function__return
usdt:/usr/local/cpython/python:import__find__load__start
usdt:/usr/local/cpython/python:import__find__load__done
usdt:/usr/local/cpython/python:gc__start
usdt:/sur/local/cpython/python:gc__done
```

Instead of providing a probe description, you can use -p PID instead to list the USDT probes in a running process.

5.9.3   kprobe and kretprobe

These probe types are for kernel dynamic instrumentation. Format:

```
kprobe:function_name
kretprobe:function_name
```

kprobe instruments the start of the function (its entry), and kretprobe instruments the end (its return). The function_name is the kernel function name. For example, the vfs_read() kernel function can be instrumented using kprobe:vfs_read and kretprobe:vfs_read.

Arguments for kprobe: arg0, arg1, ..., argN are the entry arguments to the function, as unsigned 64-bit integers. If they are a pointer to a C struct, they can be cast to that struct.[6] The future BPF type format (BTF) technology may make this automatic (see Chapter 2).

Arguments for kretprobe: the retval built-in has the return value of the function. retval is always uint64; if this does not match the return type for the function, it needs to be cast to that type.

5.9.4   uprobe and uretprobe

These probe types are for user-level dynamic instrumentation. Format:

```
uprobe:binary_path:function_name
uprobe:library_path:function_name
uretprobe:binary_path:function_name
uretprobe:library_path:function_name
```

uprobe instruments the start of the function (its entry), and uretprobe instruments the end (its return). The function_name is the function name. For example, the readline() function in /bin/bash can be instrumented using uprobe:/bin/bash:readline and uretprobe:/bin/bash:readline.

Arguments for uprobe: arg0, arg1, ..., argN are the entry arguments to the function, as unsigned 64-bit integers. They can be cast to their struct types.[7]

Arguments for uretprobe: the retval built-in has the return value of the function. retval is always uint64, and it needs to be cast to match the real return type.

---

6 This is C terminology that refers to changing the type of an object in a program. For an example, see the bpftrace source to runqlen(8) in Chapter 6.

7 It's possible that BTF may be provided as user-level software in the future, so that binaries can self-describe their struct types similarly to kernel BTF.

5.9.5   software and hardware

These probe types are for predefined software and hardware events. Format:

```
software:event_name:count
software:event_name:
hardware:event_name:count
hardware:event_name:
```

Software events are similar to tracepoints but are suited for count-based metrics and sample-based instrumentation. Hardware events are a selection of PMCs for processor-level analysis.

Both event types may occur so frequently that instrumenting every event can incur significant overhead, degrading system performance. This is avoided by using sampling and the count field, which triggers the probe to fire once every [count] events. If a count is not provided, a default is used. For example, the probe software:page-faults:100 will only fire for one in every 100 page faults.

The available software events, which depend on the kernel version, are shown in Table 5-3.

Table 5-3   **Software Events**

Software Event Name	Alias	Default Sample Count	Description
cpu-clock	cpu	1000000	CPU wall-time clock
task-clock		1000000	CPU task clock (increments only when task is on-CPU)
page-faults	faults	100	Page faults
context-switches	cs	1000	Context switches
cpu-migrations		1	CPU thread migrations
minor-faults		100	Minor page faults: satisfied by memory
major-faults		1	Major page faults: satisfied by storage I/O
alignment-faults		1	Alignment faults
emulation-faults		1	Emulation faults
dummy		1	Dummy event for testing
bpf-output		1	BPF output channel

The available hardware events, which depend on the kernel version and processor type, are listed in Table 5-4.

Table 5-4 **Hardware Events**

Hardware Event Name	Alias	Default Sample Count	Description
cpu-cycles	cycles	1000000	CPU clock cycles
instructions		1000000	CPU instructions
cache-references		1000000	CPU last level cache references
cache-misses		1000000	CPU last level cache misses
branch-instructions	branches	100000	Branch instructions
bus-cycles		100000	Bus cycles
frontend-stalls		1000000	Processor frontend stalls (e.g., instruction fetches)
backend-stalls		1000000	Processor backend stalls (e.g., data loads/ stores)
ref-cycles		1000000	CPU reference cycles (unscaled by turbo)

The hardware events occur more frequently, so higher default sample counts are used.

5.9.6 profile and interval

These probe types are timer-based events. Format:

```
profile:hz:rate
profile:s:rate
profile:ms:rate
profile:us:rate
interval:s:rate
interval:ms:rate
```

The profile type fires on all CPUs and can be used for sampling CPU usage. The interval type only fires on one CPU and can be used to print interval-based output.

The second field is the units for the last field, rate. This field may be:

- **hz:** Hertz (events per second)
- **s:** Seconds
- **ms:** Milliseconds
- **us:** Microseconds

For example, the probe profile:hz:99 fires 99 times per second, across all CPUs. A a rate of 99 is often used instead of 100 to avoid issues of lockstep sampling. The probe interval:s:1 fires once per second and can be used to print per-second output.

5.10   bpftrace Flow Control

There are three types of tests in bpftrace: filters, ternary operators, and if statements. These tests conditionally change the flow of the program based on Boolean expressions, which support:

- ==: Equal to
- !=: Not equal to
- >: Greater than
- <: Less than
- >=: Greater than or equal to
- <=: Less than or equal to
- &&: And
- ||: Or

Expressions may be grouped using parentheses.

There is limited support for loops because, for safety, the BPF verifier rejects any code that might trigger an infinite loop. bpftrace supports unrolled loops, and a future version should support bounded loops.

5.10.1   Filter

Introduced earlier, these gate whether an action is executed. Format:

```
probe /filter/ { action }
```

Boolean operators may be used. The filter /pid == 123/ only executes the action if the pid built-in equals 123.

5.10.2   Ternary Operators

A ternary operator is a three-element operator composed of a test and two outcomes. Format:

```
test ? true_statement : false_statement
```

As an example, you can use a ternary operator to find the absolute value of $x:

```
$abs = $x >= 0 ? $x : - $x;
```

5.10.3   If Statements

If statements have the following syntax:

```
if (test) { true_statements }
if (test) { true_statements } else { false_statements }
```

One use case is with programs that perform different actions on IPv4 than on IPv6. For example:

```
if ($inet_family == $AF_INET) {
    // IPv4
    ...
} else {
    // IPv6
    ...
}
```

"else if" statements are not currently supported.

5.10.4   Unrolled Loops

BPF runs in a restricted environment where it must be possible to verify that a program ends and does not get stuck in an infinite loop. For programs that need some loop functionality, bpftrace supports unrolled loops with unroll().

Syntax:

```
unroll (count) { statements }
```

The count is an integer literal (constant) with a maximum of 20. Providing the count as a variable is not supported, as the number of loop iterations must be known in the BPF compile stage.

The Linux 5.3 kernel included support for BPF bounded loops. Future versions of bpftrace should support this capability, such as by providing for and while loops, in addition to unroll.

5.11   bpftrace Operators

The previous section listed Boolean operators for use in tests. bpftrace also supports the following operators:

- =: Assignment
- +, -, *, /: Addition, subtraction, multiplication, division
- ++, --: Auto-increment, auto-decrement
- &, |, ^: Binary and, binary or, binary exclusive or

- !: Logical not
- <<, >>: Shift left, shift right
- +=, -=, *=, /=, %=, &=, ^=, <<=, >>=: Compound operators

These operators were modeled after similar operators in the C programming language.

5.12   bpftrace Variables

As introduced in Section 5.7.10, there are three variable types: built-in, scratch, and map variables.

5.12.1   Built-in Variables

The built-in variables provided by bpftrace are usually for read-only access of information. The most important built-in variables are listed in Table 5-5.

Table 5-5   bpftrace Selected Built-in Variables

Built-in Variable	Type	Description
pid	integer	Process ID (kernel tgid)
tid	integer	Thread ID (kernel pid)
uid	integer	User ID
username	string	Username
nsecs	integer	Timestamp, in nanoseconds
elapsed	integer	Timestamp, in nanoseconds, since bpftrace initialization
cpu	integer	Processor ID
comm	string	Process name
kstack	string	Kernel stack trace
ustack	string	User-level stack trace
arg0, ..., argN	integer	Arguments to some probe types (see Section 5.9)
args	struct	Arguments to some probe types (see Section 5.9)
retval	integer	Return value for some probe types (see Section 5.9)
func	string	Name of the traced function
probe	string	Full name of the current probe
curtask	integer	Kernel task_struct as a unsigned 64-bit integer (can be cast)
cgroup	integer	Cgroup ID
$1, ..., $N	int, char *	Positional parameters for the bpftrace program

All integers are currently uint64. These variables all refer to the currently running thread, probe, function, and CPU when the probe fires. See the online "bpftrace Reference Guide" for the full and updated list of built-in variables [66].

5.12.2   Built-ins: pid, comm, and uid

Many built-ins are straightforward to use. This example uses pid, comm, and uid to print who is calling the setuid() syscall:

```
# bpftrace -e 't:syscalls:sys_enter_setuid {
    printf("setuid by PID %d (%s), UID %d\n", pid, comm, uid); }'
Attaching 1 probe...
setuid by PID 3907 (sudo), UID 1000
setuid by PID 14593 (evil), UID 33
^C
```

Just because a syscall was called doesn't mean it was successful. You can trace the return value by using a different tracepoint:

```
# bpftrace -e 'tracepoint:syscalls:sys_exit_setuid {
    printf("setuid by %s returned %d\n", comm, args->ret); }'
Attaching 1 probe...
setuid by sudo returned 0
setuid by evil returned -1
^C
```

This uses another built-in, args. For tracepoints, args is a struct type that provides custom fields.

5.12.3   Built-ins: kstack and ustack

kstack and ustack return kernel- and user-level stack traces as a multi-line string. They return up to 127 frames of stack trace. The kstack() and ustack() functions, covered later, allow you to select the number of frames.

For example, printing kernel stack traces on block I/O insert using kstack:

```
# bpftrace -e 't:block:block_rq_insert { printf("Block I/O by %s\n", kstack); }'
Attaching 1 probe...

Block I/O by
        blk_mq_insert_requests+203
        blk_mq_sched_insert_requests+111
        blk_mq_flush_plug_list+446
        blk_flush_plug_list+234
        blk_finish_plug+44
        dmcrypt_write+593
```

```
              kthread+289
              ret_from_fork+53

Block I/O by
              blk_mq_insert_requests+203
              blk_mq_sched_insert_requests+111
              blk_mq_flush_plug_list+446
              blk_flush_plug_list+234
              blk_finish_plug+44
              __do_page_cache_readahead+474
              ondemand_readahead+282
              page_cache_sync_readahead+46
              generic_file_read_iter+2043
              ext4_file_read_iter+86
              new_sync_read+228
              __vfs_read+41
              vfs_read+142
              kernel_read+49
              prepare_binprm+239
              do_execveat_common.isra.34+1428
              sys_execve+49
              do_syscall_64+115
              entry_SYSCALL_64_after_hwframe+61
[...]
```

Each stack trace is printed with frames in child-to-parent order and with each frame as the function name + function offset.

The stack built-ins can also be used as keys in maps, allowing them to be frequency counted. For example, counting kernel stacks that led to block I/O:

```
# bpftrace -e 't:block:block_rq_insert { @[kstack] = count(); }'
Attaching 1 probe...
^C
[...]
@[
    blk_mq_insert_requests+203
    blk_mq_sched_insert_requests+111
    blk_mq_flush_plug_list+446
    blk_flush_plug_list+234
    blk_finish_plug+44
    dmcrypt_write+593
    kthread+289
    ret_from_fork+53
]: 39
```

```
@[
    blk_mq_insert_requests+203
    blk_mq_sched_insert_requests+111
    blk_mq_flush_plug_list+446
    blk_flush_plug_list+234
    blk_finish_plug+44
    __do_page_cache_readahead+474
    ondemand_readahead+282
    page_cache_sync_readahead+46
    generic_file_read_iter+2043
    ext4_file_read_iter+86
    new_sync_read+228
    __vfs_read+41
    vfs_read+142
    sys_read+85
    do_syscall_64+115
    entry_SYSCALL_64_after_hwframe+61
]: 52
```

Only the last two stacks are shown here, with counts of 39 and 52. Counting is more efficient than printing out each stack, as the stack traces are counted in kernel context for efficiency.[8]

5.12.4   Built-ins: Positional Parameters

Positional parameters are passed to the program on the command line, and are based on positional parameters used in shell scripting. $1 refers to the first argument, $2 the second, and so on.

For example, the simple program watchconn.bt:

```
BEGIN
{
        printf("Watching connect() calls by PID %d\n", $1);
}


tracepoint:syscalls:sys_enter_connect
/pid == $1/
{
        printf("PID %d called connect()\n", $1);
}
```

8 BPF turns each stack into a unique stack ID and then frequency counts the IDs. bpftrace reads these frequency counts and then fetches the stacks for each ID.

watches the PID passed in on the command line:

```
# ./watchconn.bt 181
Attaching 2 probes...
Watching connect() calls by PID 181
PID 181 called connect()
[...]
```

These positional parameters also work with these invocation types:

```
bpftrace ./watchconn.bt 181
bpftrace -e 'program' 181
```

They are integers by default. If a string is used as an argument, it must be accessed via a str() call. For example:

```
# bpftrace -e 'BEGIN { printf("Hello, %s!\n", str($1)); }' Reader
Attaching 1 probe...
Hello, Reader!
^C
```

If a parameter that is accessed is not provided at the command line, it is zero in integer context, or "" if accessed via str().

5.12.5 Scratch

Format:

```
$name
```

These variables can be used for temporary calculations within an action clause. Their type is determined on first assignment, and they can be integers, strings, struct pointers, or structs.

5.12.6 Maps

Format:

```
@name
@name[key]
@name[key1, key2[, ...]]
```

For storage, these variables use the BPF map object, which is a hash table (associative array) that can be used for different storage types. Values can be stored using one or more keys. Maps must have consistent key and value types.

As with scratch variables, the type is determined upon first assignment, which includes assignment to special functions. With maps, the type includes the keys, if present, as well as the value. For example, consider these first assignments:

```
@start = nsecs;
@last[tid] = nsecs;
@bytes = hist(retval);
@who[pid, comm] = count();
```

Both the @start and @last maps become integer types because an integer is assigned to them: the nanosecond timestamp built-in (nsecs). The @last map also requires a key of type integer because it uses an integer key: the thread ID (tid). The @bytes map becomes a special type, a power-of-two histogram, which handles storage and the printing of the histogram. Finally, the @who map has two keys, integer (pid) and string (comm), and the value is the count() map function.

These functions are covered in Section 5.14.

5.13 bpftrace Functions

bpftrace provides built-in functions for various tasks. The most important of them are listed in Table 5-6.

Table 5-6 **bpftrace Selected Built-in Functions**

Function	Description
printf(char *fmt [, ...])	Prints formatted
time(char *fmt)	Prints formatted time
join(char *arr[])	Prints the array of strings, joined by a space character
str(char *s [, int len])	Returns the string from the pointer s, with an optional length limit
kstack(int limit)	Returns a kernel stack up to *limit* frames deep
ustack(int limit)	Returns a user stack up to *limit* frames deep
ksym(void *p)	Resolves the kernel address and returns the string symbol
usym(void *p)	Resolves the user-space address and returns the string symbol
kaddr(char *name)	Resolves the kernel symbol name to an address
uaddr(char *name)	Resolves the user-space symbol name to an address
reg(char *name)	Returns the value stored in the named register
ntop([int af,] int addr)	Returns a string representation of an IP address
system(char *fmt [, ...])	Executes a shell command
cat(char *filename)	Prints the contents of a file
exit()	Exits bpftrace

Some of these functions are asynchronous: The kernel queues the event, and a short time later it is processed in user space. The asynchronous functions are printf(), time(), cat(), join(), and system(). kstack(), ustack(), ksym(), and usym() record addresses synchronously, but they do symbol translation asynchronously.

See the online "bpftrace Reference Guide" for the full and updated list of functions [66]. A selection of these functions are discussed in the following sections.

5.13.1   printf()

The printf() call, short for print formatted, behaves as it does in C and other languages. Syntax:

```
printf(format [, arguments ...])
```

The format string can contain any text message, as well as escape sequences beginning with '\', and field descriptions beginning with '%'. If no arguments are given, no field descriptions are required.

Commonly used escape sequences are:

- \n: New line
- \": Double quote
- \\: Backslash

See the printf(1) man page for other escape sequences.

Field descriptions begin with '%', and have the format:

```
% [-] width type
```

The '-' sets the output to be left-justified. The default is right-justified.

The width is the number of characters that the field is wide.

The type is either:

- %u, %d: Unsigned int, int
- %lu, %ld: Unsigned long, long
- %llu, %lld: Unsigned long long, long long
- %hu, %hd: Unsigned short, short
- %x, %lx, %llx: Hexadecimal: unsigned int, unsigned long, unsigned long long
- %c: Character
- %s: String

This printf() call:

```
printf("%16s %-6d\n", comm, pid)
```

prints the comm built-in as a 16-character-wide string field, right-justified, and the pid built-in as a six-character-wide integer field, left-justified, followed by a new line.

5.13.2   join()

join() is a special function for joining an array of strings with a space character and printing them out. Syntax:

```
join(char *arr[])
```

For example, this one-liner shows attempted execution of commands with their arguments:

```
# bpftrace -e 'tracepoint:syscalls:sys_enter_execve { join(args->argv); }'
Attaching 1 probe...
ls -l
df -h
date
ls -l bashreadline.bt biolatency.bt biosnoop.bt bitesize.bt
```

It prints the argv array argument to the execve() syscall. Note that this is showing attempted execution: The syscalls:sys_**exit**_execve tracepoint and its args->ret value show whether the syscall succeeded.

join() may be a handy function in some circumstances, but it has limitations on the number of arguments it can join, and their size.[9] If the output appears truncated, it is likely that you have hit these limits and need to use a different approach.

There has been work to change the behavior of join() to make it return a string rather than print one out. This would change the previous bpftrace one-liner to be:

```
# bpftrace -e 'tracepoint:syscalls:sys_enter_execve {
    printf("%s\n", join(args->argv); }'
```

This change would also make join() no longer be an asynchronous function.[10]

5.13.3   str()

str() returns the string from a pointer (char *). Syntax:

```
str(char *s [, int length])
```

---

9 The current limits are 16 arguments and a size of 1 Kbyte each. It prints out all arguments until it reaches one that is NULL or hits the 16-argument limit.

10 See bpftrace issue 26 for the status of this change [67]. It has not been a priority to do, since so far join() has only had one use case: joining args->argv for the execve syscall tracepoint.

For example, the return value from the bash(1) shell readline() function is a string and can be printed using[11]:

```
# bpftrace -e 'ur:/bin/bash:readline { printf("%s\n", str(retval)); }'
Attaching 1 probe...
ls -lh
date
echo hello BPF
^C
```

This one-liner can show all bash interactive commands system-wide.

By default, the string has a size limit of 64 bytes, which can be tuned using the bpftrace environment variable BPFTRACE_STRLEN. Sizes over 200 bytes are not currently allowed; this is a known limitation, and one day the limit may be greatly increased.[12]

5.13.4   kstack() and ustack()

kstack() and ustack() are similar to the kstack and ustack built-ins, but they accept a limit argument and an optional mode argument. Syntax:

```
kstack(limit)
kstack(mode[, limit])
ustack(limit)
ustack(mode[, limit])
```

For example, showing the top three kernel frames that led to creating block I/O, by tracing the block:block_rq_insert tracepoint:

```
# bpftrace -e 't:block:block_rq_insert { @[kstack(3), comm] = count(); }'
Attaching 1 probe...
^C

@[
    __elv_add_request+231
    blk_execute_rq_nowait+160
    blk_execute_rq+80
, kworker/u16:3]: 2
@[
    blk_mq_insert_requests+203
    blk_mq_sched_insert_requests+111
    blk_mq_flush_plug_list+446
```

---

11 This assumes that readline() is in the bash(1) binary; some builds of bash(1) may call it from libreadline instead, and this one-liner will need to be modified to match. See Section 12.2.3 in Chapter 12.

12 This is tracked by bpftrace issue 305 [68]. The problem is that string storage currently uses the BPF stack, which is limited to 512 bytes and hence has a low string limit (200 bytes). String storage should be changed to use a BPF map, at which point very large strings (Mbytes) should be possible.

```
, mysqld]: 2
@[
    blk_mq_insert_requests+203
    blk_mq_sched_insert_requests+111
    blk_mq_flush_plug_list+446
, dmcrypt_write]: 961
```

The current maximum stack size allowed is 1024 frames.

The mode argument allows the stack output to be formatted differently. Only two modes are currently supported: "bpftrace", the default; and "perf", which produces a stack format similar to that of the Linux perf(1) utility. For example:

```
# bpftrace -e 'k:do_nanosleep { printf("%s", ustack(perf)); }'
Attaching 1 probe...
[...]
        7f220f1f2c60 nanosleep+64 (/lib/x86_64-linux-gnu/libpthread-2.27.so)
        7f220f653fdd g_timeout_add_full+77 (/usr/lib/x86_64-linux-gnu/libglib-
2.0.so.0.5600.3)
        7f220f64fbc0 0x7f220f64fbc0 ([unknown])
        841f0f 0x841f0f ([unknown])
```

Other modes may be supported in the future.

5.13.5   ksym() and usym()

The ksym() and usym() functions resolve addresses into their symbol names (strings). ksym() is for kernel addresses, and usym() is for user-space addresses. Syntax:

```
ksym(addr)
usym(addr)
```

For example, the timer:hrtimer_start tracepoint has a function pointer argument. Frequency counts:

```
# bpftrace -e 'tracepoint:timer:hrtimer_start { @[args->function] = count(); }'
Attaching 1 probe...
^C

@[-1169374160]: 3
@[-1168782560]: 8
@[-1167295376]: 9
@[-1067171840]: 145
@[-1169062880]: 200
@[-1169114960]: 2517
@[-1169048384]: 8237
```

These are raw addresses. Using ksym() to convert these to kernel function names:

```
# bpftrace -e 'tracepoint:timer:hrtimer_start { @[ksym(args->function)] = count(); }'
Attaching 1 probe...
^C

@[sched_rt_period_timer]: 4
@[watchdog_timer_fn]: 8
@[timerfd_tmrproc]: 15
@[intel_uncore_fw_release_timer]: 1111
@[it_real_fn]: 2269
@[hrtimer_wakeup]: 7714
@[tick_sched_timer]: 27092
```

usym() relies on symbol tables in the binary for symbol lookup.

5.13.6   kaddr() and uaddr()

kaddr() and uaddr() take a symbol name and return the address. kaddr() is for kernel symbols, and uaddr() is for user-space symbols. Syntax:

```
kaddr(char *name)
uaddr(char *name)
```

For example, looking up the user-space symbol "ps1_prompt" when a bash(1) shell function is called, and then dereferencing it and printing it as a string:

```
# bpftrace -e 'uprobe:/bin/bash:readline {
    printf("PS1: %s\n", str(*uaddr("ps1_prompt"))); }'
Attaching 1 probe...
PS1: \[\e[34;1m\]\u@\h:\w>\[\e[0m\]
PS1: \[\e[34;1m\]\u@\h:\w>\[\e[0m\]
^C
```

This is printing the contents of the symbol—in this case the bash(1) PS1 prompt.

5.13.7   system()

system() executes a command at the shell. Syntax:

```
system(char *fmt [, arguments ...])
```

Since anything can be run at the shell, system() is deemed an unsafe function and requires the --unsafe bpftrace option to be used.

For example, calling ps(1) to print details on the PID calling nanosleep():

```
# bpftrace --unsafe -e 't:syscalls:sys_enter_nanosleep { system("ps -p %d\n",
    pid); }'
Attaching 1 probe...
  PID TTY          TIME CMD
29893 tty2     05:34:22 mysqld
  PID TTY          TIME CMD
29893 tty2     05:34:22 mysqld
  PID TTY          TIME CMD
29893 tty2     05:34:22 mysqld
[...]
```

If the traced event was frequent, using system() could create a storm of new process events that consume CPU resources. Only use system() when necessary.

5.13.8 exit()

This terminates the bpftrace program. Syntax:

```
exit()
```

This function can be used in an interval probe to instrument for a fixed duration. For example:

```
# bpftrace -e 't:syscalls:sys_enter_read { @reads = count(); }
    interval:s:5 { exit(); }'
Attaching 2 probes...
@reads: 735
```

This shows that in five seconds, there were 735 read() syscalls. All maps are printed out upon bpftrace termination, as seen in this example.

5.14 bpftrace Map Functions

Maps are special hash table storage objects from BPF that can be used for different purposes—for example, as hash tables to store key/value pairs or for statistical summaries. bpftrace provides built-in functions for map assignment and manipulation, mostly for supporting statistical summary maps. The most important map functions are listed in Table 5-7.

Table 5-7   bpftrace Selected Map Functions

Function	Description
`count()`	Counts occurrences
`sum(int n)`	Sums the value
`avg(int n)`	Averages the value
`min(int n)`	Records the minimum value
`max(int n)`	Records the maximum value
`stats(int n)`	Returns the count, average, and total
`hist(int n)`	Prints a power-of-two histogram of values
`lhist(int n, int min, int max, int step)`	Prints a linear histogram of values
`delete(@m[key])`	Deletes the map key/value pair
`print(@m [, top [, div]])`	Prints the map, with optional limits and a divisor
`clear(@m)`	Deletes all keys from the map
`zero(@m)`	Sets all map values to zero

Some of these functions are asynchronous: The kernel queues the event, and a short time later, it is processed in user space. The asynchronous actions are print(), clear(), and zero(). Bear in mind this delay when you are writing programs.

See the online "bpftrace Reference Guide" for the full and updated list of functions [66]. A selection of these functions are discussed in the following sections.

5.14.1   count()

count() counts occurrences. Syntax:

```
@m = count();
```

This function can be used with probe wildcards and the probe built-in to count events:

```
# bpftrace -e 'tracepoint:block:* { @[probe] = count(); }'
Attaching 18 probes...
^C

@[tracepoint:block:block_rq_issue]: 1
@[tracepoint:block:block_rq_insert]: 1
@[tracepoint:block:block_dirty_buffer]: 24
@[tracepoint:block:block_touch_buffer]: 29
@[tracepoint:block:block_rq_complete]: 52
```

```
@[tracepoint:block:block_getrq]: 91
@[tracepoint:block:block_bio_complete]: 102
@[tracepoint:block:block_bio_remap]: 180
@[tracepoint:block:block_bio_queue]: 270
```

With the interval probe, a per-interval rate can be printed, for example:

```
# bpftrace -e 'tracepoint:block:block_rq_i* { @[probe] = count(); }
    interval:s:1 { print(@); clear(@); }'
Attaching 3 probes...
@[tracepoint:block:block_rq_issue]: 1
@[tracepoint:block:block_rq_insert]: 1

@[tracepoint:block:block_rq_insert]: 6
@[tracepoint:block:block_rq_issue]: 8

@[tracepoint:block:block_rq_issue]: 1
@[tracepoint:block:block_rq_insert]: 1
[...]
```

This basic functionality can also be accomplished by using perf(1) and `perf stat`, as well as Ftrace. bpftrace enables more customizations: A BEGIN probe could contain a printf() call to explain the output, and the interval probe could include a time() call to annotate each interval with timestamps.

5.14.2 sum(), avg(), min(), and max()

These functions store basic statistics—the sum, average, minimum, and maximum—as a map. Syntax:

```
sum(int n)
avg(int n)
min(int n)
max(int n)
```

For example, using sum() to find the total bytes read via the read(2) syscall:

```
# bpftrace -e 'tracepoint:syscalls:sys_exit_read /args->ret > 0/ {
    @bytes = sum(args->ret); }'
Attaching 1 probe...
^C

@bytes: 461603
```

The map was named "bytes" to annotate the output. Note that this example uses a filter to ensure that args->ret is positive: A positive return value from read(2) indicates the number of bytes read, whereas a negative return value is an error code. This is documented in the man page for read(2).

5.14.3   hist()

hist() stores a value in a power-of-two histogram. Syntax:

```
hist(int n)
```

For example, a histogram of successful read(2) sizes:

```
# bpftrace -e 'tracepoint:syscalls:sys_exit_read { @ret = hist(args->ret); }'
Attaching 1 probe...
^C

@ret:
(..., 0)              237 |@@@@@@@@@@@@@@                                      |
[0]                    13 |                                                    |
[1]                   859 |@@@@@@@@@@@@@@@@@@@@@@@@@@@@@@@@@@@@@@@@@@@@@@@@@@@@@@|
[2, 4)                 57 |@@@                                                 |
[4, 8)                  5 |                                                    |
[8, 16)               749 |@@@@@@@@@@@@@@@@@@@@@@@@@@@@@@@@@@@@@@@@@@@@@@@       |
[16, 32)               69 |@@@@                                                |
[32, 64)               64 |@@@                                                 |
[64, 128)              25 |@                                                   |
[128, 256)              7 |                                                    |
[256, 512)              5 |                                                    |
[512, 1K)               7 |                                                    |
[1K, 2K)               32 |@                                                   |
```

Histograms are useful for identifying distribution characteristics such as multi-modal distributions and outliers. This example histogram has multiple modes, one for reads that were 0 or less in size (less than zero will be error codes), another mode for one byte in size, and another for sizes between eight to 16 bytes.

The characters in the ranges are from interval notation:

- "[": Equal to or greater than
- "]": Equal to or less than
- "(": Greater than
- ")": Less than
- "...": Infinite

The range "[4, 8)" means between four and less-than-eight (that is, between four and 7.9999, etc.).

5.14.4 lhist()

lhist() stores a value as a linear histogram. Syntax:

```
lhist(int n, int min, int max, int step)
```

For example, a linear histogram of read(2) returns:

```
# bpftrace -e 'tracepoint:syscalls:sys_exit_read {
    @ret = lhist(args->ret, 0, 1000, 100); }'
Attaching 1 probe...
^C

@ret:
(..., 0)            101 |@@@                                              |
[0, 100)           1569 |@@@@@@@@@@@@@@@@@@@@@@@@@@@@@@@@@@@@@@@@@@@@@@@@@@@|
[100, 200)            5 |                                                 |
[200, 300)            0 |                                                 |
[300, 400)            3 |                                                 |
[400, 500)            0 |                                                 |
[500, 600)            0 |                                                 |
[600, 700)            3 |                                                 |
[700, 800)            0 |                                                 |
[800, 900)            0 |                                                 |
[900, 1000)           0 |                                                 |
[1000, ...)           5 |                                                 |
```

The output shows that most reads were between zero and (less than) 100 bytes. The ranges are printed using the same interval notation as with hist(). The "(..., 0)" line shows the error count: 101 read(2) errors while tracing. Note that error counts are better viewed differently, such as by using a frequency count of the error codes:

```
# bpftrace -e 'tracepoint:syscalls:sys_exit_read /args->ret < 0/ {
    @[- args->ret] = count(); }'
Attaching 1 probe...
^C

@[11]: 57
```

Error code 11 is EAGAIN (try again). read(2) returns it as -11.

5.14.5 delete()

delete() deletes a key/value pair from a map. Syntax:

```
delete(@map[key])
```

There may be more than one key, as needed, to match the map type.

5.14.6 clear() and zero()

clear() deletes all key/value pairs from a map, and zero() sets all values to zero. Syntax:

```
clear(@map)
zero(@map)
```

When bpftrace terminates, all maps are printed out by default. Some maps, such as those used for timestamp delta calculations, aren't intended to be part of the tool output. They can be cleaned up in an END probe to prevent their automatic printing:

```
[...]
END
{
    clear(@start);
}
```

5.14.7 print()

print() prints maps. Syntax:

```
print(@m [, top [, div]])
```

Two optional arguments can be provided: a top integer, so that only the top number of entries is printed, and a divisor integer, which divides the value.

To demonstrate the top argument, the following prints the top five kernel function calls that begin with "vfs_":

```
# bpftrace -e 'kprobe:vfs_* { @[probe] = count(); } END { print(@, 5); clear(@); }'
Attaching 55 probes...
^C
@[kprobe:vfs_getattr_nosec]: 510
@[kprobe:vfs_getattr]: 511
@[kprobe:vfs_writev]: 1595
@[kprobe:vfs_write]: 2086
@[kprobe:vfs_read]: 2921
```

While tracing, vfs_read() was called the most (2921 times).

To demonstrate the div argument, the following records time spent in vfs_read() by process name and prints it out in milliseconds:

```
# bpftrace -e 'kprobe:vfs_read { @start[tid] = nsecs; }
    kretprobe:vfs_read /@start[tid]/ {
        @ms[comm] = sum(nsecs - @start[tid]); delete(@start[tid]); }
    END { print(@ms, 0, 1000000); clear(@ms); clear(@start); }'
Attaching 3 probes...
[...]
@ms[Xorg]: 3
@ms[InputThread]: 3
@ms[chrome]: 4
@ms[Web Content]: 5
```

Why was it necessary to have the divisor? You could try writing this program like this instead:

```
@ms[comm] = sum((nsecs - @start[tid]) / 1000000);
```

However, sum() operates on integers, and decimal places are rounded down (floored). So any duration less than one millisecond is summed as zero. This results in an output ruined by rounding errors. The solution is to sum() nanoseconds, which preserves the sub-millisecond durations, and then do the divisor on the totals as the argument to print().

A future bpftrace change may allow print() to print any type, not just maps, without formatting.

5.15 bpftrace Future Work

There are a number of planned additions to bpftrace that may be available by the time you read this book. See the bpftrace release notes and documentation in the repository for these additions: https://github.com/iovisor/bpftrace.

There are no planned changes to the bpftrace source code included in this book. In case changes do become necessary, check for updates on this book's website: http://www.brendangregg.com/bpf-performance-tools-book.html.

5.15.1 Explicit Address Modes

The largest addition to bpftrace will be explicit address space access to support a future split of bpf_probe_read() into bpf_probe_read_kernel() and bpf_probe_read_user() [69]. This split is necessary to support some processor architectures.[13] It should not affect any of the tools in this book. It should result in the addition of kptr() and uptr() bpftrace functions to specify the address mode. Needing to use these should be rare: bpftrace will figure out the address space context

---

13 "They are rare, but they exist. At least sparc32 and the old 4G:4G split x86."—Linus Torvalds [70]

whenever possible from the probe type or function used. The following shows how the probe context should work:

kprobe/kretprobe (kernel context):

- **arg0...argN, retval:** When dereferenced, are kernel addresses.
- ***addr:** Dereferences a kernel address.
- **str(addr):** Fetches a NULL-terminated kernel string.
- ***uptr(addr):** Dereferences a user address.
- **str(uptr(addr)):** Fetches a null-terminated user string.

uprobe/uretprobe (user context):

- **arg0...argN, retval:** When dereferenced, are user addresses.
- ***addr:** Dereferences a user address.
- **str(addr):** Fetches a NULL-terminated user string.
- ***kptr(addr):** Dereferences a kernel address.
- **str(kptr(addr)):** Fetches a NULL-terminated kernel string.

So *addr and str() will continue to work, but will refer to the probe-context address space: kernel memory for kprobes and user memory for uprobes. To cross address spaces, the kptr() and uptr() functions must be used. Some functions, such as curtask(), will always return a kernel pointer, regardless of the context (as would be expected).

Other probe types default to kernel context, but there will be some exceptions, documented in the "bpftrace Reference Guide" [66]. One exception will be syscall tracepoints, which refer to user address space pointers, and so their probe action will be in user space context.

5.15.2 Other Additions

Other planned additions include:

- Additional probe types for memory watchpoints,[14] socket and skb programs, and raw tracepoints
- uprobe and kprobe function offset probes
- `for` and `while` loops that make use of BPF bounded loops in Linux 5.3
- Raw PMC probes (providing a umask and event select)
- uprobes to also support relative names without full paths (e.g., both uprobe:/lib/x86_64-linux-gnu/libc.so.6:... and uprobe:libc:... should work)
- `signal()` to raise a signal (including SIGKILL) to processes

---

14 Dan Xu has already developed a proof of concept implementation for memory watchpoints that is included in bpftrace [71].

- `return()` or `override()` to rewrite the return of events (using bpf_override_return())

- `ehist()` for exponential histograms. Any tool or one-liner that currently uses the power-of-two hist() could be switched to ehist() for more resolution.

- `pcomm` to return the process name. comm returns the thread name, which is usually the same, but some applications, such as Java, may set comm to per-thread names; in that case, pcomm would still return "java".

- A helper function for struct file pointers to full pathnames

Once these additions are available, you may want to switch a few tools in this book from hist() to ehist() for more resolution, and some uprobe tools to use relative library names instead of the full paths for ease of use.

5.15.3 ply

The ply BPF front end, created by Tobias Waldekranz, provides a high-level language similar to bpftrace and requires minimal dependencies (no LLVM or Clang). This makes it suited to resource-constrained environments, with the drawback that struct navigation and including header files (as required by many tools in this book) are not possible.

An example of ply instrumenting the open(2) tracepoint:

```
# ply 'tracepoint:syscalls/sys_enter_open {
    printf("PID: %d (%s) opening: %s\n", pid, comm, str(data->filename)); }'
ply: active
PID: 22737 (Chrome_IOThread) opening: /dev/shm/.org.chromium.Chromium.dh4msB
PID: 22737 (Chrome_IOThread) opening: /dev/shm/.org.chromium.Chromium.dh4msB
PID: 22737 (Chrome_IOThread) opening: /dev/shm/.org.chromium.Chromium.2mI1x4
[...]
```

The above one-liner is almost identical to the equivalent in bpftrace. A future version of ply could support the bpftrace language directly, providing a lightweight tool for running bpftrace one-liners. These one-liners typically do not use struct navigation other than the tracepoint arguments (as shown by this example), which ply already supports. In the distant future, with BTF availability, ply could use BTF for struct information, allowing it to run more of the bpftrace tools.

5.16 bpftrace Internals

Figure 5-3 shows the internal operation of bpftrace.

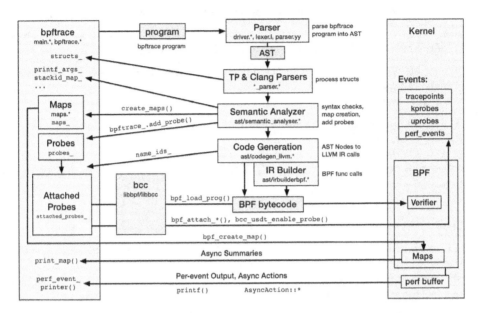

Figure 5-3   bpftrace internals

bpftrace uses libbcc and libbpf to attach to probes, load programs, and use USDT. It also uses LLVM for compiling the program to BPF bytecode.

The bpftrace language is defined by lex and yacc files that are processed by flex and bison. The output is the program as an abstract syntax tree (AST). Tracepoint and Clang parsers then process structs. A semantic analyzer checks the use of language elements, and throws errors for misuse. The next step is code generation—converting the AST nodes to LLVM IR, which LLVM finally compiles to BPF bytecode.

The next section introduces bpftrace debugging modes that show these steps in action: -d prints the AST and the LLVM IR, and -v prints the BPF bytecode.

5.17 bpftrace Debugging

There are various ways to debug and troubleshoot bpftrace programs. This section summarizes printf() statements and bpftrace debug modes. If you are here because you are troubleshooting an issue, also see Chapter 18, which covers common issues, including missing events, missing stacks, and missing symbols.

While bpftrace is a powerful language, it is really composed from a set of rigid capabilities that are designed to work safely together and to reject misuse. In comparison, BCC, which allows C and Python programs, uses a much larger set of capabilities that were not designed solely for tracing and that may not necessarily work together. The result is that bpftrace programs tend to fail with human-readable messages that do not require further debugging, whereas BCC programs can fail in unexpected ways, and require debugging modes to solve.

5.17.1   printf() Debugging

printf() statements can be added to show whether probes are really firing and whether variables are what you think they are. Consider the following program: it prints a histogram of vfs_read() duration. However, if you run it, you may discover that the output includes outliers with unbelievably high durations. Can you spot the bug?

```
kprobe:vfs_read
{
        @start[tid] = nsecs;
}


kretprobe:vfs_read
{
        $duration_ms = (nsecs - @start[tid]) / 1000000;
        @ms = hist($duration_ms);
        delete(@start[tid]);
}
```

If bpftrace begins running halfway through a vfs_read() call, then only the kretprobe will fire, and the latency calculation becomes "nsecs - 0", as @start[tid] is uninitialized. The fix is to use a filter on the kretprobe to check that @start[tid] is non-zero before you use it in the calculation. This could be debugged with a printf() statement to examine the inputs:

```
printf("$duration_ms = (%d - %d) / 1000000\n", nsecs, @start[tid]);
```

There are bpftrace debug modes (covered next), but bugs like this may be quickly solved with a well-placed printf().

5.17.2   Debug Mode

The -d option to bpftrace runs debug mode, which does not run the program but instead shows how it was parsed and converted to LLVM IR. Note that this mode may only really be of interest to developers of bpftrace itself, and it is included here for awareness.

It begins by printing an abstract syntax tree (AST) representation of the program:

```
# bpftrace -d -e 'k:vfs_read { @[pid] = count(); }'
Program
 k:vfs_read
  =
   map: @
    builtin: pid
   call: count
```

followed by the program converted to LLVM IR assembly:

```
; ModuleID = 'bpftrace'
source_filename = "bpftrace"
target datalayout = "e-m:e-p:64:64-i64:64-n32:64-S128"
target triple = "bpf-pc-linux"

; Function Attrs: nounwind
declare i64 @llvm.bpf.pseudo(i64, i64) #0

; Function Attrs: argmemonly nounwind
declare void @llvm.lifetime.start.p0i8(i64, i8* nocapture) #1

define i64 @"kprobe:vfs_read"(i8* nocapture readnone) local_unnamed_addr section
"s_kprobe:vfs_read_1" {
entry:
  %"@_val" = alloca i64, align 8
  %"@_key" = alloca [8 x i8], align 8
  %1 = getelementptr inbounds [8 x i8], [8 x i8]* %"@_key", i64 0, i64 0
  call void @llvm.lifetime.start.p0i8(i64 -1, i8* nonnull %1)
  %get_pid_tgid = tail call i64 inttoptr (i64 14 to i64 ()*)()
  %2 = lshr i64 %get_pid_tgid, 32
  store i64 %2, i8* %1, align 8
  %pseudo = tail call i64 @llvm.bpf.pseudo(i64 1, i64 1)
  %lookup_elem = call i8* inttoptr (i64 1 to i8* (i8*, i8*)*)(i64 %pseudo, [8 x i8]*
nonnull %"@_key")
  %map_lookup_cond = icmp eq i8* %lookup_elem, null
  br i1 %map_lookup_cond, label %lookup_merge, label %lookup_success

lookup_success:                                  ; preds = %entry
  %3 = load i64, i8* %lookup_elem, align 8
  %phitmp = add i64 %3, 1
  br label %lookup_merge

lookup_merge:                                    ; preds = %entry, %lookup_success
  %lookup_elem_val.0 = phi i64 [ %phitmp, %lookup_success ], [ 1, %entry ]
  %4 = bitcast i64* %"@_val" to i8*
  call void @llvm.lifetime.start.p0i8(i64 -1, i8* nonnull %4)
  store i64 %lookup_elem_val.0, i64* %"@_val", align 8
  %pseudo1 = call i64 @llvm.bpf.pseudo(i64 1, i64 1)
  %update_elem = call i64 inttoptr (i64 2 to i64 (i8*, i8*, i8*, i64)*)(i64 %pseudo1,
[8 x i8]* nonnull %"@_key", i64* nonnull %"@_val", i64 0)
```

```
    call void @llvm.lifetime.end.p0i8(i64 -1, i8* nonnull %1)
    call void @llvm.lifetime.end.p0i8(i64 -1, i8* nonnull %4)
    ret i64 0
}


; Function Attrs: argmemonly nounwind
declare void @llvm.lifetime.end.p0i8(i64, i8* nocapture) #1


attributes #0 = { nounwind }
attributes #1 = { argmemonly nounwind }
```

There is also a -dd mode, verbose debug, that prints extra information: the LLVM IR assembly
before and after optimization.

5.17.3 Verbose Mode

The -v option to bpftrace is verbose mode, printing extra information while running the
program. For example:

```
# bpftrace -v -e 'k:vfs_read { @[pid] = count(); }'
Attaching 1 probe...


Program ID: 5994


Bytecode:
0: (85) call bpf_get_current_pid_tgid#14
1: (77) r0 >>= 32
2: (7b) *(u64 *)(r10 -16) = r0
3: (18) r1 = 0xffff892f8c92be00
5: (bf) r2 = r10
6: (07) r2 += -16
7: (85) call bpf_map_lookup_elem#1
8: (b7) r1 = 1
9: (15) if r0 == 0x0 goto pc+2
 R0=map_value(id=0,off=0,ks=8,vs=8,imm=0) R1=inv1 R10=fp0
10: (79) r1 = *(u64 *)(r0 +0)
 R0=map_value(id=0,off=0,ks=8,vs=8,imm=0) R1=inv1 R10=fp0
11: (07) r1 += 1
12: (7b) *(u64 *)(r10 -8) = r1
13: (18) r1 = 0xffff892f8c92be00
15: (bf) r2 = r10
16: (07) r2 += -16
17: (bf) r3 = r10
18: (07) r3 += -8
```

```
19: (b7) r4 = 0
20: (85) call bpf_map_update_elem#2
21: (b7) r0 = 0
22: (95) exit

from 9 to 12: safe
processed 22 insns, stack depth 16

Attaching kprobe:vfs_read
Running...
^C

@[6169]: 1
@[28178]: 1
[...]
```

The program ID can be used with bpftool to print information on BPF kernel state, as shown in Chapter 2. The BPF bytecode is then printed, followed by the probe it is attaching to.

As with -d, this level of detail may only be of use to developers of bpftrace internals. Users should not need to be reading BPF bytecode while using bpftrace.

5.18   Summary

bpftrace is a powerful tracer with a concise high-level language. This chapter describes its features, tools, and example one-liners. It also covers programming and provides sections on probes, flow control, variables, and functions. The chapter finishes with debugging and internals.

The following chapters cover targets of analysis and include both BCC and bpftrace tools. An advantage of bpftrace tools is that their source code is often so concise that it can be included in this book.

Chapter 6

CPUs

CPUs execute all software and are a common starting point for performance analysis. If you find a workload to be limited by the CPUs ("CPU bound"), you can investigate further by using CPU and processor-centric tools. There are countless sampling profilers and metrics available to help you understand CPU usage. Nonetheless (if perhaps surprisingly), there are still a number of areas where BPF tracing can help even further with CPU analysis.

Learning Objectives:

- Understand CPU modes, the behavior of the CPU scheduler, and CPU caches
- Understand areas for CPU scheduler, usage, and hardware analysis with BPF
- Learn a strategy for successful analysis of CPU performance
- Solve issues of short-lived processes consuming CPU resources
- Discover and quantify issues of run queue latency
- Determine CPU usage through profiled stack traces and function counts
- Determine reasons why threads block and leave the CPU
- Understand system CPU time by tracing syscalls
- Investigate CPU consumption by soft and hard interrupts
- Use bpftrace one-liners to explore CPU usage in custom ways

This chapter begins with the background you need to understand CPU analysis, summarizing the behavior of the CPU scheduler and CPU caches. I explore what questions BPF can answer, and provide an overall strategy to follow. To avoid reinventing the wheel and to direct further analysis, I first summarize traditional CPU tools, then BPF tools, including a list of BPF one-liners. This chapter ends with optional exercises.

6.1 Background

This section covers CPU fundamentals, BPF capabilities, and a suggested strategy for CPU analysis.

6.1.1   CPU Fundamentals

CPU Modes

CPUs and other resources are managed by the kernel, which runs in a special privileged state called *system mode*. User-level applications run in user mode, which can only access resources through kernel requests. These requests can be explicit, such as system calls, or implicit, such as page faults triggered by memory loads and stores. The kernel tracks the amount of time that the CPUs are not idle, as well as CPU time spent in user mode and system mode. Various performance tools show this user/system time split.

The kernel usually only runs on demand, triggered by syscalls and interrupts. There are some exceptions, such as housekeeping threads that run in the background, consuming CPU resources. An example of this is a kernel routine to balance memory pages on non-uniform memory access (NUMA) systems, which can consume significant CPU resources without an explicit request from user-level applications. (This can be tuned or disabled.) Some file systems also have background routines, such as for periodically verifying checksums for data integrity.

CPU Scheduler

The kernel is also responsible for sharing CPU resources between consumers, which it manages via a CPU scheduler. The main consumers are threads (also called tasks) which belong to processes or kernel routines. Other CPU consumers include interrupt routines: These can be soft interrupts triggered by running software or hard interrupts triggered by hardware.

Figure 6-1 shows the CPU scheduler, picturing threads waiting their turn on run queues and how they move between different thread states.

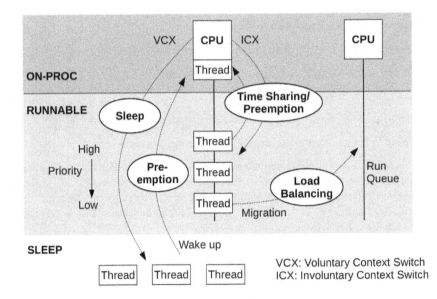

Figure 6-1   CPU scheduler

Three thread states are pictured in this diagram: ON-PROC for threads that are running on a CPU, RUNNABLE for threads that could run but are awaiting their turn, and SLEEP for threads that are blocked on another event, including uninterruptible waits. Threads waiting on a run queue are sorted by a priority value, which can be set by the kernel or by user processes to improve the performance of more important tasks. (Run queues are how scheduling was originally implemented, and the term and mental model are still used to describe waiting tasks. However, the Linux CFS scheduler actually uses a red/black tree of future task execution.)

This book uses terminology based on these thread states: "on CPU" refers to ON-PROC, and "off CPU" refers to all other states, where the thread is not running on a CPU.

Threads leave the CPU in one of two ways: (1) voluntary, if they block on I/O, a lock, or a sleep; or (2) involuntary, if they have exceeded their scheduled allocation of CPU time and are descheduled so that other threads can run or if they are preempted by a higher-priority thread. When a CPU switches from running one process or thread to another, it switches address spaces and other metadata; this is called a context switch.[1]

Figure 6-1 also pictures thread migrations. If a thread is in the runnable state and sitting in a run queue while another CPU is idle, the scheduler may migrate the thread to the idle CPU's run queue so that it can execute sooner. As a performance optimization, the scheduler uses logic to avoid migrations when the cost is expected to exceed the benefit, preferring to leave busy threads running on the same CPU where the CPU caches should still be warm.

CPU Caches

Whereas Figure 6-1 shows a software view of CPUs (the scheduler), Figure 6-2 provides a hardware view of the CPU caches.

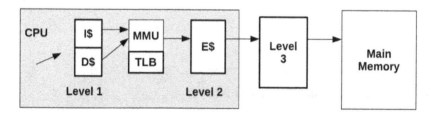

Figure 6-2 Hardware caches

Depending on the processor model and type, there are typically multiple levels of CPU cache, increasing in both size and latency. They begin with the Level 1 cache, which is split into separate instruction (I$) and data (D$) caches and is also small (Kbytes) and fast (nanoseconds). The caches end with the last-level cache (LLC), which is large (Mbytes) and much slower. On a processor with three levels of caches, the LLC is also the Level 3 cache. The Level 1 and 2 caches are usually per CPU core, and the Level 3 cache is usually shared across the socket. The memory management unit (MMU) responsible for translating virtual to physical addresses also has its own cache, the translation lookaside buffer (TLB).

---

1 There are also *mode switches*: Linux syscalls that do not block may only (depending on the processor) need to switch modes between user- and kernel-mode.

CPUs have been scaling for decades by increasing clock speed, adding cores, and adding more hardware threads. Memory bandwidth and latency have also improved, especially by adding and increasing the size of CPU caches. However, memory performance has not scaled to the same degree as the CPUs. Workloads have become limited by memory performance (termed "memory-bound") rather than the CPU cores.

Further Reading

This has been a brief summary to arm you with some essential knowledge before you use the tools. CPU software and hardware are covered in much more depth in Chapter 6 of *Systems Performance* [Gregg 13b].

6.1.2 BPF Capabilities

Traditional performance tools provide various insights for CPU usage. For example, they can show CPU utilization by process, context switch rates, and run queue lengths. These traditional tools are summarized in the next section.

BPF tracing tools can provide many additional details, answering:

- What new processes are created? What is their lifespan?
- Why is system time high? Are syscalls the culprit? What are they doing?
- How long do threads spend on-CPU for each wakeup?
- How long do threads spend waiting on the run queues?
- What is the maximum length of the run queues?
- Are the run queues balanced across the CPUs?
- Why are threads voluntarily leaving the CPU? For how long?
- What soft and hard IRQs are consuming CPUs?
- How often are CPUs idle when work is available on other run queues?
- What is the LLC hit ratio, by application request?

These questions can be answered using BPF by instrumenting tracepoints for scheduler and syscall events, kprobes for scheduler internal functions, uprobes for application-level functions, and PMCs for timed sampling and low-level CPU activity. These event sources can also be mixed: A BPF program could use uprobes to fetch application context and then associate that with instrumented PMC events. Such a program could show the LLC hit ratio by application request, for example.

Metrics that BPF provides can be examined per event or as summary statistics, with distributions shown as histograms. Stack traces can also be fetched to show the reasons for events. All these activities have been optimized using in-kernel BPF maps and output buffers for efficiency.

Event Sources

Table 6-1 lists the event sources for instrumenting CPU usage.

Table 6-1 **Event Sources for Instrumenting CPUs**

Event Type	Event Source
Kernel functions	kprobes, kretprobes
User-level functions	uprobes, uretprobes
System calls	syscall tracepoints
Soft interrupts	irq:softirq* tracepoints
Hard interrupts	irq:irq_handler* tracepoints
Workqueue events	workqueue tracepoints (see Chapter 14)
Timed sampling	PMC- or timer-based sampling
CPU power events	power tracepoints
CPU cycles	PMCs

Overhead

When tracing scheduler events, efficiency is especially important because scheduler events such as context switches may occur millions of times per second. While BPF programs are short and fast (microseconds), executing them for every context switch may cause this tiny overhead to add up to something measurable, or even significant. In the worst case, scheduler tracing can add over 10% overhead to a system. If BPF were not optimized, this overhead would be prohibitively high.

Scheduler tracing with BPF can be used for short-term, ad hoc analysis, with the understanding that there will be overhead. Such overhead can be quantified using testing or experimentation to determine: If CPU utilization is steady from second to second, what is it when the BPF tool is running and not running?

CPU tools can avoid overhead by not instrumenting frequent scheduler events. Infrequent events, such as process execution and thread migrations (with at most thousands of events per second) can be instrumented with negligible overhead. Profiling (timed sampling) also limits overhead to the fixed rate of samples, reducing overhead to negligible proportions.

6.1.3 Strategy

If you are new to CPU performance analysis, it can be difficult to know where to start—which target to begin analyzing and with which tool. Here is a suggested overall strategy that you can follow:

1. Ensure that a CPU workload is running before you spend time with analysis tools. Check system CPU utilization (e.g., using mpstat(1)) and ensure that all the CPUs are still online (and some haven't been offlined for some reason).

2. Confirm that the workload is CPU bound.

   a. Look for high CPU utilization system-wide or on a single CPU (e.g., using mpstat(1)).

   b. Look for high run queue latency (e.g., using BCC runqlat(1)). Software limits such as those used by containers can artificially limit the CPU available to processes, so an application may be CPU bound on a mostly idle system. This counterintuitive scenario can be identified by studying run queue latency.

3. Quantify CPU usage as percent utilization system-wide and then broken down by process, CPU mode, and CPU ID. This can be done using traditional tools (e.g., mpstat(1), top(1)). Look for high utilization by a single process, mode, or CPU.

   a. For high system time, frequency-count system calls by process and call type, and also examine arguments to look for inefficiencies (e.g., using perf(1), bpftrace one-liners, and BCC sysstat(8)).

4. Use a profiler to sample stack traces, which can be visualized using a CPU flame graph. Many CPU issues can be found by browsing such flame graphs.

5. For CPU consumers identified by profilers, consider writing custom tools to show more context. Profilers show the functions that are running but not the arguments and objects they are operating on, which may be needed to understand CPU usage. Examples:

   a. Kernel mode: If a file system is consuming CPU resources doing stat() on files, what are their filenames? (This could be determined, for example, using BCC statsnoop(8) or in general using tracepoints or kprobes from BPF tools.)

   b. User-mode: If an application is busy processing requests, what are the requests? (If an application-specific tool is unavailable, one could be developed using USDT or uprobes and BPF tools).

6. Measure time in hardware interrupts, since this time may not be visible in timer-based profilers (e.g., BCC hardirqs(1)).

7. Browse and execute the BPF tools listed in the BPF tools section of this chapter.

8. Measure CPU instructions per cycle (IPC) using PMCs to explain at a high level how much the CPUs are stalled (e.g., using perf(1)). This can be explored with more PMCs, which may identify low cache hit ratios (e.g., BCC llcstat), temperature stalls, and so on.

The following sections explain the tools involved in this process in more detail.

6.2   Traditional Tools

Traditional tools (see Table 6-2) can provide CPU utilization metrics for each process (thread) and for each CPU, voluntary and involuntary context switch rates, the average run queue length, and the total time spent waiting on run queues. Profilers can show and quantify the software that is running, and PMC-based tools can show how well the CPUs are operating at the cycle level.

Apart from solving issues, traditional tools can also provide clues to direct your further use of BPF tools. They have been categorized here based on their source and measurement type: kernel statistics, hardware statistics, and event tracing.

Table 6-2 **Traditional Tools**

Tool	Type	Description
uptime	Kernel statistics	Shows load averages and system uptime
top	Kernel statistics	Shows CPU time by process and CPU mode times system-wide
mpstat	Kernel statistics	Shows CPU mode time by CPU
perf	Kernel statistics, hardware statistics, event tracing	Profiles (timed sampling) of stack traces and event statistics and tracing of PMCs, tracepoints, USDT probes, kprobes, and uprobes
Ftrace	Kernel statistics, event tracing	Reports kernel function count statistics and event tracing of kprobes and uprobes

The following sections summarize key functionality of these tools. Refer to their man pages and other resources, including *Systems Performance* [Gregg 13b], for more usage and explanations.

6.2.1 Kernel Statistics

Kernel statistics tools use statistical sources in the kernel, often exposed via the /proc interface. An advantage of these tools is that the metrics are usually enabled by the kernel, so there is little additional overhead in using them. They can also often be read by non-root users.

Load Averages

uptime(1) is one of several commands that print the system load averages:

```
$ uptime
   00:34:10 up  6:29,  1 user,  load average: 20.29, 18.90, 18.70
```

The last three numbers are the 1-, 5-, and 15-minute load averages. By comparing these numbers, you can determine whether the load has been increasing, decreasing, or steady during the past 15 minutes or so. This output is from a 48-CPU production cloud instance and shows that load is increasing slightly when comparing 1-minute (20.29) to 15-minutes (18.70) load averages.

The load averages are not simple averages (means) but are exponentially damped moving sums, and reflect time beyond 1, 5, and 15 minutes. The metrics that these summarize show demand on the system: tasks in the CPU runnable state, as well as tasks in the uninterruptible wait state [72]. If you assume that the load averages are showing CPU load, you can divide them by the CPU count to see whether the system is running at CPU saturation, which would be indicated by a ratio of over 1.0. However, a number of problems with load averages, including their inclusion of uninterruptible tasks (tasks blocked in disk I/O and locks) cast doubt on this interpretation, so they are only really useful for looking at trends over time. You must use other tools, such as the BPF-based offcputime(8), to see if the load is CPU or uninterruptible time based. See Section 6.3.9 for information on offcputime(8) and Chapter 14 for more on measuring uninterruptible I/O.

top

The top(1) tool shows top CPU-consuming processes in a table of process details, along with a header summary of the system:

```
$ top
top - 00:35:49 up  6:31,  1 user,  load average: 21.35, 19.96, 19.12
Tasks: 514 total,   1 running, 288 sleeping,   0 stopped,   0 zombie
%Cpu(s): 33.2 us,  1.4 sy,  0.0 ni, 64.9 id,  0.0 wa,  0.0 hi,  0.4 si,  0.0 st
KiB Mem : 19382528+total,  1099228 free, 18422233+used,  8503712 buff/cache
KiB Swap:        0 total,        0 free,        0 used.  7984072 avail Mem

  PID USER      PR  NI    VIRT    RES    SHR S  %CPU %MEM     TIME+ COMMAND
 3606 www       20   0  0.197t 0.170t  38776 S  1681 94.2   7186:36 java
 5737 snmp      20   0   22712   6676   4256 S   0.7  0.0   0:57.96 snmp-pass
  403 root      20   0       0      0      0 I   0.3  0.0   0:00.17 kworker/41:1
  983 root      20   0    9916    128      0 S   0.3  0.0   1:29.95 rngd
29535 bgregg    20   0   41020   4224   3072 R   0.3  0.0   0:00.11 top
    1 root      20   0  225308   8988   6656 S   0.0  0.0   0:03.09 systemd
    2 root      20   0       0      0      0 S   0.0  0.0   0:00.01 kthreadd
[...]
```

This output is from a production instance and shows only one process that is CPU busy: A java process that is consuming a total of 1681% CPU, summed across all CPUs. For this 48-CPU system, the output shows that this java process is consuming 35% of overall CPU capacity. This concurs with the system-wide CPU average of 34.6% (shown in the header summary: 33.2% user and 1.4% system).

top(1) is especially useful for identifying issues of CPU load by an unexpected process. A common type of software bug causes a thread to become stuck in an infinite loop, which is easily found using top(1) as a process running at 100% CPU. Further analysis with profilers and BPF tools can confirm that the process is stuck in a loop, rather than busy processing work.

top(1) refreshes the screen by default so that the screen acts as a real-time dashboard. This is a problem: Issues can appear and then disappear before you are able to collect a screenshot. It can be important to add tool output and screenshots to ticketing systems to track work on performance issues and to share the information with others. Tools such as pidstat(1) can be used to print rolling output of process CPU usage for this purpose; CPU usage by process may also be already recorded by monitoring systems, if they are in use.

There are other top(1) variants, such as htop(1), that have more customization options. Unfortunately, many top(1) variants focus on visual enhancements rather than performance metrics, making them prettier but unable to shed light on issues beyond the original top(1). Exceptions include tiptop(1), which sources PMCs; atop(1), which uses process events to display short-lived processes; and the biotop(8) and tcptop(8) tools, which use BPF (and which I developed).

mpstat(1)

mpstat(1) can be used to examine per-CPU metrics:

```
$ mpstat -P ALL 1
Linux 4.15.0-1027-aws (api-...)      01/19/2019     _x86_64_      (48 CPU)

12:47:47 AM  CPU   %usr %nice %sys %iowait  %irq  %soft %steal %guest %gnice  %idle
12:47:48 AM  all  35.25  0.00 1.47    0.00  0.00   0.46   0.00   0.00   0.00  62.82
12:47:48 AM    0  44.55  0.00 1.98    0.00  0.00   0.99   0.00   0.00   0.00  52.48
12:47:48 AM    1  33.66  0.00 1.98    0.00  0.00   0.00   0.00   0.00   0.00  64.36
12:47:48 AM    2  30.21  0.00 2.08    0.00  0.00   0.00   0.00   0.00   0.00  67.71
12:47:48 AM    3  31.63  0.00 1.02    0.00  0.00   0.00   0.00   0.00   0.00  67.35
12:47:48 AM    4  26.21  0.00 0.00    0.00  0.00   0.97   0.00   0.00   0.00  72.82
12:47:48 AM    5  68.93  0.00 1.94    0.00  0.00   3.88   0.00   0.00   0.00  25.24
12:47:48 AM    6  26.26  0.00 3.03    0.00  0.00   0.00   0.00   0.00   0.00  70.71
12:47:48 AM    7  32.67  0.00 1.98    0.00  0.00   1.98   0.00   0.00   0.00  63.37
[...]
```

This output has been truncated because on this 48-CPU system it prints 48 lines of output per second: 1 line to summarize each CPU. This output can be used to identify issues of balance, where some CPUs have high utilization while others are idle. A CPU imbalance can occur for a number of reasons, such as misconfigured applications with a thread pool size too small to utilize all CPUs; software limits that limit a process or container to a subset of CPUs; and software bugs.

Time is broken down across the CPUs into many modes, including time in hard interrupts (%irq) and time in soft interrupts (%soft). These can be further investigated using the hardirqs(8) and softirqs(8) BPF tools.

6.2.2 Hardware Statistics

Hardware can also be a useful source of statistics—especially the performance monitoring counters (PMCs) available on the CPUs. PMCs were introduced in Chapter 2.

perf(1)

Linux perf(1) is a multi-tool that supports different instrumentation sources and presentations of data. First added to Linux in 2.6.31 (2009), it is considered the standard Linux profiler, and its code can be found in the Linux source code under tools/perf. I've published a detailed guide on how to use perf [73]. Among its many powerful capabilities is the ability to use PMCs in counting mode:

```
$ perf stat -d gzip file1

Performance counter stats for 'gzip file1':

    3952.239208   task-clock (msec)       #    0.999 CPUs utilized
              6   context-switches        #    0.002 K/sec
              0   cpu-migrations          #    0.000 K/sec
            127   page-faults             #    0.032 K/sec
 14,863,135,172   cycles                  #    3.761 GHz                      (62.35%)
 18,320,918,801   instructions            #    1.23  insn per cycle          (74.90%)
  3,876,390,410   branches                # 980.809 M/sec                    (74.90%)
    135,062,519   branch-misses           #    3.48% of all branches         (74.97%)
  3,725,936,639   L1-dcache-loads         # 942.741 M/sec                    (75.09%)
    657,864,906   L1-dcache-load-misses   #   17.66% of all L1-dcache hits   (75.16%)
     50,906,146   LLC-loads               #   12.880 M/sec                   (50.01%)
      1,411,636   LLC-load-misses         #    2.77% of all LL-cache hits    (49.87%)
```

The perf stat command counts events specified with -e arguments. If no such arguments are
supplied, it defaults to a basic set of PMCs, or it uses an extended set if -d is used, as shown here.
The output and usage varies a little depending on the version of Linux you are using and the
PMCs available for your processor type. This example shows perf(1) on Linux 4.15.

Depending on your processor type and perf version, you may find a detailed list of PMCs by using
perf list:

```
$ perf list
[...]
  mem_load_retired.l3_hit
        [Retired load instructions with L3 cache hits as data sources Supports address
when precise (Precise event)]
  mem_load_retired.l3_miss
        [Retired load instructions missed L3 cache as data sources Supports address
when precise (Precise event)]
[...]
```

This output shows the alias names you can use with -e. For example, you can count these events
on all CPUs (using -a, which recently became the default) and print output with an interval of
1000 milliseconds (-I 1000):

```
# perf stat -e mem_load_retired.l3_hit -e mem_load_retired.l3_miss -a -I 1000
#           time             counts unit events
     1.001228842            675,693      mem_load_retired.l3_hit
     1.001228842            868,728      mem_load_retired.l3_miss
     2.002185329            746,869      mem_load_retired.l3_hit
     2.002185329            965,421      mem_load_retired.l3_miss
     3.002952548          1,723,796      mem_load_retired.l3_hit
[...]
```

This output shows per-second rates for these events system-wide.

There are hundreds of PMCs available, documented in the processor vendor guides [Intel 16] [AMD 10]. You can use PMCs together with model-specific registers (MSRs) to determine how CPU internal components are performing, the current clock rates of the CPUs, their temperatures and energy consumption, the throughput on CPU interconnects and memory buses, and more.

tlbstat

As an example use of PMCs, I developed the tlbstat tool to count and summarize translation lookaside buffer (TLB)–related PMCs. My goal was to analyze the performance impact of the Linux kernel page table isolation (KPTI) patches that work around the Meltdown vulnerability [74] [75]:

```
# tlbstat -C0 1
K_CYCLES  K_INSTR   IPC DTLB_WALKS ITLB_WALKS K_DTLBCYC  K_ITLBCYC   DTLB% ITLB%
2875793   276051   0.10 89709496   65862302   787913     650834      27.40 22.63
2860557   273767   0.10 88829158   65213248   780301     644292      27.28 22.52
2885138   276533   0.10 89683045   65813992   787391     650494      27.29 22.55
2532843   243104   0.10 79055465   58023221   693910     573168      27.40 22.63
[...]
```

tlbstat prints the following columns:

- **K_CYCLES:** CPU cycles (in lots of 1000)
- **K_INSTR:** CPU Instructions (in lots of 1000)
- **IPC:** Instructions per cycle
- **DTLB_WALKS:** Data TLB walks (count)
- **ITLB_WALKS:** Instruction TLB walks (count)
- **K_DTLBCYC:** Cycles (in lots of 1000) when at least one page-miss handler (PMH) is active with data TLB walks
- **K_ITLBCYC:** Cycles (in lots of 1000) when at least one PMH is active with instruction TLB walks
- **DTLB%:** Data TLB active cycles as a ratio of total cycles
- **ITLB%:** Instruction TLB active cycles as a ratio of total cycles

The output shown earlier is from a stress test where the KPTI overhead was the worst: It shows 27% of CPU cycles in the DTLB and 22% in the ITLB. This means that half of the system-wide CPU resources were consumed by the memory management unit servicing virtual-to-physical address translations. If tlbstat showed similar numbers for production workloads, you would want to direct your tuning efforts toward the TLB.

6.2.3   Hardware Sampling

perf(1) can use PMCs in a different mode, where a count is chosen and, at a rate of one in every count, a PMC event causes an interrupt to be sent to the kernel so that it can capture event state. For example, the command below records the stack trace (-g) for L3 cache-miss events (-e ...) on all CPUs (-a) for 10 seconds (sleep 10, a dummy command used to set the duration):

```
# perf record -e mem_load_retired.l3_miss -c 50000 -a -g -- sleep 10
[ perf record: Woken up 1 times to write data ]
[ perf record: Captured and wrote 3.355 MB perf.data (342 samples) ]
```

The samples can be summarized using perf report or dumped using perf list:

```
# perf list
kworker/u17:4 11563 [007] 2707575.286552: mem_load_retired.l3_miss:
            7fffba5d8c52 move_freepages_block ([kernel.kallsyms])
            7fffba5d8e02 steal_suitable_fallback ([kernel.kallsyms])
            7fffba5da4a8 get_page_from_freelist ([kernel.kallsyms])
            7fffba5dc3fb __alloc_pages_nodemask ([kernel.kallsyms])
            7fffba63a8ea alloc_pages_current ([kernel.kallsyms])
            7fffc01faa5b crypt_page_alloc ([kernel.kallsyms])
            7fffba5d3781 mempool_alloc ([kernel.kallsyms])
            7fffc01fd870 kcryptd_crypt ([kernel.kallsyms])
            7fffba4a983e process_one_work ([kernel.kallsyms])
            7fffba4a9aa2 worker_thread ([kernel.kallsyms])
            7fffba4b0661 kthread ([kernel.kallsyms])
            7fffbae02205 ret_from_fork ([kernel.kallsyms])
[...]
```

This output shows a single stack trace sample. The stack is listed in order from child to parent, and in this case it shows the kernel functions that led to the L3 cache-miss event.

Note that you will want to use PMCs that support precise event-based sampling (PEBS) wherever possible to minimize issues of interrupt skid.

PMC hardware sampling can also trigger BPF programs. For example, instead of dumping all sampled stack traces to user space via the perf buffer, BPF can frequency-count them in kernel context to improve efficiency.

6.2.4   Timed Sampling

Many profilers support timer-based sampling (capturing the instruction pointer or stack trace at a timed interval). Such profilers provide a coarse, cheap-to-collect view of which software is consuming CPU resources. There are different types of profilers, some operating in user mode only and some in kernel mode. Kernel-mode profilers are usually preferred, as they can capture both kernel- and user-level stacks, providing a more complete picture.

perf

perf(1) is a kernel-based profiler that supports timed sampling through software events or PMCs: it defaults to the most accurate technique available. In this example, it is capturing stacks across all CPUs at 99 Hertz (samples per second per CPU) for 30 seconds:

```
# perf record -F 99 -a -g -- sleep 30
[ perf record: Woken up 1 times to write data ]
[ perf record: Captured and wrote 0.661 MB perf.data (2890 samples) ]
```

99 Hertz was chosen instead of 100 to avoid lockstep sampling with other software routines, which would otherwise skew the samples. (This is explained in more detail in Chapter 18.) Roughly 100 was chosen instead of, say, 10 or 10,000 as a balance between detail and overhead: Too low, and you don't get enough samples to see the full picture of execution, including large and small code paths; too high, and the overhead of samples skews performance and results.

When this perf(1) command is run, it writes the samples to a perf.data file: this has been optimized by use of a kernel buffer and an optimal number of writes to the file system. The output tells us it only needed to wake up once to write this data.

The output can be summarized using perf report, or each sample can be dumped using perf script. For example:

```
# perf report -n --stdio
[...]
# Children      Self       Samples  Command  Shared Object       Symbol
# ........     ........   ..........  .......  ..................  ....................
.......................
#
    99.41%    0.08%            2  iperf    libpthread-2.27.so  [.] __libc_write
            |
             --99.33%--__libc_write
                       |
                        --98.51%--entry_SYSCALL_64_after_hwframe
                                 |
                                  --98.38%--do_syscall_64
                                           |
                                            --98.29%--sys_write
                                                     |
                                                      --97.78%--vfs_write
                                                               |
[...]
```

The perf report summary shows a tree of functions from root to child. (The order can be reversed, as it was by default in earlier versions.) Unfortunately, there is not much conclusive to say from this sample of output—and the full output was six thousand lines. The full output of perf script, dumping every event, was over sixty thousand lines. These profiles can easily be 10 times this size on busier systems. A solution in such a case is to visualize the stack samples as a flame graph.

CPU Flame Graphs

Flame graphs, introduced in Chapter 2, enable visualization of stack traces. They are well suited for CPU profiles and are now commonly used for CPU analysis.

The flame graph in Figure 6-3 summarizes the same profile data captured in the previous section.

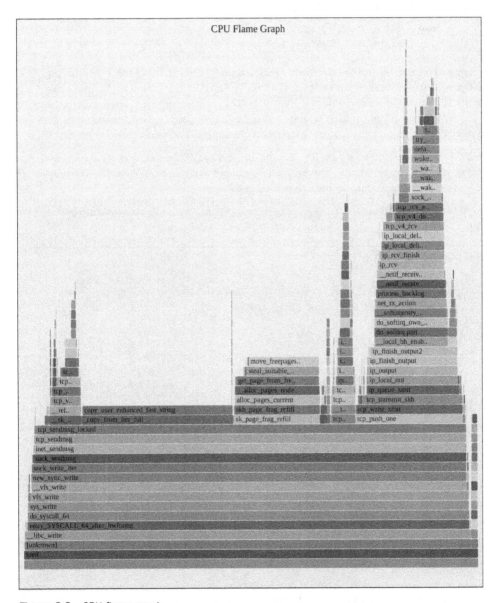

Figure 6-3   CPU flame graph

When this data is presented as a flame graph, it is easy to see that the process named iperf was consuming all CPU and exactly how: via sock_sendmsg(), which led to two hot on-CPU functions, copy_user_enhanced_fast_string() and move_freepages_block(), seen as the two plateaus. On the right is a tower that continues back into the TCP receive path; this is iperf doing a loopback test.

Below are the steps to create CPU flame graphs using perf(1) to sample stacks at 49 Hertz for 30 seconds, and my original flame graph implementation:

```
# git clone https://github.com/brendangregg/FlameGraph
# cd FlameGraph
# perf record -F 49 -ag -- sleep 30
# perf script --header | ./stackcollapse-perf.pl | ./flamegraph.pl > flame1.svg
```

The stackcollapse-perf.pl program converts `perf script` output into a standard format to be read by the flamegraph.pl program. There are converters in the FlameGraph repository for many other profilers. The flamegraph.pl program creates the flame graph as an SVG file with embedded JavaScript for interactivity when loaded in a browser. flamegraph.pl supports many options for customizations: run flamegraph.pl –help for details.

I recommend that you save the output of `perf script --header` for later analysis. Netflix has developed a newer flame graph implementation using d3, along with an additional tool that can read `perf script` output, FlameScope, which visualizes profiles as subsecond offset heatmaps from which time ranges can be selected to see the flame graph. [76] [77]

Internals

When perf(1) does timed sampling, it tries to use PMC-based hardware CPU cycle overflow events that trigger a non-maskable interrupt (NMI) to perform the sampling. In the cloud, however, many instance types do not have PMCs enabled. This may be visible in dmesg(1):

```
# dmesg | grep PMU
[    2.827349] Performance Events: unsupported p6 CPU model 85 no PMU driver,
software events only.
```

On these systems, perf(1) falls back to an hrtimer-based software interrupt. You can see this when running perf with -v:

```
# perf record -F 99 -a -v
Warning:
The cycles event is not supported, trying to fall back to cpu-clock-ticks
[...]
```

This software interrupt is generally sufficient, although be aware that there are some kernel code paths that it cannot interrupt: those with IRQs disabled (including some code paths in scheduling and hardware events). Your resulting profile will be missing samples from these code paths.

For more about how PMCs work, see Section 2.12 in Chapter 2.

6.2.5   Event Statistics and Tracing

Tools that trace events can also be used for CPU analysis. The traditional Linux tools that do this are perf(1) and Ftrace. These tools can not only trace events and save per-event details but can also count events in kernel context.

perf

perf(1) can instrument tracepoints, kprobes, uprobes, and (as of recently) USDT probes. These can provide some logical context for why CPU resources were consumed.

As an example, consider an issue where system-wide CPU utilization is high, but there is no visible process responsible in top(1). The issue could be short-lived processes. To test this hypothesis, count the sched_process_exec tracepoint system-wide using `perf script` to show the rate of exec() family syscalls:

```
# perf stat -e sched:sched_process_exec -I 1000
#          time            counts unit events
    1.000258841               169         sched:sched_process_exec
    2.000550707               168         sched:sched_process_exec
    3.000676643               167         sched:sched_process_exec
    4.000880905               167         sched:sched_process_exec
[...]
```

This output shows that there were over 160 execs per second. You can record each event using `perf record`, then dump the events using `perf script`[2]:

```
# perf record -e sched:sched_process_exec -a
^C[ perf record: Woken up 1 times to write data ]
[ perf record: Captured and wrote 3.464 MB perf.data (95 samples) ]
# perf script
    make 28767 [007] 712132.535241: sched:sched_process_exec: filename=/usr/bin/make
pid=28767 old_pid=28767
      sh 28768 [004] 712132.537036: sched:sched_process_exec: filename=/bin/sh
pid=28768 old_pid=28768
   cmake 28769 [007] 712132.538138: sched:sched_process_exec: filename=/usr/bin/cmake
pid=28769 old_pid=28769
    make 28770 [001] 712132.548034: sched:sched_process_exec: filename=/usr/bin/make
pid=28770 old_pid=28770
      sh 28771 [004] 712132.550399: sched:sched_process_exec: filename=/bin/sh
pid=28771 old_pid=28771
[...]
```

---

2 In case anyone is wondering why I don't use strace(1) for this. The current implementation of strace(1) uses breakpoints that can greatly slow the target (over 100x), making it dangerous for production use. More than one replacement is in development, including the perf trace subcommand, and another that is BPF based. Also, this example traces the exec() syscall system-wide, which strace(1) currently cannot do.

The output shows that the processes executed had names including make, sh, and cmake, which leads me to suspect that a software build is the culprit. Short-lived processes are such a common issue that there is a dedicated BPF tool for it: execsnoop(8). The fields in this output are: process name, PID, [CPU], timestamp (seconds), event name, and event arguments .

perf(1) has a special subcommand for CPU scheduler analysis called `perf sched`. It uses a dump-and-post-process approach for analyzing scheduler behavior and provides various reports that can show the CPU runtime per wakeup, the average and maximum scheduler latency (delay), and ASCII visualizations to show thread execution per CPU and migrations. Some example output:

```
# perf sched record -- sleep 1
[ perf record: Woken up 1 times to write data ]
[ perf record: Captured and wrote 1.886 MB perf.data (13502 samples) ]
# perf sched timehist
Samples do not have callchains.
           time    cpu  task name              wait time  sch delay   run time
                        [tid/pid]                 (msec)     (msec)     (msec)
--------------- ------ ----------------------  --------- ---------  ---------
[...]
 991963.885740 [0001]  :17008[17008]             25.613      0.000      0.057
 991963.886009 [0001]  sleep[16999]            1000.104      0.006      0.269
 991963.886018 [0005]  cc1[17083]                19.908      0.000      9.948
[...]
```

The output is verbose, showing all scheduler context switch events as a line summary with the time sleeping (wait time), scheduler latency (sch delay), and time spent on CPU (runtime), all in milliseconds. This output shows a sleep(1) command that slept for 1 second, and a cc1 process that ran for 9.9 milliseconds and slept for 19.9 milliseconds.

The `perf sched` subcommand can help solve many types of scheduler issues, including problems with the kernel scheduler implementation (the kernel scheduler is complex code that balances many requirements). However, the dump-and-post-process style is costly: This example recorded scheduler events for 1 second on an eight-CPU system, resulting in a 1.9 Mbyte perf.data file. On a larger, busier system, and for a longer duration, that file could be hundreds of Mbytes, which can become a problem with the CPU time needed to generate the file and the file system I/O to write it to disk.

To make sense of so many scheduler events, perf(1) output is often visualized. perf(1) also has a timechart subcommand for its own visualization.

Where possible, I recommend using BPF instead of `perf sched` as it can do in-kernel summaries that answer similar questions and emit the results (for example, the runqlat(8) and runqlen(8) tools, covered in Sections 6.3.3 and 6.3.4).

Ftrace

Ftrace is a collection of different tracing capabilities, developed by Steven Rostedt and first added to Linux 2.6.27 (2008). As with perf(1), it can also be used to explore the context of CPU usage via tracepoints and other events.

As an example, my perf-tools collection [78] mostly uses Ftrace for instrumentation, and includes funccount(8) for counting functions. This example counts the ext4 file system calls by matching those that begin with "ext":

```
# perf-tools/bin/funccount 'ext*'
Tracing "ext*"... Ctrl-C to end.
^C
FUNC                          COUNT
[...]
ext4_do_update_inode            523
ext4_inode_csum.isra.56         523
ext4_inode_csum_set             523
ext4_mark_iloc_dirty            523
ext4_reserve_inode_write        523
ext4_inode_table                551
ext4_get_group_desc             564
ext4_nonda_switch               586
ext4_bio_write_page             604
ext4_journal_check_start       1001
ext4_es_can_be_merged          1111
ext4_file_getattr              7159
ext4_getattr                   7285
```

The output here has been truncated to show only the most frequently used functions. The most frequent was ext4_getattr(), with 7285 calls while tracing.

Function calls consume CPU, and their names often provide clues as to the workload performed. In cases where the function name is ambiguous, it is often possible to find the source code to the function online and read it to understand what it does. This is especially true of Linux kernel functions, which are open source.

Ftrace has many useful canned capabilities, and recent enhancements have added histograms and more frequency counts ("hist triggers"). Unlike BPF, it is not fully programmable, so it cannot be used to fetch data and present it in completely custom ways.

6.3 BPF Tools

This section covers the BPF tools you can use for CPU performance analysis and troubleshooting. They are shown in Figure 6-4 and listed in Table 6-3.

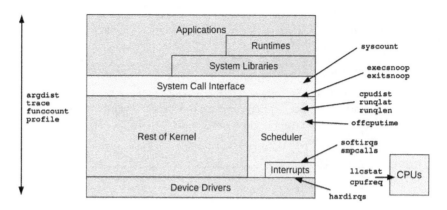

Figure 6-4   BPF tools for CPU analysis

These tools are either from the BCC and bpftrace repositories covered in Chapters 4 and 5, or were created for this book. Some tools appear in both BCC and bpftrace. Table 6-3 lists the origins of the tools covered in this section (BT is short for bpftrace.)

Table 6-3   **CPU-Related Tools**

Tool	Source	Target	Description
execsnoop	BCC/BT	Sched	Lists new process execution
exitsnoop	BCC	Sched	Shows process lifespan and exit reason
runqlat	BCC/BT	Sched	Summarizes CPU run queue latency
runqlen	BCC/BT	Sched	Summarizes CPU run queue length
runqslower	BCC	Sched	Prints run queue waits slower than a threshold
cpudist	BCC	Sched	Summarizes on-CPU time
cpufreq	Book	CPUs	Samples CPU frequency by process
profile	BCC	CPUs	Samples CPU stack traces
offcputime	BCC/book	Sched	Summarizes off-CPU stack traces and times
syscount	BCC/BT	Syscalls	Counts system calls by type and process
argdist	BCC	Syscalls	Can be used for syscall analysis
trace	BCC	Syscalls	Can be used for syscall analysis
funccount	BCC	Software	Counts function calls
softirqs	BCC	Interrupts	Summarizes soft interrupt time
hardirqs	BCC	Interrupts	Summarizes hard interrupt time
smpcalls	Book	Kernel	Times SMP remote CPU calls
llcstat	BCC	PMCs	Summarizes LLC hit ratio by process

For the tools from BCC and bpftrace, see their repositories for full and updated lists of tool options and capabilities. A selection of the most important capabilities are summarized here.

6.3.1 execsnoop

execsnoop(8)[3] is a BCC and bpftrace tool that traces new process execution system-wide. It can find issues of short-lived processes that consume CPU resources and can also be used to debug software execution, including application start scripts.

Example output from the BCC version:

```
# execsnoop
PCOMM            PID    PPID   RET ARGS
sshd             33096  2366     0 /usr/sbin/sshd -D -R
bash             33118  33096    0 /bin/bash
groups           33121  33119    0 /usr/bin/groups
ls               33123  33122    0 /bin/ls /etc/bash_completion.d
lesspipe         33125  33124    0 /usr/bin/lesspipe
basename         33126  33125    0 /usr/bin/basename /usr/bin/lesspipe
dirname          33129  33128    0 /usr/bin/dirname /usr/bin/lesspipe
tput             33130  33118    0 /usr/bin/tput setaf 1
dircolors        33132  33131    0 /usr/bin/dircolors -b
ls               33134  33133    0 /bin/ls /etc/bash_completion.d
mesg             33135  33118    0 /usr/bin/mesg n
sleep            33136  2015     0 /bin/sleep 30
sh               33143  33139    0 /bin/sh -c command -v debian-sa1 > /dev/null &&...
debian-sa1       33144  33143    0 /usr/lib/sysstat/debian-sa1 1 1
sa1              33144  33143    0 /usr/lib/sysstat/sa1 1 1
sadc             33144  33143    0 /usr/lib/sysstat/sadc -F -L -S DISK 1 1 /var/lo...
sleep            33148  2015     0 /bin/sleep 30
[...]
```

This tool captured the moment that a user logged into the system using SSH and the processes launched, including sshd(8), groups(1), and mesg(1). It also shows processes from the system activity recorder, sar, writing metrics to its log, including sa1(8) and sadc(8).

---

3 Origin: I created the first execsnoop using DTrace on 24-Mar-2004, to solve a common performance problem I was seeing with short-lived processes in Solaris environments. My prior analysis technique was to enable process accounting or BSM auditing and pick the exec events out of the logs, but both of these came with caveats: Process accounting truncated the process name and arguments to only eight characters. By comparison, my execsnoop tool could be run on a system immediately, without needing special audit modes, and could show much more of the command string. execsnoop is installed by default on OS X, and some Solaris and BSD versions. I also developed the BCC version on 7-Feb-2016, and the bpftrace version on 15-Nov-2017, and for that I added the join() built-in to bpftrace.

Use execsnoop(8) to look for high rates of short-lived processes that are consuming resources. They can be hard to spot as they may be very short-lived and may vanish before tools like top(1) or monitoring agents have a chance to see them. Chapter 1 shows an example of this, where a start script was failing to launch an application in a loop, perturbing the performance on the system. It was easily discovered using execsnoop(8). execsnoop(8) has been used to debug many production issues: perturbations from background jobs, slow or failing application startup, slow or failing container startup, and so on.

execsnoop(8) traces the execve(2) system call (the commonly used exec(2) variant) and shows details of the execve(2) arguments and return value. This catches new processes that follow the fork(2)/clone(2)->exec(2) sequence, as well as processes that re-exec(2) themselves. Some applications create new processes without calling exec(2), for example, when creating a pool of worker processes using fork(2) or clone(2) alone. These are not included in the execsnoop(8) output since they do not call execve(2). This situation should be uncommon: Applications should be creating pools of worker threads, not processes.

Since the rate of process execution is expected to be relatively low (<1000/second), the overhead of this tool is expected to be negligible.

BCC

The BCC version supports various options, including:

- **-x**: Includes failed exec()s
- **-n pattern**: Prints only commands containing patterns
- **-l pattern**: Prints only commands where arguments contain patterns
- **--max-args args**: Specifies the maximum number of arguments to print (with a default of 20)

bpftrace

The following is the code for the bpftrace version of execsnoop(8), which summarizes its core functionality. This version prints basic columns and does not support options:

```
#!/usr/local/bin/bpftrace

BEGIN
{
        printf("%-10s %-5s %s\n", "TIME(ms)", "PID", "ARGS");
}

tracepoint:syscalls:sys_enter_execve
{
        printf("%-10u %-5d ", elapsed / 1000000, pid);
        join(args->argv);
}
```

BEGIN prints a header. To capture exec() events, the syscalls:sys_enter_execve tracepoint is instrumented to print a time since the program began running, the process ID, and the command name and arguments. It uses the join() function on the args->argv field from the tracepoint so that the command name and arguments can be printed on one line.

A future version of bpftrace may change join() to return a string rather than print it out,[4] which would make this code:

```
tracepoint:syscalls:sys_enter_execve
{
        printf("%-10u %-5d %s\n", elapsed / 1000000, pid, join(args->argv));
}
```

The BCC version instruments both the entry and the return of the execve() syscall so that the return value can be printed. The bpftrace program could be easily enhanced to do this as well.[5]

See Chapter 13 for a similar tool, threadsnoop(8), which traces the creation of threads rather than process execution.

6.3.2 exitsnoop

exitsnoop(8)[6] is a BCC tool that traces when processes exit, showing their age and exit reason. The age is the time from process creation to termination, and includes time both on and off CPU. Like execsnoop(8), exitsnoop(8) can help debug issues of short-lived processes, providing different information to help understand this type of workload. For example:

```
# exitsnoop
PCOMM          PID     PPID    TID     AGE(s)  EXIT_CODE
cmake          8994    8993    8994    0.01    0
sh             8993    8951    8993    0.01    0
sleep          8946    7866    8946    1.00    0
cmake          8997    8996    8997    0.01    0
sh             8996    8995    8996    0.01    0
make           8995    8951    8995    0.02    0
cmake          9000    8999    9000    0.02    0
sh             8999    8998    8999    0.02    0
git            9003    9002    9003    0.00    0
DOM Worker     5111    4183    8301    221.25  0
sleep          8967    26663   8967    7.31    signal 9 (KILL)
git            9004    9002    9004    0.00    0
[...]
```

---

4 See bpftrace issue #26 [67].

5 This and later bpftrace programs can easily be enhanced to show more and more details. I've resisted doing so here to keep them short and to the point, as well as more easily understood.

6 Origin: This was created by Arturo Martin-de-Nicolas on 4-May-2019.

This output shows many short-lived processes exiting, such as cmake(1), sh(1), and make(1): a software build was running. A sleep(1) process exited successfully (exit code 0) after 1.00 seconds, and another sleep(1) process exited after 7.31 seconds due to a KILL signal. This also caught a "DOM Worker" thread exiting after 221.25 seconds.

This tool works by instrumenting the sched:sched_process_exit tracepoint and its arguments, and it also uses bpf_get_current_task() so that the start time can be read from the task struct (an unstable interface detail). Since this tracepoint should fire infrequently, the overhead of this tool should be negligible.

Command line usage:

```
exitsnoop [options]
```

Options include:

- **-p PID**: Measures this process only
- **-t**: Includes timestamps
- **-x**: Only trace fails (a non-zero exit reason)

There is not currently a bpftrace version of exitsnoop(8), but it might be a useful exercise to create one for those learning bpftrace programming.[7]

6.3.3 runqlat

runqlat(8)[8] is a BCC and bpftrace tool for measuring CPU scheduler latency, often called run queue latency (even when no longer implemented using run queues). It is useful for identifying and quantifying issues of CPU saturation, where there is more demand for CPU resources than they can service. The metric measured by runqlat(8) is the time each thread (task) spends waiting for its turn on CPU.

The following shows BCC runqlat(8) running on a 48-CPU production API instance operating at about 42% CPU utilization system-wide. The arguments to runqlat(8) are "10 1" to set a 10-second interval and output only once:

```
# runqlat 10 1
Tracing run queue latency... Hit Ctrl-C to end.

     usecs               : count    distribution
        0 -> 1           : 3149     |                                        |
        2 -> 3           : 304613   |****************************************|
        4 -> 7           : 274541   |************************************    |
```

---

7 If you publish it, remember to credit the original BCC author: Arturo Martin-de-Nicolas.

8 Origin: I created the first version using DTrace as dispqlat.d, published on 13-Aug-2012, inspired by the DTrace sched provider probes and examples in the "Dynamic Tracing Guide," Jan 2005 [Sun 05]. dispq is short for dispatcher queue, another term for run queue. I developed the BCC runqlat version on 7-Feb-2016, and bpftrace on 17-Sep-2018.

```
   8 -> 15       : 58576    |*******                                  |
  16 -> 31       : 15485    |**                                       |
  32 -> 63       : 24877    |***                                      |
  64 -> 127      : 6727     |                                         |
 128 -> 255      : 1214     |                                         |
 256 -> 511      : 606      |                                         |
 512 -> 1023     : 489      |                                         |
1024 -> 2047     : 315      |                                         |
2048 -> 4095     : 122      |                                         |
4096 -> 8191     : 24       |                                         |
8192 -> 16383    : 2        |                                         |
```

This output shows that, most of the time, threads were waiting less than 15 microseconds, with a mode in the histogram between two and 15 microseconds. This is relatively fast—an example of a healthy system—and is expected for a system running at 42% CPU utilization. Occasionally run queue latency reached as high as the eight- to 16-millisecond bucket in this example, but those were outliers.

runqlat(8) works by instrumenting scheduler wakeup and context switch events to determine the time from wakeup to running. These events can be very frequent on busy production systems, exceeding one million events per second. Even though BPF is optimized, at these rates even adding one microsecond per event can cause noticeable overhead.[9] Use with caution.

Misconfigured Build

Here is a different example for comparison. This time a 36-CPU build server is doing a software build, where the number of parallel jobs has been set to 72 by mistake, causing the CPUs to be overloaded:

```
# runqlat 10 1
Tracing run queue latency... Hit Ctrl-C to end.

     usecs        : count    distribution
     0 -> 1       : 1906     |***                                      |
     2 -> 3       : 22087    |*****************************************|
     4 -> 7       : 21245    |****************************************|
     8 -> 15      : 7333     |*************                            |
    16 -> 31      : 4902     |********                                 |
    32 -> 63      : 6002     |**********                               |
    64 -> 127     : 7370     |*************                            |
   128 -> 255     : 13001    |***********************                  |
```

---

9 As a simple exercise, if you had a context switch rate of 1M/sec across a 10-CPU system, adding 1 microsecond per context switch would consume 10% of CPU resources (100% × (1 × 1000000 / 10 × 1000000)). See Chapter 18 for some real measurements of BPF overhead, which is typically much less than one microsecond per event.

```
     256 -> 511        : 4823    |********                           |
     512 -> 1023       : 1519    |**                                 |
    1024 -> 2047       : 3682    |******                             |
    2048 -> 4095       : 3170    |*****                              |
    4096 -> 8191       : 5759    |**********                         |
    8192 -> 16383      : 14549   |***************************        |
   16384 -> 32767      : 5589    |**********                         |
   32768 -> 65535      : 372     |                                   |
   65536 -> 131071     : 10      |                                   |
```

The distribution is now tri-modal, with the slowest mode centered in the 8- to 16-millisecond bucket. This shows significant waiting by threads.

This particular issue is straightforward to identify from other tools and metrics. For example, sar(1) can show CPU utilization (-u) and run queue metrics (-q):

```
# sar -uq 1
Linux 4.18.0-virtual (...)    01/21/2019    _x86_64_      (36 CPU)

11:06:25 PM     CPU      %user     %nice    %system    %iowait     %steal     %idle
11:06:26 PM     all      88.06      0.00      11.94       0.00       0.00      0.00

11:06:25 PM    runq-sz  plist-sz   ldavg-1   ldavg-5   ldavg-15   blocked
11:06:26 PM         72      1030     65.90     41.52      34.75         0
[...]
```

This sar(1) output shows 0% CPU idle and an average run queue size of 72 (which includes both running and runnable)—more than the 36 CPUs available.

Chapter 15 has a runqlat(8) example showing per-container latency.

BCC

Command line usage for the BCC version:

```
runqlat [options] [interval [count]]
```

Options include:

- **-m:** Prints output in milliseconds
- **-P:** Prints a histogram per process ID
- **--pidnss:** Prints a histogram per PID namespace
- **-p PID:** Traces this process ID only
- **-T:** Includes timestamps on output

The -T option is useful for annotating per-interval output with the time. For example, runqlat -T 1 for timestamped per-second output.

bpftrace

The following is the code for the bpftrace version of runqlat(8), which summarizes its core functionality. This version does not support options.

```
#!/usr/local/bin/bpftrace

#include <linux/sched.h>

BEGIN
{
        printf("Tracing CPU scheduler... Hit Ctrl-C to end.\n");
}

tracepoint:sched:sched_wakeup,
tracepoint:sched:sched_wakeup_new
{
        @qtime[args->pid] = nsecs;
}

tracepoint:sched:sched_switch
{
        if (args->prev_state == TASK_RUNNING) {
                @qtime[args->prev_pid] = nsecs;
        }

        $ns = @qtime[args->next_pid];
        if ($ns) {
                @usecs = hist((nsecs - $ns) / 1000);
        }
        delete(@qtime[args->next_pid]);
}

END
{
        clear(@qtime);
}
```

The program records a timestamp on the sched_wakeup and sched_wakeup_new tracepoints, keyed by args->pid, which is the kernel thread ID.

The sched_switch action stores a timestamp on args->prev_pid if that state was still runnable (TASK_RUNNING). This is handling an involuntary context switch where, the moment the thread leaves the CPU, it is returned to a run queue. That action also checks whether a timestamp was stored for the next runnable process and, if so, calculates the time delta and stores it in the @usecs histogram.

Since TASK_RUNNING was used, the linux/sched.h header file was read (#include) so that its definition was available.

The BCC version can break down by PID, which this bpftrace version can easily be modified to do by adding a pid key to the @usecs map. Another enhancement in BCC is to skip recording run queue latency for PID 0 to exclude the latency of scheduling the kernel idle thread.[10] Again, this program can easily be modified to do the same.

6.3.4 runqlen

runqlen(8)[11] is a BCC and bpftrace tool for sampling the length of the CPU run queues, counting how many tasks are waiting their turn, and presenting this as a linear histogram. This can be used to further characterize issues of run queue latency or as a cheaper approximation.

The following shows runqlet(8) from BCC running on a 48-CPU production API instance that is at about 42% CPU utilization system-wide (the same instance shown earlier with runqlat(8)). The arguments to runqlen(8) are "10 1" to set a 10-second interval and output only once:

```
# runqlen 10 1
Sampling run queue length... Hit Ctrl-C to end.

    runqlen       : count    distribution
       0          : 47284    |****************************************|
       1          : 211      |                                        |
       2          : 28       |                                        |
       3          : 6        |                                        |
       4          : 4        |                                        |
       5          : 1        |                                        |
       6          : 1        |                                        |
```

This shows that most of the time, the run queue length was zero, meaning that threads did not need to wait their turn.

I describe run queue length as a secondary performance metric and run queue latency as primary. Unlike length, latency directly and proportionately affects performance. Imagine joining a checkout line at a grocery store. What matters more to you: the length of the line or the time you actually spend waiting? runqlat(8) matters more. So why use runqlen(8)?

---

10 Thanks, Ivan Babrou, for adding that.

11 Origin: I created the first version, called dispqlen.d, on 27-Jun-2005, to help characterize run queue lengths by CPU. I developed the BCC version on 12-Dec-2016 and the bpftrace version on 7-Oct-2018.

First, runqlen(8) can be used to further characterize issues found in runqlat(8) and explain how latencies become high. Second, runqlen(8) employs timed sampling at 99 Hertz, whereas runqlat(8) traces scheduler events. This timed sampling has negligible overhead compared to runqlat(8)'s scheduler tracing. For 24x7 monitoring, it may be preferable to use runqlen(8) first to identify issues (since it is cheaper to run) and then use runqlat(8) ad hoc to quantify the latency.

Four Threads, One CPU

In this example, a CPU workload of four busy threads was bound to CPU 0. runqlen(8) was executed with -C to show per-CPU histograms:

```
# runqlen -C
Sampling run queue length... Hit Ctrl-C to end.
^C

cpu = 0
    runqlen       : count     distribution
       0          : 0         |                                         |
       1          : 0         |                                         |
       2          : 0         |                                         |
       3          : 551       |*****************************************|

cpu = 1
    runqlen       : count     distribution
       0          : 41        |*****************************************|

cpu = 2
    runqlen       : count     distribution
       0          : 126       |*****************************************|
[...]
```

The run queue length on CPU 0 was three: one thread on-CPU and three threads waiting. This per-CPU output is useful for checking scheduler balance.

BCC

Command line usage for the BCC version:

```
runqlen [options] [interval [count]]
```

Options include:

- **-C**: Prints a histogram per CPU
- **-O**: Prints run queue occupancy
- **-T**: Includes timestamps on output

Run queue occupancy is a separate metric that shows the percentage of time that there were threads waiting. This is sometimes useful when a single metric is needed for monitoring, alerting, and graphing.

bpftrace

The following is the code for the bpftrace version of runqlen(8), which summarizes its core functionality. This version does not support options.

```
#!/usr/local/bin/bpftrace

#include <linux/sched.h>

struct cfs_rq_partial {
        struct load_weight load;
        unsigned long runnable_weight;
        unsigned int nr_running;
};

BEGIN
{
        printf("Sampling run queue length at 99 Hertz... Hit Ctrl-C to end.\n");
}

profile:hz:99
{
        $task = (struct task_struct *)curtask;
        $my_q = (struct cfs_rq_partial *)$task->se.cfs_rq;
        $len = $my_q->nr_running;
        $len = $len > 0 ? $len - 1 : 0;          // subtract currently running task
        @runqlen = lhist($len, 0, 100, 1);
}
```

The program needs to reference the nr_running member of the cfs_rq struct, but this struct is not available in the standard kernel headers. So the program begins by defining a cfs_rq_partial struct, enough to fetch the needed member. This workaround may no longer be needed once BTF is available (see Chapter 2).

The main event is the profile:hz:99 probe, which samples the run queue length at 99 Hertz on all CPUs. The length is fetched by walking from the current task struct to the run queue it is on and then reading the length of the run queue. These struct and member names may need to be adjusted if the kernel source changes.

You can have this bpftrace version break down by CPU by adding a cpu key to @runqlen.

6.3.5   runqslower

runqslower(8)[12] is a BCC tool that lists instances of run queue latency exceeding a configurable threshold and shows the process that suffered the latency and its duration. The following example is from a 48-CPU production API instance currently running at 45% CPU utilization system-wide:

```
# runqslower
Tracing run queue latency higher than 10000 us
TIME      COMM             PID        LAT(us)
17:42:49 python3          4590         16345
17:42:50 pool-25-thread-  4683         50001
17:42:53 ForkJoinPool.co  5898         11935
17:42:56 python3          4590         10191
17:42:56 ForkJoinPool.co  5912         13738
17:42:56 ForkJoinPool.co  5908         11434
17:42:57 ForkJoinPool.co  5890         11436
17:43:00 ForkJoinPool.co  5477         10502
17:43:01 grpc-default-wo  5794         11637
17:43:02 tomcat-exec-296  6373         12083
[...]
```

This output shows that over a period of 13 seconds, there were 10 cases of run queue latency exceeding the default threshold of 10000 microseconds (10 milliseconds). This might seem surprising for a server with 55% idle CPU headroom, but this is a busy multi-threaded application, and some run queue imbalance is likely until the scheduler can migrate threads to idle CPUs. This tool can confirm the affected applications.

This tool currently works by using kprobes for the kernel functions ttwu_do_wakeup(), wake_up_new_task(), and finish_task_switch(). A future version should switch to scheduler tracepoints, using code similar to the earlier bpftrace version of runqlat(8). The overhead is similar to that of runqlat(8); it can cause noticeable overhead on busy systems due to the cost of the kprobes, even while runqslower(8) is not printing any output.

Command line usage:

```
runqslower [options] [min_us]
```

Options include:

- -p PID: Measures this process only

The default threshold is 10000 microseconds.

---

12 Origin: This was created by Ivan Babrou on 2-May-2018.

6.3.6   cpudist

cpudist(8)[13] is a BCC tool for showing the distribution of on-CPU time for each thread wakeup. This can be used to help characterize CPU workloads, providing details for later tuning and design decisions. For example, from a 48-CPU production instance:

```
# cpudist 10 1
Tracing on-CPU time... Hit Ctrl-C to end.

     usecs               : count    distribution
        0 -> 1           : 103865   |***************************             |
        2 -> 3           : 91142    |***********************                 |
        4 -> 7           : 134188   |***********************************     |
        8 -> 15          : 149862   |****************************************|
       16 -> 31          : 122285   |********************************        |
       32 -> 63          : 71912    |******************                      |
       64 -> 127         : 27103    |*******                                 |
      128 -> 255         : 4835     |*                                       |
      256 -> 511         : 692      |                                        |
      512 -> 1023        : 320      |                                        |
     1024 -> 2047        : 328      |                                        |
     2048 -> 4095        : 412      |                                        |
     4096 -> 8191        : 356      |                                        |
     8192 -> 16383       : 69       |                                        |
    16384 -> 32767       : 42       |                                        |
    32768 -> 65535       : 30       |                                        |
    65536 -> 131071      : 22       |                                        |
   131072 -> 262143      : 20       |                                        |
   262144 -> 524287      : 4        |                                        |
```

This output shows that the production application usually spends only a short amount of time on CPU: from 0 to 127 microseconds.

Here is a CPU-heavy workload, with more busy threads than CPUs available, and with a histogram in milliseconds (-m):

```
# cpudist -m
Tracing on-CPU time... Hit Ctrl-C to end.
^C
     msecs               : count    distribution
        0 -> 1           : 521      |****************************************|
        2 -> 3           : 60       |****                                    |
```

---

13 Origin: I created cpudists on 27-Apr-2005, showing CPU runtime distributions for processes, the kernel, and the idle thread. Sasha Goldshtein developed the BCC cpudist(8) on 29-Jun-2016, with options for per-process distributions.

```
    4 -> 7        : 272    |********************          |
    8 -> 15       : 308    |***********************       |
   16 -> 31       : 66     |*****                         |
   32 -> 63       : 14     |*                             |
```

Now there is a mode of on-CPU durations from 4 to 15 milliseconds: this is likely threads exhausting their scheduler time quanta and then encountering an involuntary context switch.

This tool was used to help understand a Netflix production change, where a machine learning application began running three times faster. The perf(1) command was used to show that the context switch rate had dropped, and cpudist(8) was used to explain the affect this had: the application was now usually running for two to four milliseconds between context switches, whereas earlier it could only run for between zero and three microseconds before being interrupted with a context switch.

cpudist(8) works by tracing scheduler context switch events, which can be very frequent on busy production workloads (over one million events/sec). As with runqlat(8), the overhead of this tool could be significant, so use it with caution.

Command line usage:

```
cpudist [options] [interval [count]]
```

Options include:

- **-m**: Prints output in milliseconds (default is microseconds)
- **-O**: Shows off-CPU time instead of on-CPU time
- **-P**: Prints a histogram per process
- **-p PID**: Measures this process only

There is currently no bpftrace version of cpudist(8). I've resisted creating one and instead have added it as an optional exercise at the end of this chapter.

6.3.7 cpufreq

cpufreq(8)[14] samples the CPU frequency and shows it as a system-wide histogram, with per-process name histograms. This only works for CPU scaling governors that change the frequency, such as powersave, and can be used to determine the clock speed at which your applications are running. For example:

---

14 Origin: I created it for this book on 24-Apr-2019, inspired by the time_in_state BPF tool from Android by Connor O'Brien, with some initial work by Joel Fernandes; it uses sched tracepoints to track the frequency more precisely.

```
# cpufreq.bt
Sampling CPU freq system-wide & by process. Ctrl-C to end.
^C
[...]


@process_mhz[snmpd]:
[1200, 1400)           1 |@@@@@@@@@@@@@@@@@@@@@@@@@@@@@@@@@@@@@@@@@@@@@@@@@@@@|

@process_mhz[python3]:
[1600, 1800)           1 |@                                                 |
[1800, 2000)           0 |                                                  |
[2000, 2200)           0 |                                                  |
[2200, 2400)           0 |                                                  |
[2400, 2600)           0 |                                                  |
[2600, 2800)           2 |@@@                                               |
[2800, 3000)           0 |                                                  |
[3000, 3200)          29 |@@@@@@@@@@@@@@@@@@@@@@@@@@@@@@@@@@@@@@@@@@@@@@@@@@@@|

@process_mhz[java]:
[1200, 1400)         216 |@@@@@@@@@@@@@@@@@@@@@@@@@@@@@@@@@@@@@@@@@@@@@@@@@@@@|
[1400, 1600)          23 |@@@@@                                             |
[1600, 1800)          18 |@@@@                                              |
[1800, 2000)          16 |@@@                                               |
[2000, 2200)          12 |@@                                                |
[2200, 2400)           0 |                                                  |
[2400, 2600)           4 |                                                  |
[2600, 2800)           2 |                                                  |
[2800, 3000)           1 |                                                  |
[3000, 3200)          18 |@@@@                                              |


@system_mhz:
[1200, 1400)       22041 |@@@@@@@@@@@@@@@@@@@@@@@@@@@@@@@@@@@@@@@@@@@@@@@@@@@@|
[1400, 1600)         903 |@@                                                |
[1600, 1800)         474 |@                                                 |
[1800, 2000)         368 |                                                  |
[2000, 2200)          30 |                                                  |
[2200, 2400)           3 |                                                  |
[2400, 2600)          21 |                                                  |
[2600, 2800)          33 |                                                  |
[2800, 3000)          15 |                                                  |
[3000, 3200)         270 |                                                  |
[...]
```

This shows that, system-wide, the CPU frequency was usually in the 1200 to 1400 MHz range, so this is a mostly idle system. Similar frequencies were encountered by the java process, with only some samples (18 while sampling) reaching the 3.0 to 3.2 GHz range. This application was mostly doing disk I/O, causing the CPUs to enter a power saving state. python3 processes were usually running at full speed.

This tool works by tracing frequency change tracepoints to determine the speed of each CPU, and then samples that speed at 100 Hertz. The performance overhead should be low to negligible. The previous output is from a system using the powersave scaling governor, as set in /sys/devices/system/cpu/cpufreq/.../scaling_governor. When the system is set to the performance governor, this tool shows nothing as there are no more frequency changes to instrument: the CPUs are pinned at the highest frequency.

Here is an excerpt from a production workload I just discovered:

```
@process_mhz[nginx]:
[1200, 1400)          35 |@@@@@@@@@@@@@@@@@@@@@@@@@@@@@@@@@@@@@          |
[1400, 1600)          17 |@@@@@@@@@@@@@@@@@                             |
[1600, 1800)          16 |@@@@@@@@@@@@@@@@                              |
[1800, 2000)          17 |@@@@@@@@@@@@@@@@@                             |
[2000, 2200)           0 |                                             |
[2200, 2400)           0 |                                             |
[2400, 2600)           0 |                                             |
[2600, 2800)           0 |                                             |
[2800, 3000)           0 |                                             |
[3000, 3200)           0 |                                             |
[3200, 3400)           0 |                                             |
[3400, 3600)           0 |                                             |
[3600, 3800)          50 |@@@@@@@@@@@@@@@@@@@@@@@@@@@@@@@@@@@@@@@@@@@@@@@@@@@@|
```

It shows that the production application, nginx, was often running at low CPU clock frequencies. The CPU scaling_governor had not been set to performance and had defaulted to powersave.

The source for cpufreq(8) is:

```
#!/usr/local/bin/bpftrace

BEGIN
{
        printf("Sampling CPU freq system-wide & by process. Ctrl-C to end.\n");
}

tracepoint:power:cpu_frequency
{
        @curfreq[cpu] = args->state;
}
```

```
profile:hz:100
/@curfreq[cpu]/
{
        @system_mhz = lhist(@curfreq[cpu] / 1000, 0, 5000, 200);
        if (pid) {
                @process_mhz[comm] = lhist(@curfreq[cpu] / 1000, 0, 5000, 200);
        }
}


END
{
        clear(@curfreq);
}
```

The frequency changes are traced using the power:cpu_frequency tracepoint and saved in a @curfreq BPF map by CPU, for later lookup while sampling. The histograms track frequencies from 0 to 5000 MHz in steps of 200 MHz; these parameters can be adjusted in the tool if needed.

6.3.8 profile

profile(8)[15] is a BCC tool that samples stack traces at a timed interval and reports a frequency count of stack traces. This is the most useful tool in BCC for understanding CPU consumption as it summarizes almost all code paths that are consuming CPU resources. (See the hardirqs(8) tool in Section 6.3.14 for more CPU consumers.) It can also be used with relatively negligible overhead, as the event rate is fixed to the sample rate, which can be tuned.

By default, this tool samples both user and kernel stack traces at 49 Hertz across all CPUs. This can be customized using options, and the settings are printed at the start of the output. For example:

```
# profile
Sampling at 49 Hertz of all threads by user + kernel stack... Hit Ctrl-C to end.
^C

    sk_stream_alloc_skb
    sk_stream_alloc_skb
    tcp_sendmsg_locked
    tcp_sendmsg
    sock_sendmsg
```

---

15 Origin: there have been many profilers in the past, including gprof from 1982 [Graham 82] (rewritten in 1988 by Jay Fenlason for the GNU project). I developed this version for BCC on 15-Jul-2016, based on code from Sasha Goldshtein, Andrew Birchall, Evgeny Vereshchagin, and Teng Qin. My first version predated kernel support and worked by using a hack: I added a tracepoint on perf samples, to be used in conjunction with perf_event_open(). My patch to add this tracepoint to Linux was rejected by Peter Zijlstra, in favor of developing proper profiling support with BPF, which Alexei Starovoitov added.

```
    sock_write_iter
    __vfs_write
    vfs_write
    ksys_write
    do_syscall_64
    entry_SYSCALL_64_after_hwframe
    __GI___write
    [unknown]
    -               iperf (29136)
        1
```

[...]

```
    __free_pages_ok
    __free_pages_ok
    skb_release_data
    __kfree_skb
    tcp_ack
    tcp_rcv_established
    tcp_v4_do_rcv
    __release_sock
    release_sock
    tcp_sendmsg
    sock_sendmsg
    sock_write_iter
    __vfs_write
    vfs_write
    ksys_write
    do_syscall_64
    entry_SYSCALL_64_after_hwframe
    __GI___write
    [unknown]
    -               iperf (29136)
        1889

    get_page_from_freelist
    get_page_from_freelist
    __alloc_pages_nodemask
    skb_page_frag_refill
    sk_page_frag_refill
    tcp_sendmsg_locked
    tcp_sendmsg
    sock_sendmsg
```

```
sock_write_iter
__vfs_write
vfs_write
ksys_write
do_syscall_64
entry_SYSCALL_64_after_hwframe
__GI___write
[unknown]
-                    iperf (29136)
    2673
```

The output shows the stack traces as a list of functions, followed by a dash ("-") and the process name and PID in parentheses, and finally a count for that stack trace. The stack traces are printed in frequency count order, from least to most frequent.

The full output in this example was 17,254 lines long and has been truncated here to show only the first and final two stack traces. The most frequent stack trace, showing a path through vfs_write() and ending with get_page_from_freelist() on CPU, was seen 2673 times while sampling.

CPU Flame Graphs

Flame graphs are visualizations of stack traces that can help you quickly understand profile(8) output. They were introduced in Chapter 2.

To support flame graphs, profile(8) can produce output in folded format using -f: Stack traces are printed on one line, with functions separated by semicolons. For example, writing a 30-second profile to an out.stacks01 file and including kernel annotations (-a):

```
# profile -af 30 > out.stacks01
# tail -3 out.stacks01
iperf;
[unknown];__GI___write;entry_SYSCALL_64_after_hwframe_[k];do_syscall_64_[k];ksys_writ
e_[k];vfs_write_[k];__vfs_write_[k];sock_write_iter_[k];sock_sendmsg_[k];tcp_sendmsg_
[k];tcp_sendmsg_locked_[k];_copy_from_iter_full_[k];copyin_[k];copy_user_enhanced_fas
t_string_[k];copy_user_enhanced_fast_string_[k] 5844
iperf;
[unknown];__GI___write;entry_SYSCALL_64_after_hwframe_[k];do_syscall_64_[k];ksys_writ
e_[k];vfs_write_[k];__vfs_write_[k];sock_write_iter_[k];sock_sendmsg_[k];tcp_sendmsg_
[k];release_sock_[k];__release_sock_[k];tcp_v4_do_rcv_[k];tcp_rcv_established_[k];tcp
_ack_[k];__kfree_skb_[k];skb_release_data_[k];__free_pages_ok_[k];__free_pages_ok_[k]
10713
iperf;
[unknown];__GI___write;entry_SYSCALL_64_after_hwframe_[k];do_syscall_64_[k];ksys_writ
e_[k];vfs_write_[k];__vfs_write_[k];sock_write_iter_[k];sock_sendmsg_[k];tcp_sendmsg_
[k];tcp_sendmsg_locked_[k];sk_page_frag_refill_[k];skb_page_frag_refill_[k];__alloc_p
ages_nodemask_[k];get_page_from_freelist_[k];get_page_from_freelist_[k] 15088
```

Only the last three lines are shown here. This output can be fed into my original flame graph software to generate a CPU flame graph:

```
$ git clone https://github.com/brendangregg/FlameGraph
$ cd FlameGraph
$ ./flamegraph.pl --color=java < ../out.stacks01 > out.svg
```

flamegraph.pl supports different color palettes. The java palette used here makes use of the kernel annotations ("_[k]") for choosing color hues. The generated SVG is shown in Figure 6-5.

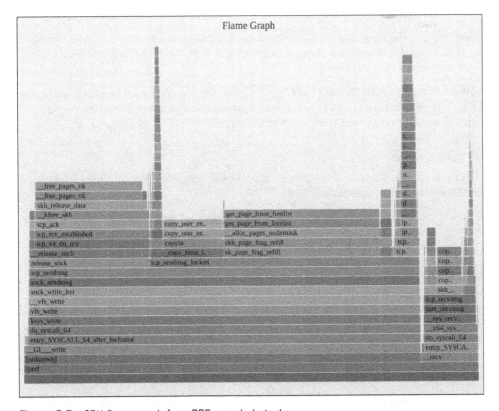

Figure 6-5   CPU flame graph from BPF sampled stacks

This flame graph shows that the hottest code paths ended in get_page_from_freelist_() and __free_pages_ok_()—these are the widest towers, with width proportional to their frequency in the profile. In a browser, this SVG supports click-to-zoom so that narrow towers can be expanded and their functions read.

What makes profile(8) different from other CPU profilers is that this frequency count is calculated in kernel space for efficiency. Other kernel-based profilers, such as perf(1), send every sampled stack trace to user space, where it is post-processed into a summary. This can be CPU expensive and, depending on the invocation, it can also involve file system and disk I/O to record the samples. profile(8) avoids those expenses.

Command line usage:

```
profile [options] [-F frequency]
```

Options include:

- **-U**: Includes user-level stacks only
- **-K**: Includes kernel-level stacks only
- **-a:** Includes frame annotations (e.g., "_[k]" for kernel frames)
- **-d:** Includes delimiters between kernel/user stacks
- **-f:** Provides output in folded format
- **-p PID**: Profiles this process only

bpftrace

The core functionality of profile(8) can be implemented as a bpftrace one-liner:

```
bpftrace -e 'profile:hz:49 /pid/ { @samples[ustack, kstack, comm] = count(); }'
```

This frequency-counts using the user stack, kernel stack, and process name as the key. A filter on the pid is included to ensure that it is non-zero: this excludes the CPU idle thread stacks. This one-liner can be customized as desired.

6.3.9   offcputime

offcputime(8)[16] is a BCC and bpftrace tool to summarize time spent by threads blocked and off CPU, showing stack traces to explain why. For CPU analysis, this tool explains why threads are not running on a CPU. It's a counterpart to profile(8); between them, they show the entire time spent by threads on the system: on-CPU time with profile(8) and off-CPU time with offcputime(8).

The following example shows offcputime(8) from BCC, tracing for five seconds:

```
# offcputime 5
Tracing off-CPU time (us) of all threads by user + kernel stack for 5 secs.

[...]
```

---

16 Origin: I created off-CPU analysis as a methodology, and DTrace one-liners to apply it, in 2005, after exploring uses of the DTrace sched provider and its sched:::off-cpu probe. When I first explained this to a Sun engineer in Adelaide, he said I should not call it "off-CPU" since the CPU isn't off! My first off-CPU tools were uoffcpu.d and koffcpu.d in 2010 for my DTrace book [Gregg 11]. For Linux, I published off-CPU analysis using perf(1), with extremely high overhead, on 26-Feb-2015. I finally developed offcputime efficiently using BCC on 13-Jan-2016, and bpftrace for this book on 16-Feb-2019.

```
finish_task_switch
schedule
schedule_timeout
wait_woken
sk_stream_wait_memory
tcp_sendmsg_locked
tcp_sendmsg
inet_sendmsg
sock_sendmsg
sock_write_iter
new_sync_write
__vfs_write
vfs_write
SyS_write
do_syscall_64
entry_SYSCALL_64_after_hwframe
__write
[unknown]
-               iperf (14657)
    5625
```

[...]

```
finish_task_switch
schedule
schedule_timeout
wait_woken
sk_wait_data
tcp_recvmsg
inet_recvmsg
sock_recvmsg
SYSC_recvfrom
sys_recvfrom
do_syscall_64
entry_SYSCALL_64_after_hwframe
recv
-               iperf (14659)
    1021497
```

[...]

```
finish_task_switch
schedule
schedule_hrtimeout_range_clock
schedule_hrtimeout_range
poll_schedule_timeout
do_select
core_sys_select
sys_select
do_syscall_64
entry_SYSCALL_64_after_hwframe
__libc_select
[unknown]
-                      offcputime (14667)
    5004039
```

The output has been truncated to only show three stacks from the hundreds that were printed. Each stack shows the kernel frames (if present), then user-level frames, then the process name and PID, and finally the total time this combination was seen, in microseconds. The first stack shows iperf(1) blocking in sk_stream_wait_memory() for memory, for a total of 5 milliseconds. The second shows iperf(1) waiting for data on a socket via sk_wait_data(), for a total of 1.02 seconds. The last shows the offcputime(8) tool itself waiting in a select(2) syscall for 5.00 seconds; this is likely for the 5-second timeout specified at the command line.

Note that, in all three stacks, the user-level stack traces are incomplete. This is because they ended at libc, and this version does not support the frame pointer. This is more evident in offcputime(8) than profile(8), since blocking stacks often pass through system libraries such as libc or libpthread. See the discussions on broken stack traces and solutions in Chapters 2, 12, 13, and 18, in particular Section 13.2.9.

offcputime(8) has been used to find various production issues, including finding unexpected time blocked in lock acquisition and the stack traces responsible.

offcputime(8) works by instrumenting context switches and recording the time from when a thread leaves the CPU to when it returns, along with the stack trace. The times and stack traces are frequency-counted in kernel context for efficiency. Context switch events can nonetheless be very frequent, and the overhead of this tool can become significant (say, >10%) for busy production workloads. This tool is best run for only short durations to minimize production impact.

Off-CPU Time Flame Graphs

As with profile(8), the output of offcputime(8) can be so verbose that you may find it preferable to examine it as a flame graph, though of a different type than introduced in Chapter 2. Instead of a CPU flame graph, offcputime(8) can be visualized as an off-CPU time flame graph.[17]

---

17 These were first published by Yichun Zhang [80].

This example creates an off-CPU time flame graph of kernel stacks for five seconds:

```
# offcputime -fKu 5 > out.offcputime01.txt
$ flamegraph.pl --hash --bgcolors=blue --title="Off-CPU Time Flame Graph" \
    < out.offcputime01.txt > out.offcputime01.svg
```

I used `--bgcolors` to change the background color to blue as a visual differentiator from CPU flame graphs. You can also change the frame colors with `--colors`, and I've published many off-CPU flame graphs using a blue palette for the frames[18].

These commands produced the flame graph shown in Figure 6-6.

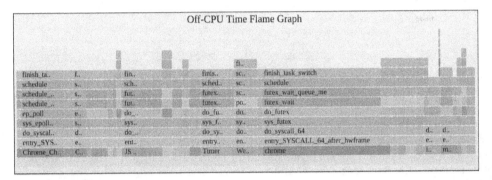

Figure 6-6   Off-CPU time flame graph

This flame graph is dominated by threads sleeping, waiting for work. Applications of interest can be examined by clicking their names to zoom in. For more on off-CPU flame graphs, including examples with full user stack traces, see Chapters 12, 13, and 14.

BCC

Command line usage:

```
offcputime [options] [duration]
```

Options include:

- **-f**: Prints output in folded format
- **-p PID**: Measures this process only
- **-u**: Traces only user threads
- **-k**: Traces only kernel threads
- **-U**: Shows only user stack traces
- **-K**: Shows only kernel stack traces

---

18 Nowadays, I prefer to just change the background color to blue, which leaves the frame color to use the same palette as CPU flame graphs for consistency.

Some of these options can help reduce overhead by filtering to record only one PID or stack type.

bpftrace

The following is the code for the bpftrace version of offcputime(8), which summarizes its core functionality. This version supports an optional PID argument for the target to trace:

```
#!/usr/local/bin/bpftrace

#include <linux/sched.h>

BEGIN
{
        printf("Tracing nanosecond time in off-CPU stacks. Ctrl-C to end.\n");
}

kprobe:finish_task_switch
{
        // record previous thread sleep time
        $prev = (struct task_struct *)arg0;
        if ($1 == 0 || $prev->tgid == $1) {
                @start[$prev->pid] = nsecs;
        }

        // get the current thread start time
        $last = @start[tid];
        if ($last != 0) {
                @[kstack, ustack, comm] = sum(nsecs - $last);
                delete(@start[tid]);
        }
}

END
{
        clear(@start);
}
```

This program records a timestamp for the thread that is leaving the CPU and also sums the off-CPU time for the thread that is starting, in the one finish_task_switch() kprobe.

6.3.10 syscount

syscount(8)[19] is a BCC and bpftrace tool for counting system calls system-wide. It is included in this chapter because it can be a starting point for investigating cases of high system CPU time.

The following output shows syscount(8) from BCC printing per-second syscall rates (-i 1) on a production instance:

```
# syscount -i 1
Tracing syscalls, printing top 10... Ctrl+C to quit.
[00:04:18]
SYSCALL                COUNT
futex                 152923
read                   29973
epoll_wait             27865
write                  21707
epoll_ctl               4696
poll                    2625
writev                  2460
recvfrom                1594
close                   1385
sendto                  1343

[...]
```

This output shows the top 10 syscalls every second, with a timestamp. The most frequent syscall is futex(2), at more than 150,000 calls per second. To further explore each syscall, check the man pages for documentation, and use more BPF tools to trace and inspect their arguments (e.g., BCC trace(8) or bpftrace one-liners). In some situations, running strace(1) can be the quickest path for understanding how a given syscall is used, but keep in mind that the current ptrace-based implementation of strace(1) can slow the target application one hundredfold, which can cause serious issues in many production environments (e.g., exceeding latency SLOs, or triggering failovers). strace(1) should be considered a last resort after you've tried BPF tooling.

The -P option can be used to count by process ID instead:

```
# syscount -Pi 1
Tracing syscalls, printing top 10... Ctrl+C to quit.
[00:04:25]
PID    COMM            COUNT
3622   java           294783
990    snmpd             124
2392   redis-server       64
```

---

19 Origin: I first created this using Ftrace and perf(1) for the perf-tools collection on 7-Jul-2014, and Sasha Goldshtein developed the BCC version on 15-Feb-2017.

```
4790    snmp-pass           32
27035   python              31
26970   sshd                24
2380    svscan              11
2441    atlas-system-ag      5
2453    apache2              2
4786    snmp-pass            1
```

[...]

The java process is making almost 300,000 syscalls per second. Other tools show that this is consuming only 1.6% system time across this 48-CPU system.

This tool works by instrumenting the raw_syscalls:sys_enter tracepoint rather than the usual syscalls:sys_enter_* tracepoints. The reason is that this is one tracepoint that can see all syscalls, making it quicker to initialize instrumentation. The downside is that it only provides syscall IDs, which must be translated back into the names. BCC provides a library call, syscall_name(), to do this.

The overhead of this tool may become noticeable for very high syscall rates. As an example, I stress-tested one CPU with a syscall rate of 3.2 million syscalls/second/CPU. While running syscount(8), the workload suffered a 30% slowdown. This helps estimate the overhead for production: The 48-CPU instance with a rate of 300,000 syscalls/second is performing about 6000 syscalls/second/CPU, so it would be expected to suffer a 0.06% slowdown (30% × 6250 / 3200000). I tried to measure this directly in production, but it was too small to measure with a variable workload.

BCC

Command line usage:

```
syscount [options] [-i interval] [-d duration]
```

Options include:

- **-T TOP:** Prints the specified number of top entries
- **-L:** Shows the total time (latency) in syscalls
- **-P:** Counts by process
- **-p PID:** Measures this process only

An example of the -L option is shown in Chapter 13.

bpftrace

There is a bpftrace version of syscount(8) that has the core functionality, but you can also use this one-liner:

```
# bpftrace -e 't:syscalls:sys_enter_* { @[probe] = count(); }'
Attaching 316 probes...
^C

[...]
@[tracepoint:syscalls:sys_enter_ioctl]: 9465
@[tracepoint:syscalls:sys_enter_epoll_wait]: 9807
@[tracepoint:syscalls:sys_enter_gettid]: 10311
@[tracepoint:syscalls:sys_enter_futex]: 14062
@[tracepoint:syscalls:sys_enter_recvmsg]: 22342
```

In this case, all 316 syscall tracepoints were instrumented (for this kernel version), and a frequency count was performed on the probe name. Currently there is a delay during program startup and shutdown to instrument all 316 tracepoints. It's preferable to use the single raw_syscalls:sys_enter tracepoint, as BCC does, but that then requires an extra step to translate from syscall ID back to syscall name. This is included as an example in Chapter 14.

6.3.11   argdist and trace

argdist(8) and trace(8) are introduced in Chapter 4, and are BCC tools that can examine events in custom ways. As a follow-on from syscount(8), if a syscall was found to be called frequently, you can use these tools to examine it in more detail.

For example, the read(2) syscall was frequent in the previous syscount(8) output. You can use argdist(8) to summarize its arguments and return value by instrumenting either the syscall tracepoint or its kernel functions. For the tracepoint, you need to find the argument names, which the BCC tool tplist(8) prints out with the -v option:

```
# tplist -v syscalls:sys_enter_read
syscalls:sys_enter_read
    int __syscall_nr;
    unsigned int fd;
    char * buf;
    size_t count;
```

The count argument is the size of the read(2). Summarizing this using argdist(8) as a histogram (-H):

```
# argdist -H 't:syscalls:sys_enter_read():int:args->count'
[09:08:31]
     args->count        : count    distribution
         0 -> 1         : 169      |****************                       |
```

```
     2 -> 3        : 243    |************************               |
     4 -> 7        : 1      |                                       |
     8 -> 15       : 0      |                                       |
    16 -> 31       : 384    |****************************************|
    32 -> 63       : 0      |                                       |
    64 -> 127      : 0      |                                       |
   128 -> 255      : 0      |                                       |
   256 -> 511      : 0      |                                       |
   512 -> 1023     : 0      |                                       |
  1024 -> 2047     : 267    |***************************            |
  2048 -> 4095     : 2      |                                       |
  4096 -> 8191     : 23     |**                                     |
```

[...]

This output shows that there were many reads in the 16- to 31-byte range, as well as the 1024- to 2047-byte range. The –C option to argdist(8) can be used instead of –H to summarize as a frequency count of sizes rather than a histogram.

This is showing the read requested size since the entry to the syscall was instrumented. Compare it with the return value from the syscall exit, which is the number of bytes actually read:

```
# argdist -H 't:syscalls:sys_exit_read():int:args->ret'
[09:12:58]
     args->ret        : count   distribution
         0 -> 1        : 481    |****************************************|
         2 -> 3        : 116    |*********                               |
         4 -> 7        : 1      |                                        |
         8 -> 15       : 29     |**                                      |
        16 -> 31       : 6      |                                        |
        32 -> 63       : 31     |**                                      |
        64 -> 127      : 8      |                                        |
       128 -> 255      : 2      |                                        |
       256 -> 511      : 1      |                                        |
       512 -> 1023     : 2      |                                        |
      1024 -> 2047     : 13     |*                                       |
      2048 -> 4095     : 2      |                                        |
```

[...]

These are mostly zero- or one-byte reads.

Thanks to its in-kernel summary, argdist(8) is useful for examining syscalls that were called frequently. trace(8) prints per-event output and is suited for examining less-frequent syscalls, showing per-event timestamps and other details.

bpftrace

This level of syscall analysis is possible using bpftrace one-liners. For example, examining the
requested read size as a histogram:

```
# bpftrace -e 't:syscalls:sys_enter_read { @ = hist(args->count); }'
Attaching 1 probe...
^C

@:
[1]                1102 |@@@@@@@@@@@@@@@@@@@@@@@@@@@@@@@@@@@@@@@@@@@@@@@@@@@@|
[2, 4)              902 |@@@@@@@@@@@@@@@@@@@@@@@@@@@@@@@@@@@@@@@@@@@@        |
[4, 8)               20 |                                                  |
[8, 16)              17 |                                                  |
[16, 32)            538 |@@@@@@@@@@@@@@@@@@@@@@@@@@@                        |
[32, 64)             56 |@@                                                |
[64, 128)             0 |                                                  |
[128, 256)            0 |                                                  |
[256, 512)            0 |                                                  |
[512, 1K)             0 |                                                  |
[1K, 2K)            119 |@@@@@                                             |
[2K, 4K)             26 |@                                                 |
[4K, 8K)            334 |@@@@@@@@@@@@@@@                                   |
```

And the return value:

```
# bpftrace -e 't:syscalls:sys_exit_read { @ = hist(args->ret); }'
Attaching 1 probe...
^C

@:
(..., 0)            105 |@@@@                                              |
[0]                  18 |                                                  |
[1]                1161 |@@@@@@@@@@@@@@@@@@@@@@@@@@@@@@@@@@@@@@@@@@@@@@@@@@@@|
[2, 4)              196 |@@@@@@@@                                          |
[4, 8)                8 |                                                  |
[8, 16)             384 |@@@@@@@@@@@@@@@@                                  |
[16, 32)             87 |@@@                                               |
[32, 64)            118 |@@@@@                                             |
[64, 128)            37 |@                                                 |
[128, 256)            6 |                                                  |
[256, 512)           13 |                                                  |
[512, 1K)             3 |                                                  |
[1K, 2K)              3 |                                                  |
[2K, 4K)             15 |                                                  |
```

bpftrace has a separate bucket for negative values ("(..., 0)"), which are error codes returned by read(2) to indicate an error. You can craft a bpftrace one-liner to print these as a frequency count (as shown in Chapter 5) or a linear histogram so that the individual numbers can be seen:

```
# bpftrace -e 't:syscalls:sys_exit_read /args->ret < 0/ {
    @ = lhist(- args->ret, 0, 100, 1); }'
Attaching 1 probe...
^C

@:
[11, 12)            123 |@@@@@@@@@@@@@@@@@@@@@@@@@@@@@@@@@@@@@@@@@@@@@@@@@@@@|
```

This output shows that error code 11 was always returned. Checking the Linux headers (asm-generic/errno-base.h):

```
#define EAGAIN        11      /* Try again */
```

Error code 11 is for "try again," an error state that can occur in normal operation.

6.3.12 funccount

funccount(8), introduced in Chapter 4, is a BCC tool that can frequency-count functions and other events. It can be used to provide more context for software CPU usage, showing which functions are called and how frequently. profile(8) may be able to show that a function is hot on CPU, but it can't explain why[20]: whether the function is slow, or whether it was simply called millions of times per second.

As an example, this frequency-counts kernel TCP functions on a busy production instance by matching those that begin with "tcp_":

```
# funccount 'tcp_*'
Tracing 316 functions for "tcp_*"... Hit Ctrl-C to end.
^C
FUNC                              COUNT
[...]
tcp_stream_memory_free            368048
tcp_established_options           381234
tcp_v4_md5_lookup                 402945
tcp_gro_receive                   484571
tcp_md5_do_lookup                 510322
Detaching...
```

---

20 profile(8) can't explain this easily. Profilers including profile(8) sample the CPU instruction pointer, and so a comparison with the function's disassembly may show whether it was stuck in a loop or called many times. In practice, it can be harder than it sounds: see Section 2.12.2 in Chapter 2.

This output shows that tcp_md5_do_lookup() was most frequent, with 510,000 calls while tracing.

Per-interval output can be generated using -i. For example, the earlier profile(8) output shows that the function get_page_from_freelist() was hot on CPU. Was that because it was called often or because it was slow? Measuring its per-second rate:

```
# funccount -i 1 get_page_from_freelist
Tracing 1 functions for "get_page_from_freelist"... Hit Ctrl-C to end.

FUNC                            COUNT
get_page_from_freelist          586452

FUNC                            COUNT
get_page_from_freelist          586241
[...]
```

The function was called over half a million times per second.

This works by using dynamic tracing of the function: It uses kprobes for kernel functions and uprobes for user-level functions (kprobes and uprobes are explained in Chapter 2). The overhead of this tool is relative to the rate of the functions. Some functions, such as malloc() and get_page_from_freelist(), tend to occur frequently, so tracing them can slow down the target application significantly, in excess of 10 percent—use caution. See Section 18.1 in Chapter 18 for more about understanding overhead.

Command line usage:

```
funccount [options] [-i interval] [-d duration] pattern
```

Options include:

- **-r**: Use regular expressions for the pattern match
- **-p PID**: Measures this process only

Patterns:

- **name** or **p:name**: Instrument the kernel function called *name*()
- **lib:name**: Instrument the user-level function called *name*() in library *lib*
- **path:name**: Instrument the user-level function called *name*() in the file at *path*
- **t:system:name**: Instruments the tracepoint called *system:name*
- *****: A wildcard to match any string (globbing)

See Section 4.5 in Chapter 4 for more examples.

bpftrace

The core functionality of funccount(8) can be implemented as a bpftrace one-liner:

```
# bpftrace -e 'k:tcp_* { @[probe] = count(); }'
Attaching 320 probes...
[...]
@[kprobe:tcp_release_cb]: 153001
@[kprobe:tcp_v4_md5_lookup]: 154896
@[kprobe:tcp_gro_receive]: 177187
```

This can be adjusted to do per-interval output, for example, with this addition:

```
interval:s:1 { print(@); clear(@); }
```

As with BCC, use caution when tracing frequent functions, as they may incur significant overhead.

6.3.13   softirqs

softirqs(8) is a BCC tool that shows the time spent servicing soft IRQs (soft interrupts). The system-wide time in soft interrupts is readily available from different tools. For example, mpstat(1) shows it as %soft. There is also /proc/softirqs to show counts of soft IRQ events. The BCC softirqs(8) tool differs in that it can show time per soft IRQ rather than event count.

For example, from a 48-CPU production instance and a 10-second trace:

```
# softirqs 10 1
Tracing soft irq event time... Hit Ctrl-C to end.

SOFTIRQ         TOTAL_usecs
net_tx                  633
tasklet               30939
rcu                  143859
sched                185873
timer                389144
net_rx              1358268
```

This output shows that the most time was spent servicing net_rx, totaling 1358 milliseconds. This is significant, as it works out to be 3 percent of the CPU time on this 48-CPU system.

softirqs(8) works by using the irq:softirq_enter and irq:softirq_exit tracepoints. The overhead of this tool is relative to the event rate, which could be high for busy production systems and high network packet rates. Use caution and check overhead.

Command line usage:

```
softirqs [options] [interval [count]]
```

Options include:

- **-d**: Shows IRQ time as histograms
- **-T**: Includes timestamps on output

The -d option can be used to explore the distribution and identify whether there are latency outliers while servicing these interrupts.

bpftrace

A bpftrace version of softirqs(8) does not exist, but could be created. The following one-liner is a starting point, counting IRQs by vector ID:

```
# bpftrace -e 'tracepoint:irq:softirq_entry { @[args->vec] = count(); }'
Attaching 1 probe...
^C

@[3]: 11
@[6]: 45
@[0]: 395
@[9]: 405
@[1]: 524
@[7]: 561
```

These vector IDs can be translated to the softirq names in the same way the BCC tool does this: by using a lookup table. Determining the time spent in soft IRQs involves tracing the irq:softirq_exit tracepoint as well.

6.3.14   hardirqs

hardirqs(8)[21] is a BCC tool that shows time spent servicing hard IRQs (hard interrupts). The system-wide time in hard interrupts is readily available from different tools. For example, mpstat(1) shows it as %irq. There is also /proc/interrupts to show counts of hard IRQ events. The BCC hardirqs(8) tool differs in that it can show time per hard IRQ rather than event count.

---

21 Origin: I first created this as inttimes.d on 28-Jun-2005, for printing time sums and intoncpu.d for printing histograms on 9-May-2005, which was based on intr.d from the "Dynamic Tracing Guide," Jan 2005 [Sun 05]. I also developed a DTrace tool to show interrupts by CPU but have not ported it to BPF since Linux has /proc/interrupts for that task. I developed this BCC version that does both sums and histograms on 20-Oct-2015.

For example, from a 48-CPU production instance and a 10-second trace:

```
# hardirqs 10 1
Tracing hard irq event time... Hit Ctrl-C to end.

HARDIRQ                        TOTAL_usecs
ena-mgmnt@pci:0000:00:05.0             43
nvme0q0                               46
eth0-Tx-Rx-7                       47424
eth0-Tx-Rx-6                       48199
eth0-Tx-Rx-5                       48524
eth0-Tx-Rx-2                       49482
eth0-Tx-Rx-3                       49750
eth0-Tx-Rx-0                       51084
eth0-Tx-Rx-4                       51106
eth0-Tx-Rx-1                       52649
```

This output shows that several hard IRQs named eth0-Tx-Rx* had total times of around 50 milliseconds for this 10-second trace.

hardirqs(8) can provide insight for CPU usage that is not visible to CPU profilers. See the Internals section of Section 6.2.4 for profiling on cloud instances that lack a hardware PMU.

This tool currently works by using dynamic tracing of the handle_irq_event_percpu() kernel function, although a future version should switch to the irq:irq_handler_entry and irq:irq_handler_exit tracepoints.

Command line usage:

```
hardirqs [options] [interval [count]]
```

Options include:

- **-d**: Shows IRQ time as histograms
- **-T**: Includes timestamps on output

The -d option can be used to explore the distribution and identify whether there are latency outliers while servicing these interrupts.

6.3.15   smpcalls

smpcalls(8)[22] is a bpftrace tool to trace and summarize time in the SMP call functions (also known as cross calls). These are a way for one CPU to run functions on other CPUs, including all other

---

22 Origin: I created smpcalls.bt for this book on 23-Jan-2019. The name comes from my earlier tool, xcallsbypid.d (named after CPU cross calls), which I created on 17-Sep-2005.

CPUs, which can become an expensive activity on large multi-processor systems. For example, on a 36-CPU system:

```
# smpcalls.bt
Attaching 8 probes...
Tracing SMP calls. Hit Ctrl-C to stop.
^C

@time_ns[do_flush_tlb_all]:
[32K, 64K)             1 |@@@@@@@@@@@@@@@@@@@@@@@@@@@@@@@@@@@@@@@@@@@@@@@@@@@@|
[64K, 128K)            1 |@@@@@@@@@@@@@@@@@@@@@@@@@@@@@@@@@@@@@@@@@@@@@@@@@@@@|

@time_ns[remote_function]:
[4K, 8K)               1 |@@@@@@@@@@@@@@@@@@@@@@@@@@@             |
[8K, 16K)              1 |@@@@@@@@@@@@@@@@@@@@@@@@@@@             |
[16K, 32K)             0 |                                      |
[32K, 64K)             2 |@@@@@@@@@@@@@@@@@@@@@@@@@@@@@@@@@@@@@@@@@@@@@@@@@@@@|

@time_ns[do_sync_core]:
[32K, 64K)            15 |@@@@@@@@@@@@@@@@@@@@@@@@@@@@@@@@@@@@@@@@@@@@@@@@@@@@|
[64K, 128K)            9 |@@@@@@@@@@@@@@@@@@@@@@@@@@@@@@@           |

@time_ns[native_smp_send_reschedule]:
[2K, 4K)               7 |@@@@@@@@@@@@@@@@@@            |
[4K, 8K)               3 |@@@@@@@@                     |
[8K, 16K)             19 |@@@@@@@@@@@@@@@@@@@@@@@@@@@@@@@@@@@@@@@@@@@@@@@@@@@@|
[16K, 32K)             3 |@@@@@@@@                     |

@time_ns[aperfmperf_snapshot_khz]:
[1K, 2K)               5 |@                            |
[2K, 4K)              12 |@@@                          |
[4K, 8K)              12 |@@@                          |
[8K, 16K)             6 |@                            |
[16K, 32K)            1 |                             |
[32K, 64K)          196 |@@@@@@@@@@@@@@@@@@@@@@@@@@@@@@@@@@@@@@@@@@@@@@@@@@@@|
[64K, 128K)          20 |@@@@@                        |
```

This is the first time I've run this tool, and it's identified an issue right away: The aperfmperf_snapshot_khz cross call is relatively frequent and slow, taking up to 128 microseconds.

The source to smpcalls(8) is:

```
#!/usr/local/bin/bpftrace

BEGIN
{
        printf("Tracing SMP calls. Hit Ctrl-C to stop.\n");
}

kprobe:smp_call_function_single,
kprobe:smp_call_function_many
{
        @ts[tid] = nsecs;
        @func[tid] = arg1;
}

kretprobe:smp_call_function_single,
kretprobe:smp_call_function_many
/@ts[tid]/
{
        @time_ns[ksym(@func[tid])] = hist(nsecs - @ts[tid]);
        delete(@ts[tid]);
        delete(@func[tid]);
}

kprobe:native_smp_send_reschedule
{
        @ts[tid] = nsecs;
        @func[tid] = reg("ip");
}

kretprobe:native_smp_send_reschedule
/@ts[tid]/
{
        @time_ns[ksym(@func[tid])] = hist(nsecs - @ts[tid]);
        delete(@ts[tid]);
        delete(@func[tid]);
}

END
{
        clear(@ts);
        clear(@func);
}
```

Many of the SMP calls are traced via kprobes for the smp_call_function_single() and smp_call_function_many() kernel functions. The entry to these functions has the remote CPU function as the second argument, which bpftrace accesses as arg1 and stores keyed by thread ID for lookup in the kretprobe. It is then converted into the human-readable symbol by the bpftrace ksym() built-in.

There is a special SMP call not covered by those functions, smp_send_reschedule(), which is traced via native_smp_send_reschedule(). I hope that a future kernel version supports SMP call tracepoints to simplify tracing of these calls.

The @time_ns histogram key can be modified to include the kernel stack trace and process name:

```
@time_ns[comm, kstack, ksym(@func[tid])] = hist(nsecs - @ts[tid]);
```

This includes more details for the slow call:

```
@time_ns[snmp-pass,
    smp_call_function_single+1
    aperfmperf_snapshot_cpu+90
    arch_freq_prepare_all+61
    cpuinfo_open+14
    proc_reg_open+111
    do_dentry_open+484
    path_openat+692
    do_filp_open+153
    do_sys_open+294
    do_syscall_64+85
    entry_SYSCALL_64_after_hwframe+68
, aperfmperf_snapshot_khz]:
[2K, 4K)            2 |@@                                                      |
[4K, 8K)            0 |                                                        |
[8K, 16K)           1 |@                                                       |
[16K, 32K)          1 |@                                                       |
[32K, 64K)         51 |@@@@@@@@@@@@@@@@@@@@@@@@@@@@@@@@@@@@@@@@@@@@@@@@@@@@@@@@@@|
[64K, 128K)        17 |@@@@@@@@@@@@@@@@@                                        |
```

This output shows that the process was snmp-pass, a monitoring agent, and it was doing an open() syscall that ends up in cpuinfo_open() and an expensive cross call.

Using another BPF tool, opensnoop(8), quickly confirms this behavior:

```
# opensnoop.py -Tn snmp-pass
TIME(s)         PID     COMM           FD ERR PATH
0.000000000     2440    snmp-pass       4   0 /proc/cpuinfo
0.000841000     2440    snmp-pass       4   0 /proc/stat
1.022128000     2440    snmp-pass       4   0 /proc/cpuinfo
```

```
1.024696000   2440   snmp-pass        4   0 /proc/stat
2.046133000   2440   snmp-pass        4   0 /proc/cpuinfo
2.049020000   2440   snmp-pass        4   0 /proc/stat
3.070135000   2440   snmp-pass        4   0 /proc/cpuinfo
3.072869000   2440   snmp-pass        4   0 /proc/stat
[...]
```

This output shows that snmp-pass is reading the /proc/cpuinfo file every second! Most of the details in this file will not change, with the exception of the "cpu MHz" field.

Inspection of the software showed that it was reading /proc/cpuinfo merely to count the number of processors; the "cpu MHz" field was not used at all. This is an example of unnecessary work, and eliminating it should provide a small but easy win.

On Intel processors, these SMP calls are ultimately implemented as x2APIC IPI (inter-processor interrupt) calls, including x2apic_send_IPI(). These can also be instrumented, as shown in Section 6.4.2.

6.3.16 llcstat

llcstat(8)[23] is a BCC tool that uses PMCs to show last-level cache (LLC) miss rates and hit ratios by process. PMCs are introduced in Chapter 2.

For example, from a 48-CPU production instance:

```
# llcstat
Running for 10 seconds or hit Ctrl-C to end.
PID       NAME         CPU   REFERENCE      MISS   HIT%
0         swapper/15   15     1007300       1000   99.90%
4435      java         18       22000        200   99.09%
4116      java          7       11000        100   99.09%
4441      java         38       32200        300   99.07%
17387     java         17       10800        100   99.07%
4113      java         17       10500        100   99.05%
[...]
```

This output shows that the java processes (threads) were running with a very high hit ratio, over 99%.

This tool works by using overflow sampling of PMCs, where one in every so many cache references or misses triggers a BPF program to read the currently running process and record stats. The default threshold is 100, and it can be tuned using -c. This one-in-a-hundred sampling helps keep the overhead low (and can be tuned to higher numbers, if needed); however, there are some issues related to sampling with it. For example, a process could by chance overflow misses more often than references, which doesn't make sense (as misses are a subset of references).

---

23 Origin: This was created by Teng Qin on 19-Oct-2016, and is the first tool in BCC to use PMCs.

Command line usage:

```
llcstat [options] [duration]
```

Options include:

- **-c SAMPLE_PERIOD**: Sample one in this many events only

llcstat(8) is interesting in that it was the first BCC tool to use PMCs, outside of timed sampling.

6.3.17   Other Tools

Other BPF tools worth mentioning:

- **cpuwalk(8)** from bpftrace samples which processes CPUs were running on and prints the result as a linear histogram. This provides a histogram view of CPU balance.
- **cpuunclaimed(8)** from BCC is an experimental tool that samples CPU run queue lengths and determines how often there are idle CPUs yet threads in a runnable state on a different run queue. This sometimes happens due to CPU affinity, but if it happens often, it may be a sign of a scheduler misconfiguration or bug.
- **loads(8)** from bpftrace is an example of fetching the load averages from a BPF tool. As discussed earlier, these numbers are misleading.
- **vltrace** is a tool in development by Intel that will be a BPF-powered version of strace(1) that can be used for further characterization of syscalls that are consuming CPU time [79].

6.4   BPF One-Liners

This section provides BCC and bpftrace one-liners. Where possible, the same one-liner is implemented using both BCC and bpftrace.

6.4.1   BCC

Trace new processes with arguments:

```
execsnoop
```

Show who is executing what:

```
trace 't:syscalls:sys_enter_execve "-> %s", args->filename'
```

Show the syscall count by process:

```
syscount -P
```

Show the syscall count by syscall name:

```
syscount
```

Sample user-level stacks at 49 Hertz, for PID 189:

```
profile -F 49 -U -p 189
```

Sample all stack traces and process names:

```
profile
```

Count kernel functions beginning with "vfs_":

```
funccount 'vfs_*'
```

Trace new threads via pthread_create():

```
trace /lib/x86_64-linux-gnu/libpthread-2.27.so:pthread_create
```

6.4.2 bpftrace

Trace new processes with arguments:

```
bpftrace -e 'tracepoint:syscalls:sys_enter_execve { join(args->argv); }'
```

Show who is executing what:

```
bpftrace -e 'tracepoint:syscalls:sys_enter_execve { printf("%s -> %s\n", comm,
    str(args->filename)); }'
```

Show the syscall count by program:

```
bpftrace -e 'tracepoint:raw_syscalls:sys_enter { @[comm] = count(); }'
```

Show the syscall count by process:

```
bpftrace -e 'tracepoint:raw_syscalls:sys_enter { @[pid, comm] = count(); }'
```

Show the syscall count by syscall probe name:

```
bpftrace -e 'tracepoint:syscalls:sys_enter_* { @[probe] = count(); }'
```

Show the syscall count by syscall function:

```
bpftrace -e 'tracepoint:raw_syscalls:sys_enter {
    @[sym(*(kaddr("sys_call_table") + args->id * 8))] = count(); }'
```

Sample running process names at 99 Hertz:

```
bpftrace -e 'profile:hz:99 { @[comm] = count(); }'
```

Sample user-level stacks at 49 Hertz, for PID 189:

```
bpftrace -e 'profile:hz:49 /pid == 189/ { @[ustack] = count(); }'
```

Sample all stack traces and process names:

```
bpftrace -e 'profile:hz:49 { @[ustack, stack, comm] = count(); }'
```

Sample the running CPU at 99 Hertz and show it as a linear histogram:

```
bpftrace -e 'profile:hz:99 { @cpu = lhist(cpu, 0, 256, 1); }'
```

Count kernel functions beginning with vfs_:

```
bpftrace -e 'kprobe:vfs_* { @[func] = count(); }'
```

Count SMP calls by name and kernel stack:

```
bpftrace -e 'kprobe:smp_call* { @[probe, kstack(5)] = count(); }'
```

Count Intel x2APIC calls by name and kernel stack:

```
bpftrace -e 'kprobe:x2apic_send_IPI* { @[probe, kstack(5)] = count(); }'
```

Trace new threads via pthread_create():

```
bpftrace -e 'u:/lib/x86_64-linux-gnu/libpthread-2.27.so:pthread_create {
    printf("%s by %s (%d)\n", probe, comm, pid); }'
```

6.5 Optional Exercises

If not specified, these can be completed using either bpftrace or BCC:

1. Use execsnoop(8) to show the new processes for the man ls command.

2. Run execsnoop(8) with -t and output to a log file for 10 minutes on a production or local system. What new processes did you find?

3. On a test system, create an overloaded CPU. This creates two CPU-bound threads that are bound to CPU 0:

    ```
    taskset -c 0 sh -c 'while :; do :; done' &
    taskset -c 0 sh -c 'while :; do :; done' &
    ```

    Now use uptime(1) (load averages), mpstat(1) (-P ALL), runqlen(8), and runqlat(8) to characterize the workload on CPU 0. (Remember to kill the workload when you are done.)

4. Develop a tool/one-liner to sample kernel stacks on CPU 0 only.

5. Use profile(8) to capture kernel CPU stacks to determine where CPU time is spent by the following workload:

    ```
    dd if=/dev/nvme0n1p3 bs=8k iflag=direct | dd of=/dev/null bs=1
    ```

    Modify the infile (if=) device to be a local disk (see df -h for a candidate). You can either profile system-wide or filter for each of those dd(1) processes.

6. Generate a CPU flame graph of the Exercise 5 output.

7. Use offcputime(8) to capture kernel CPU stacks to determine where blocked time is spent for the workload of Exercise 5.

8. Generate an off-CPU time flame graph for the output of Exercise 7.

9. execsnoop(8) only sees new processes that call exec(2) (execve(2)), although some may fork(2) or clone(2) and not exec(2) (e.g., the creation of worker processes). Write a new tool called procsnoop(8) to show all new processes with as many details as possible. You could trace fork() and clone(), or use the sched tracepoints, or do something else.

10. Develop a bpftrace version of softirqs(8) that prints the softirq name.

11. Implement cpudist(8) in bpftrace.

12. With cpudist(8) (either version), show separate histograms for voluntary and involuntary context switches.

13. (Advanced, unsolved) Develop a tool to show a histogram of time spent by tasks in CPU affinity wait: runnable while other CPUs are idle but not migrated due to cache warmth (see kernel.sched_migration_cost_ns, task_hot()—which may be inlined and not traceable, and can_migrate_task()).

6.6   Summary

This chapter summarizes how CPUs are used by a system, and how to analyze them using traditional tools: statistics, profilers, and tracers. This chapter also shows how to use BPF tools to uncover issues of short-lived processes, examine run queue latency in detail, profile CPU usage efficiency, count function calls, and show CPU usage by soft and hard interrupts.

Chapter 7

Memory

Linux is a virtual memory–based system where each process has its own virtual address space, and mappings to physical memory are made on demand. Its design allows for over-subscription of physical memory, which Linux manages with a page out daemon and physical swap devices and (as a last resort) the out-of-memory (OOM) killer. Linux uses spare memory as a file system cache, a topic covered in Chapter 8.

This chapter shows how BPF can expose application memory usage in new ways and help you examine how the kernel is responding to memory pressure. As CPU scalability has grown faster than memory speeds, memory I/O has become the new bottleneck. Understanding memory usage can lead to finding many performance wins.

Learning Objectives:

- Understand memory allocation and paging behavior
- Learn a strategy for successful analysis of memory behavior using tracers
- Use traditional tools to understand memory capacity usage
- Use BPF tools to identify code paths causing heap and RSS growth
- Characterize page faults by filename and stack trace
- Analyze the behavior of the VM scanner
- Determine the performance impact of memory reclaim
- Identify which processes are waiting for swap-ins
- Use bpftrace one-liners to explore memory usage in custom ways

This chapter begins with some necessary background for memory analysis, with a focus on application usage, summarizing virtual and physical allocation, and paging. Questions that BPF can answer are explored, as well as an overall strategy to follow. Traditional memory analysis tools are summarized first, and then BPF tools are covered, including a list of BPF one-liners. This chapter ends with optional exercises.

Chapter 14 provides additional tools for kernel memory analysis.

7.1 Background

This section covers memory fundamentals, BPF capabilities, and a suggested strategy for memory analysis.

7.1.1 Memory Fundamentals

Memory Allocators

Figure 7-1 shows commonly used memory allocation systems for user- and kernel-level software. For processes using libc for memory allocation, memory is stored on a dynamic segment of the process's virtual address space called the *heap*. libc provides functions for memory allocation, including malloc() and free(). When memory is freed, libc tracks its location and can use that location information to fulfill a subsequent malloc(). libc needs to extend the size of the heap only when there is no available memory. There is usually no reason for libc to shrink the size of the heap as this is all virtual memory, not real physical memory.

The kernel and processor are responsible for mapping virtual memory to physical memory. For efficiency, memory mappings are created in groups of memory called *pages*, where the size of each page is a processor detail; four Kbytes is common, although most processors also support larger sizes—what Linux terms *huge pages*. The kernel can service physical memory page requests from its own free lists, which it maintains for each DRAM group and CPU for efficiency. The kernel's own software also consumes memory from these free lists as well, usually via a kernel allocator such as the slab allocator.

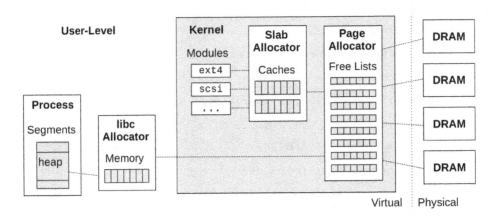

Figure 7-1   Memory allocators

Other user allocation libraries include tcmalloc and jemalloc, and runtimes such as the JVM often provide their own allocator along with garbage collection. Other allocators may also map private segments for allocation outside of the heap.

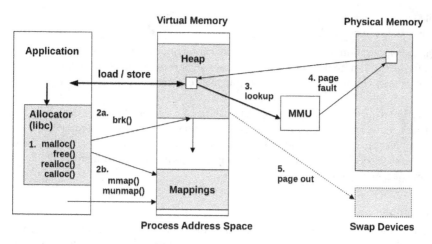

Figure 7-2 Memory page life cycle

Memory Pages and Swapping

The life cycle of a typical user memory page is shown in Figure 7-2, with the following steps enumerated:

1. The application begins with an allocation request for memory (e.g., libc malloc()).

2. The allocation library can either service the memory request from its own free lists, or it may need to expand virtual memory to accommodate. Depending on the allocation library, it will either:

    a. Extend the size of the heap by calling a brk() syscall and using the heap memory for the allocation.

    b. Create a new memory segment via the mmap() syscall.

3. Sometime later, the application tries to use the allocated memory range through store and load instructions, which involves calling in to the processor memory management unit (MMU) for virtual-to-physical address translation. At this point, the lie of virtual memory is revealed: There is no mapping for this address! This causes an MMU error called a page fault.

4. The page fault is handled by the kernel, which establishes a mapping from its physical memory free lists to virtual memory and then informs the MMU of this mapping for later lookups. The process is now consuming an extra page of physical memory. The amount of physical memory in use by the process is called its resident set size (RSS).

5. When there is too much memory demand on the system, the kernel page-out daemon (kswapd) may look for memory pages to free. It will free one of three types of memory (though only (c) is pictured in Figure 7-2, as it is showing a user memory page life cycle):

    a. File system pages that were read from disk and not modified (termed "backed by disk"): These can be freed immediately and simply reread back when needed. These pages are application-executable text, data, and file system metadata.

b. File system pages that have been modified: These are "dirty" and must be written to disk before they can be freed.

c. Pages of application memory: These are called anonymous memory because they have no file origin. If swap devices are in use, these can be freed by first being stored on a swap device. This writing of pages to a swap device is termed *swapping* (on Linux).

Memory allocation requests are typically frequent activities: User-level allocations can occur millions of times per second for a busy application. Load and store instructions and MMU lookups are even more frequent; they can occur billions of times per second. In Figure 7-2, these arrows are drawn in bold. Other activities are relatively infrequent: brk() and mmap() calls, page faults, and page-outs (lighter arrows).

Page-Out Daemon

The page-out daemon (kswapd) is activated periodically to scan LRU lists of inactive and active pages in search of memory to free. It is woken up when free memory crosses a low threshold and goes back to sleep when it crosses a high threshold, as shown in Figure 7-3.

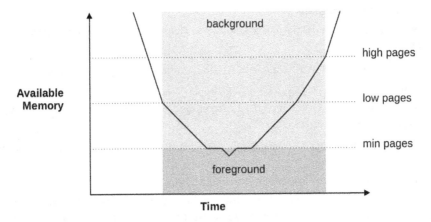

Figure 7-3   kswapd wakeups and modes

kswapd coordinates background page-outs; apart from CPU and disk I/O contention, these should not directly harm application performance. If kswapd cannot free memory quickly enough, a tunable minimum pages threshold is crossed, and direct reclaim is used; this is a foreground mode of freeing memory to satisfy allocations. In this mode, allocations block (stall) and synchronously wait for pages to be freed [Gorman 04] [81].

Direct reclaim can call kernel module shrinker functions: These free up memory that may have been kept in caches, including the kernel slab caches.

Swap Devices

Swap devices provide a degraded mode of operation for a system running out of memory: Processes can continue to allocate, but less frequently used pages are now moved to and from their swap devices, which usually causes applications to run much more slowly. Some production systems run without swap; the rationale is that the degraded mode of operation is never acceptable for those critical systems, which may have numerous redundant (and healthy!) servers that would be much better to use than one that has begun swapping. (This is usually the case for Netflix cloud instances, for example.) If a swap-less system runs out of memory, the kernel out-of-memory killer sacrifices a process. Applications are configured to never exceed the memory limits of the system, to avoid this.

OOM Killer

The Linux out-of-memory killer is a last resort to free up memory: It will find victim processes using a heuristic, and sacrifice them by killing them. The heuristic looks for the largest victim that will free many pages, and that isn't a critical task such as kernel threads or init (PID 1). Linux provides ways to tune the behavior of the OOM killer system-wide and per-process.

Page Compaction

Over time, the freed pages become fragmented, making it difficult for the kernel to allocate a large contiguous chunk, if needed. The kernel uses a compaction routine to move pages, freeing up contiguous regions [81].

File System Caching and Buffering

Linux borrows free memory for file system caching and returns it to the free status when there is demand. A consequence of such borrowing is that the free memory reported by the system rushes toward zero after Linux boots, which may cause a user to worry that the system is running out of memory when actually it's just warming up its file system cache. In addition, the file system uses memory for write-back buffering.

Linux can be tuned to prefer freeing from the file system cache or freeing memory via swapping (vm.swappiness).

Caching and buffering are discussed further in Chapter 8.

Further Reading

This is a brief summary to arm you with essential knowledge before using the tools. Additional topics, including kernel page allocation and NUMA, are covered in Chapter 14. Memory allocation and paging are covered in much more depth in Chapter 7 of *Systems Performance* [Gregg 13b].

7.1.2 BPF Capabilities

Traditional performance tools provide some insight for memory internals. For example, they can show breakdowns of virtual and physical memory usage and the rates of page operations. These traditional tools are summarized in the next section.

BPF tracing tools can provide additional insight for memory activity, answering:

- Why does the process physical memory (RSS) keep growing?
- What code paths are causing page faults? For which files?

- What processes are blocked waiting on swap-ins?

- What memory mappings are being created system-wide?

- What is the system state at the time of an OOM kill?

- What application code paths are allocating memory?

- What types of objects are allocated by applications?

- Are there memory allocations that are not freed after a while? (They could indicate potential leaks.)

These can be answered with BPF by instrumenting software events or tracepoints for faults and syscalls; kprobes for kernel memory allocation functions; uprobes for library, runtime, and application allocators; USDT probes for libc allocator events; and PMCs for overflow sampling of memory accesses. These event sources can also be mixed in one BPF program to share context between different systems.

Memory events including allocations, memory mappings, faults, and swapping, can all be instrumented using BPF. Stack traces can be fetched to show the reasons for many of these events.

Event Sources

Table 7-1 lists the event sources for instrumenting memory.

Table 7-1   **Event Sources for Instrumenting Memory**

Event Type	Event Source
User memory allocations	uprobes on allocator functions and libc USDT probes
Kernel memory allocations	kprobes on allocator functions and kmem tracepoints
Heap expansions	brk syscall tracepoints
Shared memory functions	syscall tracepoints
Page faults	kprobes, software events, and exception tracepoints
Page migrations	migration tracepoints
Page compaction	compaction tracepoints
VM scanner	vmscan tracepoints
Memory access cycles	PMCs

Here are the USDT probes available in libc:

```
# bpftrace -l usdt:/lib/x86_64-linux-gnu/libc-2.27.so
[...]
usdt:/lib/x86_64-linux-gnu/libc-2.27.so:libc:memory_mallopt_arena_max
usdt:/lib/x86_64-linux-gnu/libc-2.27.so:libc:memory_mallopt_arena_test
usdt:/lib/x86_64-linux-gnu/libc-2.27.so:libc:memory_tunable_tcache_max_bytes
```

```
usdt:/lib/x86_64-linux-gnu/libc-2.27.so:libc:memory_tunable_tcache_count
usdt:/lib/x86_64-linux-gnu/libc-2.27.so:libc:memory_tunable_tcache_unsorted_limit
usdt:/lib/x86_64-linux-gnu/libc-2.27.so:libc:memory_mallopt_trim_threshold
usdt:/lib/x86_64-linux-gnu/libc-2.27.so:libc:memory_mallopt_top_pad
usdt:/lib/x86_64-linux-gnu/libc-2.27.so:libc:memory_mallopt_mmap_threshold
usdt:/lib/x86_64-linux-gnu/libc-2.27.so:libc:memory_mallopt_mmap_max
usdt:/lib/x86_64-linux-gnu/libc-2.27.so:libc:memory_mallopt_perturb
usdt:/lib/x86_64-linux-gnu/libc-2.27.so:libc:memory_heap_new
usdt:/lib/x86_64-linux-gnu/libc-2.27.so:libc:memory_sbrk_less
usdt:/lib/x86_64-linux-gnu/libc-2.27.so:libc:memory_arena_reuse
usdt:/lib/x86_64-linux-gnu/libc-2.27.so:libc:memory_arena_reuse_wait
usdt:/lib/x86_64-linux-gnu/libc-2.27.so:libc:memory_arena_new
usdt:/lib/x86_64-linux-gnu/libc-2.27.so:libc:memory_arena_reuse_free_list
usdt:/lib/x86_64-linux-gnu/libc-2.27.so:libc:memory_arena_retry
usdt:/lib/x86_64-linux-gnu/libc-2.27.so:libc:memory_heap_free
usdt:/lib/x86_64-linux-gnu/libc-2.27.so:libc:memory_heap_less
usdt:/lib/x86_64-linux-gnu/libc-2.27.so:libc:memory_heap_more
usdt:/lib/x86_64-linux-gnu/libc-2.27.so:libc:memory_sbrk_more
usdt:/lib/x86_64-linux-gnu/libc-2.27.so:libc:memory_mallopt_free_dyn_thresholds
usdt:/lib/x86_64-linux-gnu/libc-2.27.so:libc:memory_malloc_retry
usdt:/lib/x86_64-linux-gnu/libc-2.27.so:libc:memory_memalign_retry
usdt:/lib/x86_64-linux-gnu/libc-2.27.so:libc:memory_realloc_retry
usdt:/lib/x86_64-linux-gnu/libc-2.27.so:libc:memory_calloc_retry
usdt:/lib/x86_64-linux-gnu/libc-2.27.so:libc:memory_mallopt
usdt:/lib/x86_64-linux-gnu/libc-2.27.so:libc:memory_mallopt_mxfast
```

These probes provide insight into the internal operation of the libc allocator.

Overhead

As mentioned earlier, memory allocation events can occur millions of times per second. Although BPF programs are optimized to be fast, calling them millions of times per second can add up to significant overhead, slowing the target software by more than 10%, and in some cases by 10 times (10x), depending on the rate of events traced and the BPF program used.

To work around this overhead, Figure 7-2 shows which paths are frequent by using bold arrows and which are infrequent by using lighter arrows. Many questions about memory usage can be answered, or approximated, by tracing the infrequent events: page faults, page outs, brk() calls, and mmap() calls. The overhead of tracing these events can be negligible.

One reason to trace the malloc() calls is to show the code paths that led to malloc(). These code paths can be revealed using a different technique: timed sampling of CPU stacks, as covered in Chapter 6. Searching for "malloc" in a CPU flame graph is a coarse but cheap way to identify the code paths calling this function frequently, without needing to trace the function directly.

The performance of uprobes may be greatly improved in the future (10x to 100x) through dynamic libraries involving user-to-user-space jumps rather than kernel traps (see Section 2.8.4 in Chapter 2).

7.1.3   Strategy

If you are new to memory performance analysis, here is a suggested overall strategy to follow:

1. Check system messages to see if the OOM killer has recently killed processes (e.g., using dmesg(1)).

2. Check whether the system has swap devices and the amount of swap in use; also check whether those devices have active I/O (e.g., using swap(1), iostat(1), and vmstat(1)).

3. Check the amount of free memory on the system and system-wide usage by caches (e.g., free(1)).

4. Check per-process memory usage (e.g., using top(1) and ps(1)).

5. Check the page fault rate and examine stack traces on page faults, which can explain RSS growth.

6. Check the files that were backing page faults.

7. Trace brk() and mmap() calls for a different view of memory usage.

8. Browse and execute the BPF tools listed in the BPF tools section of this chapter.

9. Measure hardware cache misses and memory accesses using PMCs (especially with PEBS enabled) to determine functions and instructions causing memory I/O (e.g., using perf(1)).

The following sections explain these tools in more detail.

7.2   Traditional Tools

Traditional performance tools provide many capacity-based memory usage statistics, including how much virtual and physical memory is in use by each process and system-wide, with some breakdowns such as by process segment or slab. Analyzing memory usage beyond basics such as the page fault rate required built-in instrumentation for each allocation by the allocation library, runtime, or application; or a virtual machine analyzer like Valgrind could be used; this latter approach can cause the target application to run over 10 times slower while instrumented. BPF tools are more efficient and cost smaller overheads.

Even where they are not sufficient on their own to solve issues, traditional tools can provide clues to direct your use of BPF tools. The traditional tools listed in Table 7-2 have been categorized here based on their source and measurement type.

Table 7-2 **Traditional Tools**

Tool	Type	Description
dmesg	Kernel log	OOM killer event details
swapon	Kernel statistics	Swap device usage
free	Kernel statistics	System-wide memory usage
ps	Kernel statistics	Process statistics, including memory usage
pmap	Kernel statistics	Process memory usage by segment
vmstat	Kernel statistics	Various statistics, including memory
sar	Kernel statistics	Can show page fault and page scanner rates
perf	Software events, hardware statistics, hardware sampling	Memory-related PMC statistics and event sampling

The following sections summarize the key functionality of these tools. Refer to their man pages and other resources, including *Systems Performance* [Gregg 13b], for more usage and explanations. Chapter 14 includes slabtop(1) for kernel slab allocations.

7.2.1 Kernel Log

The kernel out-of-memory killer writes details to the system log, viewable using dmesg(1), for each time it needs to kill a process. For example:

```
# dmesg
[2156747.865271] run invoked oom-killer: gfp_mask=0x24201ca, order=0, oom_score_adj=0
[...]
[2156747.865330] Mem-Info:
[2156747.865333] active_anon:3773117 inactive_anon:20590 isolated_anon:0
[2156747.865333]  active_file:3 inactive_file:0 isolated_file:0
[2156747.865333]  unevictable:0 dirty:0 writeback:0 unstable:0
[2156747.865333]  slab_reclaimable:3980 slab_unreclaimable:5811
[2156747.865333]  mapped:36 shmem:20596 pagetables:10620 bounce:0
[2156747.865333]  free:18748 free_pcp:455 free_cma:0
[...]
[2156747.865385] [ pid ]   uid  tgid total_vm      rss nr_ptes nr_pmds swapents
oom_score_adj name
[2156747.865390] [  510]    0   510    4870       67      15       3       0
0 upstart-udev-br
[2156747.865392] [  524]    0   524   12944      237      28       3       0
-1000 systemd-udevd
[...]
[2156747.865574] Out of memory: Kill process 23409 (perl) score 329 or sacrifice child
[2156747.865583] Killed process 23409 (perl) total-vm:5370580kB, anon-rss:5224980kB,
file-rss:4kB
```

The output includes a summary of system-wide memory usage, the process table, and the target process that was sacrificed.

You should always check dmesg(1) before getting into deeper memory analysis.

7.2.2 Kernel Statistics

Kernel statistics tools use statistical sources in the kernel, often exposed via the /proc interface (e.g., /proc/meminfo, /proc/swaps). An advantage of these tools is that the metrics are usually always enabled by the kernel, so there is little additional overhead involved in using them. They can also often be read by non-root users.

swapon

swapon(1) can show whether swap devices have been configured and how much of their volume is in use. For example:

```
$ swapon
NAME        TYPE      SIZE USED PRIO
/dev/dm-2 partition 980M    0B   -2
```

This output shows a system with one swap partition of 980 Mbytes, which is not in use at all. Many systems nowadays do not have swap configured, and if this is the case, swapon(1) does not print any output.

If a swap device has active I/O, it can be seen in the "si" and "so" columns in vmstat(1), and as device I/O in iostat(1).

free

The free(1) tool summarizes memory usage and shows available free memory system-wide. This example uses -m for Mbytes:

```
$ free -m
              total        used        free      shared  buff/cache   available
Mem:         189282      183022        1103           4        5156        4716
Swap:             0           0           0
```

The output from free(1) has improved in recent years to be less confusing; it now includes an "available" column that shows how much memory is available for use, including the file system cache. This is less confusing than the "free" column, which only shows memory that is completely unused. If you think the system is running low on memory because "free" is low, you need to consider "available" instead.

The file system cached pages are seen in the "buff/cache" column, which sums two types: I/O buffers and file system cached pages. You can view these pages in separate columns by using the -w option (wide).

This particular example is from a production system with 184 Gbytes of total main memory, of which about 4 Gbytes is currently available. For more breakdowns of system-wide memory, cat /proc/meminfo.

ps

The ps(1) process status command can show memory usage by process:

```
$ ps aux
USER    PID  %CPU %MEM     VSZ      RSS TTY       STAT START   TIME COMMAND
[...]
root    2499  0.0  0.0   30028     2720 ?         Ss   Jan25   0:00 /usr/sbin/cron -f
root    2703  0.0  0.0       0        0 ?         I    04:13   0:00 [kworker/41:0]
pcp     2951  0.0  0.0  116716     3572 ?         S    Jan25   0:00 /usr/lib/pcp/bin/pmwe...
root    2992  0.0  0.0       0        0 ?         I    Jan25   0:00 [kworker/17:2]
root    3741  0.0  0.0       0        0 ?         I    Jan25   0:05 [kworker/0:3]
www     3785 1970 95.7 213734052 185542800 ? Sl   Jan25 15123:15 /apps/java/bin/java...
[...]
```

This output has columns for:

- **%MEM:** The percentage of the system's physical memory in use by this process
- **VSZ:** Virtual memory size
- **RSS:** Resident set size: the total physical memory in use by this process

This output shows that the java process is consuming 95.7% of the physical memory on the system. The ps(1) command can print custom columns to focus only on memory statistics (e.g., ps -eo pid, pmem, vsz, rss). These statistics and more can be found in the /proc files: /proc/PID/status.

pmap

The pmap(1) command can show process memory usage by address space segment. For example:

```
$ pmap -x 3785
3785:   /apps/java/bin/java -Dnop -XX:+UseG1GC -...
XX:+ParallelRefProcEnabled -XX:+ExplicitGCIn
Address            Kbytes    RSS  Dirty Mode  Mapping
0000000000400000        4      0      0 r-x-- java
0000000000400000        0      0      0 r-x-- java
0000000000600000        4      4      4 rw--- java
0000000000600000        0      0      0 rw--- java
00000000006c2000     5700   5572   5572 rw---  [ anon ]
00000000006c2000        0      0      0 rw---  [ anon ]
[...]
```

```
00007f2ce5e61000         0        0         0 ----- libjvm.so
00007f2ce6061000       832      832       832 rw--- libjvm.so
00007f2ce6061000         0        0         0 rw--- libjvm.so
[...]
ffffffffff600000         4        0         0 r-x--  [ anon ]
ffffffffff600000         0        0         0 r-x--  [ anon ]
---------------- ------- ------- -------
total kB         213928940 185743916 185732800
```

This view can identify large memory consumers by libraries or mapped files. This extended (-x) output includes a column for "dirty" pages: pages that have changed in memory and are not yet saved on disk.

vmstat

The vmstat(1) command shows various system-wide statistics over time, including statistics for memory, CPUs, and storage I/O. For example, printing a summary line every one second:

```
$ vmstat 1
procs -----------memory---------- ---swap-- -----io---- -system-- ------cpu-----
 r  b   swpd    free   buff  cache   si   so    bi    bo   in   cs us sy id wa st
12  0      0 1075868 13232 5288396    0    0    14    26   16   19 38  2 59  0  0
14  0      0 1075000 13232 5288932    0    0     0     0 28751 77964 22  1 77  0  0
 9  0      0 1074452 13232 5289440    0    0     0     0 28511 76371 18  1 81  0  0
15  0      0 1073824 13232 5289828    0    0     0     0 32411 86088 26  1 73  0  0
```

The "free", "buff", and "cache" columns show memory in Kbytes that is free, used by storage I/O buffers, and used for the file system cache. The "si" and "so" columns show memory swapped in and out from disk, if active.

The first line of output is the "summary since boot," where most columns are an average since the system booted; however, the memory columns show the current state. The second and subsequent lines are the one-second summaries.

sar

The sar(1) command is a multi-tool that prints metrics for different targets. The -B option shows page statistics:

```
# sar -B 1
Linux 4.15.0-1031-aws (...)        01/26/2019        _x86_64_   (48 CPU)

06:10:38 PM  pgpgin/s pgpgout/s   fault/s  majflt/s  pgfree/s pgscank/s pgscand/s
pgsteal/s    %vmeff
06:10:39 PM     0.00      0.00    286.00      0.00  16911.00      0.00      0.00
0.00      0.00
```

```
06:10:40 PM       0.00       0.00      90.00      0.00  19178.00       0.00       0.00
  0.00        0.00
06:10:41 PM       0.00       0.00     187.00      0.00  18949.00       0.00       0.00
  0.00        0.00
06:10:42 PM       0.00       0.00     110.00      0.00  24266.00       0.00       0.00
  0.00        0.00
[...]
```

This output is from a busy production server. The output is very wide, so the columns have wrapped and are a little hard to read here. The page fault rate ("fault/s") is low—less than 300 per second. There also isn't any page scanning (the "pgscan" columns), indicating that the system is likely not running at memory saturation.

Here is output from a server doing a software build:

```
# sar -B 1
Linux 4.18.0-rc6-virtual (...)   01/26/2019           _x86_64_    (36 CPU)

06:16:08 PM  pgpgin/s pgpgout/s    fault/s  majflt/s  pgfree/s pgscank/s pgscand/s
pgsteal/s    %vmeff
06:16:09 PM    1968.00     302.00 1454167.00      0.00 1372222.00       0.00       0.00
  0.00        0.00
06:16:10 PM    1680.00     171.00 1374786.00      0.00 1203463.00       0.00       0.00
  0.00        0.00
06:16:11 PM    1100.00     581.00 1453754.00      0.00 1457286.00       0.00       0.00
  0.00        0.00
06:16:12 PM    1376.00     227.00 1527580.00      0.00 1364191.00       0.00       0.00
  0.00        0.00
06:16:13 PM     880.00      68.00 1456732.00      0.00 1315536.00       0.00       0.00
  0.00        0.00
[...]
```

Now the page fault rate is huge—over one million faults per second. This is because the software build involves many short-lived processes, and each new process is faulting in its address space on first execution.

7.2.3 Hardware Statistics and Sampling

There are many PMCs for memory I/O events. To be clear, this is I/O from the CPU units on the processor to the banks of main memory, via the CPU caches. PMCs, introduced in Chapter 2, can be used in two modes: counting and sampling. Counting provides statistical summaries, and costs virtually zero overhead to use. Sampling records some of the events to a file for later analysis.

This example uses perf(1) in counting mode to measure last-level cache (LLC) loads and misses, system-wide (-a), with interval output every 1 second (-I 1000):

```
# perf stat -e LLC-loads,LLC-load-misses -a -I 1000
#          time       counts unit events
     1.000705801    8,402,738      LLC-loads
     1.000705801    3,610,704      LLC-load-misses  #   42.97% of all LL-cache hits
     2.001219292    8,265,334      LLC-loads
     2.001219292    3,526,956      LLC-load-misses  #   42.32% of all LL-cache hits
     3.001763602    9,586,619      LLC-loads
     3.001763602    3,842,810      LLC-load-misses  #   43.91% of all LL-cache hits
[...]
```

For convenience, perf(1) has recognized how these PMCs are related and printed a percentage miss ratio. LLC misses are one measure of I/O to main memory, since once a memory load or store misses the LLC, it becomes a main memory access.

Now perf(1) is used in sampling mode to record details from every one in one hundred thousand L1 data cache misses:

```
# perf record -e L1-dcache-load-misses -c 100000 -a
^C[ perf record: Woken up 1 times to write data ]
[ perf record: Captured and wrote 3.075 MB perf.data (612 samples) ]
# perf report -n --stdio
# Overhead  Samples  Command  Shared Object        Symbol
# ........  .......  .......  ...................  ..................................
#
    30.56%      187  cksum    [kernel.kallsyms]    [k] copy_user_enhanced_fast_string
     8.33%       51  cksum    cksum                [.] 0x0000000000001cc9
     2.78%       17  cksum    cksum                [.] 0x0000000000001cb4
     2.45%       15  cksum    [kernel.kallsyms]    [k] generic_file_read_iter
     2.12%       13  cksum    cksum              ·  [.] 0x0000000000001cbe
[...]
```

Such a large sampling threshold (-c 100000) was used because L1 accesses are very frequent, and a lower threshold might collect so many samples that it would perturb the performance of running software. If you are unsure of the rate of a PMC, use counting mode first (perf stat) to find it, and from that you can calculate an appropriate threshold.

The output of perf report shows the symbols for the L1 dcache misses. It is recommended to use PEBS with memory PMCs so that the sample instruction pointers are accurate. With perf, add :p, or :pp (better), or :ppp (best) to the end of the event name to enable PEBS; the more *p*s, the more accurate. (See the p modifier section of the perf-list(1) man page.)

7.3 BPF Tools

This section covers the BPF tools you can use for memory performance analysis and troubleshooting (see Figure 7-4).

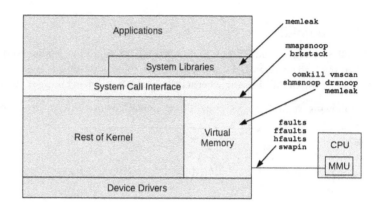

Figure 7-4   BPF tools for memory analysis

These tools are either from the BCC and bpftrace repositories covered in Chapters 4 and 5, or were created for this book. Some tools appear in both BCC and bpftrace. Table 7-3 lists the origins of the tools covered in this section (BT is short for bpftrace.)

Table 7-3   **Memory-Related Tools**

Tool	Source	Target	Description
oomkill	BCC/BT	OOM	Shows extra info on OOM kill events
memleak	BCC	Sched	Shows possible memory leak code paths
mmapsnoop	Book	Syscalls	Traces mmap(2) calls system-wide
brkstack	Book	Syscalls	Shows brk() calls with user stack traces
shmsnoop	BCC	Syscalls	Traces shared memory calls with details
faults	Book	Faults	Shows page faults, by user stack trace
ffaults	Book	Faults	Shows page faults, by filename
vmscan	Book	VM	Measures VM scanner shrink and reclaim times
drsnoop	BCC	VM	Traces direct reclaim events, showing latency
swapin	Book	VM	Shows swap-ins by process
hfaults	Book	Faults	Shows huge page faults, by process

For tools from BCC and bpftrace, see their repositories for full and updated lists of tool options and capabilities. Some of the most important capabilities are summarized here.

Chapter 14 provides more BPF tools for kernel memory analysis: kmem(8), kpages(8), slabratetop(8), and numamove(8).

7.3.1   oomkill

oomkill(8)[1] is a BCC and bpftrace tool for tracing out-of-memory killer events and printing details such as the load averages. Load averages provide some additional context for the system state at the time of the OOM, showing whether the system was getting busier or whether it was steady.

The following example shows oomkill(8) from BCC, from a 48-CPU production instance:

```
# oomkill
Tracing OOM kills... Ctrl-C to stop.
08:51:34 Triggered by PID 18601 ("perl"), OOM kill of PID 1165 ("java"), 18006224
pages, loadavg: 10.66 7.17 5.06 2/755 18643
[...]
```

This output shows that PID 18601 (perl) needed memory, which triggered an OOM kill of PID 1165 (java). PID 1165 had reached 18006224 pages in size; these are usually 4 Kbytes per page, depending on the processor and process memory settings. The load averages show that the system was getting busier at the time of the OOM kill.

This tool works by tracing the oom_kill_process() function using kprobes and printing various details. In this case, the load averages are fetched by simply reading /proc/loadavg. This tool can be enhanced to print other details, as desired, when debugging OOM events. In addition, oom tracepoints that can reveal more details about how tasks are selected are not yet used by this tool.

The BCC version currently does not use command line arguments.

bpftrace

The following is the code for the bpftrace version of oomkill(8):

```
#!/usr/local/bin/bpftrace

#include <linux/oom.h>

BEGIN
{
        printf("Tracing oom_kill_process()... Hit Ctrl-C to end.\n");
}
```

---

1 Origin: I created it on 9-Feb-2016, for BCC, to have a tool for launching extra debug info for the production OOM events I sometimes see. I wrote the bpftrace version on 7-Sep-2018.

```
kprobe:oom_kill_process
{
        $oc = (struct oom_control *)arg1;
        time("%H:%M:%S ");
        printf("Triggered by PID %d (\"%s\"), ", pid, comm);
        printf("OOM kill of PID %d (\"%s\"), %d pages, loadavg: ",
            $oc->chosen->pid, $oc->chosen->comm, $oc->totalpages);
        cat("/proc/loadavg");
}
```

The program traces oom_kill_process() and casts the second argument as a struct oom_control, which contains details of the sacrificial process. It prints details of the current process (pid, comm) that led to the OOM event, and then the target details, and finally a system() call is used to print the load averages.

7.3.2 memleak

memleak(8)[2] is a BCC tool that traces memory allocation and free events along with the allocation stack traces. Over time, it can show the long-term survivors—the allocations that have not been freed. This example shows memleak(8) running on a bash shell process[3]:

```
# memleak -p 3126
Attaching to pid 3228, Ctrl+C to quit.

[09:14:15] Top 10 stacks with outstanding allocations:
[...]
        960 bytes in 1 allocations from stack
                xrealloc+0x2a [bash]
                strvec_resize+0x2b [bash]
                maybe_make_export_env+0xa8 [bash]
                execute_simple_command+0x269 [bash]
                execute_command_internal+0x862 [bash]
                execute_connection+0x109 [bash]
                execute_command_internal+0xc18 [bash]
                execute_command+0x6b [bash]
                reader_loop+0x286 [bash]
                main+0x969 [bash]
                __libc_start_main+0xe7 [libc-2.27.so]
                [unknown]
```

---

2 Origin: This was created by Sasha Goldshtein and published on 7-Feb-2016.

3 To ensure that frame pointer–based stack traces work and regular malloc routines are used, this bash was compiled with CFLAGS=-fno-omit-frame-pointer ./configure --without-gnu-malloc.

```
      1473 bytes in 51 allocations from stack
            xmalloc+0x18 [bash]
            make_env_array_from_var_list+0xc8 [bash]
            make_var_export_array+0x3d [bash]
            maybe_make_export_env+0x12b [bash]
            execute_simple_command+0x269 [bash]
            execute_command_internal+0x862 [bash]
            execute_connection+0x109 [bash]
            execute_command_internal+0xc18 [bash]
            execute_command+0x6b [bash]
            reader_loop+0x286 [bash]
            main+0x969 [bash]
            __libc_start_main+0xe7 [libc-2.27.so]
            [unknown]

[...]
```

By default it prints output every five seconds, showing the allocation stacks and total bytes yet to be freed. The last stack shows that 1473 bytes were allocated via execute_command() and make_env_array_from_var_list().

memleak(8) alone cannot tell you whether these allocations are a genuine memory leak (that is, allocated memory with no references and which will never be freed), or memory growth, or just a long-term allocation. To differentiate between them, the code paths need to be studied and understood.

Without a -p PID provided, memleak(8) traces kernel allocations:

```
# memleak
Attaching to kernel allocators, Ctrl+C to quit.
[...]
[09:19:30] Top 10 stacks with outstanding allocations:
[...]
      15384576 bytes in 3756 allocations from stack
            __alloc_pages_nodemask+0x209 [kernel]
            alloc_pages_vma+0x88 [kernel]
            handle_pte_fault+0x3bf [kernel]
            __handle_mm_fault+0x478 [kernel]
            handle_mm_fault+0xb1 [kernel]
            __do_page_fault+0x250 [kernel]
            do_page_fault+0x2e [kernel]
            page_fault+0x45 [kernel]
[...]
```

For process targets, memleak(8) works by tracing the user-level allocation functions: malloc(), calloc(), free(), and so on. For the kernel, it uses the kmem tracepoints: kmem:kmalloc, kmem:kfree, and so on.

Command line usage:

```
memleak [options] [-p PID] [-c COMMAND] [interval [count]]
```

Options include:

- **-s RATE:** Samples one in every RATE allocations to lower overhead
- **-o OLDER:** Prunes allocations younger than OLDER, in milliseconds

Allocations, especially user-level allocations, can be extremely frequent—millions of times per second. This can slow the target application by as much as 10x or more, depending on how busy it is. For now, this means memleak(8) is more of a troubleshooting or debugging tool than an everyday production analysis tool. As mentioned earlier, this will be the case until the performance of uprobes is greatly improved.

7.3.3 mmapsnoop

mmapsnoop(8)[4] traces the mmap(2) syscall system-wide and prints details of the requested mappings. This is useful for general debugging of memory mapping usage. Example output:

```
# mmapsnoop.py
PID    COMM           PROT MAP   OFFS(KB) SIZE(KB) FILE
6015   mmapsnoop.py   RW-  S---  0        260      [perf_event]
6015   mmapsnoop.py   RW-  S---  0        260      [perf_event]
[...]
6315   java           R-E  -P--  0        2222     libjava.so
6315   java           RW-  -PF-  168      8        libjava.so
6315   java           R--  -P--  0        43       ld.so.cache
6315   java           R-E  -P--  0        2081     libnss_compat-2.23.so
6315   java           RW-  -PF-  28       8        libnss_compat-2.23.so
6315   java           R-E  -P--  0        2146     libnsl-2.23.so
6315   java           RW-  -PF-  84       8        libnsl-2.23.so
6315   java           R--  -P--  0        43       ld.so.cache
6315   java           R-E  -P--  0        2093     libnss_nis-2.23.so
6315   java           RW-  -PF-  40       8        libnss_nis-2.23.so
6315   java           R-E  -P--  0        2117     libnss_files-2.23.so
6315   java           RW-  -PF-  40       8        libnss_files-2.23.so
6315   java           R--  S---  0        2        passwd
[...]
```

---

4 Origin: I first created this as mmap.d for *DTrace: Dynamic Tracing in Oracle Solaris, Mac OS X and FreeBSD* in 2010 [Gregg 11], and I created this BCC version for this book on 3-Feb-2019.

This output begins with mappings to the perf_event ring buffers that this BCC tool uses for fetching event output. Then java mappings can be seen for a new process startup, along with the protection and mapping flags.

Protection flags (PROT):

- **R**: PROT_READ
- **W**: PROT_WRITE
- **E**: PROT_EXEC

Map flags (MAP):

- **S**: MAP_SHARED
- **P**: MAP_PRIVATE
- **F**: MAP_FIXED
- **A**: MAP_ANON

mmapsnoop(8) supports a -T option for printing a time column.

This tool works by instrumenting the syscalls:sys_enter_mmap tracepoint. The overhead of this tool should be negligible as the rate of new mappings should be relatively low.

Chapter 8 continues the analysis of memory-mapped files and includes the mmapfiles(8) and fmapfaults(8) tools.

7.3.4 brkstack

The usual memory store for application data is the heap, which grows via calls to the brk(2) syscall. It can be useful to trace brk(2) and show the user-level stack trace that led to this growth. There is also an sbrk(2) variant, but on Linux, sbrk(2) is implemented as a library call that calls brk(2).

brk(2) can be traced with the syscalls:syscall_enter_brk tracepoint, and stacks for this tracepoint can be shown using BCC's trace(8) for per-event output and stackcount(8) for a frequency count, a bpftrace one-liner, and also perf(1). Examples using BCC tools:

```
# trace -U t:syscalls:sys_enter_brk
# stackcount -PU t:syscalls:sys_enter_brk
```

For example:

```
# stackcount -PU t:syscalls:sys_enter_brk
Tracing 1 functions for "t:syscalls:sys_enter_brk"... Hit Ctrl-C to end.
^C
[...]

  brk
  __sbrk
```

```
__default_morecore
sysmalloc
_int_malloc
tcache_init
__libc_malloc
malloc_hook_ini
__libc_malloc
JLI_MemAlloc
JLI_List_new
main
__libc_start_main
_start
  java [8395]
  1


[unknown]
  cron [8385]
  2
```

This truncated output shows a brk(2) stack from a "java" process, from JLI_List_new(), JLI_MemAlloc(), and via sbrk(3): it looks as if a list object triggered a heap expansion. The second stack trace from cron is broken. For the java stack to work, I had to use a libc version with frame pointers. This is discussed further in Section 13.2.9 in Chapter 13.

brk(2) growths are infrequent, and the stack trace may reveal a large and unusual allocation that needed more space than was available, or a normal code path that happened to need one byte more than was available. The code path needs to be studied to determine which is the case. Because these growths are infrequent, the overhead of tracing them is negligible, making brk tracing an inexpensive technique for finding some clues about memory growth. In comparison, tracing the much more frequent memory allocation functions directly (e.g., malloc()) can be so expensive to instrument that the overhead is prohibitive. Another low-overhead tool for analyzing memory growth is faults(8), covered in Section 7.3.6, which traces page faults.

It can be easier to remember and find tools by their filename than to remember one-liners, so here is this important functionality implemented as a bpftrace tool, brkstack(8)[5]:

```
#!/usr/local/bin/bpftrace

tracepoint:syscalls:sys_enter_brk
{
        @[ustack, comm] = count();
}
```

---

5 Origin: I created it for this book on 26-Jan-2019. Tracing brk() stacks is something I've done for years, and in the past I have published brk(2) flame graphs [82].

7.3.5 shmsnoop

shmsnoop(8)[6] is a BCC tool that traces System V shared memory syscalls: shmget(2), shmat(2), shmdt(2), and shmctl(2). It can be used for debugging shared memory usage. For example, during startup of a Java application:

```
# shmsnoop
PID     COMM      SYS         RET ARGs
12520   java      SHMGET     58c000a key: 0x0, size: 65536, shmflg: 0x380 (IPC_CREAT|0600)
12520   java      SHMAT 7fde9c033000 shmid: 0x58c000a, shmaddr: 0x0, shmflg: 0x0
12520   java      SHMCTL          0 shmid: 0x58c000a, cmd: 0, buf: 0x0
12520   java      SHMDT           0 shmaddr: 0x7fde9c033000
1863    Xorg      SHMAT 7f98cd3b9000 shmid: 0x58c000a, shmaddr: 0x0, shmflg: 0x1000
(SHM_RDONLY)
1863    Xorg      SHMCTL          0 shmid: 0x58c000a, cmd: 2, buf: 0x7ffdddd9e240
1863    Xorg      SHMDT           0 shmaddr: 0x7f98cd3b9000
[...]
```

This output shows Java allocating shared memory using shmget(2), followed by various shared-memory operations and their arguments. The return of shmget(2) is 0x58c000a, the identifier, which is used in subsequent calls by both Java and Xorg; in other words, they are sharing memory.

This tool works by tracing the shared memory syscalls, which should be infrequent enough that the overhead of the tool is negligible.

Command line usage:

```
shmsnoop [options]
```

Options include:

- **-T**: Included timestamps
- **-p PID**: Measured this process only

7.3.6 faults

Tracing page faults and their stack traces provides a particular view of memory usage: not the code paths that allocated memory, but the code paths that first used it and triggered a page fault. These page faults cause RSS growth, so the stack traces can explain why a process is growing. As with brk(), it's possible to trace this event by using a one-liner with other tools, such as using BCC and stackcount(8) to frequency-count page user and kernel page faults with stack traces:

```
# stackcount -U t:exceptions:page_fault_user
# stackcount t:exceptions:page_fault_kernel
```

---

6 Origin: This was created by Jiri Olsa on 8-Oct-2018.

Example output, with -P for process details:

```
# stackcount -PU t:exceptions:page_fault_user
Tracing 1 functions for "t:exceptions:page_fault_user"... Hit Ctrl-C to end.
^C
[...]

  PhaseIdealLoop::Dominators()
  PhaseIdealLoop::build_and_optimize(LoopOptsMode)
  Compile::optimize_loops(PhaseIterGVN&, LoopOptsMode) [clone .part.344]
  Compile::Optimize()
  Compile::Compile(ciEnv*, C2Compiler*, ciMethod*, int, bool, bool, bool, Directiv...
  C2Compiler::compile_method(ciEnv*, ciMethod*, int, DirectiveSet*)
  CompileBroker::invoke_compiler_on_method(CompileTask*)
  CompileBroker::compiler_thread_loop()
  JavaThread::thread_main_inner()
  Thread::call_run()
  thread_native_entry(Thread*)
  start_thread
  __clone
    C2 CompilerThre [9124]
    1824


  __memset_avx2_erms
  PhaseCFG::global_code_motion()
  PhaseCFG::do_global_code_motion()
  Compile::Code_Gen()
  Compile::Compile(ciEnv*, C2Compiler*, ciMethod*, int, bool, bool, bool, Directiv...
  C2Compiler::compile_method(ciEnv*, ciMethod*, int, DirectiveSet*)
  CompileBroker::invoke_compiler_on_method(CompileTask*)
  CompileBroker::compiler_thread_loop()
  JavaThread::thread_main_inner()
  Thread::call_run()
  thread_native_entry(Thread*)
  start_thread
  __clone
    C2 CompilerThre [9124]
    2934
```

This output shows the start of a Java process and its C2 compiler thread faulting memory as it compiled code to instruction text.

Page Fault Flame Graphs

Page fault stack traces can be visualized as a flame graph to aid navigation. (Flame graphs are introduced in Chapter 2.) These instructions use my original flame graph software [37] and result in a page fault flame graph, an area of which is shown in Figure 7-5:

```
# stackcount -f -PU t:exceptions:page_fault_user > out.pagefaults01.txt
$ flamegraph.pl --hash --width=800 --title="Page Fault Flame Graph" \
    --colors=java --bgcolor=green < out.pagefaults01.txt > out.pagefaults01.svg
```

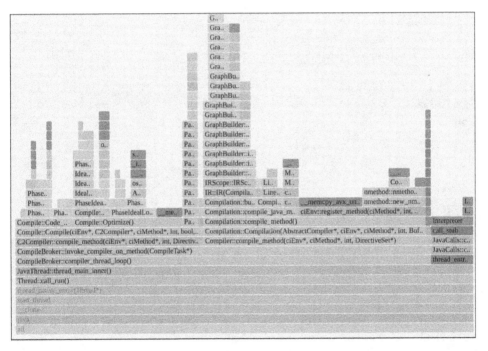

Figure 7-5   Page fault flame graph

This zoomed area shows the code paths from the Java compiler thread that grew main memory and triggered a page fault.

Netflix has automated page fault flame graph generation from Vector, an instance analysis tool, so that Netflix developers can generate these graphs with the click of a button (see Chapter 17).

bpftrace

For ease of use, here is a bpftrace tool, faults(8)[7], for tracing page faults with stacks:

```
#!/usr/local/bin/bpftrace

software:page-faults:1
{
        @[ustack, comm] = count();
}
```

This tool instruments the software event page faults with an overflow count of one: it runs the BPF program for every page fault and frequency-counts the user-level stack trace and process name.

7.3.7 ffaults

ffaults(8)[8] traces page faults by filename. For example, from a software build:

```
# ffaults.bt
Attaching 1 probe...

[...]
@[cat]: 4576
@[make]: 7054
@[libbfd-2.26.1-system.so]: 8325
@[libtinfo.so.5.9]: 8484
@[libdl-2.23.so]: 9137
@[locale-archive]: 21137
@[cc1]: 23083
@[ld-2.23.so]: 27558
@[bash]: 45236
@[libopcodes-2.26.1-system.so]: 46369
@[libc-2.23.so]: 84814
@[]: 537925
```

This output shows that the most page faults were to regions without a filename—which would be process heaps—with 537,925 faults occurring during tracing. The libc library encountered 84,814 faults while tracing. This is happening because the software build is creating many short-lived processes, which are faulting in their new address spaces.

---

7 Origin: I created it for this book on 27-Jan-2019, and I've traced page fault stacks in the past with other tracers [82].
8 Origin: I created it for this book on 26-Jan-2019.

The source to ffaults(8) is:

```
#!/usr/local/bin/bpftrace

#include <linux/mm.h>

kprobe:handle_mm_fault
{
        $vma = (struct vm_area_struct *)arg0;
        $file = $vma->vm_file->f_path.dentry->d_name.name;
        @[str($file)] = count();
}
```

This tool uses kprobes to trace the handle_mm_fault() kernel function and, from its arguments, determine the filename for the fault. The rate of file faults varies depending on the workload; you can check it using tools such as perf(1) or sar(1). For high rates, the overhead of this tool may begin to become noticeable.

7.3.8 vmscan

vmscan(8)[9] uses the vmscan tracepoints to instrument the page-out daemon (kswapd), which frees memory for reuse when the system is under memory pressure. Note that, while the term *scanner* is still used to refer to this kernel function, for efficiency, Linux nowadays manages memory via linked lists of active and inactive memory.

Running vmscan on a 36-CPU system while it runs out of memory:

```
# vmscan.bt
Attaching 10 probes...
TIME          S-SLABms   D-RECLAIMms   M-RECLAIMms  KSWAPD  WRITEPAGE
21:30:25             0             0             0       0          0
21:30:26             0             0             0       0          0
21:30:27           276           555             0       2          1
21:30:28          5459          7333             0      15         72
21:30:29            41             0             0      49         35
21:30:30             1           454             0       2          2
21:30:31             0             0             0       0          0
^C

@direct_reclaim_ns:
[256K, 512K)          5 |@                                                    |
[512K, 1M)           83 |@@@@@@@@@@@@@@@@@@@@@@@@@@@@@                         |
```

---

9 Origin: I created it for this book on 26-Jan-2019. For an earlier tool that uses these tracepoints, see Mel Gorman's trace-vmscan-postprocess.pl, which has been in the Linux source since 2009.

```
[1M, 2M)          174 |@@@@@@@@@@@@@@@@@@@@@@@@@@@@@@@@@@@@@@@@@@@@@@@@@@@@|
[2M, 4M)          136 |@@@@@@@@@@@@@@@@@@@@@@@@@@@@@@@@@@@@@@@@@@            |
[4M, 8M)           66 |@@@@@@@@@@@@@@@@@@@@                                 |
[8M, 16M)          68 |@@@@@@@@@@@@@@@@@@@@                                 |
[16M, 32M)          8 |@@                                                  |
[32M, 64M)          3 |                                                    |
[64M, 128M)         0 |                                                    |
[128M, 256M)        0 |                                                    |
[256M, 512M)       18 |@@@@@                                               |

@shrink_slab_ns:
[128, 256)      12228 |@@@@@@@@@@@@@@@@@@@@@@@@@@@@@@@@                     |
[256, 512)      19859 |@@@@@@@@@@@@@@@@@@@@@@@@@@@@@@@@@@@@@@@@@@@@@@@@@@@@@@|
[512, 1K)        1899 |@@@@                                                |
[1K, 2K)         1052 |@@                                                  |
[2K, 4K)          546 |@                                                   |
[4K, 8K)          241 |                                                    |
[8K, 16K)         122 |                                                    |
[16K, 32K)        518 |@                                                   |
[32K, 64K)        600 |@                                                   |
[64K, 128K)        49 |                                                    |
[128K, 256K)       19 |                                                    |
[256K, 512K)        7 |                                                    |
[512K, 1M)          6 |                                                    |
[1M, 2M)            8 |                                                    |
[2M, 4M)            4 |                                                    |
[4M, 8M)            7 |                                                    |
[8M, 16M)          29 |                                                    |
[16M, 32M)         11 |                                                    |
[32M, 64M)          3 |                                                    |
[64M, 128M)         0 |                                                    |
[128M, 256M)        0 |                                                    |
[256M, 512M)       19 |                                                    |
```

The per-second columns show:

- **S-SLABms:** Total time in shrink slab, in milliseconds. This is reclaiming memory from various kernel caches.

- **D-RECLAIMms:** Total time in direct reclaim, in milliseconds. This is foreground reclaim, which blocks memory allocations while memory is written to disk.

- **M-RECLAIMms:** Total time in memory cgroup reclaim, in milliseconds. If memory cgroups are in use, this shows when one cgroup has exceeded its limit and its own cgroup memory is reclaimed.

- **KSWAPD:** Number of kswapd wakeups.
- **WRITEPAGE:** Number of kswapd page writes.

The times are totals across all CPUs, which provides a measure of cost beyond the counts seen by other tools, such as vmstat(1).

Look out for time in direct reclaims (D-RECLAIMms): This type of reclaim is "bad" but necessary, and will cause performance issues. It can hopefully be eliminated by tuning the other vm sysctl tunables to engage background reclaim sooner, before direct reclaim is necessary.

The output histograms show per-event times in direct reclaim and shrink slab, in nanoseconds.

The source to vmscan(8) is:

```
#!/usr/local/bin/bpftrace

tracepoint:vmscan:mm_shrink_slab_start { @start_ss[tid] = nsecs; }
tracepoint:vmscan:mm_shrink_slab_end /@start_ss[tid]/
{
        $dur_ss = nsecs - @start_ss[tid];
        @sum_ss = @sum_ss + $dur_ss;
        @shrink_slab_ns = hist($dur_ss);
        delete(@start_ss[tid]);
}


tracepoint:vmscan:mm_vmscan_direct_reclaim_begin { @start_dr[tid] = nsecs; }
tracepoint:vmscan:mm_vmscan_direct_reclaim_end /@start_dr[tid]/
{
        $dur_dr = nsecs - @start_dr[tid];
        @sum_dr = @sum_dr + $dur_dr;
        @direct_reclaim_ns = hist($dur_dr);
        delete(@start_dr[tid]);
}



tracepoint:vmscan:mm_vmscan_memcg_reclaim_begin { @start_mr[tid] = nsecs; }
tracepoint:vmscan:mm_vmscan_memcg_reclaim_end /@start_mr[tid]/
{
        $dur_mr = nsecs - @start_mr[tid];
        @sum_mr = @sum_mr + $dur_mr;
        @memcg_reclaim_ns = hist($dur_mr);
        delete(@start_mr[tid]);
}
```

```
tracepoint:vmscan:mm_vmscan_wakeup_kswapd { @count_wk++; }

tracepoint:vmscan:mm_vmscan_writepage { @count_wp++; }

BEGIN
{
        printf("%-10s %10s %12s %12s %6s %9s\n", "TIME",
            "S-SLABms", "D-RECLAIMms", "M-RECLAIMms", "KSWAPD", "WRITEPAGE");

}

interval:s:1
{
        time("%H:%M:%S");
        printf("   %10d %12d %12d %6d %9d\n",
            @sum_ss / 1000000, @sum_dr / 1000000, @sum_mr / 1000000,
            @count_wk, @count_wp);
        clear(@sum_ss);
        clear(@sum_dr);
        clear(@sum_mr);
        clear(@count_wk);
        clear(@count_wp);
}
```

This tool uses various vmscan tracepoints to record times when events begin so that duration histograms and running totals can be maintained.

7.3.9 drsnoop

drsnoop(8)[10] is a BCC tool for tracing the direct reclaim approach to freeing memory, showing the process affected and the latency: the time taken for the reclaim. It can be used to quantify the application performance impact of a memory-constrained system. For example:

```
# drsnoop -T
TIME(s)        COMM        PID     LAT(ms)  PAGES
0.000000000    java        11266    1.72    57
0.004007000    java        11266    3.21    57
0.011856000    java        11266    2.02    43
0.018315000    java        11266    3.09    55
0.024647000    acpid       1209     6.46    73
[...]
```

---

10 Origin: This was created by Ethercflow on 10-Feb-2019.

This output shows some direct reclaims for Java, taking between one and seven milliseconds. The rates of these reclaims and their duration can be considered in quantifying the application impact.

This tool works by tracing the vmscan mm_vmscan_direct_reclaim_begin and mm_vmscan_direct_reclaim_end tracepoints. These are expected to be low-frequency events (usually happening in bursts), so the overhead should be negligible.

Command line usage:

```
drsnoop [options]
```

Options include:

- **-T**: Includes timestamps
- **-p PID**: Measures this process only

7.3.10 swapin

swapin(8)[11] shows which processes are being swapped in from the swap devices, if they exist and are in use. For example, this system swapped out some memory and had 36 Kbytes swapped back in ("si" column) while I was watching it with vmstat(1):

```
# vmstat 1
procs -----------memory---------- ---swap-- -----io---- -system-- ------cpu-----
 r  b   swpd   free   buff  cache   si   so    bi    bo   in   cs us sy id wa st
[...]
46 11  29696 1585680  4384 1828440    0    0 88047  2034 21809 37316 81 18  0  1  0
776 57 29696 2842156  7976 1865276   36    0 52832  2283 18678 37025 85 15  0  1  0
294 135 29696 448580  4620 1860144    0    0 36503  5393 16745 35235 81 19  0  0  0
[...]
```

swapin(8) identifies the process that was swapped in. At the same time:

```
# swapin.bt
Attaching 2 probes...

[...]
06:57:43

06:57:44
```

---

11 Origin: I first created a similar tool called anonpgpid.d on 25-Jul-2005, with help from James Dickens. This was one of the long-standing performance issues I wrestled with beforehand: I could see that the system was swapping, but I wanted to show which processes were affected. I created this bpftrace version for this book on 26-Jan-2019.

```
@[systemd-logind, 1354]: 9

06:57:45
[...]
```

This output shows that systemd-logind (PID 1354) had 9 swap-ins. With a 4 Kbyte page size, this adds up to the 36 Kbytes seen in vmstat(1). I logged into the system using ssh(1), and this component in the login software had been swapped out, so the login took longer than usual.

Swap-ins occur when an application tries to use memory that has been moved to the swap device. This is an important measure of the performance pain suffered by an application due to swapping. Other swap metrics, like scanning and swap-outs, may not directly affect application performance.

The source to swapin(8) is:

```
#!/usr/local/bin/bpftrace

kprobe:swap_readpage
{
        @[comm, pid] = count();
}

interval:s:1
{
        time();
        print(@);
        clear(@);
}
```

This tool uses kprobes to trace the swap_readpage() kernel function, which runs in the context of the swapping thread, so the bpftrace built-ins for comm and pid reflect the swapping process.

7.3.11   hfaults

hfaults(8)[12] traces huge page faults by their process details and can be used to confirm that huge pages are in use. For example:

```
# hfaults.bt
Attaching 2 probes...
Tracing Huge Page faults per process... Hit Ctrl-C to end.
^C
@[884, hugemmap]: 9
```

---

12 Origin: Amer Ather created it for this book on 6-May-2019.

This output includes a test program, hugemmap, with PID 884, which triggered nine huge page faults.

The source to hfaults(8) is:

```
#!/usr/local/bin/bpftrace

BEGIN
{
        printf("Tracing Huge Page faults per process... Hit Ctrl-C to end.\n");
}

kprobe:hugetlb_fault
{
        @[pid, comm] = count();
}
```

If needed, more details can be fetched from function arguments, including struct mm_struct and struct vm_area_struct. The ffaults(8) tool (see Section 7.3.7) fetched the filename from the vm_area_struct.

7.3.12   Other Tools

Two other BPF tools are worth mentioning:

- **llcstat(8)** from BCC is covered in Chapter 5; it shows the last-level cache hit ratio, by process.
- **profile(8)** from BCC is covered in Chapter 5; it samples stack traces and can be used as a coarse and cheap way to find malloc() code paths.

7.4   BPF One-Liners

This section shows BCC and bpftrace one-liners. Where possible, the same one-liner is implemented using both BCC and bpftrace.

7.4.1   BCC

Count process heap expansion (brk()) by user-level stack trace:

```
stackcount -U t:syscalls:sys_enter_brk
```

Count user page faults by user-level stack trace:

```
stackcount -U t:exceptions:page_fault_user
```

Count vmscan operations by tracepoint:

```
funccount 't:vmscan:*'
```

Show hugepage_madvise() calls by process:

```
trace hugepage_madvise
```

Count page migrations:

```
funccount t:migrate:mm_migrate_pages
```

Trace compaction events:

```
trace t:compaction:mm_compaction_begin
```

7.4.2 bpftrace

Count process heap expansion (brk()) by code path:

```
bpftrace -e tracepoint:syscalls:sys_enter_brk { @[ustack, comm] = count(); }
```

Count page faults by process:

```
bpftrace -e 'software:page-fault:1 { @[comm, pid] = count(); }'
```

Count user page faults by user-level stack trace:

```
bpftrace -e 'tracepoint:exceptions:page_fault_user { @[ustack, comm] = count(); }'
```

Count vmscan operations by tracepoint:

```
bpftrace -e 'tracepoint:vmscan:* { @[probe] = count(); }'
```

Show hugepage_madvise() calls by process:

```
bpftrace -e 'kprobe:hugepage_madvise { printf("%s by PID %d\n", probe, pid); }'
```

Count page migrations:

```
bpftrace -e 'tracepoint:migrate:mm_migrate_pages { @ = count(); }'
```

Trace compaction events:

```
bpftrace -e 't:compaction:mm_compaction_begin { time(); }'
```

7.5 Optional Exercises

If not specified, these can be completed using either bpftrace or BCC:

1. Run vmscan(8) for ten minutes on a production or local server. If any time was spent in direct reclaim (D-RECLAIMms), also run drsnoop(8) to measure this on a per-event basis.

2. Modify vmscan(8) to print the header every 20 lines so that it remains onscreen.

3. During application startup (either a production or desktop application) use fault(8) to count page fault stack traces. This may involve fixing or finding an application that supports stack traces and symbols (see Chapters 13 and 18).

4. Create a page fault flame graph from the output of Exercise 3.

5. Develop a tool to trace process virtual memory growth via both brk(2) and mmap(2).

6. Develop a tool to print the size of expansions via brk(2). It may use syscall tracepoints, kprobes, or libc USDT probes, as desired.

7. Develop a tool to show the time spent in page compaction. You can use the compaction:mm_compaction_begin and compaction:mm_compaction_end tracepoints. Print the time per event and summarize it as a histogram.

8. Develop a tool to show time spent in shrink slab, broken down by slab name (or shrinker function name).

9. Use memleak(8) to find long-term survivors on some sample software in a test environment. Also estimate the performance overhead with and without memleak(8) running.

10. (Advanced, unsolved) Develop a tool to investigate swap thrashing: Show the time spent by pages on the swap device as a histogram. This is likely to involve measuring the time from swap-out to swap-in.

7.6 Summary

This chapter summarizes how virtual and physical memory is used by processes and covers memory analysis using traditional tools, which focus on showing memory volumes by usage types. This chapter also shows how to use BPF tools to measure rates and time durations for memory activity by the OOM killer, user-level allocations, memory maps, page faults, vmscan, direct reclaim, and swap-ins.

Chapter 8

File Systems

Analysis of file systems has historically focused on disk I/O and its performance, but file systems are often a more relevant target for beginning your analysis. It is the file system that applications usually interact with directly, and file systems can use caching, read-ahead, buffering, and asynchronous I/O to avoid exposing disk I/O latency to the application.

Since there are few traditional tools for file system analysis, it is an area where BPF tracing can really help. File system tracing can measure the full time an application was waiting on I/O, including disk I/O, locks, or other CPU work. It can show the process responsible, and the files operated upon: useful context that can be much harder to fetch from down at the disk level.

Learning Objectives:

- Understand file system components: VFS, caches, and write-back
- Understand targets for file system analysis with BPF
- Learn a strategy for successful analysis of file system performance
- Characterize file system workloads by file, operation type, and by process
- Measure latency distributions for file system operations, and identify bi-modal distributions and issues of latency outliers
- Measure the latency of file system write-back events
- Analyze page cache and read ahead performance
- Observe directory and inode cache behavior
- Use bpftrace one-liners to explore file system usage in custom ways

This chapter begins with the necessary background for file system analysis, summarizing the I/O stack and caching. I explore the questions that BPF can answer, and provide an overall strategy to follow. I then focus on tools, starting with traditional file system tools and then BPF tools, including a list of BPF one-liners. This chapter ends with optional exercises.

8.1   Background

This section covers file system fundamentals, BPF capabilities, and a suggested strategy for file system analysis.

8.1.1   File Systems Fundamentals

I/O Stack

A generic I/O stack is shown in Figure 8-1, showing the path of I/O from the application to disk devices.

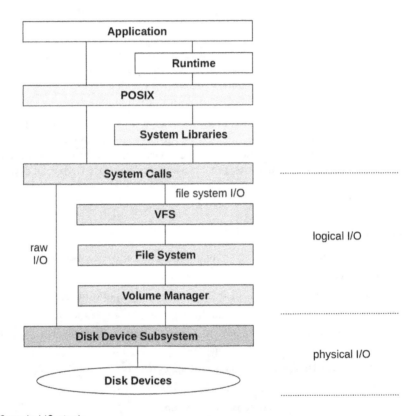

Figure 8-1   Generic I/O stack

Some terminology has been included in the diagram: *logical I/O* describes requests to the file system. If these requests must be served from the storage devices, they become *physical I/O*. Not all I/O will; many logical read requests may be returned from the file system cache, and never become physical I/O. Raw I/O is included on the diagram, though it is rarely used nowadays: it is a way for applications to use disk devices with no file system.

File systems are accessed via a virtual file system (VFS), a generic kernel interface allowing multiple different file systems to be supported using the same calls, and new file systems to be easily added. It provides operations for read, write, open, close, etc., which are mapped by file systems to their own internal functions.

After the file system, a volume manager may also be in use to manage the storage devices. There is also a block I/O subsystem for managing I/O to devices, including a queue, merge capabilities, and more. These are covered in Chapter 9.

File System Caches

Linux uses multiple caches to improve the performance of storage I/O via the file system, as shown in Figure 8-2.

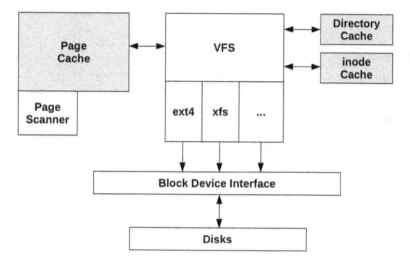

Figure 8-2   Linux FS caches

These caches are:

- **Page cache:** This contains virtual memory pages including the contents of files and I/O buffers (what was once a separate "buffer cache"), and improves the performance of file and directory I/O.

- **Inode cache:** Inodes (index nodes) are data structures used by file systems to describe their stored objects. VFS has its own generic version of an inode, and Linux keeps a cache of these because they are frequently read for permission checks and other metadata.

- **Directory cache:** Called the dcache, this caches mappings from directory entry names to VFS inodes, improving the performance of path name lookups.

The page cache grows to be the largest of all these, because it not only caches the contents of files, but also includes "dirty" pages that have been modified but not yet written to disk. Various situations can trigger a write of these dirty pages, including a set interval (e.g., 30 seconds), an explicit sync() call, and the page-out deamon (kswapd) explained in Chapter 7.

Read-Ahead

A file system feature called read ahead or prefetch, involves detecting a sequential read workload, predicting the next pages that will be accessed, and loading them into the page cache. This pre-warming improves read performance only for sequential access workloads, not random access workloads. Linux also supports an explicit readahead() syscall.

Write-Back

Linux supports file system writes in write-back mode, where buffers are dirtied in memory and flushed to disk sometime later by kernel worker threads, so as not to block applications directly on slow disk I/O.

Further Reading

This was a brief summary intended to arm you with essential knowledge before you use the tools. File systems are covered in much more depth in Chapter 8 of *Systems Performance* [Gregg 13b].

8.1.2 BPF Capabilities

Traditional performance tools have focused on disk I/O performance, not file system performance. BPF tools can provide this missing observability, showing operations, latencies, and internal functions of each file system.

Questions that BPF can help answer include:

- What are the file system requests? Counts by type?
- What are the read sizes to the file system?
- How much write I/O was synchronous?
- What is the file workload access pattern: random or sequential?
- What files are accessed? By what process or code path? Bytes, I/O counts?
- What file system errors occurred? What type, and for whom?
- What is the source of file system latency? Is it disks, the code path, locks?
- What is the distribution of file system latency?
- What is the ratio of Dcache and Icache hits vs misses?
- What is the page cache hit ratio for reads?
- How effective is prefetch/read-ahead? Should this be tuned?

As shown in the previous figures, you can trace the I/O involved to find the answers to many of these questions.

Event Sources

I/O types are listed in Table 8-1 with the event sources that can instrument them.

Table 8-1 I/O Types and Event Sources

I/O Type	Event Source
Application and library I/O	uprobes
System call I/O	syscalls tracepoints
File system I/O	ext4 (...) tracepoints, kprobes
Cache hits (reads), write-back (writes)	kprobes
Cache misses (reads), write-through (writes)	kprobes
Page cache write-back	writeback tracepoints
Physical disk I/O	block tracepoints, kprobes
Raw I/O	kprobes

This provides visibility from the application to devices. File system I/O may be visible from file system tracepoints, depending on the file system. For example, ext4 provides over one hundred tracepoints.

Overhead

Logical I/O, especially reads and writes to the file system cache, can be very frequent: over 100k events per second. Use caution when tracing these, since the performance overhead at this rate may begin to become noticeable. Also be careful with VFS tracing: VFS is also used by many network I/O paths, so this adds overhead to packets as well, which may also have a high rate.[1]

Physical disk I/O on most servers is typically so low (less than 1000 IOPS), that tracing it incurs negligible overhead. Some storage and database servers may be exceptions: check the I/O rate beforehand with iostat(1).

8.1.3 Strategy

If you are new to file system performance analysis, here is a suggested overall strategy that you can follow. The next sections explain these tools in more detail.

1. Identify the mounted file systems: see df(1) and mount(8).

2. Check the capacity of mounted file systems: in the past, there have been performance issues when certain file systems approach 100% full, due to the use of different free-block-finding algorithms (e.g., FFS, ZFS[2]).

---

1 Although Linux uses software or hardware segmentation offload to reduce the number of packets at this layer, so the event rate may be much lower than the wire-packet rate; see the netsize(8) tool in Chapter 10.

2 The zpool 80% rule, although from memory I was able to move that to 99% when building storage products. Also see "Pool performance can degrade when a pool is very full" from the ZFS Recommended Storage Pool Practices guide [83].

3. Instead of using unfamiliar BPF tools to understand an unknown production workload, first use those on a known workload. On an idle system, create a known file system workload, e.g., using the fio(1) tool.

4. Run opensnoop(8) to see which files are being opened.

5. Run filelife(8) to check for issues of short-lived files.

6. Look for unusually slow file system I/O, and examine process and file details (e.g., using ext4slower(8), btrfsslower(8), zfsslower(8), etc., or as a catch-all with possibly higher overhead, fileslower(8)). It may reveal a workload that can be eliminated, or quantify a problem to aid file system tuning.

7. Examine the distribution of latency for your file systems (e.g., using ext4dist(8), btrfsdist(8), zfsdist(8), etc.). This may reveal bi-modal distributions or latency outliers that are causing performance problems, that can be isolated and investigated more with other tools.

8. Examine the page cache hit ratio over time (e.g., using cachestat(8)): does any other workload perturb the hit ratio, or does any tuning improve it?

9. Use vfsstat(8) to compare logical I/O rates to physical I/O rates from iostat(1): ideally, there is a much higher rate of logical than physical I/O, indicating that caching is effective.

10. Browse and execute the BPF tools listed in the BPF tools section of this book.

8.2 Traditional Tools

Because analysis has historically focused on the disks, there are few traditional tools for observing file systems. This section summarizes file system analysis using df(1), mount(1), strace(1), perf(1), and fatrace(1).

Note that file system performance analysis has often been the domain of micro-benchmark tools, rather than observability tools. A recommended example of a file system micro-benchmark tool is fio(1).

8.2.1 df

df(1) shows file system disk usage:

```
$ df -h
Filesystem      Size  Used Avail Use% Mounted on
udev             93G     0   93G   0% /dev
tmpfs            19G  4.0M   19G   1% /run
/dev/nvme0n1    9.7G  5.1G  4.6G  53% /
tmpfs            93G     0   93G   0% /dev/shm
tmpfs           5.0M     0  5.0M   0% /run/lock
tmpfs            93G     0   93G   0% /sys/fs/cgroup
/dev/nvme1n1    120G   18G  103G  15% /mnt
tmpfs            19G     0   19G   0% /run/user/60000
```

The output includes some virtual physical systems, mounted using the tmpfs device, which are used for containing system state.

Check disk-based file systems for their percent utilization ("Use%" column). For example, in the above output this is "/" and "/mnt", at 53% and 15% full. Once a file system exceeds about 90% full, it may begin to suffer performance issues as available free blocks become fewer and more scattered, turning sequential write workloads into random write workloads. Or it may not: this is really dependent on the file system implementation. It's just worth a quick look.

8.2.2 mount

The mount(1) command makes file systems accessible, and can also list their type and mount flags:

```
$ mount
sysfs on /sys type sysfs (rw,nosuid,nodev,noexec,relatime)
proc on /proc type proc (rw,nosuid,nodev,noexec,relatime,gid=60243,hidepid=2)
udev on /dev type devtmpfs
(rw,nosuid,relatime,size=96902412k,nr_inodes=24225603,mode=755)
devpts on /dev/pts type devpts
(rw,nosuid,noexec,relatime,gid=5,mode=620,ptmxmode=000)
tmpfs on /run type tmpfs (rw,nosuid,noexec,relatime,size=19382532k,mode=755)
/dev/nvme0n1 on / type ext4 (rw,noatime,nobarrier,data=ordered)
[...]
```

This output shows that the "/" (root) file system is ext4, mounted with options including "noatime," a performance tuning that skips recording access timestamps.

8.2.3 strace

strace(1) can trace system calls, which provides a view of file system operations. In this example, the -ttt option is used to print wall timestamps with microsecond resolution as the first field, and -T to print the time spent in syscalls as the last field. All times are printed in seconds.

```
$ strace cksum -tttT /usr/bin/cksum
[...]
1548892204.789115 openat(AT_FDCWD, "/usr/bin/cksum", O_RDONLY) = 3 <0.000030>
1548892204.789202 fadvise64(3, 0, 0, POSIX_FADV_SEQUENTIAL) = 0 <0.000049>
1548892204.789308 fstat(3, {st_mode=S_IFREG|0755, st_size=35000, ...}) = 0 <0.000025>
1548892204.789397 read(3, "\177ELF\2\1\1\0\0\0\0\0\0\0\0\0\3\0>
\0\1\0\0\0\0\33\0\0\0\0\0\0\0"..., 65536) = 35000 <0.000072>
1548892204.789526 read(3, "", 28672)    = 0 <0.000024>
1548892204.790011 lseek(3, 0, SEEK_CUR) = 35000 <0.000024>
1548892204.790087 close(3)              = 0 <0.000025>
[...]
```

strace(1) formats the arguments to syscalls in a human-readable way.

All this information should be extremely valuable for performance analysis, but there's a catch: strace(1) has historically been implemented to use ptrace(2), which operates by inserting breakpoints at the start and end of syscalls. This can massively slow down target software, by as much as over 100 fold, making strace(1) dangerous for use in production environments. It is more useful as a troubleshooting tool, where such slowdowns can be tolerated.

There have been multiple projects to develop an strace(1) replacement using buffered tracing. One is for perf(1), covered next.

8.2.4 perf

The Linux perf(1) multi-tool can trace file system tracepoints, use kprobes to inspect VFS and file system internals, and has a `trace` subcommand as a more efficient version of strace(1). For example:

```
# perf trace cksum /usr/bin/cksum
[...]
0.683 ( 0.013 ms): cksum/20905 openat(dfd: CWD, filename: 0x4517a6cc)          = 3
0.698 ( 0.002 ms): cksum/20905 fadvise64(fd: 3, advice: 2)                     = 0
0.702 ( 0.002 ms): cksum/20905 fstat(fd: 3, statbuf: 0x7fff45169610)           = 0
0.713 ( 0.059 ms): cksum/20905 read(fd: 3, buf: 0x7fff45169790, count: 65536)  = 35000
0.774 ( 0.002 ms): cksum/20905 read(fd: 3, buf: 0x7fff45172048, count: 28672)  = 0
0.875 ( 0.002 ms): cksum/20905 lseek(fd: 3, whence: CUR)                       = 35000
0.879 ( 0.002 ms): cksum/20905 close(fd: 3)                                    = 0
[...]
```

The output of perf trace has been improving in each Linux version (the above demonstrates Linux 5.0). Arnaldo Carvalho de Melo has been improving this further, using kernel header parsing and BPF to improve the output [84]; future versions should, for example, show the filename string for the openat() call, instead of just the filename pointer address.

The more commonly used perf(1) subcommands, stat and record, can be used with file system tracepoints, when such tracepoints for a file system are available. For example, counting ext4 calls system-wide via ext4 tracepoints:

```
# perf stat -e 'ext4:*' -a
^C
 Performance counter stats for 'system wide':

               0      ext4:ext4_other_inode_update_time
               1      ext4:ext4_free_inode
               1      ext4:ext4_request_inode
               1      ext4:ext4_allocate_inode
               1      ext4:ext4_evict_inode
               1      ext4:ext4_drop_inode
             163      ext4:ext4_mark_inode_dirty
               1      ext4:ext4_begin_ordered_truncate
               0      ext4:ext4_write_begin
```

```
      260        ext4:ext4_da_write_begin
        0        ext4:ext4_write_end
        0        ext4:ext4_journalled_write_end
      260        ext4:ext4_da_write_end
        0        ext4:ext4_writepages
        0        ext4:ext4_da_write_pages
[...]
```

The ext4 file system provides around one hundred tracepoints for visibility into its requests and internals. Each of these has format strings for associated information, for example (**do not run this command**):

```
# perf record -e ext4:ext4_da_write_begin -a
^C[ perf record: Woken up 1 times to write data ]
[ perf record: Captured and wrote 1376.293 MB perf.data (14394798 samples) ]
```

Well, this is embarrassing, but it's an important lesson for file system tracing. Because perf record will write events to the file system, if you trace file system (or disk) writes you can create a feedback loop, as I just did here, resulting in 14 million samples and a 1.3 Gbyte perf.data file!

The format string for this example looks like this:

```
# perf script
[...]
  perf 26768 [005] 275068.339717: ext4:ext4_da_write_begin: dev 253,1 ino 1967479 pos
5260704 len 192 flags 0
  perf 26768 [005] 275068.339723: ext4:ext4_da_write_begin: dev 253,1 ino 1967479 pos
5260896 len 8 flags 0
  perf 26768 [005] 275068.339729: ext4:ext4_da_write_begin: dev 253,1 ino 1967479 pos
5260904 len 192 flags 0
  perf 26768 [005] 275068.339735: ext4:ext4_da_write_begin: dev 253,1 ino 1967479 pos
5261096 len 8 flags 0
[...]
```

The format string (one has been highlighted in bold) includes the device, inode, position, length, and flags for the write.

File systems may support many tracepoints, or some, or none. XFS, for example, has around 500. If your file system does not have tracepoints, you can try to instrument its internals using kprobes instead.

For comparison with later BPF tools, consider the same tracepoint instrumented using bpftrace to summarize the length argument as a histogram:

```
# bpftrace -e 'tracepoint:ext4:ext4_da_write_begin { @ = hist(args->len); }'
Attaching 1 probe...
^C
```

```
@:
[16, 32)              26 |@@@@@@@@                                             |
[32, 64)               4 |@                                                    |
[64, 128)             27 |@@@@@@@@                                             |
[128, 256)            15 |@@@@                                                 |
[256, 512)            10 |@@@                                                  |
[512, 1K)              0 |                                                     |
[1K, 2K)               0 |                                                     |
[2K, 4K)              20 |@@@@@@                                               |
[4K, 8K)             164 |@@@@@@@@@@@@@@@@@@@@@@@@@@@@@@@@@@@@@@@@@@@@@@@@@@@@@@@|
```

This shows that most of the lengths were between four and eight Kbytes. This summary is performed in kernel context, and does not require writing a perf.data file to the file system. This avoids not only the overhead of those writes and additional overhead to post-process, but also the risk of a feedback loop.

8.2.5 fatrace

fatrace(1) is a specialized tracer that uses the Linux fanotify API (file access notify). Example output:

```
# fatrace
cron(4794): CW /tmp/#9346 (deleted)
cron(4794): RO /etc/login.defs
cron(4794): RC /etc/login.defs
rsyslogd(872): W /var/log/auth.log
sshd(7553): O /etc/motd
sshd(7553): R /etc/motd
sshd(7553): C /etc/motd
[...]
```

Each line shows the process name, PID, type of event, full path, and optional status. The type of event can be opens (O), reads (R), writes (W), and closes (C). fatrace(1) can be used for workload characterization: understanding the files accessed, and looking for unnecessary work that could be eliminated.

However, for a busy file system workload, fatrace(1) can produce tens of thousands of lines of output every second, and can cost significant CPU resources. This may be alleviated somewhat by filtering to one type of event, for example, opens only:

```
# fatrace -f O
run(6383): O /bin/sleep
run(6383): RO /lib/x86_64-linux-gnu/ld-2.27.so
sleep(6383): O /etc/ld.so.cache
sleep(6383): RO /lib/x86_64-linux-gnu/libc-2.27.so
[...]
```

In the following BPF section, a dedicated BPF tool is provided for this: opensnoop(8), which provides more command line options and is also much more efficient. Comparing the CPU overhead of `fatrace -f O` vs BCC opensnoop(8) for the same heavy file system workload:

```
# pidstat 10
[...]
09:38:54 PM   UID    PID    %usr %system  %guest    %wait    %CPU   CPU  Command
09:39:04 PM     0   6075   11.19   56.44    0.00     0.20   67.63     1  fatrace
[...]
09:50:32 PM     0   7079    0.90    0.20    0.00     0.00    1.10     2  opensnoop
[...]
```

opensnoop(8) is consuming 1.1% CPU vs fatrace(1)'s 67%.[3]

8.3 BPF Tools

This section covers the BPF tools you can use for file system performance analysis and troubleshooting (see Figure 8-3).

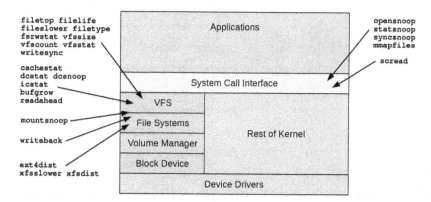

Figure 8-3   BPF tools for file system analysis

These tools are either from the BCC and bpftrace repositories (covered in Chapters 4 and 5), or were created for this book. Some tools appear in both BCC and bpftrace. Table 8-2 lists the origins of the tools covered in this section (BT is short for bpftrace).

---

3 This is running BCC opensnoop(8) as-is. By tuning the polling loop (inserting a delay to increase buffering), I was able to take the overhead down to 0.6%.

Table 8-2 **File System–Related Tools**

Tool	Source	Target	Description
opensnoop	BCC/BT	Syscalls	Trace files opened
statsnoop	BCC/BT	Syscalls	Trace calls to stat(2) varieties
syncsnoop	BCC/BT	Syscalls	Trace sync(2) and variety calls with timestamps
mmapfiles	Book	Syscalls	Count mmap(2) files
scread	Book	Syscalls	Count read(2) files
fmapfault	Book	Page cache	Count file map faults
filelife	BCC/book	VFS	Trace short-lived files with their lifespan in seconds
vfsstat	BCC/BT	VFS	Common VFS operation statistics
vfscount	BCC/BT	VFS	Count all VFS operations
vfssize	Book	VFS	Show VFS read/write sizes
fsrwstat	Book	VFS	Show VFS reads/writes by file system type
fileslower	BCC/book	VFS	Show slow file reads/writes
filetop	BCC	VFS	Top files in use by IOPS and bytes
filetype	Book	VFS	Show VFS reads/writes by file type and process
writesync	Book	VFS	Show regular file writes by sync flag
cachestat	BCC	Page cache	Page cache statistics
writeback	BT	Page cache	Show write-back events and latencies
dcstat	BCC/book	Dcache	Directory cache hit statistics
dcsnoop	BCC/BT	Dcache	Trace directory cache lookups
mountsnoop	BCC	VFS	Trace mount and umounts system-wide
xfsslower	BCC	XFS	Show slow XFS operations
xfsdist	BCC	XFS	Common XFS operation latency histograms
ext4dist	BCC/book	ext4	Common ext4 operation latency histograms
icstat	Book	Icache	Inode cache hit statistics
bufgrow	Book	Buffer cache	Buffer cache growth by process and bytes
readahead	Book	VFS	Show read ahead hits and efficiency

For the tools from BCC and bpftrace, see their repositories for full and updated lists of tool options and capabilities. A selection of the most important capabilities are summarized here.

The following tool summaries include a discussion on translating file descriptors to filenames (see scread(8)).

8.3.1 opensnoop

opensnoop(8)[4] was shown in Chapters 1 and 4, and is provided by BCC and bpftrace. It traces file opens and is useful for discovering the location of data files, log files, and configuration files. It can also discover performance problems caused by frequent opens, or help troubleshoot issues caused by missing files. Example output from a production system, with -T to include timestamps:

```
# opensnoop -T
TIME(s)         PID    COMM      FD ERR PATH
0.000000000     3862   java    5248   0 /proc/loadavg
0.000036000     3862   java    5248   0 /sys/fs/cgroup/cpu,cpuacct/.../cpu.cfs_quota_us
0.000051000     3862   java    5248   0 /sys/fs/cgroup/cpu,cpuacct/.../cpu.cfs_period_us
0.000059000     3862   java    5248   0 /sys/fs/cgroup/cpu,cpuacct/.../cpu.shares
0.012956000     3862   java    5248   0 /proc/loadavg
0.012995000     3862   java    5248   0 /sys/fs/cgroup/cpu,cpuacct/.../cpu.cfs_quota_us
0.013012000     3862   java    5248   0 /sys/fs/cgroup/cpu,cpuacct/.../cpu.cfs_period_us
0.013020000     3862   java    5248   0 /sys/fs/cgroup/cpu,cpuacct/.../cpu.shares
0.021259000     3862   java    5248   0 /proc/loadavg
0.021301000     3862   java    5248   0 /sys/fs/cgroup/cpu,cpuacct/.../cpu.cfs_quota_us
0.021317000     3862   java    5248   0 /sys/fs/cgroup/cpu,cpuacct/.../cpu.cfs
0.021325000     3862   java    5248   0 /sys/fs/cgroup/cpu,cpuacct/.../cpu.shares
0.022079000     3862   java    5248   0 /proc/loadavg
[...]
```

The output rate was high, and shows that a group of four files are read at a rate of one hundred times per second by Java (I just discovered this[5]). The filename has been partially truncated in this book to fit. These are in-memory files of system metrics, and reading them should be fast, but does Java really need to read them one hundred times every second? My next step in analysis was to fetch the stack responsible. Since these were the only file opens that this Java process was performing, I simply counted stacks for the open tracepoint for this PID using:

```
stackcount -p 3862 't:syscalls:sys_enter_openat'
```

This showed the full stack trace, including the Java methods[6] responsible. The culprit turned out to be new load balancing software.

opensnoop(8) works by tracing the open(2) variant syscalls: open(2) and openat(2). The overhead is expected to be negligible as the open(2) rate is typically infrequent.

---

4 Origin: I created the first version as opensnoop.d on 9-May-2004, it was simple, useful, and being able to see opens system-wide was amazing. My prior approaches to achieve this had been to use truss(1M) on a single process only, or BSM auditing, which required changing the state of the system. The name "snoop" comes from the Solaris network sniffer, snoop(1M), and the terminology "snooping events." opensnoop has since been ported to many other tracers, by myself and others. I wrote the BCC version on 17-Sep-2015, and bpftrace on 8-Sep-2018.

5 I intended to run opensnoop on several production servers to find some interesting output to include here. I saw this on the first one I tried.

6 See Chapter 18 for how to get Java stacks and symbols to work.

BCC

Command line usage:

```
opensnoop [options]
```

Options include:

- **-x**: Show only failed opens
- **-p PID**: Measure this process only
- **-n NAME**: Only show opens when the process name contains NAME

bpftrace

The following is the code for the bpftrace version, which summarizes its core functionality. This version does not support options.

```
#!/usr/local/bin/bpftrace

BEGIN
{
        printf("Tracing open syscalls... Hit Ctrl-C to end.\n");
        printf("%-6s %-16s %4s %3s %s\n", "PID", "COMM", "FD", "ERR", "PATH");
}

tracepoint:syscalls:sys_enter_open,
tracepoint:syscalls:sys_enter_openat
{
        @filename[tid] = args->filename;
}

tracepoint:syscalls:sys_exit_open,
tracepoint:syscalls:sys_exit_openat
/@filename[tid]/
{
        $ret = args->ret;
        $fd = $ret > 0 ? $ret : -1;
        $errno = $ret > 0 ? 0 : - $ret;

        printf("%-6d %-16s %4d %3d %s\n", pid, comm, $fd, $errno,
            str(@filename[tid]));
        delete(@filename[tid]);
}

END
{
        clear(@filename);
}
```

This program traces open(2) and openat(2) syscalls, and teases apart the file descriptor or error number from the return value. The filename is cached on the entry probe so that it can be fetched and printed on syscall exit, along with the return value.

8.3.2 statsnoop

statsnoop(8)[7] is a BCC and bpftrace tool similar to opensnoop(8) but for the stat(2) family syscalls. stat(2) returns file statistics. This tool is useful for the same reasons as opensnoop(8): discovering file locations, finding performance issues of load, and troubleshooting missing files. Example production output, with -t for timestamps:

```
# statsnoop -t
TIME(s)         PID    COMM             FD ERR PATH
0.000366347     9118   statsnoop        -1  2 /usr/lib/python2.7/encodings/ascii
0.238452415     744    systemd-resolve   0  0 /etc/resolv.conf
0.238462451     744    systemd-resolve   0  0 /run/systemd/resolve/resolv.conf
0.238470518     744    systemd-resolve   0  0 /run/systemd/resolve/stub-resolv.conf
0.238497017     744    systemd-resolve   0  0 /etc/resolv.conf
0.238506760     744    systemd-resolve   0  0 /run/systemd/resolve/resolv.conf
0.238514099     744    systemd-resolve   0  0 /run/systemd/resolve/stub-resolv.conf
0.238645046     744    systemd-resolve   0  0 /etc/resolv.conf
0.238659277     744    systemd-resolve   0  0 /run/systemd/resolve/resolv.conf
0.238667182     744    systemd-resolve   0  0 /run/systemd/resolve/stub-resolv.conf
[...]
```

This output shows systemd-resolve (which is really "systemd-resolved" truncated) calling stat(2) on the same three files in a loop.

I found a number of occasions when stat(2)s were called tens of thousands of times per second on production servers without a good reason; fortunately, it's a fast syscall, so these were not causing major performance issues. There was one exception, however, where a Netflix microservice hit 100% disk utilization, which I found was caused by a disk usage monitoring agent calling stat(2) continually on a large file system where the metadata did not fully cache, and the stat(2) calls became disk I/O.

This tool works by tracing stat(2) variants via tracepoints: statfs(2), statx(2), newstat(2), and newlstat(2). The overhead of this tool is expected to be negligible, unless the stat(2) rate was very high.

BCC

Command line usage:

```
statsnoop [options]
```

---

7 Origin: I first created this using DTrace on 9-Sep-2007 as a companion to opensnoop. I wrote the BCC version on 8-Feb-2016 and bpftrace on 8-Sep-2018.

Options include:

- **-x:** Show only failed stats
- **-t:** Include a column of timestamps (seconds)
- **-p PID:** Measure this process only

bpftrace

The following is the code for the bpftrace version, which summarizes its core functionality. This version does not support options.

```
#!/usr/local/bin/bpftrace

BEGIN
{
        printf("Tracing stat syscalls... Hit Ctrl-C to end.\n");
        printf("%-6s %-16s %3s %s\n", "PID", "COMM", "ERR", "PATH");
}

tracepoint:syscalls:sys_enter_statfs
{
        @filename[tid] = args->pathname;
}

tracepoint:syscalls:sys_enter_statx,
tracepoint:syscalls:sys_enter_newstat,
tracepoint:syscalls:sys_enter_newlstat
{
        @filename[tid] = args->filename;
}

tracepoint:syscalls:sys_exit_statfs,
tracepoint:syscalls:sys_exit_statx,
tracepoint:syscalls:sys_exit_newstat,
tracepoint:syscalls:sys_exit_newlstat
/@filename[tid]/
{
        $ret = args->ret;
        $errno = $ret >= 0 ? 0 : - $ret;

        printf("%-6d %-16s %3d %s\n", pid, comm, $errno,
            str(@filename[tid]));
        delete(@filename[tid]);
}

END
{
        clear(@filename);
}
```

The program stashes the filename on syscall entry, and fetches it on return to display with return details.

8.3.3 syncsnoop

syncsnoop(8)[8] is a BCC and bpftrace tool to show sync(2) calls with timestamps. sync(2) flushes dirty data to disk. Here is some output from the bpftrace version:

```
# syncsnoop.bt
Attaching 7 probes...
Tracing sync syscalls... Hit Ctrl-C to end.
TIME      PID    COMM             EVENT
08:48:31  14172  TaskSchedulerFo  tracepoint:syscalls:sys_enter_fdatasync
08:48:31  14172  TaskSchedulerFo  tracepoint:syscalls:sys_enter_fdatasync
08:48:31  14172  TaskSchedulerFo  tracepoint:syscalls:sys_enter_fdatasync
08:48:31  14172  TaskSchedulerFo  tracepoint:syscalls:sys_enter_fdatasync
08:48:31  14172  TaskSchedulerFo  tracepoint:syscalls:sys_enter_fdatasync
08:48:40  17822  sync             tracepoint:syscalls:sys_enter_sync
[...]
```

This output shows "TaskSchedulerFo" (a truncated name) calling fdatasync(2) five times in a row. sync(2) calls can trigger bursts of disk I/O, perturbing performance on the system. Timestamps are printed so that they can be correlated with performance issues seen in monitoring software, which would be a clue that sync(2) and the disk I/O it triggers is responsible.

This tool works by tracing sync(2) variants via tracepoints: sync(2), syncfs(2), fsync(2), fdatasync(2), sync_file_range(2), and msync(2). The overhead of this tool is expected to be negligible, as the rate of sync(2) is typically very infrequent.

BCC

The BCC version currently does not support options, and works similarly to the bpftrace version.

bpftrace

The following is the code for the bpftrace version:

```
#!/usr/local/bin/bpftrace

BEGIN
{
        printf("Tracing sync syscalls... Hit Ctrl-C to end.\n");
        printf("%-9s %-6s %-16s %s\n", "TIME", "PID", "COMM", "EVENT");
}
```

---

8 Origin: In the past, I've debugged issues of syncs causing application latency spikes, where disk reads then queued behind a bunch of writes from the sync. These syncs are usually infrequent, so it's always been sufficient to have the second offset of when they occurred to correlate with performance monitoring dashboards. I created this tool for BCC on 13-Aug-2015 and bpftrace on 6-Sep-2018.

```
tracepoint:syscalls:sys_enter_sync,
tracepoint:syscalls:sys_enter_syncfs,
tracepoint:syscalls:sys_enter_fsync,
tracepoint:syscalls:sys_enter_fdatasync,
tracepoint:syscalls:sys_enter_sync_file_range,
tracepoint:syscalls:sys_enter_msync
{
        time("%H:%M:%S  ");
        printf("%-6d %-16s %s\n", pid, comm, probe);
}
```

If sync(2) related calls were found to be a problem, they can be examined further with custom bpftrace, showing the arguments and return value, and issued disk I/O.

8.3.4   mmapfiles

mmapfiles(8)[9] traces mmap(2) and frequency counts the file that is mapped to memory address ranges. For example:

```
# mmapfiles.bt
Attaching 1 probe...
^C

@[usr, bin, x86_64-linux-gnu-ar]: 2
@[lib, x86_64-linux-gnu, libreadline.so.6.3]: 2
@[usr, bin, x86_64-linux-gnu-objcopy]: 2
[...]
@[usr, bin, make]: 226
@[lib, x86_64-linux-gnu, libz.so.1.2.8]: 296
@[x86_64-linux-gnu, gconv, gconv-modules.cache]: 365
@[/, bin, bash]: 670
@[lib, x86_64-linux-gnu, libtinfo.so.5.9]: 672
@[/, bin, cat]: 1152
@[lib, x86_64-linux-gnu, libdl-2.23.so]: 1240
@[lib, locale, locale-archive]: 1424
@[/, etc, ld.so.cache]: 1449
@[lib, x86_64-linux-gnu, ld-2.23.so]: 2879
@[lib, x86_64-linux-gnu, libc-2.23.so]: 2879
@[, , ]: 8384
```

This example has traced a software build. Each file is shown by the filename and two parent directories. The last entry in the output above has no names: it is anonymous mappings for program private data.

---

9 Origin: I created this for DTrace on 18-Oct-2005, and this bpftrace version for this book on 26-Jan-2019.

The source to mmapfiles(8) is:

```
#!/usr/local/bin/bpftrace

#include <linux/mm.h>

kprobe:do_mmap
{
        $file = (struct file *)arg0;
        $name = $file->f_path.dentry;
        $dir1 = $name->d_parent;
        $dir2 = $dir1->d_parent;
        @[str($dir2->d_name.name), str($dir1->d_name.name),
            str($name->d_name.name)] = count();
}
```

It uses kprobes to trace the kernel do_mmap() function, and reads the filename from its struct file * argument, via a struct dentry (directory entry). The dentry only has one component of the path name, so to provide more context on where this file is located, the parent directory and grandparent directory are read and included in the output.[10] Since the mmap() call is expected to be relatively infrequent, the overhead of this tool is expected to be negligible.

The aggregation key can be easily modified to include the process name, to show who is making these mappings ("@[comm, ...]"), and the user-level stack as well to show the code path ("@[comm, ustack, ...]").

Chapter 7 includes a per-event mmap() analysis tool: mmapsnoop(8).

8.3.5   scread

scread(8)[11] traces the read(2) system call and shows the filename it is operating on. For example:

```
# scread.bt
Attaching 1 probe...
^C
@filename[org.chromium.BkPmzg]: 1
@filename[locale.alias]: 2
@filename[chrome_200_percent.pak]: 4
@filename[passwd]: 7
@filename[17]: 44
@filename[scriptCache-current.bin]: 48
[...]
```

---

10 I've suggested adding a BPF kernel helper that takes a struct file or struct dentry, and returns the full path, similar to the kernel d_path().

11 Origin: I created it for this book on 26-Jan-2019.

This shows the "scriptCache-current.bin" file was read(2) 48 times while tracing. This is a syscall-based view into file I/O; see the later filetop(8) tool for a VFS-level view. These tools help characterize file usage, so you can look for inefficiencies.

The source to scread(8) is:

```
#!/usr/local/bin/bpftrace

#include <linux/sched.h>
#include <linux/fs.h>
#include <linux/fdtable.h>

tracepoint:syscalls:sys_enter_read
{
        $task = (struct task_struct *)curtask;
        $file = (struct file *)*($task->files->fdt->fd + args->fd);
        @filename[str($file->f_path.dentry->d_name.name)] = count();
}
```

This pulls the filename from the file descriptor table.

File Descriptor to Filename

This tool has also been included as an example of fetching the filename from a file descriptor (FD) integer. There are at least two ways to do this:

1. Walk from the task_struct to the file descriptor table, and use the FD as the index to find the struct file. The filename can then be found from this struct. This is used by scread(2). This is an unstable technique: the way the file descriptor table is found (task->files->fdt->fd) refers to kernel internals that may change between kernel versions, which would break this script.[12]

2. Trace the open(2) syscall(s), and build a lookup hash with the PID and FD as the keys, and the file/pathname as the value. This can then be queried during read(2) and other syscalls. While this adds additional probes (and overhead), it is a stable technique.

There are many other tools in this book (fmapfault(8), filelife(8), vfssize(8), etc.) that refer to the filename for different operations; however, those work by tracing via the VFS layer, which provides the struct file immediately. While that is also an unstable interface, it makes it possible to find the filename string in fewer steps. Another advantage of VFS tracing is that there is usually only one function per type of operation, whereas with syscalls there can be variants (e.g., read(2), readv(2), preadv(2), pread64(), etc.) that may all need to be traced.

---

12 Some changes are already being considered. Dave Watson has been considering rearranging it to improve performance. Matthew Wilox is also working on changing it to task_struct->files_struct->maple_node->fd[i]. [85] [86]

8.3.6   fmapfault

fmapfault(8)[13] traces page faults for memory mapped files, and counts the process name and filename. For example:

```
# fmapfault.bt
Attaching 1 probe...
^C

@[dirname, libc-2.23.so]: 1
@[date, libc-2.23.so]: 1
[...]
@[cat, libc-2.23.so]: 901
@[sh, libtinfo.so.5.9]: 962
@[sed, ld-2.23.so]: 984
@[sh, libc-2.23.so]: 997
@[cat, ld-2.23.so]: 1252
@[sh, ld-2.23.so]: 1427
@[as, libbfd-2.26.1-system.so]: 3984
@[as, libopcodes-2.26.1-system.so]: 68455
```

This traced a software build, and shows the build processes and libraries in which they were faulting.

Later tools in this book, such as filetop(8), fileslower(8), xfsslower(8), and ext4dist(8), show file I/O via the read(2) and write(2) syscalls (and their variants). But these are not the only way that files can be read and written to: file mappings are another method, which avoids explicit syscalls. fmapfault(8) provides a view of their use, by tracing file page faults and the creation of new page maps. Note that the actual reads and writes to a file may be far higher than the fault rate.

The source to fmapfault(8) is:

```
#!/usr/local/bin/bpftrace

#include <linux/mm.h>

kprobe:filemap_fault
{
        $vf = (struct vm_fault *)arg0;
        $file = $vf->vma->vm_file->f_path.dentry->d_name.name;
        @[comm, str($file)] = count();
}
```

This works by using kprobes to trace the filemap_fault() kernel function and, from its struct vm_fault argument, determine the filename for the mapping. These details will need to be updated as the kernel changes. The overhead of this tool may be noticeable for systems with high fault rates.

---

13 Origin: I created it for this book on 26-Jan-2019.

8.3.7   filelife

filelife(8)[14] is a BCC and bpftrace tool to show the lifespan of short-lived files: those that were created and then deleted while tracing.

The following shows filelife(8) from BCC, during a software build:

```
# filelife
TIME      PID    COMM              AGE(s)    FILE
17:04:51  3576   gcc               0.02      cc9JENsb.s
17:04:51  3632   rm                0.00      kernel.release.tmp
17:04:51  3656   rm                0.00      version.h.tmp
17:04:51  3678   rm                0.00      utsrelease.h.tmp
17:04:51  3698   gcc               0.01      ccTtEADr.s
17:04:51  3701   rm                0.00      .3697.tmp
17:04:51  736    systemd-udevd     0.00      queue
17:04:51  3703   gcc               0.16      cc05cPSr.s
17:04:51  3708   rm                0.01      .purgatory.o.d
17:04:51  3711   gcc               0.01      ccgk4xfE.s
17:04:51  3715   rm                0.01      .stack.o.d
17:04:51  3718   gcc               0.01      ccPiKOgD.s
17:04:51  3722   rm                0.01      .setup-x86_64.o.d
[...]
```

This output shows the many short-lived files created during the build process, which were removed at an age ("AGE(s)") of less than one second.

This tool has been used to find some small performance wins: discovering cases where applications were using temporary files which could be avoided.

This works by using kprobes to trace file creation and deletion via the VFS calls vfs_create() and vfs_unlink(). The overhead of this tool should be negligible as the rate of these should be relatively low.

BCC

Command line usage:

```
filelife [options]
```

Options include:

- **-p** **PID**: Measure this process only

---

14 Origin: I first created it for BCC on 8-Feb-2015 to debug short-lived file usage, and for bpftrace for this book on 31-Jan-2019. It's inspired by my vfslife.d tool from the 2011 DTrace book [Gregg 11].

bpftrace

The following is the code for the bpftrace version:

```
#!/usr/local/bin/bpftrace

#include <linux/fs.h>

BEGIN
{
        printf("%-6s %-16s %8s %s\n", "PID", "COMM", "AGE(ms)", "FILE");
}

kprobe:vfs_create,
kprobe:security_inode_create
{
        @birth[arg1] = nsecs;
}

kprobe:vfs_unlink
/@birth[arg1]/
{
        $dur = nsecs - @birth[arg1];
        delete(@birth[arg1]);
        $dentry = (struct dentry *)arg1;
        printf("%-6d %-16s %8d %s\n", pid, comm, $dur / 1000000,
            str($dentry->d_name.name));
}
```

Newer kernels may not use vfs_create(), so file creation can also be fetched via security_inode_create(), the access-control hook (LSM) for inode creation (if both events occur for the same file, then the birth timestamp is overwritten, but this should not noticeably affect the file lifespan measurement). The birth timestamp is stored keyed on arg1 of those functions, which is the struct dentry pointer, and is used as a unique ID. The filename is also fetched from struct dentry.

8.3.8 vfsstat

vfsstat(8)[15] is a BCC and bpftrace tool to summarize statistics for some common VFS calls: reads and writes (I/O), creates, opens, and fsyncs. This provides the highest-level workload characterization of virtual file system operations. The following shows vfsstat(8) from BCC on a 36-CPU production Hadoop server:

```
# vfsstat
TIME        READ/s  WRITE/s CREATE/s   OPEN/s  FSYNC/s
02:41:23:  1715013    38717        0     5379        0
02:41:24:   947879    30903        0    10547        0
```

---

15 Origin: I first created this for BCC on 14-Aug-2015 and for bpftrace on 6-Sep-2018.

```
02:41:25:   1064800    34387        0    57883        0
02:41:26:   1150847    36104        0     5105        0
02:41:27:   1281686    33610        0     2703        0
02:41:28:   1075975    31496        0     6204        0
02:41:29:    868243    34139        0     5090        0
02:41:30:    889394    31388        0     2730        0
02:41:31:   1124013    35483        0     8121        0
17:21:47:     11443     7876        0      507        0
[...]
```

This output shows a workload reaching over one million reads/second. A surprising detail is the number of file opens per second: over five thousand. These are a slower operation, requiring path name lookups by the kernel and creating file descriptors, plus additional file metadata structs if they weren't already cached. This workload can be investigated further using opensnoop(8) to find ways to reduce the number of opens.

vfsstat(8) works by using kprobes for the functions: vfs_read(), vfs_write(), vfs_fsync(), vfs_open(), and vfs_create(), and printing them as per-second summaries in a table. VFS functions can be very frequent, as shown by this real-world example and, at rates of over one million events per second, the overhead of this tool is expected to be measurable (e.g., 1–3% at this rate). This tool is suited for ad hoc investigations, not 24x7 monitoring, where we'd prefer the overhead to be less than 0.1%.

This tool is only useful for the beginning of your investigation. VFS operations include file systems and networking, and you will need to drill down using other tools (e.g., the following vfssize(8)) to differentiate between them.

BCC

Command line usage:

```
vfsstat [interval [count]]
```

This is modeled on other traditional tools (vmstat(1)).

bpftrace

There is a bpftrace version of vfsstat(8) which prints the same data:

```
#!/usr/local/bin/bpftrace

BEGIN
{
        printf("Tracing key VFS calls... Hit Ctrl-C to end.\n");
}

kprobe:vfs_read*,
kprobe:vfs_write*,
kprobe:vfs_fsync,
kprobe:vfs_open,
kprobe:vfs_create
```

```
{
        @[func] = count();
}


interval:s:1
{
        time();
        print(@);
        clear(@);
}


END
{
        clear(@);
}
```

This outputs every one second, formatted as a list of counts. Wildcards have been used to match variants of vfs_read() and vfs_write(): vfs_readv(), etc. If desired, this could be enhanced to use positional parameters to allow a custom interval to be specified.

8.3.9   vfscount

Instead of these five VFS functions counted by vfsstat(8), you can count all of them (there are over 50) and print a frequency count of their calls using the vfscount(8)[16] tool in BCC and bpftrace. For example, from BCC:

```
# vfscount
Tracing... Ctrl-C to end.
^C
ADDR                FUNC                       COUNT
ffffffffb8473d01 vfs_fallocate                  1
ffffffffb849d301 vfs_kern_mount                 1
ffffffffb84b0851 vfs_fsync_range                2
ffffffffb8487271 vfs_mknod                      3
ffffffffb8487101 vfs_symlink                   68
ffffffffb8488231 vfs_unlink                   376
ffffffffb8478161 vfs_writev                   525
ffffffffb8486d51 vfs_rmdir                    638
ffffffffb8487971 vfs_rename                   762
ffffffffb84874c1 vfs_mkdir                    768
ffffffffb84a2d61 vfs_getxattr                 894
ffffffffb84da761 vfs_lock_file               1601
ffffffffb848c861 vfs_readlink                3309
```

---

16 Origin: I first created this for BCC on 14-Aug-2015 and bpftrace on 6-Sep-2018.

```
ffffffffb84b2451 vfs_statfs                    18346
ffffffffb8475ea1 vfs_open                     108173
ffffffffb847dbf1 vfs_statx_fd                 193851
ffffffffb847dc71 vfs_statx                    274022
ffffffffb847dbb1 vfs_getattr                  330689
ffffffffb847db21 vfs_getattr_nosec            331766
ffffffffb84790a1 vfs_write                    355960
ffffffffb8478df1 vfs_read                     712610
```

While tracing, vfs_read() was most frequent with 712,610 calls, and vfs_fallocate() was called once. The overhead of this tool, like vfsstat(8), can become noticeable at high rates of VFS calls.

Its functionality can also be implemented using funccount(8) from BCC, and bpftrace(8) directly:

```
# funccount 'vfs_*'
# bpftrace -e 'kprobe:vfs_* { @[func] = count(); }'
```

Counting VFS calls like this is only useful as a high-level view, before digging deeper. These calls can be for any subsystem that operates via VFS, including sockets (networking), /dev files, and /proc. The fsrwstat(8) tool, covered next, shows one way to separate these types.

8.3.10 vfssize

vfssize(8)[17] is a bpftrace tool that shows VFS read and write sizes as histograms, broken down by process name and VFS filename or type. Example output from a 48-CPU production API server:

```
# vfssize
Attaching 5 probes...

@[tomcat-exec-393, tomcat_access.log]:
[8K, 16K)              31 |@@@@@@@@@@@@@@@@@@@@@@@@@@@@@@@@@@@@@@@@@@@@@@@@@@@@|

[...]

@[kafka-producer-, TCP]:
[4, 8)               2061 |@@@@@@@@@@@@@@@@@@@@@@@@@@@@@@@@@@@@@@@@@@@@@@@@@@@@|
[8, 16)                 0 |                                                  |
[16, 32)                0 |                                                  |
[32, 64)             2032 |@@@@@@@@@@@@@@@@@@@@@@@@@@@@@@@@@@@@@@@@@@@@@@@@@@@ |

@[EVCACHE_...., FIFO]:
[1]                  6376 |@@@@@@@@@@@@@@@@@@@@@@@@@@@@@@@@@@@@@@@@@@@@@@@@@@@@|

[...]
```

---

17 Origin: I created it for this book on 17-Apr-2019.

```
@[grpc-default-wo, TCP]:
[4, 8)                 101 |                                                              |
[8, 16)              12062 |@@@@@@@@@@@@@@@@@@@@@@@@@@@@@@@@@@@@@@@@@@@@@@@@@@@@@@@@@@@@@@@@|
[16, 32)              8217 |@@@@@@@@@@@@@@@@@@@@@@@@@@@@@@@@@@@@@@@@@@                      |
[32, 64)              7459 |@@@@@@@@@@@@@@@@@@@@@@@@@@@@@@@@@@@@@@                          |
[64, 128)             5488 |@@@@@@@@@@@@@@@@@@@@@@@@@@@@                                   |
[128, 256)            2567 |@@@@@@@@@@@@                                                  |
[256, 512)           11030 |@@@@@@@@@@@@@@@@@@@@@@@@@@@@@@@@@@@@@@@@@@@@@@@@@@@@@@@@@       |
[512, 1K)             9022 |@@@@@@@@@@@@@@@@@@@@@@@@@@@@@@@@@@@@@@@@@@@@@@@                 |
[1K, 2K)              6131 |@@@@@@@@@@@@@@@@@@@@@@@@@@@@@@                                 |
[2K, 4K)              6276 |@@@@@@@@@@@@@@@@@@@@@@@@@@@@@@@                                |
[4K, 8K)              2581 |@@@@@@@@@@@@                                                  |
[8K, 16K)              950 |@@@@                                                          |


@[grpc-default-wo, FIFO]:
[1]                 266897 |@@@@@@@@@@@@@@@@@@@@@@@@@@@@@@@@@@@@@@@@@@@@@@@@@@@@@@@@@@@@@@@@|
```

This highlights how VFS handles networking and FIFO as well. Processes named "grpc-default-wo" (truncated) did 266,897 one-byte reads or writes while tracing: this sounds like an opportunity for a performance optimization, by increasing the I/O size. The same process names also performed many TCP reads and writes, with a bi-modal distribution of sizes. The output has only a single example of a file system file, "tomcat_access.log," with 31 total reads and writes by tomcat-exec-393.

Source for vfssize(8):

```
#!/usr/local/bin/bpftrace

#include <linux/fs.h>

kprobe:vfs_read,
kprobe:vfs_readv,
kprobe:vfs_write,
kprobe:vfs_writev
{
        @file[tid] = arg0;
}

kretprobe:vfs_read,
kretprobe:vfs_readv,
kretprobe:vfs_write,
kretprobe:vfs_writev
/@file[tid]/
{
        if (retval >= 0) {
                $file = (struct file *)@file[tid];
                $name = $file->f_path.dentry->d_name.name;
```

```
                if ((($file->f_inode->i_mode >> 12) & 15) == DT_FIFO) {
                        @[comm, "FIFO"] = hist(retval);
                } else {
                        @[comm, str($name)] = hist(retval);
                }
        }
        delete(@file[tid]);
}


END
{
        clear(@file);
}
```

This fetches the struct file from the first argument to vfs_read(), vfs_readv(), vfs_write(), and vfs_writev(), and gets the resulting size from the kretprobe. Fortunately, for network protocols, the protocol name is stored in the filename. (This originates from struct proto: see Chapter 10 for more about this.) For FIFOs, there is nothing currently stored in the filename, so the text "FIFO" is hardcoded in this tool.

vfssize(8) can be enhanced to include the type of call (read or write) by adding "probe" as a key, the process ID ("pid"), and other details as desired.

8.3.11   fsrwstat

fsrwstat(8)[18] shows how to customize vfsstat(8) to include the file system type. Example output:

```
# fsrwstat
Attaching 7 probes...
Tracing VFS reads and writes... Hit Ctrl-C to end.

18:29:27
@[sockfs, vfs_write]: 1
@[sysfs, vfs_read]: 4
@[sockfs, vfs_read]: 5
@[devtmpfs, vfs_read]: 57
@[pipefs, vfs_write]: 156
@[pipefs, vfs_read]: 160
@[anon_inodefs, vfs_read]: 164
@[sockfs, vfs_writev]: 223
@[anon_inodefs, vfs_write]: 292
@[devpts, vfs_write]: 2634
```

---

18 Origin: I created it for this book on 1-Feb-2019, inspired by my fsrwcount.d tool from the 2011 DTrace book [Gregg 11].

```
@[ext4, vfs_write]: 104268
@[ext4, vfs_read]: 10495

[...]
```

This shows the different file system types as the first column, separating socket I/O from ext4 file system I/O. This particular output shows a heavy (over 100,000 IOPS) ext4 read and write workload.

Source for fsrwstat(8):

```
#!/usr/local/bin/bpftrace

#include <linux/fs.h>

BEGIN
{
        printf("Tracing VFS reads and writes... Hit Ctrl-C to end.\n");
}

kprobe:vfs_read,
kprobe:vfs_readv,
kprobe:vfs_write,
kprobe:vfs_writev
{
        @[str(((struct file *)arg0)->f_inode->i_sb->s_type->name), func] =
            count();
}

interval:s:1
{
        time(); print(@); clear(@);
}

END
{
        clear(@);
}
```

The program traces four VFS functions and frequency counts the file system type and the function name. Since struct file * is the first argument to these functions, it can be cast from arg0, and then members walked until the file system type name is read. The path walked is file -> inode -> superblock -> file_system_type -> name. Because it uses kprobes, this path is an unstable interface, and will need to be updated to match kernel changes.

fsrwstat(8) can be enhanced to include other VFS calls, so long as there is a path to the file system type from the instrumented function arguments (from arg0, or arg1, or arg2, etc.).

8.3.12   fileslower

fileslower(8)[19] is a BCC and bpftrace tool to show synchronous file reads and writes slower than a given threshold. The following shows fileslower(8) from BCC, tracing reads/writes slower than 10 milliseconds (the default threshold), on a 36-CPU production Hadoop server:

```
# fileslower
Tracing sync read/writes slower than 10 ms
TIME(s)    COMM        TID     D BYTES    LAT(ms)  FILENAME
0.142      java        111264  R 4096       25.53  part-00762-37d00f8d...
0.417      java        7122    R 65536      22.80  file.out.index
1.809      java        70560   R 8192       21.71  temp_local_3c9f655b...
2.592      java        47861   W 64512      10.43  blk_2191482458
2.605      java        47785   W 64512      34.45  blk_2191481297
4.454      java        47799   W 64512      24.84  blk_2191482039
4.987      java        111264  R 4096       10.36  part-00762-37d00f8d...
5.091      java        47895   W 64512      15.72  blk_2191483348
5.130      java        47906   W 64512      10.34  blk_2191484018
5.134      java        47799   W 504        13.73  blk_2191482039_1117768266.meta
5.303      java        47984   R 30         12.50  spark-core_2.11-2.3.2...
5.383      java        47899   W 64512      11.27  blk_2191483378
5.773      java        47998   W 64512      10.83  blk_2191487052
[...]
```

This output shows a Java process encountering writes as slow as 34 milliseconds, and displays the names of the files read and written. The direction is the "D" column: "R" for read or "W" for write. The "TIME(s)" column reveals that these slow reads and writes were not very frequent—only a few per second.

Synchronous reads and writes are important as processes block on them and suffer their latency directly. The introduction to this chapter discussed how file system analysis can be more relevant than disk I/O analysis, and this is an example case. In the next chapter, disk I/O latency will be measured, but at that level, applications may not be directly affected by latency issues. With disk I/O, it's easy to find phenomena that look like problems of latency but aren't really problems at all. However, if fileslower(8) shows a latency problem, it's probably an actual problem.

Synchronous reads and writes will block a process. It is likely—but not certain—that this also causes application-level problems. The application could be using a background I/O thread for write flushing and cache warming, which is performing synchronous I/O but without an application request blocking on it.

This tool has been used to prove production latency originated from the file system, and in other cases exonerate the file system: showing no I/O was slow as was assumed.

fileslower(8) works by tracing the synchronous read and write codepath from VFS. The current implementation traces all VFS reads and writes and then filters on those that are synchronous, so the overhead may be higher than expected.

---

19 Origin: I first created this for BCC on 6-Feb-2016, and the bpftrace version for this book on 31 Jan-2019.

BCC

Command line usage:

```
fileslower [options] [min_ms]
```

Options include:

- **-p PID**: Measure this process only

The min_ms argument is the minimum time in milliseconds. If 0 is provided, then all synchronous reads and writes are printed out. This output may be thousands of lines per second, depending on their rate, and unless you have a good reason to see them all, that's not likely something you want to do. A default of 10 milliseconds is used if no argument is provided.

bpftrace

The following is the code for the bpftrace version:

```
#!/usr/local/bin/bpftrace

#include <linux/fs.h>

BEGIN
{
        printf("%-8s %-16s %-6s T %-7s %7s %s\n", "TIMEms", "COMM", "PID",
            "BYTES", "LATms", "FILE");
}

kprobe:new_sync_read,
kprobe:new_sync_write
{
        $file = (struct file *)arg0;
        if ($file->f_path.dentry->d_name.len != 0) {
                @name[tid] = $file->f_path.dentry->d_name.name;
                @size[tid] = arg2;
                @start[tid] = nsecs;
        }
}

kretprobe:new_sync_read
/@start[tid]/
{
        $read_ms = (nsecs - @start[tid]) / 1000000;
        if ($read_ms >= 1) {
                printf("%-8d %-16s %-6d R %-7d %7d %s\n", nsecs / 1000000,
                    comm, pid, @size[tid], $read_ms, str(@name[tid]));
        }
        delete(@start[tid]); delete(@size[tid]); delete(@name[tid]);
}
```

```
kretprobe:new_sync_write
/@start[tid]/
{
        $write_ms = (nsecs - @start[tid]) / 1000000;
        if ($write_ms >= 1) {
                printf("%-8d %-16s %-6d W %-7d %7d %s\n", nsecs / 1000000,
                    comm, pid, @size[tid], $write_ms, str(@name[tid]));
        }
        delete(@start[tid]); delete(@size[tid]); delete(@name[tid]);
}


END
{
        clear(@start); clear(@size); clear(@name);
}
```

This uses kprobes to trace the new_sync_read() and new_sync_write() kernel functions. As kprobes is an unstable interface, there's no guarantee that these will work across different kernel versions, and I've already encountered kernels where they are not available for tracing (inlined). The BCC version employs the workaround, by tracing higher-level __vfs_read() and __vfs_write() internal functions and then filtering for those that are synchronous.

8.3.13 filetop

filetop(8)[20] is BCC tool that is like top(1) for files, showing the most frequently read or written filenames. Example output on a 36-CPU production Hadoop server:

```
# filetop
Tracing... Output every 1 secs. Hit Ctrl-C to end

02:31:38 loadavg: 39.53 36.71 32.66 26/3427 30188

TID     COMM           READS  WRITES  R_Kb    W_Kb   T FILE
113962  java           15171  0       60684   0      R part-00903-37d00f8d-ecf9-4...
23110   java           7      0       7168    0      R temp_local_6ba99afa-351d-4...
25836   java           48     0       3072    0      R map_4141.out
26890   java           46     0       2944    0      R map_5827.out
26788   java           42     0       2688    0      R map_4363.out
26788   java           18     0       1152    0      R map_4756.out.merged
70560   java           130    0       1085    0      R temp_local_1bd4386b-b33c-4...
70560   java           130    0       1079    0      R temp_local_a3938a84-9f23-4...
70560   java           127    0       1053    0      R temp_local_3c9f655b-06e4-4...
26890   java           16     0       1024    0      R map_11374.out.merged
26890   java           15     0       960     0      R map_5262.out.merged
```

_____

20 Origin: I created this for BCC on 6-Feb-2016, inspired by top(1) by William LeFebvre.

```
26788   java              15    0    960    0       R map_20423.out.merged
26788   java              14    0    896    0       R map_4371.out.merged
26890   java              14    0    896    0       R map_10138.out.merged
26890   java              13    0    832    0       R map_4991.out.merged
25836   java              13    0    832    0       R map_3994.out.merged
25836   java              13    0    832    0       R map_4651.out.merged
25836   java              13    0    832    0       R map_16267.out.merged
25836   java              13    0    832    0       R map_15255.out.merged
26788   java              12    0    768    0       R map_6917.out.merged
[...]
```

By default, the top twenty files are shown, sorted by the read bytes column, and the screen redraws every second. This particular output shows that a "part-00903-37d00f8d" file (file-name truncated) had the most read bytes at around 60 Mbytes during that one-second interval, from about 15k reads. Not shown is the average read size, but that can be calculated from those numbers to be 4.0 Kbytes.

This tool is used for workload characterization and general file system observability. Just as you can discover an unexpected CPU-consuming process using top(1), this may help you discover an unexpected I/O-busy file.

filetop by default also only shows regular files.[21] The -a option shows all files, including TCP sockets:

```
# filetop -a
[...]
TID      COMM          READS  WRITES  R_Kb   W_Kb   T FILE
32857    java          718    0       15756  0      S TCP
120597   java          12     0       12288  0      R temp_local_3807d4ca-b41e-3...
32770    java          502    0       10118  0      S TCP
32507    java          199    0       4212   0      S TCP
88371    java          186    0       1775   0      R temp_local_215ae692-35a4-2...
[...]
```

The columns are:

- **TID:** Thread ID
- **COMM:** Process/thread name
- **READS:** Number of reads during interval
- **WRITES:** Number of writes during interval
- **R_Kb:** Total read Kbytes during interval
- **W_Kb:** Total write Kbytes during interval
- **T:** Type: R == Regular file, S == Socket, O == Other
- **FILE:** Filename

---

21 "regular" refers to the file type: DT_REG in the kernel source. Other file types include DT_DIR for directories, DT_BLK for block special devices, etc.

This works by using kprobes to trace the vfs_read() and vfs_write() kernel functions. The file type is read from the inode mode, via the S_ISREG() and S_ISSOCK() macros.

The overhead of this tool, like earlier ones, can begin to be noticeable because VFS reads/writes can be frequent. This also traces various statistics, including the filename, which makes its overhead a little higher than for other tools.

Command line usage:

```
filetop [options] [interval [count]]
```

Options include:

- **-C**: Don't clear the screen: rolling output
- **-r ROWS**: Print this many rows (default 20)
- **-p PID**: Measure this process only

The -C option is useful for preserving the terminal's scroll-back buffer, so that patterns over time can be examined.

8.3.14   writesync

writesync(8)[22] is a bpftrace tool that traces VFS writes to regular files and shows which were using a synchronous write flag (O_SYNC or O_DSYNC). For example:

```
# writesync.bt
Attaching 2 probes...
Tracing VFS write sync flags... Hit Ctrl-C to end.
^C

@regular[cronolog, output_20190520_06.log]: 1
@regular[VM Thread, gc.log]: 2
@regular[cronolog, catalina_20190520_06.out]: 9
@regular[tomcat-exec-142, tomcat_access.log]: 15
[...]

@sync[dd, outfile]: 100
```

This output shows shows a number of regular writes to files, and one hundred writes from a "dd" process to a file called "outfile1." The dd(1) was an artificial test using:

```
dd if=/dev/zero of=outfile oflag=sync count=100
```

Synchronous writes must wait for the storage I/O to complete (write through), unlike normal I/O which can complete from cache (write-back). This makes synchronous I/O slow, and if the synchronous flag is unnecessary, removing it can greatly improve performance.

---

22 Origin: I created it for this book on 19-May-2019.

The source to writesync(8) is:

```
#!/usr/local/bin/bpftrace

#include <linux/fs.h>
#include <asm-generic/fcntl.h>

BEGIN
{
        printf("Tracing VFS write sync flags... Hit Ctrl-C to end.\n");
}

kprobe:vfs_write,
kprobe:vfs_writev
{
        $file = (struct file *)arg0;
        $name = $file->f_path.dentry->d_name.name;
        if ((($file->f_inode->i_mode >> 12) & 15) == DT_REG) {
                if ($file->f_flags & O_DSYNC) {
                        @sync[comm, str($name)] = count();
                } else {
                        @regular[comm, str($name)] = count();
                }
        }
}
```

This checks that the file is a regular file (DT_REG), and then checks for the presence of the O_DSYNC flag (which is also set by O_SYNC).

8.3.15   filetype

filetype(8)[23] is a bpftrace tool that traces VFS reads and writes along with the type of the file and process name. For example, on a 36-CPU system during a software build:

```
# filetype.bt
Attaching 4 probes...
^C

@[regular, vfs_read, expr]: 1
@[character, vfs_read, bash]: 10
[...]
@[socket, vfs_write, sshd]: 435
@[fifo, vfs_write, cat]: 464
```

---

23 Origin: I created it for this book on 2-Feb-2019.

```
@[regular, vfs_write, sh]: 697
@[regular, vfs_write, as]: 785
@[regular, vfs_read, objtool]: 932
@[fifo, vfs_read, make]: 1033
@[regular, vfs_read, as]: 1437
@[regular, vfs_read, gcc]: 1563
@[regular, vfs_read, cat]: 2196
@[regular, vfs_read, sh]: 8391
@[regular, vfs_read, fixdep]: 11299
@[fifo, vfs_read, sh]: 15422
@[regular, vfs_read, cc1]: 16851
@[regular, vfs_read, make]: 39600
```

This output shows that most of the file types were "regular", for normal files, which were read and written by build software (make(1), cc1(1), gcc(1), etc.). The output also includes socket writes for sshd, which is the SSH server sending packets, and character reads from bash, which would be the bash shell reading input from the /dev/pts/1 character device.

The output also includes FIFO[24] reads and writes. Here's a short demo to illustrate their role:

```
window1$ tar cf - dir1 | gzip > dir1.tar.gz
window2# filetype.bt
Attaching 4 probes...
^C
[...]
@[regular, vfs_write, gzip]: 36
@[fifo, vfs_write, tar]: 191
@[fifo, vfs_read, gzip]: 191
@[regular, vfs_read, tar]: 425
```

The FIFO type is for shell pipes. Here the tar(1) command is performing reads of regular files, and then writing them to a FIFO. gzip(1) is reading from the FIFO, and writing to a regular file. This is all visible in the output.

The source to filetype(8) is:

```
#!/usr/local/bin/bpftrace

#include <linux/fs.h>

BEGIN
{
        // from uapi/linux/stat.h:
        @type[0xc000] = "socket";
        @type[0xa000] = "link";
```

---

24 FIFO: first-in, first-out special file (named pipe). See the FIFO(7) man page.

```
        @type[0x8000] = "regular";
        @type[0x6000] = "block";
        @type[0x4000] = "directory";
        @type[0x2000] = "character";
        @type[0x1000] = "fifo";
        @type[0] = "other";
}

kprobe:vfs_read,
kprobe:vfs_readv,
kprobe:vfs_write,
kprobe:vfs_writev
{
        $file = (struct file *)arg0;
        $mode = $file->f_inode->i_mode;
        @[@type[$mode & 0xf000], func, comm] = count();
}

END
{
        clear(@type);
}
```

The BEGIN program sets up a hash table (@type) for inode file modes to strings, which are then looked up in the kprobes for the VFS functions.

Two months after writing this tool, I was developing socket I/O tools and noticed that I had not written a VFS tool to expose the file modes from include/linux/fs.h (DT_FIFO, DT_CHR, etc.). I developed this tool to do it (dropping the "DT_" prefix):

```
#!/usr/local/bin/bpftrace

#include <linux/fs.h>

BEGIN
{
        printf("Tracing VFS reads and writes... Hit Ctrl-C to end.\n");
        // from include/linux/fs.h:
        @type2str[0] = "UNKNOWN";
        @type2str[1] = "FIFO";
        @type2str[2] = "CHR";
        @type2str[4] = "DIR";
        @type2str[6] = "BLK";
        @type2str[8] = "REG";
        @type2str[10] = "LNK";
```

```
        @type2str[12] = "SOCK";
        @type2str[14] = "WHT";
}


kprobe:vfs_read,
kprobe:vfs_readv,
kprobe:vfs_write,
kprobe:vfs_writev
{
        $file = (struct file *)arg0;
        $type = ($file->f_inode->i_mode >> 12) & 15;
        @[@type2str[$type], func, comm] = count();

}


END
{
        clear(@type2str);

}
```

When I went to add it to this chapter, I discovered I had accidentally written a second version of filetype(8), this time using a different header file for file type lookups. I've included the source here as a lesson that sometimes there is more than one way to write these tools.

8.3.16 cachestat

cachestat(8)[25] is a BCC tool that shows page cache hit and miss statistics. This can be used to check the hit ratio and efficiency of the page cache, and run while investigating system and application tuning for feedback on cache performance. For example, from a 36-CPU production Hadoop instance:

```
# cachestat
   HITS   MISSES  DIRTIES HITRATIO  BUFFERS_MB  CACHED_MB
  53401    2755    20953   95.09%          14      90223
  49599    4098    21460   92.37%          14      90230
  16601    2689    61329   86.06%          14      90381
  15197    2477    58028   85.99%          14      90522
  18169    4402    51421   80.50%          14      90656
  57604    3064    22117   94.95%          14      90693
  76559    3777     3128   95.30%          14      90692
  49044    3621    26570   93.12%          14      90743
[...]
```

25 Origin: I first created this as an experimental tool using Ftrace for my perf-tools collection on 28-Dec-2014, while I was on vacation in Yulara, near Uluru, in the outback of Australia [87]. Since it's so tied to kernel internals, it contains a block comment in the header to describe it as a sand castle: a new kernel version can easily break it and wash it away. Allan McAleavy ported it to BCC on 6-Nov-2015.

This output shows a hit ratio often exceeding 90%. Tuning the system and application to bring this 90% close to 100% can result in very large performance wins (much larger than the 10% difference in hit ratio), as the application more often runs from memory without waiting on disk I/O.

Large-scale cloud databases such as Cassandra, Elasticsearch, and PostgreSQL often make heavy usage of the page cache to ensure that the hot dataset is always live in memory. This means that one of the most important questions in provisioning datastores is if the working set fits into the provisioned memory capacity. Netflix teams managing stateful services use this cachestat(8) tool to help answer this question and inform decisions such as what data compression algorithms to use and if adding more memory to a cluster would actually help performance.

A couple of simple examples can better explain the cachestat(8) output. Here is an idle system, where a one-Gbyte file is created. The -T option is now used to show a timestamp column:

```
# cachestat -T
TIME       HITS   MISSES  DIRTIES HITRATIO    BUFFERS_MB  CACHED_MB
21:06:47      0        0        0    0.00%             9        191
21:06:48      0        0   120889    0.00%             9        663
21:06:49      0        0   141167    0.00%             9       1215
21:06:50    795        0        1  100.00%             9       1215
21:06:51      0        0        0    0.00%             9       1215
```

The DIRTIES column shows pages being written to the page cache (they are "dirty"), and the CACHED_MB column increases by 1024 Mbytes: the size of the newly created file.

This file is then flushed to disk and dropped from the page cache (this drops all pages from the page cache):

```
# sync
# echo 3 > /proc/sys/vm/drop_caches
```

Now the file is read twice. This time a cachestat(8) interval of 10 seconds is used:

```
# cachestat -T 10
TIME       HITS   MISSES  DIRTIES HITRATIO    BUFFERS_MB  CACHED_MB
21:08:58    771        0        1  100.00%             8        190
21:09:08  33036    53975       16   37.97%             9        400
21:09:18     15    68544        2    0.02%             9        668
21:09:28    798    65632        1    1.20%             9        924
21:09:38      5    67424        0    0.01%             9       1187
21:09:48   3757    11329        0   24.90%             9       1232
21:09:58   2082        0        1  100.00%             9       1232
21:10:08 268421       11       12  100.00%             9       1232
21:10:18      6        0        0  100.00%             9       1232
21:10:19    784        0        1  100.00%             9       1232
```

The file is read between 21:09:08 and 21:09:48, seen by the high rate of MISSES, a low HITRATIO, and the increase in the page cache size in CACHED_MB by 1024 Mbytes. At 21:10:08 the file was read the second time, now hitting entirely from the page cache (100%).

cachestat(8) works by using kprobes to instrument these kernel functions:

- **mark_page_accessed()**: For measuring cache accesses
- **mark_buffer_dirty()**: For measuring cache writes
- **add_to_page_cache_lru()**: For measuring page additions
- **account_page_dirtied()**: For measuring page dirties

While this tool provides crucial insight for the page cache hit ratio, it is also tied to kernel implementation details via these kprobes and will need maintenance to work on different kernel versions. Its best use may be simply to show that that such a tool is possible.[26]

These page cache functions can be very frequent: they can be called millions of times a second. The overhead for this tool for extreme workloads can exceed 30%, though for normal workloads it will be much less. You should test in a lab environment and quantify before production use.

Command line usage:

```
cachestat [options] [interval [count]]
```

There is a -T option to include the timestamp on the output.

There is another BCC tool, cachetop(8),[27] that prints the cachestat(8) statistics by process in a top(1)-style display using the curses library.

8.3.17 writeback

writeback(8)[28] is a bpftrace tool that shows the operation of page cache write-back: when pages are scanned, when dirty pages are flushed to disk, the type of write-back event, and the duration. For example, on a 36-CPU system:

```
# writeback.bt
Attaching 4 probes...
Tracing writeback... Hit Ctrl-C to end.
TIME      DEVICE   PAGES   REASON       ms
03:42:50  253:1    0       periodic     0.013
03:42:55  253:1    40      periodic     0.167
03:43:00  253:1    0       periodic     0.005
```

26 When I presented cachestat(8) in my LSFMM keynote, the mm engineers stressed that it will break, and later explained some of the challenges in doing this correctly for future kernels (thanks, Mel Gorman). Some of us, like at Netflix, have it working well enough for our kernels and workloads. But to become a robust tool for everyone, I think either (A) someone needs to spend a few weeks studying the kernel source, trying different workloads, and working with the mm engineers to truly solve it; or perhaps even better, (B) add /proc statistics so this can switch to being a counter-based tool.

27 Origin: cachetop(8) was created by Emmanuel Bretelle on 13-Jul-2016.

28 Origin: I created it for bpftrace on 14-Sep-2018.

```
03:43:01   253:1    11268    background       6.112
03:43:01   253:1    11266    background       7.977
03:43:01   253:1    11314    background       22.209
03:43:02   253:1    11266    background       20.698
03:43:02   253:1    11266    background       7.421
03:43:02   253:1    11266    background       11.382
03:43:02   253:1    11266    background       6.954
03:43:02   253:1    11266    background       8.749
03:43:02   253:1    11266    background       14.518
03:43:04   253:1    38836    sync             64.655
03:43:04   253:1    0        sync             0.004
03:43:04   253:1    0        sync             0.002
03:43:09   253:1    0        periodic         0.012
03:43:14   253:1    0        periodic         0.016
[...]
```

This output begins by showing a periodic write-back every five seconds. These were not writing many pages (0, 40, 0). Then there was a burst of background write-backs, writing tens of thousands of pages, and taking between 6 and 22 milliseconds for each write-back. This is asynchronous page flushing for when the system is running low on free memory. If the timestamps were correlated with application performance problems seen by other monitoring tools (e.g., cloud-wide performance monitoring), this would be a clue that the application problem was caused by file system write-back. The behavior of the write-back flushing is tunable (e.g., sysctl(8) and vm.dirty_writeback_centisecs). A sync write-back occurred at 3:43:04, writing 38,836 pages in 64 milliseconds.

The source to writeback(8) is:

```
#!/usr/local/bin/bpftrace

BEGIN
{
        printf("Tracing writeback... Hit Ctrl-C to end.\n");
        printf("%-9s %-8s %-8s %-16s %s\n", "TIME", "DEVICE", "PAGES",
            "REASON", "ms");

        // see /sys/kernel/debug/tracing/events/writeback/writeback_start/format
        @reason[0] = "background";
        @reason[1] = "vmscan";
        @reason[2] = "sync";
        @reason[3] = "periodic";
        @reason[4] = "laptop_timer";
        @reason[5] = "free_more_memory";
        @reason[6] = "fs_free_space";
        @reason[7] = "forker_thread";
}
```

```
tracepoint:writeback:writeback_start
{
        @start[args->sb_dev] = nsecs;
        @pages[args->sb_dev] = args->nr_pages;
}

tracepoint:writeback:writeback_written
/@start[args->sb_dev]/
{
        $sb_dev = args->sb_dev;
        $s = @start[$sb_dev];
        $lat = $s ? (nsecs - $s) / 1000 : 0;
        $pages = @pages[args->sb_dev] - args->nr_pages;

        time("%H:%M:%S  ");
        printf("%-8s %-8d %-16s %d.%03d\n", args->name, $pages,
            @reason[args->reason], $lat / 1000, $lat % 1000);

        delete(@start[$sb_dev]);
        delete(@pages[$sb_dev]);
}

END
{
        clear(@reason);
        clear(@start);
}
```

This populates @reason to map the reason identifiers to human-readable strings. The time during write-back is measured, keyed on the device, and all details are printed in the writeback_written tracepoint. The page count is determined by a drop in the args->nr_pages argument, following how the kernel accounts for this (see the wb_writeback() source in fs/fs-writeback.c).

8.3.18   dcstat

dcstat(8)[29] is a BCC and bpftrace tool that shows directory entry cache (dcache) statistics. The following shows dcstat(8) from BCC, on a 36-CPU production Hadoop instance:

```
# dcstat
TIME        REFS/s    SLOW/s    MISS/s    HIT%
22:48:20:   661815    27942     20814     96.86
22:48:21:   540677    87375     80708     85.07
```

---

29 Origin: I first created a similar tool called dnlcstat on 10-Mar-2004 to instrument the Solaris directory name lookup cache, using the kernel Kstat statistics. I created the BCC dcstat(8) on 9-Feb-2016, and the bpftrace version for this book on 26-Mar-2019.

```
22:48:22:    271719    4042     914    99.66
22:48:23:    434353    4765      37    99.99
22:48:24:    766316    5860     607    99.92
22:48:25:    567078    7866    2279    99.60
22:48:26:    556771   26845   20431    96.33
22:48:27:    558992    4095     747    99.87
22:48:28:    299356    3785     105    99.96
[...]
```

This output shows hit ratios of over 99%, and a workload of over 500k references per second. The columns are:

- **REFS/s:** dcache references.
- **SLOW/s:** Since Linux 2.5.11, the dcache has an optimization to avoid cacheline bouncing during lookups of common entries ("/", "/usr") [88]. This column shows when this optimization was not used, and the dcache lookup took the "slow" path.
- **MISS/s:** The dcache lookup failed. The directory entry may still be memory as part of the page cache, but the specialized dcache did not return it.
- **HIT%:** Ratio of hits to references.

This works by using kprobes to instrument the lookup_fast() kernel function, and kretprobes for d_lookup(). The overhead of this tool may become noticeable depending on the workload, since these functions can be frequently called as seen in the example output. Test and quantify in a lab environment.

BCC

Command line usage:

```
dcstat [interval [count]]
```

This is modeled on other traditional tools (e.g., vmstat(1)).

bpftrace

Example output from the bpftrace version:

```
# dcstat.bt
Attaching 4 probes...
Tracing dcache lookups... Hit Ctrl-C to end.
    REFS    MISSES   HIT%
   234096    16111   93%
   495104    36714   92%
   461846    36543   92%
   460245    36154   92%
[...]
```

Source code:

```
#!/usr/local/bin/bpftrace

BEGIN
{
        printf("Tracing dcache lookups... Hit Ctrl-C to end.\n");
        printf("%10s %10s %5s%\n", "REFS", "MISSES", "HIT%");
}


kprobe:lookup_fast { @hits++; }


kretprobe:d_lookup /retval == 0/ { @misses++; }


interval:s:1
{
        $refs = @hits + @misses;
        $percent = $refs > 0 ? 100 * @hits / $refs : 0;
        printf("%10d %10d %4d%%\n", $refs, @misses, $percent);
        clear(@hits);
        clear(@misses);
}


END
{
        clear(@hits);
        clear(@misses);
}
```

This uses a ternary operator to avoid a divide-by-zero condition, in the unlikely case that there were zero hits and misses measured.[30]

8.3.19   dcsnoop

dcsnoop(8).[31] is a BCC and bpftrace tool to trace directory entry cache (dcache) lookups, showing details on every lookup. The output can be verbose, thousands of lines per second, depending on the lookup rate. The following shows dcsnoop(8) from BCC, with -a to show all lookups:

```
# dcsnoop -a
TIME(s)      PID     COMM          T FILE
0.005463     2663    snmpd         R proc/sys/net/ipv6/conf/eth0/forwarding
```

---

30 Note that BPF does have protections against divide-by-zero [89]; it is still a good idea to check before sending a program to BPF, to avoid being rejected by the BPF verifier.
31 Origin: I first created this as dnlcsnoop using DTrace on 17-Mar-2004, the BCC version on 9-Feb-2016, and the bpftrace version on 8-Sep-2018.

```
0.005471    2663    snmpd           R sys/net/ipv6/conf/eth0/forwarding
0.005479    2663    snmpd           R net/ipv6/conf/eth0/forwarding
0.005487    2663    snmpd           R ipv6/conf/eth0/forwarding
0.005495    2663    snmpd           R conf/eth0/forwarding
0.005503    2663    snmpd           R eth0/forwarding
0.005511    2663    snmpd           R forwarding
[...]
```

This output shows a /proc/sys/net/ipv6/conf/eth0/forwarding path lookup by snmpd, and shows how the path is walked looking up each component. The "T" column is the type: R == reference, M == miss.

This works the same way as dcstat(8), using kprobes. The overhead of this tool is expected to be high for any moderate workload, as it is printing a line of output per event. It is intended to be used for short periods to investigate misses seen in dcstat(8).

BCC

The BCC version supports only one command line option: -a, to show both references and misses. By default, only misses are shown.

bpftrace

The following is the code for the bpftrace version:

```
#!/usr/local/bin/bpftrace

#include <linux/fs.h>
#include <linux/sched.h>

// from fs/namei.c:
struct nameidata {
        struct path      path;
        struct qstr      last;
        // [...]
};

BEGIN
{
        printf("Tracing dcache lookups... Hit Ctrl-C to end.\n");
        printf("%-8s %-6s %-16s %1s %s\n", "TIME", "PID", "COMM", "T", "FILE");
}

// comment out this block to avoid showing hits:
kprobe:lookup_fast
```

```
{
        $nd = (struct nameidata *)arg0;
        printf("%-8d %-6d %-16s R %s\n", elapsed / 1000000, pid, comm,
            str($nd->last.name));
}


kprobe:d_lookup
{
        $name = (struct qstr *)arg1;
        @fname[tid] = $name->name;
}


kretprobe:d_lookup
/@fname[tid]/
{
        if (retval == 0) {
                printf("%-8d %-6d %-16s M %s\n", elapsed / 1000000, pid, comm,
                    str(@fname[tid]));
        }
        delete(@fname[tid]);
}
```

This program needed to reference the "last" member from the nameidata struct, which was not available in kernel headers, so enough of it was declared in this program to find that member.

8.3.20 mountsnoop

mountsnoop(8)[32] is a BCC tool that shows when file systems are mounted. This can be used for troubleshooting, especially for container environments that mount file systems on container startup. Example output:

```
# mountsnoop
COMM             PID    TID    MNT_NS       CALL
systemd-logind   1392   1392   4026531840   mount("tmpfs", "/run/user/116", "tmpfs",
MS_NOSUID|MS_NODEV, "mode=0700,uid=116,gid=65534,size=25778348032") = 0
systemd-logind   1392   1392   4026531840   umount("/run/user/116", MNT_DETACH) = 0
[...]
```

This output shows systemd-logind performing a mount(2) and umount(2) of a tmpfs at /run/user/116.

This works by tracing the mount(2) and unmount(2) syscalls, using kprobes for the functions that perform these. Since mounts should be an infrequent activity, the overhead of this tool is expected to be negligible.

---

32 Origin: It was created by Omar Sandoval on 14-Oct-2016.

8.3.21 xfsslower

xfsslower(8)[33] is a BCC tool to trace common XFS file system operations; it prints per-event details for those operations that were slower than a given threshold. The operations traced are reads, writes, opens, and fsync.

The following shows xfsslower(8) from BCC tracing these operations slower than 10 milliseconds (the default) from a 36-CPU production instance:

```
# xfsslower
Tracing XFS operations slower than 10 ms
TIME      COMM         PID    T BYTES   OFF_KB   LAT(ms)  FILENAME
02:04:07 java          5565   R 63559   360237    17.16 shuffle_2_63762_0.data
02:04:07 java          5565   R 44203   151427    12.59 shuffle_0_12138_0.data
02:04:07 java          5565   R 39911   106647    34.96 shuffle_0_12138_0.data
02:04:07 java          5565   R 65536   340788    14.80 shuffle_2_101288_0.data
02:04:07 java          5565   R 65536   340744    14.73 shuffle_2_103383_0.data
02:04:07 java          5565   R 64182   361925    59.44 shuffle_2_64928_0.data
02:04:07 java          5565   R 44215   108517    12.14 shuffle_0_12138_0.data
02:04:07 java          5565   R 63370   338650    23.23 shuffle_2_104532_0.data
02:04:07 java          5565   R 63708   360777    22.61 shuffle_2_65806_0.data
[...]
```

This output shows frequent reads by Java that exceed 10 milliseconds.

Similar to fileslower(8), this is instrumenting close to the application, and latency seen here is likely suffered by the application.

This works by using kprobes to trace the kernel functions in the file system's struct file_operations, which is its interface to VFS. From Linux fs/xfs/xfs_file.c:

```
const struct file_operations xfs_file_operations = {
        .llseek         = xfs_file_llseek,
        .read_iter      = xfs_file_read_iter,
        .write_iter     = xfs_file_write_iter,
        .splice_read    = generic_file_splice_read,
        .splice_write   = iter_file_splice_write,
        .unlocked_ioctl = xfs_file_ioctl,
#ifdef CONFIG_COMPAT
        .compat_ioctl   = xfs_file_compat_ioctl,
#endif
        .mmap           = xfs_file_mmap,
        .mmap_supported_flags = MAP_SYNC,
        .open           = xfs_file_open,
        .release        = xfs_file_release,
        .fsync          = xfs_file_fsync,
```

---

33 Origin: I created this on 11-Feb-2016, inspired by my zfsslower.d tool from the 2011 DTrace book [Gregg 11].

```
        .get_unmapped_area = thp_get_unmapped_area,
        .fallocate        = xfs_file_fallocate,
        .remap_file_range = xfs_file_remap_range,
};
```

The xfs_file_read_iter() function is traced for reads, and xfs_file_write_iter() for writes, and so on. These functions may change from kernel version to version, and so this tool will need maintenance. The overhead of this tool is relative to the rate of the operations, plus the rate of events printed that exceeded the threshold. The rate of operations for busy workloads can be high enough that the overhead is noticeable, even when there are no operations slower than the threshold so that no output is printed.

Command line usage:

```
xfsslower [options] [min_ms]
```

Options include:

- **-p PID**: Measure this process only

The min_ms argument is the minimum time in milliseconds. If 0 is provided, then all traced operations are printed out. This output may be thousands of lines per second, depending on their rate, and unless you have a good reason to see them all, it is likely undesirable. A default of 10 milliseconds is used if no argument is provided.

The next tool shows a bpftrace program instrumenting the same functions for latency histograms, rather than per-event output.

8.3.22 xfsdist

xfsdist(8)[34] is a BCC and bpftrace tool to instrument the XFS file system and show the distribution of latencies as histograms for common operations: reads, writes, opens, and fsync. The following shows xfsdist(8) from BCC, running on a 36-CPU production Hadoop instance for 10 seconds:

```
# xfsdist 10 1
Tracing XFS operation latency... Hit Ctrl-C to end.

23:55:23:

operation = 'read'
     usecs             : count    distribution
         0 -> 1        : 5492     |****************************            |
         2 -> 3        : 4384     |**********************                  |
         4 -> 7        : 3387     |*****************                       |
         8 -> 15       : 1675     |********                                |
        16 -> 31       : 7429     |****************************************|
```

---

34 Origin: I created this for BCC on 12-Feb-2016 and bpftrace on 8-Sep-2018. The tool is inspired by my 2012 zfsdist.d DTrace tool.

```
        32 -> 63       : 574     |***                                    |
        64 -> 127      : 407     |**                                     |
       128 -> 255      : 163     |                                       |
       256 -> 511      : 253     |*                                      |
       512 -> 1023     : 98      |                                       |
      1024 -> 2047     : 89      |                                       |
      2048 -> 4095     : 39      |                                       |
      4096 -> 8191     : 37      |                                       |
      8192 -> 16383    : 27      |                                       |
     16384 -> 32767    : 11      |                                       |
     32768 -> 65535    : 21      |                                       |
     65536 -> 131071   : 10      |                                       |

operation = 'write'
    usecs              : count    distribution
         0 -> 1        : 414     |                                       |
         2 -> 3        : 1327    |                                       |
         4 -> 7        : 3367    |**                                     |
         8 -> 15       : 22415   |*************                          |
        16 -> 31       : 65348   |****************************************|
        32 -> 63       : 5955    |***                                    |
        64 -> 127      : 1409    |                                       |
       128 -> 255      : 28      |                                       |

operation = 'open'
    usecs              : count    distribution
         0 -> 1        : 7557    |****************************************|
         2 -> 3        : 263     |*                                      |
         4 -> 7        : 4       |                                       |
         8 -> 15       : 6       |                                       |
        16 -> 31       : 2       |                                       |
```

This output shows separate histograms for reads, writes, and opens, with counts indicating that the workload is currently write-heavy. The read histogram shows a bi-modal distribution, with many taking less than seven microseconds, and another mode at 16 to 31 microseconds. The speed of both these modes suggested they were served from the page cache. This difference between them may be caused by the size of the data read, or different types of reads that take different code paths. The slowest reads reached the 65- to 131-millisecond bucket: these may be from storage devices, and also involve queueing.

The write histogram showed that most writes were in the 16- to 31-microsecond range: also fast, and likely using write-back buffering.

BCC

Command line usage:

```
xfsdist [options] [interval [count]]
```

Options include:

- **-m:** Print output in milliseconds (default is microseconds)
- **-p PID:** Measure this process only

The interval and count arguments allow these histograms to be studied over time.

bpftrace

The following is the code for the bpftrace version, which summarizes its core functionality. This version does not support options.

```
#!/usr/local/bin/bpftrace

BEGIN
{
        printf("Tracing XFS operation latency... Hit Ctrl-C to end.\n");
}

kprobe:xfs_file_read_iter,
kprobe:xfs_file_write_iter,
kprobe:xfs_file_open,
kprobe:xfs_file_fsync
{
        @start[tid] = nsecs;
        @name[tid] = func;
}

kretprobe:xfs_file_read_iter,
kretprobe:xfs_file_write_iter,
kretprobe:xfs_file_open,
kretprobe:xfs_file_fsync
/@start[tid]/
{
        @us[@name[tid]] = hist((nsecs - @start[tid]) / 1000);
        delete(@start[tid]);
        delete(@name[tid]);
}

END
{
        clear(@start);
        clear(@name);
}
```

This makes use of the functions from the XFS struct file_operations. Not all file systems have such a simple mapping, as discussed in the next section about ext4.

8.3.23 ext4dist

There is a ext4dist(8)[35] tool in BCC that works like xfsdist(8), but for the ext4 file system instead. See the xfsdist(8) section for output and usage.

There is one difference, and it is an example of the difficulty of using kprobes. Here is the ext4_file_operations struct from Linux 4.8:

```
const struct file_operations ext4_file_operations = {
        .llseek         = ext4_llseek,
        .read_iter      = generic_file_read_iter,
        .write_iter     = ext4_file_write_iter,
        .unlocked_ioctl = ext4_ioctl,
[...]
```

The read function highlighted in bold is generic_file_read_iter(), and not an ext4 specific one. This is a problem: if you trace this generic one, you are also tracing operations from other file system types, and the output will be polluted.

The workaround used was to trace generic_file_read_iter() and examine its arguments to determine if it came from ext4 or not. The BPF code examined the struct kiocb *icb argument in this way, returning from the tracing function if the file system operations were not for ext4:

```
    // ext4 filter on file->f_op == ext4_file_operations
    struct file *fp = iocb->ki_filp;
    if ((u64)fp->f_op != EXT4_FILE_OPERATIONS)
        return 0;
```

The EXT4_FILE_OPERATIONS was replaced with the actual address of the ext4_file_operations struct, found by reading /proc/kallsyms during program startup. It's something of a hack, but it works. It comes with the performance cost of tracing all generic_file_read_iter() calls, affecting other file systems that use it, as well as the additional test in the BPF program.

Then came Linux 4.10, which changed the functions used. Now we can examine a real kernel change and its affect on kprobes, instead of hypothetically warning about the possibility. The file_operations struct became:

```
const struct file_operations ext4_file_operations = {
        .llseek         = ext4_llseek,
        .read_iter      = ext4_file_read_iter,
        .write_iter     = ext4_file_write_iter,
        .unlocked_ioctl = ext4_ioctl,
[...]
```

Compare this to the earlier version. Now there is an ext4_file_read_iter() function that you can trace directly, so you no longer need to tease apart ext4 calls from the generic function.

---

35 Origin: I created this on 12-Feb-2016, inspired by my 2012 zfsdist.d DTrace tool, and the bpftrace version for this book on 2-Feb-2019.

bpftrace

To celebrate this change, I developed ext4dist(8) for Linux 4.10 and later (until it changes again). Example output:

```
# ext4dist.bt
Attaching 9 probes...
Tracing ext4 operation latency... Hit Ctrl-C to end.
^C

@us[ext4_sync_file]:
[1K, 2K)               2 |@@@@@@@@@@@@@@@@@@@@@@@@@@@@@@@@@@@@@@@@@@@@@@@@@@@@|
[2K, 4K)               1 |@@@@@@@@@@@@@@@@@@@@@@@@@@@                        |
[4K, 8K)               0 |                                                  |
[8K, 16K)              1 |@@@@@@@@@@@@@@@@@@@@@@@@@@@                        |

@us[ext4_file_write_iter]:
[1]                   14 |@@@@@@                                            |
[2, 4)                28 |@@@@@@@@@@@@                                      |
[4, 8)                72 |@@@@@@@@@@@@@@@@@@@@@@@@@@@@@@@@                   |
[8, 16)              114 |@@@@@@@@@@@@@@@@@@@@@@@@@@@@@@@@@@@@@@@@@@@@@@@@@@@@|
[16, 32)              26 |@@@@@@@@@@@                                       |
[32, 64)              61 |@@@@@@@@@@@@@@@@@@@@@@@@@@                         |
[64, 128)              5 |@@                                                |
[128, 256)             0 |                                                  |
[256, 512)             0 |                                                  |
[512, 1K)              1 |                                                  |

@us[ext4_file_read_iter]:
[0]                    1 |                                                  |
[1]                    1 |                                                  |
[2, 4)               768 |@@@@@@@@@@@@@@@@@@@@@@@@@@@@@@@@@@@@@@@@@@@@@@@@@@@@|
[4, 8)               385 |@@@@@@@@@@@@@@@@@@@@@@@@@@@                        |
[8, 16)              112 |@@@@@@@                                           |
[16, 32)              18 |@                                                 |
[32, 64)               5 |                                                  |
[64, 128)              0 |                                                  |
[128, 256)           124 |@@@@@@@@                                          |
[256, 512)            70 |@@@@                                              |
[512, 1K)              3 |                                                  |

@us[ext4_file_open]:
[0]                 1105 |@@@@@@@@@@                                        |
[1]                  221 |@@                                                |
```

```
[2, 4)                 5377 |@@@@@@@@@@@@@@@@@@@@@@@@@@@@@@@@@@@@@@@@@@@@@@@@@@@@|
[4, 8)                  359 |@@@                                              |
[8, 16)                  42 |                                                 |
[16, 32)                  5 |                                                 |
[32, 64)                  1 |                                                 |
```

The histograms are in microseconds, and this output all shows sub-millisecond latencies.

Source:

```
#!/usr/local/bin/bpftrace

BEGIN
{
        printf("Tracing ext4 operation latency... Hit Ctrl-C to end.\n");
}

kprobe:ext4_file_read_iter,
kprobe:ext4_file_write_iter,
kprobe:ext4_file_open,
kprobe:ext4_sync_file
{
        @start[tid] = nsecs;
        @name[tid] = func;
}

kretprobe:ext4_file_read_iter,
kretprobe:ext4_file_write_iter,
kretprobe:ext4_file_open,
kretprobe:ext4_sync_file
/@start[tid]/
{
        @us[@name[tid]] = hist((nsecs - @start[tid]) / 1000);
        delete(@start[tid]);
        delete(@name[tid]);
}

END
{
        clear(@start);
        clear(@name);
}
```

The map was named "@us" to decorate the output with the units (microseconds).

8.3.24   icstat

icstat(8)[36] traces inode cache references and misses and prints statistics every second. For example:

```
# icstat.bt
Attaching 3 probes...
Tracing icache lookups... Hit Ctrl-C to end.
     REFS    MISSES  HIT%
        0         0   0%
    21647         0 100%
    38925     35250   8%
    33781     33780   0%
      815       806   1%
        0         0   0%
        0         0   0%
[...]
```

This output shows an initial second of hits, followed by a few seconds of mostly misses. The workload was a find /var -ls, to walk inodes and print their details.

The source to icstat(8) is:

```
#!/usr/local/bin/bpftrace

BEGIN
{
        printf("Tracing icache lookups... Hit Ctrl-C to end.\n");
        printf("%10s %10s %5s\n", "REFS", "MISSES", "HIT%");
}


kretprobe:find_inode_fast
{
        @refs++;
        if (retval == 0) {
                @misses++;
        }
}


interval:s:1
{
        $hits = @refs - @misses;
        $percent = @refs > 0 ? 100 * $hits / @refs : 0;
        printf("%10d %10d %4d%%\n", @refs, @misses, $percent);
```

---

36 Origin: I created it for this book on 2-Feb-2019. My first inode cache stat tool was inodestat7 on 11-Mar-2004, and I'm sure there were earlier inode stat tools (from memory, the SE Toolkit).

```
        clear(@refs);
        clear(@misses);
}


END
{
        clear(@refs);
        clear(@misses);
}
```

As with dcstat(8), for the percent calculation a division by zero is avoided by checking whether @refs is zero.

8.3.25 bufgrow

bufgrow(8)[37] is a bpftrace tool that provides some insight into operation of the buffer cache. This shows page cache growth for block pages only (the buffer cache, used for block I/O buffers), showing which processes grew the cache by how many Kbytes. For example:

```
# bufgrow.bt
Attaching 1 probe...
^C

@kb[dd]: 101856
```

While tracing, "dd" processes increased the buffer cache by around 100 Mbytes. This was a synthetic test involving a dd(1) from a block device, during which the buffer cache did grow by 100 Mbytes:

```
# free -wm
            total      used      free    shared   buffers     cache   available
Mem:        70336       471     69328        26         2       534       68928
Swap:           0         0         0
[...]
# free -wm
            total      used      free    shared   buffers     cache   available
Mem:        70336       473     69153        26       102       607       68839
Swap:           0         0         0
```

The source to bufgrow(8) is:

```
#!/usr/local/bin/bpftrace

#include <linux/fs.h>
```

---

37 Origin: I created it for this book on 3-Feb-2019.

```
kprobe:add_to_page_cache_lru
{
        $as = (struct address_space *)arg1;
        $mode = $as->host->i_mode;
        // match block mode, uapi/linux/stat.h:
        if ($mode & 0x6000) {
                @kb[comm] = sum(4);          // page size
        }
}
```

This works by using kprobes to instrument the add_to_page_cache_lru() function, and filters on the block type. Since the block type requires a struct cast and dereference, it is tested in an if-statement rather than the probe filter. This is a frequent function, so running this tool can cost noticeable overhead for busy workloads.

8.3.26 readahead

readahead(8)[38] traces file system automatic read-ahead (not the readahead(2) syscall) and shows whether the read-ahead pages were used during tracing, and the time between reading the page and its use. For example:

```
# readahead.bt
Attaching 5 probes...
^C
Readahead unused pages: 128

Readahead used page age (ms):
@age_ms:
[1]                      2455 |@@@@@@@@@@@@@@@@                                    |
[2, 4)                   8424 |@@@@@@@@@@@@@@@@@@@@@@@@@@@@@@@@@@@@@@@@@@@@@@@@@@@@@@|
[4, 8)                   4417 |@@@@@@@@@@@@@@@@@@@@@@@@@@@@@@                       |
[8, 16)                  7680 |@@@@@@@@@@@@@@@@@@@@@@@@@@@@@@@@@@@@@@@@@@@@@@@@     |
[16, 32)                 4352 |@@@@@@@@@@@@@@@@@@@@@@@@@@@@                        |
[32, 64)                    0 |                                                   |
[64, 128)                   0 |                                                   |
[128, 256)                384 |@@                                                 |
```

This shows that during tracing there were 128 pages read ahead but unused (that's not many). The histogram shows thousands of pages were read and used, mostly within 32 milliseconds. If that time was in the many seconds, it could be a sign that read-ahead is loading too aggressively, and should be tuned.

This tool was created to help analyze read-ahead behavior on Netflix production instances that were using solid state drives, where read ahead is far less useful than it is for rotational disks, and

---

38 Origin: I created it for this book on 3-Feb-2019. I've talked about writing this tool for years, and now I've finally gotten around to it.

can negatively affect performance. This particular production issue is also described in the biosnoop(8) section in Chapter 9, as biosnoop(8) had previously been used for this analysis.

The source to readahead(8) is:

```
#!/usr/local/bin/bpftrace

kprobe:__do_page_cache_readahead    { @in_readahead[tid] = 1; }
kretprobe:__do_page_cache_readahead { @in_readahead[tid] = 0; }

kretprobe:__page_cache_alloc
/@in_readahead[tid]/
{
        @birth[retval] = nsecs;
        @rapages++;
}

kprobe:mark_page_accessed
/@birth[arg0]/
{
        @age_ms = hist((nsecs - @birth[arg0]) / 1000000);
        delete(@birth[arg0]);
        @rapages--;
}

END
{
        printf("\nReadahead unused pages: %d\n", @rapages);
        printf("\nReadahead used page age (ms):\n");
        print(@age_ms); clear(@age_ms);
        clear(@birth); clear(@in_readahead); clear(@rapages);
}
```

This works by using kprobes to instrument various kernel functions. It sets a per-thread flag during __do_page_cache_readahead(), which is checked during page allocation to know whether the page was for read-ahead. If so, a timestamp is saved for the page, keyed on the page struct address. This is read later on page access, if set, for the time histogram. The count of unused pages is an entropy count of read-ahead page allocations minus their use, for the duration of the program.

If the kernel implementation changes, this tool will need to be updated to match. Also, tracing page functions and storing extra metadata per page will likely add up to significant overhead, as these page functions are frequent. The overhead of this tool may reach 30% or higher on very busy systems. It is intended for short-term analysis.

At the end of Chapter 9, a bpftrace one-liner is shown that can count the ratio of read vs read-ahead block I/O.

8.3.27   Other Tools

Other BPF tools worth mentioning:

- **ext4slower(8), ext4dist(8)**: ext4 versions of xfsslower(8) and xfsdist(8), in BCC
- **btrfsslower(8), btrfsdist(8)**: btrfs versions of xfsslower(8) and xfsdist(8), in BCC
- **zfsslower(8), zfsdist(8)**: zfs versions of xfsslower(8) and xfsdist(8), in BCC
- **nfsslower(8), nfsdist(8)**: NFS versions of xfsslower(8) and xfsdist(8), in BCC, for NFSv3 and NFSv4

8.4   BPF One-Liners

These sections show BCC and bpftrace one-liners. Where possible, the same one-liner is implemented using both BCC and bpftrace.

8.4.1   BCC

Trace files opened via open(2) with process name:

```
opensnoop
```

Trace files created via creat(2) with process name:

```
trace 't:syscalls:sys_enter_creat "%s", args->pathname'
```

Count newstat(2) calls by filename:

```
argdist -C 't:syscalls:sys_enter_newstat():char*:args->filename'
```

Count read syscalls by syscall type:

```
funccount 't:syscalls:sys_enter_*read*'
```

Count write syscalls by syscall type:

```
funccount 't:syscalls:sys_enter_*write*'
```

Show the distribution of read() syscall request sizes:

```
argdist -H 't:syscalls:sys_enter_read():int:args->count'
```

Show the distribution of read() syscall read bytes (and errors):

```
argdist -H 't:syscalls:sys_exit_read():int:args->ret'
```

Count read() syscall errors by error code:

```
argdist -C 't:syscalls:sys_exit_read():int:args->ret:args->ret<0'
```

Count VFS calls:

```
funccount 'vfs_*'
```

Count ext4 tracepoints:

```
funccount 't:ext4:*'
```

Count xfs tracepoints:

```
funccount 't:xfs:*'
```

Count ext4 file reads by process name and stack trace:

```
stackcount ext4_file_read_iter
```

Count ext4 file reads by process name and user-level stack only:

```
stackcount -U ext4_file_read_iter
```

Trace ZFS spa_sync() times:

```
trace -T 'spa_sync "ZFS spa_sync()"'
```

Count FS reads to storage devices via read_pages, with stacks and process names:

```
stackcount -P read_pages
```

Count ext4 reads to storage devices, with stacks and process names:

```
stackcount -P ext4_readpages
```

8.4.2   bpftrace

Trace files opened via open(2) with process name:

```
bpftrace -e 't:syscalls:sys_enter_open { printf("%s %s\n", comm,
    str(args->filename)); }'
```

Trace files created via creat(2) with process name:

```
bpftrace -e 't:syscalls:sys_enter_creat { printf("%s %s\n", comm,
    str(args->pathname)); }'
```

Count newstat(2) calls by filename:

```
bpftrace -e 't:syscalls:sys_enter_newstat { @[str(args->filename)] = count(); }'
```

Count read syscalls by syscall type:

```
bpftrace -e 'tracepoint:syscalls:sys_enter_*read* { @[probe] = count(); }'
```

Count write syscalls by syscall type:

```
bpftrace -e 'tracepoint:syscalls:sys_enter_*write* { @[probe] = count(); }'
```

Show the distribution of read() syscall request sizes:

```
bpftrace -e 'tracepoint:syscalls:sys_enter_read { @ = hist(args->count); }'
```

Show the distribution of read() syscall read bytes (and errors):

```
bpftrace -e 'tracepoint:syscalls:sys_exit_read { @ = hist(args->ret); }'
```

Count read() syscall errors by error code:

```
bpftrace -e 't:syscalls:sys_exit_read /args->ret < 0/ { @[- args->ret] = count(); }'
```

Count VFS calls:

```
bpftrace -e 'kprobe:vfs_* { @[probe] = count(); }'
```

Count ext4 tracepoints:

```
bpftrace -e 'tracepoint:ext4:* { @[probe] = count(); }'
```

Count xfs tracepoints:

```
bpftrace -e 'tracepoint:xfs:* { @[probe] = count(); }'
```

Count ext4 file reads by process name:

```
bpftrace -e 'kprobe:ext4_file_read_iter { @[comm] = count(); }'
```

Count ext4 file reads by process name and user-level stack:

```
bpftrace -e 'kprobe:ext4_file_read_iter { @[ustack, comm] = count(); }'
```

Trace ZFS spa_sync() times:

```
bpftrace -e 'kprobe:spa_sync { time("%H:%M:%S ZFS spa_sinc()\n"); }'
```

Count dcache references by process name and PID:

```
bpftrace -e 'kprobe:lookup_fast { @[comm, pid] = count(); }'
```

Count FS reads to storage devices via read_pages, with kernel stacks:

```
bpftrace -e 'kprobe:read_pages { @[kstack] = count(); }'
```

Count ext4 reads to storage devices via read_pages, with kernel stacks:

```
bpftrace -e 'kprobe:ext4_readpages { @[kstack] = count(); }'
```

8.4.3 BPF One-Liners Examples

Including some sample output, as I did previously for each tool, is also useful for illustrating one-liners. These are some selected one-liners with example output.

Counting Read Syscalls by Syscall Type

```
# funccount -d 10 't:syscalls:sys_enter_*read*'
Tracing 9 functions for "t:syscalls:sys_enter_*read*"... Hit Ctrl-C to end.

FUNC                              COUNT
syscalls:sys_enter_pread64            3
syscalls:sys_enter_readlinkat        34
syscalls:sys_enter_readlink         294
syscalls:sys_enter_read         9863782
Detaching...
```

This example uses –d 10 to run for 10 seconds. This one-liner, and similar ones using "*write*" and "*open*", are useful for determining which syscall variants are in use, so that they can then be studied. This output is from a 36-CPU production server, which is almost always using read(2), with nearly 10 million calls in the 10 seconds of tracing.

Showing the Distribution of read() Syscall Read Bytes (and Errors)

```
# bpftrace -e 'tracepoint:syscalls:sys_exit_read { @ = hist(args->ret); }'
Attaching 1 probe...
^C

@:
(..., 0)             279 |                                                       |
[0]                 2899 |@@@@@@                                                  |
[1]                15609 |@@@@@@@@@@@@@@@@@@@@@@@@@@@@@@@@@@@                      |
[2, 4)                73 |                                                       |
[4, 8)               179 |                                                       |
[8, 16)              374 |                                                       |
[16, 32)            2184 |@@@@                                                   |
[32, 64)            1421 |@@@                                                    |
[64, 128)           2758 |@@@@@                                                  |
[128, 256)          3899 |@@@@@@@@                                               |
[256, 512)          8913 |@@@@@@@@@@@@@@@@@@@                                     |
[512, 1K)          16498 |@@@@@@@@@@@@@@@@@@@@@@@@@@@@@@@@@@@@                     |
[1K, 2K)           16170 |@@@@@@@@@@@@@@@@@@@@@@@@@@@@@@@@@@@@                     |
[2K, 4K)           19885 |@@@@@@@@@@@@@@@@@@@@@@@@@@@@@@@@@@@@@@@@@@@@             |
[4K, 8K)           23926 |@@@@@@@@@@@@@@@@@@@@@@@@@@@@@@@@@@@@@@@@@@@@@@@@@@@@@@@@@@|
[8K, 16K)           9974 |@@@@@@@@@@@@@@@@@@@@@@                                  |
[16K, 32K)          7569 |@@@@@@@@@@@@@@@@                                       |
[32K, 64K)          1909 |@@@@                                                   |
[64K, 128K)          551 |@                                                      |
[128K, 256K)         149 |                                                       |
[256K, 512K)           1 |                                                       |
```

This output shows a large mode of reads between 512 bytes and 8 Kbytes. It also shows that 15,609 reads returned one byte only, which could be a target for performance optimizations. These can be investigated further by fetching the stack for these one-byte reads like this:

```
bpftrace -e 'tracepoint:syscalls:sys_exit_read /args->ret == 1/ { @[ustack] =
    count(); }'
```

There were also 2,899 reads of zero bytes, which may be normal based on the target of the read, and if there are no further bytes to read. The 279 events with a negative return value are error codes, which can also be investigated separately.

Counting XFS Tracepoints

```
# funccount -d 10 't:xfs:*'
Tracing 496 functions for "t:xfs:*"... Hit Ctrl-C to end.
FUNC                              COUNT
xfs:xfs_buf_delwri_queued             1
xfs:xfs_irele                         1
xfs:xfs_inactive_symlink              2
xfs:xfs_dir2_block_addname            4
xfs:xfs_buf_trylock_fail              5
[...]
xfs:xfs_trans_read_buf             9548
xfs:xfs_trans_log_buf             11800
xfs:xfs_buf_read                  13320
xfs:xfs_buf_find                  13322
xfs:xfs_buf_get                   13322
xfs:xfs_buf_trylock               15740
xfs:xfs_buf_unlock                15836
xfs:xfs_buf_rele                  20959
xfs:xfs_perag_get                 21048
xfs:xfs_perag_put                 26230
xfs:xfs_file_buffered_read        43283
xfs:xfs_getattr                   80541
xfs:xfs_write_extent             121930
xfs:xfs_update_time              137315
xfs:xfs_log_reserve              140053
xfs:xfs_log_reserve_exit         140066
xfs:xfs_log_ungrant_sub          140094
xfs:xfs_log_ungrant_exit         140107
xfs:xfs_log_ungrant_enter        140195
xfs:xfs_log_done_nonperm         140264
xfs:xfs_iomap_found              188507
xfs:xfs_file_buffered_write      188759
xfs:xfs_writepage                476196
xfs:xfs_releasepage              479235
xfs:xfs_ilock                    581785
xfs:xfs_iunlock                  589775
Detaching...
```

XFS has so many tracepoints that this output example was truncated to save space. These provide many ways to investigate XFS internals as needed, and get to the bottom of problems.

Counting ext4 Reads to Storage Devices, with Stacks and Process Names

```
# stackcount -P ext4_readpages
Tracing 1 functions for "ext4_readpages"... Hit Ctrl-C to end.
^C
  ext4_readpages
  read_pages
  __do_page_cache_readahead
  filemap_fault
  ext4_filemap_fault
  __do_fault
  __handle_mm_fault
  handle_mm_fault
  __do_page_fault
  async_page_fault
  __clear_user
  load_elf_binary
  search_binary_handler
  __do_execve_file.isra.36
  __x64_sys_execve
  do_syscall_64
  entry_SYSCALL_64_after_hwframe
  [unknown]
    head [28475]
    1

  ext4_readpages
  read_pages
  __do_page_cache_readahead
  ondemand_readahead
  generic_file_read_iter
  __vfs_read
  vfs_read
  kernel_read
  prepare_binprm
  __do_execve_file.isra.36
  __x64_sys_execve
  do_syscall_64
  entry_SYSCALL_64_after_hwframe
  [unknown]
    bash [28475]
    1

Detaching...
```

This output has only two events, but it was the two I was hoping to capture for an example: the first shows a page fault and how it leads to calling ext4_readpages() and reading from disk (it's actually from an execve(2) call loading its binary program); the second shows a normal read(2) that reaches ext4_readpages() via readahead functions. They are examples of an address space operations read, and a file operations read. The output also shows how the kernel stack trace can provide more information about an event. These stacks are from Linux 4.18, and may change between Linux kernel versions.

8.5 Optional Exercises

If not specified, these can be completed using either bpftrace or BCC:

1. Rewrite filelife(8) to use the syscall tracepoints for creat(2) and unlink(2).

2. What are the pros and cons of switching filelife(8) to these tracepoints?

3. Develop a version of vfsstat(8) that prints separate rows for your local file system and TCP. (See vfssize(8) and fsrwstat(8).) Mock output:

```
# vfsstatx
TIME          FS    READ/s  WRITE/s CREATE/s   OPEN/s  FSYNC/s
02:41:23:    ext4  1715013   38717        0     5379        0
02:41:23:     TCP     1431    1311        0        5        0
02:41:24:    ext4   947879   30903        0    10547        0
02:41:24:     TCP     1231     982        0        4        0
[...]
```

4. Develop a tool to show the ratio of logical file system I/O (via VFS or the file system interface) vs physical I/O (via block tracepoints).

5. Develop a tool to analyze file descriptor leaks: those that were allocated during tracing but not freed. One possible solution may be to trace the kernel functions __alloc_fd() and __close_fd().

6. (Advanced) Develop a tool to show file system I/O broken down by mountpoint.

7. (Advanced, unsolved) Develop a tool to show the time between accesses in the page cache as a distribution. What are the challenges with this tool?

8.6 Summary

This chapter summarizes BPF tools for file system analysis, instrumenting: system calls, VFS calls, file system calls, and file system tracepoints; the operation of write-back and read-ahead; and the page cache, the dentry cache, the inode cache, and the buffer cache. I included tools that show histograms of file system operation latency to identify multi-modal distributions and outliers, to help solve application performance issues.

Chapter 9

Disk I/O

Disk I/O is a common source of performance issues because I/O latency to a heavily loaded disk can reach tens of milliseconds or more—orders of magnitude slower than the nanosecond or microsecond speed of CPU and memory operations. Analysis with BPF tools can help find ways to tune or eliminate this disk I/O, leading to some of the largest application performance wins.

The term *disk I/O* refers to any storage I/O type: rotational magnetic media, flash-based storage, and network storage. These can all be exposed in Linux in the same way, as storage devices, and analyzed using the same tools.

Between an application and a storage device is usually a file system. File systems employ caching, read ahead, buffering, and asynchronous I/O to avoid blocking applications on slow disk I/O. I therefore suggest that you begin your analysis at the file system, covered in Chapter 8.

Tracing tools have already become a staple for disk I/O analysis: I wrote the first popular disk I/O tracing tools, iosnoop(8) in 2004 and iotop(8) in 2005, which are now shipped with different OSes. I also developed the BPF versions, called biosnoop(8) and biotop(8), finally adding the long-missing "b" for block device I/O. These and other disk I/O analysis tools are covered in this chapter.

Learning Objectives:

- Understand the I/O stack and the role of Linux I/O schedulers
- Learn a strategy for successful analysis of disk I/O performance
- Identify issues of disk I/O latency outliers
- Analyze multi-modal disk I/O distributions
- Identify which code paths are issuing disk I/O, and their latency
- Analyze I/O scheduler latency
- Use bpftrace one-liners to explore disk I/O in custom ways

This chapter begins with the necessary background for disk I/O analysis, summarizing the I/O stack. I explore the questions that BPF can answer, and provide an overall strategy to follow. I then focus on tools, starting with traditional disk tools and then BPF tools, including a list of BPF one-liners. This chapter ends with optional exercises.

9.1 Background

This section covers disk fundamentals, BPF capabilities, and a suggested strategy for disk analysis.

9.1.1 Disk Fundamentals

Block I/O Stack

The main components of the Linux block I/O stack are shown in Figure 9-1.

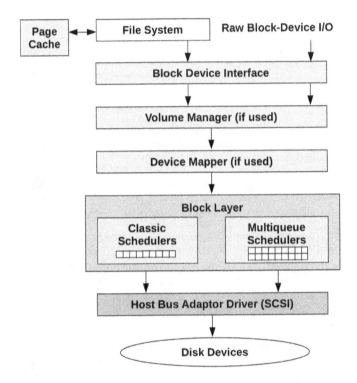

Figure 9-1   Linux block I/O stack

The term *block I/O* refers to device access in blocks, traditionally 512-byte sectors. The block device interface originated from Unix. Linux has enhanced block I/O with the addition of schedulers for improving I/O performance, volume managers for grouping multiple devices, and a device mapper for creating virtual devices.

Internals

Later BPF tools will refer to some kernel types used by the I/O stack. To introduce them here: I/O is passed through the stack as type struct request (from include/linux/blkdev.h) and, for lower levels, as struct bio (from include/linux/blk_types.h).

rwbs

For tracing observability, the kernel provides a way to describe the type of each I/O using a character string named rwbs. This is defined in the kernel blk_fill_rwbs() function and uses the characters:

- **R:** Read
- **W:** Write
- **M:** Metadata
- **S:** Synchronous
- **A:** Read-ahead
- **F:** Flush or force unit access
- **D:** Discard
- **E:** Erase
- **N:** None

The characters can be combined. For example, "WM" is for writes of metadata.

I/O Schedulers

I/O is queued and scheduled in the block layer, either by classic schedulers (only present in Linux versions older than 5.0) or by the newer multi-queue schedulers. The classic schedulers are:

- **Noop:** No scheduling (a no-operation)
- **Deadline:** Enforce a latency deadline, useful for real-time systems
- **CFQ:** The completely fair queueing scheduler, which allocates I/O time slices to processes, similar to CPU scheduling

A problem with the classic schedulers was their use of a single request queue, protected by a single lock, which became a performance bottleneck at high I/O rates. The multi-queue driver (blk-mq, added in Linux 3.13) solves this by using separate submission queues for each CPU, and multiple dispatch queues for the devices. This delivers better performance and lower latency for I/O versus classic schedulers, as requests can be processed in parallel and on the same CPU as the I/O was initiated. This was necessary to support flash memory-based and other device types capable of handling millions of IOPS [90].

Multi-queue schedulers available include:

- **None:** No queueing
- **BFQ:** The budget fair queueing scheduler, similar to CFQ, but allocates bandwidth as well as I/O time
- **mq-deadline:** A blk-mq version of deadline
- **Kyber:** A scheduler that adjusts read and write dispatch queue lengths based on performance, so that target read or write latencies can be met

The classic schedulers and the legacy I/O stack were removed in Linux 5.0. All schedulers are now multi-queue.

Disk I/O Performance

Figure 9-2 shows a disk I/O with operating system terminology.

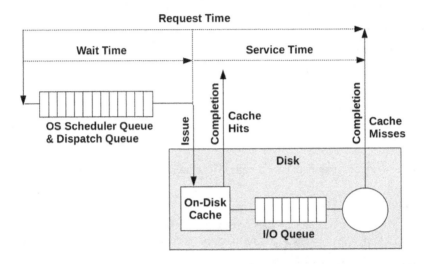

Figure 9-2   Disk I/O

From the operating system, wait time is the time spent in the block layer scheduler queues and device dispatcher queues. Service time is the time from device issue to completion. This may include time spent waiting on an on-device queue. Request time is the overall time from when an I/O was inserted into the OS queues to its completion. The request time matters the most, as that is the time that applications must wait if I/O is synchronous.

A metric not included in this diagram is disk utilization. It may seem ideal for capacity planning: when a disk approaches 100% utilization, you may assume there is a performance problem. However, utilization is calculated by the OS as the time that disk was *doing something,* and does not account for virtual disks that may be backed by multiple devices, or on-disk queues. This can make the disk utilization metric misleading in some situations, including when a disk at 90% may be able to accept much more than an extra 10% of workload. Utilization is still useful as a clue, and is a readily available metric. However, saturation metrics, such as time spent waiting, are better measures of disk performance problems.

9.1.2 BPF Capabilities

Traditional performance tools provide some insight for storage I/O, including IOPS rates, average latency and queue lengths, and I/O by process. These traditional tools are summarized in the next section.

BPF tracing tools can provide additional insight for disk activity, answering:

- What are the disk I/O requests? What type, how many, and what I/O size?
- What were the request times? Queued times?
- Were there latency outliers?
- Is the latency distribution multi-modal?
- Were there any disk errors?
- What SCSI commands were sent?
- Were there any timeouts?

To answer these, trace I/O throughout the block I/O stack.

Event Sources

Table 9-1 lists the event sources for instrumenting disk I/O.

Table 9-1   **Event Sources for Instrumenting Disk I/O**

Event Type	Event Source
Block interface and block layer I/O	block tracepoints, kprobes
I/O scheduler events	kprobes
SCSI I/O	scsi tracepoints, kprobes
Device driver I/O	kprobes

These provide visibility from the block I/O interface down to the device driver.

As an example event, here are the arguments to block:block_rq_issue, which sends a block I/O to a device:

```
# bpftrace -lv tracepoint:block:block_rq_issue
tracepoint:block:block_rq_issue
    dev_t dev;
    sector_t sector;
    unsigned int nr_sector;
    unsigned int bytes;
    char rwbs[8];
    char comm[16];
    __data_loc char[] cmd;
```

Questions such as "what are the I/O sizes for requests?" can be answered via a one-liner using this tracepoint:

```
bpftrace -e 'tracepoint:block:block_rq_issue { @bytes = hist(args->bytes); }'
```

Combinations of tracepoints allow the time between events to be measured.

9.1.3   Strategy

If you are new to disk I/O analysis, here is a suggested overall strategy that you can follow. The next sections explain these tools in more detail.

1. For application performance issues, begin with file system analysis, covered in Chapter 8.

2. Check basic disk metrics: request times, IOPS, and utilization (e.g., iostat(1)). Look for high utilization (which is a clue) and higher-than-normal request times (latency) and IOPS.

   a. If you are unfamiliar with what IOPS rates or latencies are normal, use a microbenchmark tool such as fio(1) on an idle system with some known workloads and run iostat(1) to examine them.

3. Trace block I/O latency distributions and check for multi-modal distributions and latency outliers (e.g., using BCC biolatency(8)).

4. Trace individual block I/O and look for patterns such as reads queueing behind writes (you can use BCC biosnoop(8)).

5. Use other tools and one-liners from this chapter.

To explain that first step some more: if you begin with disk I/O tools, you may quickly identify cases of high latency, but the question then becomes: how much does this matter? I/O may be asynchronous to the application. If so, that's interesting to analyze, but for different reasons: understanding contention with other synchronous I/O, and device capacity planning.

9.2   Traditional Tools

This section covers iostat(1) for disk activity summaries, perf(1) for block I/O tracing, blktrace(8), and the SCSI log.

9.2.1   iostat

iostat(1) summarizes per-disk I/O statistics, providing metrics for IOPS, throughput, I/O request times, and utilization. It can be executed by any user, and is typically the first command used to investigate disk I/O issues at the command line. The statistics it sources are maintained by the kernel by default, so the overhead of this tool is considered negligible.

iostat(1) provides many options for customizing the output. A useful combination is -dxz 1, to show disk utilization only (-d), extended columns (-x), skipping devices with zero metrics (-z), and per-second output (1). The output is so wide that I'll show a left portion and then the right portion; this is from a production issue I helped debug:

```
# iostat -dxz 1
Linux 4.4.0-1072-aws (...)        12/18/2018      _x86_64_        (16 CPU)

Device:         rrqm/s   wrqm/s     r/s     w/s     rkB/s     wkB/s \ ...
xvda              0.00     0.29    0.21    0.17      6.29      3.09 / ...
xvdb              0.00     0.08   44.39    9.98   5507.39   1110.55 \ ...
```

						/ ...
Device:	rrqm/s	wrqm/s	r/s	w/s	rkB/s	wkB/s \ ...
xvdb	0.00	0.00	745.00	0.00	91656.00	0.00 / ...
						\ ...
Device:	rrqm/s	wrqm/s	r/s	w/s	rkB/s	wkB/s / ...
xvdb	0.00	0.00	739.00	0.00	92152.00	0.00 \ ...

These columns summarize the workload applied, and are useful for workload characterization. The first two provide insight into disk merges: this is where a new I/O is found to be reading or writing to a disk location adjacent (front or back) to another queued I/O, so they are merged for efficiency.

The columns are:

- **rrqm/s:** Read requests queued and merged per second

- **wrqm/s:** Write requests queued and merged per second

- **r/s:** Read requests completed per second (after merges)

- **w/s:** Write requests completed per second (after merges)

- **rkB/s:** Kbytes read from the disk device per second

- **wkB/s:** Kbytes written to the disk device per second

The first group of output (showing both xvda and xvdb devices) is the summary since boot, and can be used for comparison with the subsequent one-second summaries. This output shows that xvdb normally has a read throughput of 5,507 Kbytes/sec, but the current one-second summaries show over 90,000 read Kbytes/sec. The system has a heavier-than-normal read workload.

Some math can be applied to these columns to figure out the average read and write size. Dividing the rkB/s column by the r/s column shows the average read size is about 124 Kbytes. A newer version of iostat(1) includes average sizes as the rareq-sz (read average request size) and wareq-sz columns.

The right columns show:

... \	avgrq-sz	avgqu-sz	await	r_await	w_await	svctm	%util
... /	49.32	0.00	12.74	6.96	19.87	3.96	0.15
... \	243.43	2.28	41.96	41.75	42.88	1.52	8.25
... /							
... \	avgrq-sz	avgqu-sz	await	r_await	w_await	svctm	%util
... /	246.06	25.32	33.84	33.84	0.00	1.35	100.40
... \							
... /	avgrq-sz	avgqu-sz	await	r_await	w_await	svctm	%util
... \	249.40	24.75	33.49	33.49	0.00	1.35	100.00

These show the resulting performance by the device. The columns are:

- **avgrq-sz:** Average request size in sectors (512 bytes).

- **avgqu-sz:** Average number of requests both waiting in the driver request queue and active on the device.

- **await:** Average I/O request time (aka response time), including time waiting in the driver request queue and the I/O response time of the device (ms).

- **r_await:** Same as await, but for reads only (ms).

- **w_await:** Same as await, but for writes only (ms).

- **svctm:** Average (inferred) I/O response time for the disk device (ms).

- **%util:** Percentage of time device was busy processing I/O requests (utilization).

The most important metric for delivered performance is await. If the application and file system use a technique to mitigate write latency (e.g., write through), then w_await may not matter as much, and you can focus on r_await instead.

For resource usage and capacity planning, %util is important, but keep in mind that it is only a measure of busy-ness (non-idle time), and may mean little for virtual devices backed by multiple disks. Those devices may be better understood by the load applied: IOPS (r/s + w/s) and through-put (rkB/s + wkB/s).

This example output shows the disk hitting 100% utilization, and an average read I/O time of 33 milliseconds. For the workload applied and the disk device, this turned out to be expected performance. The real issue was that the files being read had become so large they could no longer be cached in the page cache, and were read from disk instead.

9.2.2 perf

perf(1) was introduced in Chapter 6 for PMC analysis and timed stack sampling. Its tracing capabilities can also be used for disk analysis, especially using the block tracepoints.

For example, tracing the queuing of requests (block_rq_insert), their issue to a storage device (block_rq_issue), and their completions (block_rq_complete):

```
# perf record -e block:block_rq_insert,block:block_rq_issue,block:block_rq_complete -a
^C[ perf record: Woken up 7 times to write data ]
[ perf record: Captured and wrote 6.415 MB perf.data (20434 samples) ]
# perf script
    kworker/u16:3 25003 [004] 543348.164811:  block:block_rq_insert: 259,0 RM 4096 ()
2564656 + 8 [kworker/u16:3]
    kworker/4:1H    533 [004] 543348.164815:  block:block_rq_issue: 259,0 RM 4096 ()
2564656 + 8 [kworker/4:1H]
        swapper      0 [004] 543348.164887:  block:block_rq_complete: 259,0 RM ()
2564656 + 8 [0]
  kworker/u17:0 23867 [005] 543348.164960:  block:block_rq_complete: 259,0 R ()
3190760 + 256 [0]
            dd 25337 [001] 543348.165046:  block:block_rq_insert: 259,0 R 131072 ()
3191272 + 256 [dd]
            dd 25337 [001] 543348.165050:  block:block_rq_issue: 259,0 R 131072 ()
3191272 + 256 [dd]
```

```
            dd 25337   [001] 543348.165111:   block:block_rq_complete: 259,0 R ()
3191272 + 256 [0]
[...]
```

The output contains many details, beginning with the process that was on-CPU when the event occurred, which may or may not be the process responsible for the event. Other details include a timestamp, disk major and minor numbers, a string encoding the type of I/O (rwbs, described earlier), and other details about the I/O.

I have in the past built tools that post-process these events for calculating latency histograms, and visualizing access patterns.[1] However, for busy systems this means dumping all block events to user space for post-processing. BPF can do this processing in the kernel more efficiently, and then emit only the desired output. See the later biosnoop(8) tool as an example.

9.2.3 blktrace

blktrace(8) is a specialized utility for tracing block I/O events. Using its btrace(8) front-end to trace all events:

```
# btrace /dev/nvme2n1
259,0    2      1     0.000000000    430  Q  WS 2163864 + 8 [jbd2/nvme2n1-8]
259,0    2      2     0.000009556    430  G  WS 2163864 + 8 [jbd2/nvme2n1-8]
259,0    2      3     0.000011109    430  P  N [jbd2/nvme2n1-8]
259,0    2      4     0.000013256    430  Q  WS 2163872 + 8 [jbd2/nvme2n1-8]
259,0    2      5     0.000015740    430  M  WS 2163872 + 8 [jbd2/nvme2n1-8]
[...]
259,0    2     15     0.000026963    430  I  WS 2163864 + 48 [jbd2/nvme2n1-8]
259,0    2     16     0.000046155    430  D  WS 2163864 + 48 [jbd2/nvme2n1-8]
259,0    2     17     0.000699822    430  Q  WS 2163912 + 8 [jbd2/nvme2n1-8]
259,0    2     18     0.000701539    430  G  WS 2163912 + 8 [jbd2/nvme2n1-8]
259,0    2     19     0.000702820    430  I  WS 2163912 + 8 [jbd2/nvme2n1-8]
259,0    2     20     0.000704649    430  D  WS 2163912 + 8 [jbd2/nvme2n1-8]
259,0   11      1     0.000664811      0  C  WS 2163864 + 48 [0]
259,0   11      2     0.001098435      0  C  WS 2163912 + 8 [0]
[...]
```

Multiple event lines are printed for each I/O. The columns are:

1. Device major, minor number

2. CPU ID

3. Sequence number

4. Action time, in seconds

---

1 See iolatency(8) in perf-tools [78]: this uses Ftrace to access the same per-event tracepoint data from the trace buffer, which avoids the overhead of creating and writing a perf.data file.

5. Process ID

6. Action identifier (see blkparse(1)): Q == queued, G == get request, P == plug, M == merge, D == issued, C == completed, etc.

7. RWBS description (see the "rwbs" section earlier in this chapter): W == write, S == synchronous, etc.

8. Address + size [device]

The output can be post-processed and visualized using Chris Mason's seekwatcher [91].

As with perf(1) per-event dumping, the overhead of blktrace(8) can be a problem for busy disk I/O workloads. In-kernel summaries using BPF can greatly reduce this overhead.

9.2.4 SCSI Logging

Linux also has a built-in facility for SCSI event logging. It can be enabled via sysctl(8) or /proc. For example, both of these commands set the logging to the maximum for all event types (warning: depending on your disk workload, this may flood your system log):

```
# sysctl -w dev.scsi.logging_level=0x1b6db6db
# echo 0x1b6db6db > /proc/sys/dev/scsi/logging_level
```

The format of the number is a bitfield that sets the logging level from 1 to 7 for 10 different event types. It is defined in drivers/scsi/scsi_logging.h. The sg3-utils package provides a scsi_logging_level(8) tool for setting these. For example:

```
scsi_logging_level -s --all 3
```

Example events:

```
# dmesg
[...]
[542136.259412] sd 0:0:0:0: tag#0 Send: scmd 0x0000000001fb89dc
[542136.259422] sd 0:0:0:0: tag#0 CDB: Test Unit Ready 00 00 00 00 00 00
[542136.261103] sd 0:0:0:0: tag#0 Done: SUCCESS Result: hostbyte=DID_OK
driverbyte=DRIVER_OK
[542136.261110] sd 0:0:0:0: tag#0 CDB: Test Unit Ready 00 00 00 00 00 00
[542136.261115] sd 0:0:0:0: tag#0 Sense Key : Not Ready [current]
[542136.261121] sd 0:0:0:0: tag#0 Add. Sense: Medium not present
[542136.261127] sd 0:0:0:0: tag#0 0 sectors total, 0 bytes done.
[...]
```

This can be used to help debug errors and timeouts. While timestamps are provided (the first column), using them to calculate I/O latency is difficult without unique identifying details.

BPF tracing can be used to produce custom SCSI-level and other I/O stack-level logs, with more I/O details including latency calculated in the kernel.

9.3 BPF Tools

This section covers the BPF tools you can use for disk performance analysis and troubleshooting. They are shown in Figure 9-3.

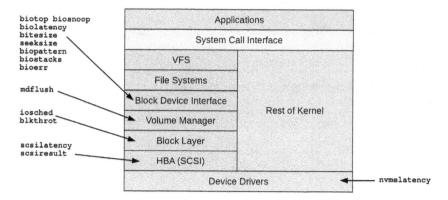

Figure 9-3 BPF tools for disk analysis

These tools are either from the BCC and bpftrace repositories covered in Chapters 4 and 5, or were created for this book. Some tools appear in both BCC and bpftrace. Table 9-2 lists the origins of the tools covered in this section (BT is short for bpftrace).

Table 9-2 **Disk-Related Tools**

Tool	Source	Target	Description
biolatency	BCC/BT	Block I/O	Summarize block I/O latency as a histogram
biosnoop	BCC/BT	Block I/O	Trace block I/O with PID and latency
biotop	BCC	Block I/O	Top for disks: summarize block I/O by process
bitesize	BCC/BT	Block I/O	Show disk I/O size histogram by process
seeksize	Book	Block I/O	Show requested I/O seek distances
biopattern	Book	Block I/O	Identify random/sequential disk access patterns
biostacks	Book	Block I/O	Show disk I/O with initialization stacks
bioerr	Book	Block I/O	Trace disk errors
mdflush	BCC/BT	MD	Trace md flush requests
iosched	Book	I/O sched	Summarize I/O scheduler latency
scsilatency	Book	SCSI	Show SCSI command latency distributions
scsiresult	Book	SCSI	Show SCSI command result codes
nvmelatency	Book	NVME	Summarize NVME driver command latency

For the tools from BCC and bpftrace, see their repositories for full and updated lists of tool
options and capabilities. A selection of the most important capabilities are summarized here.
See Chapter 8 for file system tools.

9.3.1 biolatency

biolatency(8)[2] is a BCC and bpftrace tool to show block I/O device latency as a histogram. The
term *device latency* refers to the time from issuing a request to the device, to when it completes,
including time spent queued in the operating system.

The following shows biolatency(8) from BCC, on a production Hadoop instance, tracing block
I/O for 10 seconds:

```
# biolatency 10 1
Tracing block device I/O... Hit Ctrl-C to end.

     usecs               : count    distribution
         0 -> 1          : 0        |                                        |
         2 -> 3          : 0        |                                        |
         4 -> 7          : 0        |                                        |
         8 -> 15         : 0        |                                        |
        16 -> 31         : 0        |                                        |
        32 -> 63         : 0        |                                        |
        64 -> 127        : 15       |                                        |
       128 -> 255        : 4475     |***********                             |
       256 -> 511        : 14222    |****************************************|
       512 -> 1023       : 12303    |**********************************      |
      1024 -> 2047       : 5649     |***************                         |
      2048 -> 4095       : 995      |**                                      |
      4096 -> 8191       : 1980     |*****                                   |
      8192 -> 16383      : 3681     |**********                              |
     16384 -> 32767      : 1895     |*****                                   |
     32768 -> 65535      : 721      |**                                      |
     65536 -> 131071     : 394      |*                                       |
    131072 -> 262143     : 65       |                                        |
    262144 -> 524287     : 17       |                                        |
```

This output shows a bi-modal distribution, with one mode between 128 and 2047 microseconds
and the other between about 4 and 32 milliseconds. Now that I know that the device latency is
bi-modal, understanding why may lead to tuning that moves more I/O to the faster mode. For
example, the slower I/O could be random I/O, or larger-size I/O (which can be determined using

---

2 Origin: I created this as iolatency.d for the 2011 DTrace book [Gregg 11], following the same name as my other
iosnoop and iotop tools. This led to confusion since "io" is ambiguous, so for BPF I've added the "b" to these tools
to signify block I/O. I created biolatency for BCC on 20-Sep-2015 and bpftrace on 13-Sep-2018.

other BPF tools). The slowest I/O in this output reached the 262- to 524-millisecond range: this sounds like deep queueing on the device.

biolatency(8) and the later biosnoop(8) tool have been used to solve many production issues. They can be especially useful for the analysis of multi-tenant drives in cloud environments, which can be noisy and break latency SLOs. When running on small cloud instances, Netflix's Cloud Database team was able to use biolatency(8) and biosnoop(8) to isolate machines with unacceptably bi-modal or latent drives, and evict them from both distributed caching tiers and distributed database tiers. Upon further analysis, the team decided to change their deployment strategy based on these findings, and now deploy clusters to fewer nodes, choosing those large enough to have dedicated drives. This small change effectively eliminated the latency outliers with no additional infrastructure cost.

The biolatency(8) tool currently works by tracing various block I/O kernel functions using kprobes. It was written before tracepoint support was available in BCC, so used kprobes instead. The overhead of this tool should be negligible on most systems where the disk IOPS rate is low (<1000).

Queued Time

BCC biolatency(8) has a -Q option to include the OS queued time:

```
# biolatency -Q 10 1
Tracing block device I/O... Hit Ctrl-C to end.

      usecs               : count    distribution
         0 -> 1           : 0        |                                        |
         2 -> 3           : 0        |                                        |
         4 -> 7           : 0        |                                        |
         8 -> 15          : 0        |                                        |
        16 -> 31          : 0        |                                        |
        32 -> 63          : 0        |                                        |
        64 -> 127         : 1        |                                        |
       128 -> 255         : 2780     |**********                              |
       256 -> 511         : 10386    |****************************************|
       512 -> 1023        : 8399     |********************************        |
      1024 -> 2047        : 4154     |***************                         |
      2048 -> 4095        : 1074     |****                                    |
      4096 -> 8191        : 2078     |********                                |
      8192 -> 16383       : 7688     |*****************************           |
     16384 -> 32767       : 4111     |***************                         |
     32768 -> 65535       : 818      |***                                     |
     65536 -> 131071      : 220      |                                        |
    131072 -> 262143      : 103      |                                        |
    262144 -> 524287      : 48       |                                        |
    524288 -> 1048575     : 6        |                                        |
```

The output is not much different: this time there's some more I/O in the slower mode. iostat(1) confirms that the queue lengths are small (avgqu-sz < 1).

Disks

Systems can have mixed storage devices: disks for the OS, disks for storage pools, and drives for removable media. The -D option in biolatency(8) shows histograms for disks separately, helping you see how each type performs. For example:

```
# biolatency -D
Tracing block device I/O... Hit Ctrl-C to end.
^C
[...]
disk = 'sdb'
     usecs               : count    distribution
        0 -> 1           : 0        |                                        |
        2 -> 3           : 0        |                                        |
        4 -> 7           : 0        |                                        |
        8 -> 15          : 0        |                                        |
       16 -> 31          : 0        |                                        |
       32 -> 63          : 0        |                                        |
       64 -> 127         : 0        |                                        |
      128 -> 255         : 1        |                                        |
      256 -> 511         : 25       |**                                      |
      512 -> 1023        : 43       |****                                    |
     1024 -> 2047        : 206      |********************                    |
     2048 -> 4095        : 8        |                                        |
     4096 -> 8191        : 8        |                                        |
     8192 -> 16383       : 392      |****************************************|

disk = 'nvme0n1'
     usecs               : count    distribution
        0 -> 1           : 0        |                                        |
        2 -> 3           : 0        |                                        |
        4 -> 7           : 0        |                                        |
        8 -> 15          : 12       |                                        |
       16 -> 31          : 72       |                                        |
       32 -> 63          : 5980     |****************************************|
       64 -> 127         : 1240     |********                                |
      128 -> 255         : 74       |                                        |
      256 -> 511         : 13       |                                        |
      512 -> 1023        : 4        |                                        |
     1024 -> 2047        : 23       |                                        |
     2048 -> 4095        : 10       |                                        |
     4096 -> 8191        : 63       |                                        |
```

This output shows two very different disk devices: nvme0n1, a flash-memory based disk, with I/O latency often between 32 and 127 microseconds; and sdb, an external USB storage device, with a bimodal I/O latency distribution in the milliseconds.

Flags

BCC biolatency(8) also has a -F option to print each set of I/O flags differently. For example, with -m for millisecond histograms:

```
# biolatency -Fm
Tracing block device I/O... Hit Ctrl-C to end.
^C

[...]

flags = Read
     msecs               : count    distribution
        0 -> 1           : 180      |*************                           |
        2 -> 3           : 519      |****************************************|
        4 -> 7           : 60       |****                                    |
        8 -> 15          : 123      |*********                               |
       16 -> 31          : 68       |*****                                   |
       32 -> 63          : 0        |                                        |
       64 -> 127         : 2        |                                        |
      128 -> 255         : 12       |                                        |
      256 -> 511         : 0        |                                        |
      512 -> 1023        : 1        |                                        |

flags = Sync-Write
     msecs               : count    distribution
        0 -> 1           : 8        |***                                     |
        2 -> 3           : 26       |***********                             |
        4 -> 7           : 37       |****************                        |
        8 -> 15          : 65       |****************************            |
       16 -> 31          : 93       |****************************************|
       32 -> 63          : 20       |********                                |
       64 -> 127         : 6        |**                                      |
      128 -> 255         : 0        |                                        |
      256 -> 511         : 4        |*                                       |
      512 -> 1023        : 17       |*******                                 |

flags = Flush
     msecs               : count    distribution
        0 -> 1           : 2        |****************************************|
```

```
flags = Metadata-Read
     msecs                  : count    distribution
         0 -> 1             : 3        |****************************************|
         2 -> 3             : 2        |**************************               |
         4 -> 7             : 0        |                                         |
         8 -> 15            : 1        |************                             |
        16 -> 31            : 1        |************                             |
```

These flags may be handled differently by the storage device; separating them allows us to study them in isolation. The above output shows that synchronous writes are bi-modal, with a slower mode in the 512- to 1023-millisecond range.

These flags are also visible in the block tracepoints via the rwbs field and one-letter encodings: see the "rwbs" section, earlier in this chapter, for an explanation of this field.

BCC

Command line usage:

```
biolatency [options] [interval [count]]
```

Options include:

- **-m**: Print output in milliseconds (default is microseconds)
- **-Q**: Include OS queued time
- **-D**: Show each disk separately
- **-F**: Show each set of I/O flags separately
- **-T**: Include a timestamp on the output

Using an interval of one will print per-second histograms. This information can be visualized as a latency heat map, with a full second as columns, latency ranges as rows, and a color saturation to show the number of I/O in that time range [Gregg 10]. See Chapter 17 for an example using Vector.

bpftrace

The following is the code for the bpftrace version, which summarizes its core functionality. This version does not support options.

```
#!/usr/local/bin/bpftrace

BEGIN
{
        printf("Tracing block device I/O... Hit Ctrl-C to end.\n");
}

kprobe:blk_account_io_start
```

```
{
        @start[arg0] = nsecs;
}


kprobe:blk_account_io_done
/@start[arg0]/
{
        @usecs = hist((nsecs - @start[arg0]) / 1000);
        delete(@start[arg0]);
}


END
{
        clear(@start);
}
```

This tool needs to store a timestamp at the start of each I/O to record its duration (latency). However, multiple I/O can be in flight concurrently. A single global timestamp variable would not work: a timestamp must be associated with each I/O. In many other BPF tools, this is solved by storing timestamps in a hash with the thread ID as a key. This does not work with disk I/O, since disk I/O can initiate on one thread and complete on another, in which case the thread ID changes. The solution used here is to take arg0 of these functions, which is the address of the struct request for the I/O, and use that memory address as the hash key. So long as the kernel does not change the memory address between issue and completion, it is suitable as the unique ID.

Tracepoints

The BCC and bpftrace versions of biolatency(8) should use the block tracepoints where possible, but there is a challenge: the struct request pointer is not currently available in the tracepoint arguments, so another key must be used to uniquely identify the I/O. One approach is to use the device ID and sector number. The core of the program can be changed to the following (biolatency-tp.bt):

```
[...]
tracepoint:block:block_rq_issue
{
        @start[args->dev, args->sector] = nsecs;
}


tracepoint:block:block_rq_complete
/@start[args->dev, args->sector]/
{
        @usecs = hist((nsecs - @start[args->dev, args->sector]) / 1000);
        delete(@start[args->dev, args->sector]);
}
[...]
```

This assumes that there is not multiple concurrent I/O to the same device and sector. This is measuring the device time, not including the OS queued time.

9.3.2 biosnoop

biosnoop(8)[3] is a BCC and bpftrace tool that prints a one-line summary for each disk I/O. The following shows biosnoop(8) from BCC, running on a Hadoop production instance:

```
# biosnoop
TIME(s)       COMM        PID    DISK   T  SECTOR      BYTES   LAT(ms)
0.000000      java        5136   xvdq   R  980043184   45056    0.35
0.000060      java        5136   xvdq   R  980043272   45056    0.40
0.000083      java        5136   xvdq   R  980043360   4096     0.42
[...]
0.143724      java        5136   xvdy   R  5153784     45056    1.08
0.143755      java        5136   xvdy   R  5153872     40960    1.10
0.185374      java        5136   xvdm   R  2007186664  45056    0.34
0.189267      java        5136   xvdy   R  979232832   45056   14.00
0.190330      java        5136   xvdy   R  979232920   45056   15.05
0.190376      java        5136   xvdy   R  979233008   45056   15.09
0.190403      java        5136   xvdy   R  979233096   45056   15.12
0.190409      java        5136   xvdy   R  979233184   45056   15.12
0.190441      java        5136   xvdy   R  979233272   36864   15.15
0.190176      java        5136   xvdm   R  2007186752  45056    5.13
0.190231      java        5136   xvdm   R  2007186840  45056    5.18
[...]
```

This output shows Java with PID 5136 doing reads to different disks. There were six reads with latency of around 15 milliseconds. If you look closely at the TIME(s) column, which shows the I/O completion time, these all finished within a fraction of a millisecond and were to the same disk (xvdy). You can conclude that these were queued together: the latency creeping up from 14.00 to 15.15 milliseconds is another clue to queued I/O being completed in turn. The sector offsets are also contiguous: 45056 byte reads are 88 × 512-byte sectors.

---

3 Origin: While I was a sysadmin at the University of Newcastle, Australia, in 2000, a shared server was suffering slow disk performance, which was suspected to be caused by a researcher running a batch job. They refused to move their workload unless I could prove that they were causing the heavy disk I/O, but no tool could do this. A workaround concocted either by me or the senior admin, Doug Scott, was to SIGSTOP their process while watching iostat(1), then SIGCONT it a few seconds later: the dramatic drop in disk I/O proved that they were responsible. Wanting a less invasive method, I saw the Sun TNF/prex tracing utility in Adrian Cockcroft's *Sun Performance and Tuning* book [Cockcroft 98], and on 3-Dec-2003 I created psio(1M), a utility to print disk I/O by process [185], which also had a mode to trace per-event disk I/O. DTrace was made available in beta in the same month, and I eventually rewrote my disk I/O tracer as iosnoop(1M) on 12-Mar-2004, initially before there was an io provider. I was quoted in *The Register*'s DTrace announcement talking about this work [Vance 04]. I created the BCC version as biosnoop(8) on 16-Sep-2015, and the bpftrace version on 15-Nov-2017.

As an example of production use: teams at Netflix that run stateful services routinely use bios-noop(8) to isolate issues with read-ahead degrading the performance of I/O-intensive workloads. Linux tries to intelligently read ahead data into the OS page cache, but this can cause severe performance issues for data stores running on fast solid-state drives, especially with the default read ahead settings. After identifying aggressive read-ahead, these teams then perform targeted refactors by analyzing histograms of I/O size and latency organized by thread, and then improve performance by using an appropriate madvise option, direct I/O, or changing the default read-ahead to smaller values such as 16 Kbytes. For histograms of I/O sizes, see vfssize(8) from Chapter 8 and bitesize(8) from this chapter; also see the readahead(8) tool in Chapter 8, which was created more recently for the analysis of this issue.

The biostoop(8) columns are:

- **TIME(s):** I/O completion time in seconds
- **COMM:** Process name, if cached
- **PID:** Process ID, if cached
- **DISK:** Storage device name
- **T:** Type: R == reads, W == writes
- **SECTOR:** Address on disk in units of 512-byte sectors
- **BYTES:** Size of the I/O
- **LAT(ms):** Duration of the I/O from device issue to device completion

This works in the same way as biolatency(8): tracing kernel block I/O functions. A future version should switch to the block tracepoints. The overhead of this tool is a little higher than biolatency(8) as it is printing per-event output.

OS Queued Time

A -Q option to BCC biosnoop(8) can be used to show the time spent between the creation of the I/O and the issue to the device: this time is mostly spent on OS queues, but could also include memory allocation and lock acquisition. For example:

```
# biosnoop -Q
TIME(s)       COMM          PID     DISK    T SECTOR      BYTES   QUE(ms)  LAT(ms)
19.925329     cksum         20405   sdb     R 249631      16384    17.17    1.63
19.933890     cksum         20405   sdb     R 249663      122880   17.81    8.51
19.942442     cksum         20405   sdb     R 249903      122880   26.35    8.51
19.944161     cksum         20405   sdb     R 250143      16384    34.91    1.66
19.952853     cksum         20405   sdb     R 250175      122880   15.53    8.59
[...]
```

The queued time is shown in the QUE(ms) column. This example of high queue times for reads was from a USB flash drive using the CFQ I/O scheduler. Write I/O queues even more:

```
# biosnoop -Q
TIME(s)     COMM           PID     DISK     T SECTOR      BYTES   QUE(ms)  LAT(ms)
[...]
2.338149    ?              0                W 0           8192       0.00     2.72
2.354710    ?              0                W 0           122880     0.00    16.17
2.371236    kworker/u16:1  18754   sdb      W 486703      122880  2070.06    16.51
2.387687    cp             20631   nvme0n1  R 73365192    262144     0.01     3.23
2.389213    kworker/u16:1  18754   sdb      W 486943      122880  2086.60    17.92
2.404042    kworker/u16:1  18754   sdb      W 487183      122880  2104.53    14.81
2.421539    kworker/u16:1  18754   sdb      W 487423      122880  2119.40    17.43
[...]
```

The queue time for writes exceeds two seconds. Note that earlier I/O lacked most of the column details: they were enqueued before tracing began, and so biosnoop(8) missed caching those details and only shows the device latency.

BCC

Command line usage:

```
biosnoop [options]
```

Options include -Q for OS queued time.

bpftrace

The following is the code for the bpftrace version, which traces the full duration of the I/O, including queued time:

```
#!/usr/local/bin/bpftrace

BEGIN
{
        printf("%-12s %-16s %-6s %7s\n", "TIME(ms)", "COMM", "PID", "LAT(ms)");
}

kprobe:blk_account_io_start
{
        @start[arg0] = nsecs;
        @iopid[arg0] = pid;
        @iocomm[arg0] = comm;
}
```

```
kprobe:blk_account_io_done
/@start[arg0] != 0 && @iopid[arg0] != 0 && @iocomm[arg0] != ""/
{
        $now = nsecs;
        printf("%-12u %-16s %-6d %7d\n",
            elapsed / 1000000, @iocomm[arg0], @iopid[arg0],
            ($now - @start[arg0]) / 1000000);


        delete(@start[arg0]);
        delete(@iopid[arg0]);
        delete(@iocomm[arg0]);
}


END
{
        clear(@start);
        clear(@iopid);
        clear(@iocomm);
}
```

The blk_account_io_start() function often fires in process context and occurs when the I/O is queued. Later events, such as issuing the I/O to the device and I/O completion, may or may not happen in process context, so you cannot rely on the value of the pid and comm builtins at those later times. The solution is to store them in BPF maps during blk_account_io_start(), keyed by the request ID, so that they can be retrieved later.

As with biolatency(8), this tool can be rewritten to use the block tracepoints (see Section 9.5).

9.3.3 biotop

biotop(8)[4] is a BCC tool that is top(1) for disks. The following shows it running on a production Hadoop instance, with -C to not clear the screen between updates:

```
# biotop -C
Tracing... Output every 1 secs. Hit Ctrl-C to end
06:09:47 loadavg: 28.40 29.00 28.96 44/3812 124008

PID     COMM            D MAJ MIN  DISK     I/O   Kbytes  AVGms
123693  kworker/u258:0  W 202 4096 xvdq     1979  86148   0.93
55024   kworker/u257:8  W 202 4608 xvds     1480  64068   0.73
123693  kworker/u258:0  W 202 5376 xvdv     143   5700    0.52
5381    java            R 202 176  xvdl     81    3456    3.01
43297   kworker/u257:0  W 202 80   xvdf     48    1996    0.56
```

_____

4 Origin: I created the first iotop using DTrace on 15-Jul-2005, and wrote this BCC version 6-Feb-2016. These were inspired by top(1) by William LeFebvre.

```
5383    java              R 202 112   xvdh      27      1152   16.05
5383    java              R 202 5632  xvdw      27      1152   3.45
5383    java              R 202 224   xvdo      27      1152   6.79
5383    java              R 202 96    xvdg      24      1024   0.52
5383    java              R 202 192   xvdm      24      1024   39.45
5383    java              R 202 5888  xvdx      24      1024   0.64
5383    java              R 202 5376  xvdv      24      1024   4.74
5383    java              R 202 4096  xvdq      24      1024   3.07
5383    java              R 202 48    xvdd      24      1024   0.62
5383    java              R 202 5120  xvdu      24      1024   4.20
5383    java              R 202 208   xvdn      24      1024   2.54
5383    java              R 202 80    xvdf      24      1024   0.66
5383    java              R 202 64    xvde      24      1024   8.08
5383    java              R 202 32    xvdc      24      1024   0.63
5383    java              R 202 160   xvdk      24      1024   1.42
[...]
```

This shows that a Java process is reading from many different disks. Top of the list are kworker threads initiating writes: this is background write flushing, and the real process that dirtied the pages is not known at this point (it can be identified using the file system tools from Chapter 8).

This works using the same events as biolatency(8), with similar overhead expectations.

Command line usage:

```
biotop [options] [interval [count]]
```

Options include:

- **-C**: Don't clear the screen
- **-r ROWS**: Number of rows to print

The output is truncated to 20 rows by default, which can be tuned with -r.

9.3.4   bitesize

bitesize(8)[5] is a BCC and bpftrace tool to show the size of disk I/O. The following shows the BCC version running on a production Hadoop instance:

```
# bitesize
Tracing... Hit Ctrl-C to end.
^C
[...]
```

---

5 Origin: I first created this as bitesize.d using DTrace on 31-Mar-2004, before the io provider was available. Allan McAleavy created the BCC version on 5-Feb-2016, and I created the bpftrace one on 7-Sep-2018.

```
Process Name = kworker/u257:10
    Kbytes              : count    distribution
       0 -> 1           : 0        |                                        |
       2 -> 3           : 0        |                                        |
       4 -> 7           : 17       |                                        |
       8 -> 15          : 12       |                                        |
      16 -> 31          : 79       |*                                       |
      32 -> 63          : 3140     |****************************************|

Process Name = java
    Kbytes              : count    distribution
       0 -> 1           : 0        |                                        |
       2 -> 3           : 3        |                                        |
       4 -> 7           : 60       |                                        |
       8 -> 15          : 68       |                                        |
      16 -> 31          : 220      |**                                      |
      32 -> 63          : 3996     |****************************************|
```

This output shows that both the kworker thread and java are calling I/O mostly in the 32- to 63-Kbyte range. Checking the I/O size can lead to optimizations:

- Sequential workloads should try the largest possible I/O size for peak performance. Larger sizes sometimes encounter slightly worse performance; there may be a sweet spot (e.g., 128 Kbytes) based on memory allocators and device logic.

- Random workloads should try to match the I/O size with the application record size. Larger I/O sizes pollute the page cache with data that isn't needed; smaller I/O sizes result in more I/O overhead than needed.

This works by instrumenting the block:block_rq_issue tracepoint.

BCC

bitesize(8) currently does not support options.

bpftrace

The following is the code for the bpftrace version:

```
#!/usr/local/bin/bpftrace

BEGIN
{
        printf("Tracing block device I/O... Hit Ctrl-C to end.\n");
}
```

```
tracepoint:block:block_rq_issue
{
        @[args->comm] = hist(args->bytes);
}


END
{
        printf("\nI/O size (bytes) histograms by process name:");
}
```

The tracepoint provides the process name as args->comm, and the size as args->bytes. This insert tracepoint fires when the request is inserted on the OS queue. Later tracepoints such as completion do not provide args->comm, nor can the comm builtin be used, as they fire asynchronously to the process (e.g., on device completion interrupt).

9.3.5   seeksize

seeksize(8)[6] is a bpftrace tool to show how many sectors that processes are requesting the disks to seek. This is only a problem for rotational magnetic media,[7] where the drive heads must physically move from one sector offset to another, causing latency. Example output:

```
# seeksize.bt
Attaching 3 probes...
Tracing block I/O requested seeks... Hit Ctrl-C to end.
^C
[...]

@sectors[tar]:
[0]              8220 |@@@@@@@@@@@@@@@@@@@@@@@@@@@@@@@@@@@@@@@@@@@@@@@@@@@@|
[1]                 0 |                                                  |
[2, 4)              0 |                                                  |
[4, 8)              0 |                                                  |
[8, 16)           882 |@@@@@                                             |
[16, 32)         1897 |@@@@@@@@@@@@                                      |
[32, 64)         1588 |@@@@@@@@@@                                        |
[64, 128)        1502 |@@@@@@@@@                                         |
[128, 256)       1105 |@@@@@@                                            |
[256, 512)        734 |@@@@                                              |
```

---

6 Origin: I first created it as seeksize.d using DTrace on 11-Sep-2004, as seek issues on rotational disks were common at the time. I created the bpftrace version it for a blog post on 18-Oct-2018 and revised it for this book on 20-Mar-2019.

7 Almost. Flash drives have their flash-translation-layer logic, and I've noticed a tiny slowdown (less than 1%) when seeking across large ranges vs small: perhaps it's busting the flash equivalent of a TLB.

```
[512, 1K)            501 |@@@                                        |
[1K, 2K)             302 |@                                          |
[2K, 4K)             194 |@                                          |
[4K, 8K)              82 |                                           |
[8K, 16K)             0 |                                            |
[16K, 32K)            0 |                                            |
[32K, 64K)            6 |                                            |
[64K, 128K)          191 |@                                          |
[128K, 256K)          0 |                                            |
[256K, 512K)          0 |                                            |
[512K, 1M)            0 |                                            |
[1M, 2M)              1 |                                            |
[2M, 4M)             840 |@@@@@                                      |
[4M, 8M)             887 |@@@@@                                      |
[8M, 16M)            441 |@@                                         |
[16M, 32M)           124 |                                           |
[32M, 64M)           220 |@                                          |
[64M, 128M)          207 |@                                          |
[128M, 256M)         205 |@                                          |
[256M, 512M)          3 |                                            |
[512M, 1G)           286 |@                                          |

@sectors[dd]:
[0]                29908 |@@@@@@@@@@@@@@@@@@@@@@@@@@@@@@@@@@@@@@@@@@@@@@@@@@@@|
[1]                   0 |                                            |
[...]
[32M, 64M)            0 |                                            |
[64M, 128M)           1 |                                            |
```

This output shows that processes named "dd" usually did not request any seeking: an offset of 0 was requested 29,908 times while tracing. This is expected, as I was running a dd(1) sequential workload. I also ran a tar(1) file system backup, which generated a mixed workload: some sequential, some random.

The source to seeksize(8) is:

```
#!/usr/local/bin/bpftrace

BEGIN
{
        printf("Tracing block I/O requested seeks... Hit Ctrl-C to end.\n");
}


tracepoint:block:block_rq_issue
```

```
{
        if (@last[args->dev]) {
                // calculate requested seek distance
                $last = @last[args->dev];
                $dist = (args->sector - $last) > 0 ?
                    args->sector - $last : $last - args->sector;

                // store details
                @sectors[args->comm] = hist($dist);
        }
        // save last requested position of disk head
        @last[args->dev] = args->sector + args->nr_sector;
}


END
{
        clear(@last);
}
```

This works by looking at the requested sector offset for each device I/O and comparing it to a recorded previous location. If the script is changed to use the block_rq_completion tracepoint, it will show the actual seeks encountered by the disk. But instead it uses the block_rq_issue trace-point to answer a different question: how random is the workload the application is requesting? This randomness may change after the I/O is processed by the Linux I/O scheduler and by the on-disk scheduler. I first wrote this to prove which applications were causing random workloads, so I chose to measure the workload on requests.

The following tool, biopattern(8), measures randomness on I/O completion instead.

9.3.6 biopattern

biopattern(8)[8] is a bpftrace tool to identify the pattern of I/O: random or sequential. For example:

```
# biopattern.bt
Attaching 4 probes...
TIME       %RND  %SEQ   COUNT     KBYTES
00:05:54    83    16     2960     13312
00:05:55    82    17     3881     15524
00:05:56    78    21     3059     12232
00:05:57    73    26     2770     14204
00:05:58     0   100        1         0
```

---

8 Origin: I created the first version as iopattern using DTrace on 25-Jul-2005, based on a mockup that Ryan Matteson had sent me (which also had more columns). I created this bpftrace version for this book on 19-Mar-2019.

```
00:05:59    0    0       0           0
00:06:00    0   99    1536      196360
00:06:01    0  100   13444     1720704
00:06:02    0   99   13864     1771876
00:06:03    0  100   13129     1680640
00:06:04    0   99   13532     1731484
[...]
```

This examples begins with a file system backup workload, which caused mostly random I/O. At 6:00 I switched to a sequential disk read, which was 99 or 100% sequential, and delivered a much higher throughput (KBYTES).

The source to biopattern(8) is:

```
#!/usr/local/bin/bpftrace

BEGIN
{
        printf("%-8s %5s %5s %8s %10s\n", "TIME", "%RND", "%SEQ", "COUNT",
            "KBYTES");
}


tracepoint:block:block_rq_complete
{
        if (@lastsector[args->dev] == args->sector) {
                @sequential++;
        } else {
                @random++;
        }
        @bytes = @bytes + args->nr_sector * 512;
        @lastsector[args->dev] = args->sector + args->nr_sector;
}


interval:s:1
{
        $count = @random + @sequential;
        $div = $count;
        if ($div == 0) {
                $div = 1;
        }
        time("%H:%M:%S ");
        printf("%5d %5d %8d %10d\n", @random * 100 / $div,
            @sequential * 100 / $div, $count, @bytes / 1024);
        clear(@random); clear(@sequential); clear(@bytes);
```

```
}


END
{
        clear(@lastsector);
        clear(@random); clear(@sequential); clear(@bytes);
}
```

This works by instrumenting block I/O completion and remembering the last sector (disk address) used for each device, so that it can be compared with the following I/O to see if it carried on from the previous address (sequential) or did not (random).[9]

This tool can be changed to instrument tracepoint:block:block_rq_insert, which will show the randomness of the workload applied (similar to seeksize(8)).

9.3.7   biostacks

biostacks(8)[10] is a bpftrace tool that traces full I/O latency (from OS enqueue to device completion) with the I/O initialization stack trace. For example:

```
# biostacks.bt
Attaching 5 probes...
Tracing block I/O with init stacks. Hit Ctrl-C to end.
^C
[...]

@usecs[
    blk_account_io_start+1
    blk_mq_make_request+1069
    generic_make_request+292
    submit_bio+115
    swap_readpage+310
    read_swap_cache_async+64
    swapin_readahead+614
    do_swap_page+1086
    handle_pte_fault+725
    __handle_mm_fault+1144
    handle_mm_fault+177
    __do_page_fault+592
    do_page_fault+46
```

---

9 Prior to the tracing era, I would identify random/sequential workloads by interpreting iostat(1) output and looking for high service times with small I/O sizes (random) or low service times with high I/O sizes (sequential).

10 Origin: I created it for this book on 19-Mar-2019. I had constructed a similar tool live during an internal Facebook talk in 2018, and for the first time saw initialization stacks associated with I/O completion times.

```
        page_fault+69
]:
[16K, 32K)             1 |                                                                      |
[32K, 64K)            32 |                                                                      |
[64K, 128K)         3362 |@@@@@@@@@@@@@@@@@@@@@@@@@@@@@@@@@@@@@@@@@@@@@@@@@@@@@@@@@@@@@@@@@@@@@@@@|
[128K, 256K)          38 |                                                                      |
[256K, 512K)           0 |                                                                      |
[512K, 1M)             0 |                                                                      |
[1M, 2M)               1 |                                                                      |
[2M, 4M)               1 |                                                                      |
[4M, 8M)               1 |                                                                      |

@usecs[
    blk_account_io_start+1
    blk_mq_make_request+1069
    generic_make_request+292
    submit_bio+115
    submit_bh_wbc+384
    ll_rw_block+173
    __breadahead+68
    __ext4_get_inode_loc+914
    ext4_iget+146
    ext4_iget_normal+48
    ext4_lookup+240
    lookup_slow+171
    walk_component+451
    path_lookupat+132
    filename_lookup+182
    user_path_at_empty+54
    vfs_statx+118
    SYSC_newfstatat+53
    sys_newfstatat+14
    do_syscall_64+115
    entry_SYSCALL_64_after_hwframe+61
]:
[8K, 16K)             18 |@@@@@@@@@@                                                            |
[16K, 32K)            20 |@@@@@@@@@@@                                                           |
[32K, 64K)            10 |@@@@@@                                                                |
[64K, 128K)           56 |@@@@@@@@@@@@@@@@@@@@@@@@@@@@@@@@@@@                                    |
[128K, 256K)          81 |@@@@@@@@@@@@@@@@@@@@@@@@@@@@@@@@@@@@@@@@@@@@@@@@@@@@@@@@@@@@@@@@@@@@@@@@@|
[256K, 512K)           7 |@@@@                                                                  |
```

I have seen cases where there was mysterious disk I/O without any application causing it. The reason turned out to be background file system tasks. (In one case it was ZFS's background scrubber, which periodically verifies checksums.) biostacks(8) can identify the real reason for disk I/O by showing the kernel stack trace.

The above output has two interesting stacks. The first was triggered by a page fault that became a swap in: this is swapping.[11] The second was a newfstatat() syscall that became a readahead.

The source to biostacks(8) is:

```
#!/usr/local/bin/bpftrace

BEGIN
{
        printf("Tracing block I/O with init stacks. Hit Ctrl-C to end.\n");
}

kprobe:blk_account_io_start
{
        @reqstack[arg0] = kstack;
        @reqts[arg0] = nsecs;
}

kprobe:blk_start_request,
kprobe:blk_mq_start_request
/@reqts[arg0]/
{
        @usecs[@reqstack[arg0]] = hist(nsecs - @reqts[arg0]);
        delete(@reqstack[arg0]);
        delete(@reqts[arg0]);
}

END
{
        clear(@reqstack); clear(@reqts);
}
```

This works by saving the kernel stack and a timestamp when the I/O was initiated and retrieving that saved stack and timestamp when the I/O completed. These are saved in a map keyed by the struct request pointer, which is arg0 to the traced kernel functions. The kernel stack trace is recorded using the kstack builtin. You can change this to ustack to record the user-level stack trace or add them both.

---

11 Linux terminology, where this means switching pages with the swap device. Swapping for other kernels can mean moving entire processes.

With the Linux 5.0 switch to multi-queue only, the blk_start_request() function was removed from the kernel. On that and later kernels, this tool prints a warning:

```
Warning: could not attach probe kprobe:blk_start_request, skipping.
```

This can be ignored, or that kprobe can be deleted from the tool. The tool could also be rewritten to use tracepoints. See the "Tracepoints" subsection of Section 9.3.1.

9.3.8 bioerr

bioerr(8)[12] traces block I/O errors and prints details. For example, running bioerr(8) on my laptop:

```
# bioerr.bt
Attaching 2 probes...
Tracing block I/O errors. Hit Ctrl-C to end.
00:31:52 device: 0,0, sector: -1, bytes: 0, flags: N, error: -5
00:31:54 device: 0,0, sector: -1, bytes: 0, flags: N, error: -5
00:31:56 device: 0,0, sector: -1, bytes: 0, flags: N, error: -5
00:31:58 device: 0,0, sector: -1, bytes: 0, flags: N, error: -5
00:32:00 device: 0,0, sector: -1, bytes: 0, flags: N, error: -5
[...]
```

This output is far more interesting than I was expecting. (I wasn't expecting any errors, but ran it just in case.) Every two seconds there is a zero-byte request to device 0,0, which seems bogus, and which returns with a -5 error (EIO).

The previous tool, biostacks(8), was created to investigate this kind of issue. In this case I don't need to see the latency, and I only want to see stacks for the device 0,0 I/O. I can tweak biostacks(8) to do this, although it can also be done as a bpftrace one-liner (in this case, I'll check that the stack trace is still meaningful by the time this tracepoint is hit; if it were not still meaningful, I'd need to switch back to a kprobe of blk_account_io_start() to really catch the initialization of this I/O):

```
# bpftrace -e 't:block:block_rq_issue /args->dev == 0/ { @[kstack]++ }'
Attaching 1 probe...
^C

@[
    blk_peek_request+590
    scsi_request_fn+51
    __blk_run_queue+67
    blk_execute_rq_nowait+168
    blk_execute_rq+80
    scsi_execute+227
```

---

12 Origin: I created it for this book on 19-Mar-2019.

```
        scsi_test_unit_ready+96
        sd_check_events+248
        disk_check_events+101
        disk_events_workfn+22
        process_one_work+478
        worker_thread+50
        kthread+289
        ret_from_fork+53
]: 3
```

This shows that device 0 I/O was created from scsi_test_unit_ready(). A little more digging into the parent functions shows that it was checking for USB removable media. As an experiment, I traced scsi_test_unit_ready() while inserting a USB flash drive, which changed its return value. This was my laptop detecting USB drives.

The source to bioerr(8) is:

```
#!/usr/local/bin/bpftrace

BEGIN
{
        printf("Tracing block I/O errors. Hit Ctrl-C to end.\n");
}

tracepoint:block:block_rq_complete
/args->error != 0/
{
        time("%H:%M:%S ");
        printf("device: %d,%d, sector: %d, bytes: %d, flags: %s, error: %d\n",
            args->dev >> 20, args->dev & ((1 << 20) - 1), args->sector,
            args->nr_sector * 512, args->rwbs, args->error);
}
```

The logic for mapping the device identifier (args->dev) to the major and minor numbers comes from the format file for this tracepoint:

```
# cat /sys/kernel/debug/tracing/events/block/block_rq_complete/format
name: block_rq_complete
[...]

print fmt: "%d,%d %s (%s) %llu + %u [%d]", ((unsigned int) ((REC->dev) >> 20)),
((unsigned int) ((REC->dev) & ((1U << 20) - 1))), REC->rwbs, __get_str(cmd), (unsigned
long long)REC->sector, REC->nr_sector, REC->error
```

While bioerr(8) is a handy tool, note that perf(1) can be used for similar functionality by filtering on error. The output includes the format string as defined by the /sys format file. For example:

```
# perf record -e block:block_rq_complete --filter 'error != 0'
# perf script
     ksoftirqd/2    22 [002] 2289450.691041: block:block_rq_complete: 0,0 N ()
18446744073709551615 + 0 [-5]
[...]
```

The BPF tool can be customized to include more information, going beyond the standard capabilities of perf(1).

For example, the error returned, in this case -5 for EIO, has been mapped from a block error code. It may be interesting to see the original block error code, which can be traced from functions that handle it, for example:

```
# bpftrace -e 'kprobe:blk_status_to_errno /arg0/ { @[arg0]++ }'
Attaching 1 probe...
^C

@[10]: 2
```

It's really block I/O status 10, which is BLK_STS_IOERR. These are defined in linux/blk_types.h:

```
#define BLK_STS_OK 0
#define BLK_STS_NOTSUPP        ((__force blk_status_t)1)
#define BLK_STS_TIMEOUT        ((__force blk_status_t)2)
#define BLK_STS_NOSPC          ((__force blk_status_t)3)
#define BLK_STS_TRANSPORT      ((__force blk_status_t)4)
#define BLK_STS_TARGET         ((__force blk_status_t)5)
#define BLK_STS_NEXUS          ((__force blk_status_t)6)
#define BLK_STS_MEDIUM         ((__force blk_status_t)7)
#define BLK_STS_PROTECTION     ((__force blk_status_t)8)
#define BLK_STS_RESOURCE       ((__force blk_status_t)9)
#define BLK_STS_IOERR          ((__force blk_status_t)10)
```

bioerr(8) could be enhanced to print these BLK_STS code names instead of the error numbers. These are actually mapped from SCSI result codes, which can be traced from the scsi events. I'll demonstrate SCSI tracing in sections 9.3.11 and 9.3.12.

9.3.9 mdflush

mdflush(8)[13] is a BCC and bpftrace tool for tracing flush events from md, the multiple devices driver that is used on some systems to implement software RAID. For example, running the BCC version on a production server using md:

```
# mdflush
Tracing md flush requests... Hit Ctrl-C to end.
TIME     PID     COMM            DEVICE
23:43:37 333     kworker/0:1H    md0
23:43:37 4038    xfsaild/md0     md0
23:43:38 8751    filebeat        md0
23:43:43 5575    filebeat        md0
23:43:48 5824    filebeat        md0
23:43:53 5575    filebeat        md0
23:43:58 5824    filebeat        md0
[...]
```

md flush events are usually infrequent and cause bursts of disk writes, perturbing system performance. Knowing exactly when they occurred can be useful for correlation with monitoring dashboards, to see if they align with latency spikes or other problems.

This output shows a process called filebeat doing md flushes every five seconds (I just discovered this). filebeat is a service that sends log files to Logstash or directly to Elasticsearch.

This works by tracing the md_flush_request() function using a kprobe. Since the event frequency is low, the overhead should be negligible.

BCC

mdflush(8) currently does not support any options.

bpftrace

The following is the code for the bpftrace version:

```
#!/usr/local/bin/bpftrace

#include <linux/genhd.h>
#include <linux/bio.h>

BEGIN
{
        printf("Tracing md flush events... Hit Ctrl-C to end.\n");
        printf("%-8s %-6s %-16s %s", "TIME", "PID", "COMM", "DEVICE");
```

---

13 Origin: I created it for BCC on 13-Feb-2015 and for bpftrace on 8-Sep-2018.

```
}

kprobe:md_flush_request
{
        time("%H:%M:%S ");
        printf("%-6d %-16s %s\n", pid, comm,
            ((struct bio *)arg1)->bi_disk->disk_name);
}
```

The program digs out the disk name via the struct bio argument.

9.3.10 iosched

iosched(8)[14] traces the time that requests were queued in the I/O scheduler, and groups this by scheduler name. For example:

```
# iosched.bt
Attaching 5 probes...
Tracing block I/O schedulers. Hit Ctrl-C to end.
^C

@usecs[cfq]:
[2, 4)                 1 |                                                    |
[4, 8)                 3 |@                                                   |
[8, 16)               18 |@@@@@@@                                             |
[16, 32)               6 |@@                                                  |
[32, 64)               0 |                                                    |
[64, 128)              0 |                                                    |
[128, 256)             0 |                                                    |
[256, 512)             0 |                                                    |
[512, 1K)              6 |@@                                                  |
[1K, 2K)               8 |@@@                                                 |
[2K, 4K)               0 |                                                    |
[4K, 8K)               0 |                                                    |
[8K, 16K)             28 |@@@@@@@@@@                                          |
[16K, 32K)           131 |@@@@@@@@@@@@@@@@@@@@@@@@@@@@@@@@@@@@@@@@@@@@@@@@@@@@@@|
[32K, 64K)            68 |@@@@@@@@@@@@@@@@@@@@@@@@@@                           |
```

14 Origin: I created it for this book on 20-Mar-2019.

This shows the CFQ scheduler in use, with queueing times usually between eight and 64 milliseconds.

The source to iosched(8) is:

```
#!/usr/local/bin/bpftrace

#include <linux/blkdev.h>

BEGIN
{
        printf("Tracing block I/O schedulers. Hit Ctrl-C to end.\n");
}

kprobe:__elv_add_request
{
        @start[arg1] = nsecs;
}

kprobe:blk_start_request,
kprobe:blk_mq_start_request
/@start[arg0]/
{
        $r = (struct request *)arg0;
        @usecs[$r->q->elevator->type->elevator_name] =
            hist((nsecs - @start[arg0]) / 1000);
        delete(@start[arg0]);
}

END
{
        clear(@start);
}
```

This works by recording a timestamp when requests were added to an I/O scheduler via an elevator function, __elv_add_request(), and then calculating the time queued when the I/O was issued. This focuses tracing I/O to only those that pass via an I/O scheduler, and also focuses on tracing just the queued time. The scheduler (elevator) name is fetched from the struct request.

With the Linux 5.0 switch to multi-queue only, the blk_start_request() function was removed from the kernel. On that and later kernels this tool will print a warning about skipping the blk_start_request() kprobe, which can be ignored, or that kprobe can be removed from this program.

9.3.11   scsilatency

scsilatency(8)[15] is a tool to trace SCSI commands with latency distributions. For example:

```
# scsilatency.bt
Attaching 4 probes...
Tracing scsi latency. Hit Ctrl-C to end.
^C

@usecs[0, TEST_UNIT_READY]:
[128K, 256K)           2 |@@@@@@@@@@@@@@@@@@@@@@@@@@@@@@@@@@@   |
[256K, 512K)           2 |@@@@@@@@@@@@@@@@@@@@@@@@@@@@@@@@@@@   |
[512K, 1M)             0 |                                    |
[1M, 2M)               1 |@@@@@@@@@@@@@@@@@@                   |
[2M, 4M)               2 |@@@@@@@@@@@@@@@@@@@@@@@@@@@@@@@@@@@   |
[4M, 8M)               3 |@@@@@@@@@@@@@@@@@@@@@@@@@@@@@@@@@@@@@@@@@@@@@@@@@@@@|
[8M, 16M)              1 |@@@@@@@@@@@@@@@@@@                   |

@usecs[42, WRITE_10]:
[2K, 4K)               2 |@                                   |
[4K, 8K)               0 |                                    |
[8K, 16K)              2 |@                                   |
[16K, 32K)            50 |@@@@@@@@@@@@@@@@@@@@@@@@@@@@@@@@@@@@@@@@@@@@@@@@   |
[32K, 64K)            57 |@@@@@@@@@@@@@@@@@@@@@@@@@@@@@@@@@@@@@@@@@@@@@@@@@@@@|

@usecs[40, READ_10]:
[4K, 8K)              15 |@                                   |
[8K, 16K)            676 |@@@@@@@@@@@@@@@@@@@@@@@@@@@@@@@@@@@@@@@@@@@@@@@@@@@@|
[16K, 32K)          447 |@@@@@@@@@@@@@@@@@@@@@@@@@@@@@@@@@@@   |
[32K, 64K)             2 |                                    |
[...]
```

This has a latency histogram for each SCSI command type, showing the opcode and command name (if available).

The source to scsilatency(8) is:

```
#!/usr/local/bin/bpftrace

#include <scsi/scsi_cmnd.h>

BEGIN
```

----

15 Origin: I created it for this book on 21-Mar-2019, inspired by similar tools I created for the 2011 DTrace book [Gregg 11].

```
{
        printf("Tracing scsi latency. Hit Ctrl-C to end.\n");
        // SCSI opcodes from scsi/scsi_proto.h; add more mappings if desired:
        @opcode[0x00] = "TEST_UNIT_READY";
        @opcode[0x03] = "REQUEST_SENSE";
        @opcode[0x08] = "READ_6";
        @opcode[0x0a] = "WRITE_6";
        @opcode[0x0b] = "SEEK_6";
        @opcode[0x12] = "INQUIRY";
        @opcode[0x18] = "ERASE";
        @opcode[0x28] = "READ_10";
        @opcode[0x2a] = "WRITE_10";
        @opcode[0x2b] = "SEEK_10";
        @opcode[0x35] = "SYNCHRONIZE_CACHE";
}

kprobe:scsi_init_io
{
        @start[arg0] = nsecs;
}

kprobe:scsi_done,
kprobe:scsi_mq_done
/@start[arg0]/
{
        $cmnd = (struct scsi_cmnd *)arg0;
        $opcode = *$cmnd->req.cmd & 0xff;
        @usecs[$opcode, @opcode[$opcode]] = hist((nsecs - @start[arg0]) / 1000);
}

END
{
        clear(@start); clear(@opcode);
}
```

There are many possible SCSI commands; this tool only translates a handful into the opcode names. Since the opcode number is printed with the output, if a translation is missing it can still be determined by referring to scsi/scsi_proto.h, and this tool can be enhanced to include it.

There are scsi tracepoints, and one is used in the next tool, but these lack a unique identifier, which would be needed as a BPF map key to store a timestamp.

Due to the Linux 5.0 switch to multi-queue only, the scsi_done() function was removed, and so the kprobe:scsi_done can be removed.

With the Linux 5.0 switch to multi-queue only, scsi_done() function was removed from the kernel. On that and later kernels this tool will print a warning about skipping the scsi_done() kprobe, which can be ignored, or that kprobe can be removed from this program.

9.3.12   scsiresult

scsiresult(8)[16] summarizes SCSI command results: the host and status codes. For example:

```
# scsiresult.bt
Attaching 3 probes...
Tracing scsi command results. Hit Ctrl-C to end.
^C

@[DID_BAD_TARGET, SAM_STAT_GOOD]: 1
@[DID_OK, SAM_STAT_CHECK_CONDITION]: 10
@[DID_OK, SAM_STAT_GOOD]: 2202
```

This shows 2202 results with the codes DID_OK and SAM_STAT_GOOD and one with DID_BAD_TARGET and SAM_STAT_GOOD. These codes are defined in the kernel source, for example, from include/scsi/scsi.h:

```
#define DID_OK          0x00    /* NO error                          */
#define DID_NO_CONNECT  0x01    /* Couldn't connect before timeout period */
#define DID_BUS_BUSY    0x02    /* BUS stayed busy through time out period */
#define DID_TIME_OUT    0x03    /* TIMED OUT for other reason        */
#define DID_BAD_TARGET  0x04    /* BAD target.                       */
[...]
```

This tool can be used to identify anomalous results from SCSI devices.

The source to scsiresult(8) is:

```
#!/usr/local/bin/bpftrace

BEGIN
{
        printf("Tracing scsi command results. Hit Ctrl-C to end.\n");

        // host byte codes, from include/scsi/scsi.h:
        @host[0x00] = "DID_OK";
        @host[0x01] = "DID_NO_CONNECT";
        @host[0x02] = "DID_BUS_BUSY";
        @host[0x03] = "DID_TIME_OUT";
```

---

16 Origin: I created it for this book on 21-Mar-2019, inspired by similar tools I created for the 2011 DTrace book [Gregg 11].

```
        @host[0x04] = "DID_BAD_TARGET";
        @host[0x05] = "DID_ABORT";
        @host[0x06] = "DID_PARITY";
        @host[0x07] = "DID_ERROR";
        @host[0x08] = "DID_RESET";
        @host[0x09] = "DID_BAD_INTR";
        @host[0x0a] = "DID_PASSTHROUGH";
        @host[0x0b] = "DID_SOFT_ERROR";
        @host[0x0c] = "DID_IMM_RETRY";
        @host[0x0d] = "DID_REQUEUE";
        @host[0x0e] = "DID_TRANSPORT_DISRUPTED";
        @host[0x0f] = "DID_TRANSPORT_FAILFAST";
        @host[0x10] = "DID_TARGET_FAILURE";
        @host[0x11] = "DID_NEXUS_FAILURE";
        @host[0x12] = "DID_ALLOC_FAILURE";
        @host[0x13] = "DID_MEDIUM_ERROR";

        // status byte codes, from include/scsi/scsi_proto.h:
        @status[0x00] = "SAM_STAT_GOOD";
        @status[0x02] = "SAM_STAT_CHECK_CONDITION";
        @status[0x04] = "SAM_STAT_CONDITION_MET";
        @status[0x08] = "SAM_STAT_BUSY";
        @status[0x10] = "SAM_STAT_INTERMEDIATE";
        @status[0x14] = "SAM_STAT_INTERMEDIATE_CONDITION_MET";
        @status[0x18] = "SAM_STAT_RESERVATION_CONFLICT";
        @status[0x22] = "SAM_STAT_COMMAND_TERMINATED";
        @status[0x28] = "SAM_STAT_TASK_SET_FULL";
        @status[0x30] = "SAM_STAT_ACA_ACTIVE";
        @status[0x40] = "SAM_STAT_TASK_ABORTED";
}

tracepoint:scsi:scsi_dispatch_cmd_done
{
        @[@host[(args->result >> 16) & 0xff], @status[args->result & 0xff]] =
            count();
}

END
{
        clear(@status);
        clear(@host);
}
```

This works by tracing the scsi:scsi_dispatch_cmd_done tracepoint and fetching the host and status bytes from the result, and then mapping them to kernel names. The kernel has similar lookup tables in include/trace/events/scsi.h for the tracepoint format string.

The result also has driver and message bytes, not shown by this tool. It is of the format:

```
driver_byte << 24 | host_byte << 16 | msg_byte << 8 | status_byte
```

This tool can be enhanced to add these bytes and other details to the map as additional keys. Other details are readily available in that tracepoint:

```
# bpftrace -lv t:scsi:scsi_dispatch_cmd_done
tracepoint:scsi:scsi_dispatch_cmd_done
    unsigned int host_no;
    unsigned int channel;
    unsigned int id;
    unsigned int lun;
    int result;
    unsigned int opcode;
    unsigned int cmd_len;
    unsigned int data_sglen;
    unsigned int prot_sglen;
    unsigned char prot_op;
    __data_loc unsigned char[] cmnd;
```

Even more details are available via kprobes of scsi functions, although without the interface stability.

9.3.13 nvmelatency

nvmelatency(8)[17] traces the nvme storage driver and shows command latencies by disk and nvme command opcode. This can be useful for isolating device latency from the latency measured higher in the stack at the block I/O layer. For example:

```
# nvmelatency.bt
Attaching 4 probes...
Tracing nvme command latency. Hit Ctrl-C to end.
^C

@usecs[nvme0n1, nvme_cmd_flush]:
[8, 16)                2 |@@@@@@@@@                                          |
[16, 32)               7 |@@@@@@@@@@@@@@@@@@@@@@@@@@@@@@@@@@@@@@@             |
[32, 64)               6 |@@@@@@@@@@@@@@@@@@@@@@@@@@@@@@@@                    |
```

---

17 Origin: I created it for this book on 21-Mar-2019, inspired by similar storage driver tools that I created for the 2011 DTrace book [Gregg 11].

```
[64, 128)          11 |@@@@@@@@@@@@@@@@@@@@@@@@@@@@@@@@@@@@@@@@@@@@@@@@@@@@|
[128, 256)          0 |                                                  |
[256, 512)          0 |                                                  |
[512, 1K)           3 |@@@@@@@@@@@@@                                      |
[1K, 2K)            8 |@@@@@@@@@@@@@@@@@@@@@@@@@@@@@@@@@@@@@@              |
[2K, 4K)            1 |@@@@                                              |
[4K, 8K)            4 |@@@@@@@@@@@@@@@@@@                                 |

@usecs[nvme0n1, nvme_cmd_write]:
[8, 16)             3 |@@@@                                              |
[16, 32)           37 |@@@@@@@@@@@@@@@@@@@@@@@@@@@@@@@@@@@@@@@@@@@@@@@@@@@@|
[32, 64)           20 |@@@@@@@@@@@@@@@@@@@@@@@@@@@@                       |
[64, 128)           6 |@@@@@@@@                                          |
[128, 256)          0 |                                                  |
[256, 512)          0 |                                                  |
[512, 1K)           0 |                                                  |
[1K, 2K)            0 |                                                  |
[2K, 4K)            0 |                                                  |
[4K, 8K)            7 |@@@@@@@@@                                         |

@usecs[nvme0n1, nvme_cmd_read]:
[32, 64)         7653 |@@@@@@@@@@@@@@@@@@@@@@@@@@@@@@@@@@@@@@@@@@@@@@@@@@@@|
[64, 128)         568 |@@@                                               |
[128, 256)         45 |                                                  |
[256, 512)          4 |                                                  |
[512, 1K)           0 |                                                  |
[1K, 2K)            0 |                                                  |
[2K, 4K)            0 |                                                  |
[4K, 8K)            1 |                                                  |
```

This output showed that only one disk was in use, nvme0n1, and the latency distributions for three nvme command types.

Tracepoints for nvme were recently added to Linux, but I wrote this tool on a system that did not have them, to show what can be accomplished with kprobes and storage drivers. I began by frequency counting which nvme functions were in use during different I/O workloads:

```
# bpftrace -e 'kprobe:nvme* { @[func] = count(); }'
Attaching 184 probes...
^C

@[nvme_pci_complete_rq]: 5998
@[nvme_free_iod]: 6047
@[nvme_setup_cmd]: 6048
```

```
@[nvme_queue_rq]: 6071
@[nvme_complete_rq]: 6171
@[nvme_irq]: 6304
@[nvme_process_cq]: 12327
```

Browsing the source for these functions showed that latency could be traced as the time from nvme_setup_cmd() to nvme_complete_rq().

The existence of tracepoints can aid in tool development, even if you are on a system that lacks them. By inspecting how the nvme tracepoints worked [187], I was able to develop this tool more quickly, because the tracepoint source showed how to correctly interpret nvme opcodes.

The source to nvmelatency(8) is:

```
#!/usr/local/bin/bpftrace

#include <linux/blkdev.h>
#include <linux/nvme.h>

BEGIN
{
        printf("Tracing nvme command latency. Hit Ctrl-C to end.\n");
        // from linux/nvme.h:
        @ioopcode[0x00] = "nvme_cmd_flush";
        @ioopcode[0x01] = "nvme_cmd_write";
        @ioopcode[0x02] = "nvme_cmd_read";
        @ioopcode[0x04] = "nvme_cmd_write_uncor";
        @ioopcode[0x05] = "nvme_cmd_compare";
        @ioopcode[0x08] = "nvme_cmd_write_zeroes";
        @ioopcode[0x09] = "nvme_cmd_dsm";
        @ioopcode[0x0d] = "nvme_cmd_resv_register";
        @ioopcode[0x0e] = "nvme_cmd_resv_report";
        @ioopcode[0x11] = "nvme_cmd_resv_acquire";
        @ioopcode[0x15] = "nvme_cmd_resv_release";
}

kprobe:nvme_setup_cmd
{
        $req = (struct request *)arg1;
        if ($req->rq_disk) {
                @start[arg1] = nsecs;
                @cmd[arg1] = arg2;
        } else {
                @admin_commands = count();
```

```
        }
}

kprobe:nvme_complete_rq
/@start[arg0]/
{
        $req = (struct request *)arg0;
        $cmd = (struct nvme_command *)@cmd[arg0];
        $disk = $req->rq_disk;
        $opcode = $cmd->common.opcode & 0xff;
        @usecs[$disk->disk_name, @ioopcode[$opcode]] =
            hist((nsecs - @start[arg0]) / 1000);
        delete(@start[tid]); delete(@cmd[tid]);
}

END
{
        clear(@ioopcode); clear(@start); clear(@cmd);
}
```

If a request is created without a disk, it is an admin command. The script can be enhanced to decode and time the admin commands (see nvme_admin_opcode in include/linux/nvme.h). To keep this tool short, I simply counted admin commands so that if any are present they will be noted in the output.

9.4 BPF One-Liners

These sections show BCC and bpftrace one-liners. Where possible, the same one-liner is implemented using both BCC and bpftrace.

9.4.1 BCC

Count block I/O tracepoints:

```
funccount t:block:*
```

Summarize block I/O size as a histogram:

```
argdist -H 't:block:block_rq_issue():u32:args->bytes'
```

Count block I/O request user stack traces:

```
stackcount -U t:block:block_rq_issue
```

Count block I/O type flags:

```
argdist -C 't:block:block_rq_issue():char*:args->rwbs'
```

Trace block I/O errors with device and I/O type:

```
trace 't:block:block_rq_complete (args->error) "dev %d type %s error %d", args->dev,
args->rwbs, args->error'
```

Count SCSI opcodes:

```
argdist -C 't:scsi:scsi_dispatch_cmd_start():u32:args->opcode'
```

Count SCSI result codes:

```
argdist -C 't:scsi:scsi_dispatch_cmd_done():u32:args->result'
```

Count nvme driver functions:

```
funccount 'nvme*'
```

9.4.2   bpftrace

Count block I/O tracepoints:

```
bpftrace -e 'tracepoint:block:* { @[probe] = count(); }'
```

Summarize block I/O size as a histogram:

```
bpftrace -e 't:block:block_rq_issue { @bytes = hist(args->bytes); }'
```

Count block I/O request user stack traces:

```
bpftrace -e 't:block:block_rq_issue { @[ustack] = count(); }'
```

Count block I/O type flags:

```
bpftrace -e 't:block:block_rq_issue { @[args->rwbs] = count(); }'
```

Show total bytes by I/O type:

```
bpftrace -e 't:block:block_rq_issue { @[args->rwbs] = sum(args->bytes); }'
```

Trace block I/O errors with device and I/O type:

```
bpftrace -e 't:block:block_rq_complete /args->error/ {
    printf("dev %d type %s error %d\n", args->dev, args->rwbs, args->error); }'
```

Summarize block I/O plug time as a histogram:

```
bpftrace -e 'k:blk_start_plug { @ts[arg0] = nsecs; }
    k:blk_flush_plug_list /@ts[arg0]/ { @plug_ns = hist(nsecs - @ts[arg0]);
    delete(@ts[arg0]); }'
```

Count SCSI opcodes:

```
bpftrace -e 't:scsi:scsi_dispatch_cmd_start { @opcode[args->opcode] = count(); }'
```

Count SCSI result codes (all four bytes):

```
bpftrace -e 't:scsi:scsi_dispatch_cmd_done { @result[args->result] = count(); }'
```

Show CPU distribution of blk_mq requests:

```
bpftrace -e 'k:blk_mq_start_request { @swqueues = lhist(cpu, 0, 100, 1); }'
```

Count scsi driver functions:

```
bpftrace -e 'kprobe:scsi* { @[func] = count(); }'
```

Count nvme driver functions:

```
bpftrace -e 'kprobe:nvme* { @[func] = count(); }'
```

9.4.3 BPF One-Liners Examples

Including some sample output, as was done for each tool, is also useful for illustrating one-liners.

Counting Block I/O Type Flags

```
# bpftrace -e 't:block:block_rq_issue { @[args->rwbs] = count(); }'
Attaching 1 probe...
^C

@[N]: 2
@[WFS]: 9
@[FF]: 12
@[N]: 13
@[WSM]: 23
@[WM]: 64
@[WS]: 86
@[R]: 201
@[R]: 285
@[W]: 459
@[RM]: 1112
@[RA]: 2128
@[R]: 3635
@[W]: 4578
```

This frequency counts the rwbs field that encodes the I/O type. While tracing, where were 3635 reads ("R") and 2128 read-ahead I/O ("RA"). The "rwbs" section at the start of this chapter describes this rwbs field.

This one-liner can answer workload characterization questions such as:

- What is the ratio of read versus read-ahead block I/O?
- What is the ratio of write versus synchronous write block I/O?

By changing count() to be sum(args->bytes), this one-liner will sum the bytes by I/O type.

9.5 Optional Exercises

If not specified, these can be completed using either bpftrace or BCC:

1. Modify biolatency(8) to print a linear histogram instead, for the range 0 to 100 milliseconds and a step size of one millisecond.

2. Modify biolatency(8) to print the linear histogram summary every one second.

3. Develop a tool to show disk I/O completions by CPU, to check how these interrupts are balanced. It could be displayed as a linear histogram.

4. Develop a tool similar to biosnoop(8) to print per-event block I/O, with only the following fields, in CSV format: completion_time,direction,latency_ms. The direction is read or write.

5. Save two minutes of (4) and use plotting software to visualize it as a scatter plot, coloring reads red and writes blue.

6. Save two minutes of the output of (2) and use plotting software to display it as a latency heat map. (You can also develop some plotting software: e.g., use awk(1) to turn the count column into rows of a HTML table, with the background color scaled to the value.)

7. Rewrite biosnoop(8) to use block tracepoints.

8. Modify seeksize(8) to show the actual seek distances encountered by the storage devices: measured on completions.

9. Write a tool to show disk I/O timeouts. One solution could be to use the block tracepoints and BLK_STS_TIMEOUT (see bioerr(8)).

10. (Advanced, unsolved) Develop a tool that shows the lengths of block I/O merging as a histogram.

9.6 Summary

This chapter shows how BPF can trace at all layers of the storage I/O stack. The tools traced the block I/O layer, the I/O scheduler, SCSI, and nvme as an example driver.

Chapter 10

Networking

Networking is playing an ever-increasing role in the performance analysis of systems, with the rise of distributed cloud computing models increasing network traffic within a datacenter or cloud environment, and online applications increasing external network traffic. The need for efficient network analysis tools is also on the rise, as servers scale to processing millions of packets per second. Extended BPF began as a technology for packet processing, so it has been designed and built to operate at these rates. The Cilium project for container networking and security policies, and Facebook's Katran scalable network load balancer, are further examples of BPF's ability to handle high packet rates in production environments, including for distributed denial of service attack (DDoS) mitigation.[1]

Network I/O is processed by many different layers and protocols, including the application, protocol libraries, syscalls, TCP or UDP, IP, and device drivers for the network interface. These can all be traced with the BPF tools shown in this chapter, providing insight on the requested workloads and latencies encountered.

Learning Objectives:

- Gain a high-level view of the networking stack and scalability approaches, including receive and transmit scaling, TCP buffers, and queueing disciplines

- Learn a strategy for successful analysis of network performance

- Characterize socket, TCP, and UDP workloads to identify issues

- Measure different latency metrics: connection latency, first byte latency, connection duration

- Learn an efficient way to trace and analyze TCP retransmits

- Investigate inter-network-stack latency

- Quantify time spent in software and hardware networking queues

- Use bpftrace one-liners to explore networking in custom ways

This chapter begins with the necessary background for networking analysis, summarizing the network stack and scalability approaches. I explore questions that BPF can answer, and provide an overall strategy to follow. I then focus on tools, starting with traditional tools and then BPF tools, including a list of BPF one-liners. This chapter ends with optional exercises.

---

1 Both of these are also open source [93] [94].

10.1   Background

This section covers networking fundamentals, BPF capabilities, a suggested strategy for networking analysis, and common tracing mistakes.

10.1.1   Networking Fundamentals

A basic knowledge of IP and TCP, including the TCP three-way handshake, acknowledgment packets, and active/passive connection terminology, is assumed for this chapter.

Network Stack

The Linux network stack is pictured in Figure 10-1, which shows how data commonly moves from an application to a network interface card (NIC).

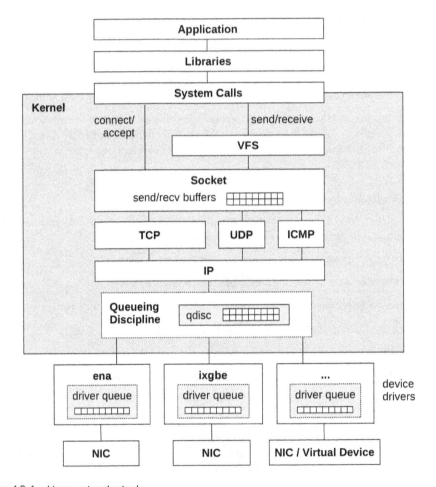

Figure 10-1   Linux network stack

Major components include:

- **Sockets:** Endpoints for sending or receiving data. These also include the send and receive buffers used by TCP.

- **TCP (Transmission Control Protocol):** A widely used transport protocol for transferring data in an ordered and reliable way, with error checking.

- **UDP (User Datagram Protocol):** A simple transport protocol for sending messages without the overhead or guarantees of TCP.

- **IP (Internet Protocol):** A network protocol for delivering packets between hosts on a network. Main versions are IPv4 and IPv6.

- **ICMP (Internet Control Message Protocol):** An IP-level protocol to support IP, relaying messages about routes and errors.

- **Queueing discipline:** An optional layer for traffic classification (tc), scheduling, manipulation, filtering, and shaping [95][2].

- **Device drivers:** Drivers that may include their own driver queues (NIC RX-ring and TX-ring).

- **NIC (network interface card):** A device that contains the physical network ports. These can also be virtual devices, such as tunnels, veths (virtual Ethernet devices), and loopback.

Figure 10-1 shows the path most commonly taken, but other paths may be used to improve the performance of certain workloads. These different paths include kernel bypass and the new BPF-based XDP.

Kernel Bypass

Applications can bypass the kernel network stack using technologies such as the Data Plane Development Kit (DPDK) for achieving higher packet rates and performance. This involves an application implementing its own network protocols in user-space, and making writes to the network driver via a DPDK library and a kernel user space I/O (UIO) or virtual function I/O (VFIO) driver. The expense of copying packet data can be avoided by directly accessing memory on the NIC.

Because the kernel network stack is bypassed, instrumentation using traditional tools and metrics is not available, making performance analysis more difficult.

XDP

The eXpress Data Path (XDP) technology provides another path for network packets: a programmable fast path that uses extended BPF, and which integrates into the existing kernel stack rather than bypassing it [Høiland-Jørgensen 18]. Because it accesses the raw network Ethernet frame as early as possible via a BPF hook inside the NIC driver, it can make early decisions about forwarding or dropping without the overhead of TCP/IP stack processing. When needed, it can also fall back to regular network stack processing. Use cases include faster DDoS mitigation, and software-defined routing.

---

2 This reference is for "Queueing in the Linux Network Stack" by Dan Siemon, published by *Linux Journal* in 2013, an excellent explanation of these queues. Coincidentally, about 90 minutes after writing this section, I found myself on an iovisor concall with Dan Siemon and was able to thank him directly.

Internals

An understanding of some kernel internals will help you understand later BPF tools. The essentials are: packets are passed through the kernel using an sk_buff struct (socket buffer). Sockets are defined by a sock struct embedded at the start of protocol variants such as tcp_sock. Network protocols are attached to sockets using a struct proto, such that there is a tcp_prot, udp_prot, etc; this struct defines callback functions for operating the protocol, including for connect, sendmsg, and recvmsg.

Receive and Transmit Scaling

Without a CPU load-balancing strategy for network packets, a NIC may only interrupt one CPU, which can drive it to 100% utilization in interrupt and network stack processing, becoming a bottleneck. Various policies are available for interrupt mitigation and distributing NIC interrupts and packet processing across multiple CPUs, improving scalability and performance. These include the new API (NAPI) interface, Receive Side Scaling (RSS),[3] Receive Packet Steering (RPS), Receive Flow Steering (RFS), Accelerated RFS, and Transmit Packet Steering (XPS). These are documented in the Linux source [96].

Socket Accept Scaling

A commonly used model to handle high rates of passive TCP connections uses a thread to process the accept(2) calls and then pass the connection to a pool of worker threads. To scale this further, a SO_REUSEPORT setsockopt(3) option was added in Linux 3.9 that allows a pool of processes or threads to bind to the same socket address, where they all can call accept(2). It is then up to the kernel to balance the new connections across the pool of bound threads. A BPF program can be supplied to steer this balancing via the SO_ATTACH_REUSEPORT_EBPF option: this was added for UDP in Linux 4.5, and TCP in Linux 4.6.

TCP Backlogs

Passive TCP connections are initiated by the kernel receiving a TCP SYN packet. The kernel must track state for this potential connection until the handshake is completed, a situation that in the past was abused by attackers using SYN floods to exhaust kernel memory. Linux uses two queues to prevent this: a SYN backlog with minimal metadata that can better survive SYN floods, and then a listen backlog for completed connections for the application to consume. This is pictured in Figure 10-2.

Packets can be dropped from the SYN backlog in the case of flooding, or the listen backlog if the application cannot accept connections quickly enough. A legitimate remote host will respond with a timer-based retransmit.

In addition to the two-queue model, the TCP listen path was also made lockless to improve scalability for SYN flood attacks [98].[4]

---

3 RSS is processed purely by NIC hardware. Some NICs support offloading of BPF networking programs (e.g., Netronome), allowing RSS to become BPF programmable [97].

4 The developer, Eric Dumazet, was able to reach six million SYN packets per second on his system after fixing a final false-sharing issue [99].

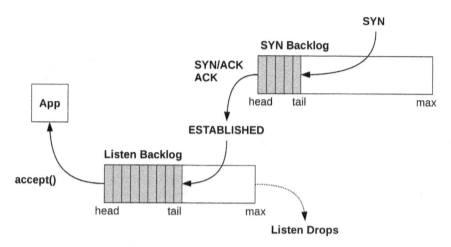

Figure 10-2   TCP SYN backlogs

TCP Retransmits

TCP detects and retransmits lost packets using one of two techniques:

- **Timer-based retransmits:** These occur when a time has passed and a packet acknowledgment has not yet been received. This time is the TCP retransmit timeout, calculated dynamically based on the connection round trip time (RTT). On Linux, this will be at least 200 ms (TCP_RTO_MIN) for the first retransmit, and subsequent retransmits will be much slower, following an exponential backoff algorithm that doubles the timeout.

- **Fast retransmits:** When duplicate ACKs arrive, TCP can assume that a packet was dropped and retransmit it immediately.

Timer-based retransmits in particular cause performance issues, injecting latencies of 200 ms and higher into network connections. Congestion control algorithms may also throttle throughput in the presence of retransmits.

Retransmits can require a sequence of packets to be resent, beginning from the lost packet, even if later packets were received correctly. Selective acknowledgments (SACK) is a TCP option commonly used to avoid this: it allows later packets to be acknowledged so that they do not need to be resent, improving performance.

TCP Send and Receive Buffers

TCP data throughput is improved by using socket send and receive buffer accounting. Linux dynamically sizes the buffers based on connection activity, and allows tuning of their minimum, default, and maximum sizes. Larger sizes improve performance at the cost of more memory per connection. They are shown in Figure 10-3.

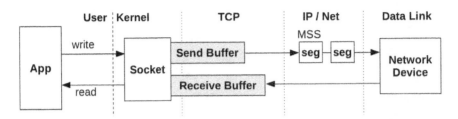

Figure 10-3   TCP send and receive buffers

Network devices and networks accept packet sizes up to a maximum segment size (MSS) that may be as small as 1500 bytes. To avoid the network stack overheads of sending many small packets, TCP uses generic segmentation offload (GSO) to send packets up to 64 Kbytes in size ("super packets"), which are split into MSS-sized segments just before delivery to the network device. If the NIC and driver support TCP segmentation offload (TSO), GSO leaves splitting to the device, further improving network stack throughput. There is also a generic receive offload (GRO) complement to GSO [100]. GRO and GSO are implemented in kernel software, and TSO is implemented by NIC hardware.

TCP Congestion Controls

Linux supports different TCP congestion control algorithms, including Cubic (the default), Reno, Tahoe, DCTCP, and BBR. These algorithms modify send and receive windows based on detected congestion to keep network connections running optimally.

Queueing Discipline

This optional layer manages traffic classification (tc), scheduling, manipulation, filtering, and shaping of network packets. Linux provides numerous queueing discipline algorithms, which can be configured using the tc(8) command. As each has a man page, the man(1) command can be used to list them:

```
# man -k tc-
tc-actions (8)          - independently defined actions in tc
tc-basic (8)            - basic traffic control filter
tc-bfifo (8)            - Packet limited First In, First Out queue
tc-bpf (8)              - BPF programmable classifier and actions for ingress/egress
queueing disciplines
tc-cbq (8)              - Class Based Queueing
tc-cbq-details (8)      - Class Based Queueing
tc-cbs (8)              - Credit Based Shaper (CBS) Qdisc
tc-cgroup (8)           - control group based traffic control filter
tc-choke (8)            - choose and keep scheduler
tc-codel (8)            - Controlled-Delay Active Queue Management algorithm
tc-connmark (8)         - netfilter connmark retriever action
tc-csum (8)             - checksum update action
```

```
tc-drr (8)              - deficit round robin scheduler
tc-ematch (8)           - extended matches for use with "basic" or "flow" filters
tc-flow (8)             - flow based traffic control filter
tc-flower (8)           - flow based traffic control filter
tc-fq (8)               - Fair Queue traffic policing
tc-fq_codel (8)         - Fair Queuing (FQ) with Controlled Delay (CoDel)
[...]
```

BPF can enhance the capabilities of this layer with the programs of type
BPF_PROG_TYPE_SCHED_CLS and BPF_PROG_TYPE_SCHED_ACT.

Other Performance Optimizations

There are other algorithms in use throughout the network stack to improve performance,
including:

- **Nagle:** This reduces small network packets by delaying their transmission, allowing more to
  arrive and coalesce.

- **Byte Queue Limits (BQL):** These automatically size the driver queues large enough to
  avoid starvation, but also small enough to reduce the maximum latency of queued packets.
  It works by pausing the addition of packets to the driver queue when necessary, and was
  added in Linux 3.3 [95].

- **Pacing:** This controls when to send packets, spreading out transmissions (pacing) to avoid
  bursts that may hurt performance.

- **TCP Small Queues (TSQ):** This controls (reduces) how much is queued by the network
  stack to avoid problems including bufferbloat [101].

- **Early Departure Time (EDT):** This uses a timing wheel to order packets sent to the
  NIC, instead of a queue. Timestamps are set on every packet based on policy and rate
  configuration. This was added in Linux 4.20, and has BQL- and TSQ-like capabilities
  [Jacobson 18].

These algorithms often work in combination to improve performance. A TCP sent packet can be
processed by any of the congestion controls, TSO, TSQ, Pacing, and queueing disciplines, before it
ever arrives at the NIC [Cheng 16].

Latency Measurements

Various networking latency measurements can be made to provide insight into performance,
helping to determine whether bottlenecks are in the sending or receiving applications, or the
network itself. These include [Gregg 13b]:

- **Name resolution latency:** The time for a host to be resolved to an IP address, usually by
  DNS resolution—a common source of performance issues.

- **Ping latency:** The time from an ICMP echo request to a response. This measures the
  network and kernel stack handling of the packet on each host.

- **TCP connection latency:** The time from when a SYN is sent to when the SYN,ACK is received. Since no applications are involved, this measures the network and kernel stack latency on each host, similar to ping latency, with some additional kernel processing for the TCP session. TCP Fast Open (TFO) is a technology to eliminate connection latency for subsequent connections by providing cryptographic cookie with the SYN to authenticate the client immediately, allowing the server to respond with data without waiting for the three-way handshake to complete.

- **TCP first byte latency:** Also known as the time-to-first-byte latency (TTFB), this measures the time from when a connection is established to when the first data byte is received by the client. This includes CPU scheduling and application think time for the host, making it a more a measure of application performance and current load than TCP connection latency.

- **Round trip time (RTT):** The time for a network packet to make a round trip between endpoints. The kernel may use such measurements with congestion control algorithms.

- **Connection lifespan:** The duration of a network connection from initialization to close. Some protocols like HTTP can use a keep-alive strategy, leaving connections open and idle for future requests, to avoid the overheads and latency of repeated connection establishment.

Using these in combination can help locate the source of latency, by process of elimination. They should also be used in combination with other metrics to understand network health, including event rates and throughput.

Further Reading

This summarized selected topics as background for network analysis tools. The implementation of the Linux network stack is described in the kernel source under Documentation/networking [102], and network performance is covered in more depth in Chapter 10 of *Systems Performance* [Gregg 13a].

10.1.2   BPF Capabilities

Traditional network performance tools operate on kernel statistics and network packet captures. BPF tracing tools can provide more insight, answering:

- What socket I/O is occurring, and why? What are the user-level stacks?
- Which new TCP sessions are created, and by which processes?
- Are there socket, TCP, or IP-level errors occurring?
- What are the TCP window sizes? Any zero-size transmits?
- What is the I/O size at different stack layers? To the devices?
- Which packets are dropped by the network stack, and why?
- What are the TCP connection latency, first byte latency, and lifespans?

- What is the kernel inter-network-stack latency?

- How long do packets spend on the qdisc queues? Network driver queues?

- What higher-level protocols are in use?

These can be answered with BPF by instrumenting tracepoints when available, and then using kprobes and uprobes when details beyond tracepoint coverage are needed.

Event Sources

Table 10-1 lists networking targets and the sources that can instrument them.

Table 10-1   **Network Events and Sources**

Network Event	Event Source
Application protocols	uprobes
Sockets	syscalls tracepoints
TCP	tcp tracepoints, kprobes
UDP	kprobes
IP and ICMP	kprobes
Packets	skb tracepoints, kprobes
QDiscs and driver queues	qdisc and net tracepoints, kprobes
XDP	xdp tracepoints
Network device drivers	kprobes

In many cases, kprobes must be used due to a lack of tracepoints. One reason that there are so few tracepoints is the historical (pre-BPF) lack of demand. Now that BPF is driving demand, the first TCP tracepoints were added in the 4.15 and 4.16 kernels. By Linux 5.2, the TCP tracepoints are:

```
# bpftrace -l 'tracepoint:tcp:*'
tracepoint:tcp:tcp_retransmit_skb
tracepoint:tcp:tcp_send_reset
tracepoint:tcp:tcp_receive_reset
tracepoint:tcp:tcp_destroy_sock
tracepoint:tcp:tcp_rcv_space_adjust
tracepoint:tcp:tcp_retransmit_synack
tracepoint:tcp:tcp_probe
```

More network protocol tracepoints may be added in future kernels. It may seem obvious to add send and receive tracepoints for the different protocols, but that involves modifying critical latency-sensitive code paths, and care must be taken to understand the not-enabled overheads that such additions would introduce.

Overhead

Network events can be frequent, exceeding several million packets per second on some servers and workloads. Fortunately, BPF originated as an efficient per-packet filter, and adds only a tiny amount of overhead to each event. Nevertheless, when multiplied by millions or 10 millions of events per second, that can add up to become a noticeable or even significant overhead.

Fortunately, many observability needs can be met without per-packet tracing, by instead tracing events that have a much lower frequency and therefore lower overhead. TCP retransmits, for example, can be traced via the tcp_retransmit_skb() kernel function alone, without needing to trace each packet. I did this for a recent production issue, where the server packet rate was over 100,000/second, and the retransmit rate was 1000/second. Whatever the overhead was for packet tracing, my choice of event to trace reduced it one hundred fold.

For times when it is necessary to trace each packet, raw tracepoints (introduced in Chapter 2) are a more efficient option than tracepoints and kprobes.

A common technique for network performance analysis involves collecting per-packet captures (tcpdump(8), libpcap, etc.), which not only adds overhead to each packet but also additional CPU, memory, and storage overheads when writing these packets to the file system, then additional overheads when reading them again for post-processing. In comparison, BPF per-packet tracing is already a large efficiency improvement. Because it emits summaries calculated in kernel memory only, without the use of capture files.

10.1.3 Strategy

If you are new to network performance analysis, here is a suggested overall strategy you can follow. The next sections explain these tools in more detail.

This strategy begins by using workload characterization to spot inefficiencies (steps 1 and 2), then checks interface limits (step 3) and different sources of latency (steps 4, 5, and 6). At this point, it may be worth trying experimental analysis (step 7)—bearing in mind, however, that it can interfere with production workloads—followed by more advanced and custom analysis (steps 8, 9, and 10).

1. Use counter-based tools to understand basic network statistics: packet rates and throughput and, if TCP is in use, TCP connection rates and TCP retransmit rates (e.g., using ss(8), nstat(8), netstat(1) and sar(1)).

2. Trace which new TCP connections are created, and their duration, to characterize the workload and look for inefficiencies (e.g., using BCC tcplife(8)). For example, you might find frequent connections to read a resource from a remote service that can be cached locally.

3. Check whether network interface throughput limits have been hit (e.g., using sar(1) or nicstat(1)'s interface utilization percent).

4. Trace TCP retransmits and other unusual TCP events (e.g., BCC tcpretrans(8), tcpdrop(8), and the skb:kfree_skb tracepoint).

5. Measure host name resolution (DNS) latency, as this is a common source of performance issues (e.g., BCC gethostlatency(8)).

6. Measure networking latency from different points: connection latency, first byte latency, inter-stack latency, etc.

    a. Note that network latency measurements can vary significantly with load due to bufferbloat in the network (an issue of excessive queueing latency). If possible, it can be useful to measure these latencies during load, and also for an idle network, for comparison.

7. Use load-generation tools to explore network throughput limits between hosts, and to examine network events against a known workload (e.g., using iperf(1) and netperf(1)).

8. Browse and execute the BPF tools listed in the BPF tools section of this book.

9. Use high-frequency CPU profiling of kernel stack traces to quantify CPU time spent in protocol and driver processing.

10. Use tracepoints and kprobes to explore network stack internals.

10.1.4 Common Tracing Mistakes

Some common mistakes when developing BPF tools for network analysis:

- Events may not happen in application context. Packets may be received when the idle thread is on-CPU, and TCP sessions may be initialized and change state at this time. Examining the on-CPU PID and process name for these events will not show the application endpoint for the connection. You need to choose different events that are in application context, or cache application context by an identifier (e.g., struct sock) that can be fetched later.

- There may be fast paths and slow paths. You may write a program that seems to work, but is only tracing one of these paths. Use known workloads and ensure that packet and byte counts match.

- In TCP there are full sockets and non-full sockets: the latter are request sockets before the three-way handshake has completed, or when the socket is in the TCP TIME_WAIT state. Some socket struct fields may not be valid for non-full sockets.

10.2 Traditional Tools

Traditional performance tools can display kernel statistics for packet rates, various events, and throughput and show the state of open sockets. Many such statistics are commonly collected and graphed by monitoring tools. Another type of tool captures packets for analysis, allowing each packet header and contents to be studied.

Apart from solving issues, traditional tools can also provide clues to direct your further use of BPF tools. They have been categorized in Table 10.2 based on their source and measurement type, kernel statistics or packet captures.

Table 10-2 **Traditional Tools**

Tool	Type	Description
ss	Kernel statistics	Socket statistics
ip	Kernel statistics	IP statistics
nstat	Kernel statistics	Network stack statistics
netstat	Kernel statistics	Multi-tool for showing network stack statistics and state
sar	Kernel statistics	Multi-tool for showing networking and other statistics
nicstat	Kernel statistics	Network interface statistics
ethtool	Driver statistics	Network interface driver statistics
tcpdump	Packet capture	Capture packets for analysis

The following sections summarize key functionality of these observability tools. Refer to their man pages and other resources, including *Systems Performance* [Gregg 13a], for more usage and explanations.

Note that there are also tools that perform experiments for network analysis. These include micro benchmarks such as iperf(1) and netperf(1), ICMP tools including ping(1), and network route discovery tools including traceroute(1) and pathchar. There is also the Flent GUI for automating network tests [103]. And there are tools for static analysis: checking the configuration of the system and hardware, without necessarily having any workload applied [Elling 00]. These experimental and static tools are covered elsewhere (e.g., [Gregg 13a]).

The ss(8), ip(8), and nstat(8) tools are covered first, as these are from the iproute2 package that is maintained by the network kernel engineers. Tools from this package are most likely to support the latest Linux kernel features.

10.2.1 ss

ss(8) is a socket statistics tool that summarizes open sockets. The default output provides high-level information about sockets, for example:

```
# ss
Netid State     Recv-Q Send-Q  Local Address:Port      Peer Address:Port
[...]
tcp   ESTAB     0      0        100.85.142.69:65264     100.82.166.11:6001
tcp   ESTAB     0      0        100.85.142.69:6028      100.82.16.200:6101
[...]
```

This output is a snapshot of the current state. The first column shows the protocol used by the sockets: these are TCP. Since this output lists all established connections with IP address information, it can be used to characterize the current workload, and answer questions including how many client connections are open, how many concurrent connections there are to a dependency service, etc.

Much more information is available using options. For example, showing TCP sockets only (-t), with TCP internal info (-i), extended socket info (-e), process info (-p), and memory usage (-m):

```
# ss -tiepm
State     Recv-Q  Send-Q    Local Address:Port     Peer Address:Port

ESTAB     0       0         100.85.142.69:65264    100.82.166.11:6001
  users:(("java",pid=4195,fd=10865)) uid:33 ino:2009918 sk:78 <->
          skmem:(r0,rb12582912,t0,tb12582912,f266240,w0,o0,bl0,d0) ts sack bbr ws
cale:9,9 rto:204 rtt:0.159/0.009 ato:40 mss:1448 pmtu:1500 rcvmss:1448 advmss:14
48 cwnd:152 bytes_acked:347681 bytes_received:1798733 segs_out:582 segs_in:1397
data_segs_out:294 data_segs_in:1318 bbr:(bw:328.6Mbps,mrtt:0.149,pacing_gain:2.8
8672,cwnd_gain:2.88672) send 11074.0Mbps lastsnd:1696 lastrcv:1660 lastack:1660
pacing_rate 2422.4Mbps delivery_rate 328.6Mbps app_limited busy:16ms rcv_rtt:39.
822 rcv_space:84867 rcv_ssthresh:3609062 minrtt:0.139
[...]
```

This output includes many details. Highlighted in bold are the endpoint addresses and the following details:

- **"java",pid=4195**: Process name "java", PID 4195
- **fd=10865**: File descriptor 10865 (for PID 4195)
- **rto:204**: TCP retransmission timeout: 204 milliseconds
- **rtt:0.159/0.009**: Average round-trip time is 0.159 milliseconds, with 0.009 milliseconds mean deviation
- **mss:1448**: Maximum segment size: 1448 bytes
- **cwnd:152**: Congestion window size: 152 × MSS
- **bytes_acked:347681**: 340 Kbytes successfully transmitted
- **bytes_received:1798733**: 1.72 Mbytes received
- **bbr:...**: BBR congestion control statistics
- **pacing_rate 2422.4Mbps**: Pacing rate of 2422.4 Mbps

This tool uses the netlink interface, which uses sockets of family AF_NETLINK to fetch information from the kernel.

10.2.2 ip

ip(8) is a tool for managing routing, network devices, interfaces, and tunnels. For observability, it can be used to print statistics on various objects: link, address, route, etc. For example, printing extra statistics (-s) on interfaces (link):

```
# ip -s link
1: lo: <LOOPBACK,UP,LOWER_UP> mtu 65536 qdisc noqueue state UNKNOWN mode DEFAULT
group default qlen 1000
    link/loopback 00:00:00:00:00:00 brd 00:00:00:00:00:00
    RX: bytes  packets  errors  dropped overrun mcast
    26550075   273178   0       0       0       0
    TX: bytes  packets  errors  dropped carrier collsns
    26550075   273178   0       0       0       0
2: eth0: <BROADCAST,MULTICAST,UP,LOWER_UP> mtu 1500 qdisc mq state UP mode DEFAULT
group default qlen 1000
    link/ether 12:c0:0a:b0:21:b8 brd ff:ff:ff:ff:ff:ff
    RX: bytes  packets  errors  dropped overrun mcast
    512473039143 568704184 0      0       0       0
    TX: bytes  packets  errors  dropped carrier collsns
    573510263433 668110321 0      0       0       0
```

Various error types can be checked from this output: for receive (RX): receive errors, drops, and overruns; for transmit (TX): transmit errors, drops, carrier errors, and collisions. Such errors can be a source of performance issues and, depending on the error, may be caused by faulty network hardware.

Printing the route object shows the routing table:

```
# ip route
default via 100.85.128.1 dev eth0
default via 100.85.128.1 dev eth0 proto dhcp src 100.85.142.69 metric 100
100.85.128.0/18 dev eth0 proto kernel scope link src 100.85.142.69
100.85.128.1 dev eth0 proto dhcp scope link src 100.85.142.69 metric 100
```

Misconfigured routes can also be a source of performance problems.

10.2.3 nstat

nstat(8) prints the various network metrics maintained by the kernel, with their SNMP names:

```
# nstat -s
#kernel
IpInReceives         462657733        0.0
IpInDelivers         462657733        0.0
IpOutRequests        497050986        0.0
```

```
[...]
TcpActiveOpens                   362997              0.0
TcpPassiveOpens                  9663983             0.0
TcpAttemptFails                  12718               0.0
TcpEstabResets                   14591               0.0
TcpInSegs                        462181482           0.0
TcpOutSegs                       938958577           0.0
TcpRetransSegs                   129212              0.0
TcpOutRsts                       52362               0.0
[...]
```

The -s option was used to avoid resetting these counters, which is the default behavior of nstat(8). Resetting is useful, as you can then run nstat(8) a second time and see counts that spanned that interval, rather than totals since boot. If you had a network problem that could be reproduced with a command, then nstat(8) can be run before and after the command to show which counters changed.

nstat(8) also has a daemon mode (-d) to collect interval statistics, which when used are shown in the last column.

10.2.4 netstat

netstat(8) is a tool traditionally used for reporting different types of network statistics based on the options used. These options include:

- **(default)**: Lists open sockets
- **-a**: Lists information for all sockets
- **-s**: Network stack statistics
- **-i**: Network interface statistics
- **-r**: Lists the route table

For example, modifying the default output with -a to show all sockets, and -n to not resolve IP addresses (otherwise, this invocation can cause a heavy name resolution workload as a side effect), and -p to show process information:

```
# netstat -anp
Active Internet connections (servers and established)
Proto Recv-Q Send-Q Local Address      Foreign Address   State         PID/Program name
tcp        0      0 192.168.122.1:53   0.0.0.0:*         LISTEN        8086/dnsmasq
tcp        0      0 127.0.0.53:53      0.0.0.0:*         LISTEN        1112/systemd-resolv
tcp        0      0 0.0.0.0:22         0.0.0.0:*         LISTEN        1440/sshd
[...]
tcp        0      0 10.1.64.90:36426   10.2.25.52:22     ESTABLISHED 24152/ssh
[...]
```

The -i option prints interface statistics. On a production cloud instance:

```
# netstat -i
Kernel Interface table
Iface   MTU      RX-OK RX-ERR RX-DRP RX-OVR    TX-OK TX-ERR TX-DRP TX-OVR Flg
eth0    1500 743442015     0    0 0      882573158     0      0      0 BMRU
lo      65536   427560     0    0 0         427560     0      0      0 LRU
```

The interface eth0 is the primary interface. The fields show receive (RX-) and transmit (TX-):

- **OK:** Packets transferred successfully

- **ERR:** Packet errors

- **DRP:** Packet drops

- **OVR:** Packet overruns

An additional -c (continuous) option prints this summary every second.

The -s option prints network stack statistics. For example, on a busy production system (output truncated):

```
# netstat -s
Ip:
    Forwarding: 2
    454143446 total packets received
    0 forwarded
    0 incoming packets discarded
    454143446 incoming packets delivered
    487760885 requests sent out
    42 outgoing packets dropped
    2260 fragments received ok
    13560 fragments created
Icmp:
[...]
Tcp:
    359286 active connection openings
    9463980 passive connection openings
    12527 failed connection attempts
    14323 connection resets received
    13545 connections established
    453673963 segments received
    922299281 segments sent out
    127247 segments retransmitted
    0 bad segments received
    51660 resets sent
```

```
Udp:
[...]
TcpExt:
    21 resets received for embryonic SYN_RECV sockets
    12252 packets pruned from receive queue because of socket buffer overrun
    201219 TCP sockets finished time wait in fast timer
    11727438 delayed acks sent
    1445 delayed acks further delayed because of locked socket
    Quick ack mode was activated 17624 times
    169257582 packet headers predicted
    76058392 acknowledgments not containing data payload received
    111925821 predicted acknowledgments
    TCPSackRecovery: 1703
    Detected reordering 876 times using SACK
    Detected reordering 19 times using time stamp
    2 congestion windows fully recovered without slow start
[...]
```

This shows totals since boot. Much can be learned by studying this output: you can calculate packet rates for different protocols, connection rates (TCP active and passive), error rates, throughput, and other events. Some of the metrics I look for first I've highlighted in bold.

This output has human-readable descriptions of the metrics; it is not supposed to be parsed by other software, such as monitoring agents. Those should read the metrics directly from /proc/net/snmp and /proc/net/netstat instead (or even nstat(8)).

10.2.5 sar

The system activity reporter, sar(1), can print various network statistics reports. sar(1) can be used live, or configured to record data periodically as a monitoring tool. The networking options to sar(1) are:

- **-n DEV**: Network interface statistics
- **-n EDEV**: Network interface errors
- **-n IP,IP6**: IPv4 and IPv6 datagram statistics
- **-n EIP,EIP6**: IPv4 and IPv6 error statistics
- **-n ICMP,ICMP6**: ICMP IPv4 and IPv6 statistics
- **-n EICMP,EICMP6**: ICMP IPv4 and IPv6 error statistics
- **-n TCP**: TCP statistics
- **-n ETCP**: TCP error statistics
- **-n SOCK,SOCK6**: IPv4 and IPv6 socket usage

As an example invocation, the following shows using four of these options on a production Hadoop instance, printed with an interval of one second:

```
# sar -n SOCK,TCP,ETCP,DEV 1
Linux 4.15.0-34-generic (...)       03/06/2019    _x86_64_      (36 CPU)


08:06:48 PM     IFACE   rxpck/s    txpck/s    rxkB/s    txkB/s   rxcmp/s   txcmp/s
rxmcst/s    %ifutil
08:06:49 PM      eth0 121615.00 108725.00 168906.73 149731.09     0.00      0.00
0.00     13.84
08:06:49 PM        lo   600.00     600.00   11879.12  11879.12    0.00      0.00
0.00      0.00


08:06:48 PM    totsck     tcpsck     udpsck     rawsck    ip-frag    tcp-tw
08:06:49 PM      2133        108          5          0          0     7134


08:06:48 PM  active/s passive/s     iseg/s     oseg/s
08:06:49 PM     16.00     134.00   15230.00 109267.00


08:06:48 PM  atmptf/s   estres/s retrans/s isegerr/s    orsts/s
08:06:49 PM      0.00       8.00      1.00      0.00      14.00
[...]
```

This multi-line output repeats for each interval. It can be used to determine:

- The number of open TCP sockets (tcpsck)
- The current TCP connection rate (active/s + passive/s)
- The TCP retransmit rate (retrans/s / oseg/s)
- Interfaces packet rates and throughput (rxpck/s + txpck/s, rxkB/s + txkB/s)

This is a cloud instance where I expect network interface errors to be zero: on physical servers, include the EDEV group to check for such errors.

10.2.6 nicstat

This tool prints network interface statistics and is modeled on iostat(1).[5] For example:

```
# nicstat 1
    Time    Int    rKB/s   wKB/s    rPk/s    wPk/s     rAvs     wAvs %Util    Sat
20:07:43    eth0   122190 81009.7  89435.8  61576.8   1399.0   1347.2  10.0   0.00
20:07:43      lo   13000.0 13000.0   646.7    646.7  20583.5  20583.5   0.00   0.00
```

---

5 Origin: I developed it for Solaris on 18-Jul-2004; Tim Cook developed the Linux version.

Time	Int	rKB/s	wKB/s	rPk/s	wPk/s	rAvs	wAvs	%Util	Sat
20:07:44	eth0	268115	42283.6	185199	40329.2	1482.5	1073.6	22.0	0.00
20:07:44	lo	1869.3	1869.3	400.3	400.3	4782.1	4782.1	0.00	0.00
Time	Int	rKB/s	wKB/s	rPk/s	wPk/s	rAvs	wAvs	%Util	Sat
20:07:45	eth0	146194	40685.3	102412	33270.4	1461.8	1252.2	12.0	0.00
20:07:45	lo	1721.1	1721.1	109.1	109.1	16149.1	16149.1	0.00	0.00

[...]

This includes a saturation statistic, which combines different errors that indicate the level of interface saturation. A -U option will print separate read and write utilization percents, to determine if one direction is hitting limits.

10.2.7 ethtool

ethtool(8) can be used to check the static configuration of the network interfaces with -i and -k options, and also print driver statistics with -S. For example:

```
# ethtool -S eth0
NIC statistics:
     tx_timeout: 0
     suspend: 0
     resume: 0
     wd_expired: 0
     interface_up: 1
     interface_down: 0
     admin_q_pause: 0
     queue_0_tx_cnt: 100219217
     queue_0_tx_bytes: 84830086234
     queue_0_tx_queue_stop: 0
     queue_0_tx_queue_wakeup: 0
     queue_0_tx_dma_mapping_err: 0
     queue_0_tx_linearize: 0
     queue_0_tx_linearize_failed: 0
     queue_0_tx_napi_comp: 112514572
     queue_0_tx_tx_poll: 112514649
     queue_0_tx_doorbells: 52759561
[...]
```

This fetches statistics from the kernel ethtool framework, which many network device drivers support. Device drivers can define their own ethtool metrics.

The -i option shows driver details, and -k shows interface tunables. For example:

```
# ethtool -i eth0
driver: ena
version: 2.0.3K
[...]
# ethtool -k eth0
Features for eth0:
rx-checksumming: on
[...]
tcp-segmentation-offload: off
        tx-tcp-segmentation: off [fixed]
        tx-tcp-ecn-segmentation: off [fixed]
        tx-tcp-mangleid-segmentation: off [fixed]
        tx-tcp6-segmentation: off [fixed]
udp-fragmentation-offload: off
generic-segmentation-offload: on
generic-receive-offload: on
large-receive-offload: off [fixed]
rx-vlan-offload: off [fixed]
tx-vlan-offload: off [fixed]
ntuple-filters: off [fixed]
receive-hashing: on
highdma: on
[...]
```

This example is a cloud instance with the ena driver, and tcp-segmentation-offload is currently off. The -K option can be used to change these tunables.

10.2.8 tcpdump

Finally, tcpdump(8) can capture packets for study. This is termed "packet sniffing." For example, sniffing interface en0 (-i) and writing (-w) to a dump file and then reading it (-r) without name resolution (-n)[6]:

```
# tcpdump -i en0 -w /tmp/out.tcpdump01
tcpdump: listening on en0, link-type EN10MB (Ethernet), capture size 262144 bytes
^C451 packets captured
477 packets received by filter
0 packets dropped by kernel
# tcpdump -nr /tmp/out.tcpdump01
reading from file /tmp/out.tcpdump01, link-type EN10MB (Ethernet)
```

---

6 It may cause additional network traffic for name resolution as an unwanted side effect of reading the file.

```
13:39:48.917870 IP 10.0.0.65.54154 > 69.53.1.1.4433: UDP, length 1357
13:39:48.921398 IP 108.177.1.2.443 > 10.0.0.65.59496: Flags [P.], seq
3108664869:3108664929, ack 2844371493, win 537, options [nop,nop,TS val 2521261
368 ecr 4065740083], length 60
13:39:48.921442 IP 10.0.0.65.59496 > 108.177.1.2.443: Flags [.], ack 60, win 505,
options [nop,nop,TS val 4065741487 ecr 2521261368], length 0
13:39:48.921463 IP 108.177.1.2.443 > 10.0.0.65.59496: Flags [P.], seq 0:60, ack 1,
win 537, options [nop,nop,TS val 2521261793 ecr 4065740083], length 60
[...]
```

tcpdump(8) output files can be read by other tools, including the Wireshark GUI [104]. Wireshark allows packet headers to be easily inspected, and TCP sessions to be "followed," reassembling the transmit and receive bytes so that client/host interactions can be studied.

While packet capture has been optimized in the kernel and the libpcap library, at high rates it can still be expensive to perform, costing additional CPU overheads to collect, and CPU, memory, and disk resources to store, and then again to post-process. These overheads can be reduced somewhat by using a filter, so that only packets with certain header details are recorded. However, there are CPU overheads even for packets that are not collected.[7] Since the filter expression must be applied to all packets, its processing must be efficient. This is the origin of Berkeley Packet Filter (BPF), which was created as a packet capture filter and later extended to become the technology I am using in this book for tracing tools. See Section 2.2 for an example of a tcpdump(8) filter program.

While packet capture tools may appear to show comprehensive details of networking, they only show details sent on the wire. They are blind to kernel state, including which processes are responsible for the packets, the stack traces, and kernel state of the sockets and TCP. Such details can be seen using BPF tracing tools.

10.2.9 /proc

Many of the prior statistic tools source metrics from /proc files, especially those in /proc/net. This directory can be explored at the command line:

```
$ ls /proc/net/
anycast6     if_inet6             ip_tables_names      ptype     sockstat6
arp          igmp                 ip_tables_targets    raw       softnet_stat
bnep         igmp6                ipv6_route           raw6      stat/
connector    ip6_flowlabel        l2cap                rfcomm    tcp
dev          ip6_mr_cache         mcfilter             route     tcp6
dev_mcast    ip6_mr_vif           mcfilter6            rt6_stats udp
dev_snmp6/   ip6_tables_matches   netfilter/           rt_acct   udp6
fib_trie     ip6_tables_names     netlink              rt_cache  udplite
fib_triestat ip6_tables_targets   netstat              sco       udplite6
```

---

7 Every skb has to be cloned before it is handed to one of the packet handlers, and only later filtered (see dev_queue_xmit_nit()). BPF-based solutions can avoid the skb copy.

```
hci                ip_mr_cache        packet           snmp       unix
icmp               ip_mr_vif          protocols        snmp6      wireless
icmp6              ip_tables_matches  psched           sockstat   xfrm_stat
$ cat /proc/net/snmp
Ip: Forwarding DefaultTTL InReceives InHdrErrors InAddrErrors ForwDatagrams
InUnknownProtos InDiscards InDelivers OutRequests OutDiscards OutNoRoutes
ReasmTimeout ReasmReqds ReasmOKs ReasmFails FragOKs FragFails FragCreates
Ip: 2 64 45794729 0 28 0 0 0 45777774 40659467 4 6429 0 0 0 0 0 0
[...]
```

The netstat(1) and sar(1) tools expose many of these metrics. As shown earlier, they include system-wide statistics for packet rates, TCP active and passive new connections, TCP retransmits, ICMP errors, and much more.

There are also /proc/interrupts and /proc/softirqs, which can show the distribution of network device interrupts across CPUs. For example, on a two-CPU system:

```
$ cat /proc/interrupts
          CPU0        CPU1
[...]
  28:    1775400          80    PCI-MSI 81920-edge      ena-mgmnt@pci:0000:00:05.0
  29:        533     5501189    PCI-MSI 81921-edge      eth0-Tx-Rx-0
  30:    4526113         278    PCI-MSI 81922-edge      eth0-Tx-Rx-1
$ cat /proc/softirqs
                    CPU0        CPU1
[...]
      NET_TX:     332966          34
      NET_RX:   10915058    11500522
[...]
```

This system has an eth0 interface that uses the ena driver. The above output shows eth0 is using a queue for each CPU, and receive softirqs are spread across both CPUs. (Transmits appear unbalanced, but the network stack often skips this softirq and transmits directly to the device.) mpstat(8) also has an -I option to print interrupt statistics.

The BPF tools that follow have been created to extend, rather than duplicate, network observability beyond these /proc and traditional tool metrics. There is a BPF sockstat(8) for system-wide socket metrics, since those particular metrics are not available in /proc. But there is not a similar tcpstat(8), udpstat(8), or ipstat(8) tool for system-wide metrics: while it is possible to write these in BPF, such tools only need to use the already-maintained metrics in /proc. It is not even necessary to write those tools: netstat(1) and sar(1) provide that observability.

The following BPF tools extend observability by breaking down statistics by process ID, process name, IP address, and ports, revealing stack traces that led to events, exposing kernel state, and by showing custom latency measurements. It might appear that these tools are comprehensive: they are not. They are designed to be used with /proc/net and the earlier traditional tools, to extend observability.

10.3 BPF Tools

This section covers the BPF tools you can use for network performance analysis and troubleshooting. They are shown in Figure 10-4.

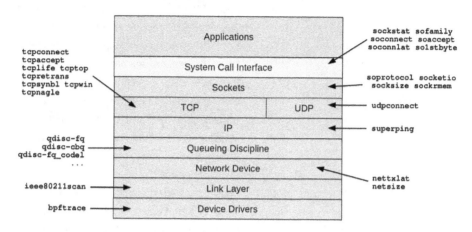

Figure 10-4   BPF tools for network analysis

bpftrace is shown in Figure 10-4 as observing device drivers. See Section 10.4.3 for examples. The other tools in this figure are from either the BCC or bpftrace repositories covered in Chapters 4 and 5, or were created for this book. Some tools appear in both BCC and bpftrace. Table 10-3 lists the origins of these tools (BT is short for bpftrace).

Table 10-3 **Network-Related Tools**

Tool	Source	Target	Description
sockstat	Book	Sockets	High-level socket statistics
sofamily	Book	Sockets	Count address families for new sockets, by process
soprotocol	Book	Sockets	Count transport protocols for new sockets, by process
soconnect	Book	Sockets	Trace socket IP-protocol connections with details
soaccept	Book	Sockets	Trace socket IP-protocol accepts with details
socketio	Book	Sockets	Summarize socket details with I/O counts
socksize	Book	Sockets	Show socket I/O sizes as per-process histograms
sormem	Book	Sockets	Show socket receive buffer usage and overflows
soconnlat	Book	Sockets	Summarize IP socket connection latency with stacks
solstbyte	Book	Sockets	Summarize IP socket first byte latency
tcpconnect	BCC/BT/book	TCP	Trace TCP active connections (connect())
tcpaccept	BCC/BT/book	TCP	Trace TCP passive connections (accept())

Tool	Source	Target	Description
`tcplife`	BCC/book	TCP	Trace TCP session lifespans with connection details
`tcptop`	BCC	TCP	Show TCP send/recv throughput by host
`tcpretrans`	BCC/BT	TCP	Trace TCP retransmits with address and TCP state
`tcpsynbl`	Book	TCP	Show TCP SYN backlog as a histogram
`tcpwin`	Book	TCP	Trace TCP send congestion window parameters
`tcpnagle`	Book	TCP	Trace TCP nagle usage and transmit delays
`udpconnect`	Book	UDP	Trace new UDP connections from localhost
`gethostlatency`	Book/BT	DNS	Trace DNS lookup latency via library calls
`ipecn`	Book	IP	Trace IP inbound explicit congestion notification
`superping`	Book	ICMP	Measure ICMP echo times from the network stack
`qdisc-fq (...)`	Book	qdiscs	Show FQ qdisc queue latency
`netsize`	Book	net	Show net device I/O sizes
`nettxlat`	Book	net	Show net device transmission latency
`skbdrop`	Book	skbs	Trace sk_buff drops with kernel stack traces
`skblife`	Book	skbs	Lifespan of sk_buff as inter-stack latency
`ieee80211scan`	Book	WiFi	Trace IEEE 802.11 WiFi scanning

For the tools from BCC and bpftrace, see their repositories for full and updated lists of tool options and capabilities. A selection of the most important capabilities is summarized here.

10.3.1   sockstat

sockstat(8)[8] prints socket statistics along with counts for socket-related system calls each second. For example, on a production edge server:

```
# sockstat.bt
Attaching 10 probes...
Tracing sock statistics. Output every 1 second.
01:11:41
@[tracepoint:syscalls:sys_enter_bind]: 1
@[tracepoint:syscalls:sys_enter_socket]: 67
@[tracepoint:syscalls:sys_enter_connect]: 67
@[tracepoint:syscalls:sys_enter_accept4]: 89
@[kprobe:sock_sendmsg]: 5280
@[kprobe:sock_recvmsg]: 10547

01:11:42
[...]
```

---

8 Origin: I created it for this book on 14-Apr-2019.

A time is printed each second (e.g., "21:22:56"), followed by counts for various socket events. This example shows 10,547 sock_recvmsg() and 5280 sock_sendmsg() events per second, and fewer than one hundred accept4(2)s and connect(2)s.

The role of this tool is to provide high-level socket statistics for workload characterization, and starting points for further analysis. The output includes the probe name so that you can investigate further; for example, if you see a higher-than-expected rate of kprobe:sock_sendmsg events, the process name can be fetched using this bpftrace one-liner[9]:

```
# bpftrace -e 'kprobe:sock_sendmsg { @[comm] = count(); }'
Attaching 1 probe...
^C

@[sshd]: 1
@[redis-server]: 3
@[snmpd]: 6
@[systemd-resolve]: 28
@[java]: 17377
```

The user-level stack trace can also be inspected by adding ustack to the map key.

The sockstat(8) tool works by tracing key socket-related syscalls using tracepoints, and the sock_recvmsg() and sock_sendmsg() kernel functions using kprobes. The overhead of the kprobes is likely to be the most noticeable, and may become measurable on high network-throughput systems.

The source to sockstat(8) is:

```
#!/usr/local/bin/bpftrace

BEGIN
{
        printf("Tracing sock statistics. Output every 1 second.\n");
}

tracepoint:syscalls:sys_enter_accept*,
tracepoint:syscalls:sys_enter_connect,
tracepoint:syscalls:sys_enter_bind,
tracepoint:syscalls:sys_enter_socket*,
kprobe:sock_recvmsg,
kprobe:sock_sendmsg
{
        @[probe] = count();
}
```

---

9 Note for this and subsequent tools: applications can override their comm string by writing to /proc/self/comm.

```
interval:s:1
{
        time();
        print(@);
        clear(@);
}
```

The use of these kprobes is a shortcut. These could be traced using syscall tracepoints instead. The recvfrom(2), recvmsg(2), sendto(2), and sendmsg(2) syscalls, and other variants, can be traced by adding more tracepoints to the code. It becomes more complex with the read(2) and write(2) family of syscalls, where the file descriptor must be processed to determine the file type, to match on socket reads and writes only.

10.3.2 sofamily

sofamily(8)[10] traces new socket connections via the accept(2) and connect(2) system calls and summarizes the process name and address family. This is useful for workload characterization: quantifying the load applied and looking for any unexpected socket usage that needs further investigation. For example, on a production edge server:

```
# sofamily.bt
Attaching 7 probes...
Tracing socket connect/accepts. Ctrl-C to end.
^C

@accept[sshd, 2, AF_INET]: 2
@accept[java, 2, AF_INET]: 420

@connect[sshd, 2, AF_INET]: 2
@connect[sshd, 10, AF_INET6]: 2
@connect[(systemd), 1, AF_UNIX]: 12
@connect[sshd, 1, AF_UNIX]: 34
@connect[java, 2, AF_INET]: 215
```

This output shows 420 AF_INET (IPv4) accepts and 215 connection attempts by Java while tracing, which is expected for this server. The output shows a map for socket accepts (@accept) and connects (@connect), with the keys process name, address family number, and the address family name for that number if known.

The address family number mappings (e.g., AF_INET == 2) is specific to Linux and is defined in the include/linux/socket.h header. (The table is included on the following pages.) Other kernels use their own number mappings.

---

10 Origin: I created this tool for this book on 10-Apr-2019.

Since the traced calls occur at a relatively low rate (compared to packet events), the overhead of this tool is expected to be negligible.

The source to sofamily(8) is:

```
#!/usr/local/bin/bpftrace

#include <linux/socket.h>

BEGIN
{
        printf("Tracing socket connect/accepts. Ctrl-C to end.\n");
        // from linux/socket.h:
        @fam2str[AF_UNSPEC] = "AF_UNSPEC";
        @fam2str[AF_UNIX] = "AF_UNIX";
        @fam2str[AF_INET] = "AF_INET";
        @fam2str[AF_INET6] = "AF_INET6";
}

tracepoint:syscalls:sys_enter_connect
{
        @connect[comm, args->uservaddr->sa_family,
            @fam2str[args->uservaddr->sa_family]] = count();
}

tracepoint:syscalls:sys_enter_accept,
tracepoint:syscalls:sys_enter_accept4
{
        @sockaddr[tid] = args->upeer_sockaddr;
}

tracepoint:syscalls:sys_exit_accept,
tracepoint:syscalls:sys_exit_accept4
/@sockaddr[tid]/
{
        if (args->ret > 0) {
                $sa = (struct sockaddr *)@sockaddr[tid];
                @accept[comm, $sa->sa_family, @fam2str[$sa->sa_family]] =
                    count();
        }
        delete(@sockaddr[tid]);
}

END
```

```
{
        clear(@sockaddr); clear(@fam2str);
}
```

The address family is read from the sa_family member of struct sockaddr. This is a number of type sa_family_t, which resolves to unsigned short. This tool includes the number on the output and also maps some common address families to string names to aid readability, based on this table from linux/socket.h:

```
/* Supported address families. */
#define AF_UNSPEC       0
#define AF_UNIX         1       /* Unix domain sockets         */
#define AF_LOCAL        1       /* POSIX name for AF_UNIX      */
#define AF_INET         2       /* Internet IP Protocol        */
#define AF_AX25         3       /* Amateur Radio AX.25         */
#define AF_IPX          4       /* Novell IPX                  */
#define AF_APPLETALK    5       /* AppleTalk DDP               */
#define AF_NETROM       6       /* Amateur Radio NET/ROM       */
#define AF_BRIDGE       7       /* Multiprotocol bridge        */
#define AF_ATMPVC       8       /* ATM PVCs                    */
#define AF_X25          9       /* Reserved for X.25 project   */
#define AF_INET6        10      /* IP version 6                */
[..]
```

This header is included when running this bpftrace program, so that this line:

```
@fam2str[AF_INET] = "AF_INET";
```

becomes:

```
@fam2str[2] = "AF_INET";
```

mapping the number two to the string "AF_INET".

For the connect(2) syscall, all details are read on the syscall entry. The accept(2) syscalls are traced differently: the sockaddr pointer is saved in a hash and then retrieved on the exit of those syscalls to read the address family. This is because the sockaddr is populated during the syscall, so must be read at the end. The accept(2) return value is also checked (was it successful or not?); otherwise, the contents of the sockaddr struct would not be valid. This script could be enhanced to do a similar check for connect(2), so that the output counts are given only for successful new connections. The soconnect(8) tool shows the different return results for these connect(2) syscalls.

10.3.3 soprotocol

soprotocol(8)[11] traces new socket connections and summarizes the process name and transport protocol. This is another workload characterization tool, for the transport protocol. For example, on a production edge server:

---

11 Origin: I created this tool for this book on 13-Apr-2019.

```
# soprotocol.bt
Attaching 4 probes...
Tracing socket connect/accepts. Ctrl-C to end.
^C

@accept[java, 6, IPPROTO_TCP, TCP]: 1171

@connect[setuidgid, 0, IPPROTO, UNIX]: 2
@connect[ldconfig, 0, IPPROTO, UNIX]: 2
@connect[systemd-resolve, 17, IPPROTO_UDP, UDP]: 79
@connect[java, 17, IPPROTO_UDP, UDP]: 80
@connect[java, 6, IPPROTO_TCP, TCP]: 559
```

This output shows 559 TCP accepts and 1171 TCP connects by Java while tracing. The output shows a map for socket accepts (@accept) and connects (@connect), with the keys: process name, protocol number, protocol name for that number if known, and protocol module name.

Since these calls happen at a relatively low rate (compared to packet events), the overhead of this tool is expected to be negligible.

The source to soprotocol(8) is:

```
#!/usr/local/bin/bpftrace

#include <net/sock.h>

BEGIN
{
        printf("Tracing socket connect/accepts. Ctrl-C to end.\n");
        // from include/uapi/linux/in.h:
        @prot2str[IPPROTO_IP] = "IPPROTO_IP";
        @prot2str[IPPROTO_ICMP] = "IPPROTO_ICMP";
        @prot2str[IPPROTO_TCP] = "IPPROTO_TCP";
        @prot2str[IPPROTO_UDP] = "IPPROTO_UDP";
}

kprobe:security_socket_accept,
kprobe:security_socket_connect
{
        $sock = (struct socket *)arg0;
        $protocol = $sock->sk->sk_protocol & 0xff;
        @connect[comm, $protocol, @prot2str[$protocol],
            $sock->sk->__sk_common.skc_prot->name] = count();
}
```

```
END
{
        clear(@prot2str);
}
```

This provides a short lookup table to translate protocol numbers into strings, and four common protocols. These are from the in.h header:

```
#if __UAPI_DEF_IN_IPPROTO
/* Standard well-defined IP protocols.  */
enum {
  IPPROTO_IP = 0,              /* Dummy protocol for TCP            */
#define IPPROTO_IP            IPPROTO_IP
  IPPROTO_ICMP = 1,            /* Internet Control Message Protocol   */
#define IPPROTO_ICMP          IPPROTO_ICMP
  IPPROTO_IGMP = 2,            /* Internet Group Management Protocol   */
#define IPPROTO_IGMP          IPPROTO_IGMP
  IPPROTO_IPIP = 4,            /* IPIP tunnels (older KA9Q tunnels use 94) */
#define IPPROTO_IPIP          IPPROTO_IPIP
  IPPROTO_TCP = 6,             /* Transmission Control Protocol       */
#define IPPROTO_TCP           IPPROTO_TCP
[...]
```

The bpftrace @prot2str table can be extended if needed.

The protocol module name, seen in the previous output as "TCP," "UDP," etc., is available as a string from the struct sock: __sk_common.skc_prot->name. This is convenient, and I've used this in other tools to print the transport protocol. Here is an an example from net/ipv4/tcp_ipv4.c:

```
struct proto tcp_prot = {
        .name           = "TCP",
        .owner          = THIS_MODULE,
        .close          = tcp_close,
        .pre_connect    = tcp_v4_pre_connect,
[...]
```

The presence of this name field (.name = "TCP") is a Linux kernel implementation detail. While convenient, it is possible that this .name member could change or vanish in future kernels. The transport protocol number, however, should always be present—which is why I included it in this tool as well.

The syscall tracepoints for accept(2) and connect(2) do not provide an easy path for fetching the protocol, and currently there are not any other tracepoints for these events. Without them, I have switched to using kprobes and chosen the LSM security_socket_* functions, which provide a struct sock as the first argument, and are a relatively stable interface.

10.3.4 soconnect

soconnect(8)[12] shows IP protocol socket connect requests. For example:

```
# soconnect.bt
Attaching 4 probes...
PID    PROCESS      FAM ADDRESS               PORT   LAT(us) RESULT
11448  ssh          2   127.0.0.1             22          43 Success
11449  ssh          2   10.168.188.1          22       45134 Success
11451  curl         2   100.66.96.2           53           6 Success
11451  curl         10  2406:da00:ff00::36d0:a866  80       3 Network unreachable
11451  curl         2   52.43.200.64          80           7 Success
11451  curl         2   52.39.122.191         80           3 Success
11451  curl         2   52.24.119.28          80          19 In progress
[...]
```

This shows two ssh(1) connections to port 22, followed by a curl(1) process that begins with a port 53 connection (DNS) and then an attempted IPv6 connection to port 80 that resulted in "network unreachable," followed by successful IPv4 connections. The columns are:

- **PID:** Process ID calling connect(2)

- **PROCESS:** Process name calling connect(2)

- **FAM:** Address family number (see the description in sofamily(8) earlier)

- **ADDRESS:** IP address

- **PORT:** Remote port

- **LAT(us):** Latency (duration) of the connect(2) syscall only (see note below)

- **RESULT:** Syscall error status

Note that IPv6 addresses can be so long that they cause the columns to overflow[13] (as seen in this example).

This works by instrumenting the connect(2) syscall tracepoints. One benefit is that these occur in process context, so you can reliably know who made the syscall. Compare this to the later tcpconnect(8) tool, which traces deeper in TCP and may or may not identify the process responsible. These connect(8) syscalls are also relatively low in frequency compared to packets and other events, and the overhead should be negligible.

The reported latency is for the connect() syscall only. For some applications, including the ssh(1) processes seen in the earlier output, this spans the network latency to establish a connection to

---

12 Origin: I created this for the 2011 DTrace book [Gregg 11] and created this bpftrace version on 9-Apr-2019.

13 You might wonder why I don't just make the columns wider. If I did, it would cause wrapping for every line of output in this example, rather than just one. I try to keep the default output of all tools to less than 80 characters wide, so that it fits without problems in books, slides, emails, ticketing systems, and chat rooms. Some tools in BCC have a wide mode available, just to fit IPv6 neatly.

the remote host. Other applications may create non-blocking sockets (SOCK_NONBLOCK), and the connect() syscall may return early before the connection is completed. This can be seen in the example output as the final curl(1) connection that results in an "In progress" result. To measure the full connection latency for these non-blocking calls requires instrumenting more events; an example is the later soconnlat(8) tool.

The source to soconnect(8) is:

```
#!/usr/local/bin/bpftrace

#include <linux/in.h>
#include <linux/in6.h>

BEGIN
{
        printf("%-6s %-16s FAM %-16s %-5s %8s %s\n", "PID", "PROCESS",
            "ADDRESS", "PORT", "LAT(us)", "RESULT");
        // connect(2) has more details:
        @err2str[0] = "Success";
        @err2str[EPERM] = "Permission denied";
        @err2str[EINTR] = "Interrupted";
        @err2str[EBADF] = "Invalid sockfd";
        @err2str[EAGAIN] = "Routing cache insuff.";
        @err2str[EACCES] = "Perm. denied (EACCES)";
        @err2str[EFAULT] = "Sock struct addr invalid";
        @err2str[ENOTSOCK] = "FD not a socket";
        @err2str[EPROTOTYPE] = "Socket protocol error";
        @err2str[EAFNOSUPPORT] = "Address family invalid";
        @err2str[EADDRINUSE] = "Local addr in use";
        @err2str[EADDRNOTAVAIL] = "No port available";
        @err2str[ENETUNREACH] = "Network unreachable";
        @err2str[EISCONN] = "Already connected";
        @err2str[ETIMEDOUT] = "Timeout";
        @err2str[ECONNREFUSED] = "Connect refused";
        @err2str[EALREADY] = "Not yet completed";
        @err2str[EINPROGRESS] = "In progress";
}

tracepoint:syscalls:sys_enter_connect
/args->uservaddr->sa_family == AF_INET ||
    args->uservaddr->sa_family == AF_INET6/
```

```
{
        @sockaddr[tid] = args->uservaddr;
        @start[tid] = nsecs;
}


tracepoint:syscalls:sys_exit_connect
/@start[tid]/
{
        $dur_us = (nsecs - @start[tid]) / 1000;
        printf("%-6d %-16s %-3d ", pid, comm, @sockaddr[tid]->sa_family);

        if (@sockaddr[tid]->sa_family == AF_INET) {
                $s = (struct sockaddr_in *)@sockaddr[tid];
                $port = ($s->sin_port >> 8) | (($s->sin_port << 8) & 0xff00);
                printf("%-16s %-5d %8d %s\n",
                    ntop(AF_INET, $s->sin_addr.s_addr),
                    $port, $dur_us, @err2str[- args->ret]);
        } else {
                $s6 = (struct sockaddr_in6 *)@sockaddr[tid];
                $port = ($s6->sin6_port >> 8) | (($s6->sin6_port << 8) & 0xff00);
                printf("%-16s %-5d %8d %s\n",
                    ntop(AF_INET6, $s6->sin6_addr.in6_u.u6_addr8),
                    $port, $dur_us, @err2str[- args->ret]);
        }

        delete(@sockaddr[tid]);
        delete(@start[tid]);
}


END
{
        clear(@start); clear(@err2str); clear(@sockaddr);
}
```

This records the struct sockaddr pointer when the syscall begins from args->uservaddr, along with a timestamp, so that these details can be fetched on the syscall exit. The sockaddr struct contains the connection details, but it must first be recast to the IPv4 sockaddr_in or the IPv6 sockaddr_in6 based on the sin_family member. A table of error codes that map to descriptions for connect(2) is used, based on the descriptions in the connect(2) man page.

The port number is flipped from network to host order using bitwise operations.

10.3.5   soaccept

soaccept(8)[14] shows IP protocol socket accepts. For example:

```
# soaccept.bt
Attaching 6 probes...
PID    PROCESS          FAM ADDRESS          PORT  RESULT
4225   java             2   100.85.215.60    65062 Success
4225   java             2   100.85.54.16     11742 Success
4225   java             2   100.82.213.228   18500 Success
4225   java             2   100.85.209.40    20150 Success
4225   java             2   100.82.21.89     27278 Success
4225   java             2   100.85.192.93    32490 Success
[...]
```

This shows many accepts by Java from different address. The port shown is the remote ephemeral port. See the later tcpaccept(8) tool for showing both endpoint ports. The columns are:

- **PID:** Process ID calling connect(2)
- **COMM:** Process name calling connect(2)
- **FAM:** Address family number (see the description in Section 10.3.2)
- **ADDRESS:** IP address
- **PORT:** Remote port
- **RESULT:** Syscall error status

This works by instrumenting the accept(2) syscall tracepoint. As with soconnect(8), this occurs in process context, so you can reliably identify who is making these accept(8) calls. These are also relatively low frequency compared to packets and other events, and the overhead should be negligible.

The source to soaccept(8) is:

```
#!/usr/local/bin/bpftrace

#include <linux/in.h>
#include <linux/in6.h>

BEGIN
{
        printf("%-6s %-16s FAM %-16s %-5s %s\n", "PID", "PROCESS",
            "ADDRESS", "PORT", "RESULT");
        // accept(2) has more details:
```

14 Origin: I created this for the 2011 DTrace book [Gregg 11] and created this bpftrace version on 13-Apr-2019.

```
        @err2str[0] = "Success";
        @err2str[EPERM] = "Permission denied";
        @err2str[EINTR] = "Interrupted";
        @err2str[EBADF] = "Invalid sockfd";
        @err2str[EAGAIN] = "None to accept";
        @err2str[ENOMEM] = "Out of memory";
        @err2str[EFAULT] = "Sock struct addr invalid";
        @err2str[EINVAL] = "Args invalid";
        @err2str[ENFILE] = "System FD limit";
        @err2str[EMFILE] = "Process FD limit";
        @err2str[EPROTO] = "Protocol error";
        @err2str[ENOTSOCK] = "FD not a socket";
        @err2str[EOPNOTSUPP] = "Not SOCK_STREAM";
        @err2str[ECONNABORTED] = "Aborted";
        @err2str[ENOBUFS] = "Memory (ENOBUFS)";
}

tracepoint:syscalls:sys_enter_accept,
tracepoint:syscalls:sys_enter_accept4
{
        @sockaddr[tid] = args->upeer_sockaddr;
}

tracepoint:syscalls:sys_exit_accept,
tracepoint:syscalls:sys_exit_accept4
/@sockaddr[tid]/
{
        $sa = (struct sockaddr *)@sockaddr[tid];
        if ($sa->sa_family == AF_INET || $sa->sa_family == AF_INET6) {
                printf("%-6d %-16s %-3d ", pid, comm, $sa->sa_family);
                $error = args->ret > 0 ? 0 : - args->ret;

                if ($sa->sa_family == AF_INET) {
                        $s = (struct sockaddr_in *)@sockaddr[tid];
                        $port = ($s->sin_port >> 8) |
                            (($s->sin_port << 8) & 0xff00);
                        printf("%-16s %-5d %s\n",
                            ntop(AF_INET, $s->sin_addr.s_addr),
                            $port, @err2str[$error]);
                } else {
                        $s6 = (struct sockaddr_in6 *)@sockaddr[tid];
                        $port = ($s6->sin6_port >> 8) |
                            (($s6->sin6_port << 8) & 0xff00);
```

```
                      printf("%-16s %-5d %s\n",
                          ntop(AF_INET6, $s6->sin6_addr.in6_u.u6_addr8),
                          $port, @err2str[$error]);
            }
        }

        delete(@sockaddr[tid]);
}

END
{
        clear(@err2str); clear(@sockaddr);
}
```

This is similar to soconnect(8), processing and recasting the sockaddr on the return of the syscall. The error code descriptions have been changed, based on the descriptions in the accept(2) man page.

10.3.6 socketio

socketio(8)[15] shows socket I/O counts by process, direction, protocol, and port. Example output:

```
# socketio.bt
Attaching 4 probes...
^C
@io[sshd, 13348, write, TCP, 49076]: 1
@io[redis-server, 2583, write, TCP, 41154]: 5
@io[redis-server, 2583, read, TCP, 41154]: 5
@io[snmpd, 1242, read, NETLINK, 0]: 6
@io[snmpd, 1242, write, NETLINK, 0]: 6
@io[systemd-resolve, 1016, read, UDP, 53]: 52
@io[systemd-resolve, 1016, read, UDP, 0]: 52
@io[java, 3929, read, TCP, 6001]: 1367
@io[java, 3929, write, TCP, 8980]: 24979
@io[java, 3929, read, TCP, 8980]: 44462
```

The final line in the output shows that Java PID 3929 performed 44,462 socket reads from TCP port 8980 while tracing. The five fields in each map key are process name, process ID, direction, protocol, and port.

---

15 Origin: I first created it as socketio.d for the 2011 DTrace book [Gregg 11], and I created the bpftrace version for this book on 11-Apr-2019.

This works by tracing the sock_recvmsg() and sock_sendmsg() kernel functions. To explain why I chose these functions, consider the socket_file_ops struct in net/socket.c:

```
/*
 *      Socket files have a set of 'special' operations as well as the generic file
 ones. These don't appear
 *      in the operation structures but are done directly via the socketcall()
 multiplexor.
 */

static const struct file_operations socket_file_ops = {
        .owner =        THIS_MODULE,
        .llseek =       no_llseek,
        .read_iter =    sock_read_iter,
        .write_iter =   sock_write_iter,
[...]
```

This code defines the socket read and write functions as sock_read_iter() and sock_write_iter(), and I tried tracing them first. But testing with a variety of workloads showed that tracing those particular functions was missing some events. The block comment in the code excerpt explains why: There are additional special operations that don't appear in the operation struct, and these can also perform I/O on sockets. These include sock_recvmsg() and sock_sendmsg(), called directly via syscalls or other code paths, including sock_read_iter() and sock_write_iter(). This makes them a common point for tracing socket I/O.

For systems with busy network I/O, these socket functions may be called very frequently, causing the overhead to become measurable.

The source to socketio(8) is:

```
#!/usr/local/bin/bpftrace

#include <net/sock.h>

kprobe:sock_recvmsg
{
        $sock = (struct socket *)arg0;
        $dport = $sock->sk->__sk_common.skc_dport;
        $dport = ($dport >> 8) | (($dport << 8) & 0xff00);
        @io[comm, pid, "read", $sock->sk->__sk_common.skc_prot->name, $dport] =
            count();
}

kprobe:sock_sendmsg
{
```

```
$sock = (struct socket *)arg0;
$dport = $sock->sk->__sk_common.skc_dport;
$dport = ($dport >> 8) | (($dport << 8) & 0xff00);
@io[comm, pid, "write", $sock->sk->__sk_common.skc_prot->name, $dport] =
    count();
}
```

The destination port is big endian, and is converted to little endian (for this x86 processor) by the tool before inclusion in the @io map.[16] This script could be modified to show the bytes transferred instead of the I/O counts; for an example, see the code in the following tool, socksize(8).

socketio(8) is based on kprobes, which instruments kernel implementation details that may change, breaking the tool. With much more effort, it would be possible to rewrite this tool using syscall tracepoints instead. It will be necessary to trace sendto(2), sendmsg(2), sendmmsg(2), recvfrom(2), recvmsg(2), and recvmmsg(2). For some socket types, such as UNIX domain sockets, the read(2) and write(2) family of syscalls must also be traced. It would be easier to instrument tracepoints for socket I/O instead, however, they do not yet exist.

10.3.7   socksize

socksize(8)[17] shows socket I/O counts and total bytes by process and direction. Example output from a 48-CPU production edge server:

```
# socksize.bt
Attaching 2 probes...
^C

@read_bytes[sshd]:
[32, 64)               1 |@@@@@@@@@@@@@@@@@@@@@@@@@@@@@@@@@@@@@@@@@@@@@@@@@@@@|

@read_bytes[java]:
[0]                  431 |@@@@@                                              |
[1]                    4 |                                                   |
[2, 4)                10 |                                                   |
[4, 8)               542 |@@@@@@                                             |
[8, 16)             3445 |@@@@@@@@@@@@@@@@@@@@@@@@@@@@@@@@@@@@@@@@@@@@@@       |
[16, 32)            2635 |@@@@@@@@@@@@@@@@@@@@@@@@@@@@@@@@@@@@                 |
[32, 64)            3497 |@@@@@@@@@@@@@@@@@@@@@@@@@@@@@@@@@@@@@@@@@@@@@@@      |
[64, 128)            776 |@@@@@@@@@                                          |
[128, 256)           916 |@@@@@@@@@@@                                        |
[256, 512)          3123 |@@@@@@@@@@@@@@@@@@@@@@@@@@@@@@@@@@@@@@@@@            |
```

---

16 For this to work on big-endian processors, the tool should test for processor endianness and use a conversion only if necessary; for example, by use of #ifdef LITTLE_ENDIAN

17 Origin: I created it for this book on 12-Apr-2019, inspired by my disk I/O bitesize tool.

```
[512, 1K)              4199 |@@@@@@@@@@@@@@@@@@@@@@@@@@@@@@@@@@@@@@@@@@@@@@@@@@@@|
[1K, 2K)               2972 |@@@@@@@@@@@@@@@@@@@@@@@@@@@@@@@@@@@@@@            |
[2K, 4K)               1863 |@@@@@@@@@@@@@@@@@@@@@@@@                        |
[4K, 8K)               2501 |@@@@@@@@@@@@@@@@@@@@@@@@@@@@@@@                 |
[8K, 16K)              1422 |@@@@@@@@@@@@@@@@@                              |
[16K, 32K)              148 |@                                             |
[32K, 64K)               29 |                                              |
[64K, 128K)               6 |                                              |

@write_bytes[sshd]:
[32, 64)                  1 |@@@@@@@@@@@@@@@@@@@@@@@@@@@@@@@@@@@@@@@@@@@@@@@@@@@@|

@write_bytes[java]:
[8, 16)                  36 |                                              |
[16, 32)                  6 |                                              |
[32, 64)               6131 |@@@@@@@@@@@@@@@@@@@@@@@@@@@@@@@@@@@@@@@@@@@@@@@@@@@@|
[64, 128)              1382 |@@@@@@@@@@@                                    |
[128, 256)               30 |                                              |
[256, 512)               87 |                                              |
[512, 1K)               169 |@                                             |
[1K, 2K)                522 |@@@@                                          |
[2K, 4K)               3607 |@@@@@@@@@@@@@@@@@@@@@@@@@@@@@                   |
[4K, 8K)               2673 |@@@@@@@@@@@@@@@@@@@@@@                         |
[8K, 16K)               394 |@@@                                           |
[16K, 32K)              815 |@@@@@@                                        |
[32K, 64K)              175 |@                                             |
[64K, 128K)               1 |                                              |
[128K, 256K)              1 |                                              |
```

The main application is Java, and both reads and writes show a bimodal distribution of socket I/O sizes. There could be different reasons causing these modes: different code paths or message contents. The tool can be modified to include stack traces and application context to answer this.

socksize(8) works by tracing the sock_recvmsg() and sock_sendmsg() kernel functions, as does socketio(8). The source to socksize(8) is:

```
#!/usr/local/bin/bpftrace

#include <linux/fs.h>
#include <net/sock.h>

kprobe:sock_recvmsg,
kprobe:sock_sendmsg
{
```

```
        @socket[tid] = arg0;
}


kretprobe:sock_recvmsg
{
        if (retval < 0x7fffffff) {
                @read_bytes[comm] = hist(retval);
        }
        delete(@socket[tid]);
}


kretprobe:sock_sendmsg
{
        if (retval < 0x7fffffff) {
                @write_bytes[comm] = hist(retval);
        }
        delete(@socket[tid]);
}


END
{
        clear(@socket);
}
```

The return value of these functions contains either the bytes transferred or a negative error code. To filter the error codes, an if (retval >= 0) test would seem appropriate; however, retval is not type-aware: it is a 64-bit unsigned integer, whereas the sock_recvmsg() and sock_sendmsg() functions return a 32-bit signed integer. The solution should be to cast retval to its correct type using (int)retval, but int casts are not yet available in bpftrace, so the 0x7fffffff test is a workaround.[18]

More keys can be added if desired, such as the PID, port number, and user stack trace. The maps can also be changed from hist() to stats() to provide a different type of summary:

```
# socksize.bt
Attaching 2 probes...
^C

@read_bytes[sshd]: count 1, average 36, total 36
@read_bytes[java]: count 19874, average 1584, total 31486578

@write_bytes[sshd]: count 1, average 36, total 36
@write_bytes[java]: count 11061, average 3741, total 41379939
```

18 bpftrace int casts have been prototyped by Bas Smit, and should be merged soon. See bpftrace PR #772.

This shows the number of I/O ("count"), the average size in bytes ("average"), and the total throughput in bytes ("total"). During tracing, Java wrote 41 Mbytes.

10.3.8   sormem

sormem(8)[19] traces the size of the socket receive queue, showing how full it is compared to the tunable limit, as histograms. If the receive queue exceeds the limit, packets are dropped, causing performance issues. For example, running this tool on a production edge server:

```
# sormem.bt
Attaching 4 probes...
Tracing socket receive buffer size. Hit Ctrl-C to end.
^C

@rmem_alloc:
[0]                  72870 |@@@@@@@@@@@@@@@@@@@@@@@@@@@@@@@@@@@          |
[1]                      0 |                                            |
[2, 4)                   0 |                                            |
[4, 8)                   0 |                                            |
[8, 16)                  0 |                                            |
[16, 32)                 0 |                                            |
[32, 64)                 0 |                                            |
[64, 128)                0 |                                            |
[128, 256)               0 |                                            |
[256, 512)               0 |                                            |
[512, 1K)           113831 |@@@@@@@@@@@@@@@@@@@@@@@@@@@@@@@@@@@@@@@@@@@@@@|
[1K, 2K)               113 |                                            |
[2K, 4K)               105 |                                            |
[4K, 8K)             99221 |@@@@@@@@@@@@@@@@@@@@@@@@@@@@@@@@@@@@@@@@      |
[8K, 16K)            26726 |@@@@@@@@@@@                                  |
[16K, 32K)           58028 |@@@@@@@@@@@@@@@@@@@@@@@                      |
[32K, 64K)           31336 |@@@@@@@@@@@@                                |
[64K, 128K)          15039 |@@@@@@                                      |
[128K, 256K)          6692 |@@@                                         |
[256K, 512K)           697 |                                            |
[512K, 1M)              91 |                                            |
[1M, 2M)                45 |                                            |
[2M, 4M)                80 |                                            |

@rmem_limit:
[64K, 128K)          14447 |@                                           |
[128K, 256K)           262 |                                            |
```

---

19 Origin: I created it for this book on 14-Apr-2019.

```
[256K, 512K)            0 |                                                        |
[512K, 1M)              0 |                                                        |
[1M, 2M)                0 |                                                        |
[2M, 4M)                0 |                                                        |
[4M, 8M)                0 |                                                        |
[8M, 16M)          410158 |@@@@@@@@@@@@@@@@@@@@@@@@@@@@@@@@@@@@@@@@@@@@@@@@@@@@@@@@@@@@|
[16M, 32M)              7 |                                                        |
```

@rmem_alloc shows how much memory has been allocated for the receive buffer. @rmem_limit is the limit size of the receive buffer, tunable using sysctl(8). This example shows that the limit is often in the eight- to 16-Mbyte range, whereas the memory actually allocated is much lower, often between 512 bytes and 256 Kbytes.

Here is a synthetic example to help explain this; an iperf(1) throughput test is performed with this sysctl(1) tcp_rmem setting (be careful when tuning this as larger sizes can introduce latency due to skb collapse and coalescing [105]):

```
# sysctl -w net.ipv4.tcp_rmem='4096 32768 10485760'
# sormem.bt
Attaching 4 probes...
Tracing socket receive buffer size. Hit Ctrl-C to end.
[...]

@rmem_limit:
[64K, 128K)            17 |                                                        |
[128K, 256K)        26319 |@@@@                                                    |
[256K, 512K)           31 |                                                        |
[512K, 1M)              0 |                                                        |
[1M, 2M)               26 |                                                        |
[2M, 4M)                0 |                                                        |
[4M, 8M)                8 |                                                        |
[8M, 16M)          320047 |@@@@@@@@@@@@@@@@@@@@@@@@@@@@@@@@@@@@@@@@@@@@@@@@@@@@@@@@@@@@|
```

And again with a reduction in the max rmem setting:

```
# sysctl -w net.ipv4.tcp_rmem='4096 32768 100000'
# sormem.bt
Attaching 4 probes...
Tracing socket receive buffer size. Hit Ctrl-C to end.
[...]

@rmem_limit:
[64K, 128K)        656221 |@@@@@@@@@@@@@@@@@@@@@@@@@@@@@@@@@@@@@@@@@@@@@@@@@@@@@@@@@@@@|
[128K, 256K)        34058 |@@                                                      |
[256K, 512K)           92 |                                                        |
```

The rmem_limit has now dropped to the 64- to 128-Kbyte range, matching the configured limit of 100 Kbytes. Note that net.ipv4.tcp_moderate_rcvbuf is enabled, which helps tune the receive buffer to reach this limit sooner.

This works by tracing the kernel sock_rcvmsg() function using kprobes, which might cause measurable overhead for busy workloads.

The source to sormem(8) is:

```
#!/usr/local/bin/bpftrace

#include <net/sock.h>

BEGIN
{
        printf("Tracing socket receive buffer size. Hit Ctrl-C to end.\n");
}

kprobe:sock_recvmsg
{
        $sock = ((struct socket *)arg0)->sk;
        @rmem_alloc = hist($sock->sk_backlog.rmem_alloc.counter);
        @rmem_limit = hist($sock->sk_rcvbuf & 0xffffffff);
}

tracepoint:sock:sock_rcvqueue_full
{
        printf("%s rmem_alloc %d > rcvbuf %d, skb size %d\n", probe,
            args->rmem_alloc, args->sk_rcvbuf, args->truesize);
}

tracepoint:sock:sock_exceed_buf_limit
{
        printf("%s rmem_alloc %d, allocated %d\n", probe,
            args->rmem_alloc, args->allocated);
}
```

There are two sock tracepoints that fire when buffer limits are exceeded, also traced in this tool.[20] If they happen, per-event lines are printed with details. (In the prior outputs, these events did not occur.)

---

20 The tracepoint:sock:sock_exceed_buf_limit tracepoint was extended in newer kernels (by 5.0) with extra arguments: you can now filter on receive events only by adding the filter /args->kind == SK_MEM_RECV/.

10.3.9 soconnlat

soconnlat(8)[21] shows socket connection latency as a histogram, with user-level stack traces. This provides a different view of socket usage: rather than identifying connections by their IP addresses and ports, as soconnect(8) does, this helps you identify connections by their code paths. Example output:

```
# soconnlat.bt
Attaching 12 probes...
Tracing IP connect() latency with ustacks. Ctrl-C to end.
^C

@us[
    __GI___connect+108
    Java_java_net_PlainSocketImpl_socketConnect+368
    Ljava/net/PlainSocketImpl;::socketConnect+197
    Ljava/net/AbstractPlainSocketImpl;::doConnect+1156
    Ljava/net/AbstractPlainSocketImpl;::connect+476
    Interpreter+5955
    Ljava/net/Socket;::connect+1212
    Lnet/sf/freecol/common/networking/Connection;::<init>+324
    Interpreter+5955
    Lnet/sf/freecol/common/networking/ServerAPI;::connect+236
    Lnet/sf/freecol/client/control/ConnectController;::login+660
    Interpreter+3856
    Lnet/sf/freecol/client/control/ConnectController$$Lambda$258/1471835655;::run+92
    Lnet/sf/freecol/client/Worker;::run+628
    call_stub+138
    JavaCalls::call_helper(JavaValue*, methodHandle const&, JavaCallArguments*, Th...
    JavaCalls::call_virtual(JavaValue*, Handle, Klass*, Symbol*, Symbol*, Thread*)...
    thread_entry(JavaThread*, Thread*)+108
    JavaThread::thread_main_inner()+446
    Thread::call_run()+376
    thread_native_entry(Thread*)+238
    start_thread+208
    __clone+63
, FreeColClient:W]:
[32, 64)               1 |@@@@@@@@@@@@@@@@@@@@@@@@@@@@@@@@@@@@@@@@@@@@@@@@@@@@|

@us[
    __connect+71
, java]:
```

---

21 Origin: I created it for this book on 12-Apr-2019, inspired by my disk I/O bitesize tool.

```
[128, 256)         69 |@@@@@@@@@@@@@@@@@@@@@@@@@@@@@@@         |
[256, 512)         28 |@@@@@@@@@@@@                          |
[512, 1K)         121 |@@@@@@@@@@@@@@@@@@@@@@@@@@@@@@@@@@@@@@@@@@@@@@@@@@@@@|
[1K, 2K)           53 |@@@@@@@@@@@@@@@@@@@@@@@                |
```

This shows two stack traces: the first is from an open source Java game, and the code path shows why it was calling connect. There was only one occurrence of this codepath, with a connect latency of between 32 and 64 microseconds. The second stack shows over 200 connections, of between 128 microseconds and 2 milliseconds, from Java. This second stack trace is broken, however, showing only one frame "__connect+71" before abruptly ending. The reason is that this Java application is using the default libc library, which has been compiled without frame pointers. See Section 13.2.9 in Chapter 13 for ways to fix this.

This connection latency shows how long it took for the connection to be established across the network, which for TCP spans the three-way TCP handshake. It also includes remote host kernel latency to process an inbound SYN and respond: this usually happens very quickly in interrupt context, so the connection latency should be dominated by the network round trip times.

This tool works by tracing the connect(2), select(2), and poll(2) family of syscalls via their tracepoints. The overhead might become measurable on busy systems that frequently call select(2) and poll(2) syscalls.

The source to soconnlat(8) is:

```
#!/usr/local/bin/bpftrace

#include <asm-generic/errno.h>
#include <linux/in.h>

BEGIN
{
        printf("Tracing IP connect() latency with ustacks. Ctrl-C to end.\n");
}

tracepoint:syscalls:sys_enter_connect
/args->uservaddr->sa_family == AF_INET ||
    args->uservaddr->sa_family == AF_INET6/
{
        @conn_start[tid] = nsecs;
        @conn_stack[tid] = ustack();
}

tracepoint:syscalls:sys_exit_connect
/@conn_start[tid] && args->ret != - EINPROGRESS/
{
```

```
        $dur_us = (nsecs - @conn_start[tid]) / 1000;
        @us[@conn_stack[tid], comm] = hist($dur_us);
        delete(@conn_start[tid]);
        delete(@conn_stack[tid]);
}

tracepoint:syscalls:sys_exit_poll*,
tracepoint:syscalls:sys_exit_epoll*,
tracepoint:syscalls:sys_exit_select*,
tracepoint:syscalls:sys_exit_pselect*
/@conn_start[tid] && args->ret > 0/
{
        $dur_us = (nsecs - @conn_start[tid]) / 1000;
        @us[@conn_stack[tid], comm] = hist($dur_us);
        delete(@conn_start[tid]);
        delete(@conn_stack[tid]);
}

END
{
        clear(@conn_start); clear(@conn_stack);
}
```

This solves the problem mentioned in the earlier description of the soconnect(8) tool. The connection latency is measured as the time for the connect(2) syscall to complete, unless it completes with an EINPROGRESS status, in which case the true connection completion occurs sometime later, when a poll(2) or select(2) syscall successfully finds an event for that file descriptor. What this tool should do is record the enter arguments of each poll(2) or select(2) syscall, then examine them again on exit to ensure that the connect socket file descriptor is the one that had the event. Instead, this tool takes a giant shortcut by assuming that the first successful poll(2) or select(2) after a connect(2) that is EINPROGRESS on the same thread is related. It probably is, but bear in mind that the tool may have a margin of error if the application called connect(2) and then—on the same thread—received an event on a different file descriptor that it was also waiting on. You can enhance the tool or investigate your application's use of those syscalls to see how plausible that scenario may be.

For example, counting how many file descriptors applications are waiting for via poll(2), on a production edge server:

```
# bpftrace -e 't:syscalls:sys_enter_poll { @[comm, args->nfds] = count(); }'
Attaching 1 probe...
^C

@[python3, 96]: 181
@[java, 1]: 10300
```

During tracing, Java only calls poll(2) on one file descriptor, so the scenario I just described seems even less likely, unless it is calling poll(2) separately for different file descriptions. Similar tests can be performed for the other poll(2) and select(2) syscalls.

This output also caught python3 calling poll(2) on...96 file descriptors? By adding pid to the map key to identify which python3 process, and then examining its file descriptors in lsof(8), I found that it really does have 96 file descriptors open, by mistake, and is frequently polling them on production servers. I should be able to fix this and get some CPU cycles back.[22]

10.3.10 so1stbyte

so1stbyte(8)[23] traces the time from issuing an IP socket connect(2) to the first read byte for that socket. While soconnlat(8) is a measure of network and kernel latency to establish a connection, so1stbyte(8) includes the time for the remote host application to be scheduled and produce data. This provides a view of how busy the remote host is and, if measured over time, may reveal times when the remote hosts are more heavily loaded, and have higher latency. For example:

```
# so1stbyte.bt
Attaching 21 probes...
Tracing IP socket first-read-byte latency. Ctrl-C to end.
^C

@us[java]:
[256, 512)             4 |                                                      |
[512, 1K)              5 |@                                                     |
[1K, 2K)              34 |@@@@@@                                                |
[2K, 4K)             212 |@@@@@@@@@@@@@@@@@@@@@@@@@@@@@@@@@@@@@@@@@@              |
[4K, 8K)             260 |@@@@@@@@@@@@@@@@@@@@@@@@@@@@@@@@@@@@@@@@@@@@@@@@@@@@@@@@|
[8K, 16K)             35 |@@@@@@@                                               |
[16K, 32K)             6 |@                                                     |
[32K, 64K)             1 |                                                      |
[64K, 128K)            0 |                                                      |
[128K, 256K)           4 |                                                      |
[256K, 512K)           3 |                                                      |
[512K, 1M)             1 |                                                      |
```

This output shows that the connections from this Java process usually received their first bytes in one to 16 milliseconds.

This works by using the syscall tracepoints to instrument the connect(2), read(2), and recv(2) family of syscalls. The overhead may be measurable while running, as these syscalls can be frequent on high-I/O systems.

---

22 Before getting too excited, I checked the server uptime, CPU count, and process CPU usage via ps(1) (the process is supposed to be idle), to calculate how much CPU resources are wasted by this: it came out to only 0.02%.

23 Origin: I first created so1stbyte.d for the 2011 DTrace book [Gregg 11]. I created this version on 16-Apr-2019.

The source to so1stbyte(8) is:

```
#!/usr/local/bin/bpftrace

#include <asm-generic/errno.h>
#include <linux/in.h>

BEGIN
{
        printf("Tracing IP socket first-read-byte latency. Ctrl-C to end.\n");
}

tracepoint:syscalls:sys_enter_connect
/args->uservaddr->sa_family == AF_INET ||
    args->uservaddr->sa_family == AF_INET6/
{
        @connfd[tid] = args->fd;
        @connstart[pid, args->fd] = nsecs;
}

tracepoint:syscalls:sys_exit_connect
{
        if (args->ret != 0 && args->ret != - EINPROGRESS) {
                // connect() failure, delete flag if present
                delete(@connstart[pid, @connfd[tid]]);
        }
        delete(@connfd[tid]);
}

tracepoint:syscalls:sys_enter_close
/@connstart[pid, args->fd]/
{
        // never called read
        delete(@connstart[pid, @connfd[tid]]);
}

tracepoint:syscalls:sys_enter_read,
tracepoint:syscalls:sys_enter_readv,
tracepoint:syscalls:sys_enter_pread*,
tracepoint:syscalls:sys_enter_recvfrom,
tracepoint:syscalls:sys_enter_recvmsg,
tracepoint:syscalls:sys_enter_recvmmsg
/@connstart[pid, args->fd]/
```

```
{
        @readfd[tid] = args->fd;
}


tracepoint:syscalls:sys_exit_read,
tracepoint:syscalls:sys_exit_readv,
tracepoint:syscalls:sys_exit_pread*,
tracepoint:syscalls:sys_exit_recvfrom,
tracepoint:syscalls:sys_exit_recvmsg,
tracepoint:syscalls:sys_exit_recvmmsg
/@readfd[tid]/
{
        $fd = @readfd[tid];
        @us[comm, pid] = hist((nsecs - @connstart[pid, $fd]) / 1000);
        delete(@connstart[pid, $fd]);
        delete(@readfd[tid]);
}


END
{
        clear(@connstart); clear(@connfd); clear(@readfd);
}
```

This tool records a starting timestamp in a @connstart map during the entry to connect(2), keyed by the process ID and file descriptor. If this connect(2) is a failure (unless it is non-blocking and returned with EINPROGRESS) or close(2) was issued, it deletes the timestamp to stop tracking that connection. When the first read or recv syscall is entered on the socket file descriptor seen earlier, it tracks the file descriptor in @readfd so that it can be fetched on syscall exit, and finally the starting time read from the @connstart map.

This timespan is similar to the TCP time to first byte described earlier, but with a small difference: the connect(2) duration is included.

Many syscall tracepoints need to be instrumented to catch the first read for the socket, adding overhead to all of those read paths. This overhead and the number of traced events could be reduced by switching instead to kprobes such as sock_recvmsg() for socket functions, and tracking the sock pointer as the unique ID rather than the PID and FD pair. The tradeoff would be that kprobes are not stable.

10.3.11   tcpconnect

tcpconnect(8)[24] is a BCC and bpftrace tool to trace new TCP active connections. Unlike the earlier socket tools, tcpconnect(8) and the following TCP tools trace deeper in the network stack in the

---

24 Origin: I created a similar tcpconnect.d tool for the 2011 DTrace book [Gregg 11], and I created the BCC version on 25-Sep-2015, and the tcpconnect-tp(8) bpftrace tracepoint version on 7-Apr-2019.

TCP code, rather than tracing the socket syscalls. tcpconnect(8) is named after the socket system call connect(2), and these are often termed *outbound* connections, although they may also be to localhost.

tcpconnect(8) is useful for workload characterization: determining who is connecting to whom, and at what rate. Here is tcpconnect(8) from BCC:

```
# tcpconnect.py -t
TIME(s)   PID    COMM        IP SADDR            DADDR            DPORT
0.000     4218   java        4  100.1.101.18     100.2.51.232     6001
0.011     4218   java        4  100.1.101.18     100.2.135.216    6001
0.072     4218   java        4  100.1.101.18     100.2.135.94     6001
0.073     4218   java        4  100.1.101.18     100.2.160.87     8980
0.124     4218   java        4  100.1.101.18     100.2.177.63     6001
0.212     4218   java        4  100.1.101.18     100.2.58.22      6001
0.214     4218   java        4  100.1.101.18     100.2.43.148     6001
[...]
```

This has caught several connections to different remote hosts with the same port, 6001. The columns are:

- **TIME(s):** The time of the accept in seconds, counting from the first event seen.
- **PID:** The process ID that accepted the connection. This is best-effort that matches on the current process; at the TCP level, these events may not happen in process context. For reliable PIDs, use socket tracing.
- **COMM:** The process name that accepted the connection. As with PID, this is best-effort, and socket tracing should be used for better reliability.
- **IP:** IP address protocol.
- **SADDR:** Source address.
- **DADDR:** Destination address.
- **DPORT:** Destination port.

Both IPv4 and IPv6 are supported, although IPv6 addresses can be so wide that they can make the output columns untidy.

This works by tracing events related to creating new TCP sessions, rather than per-packet tracing. On this production server, the packet rate is around 50,000/s, whereas the new TCP session rate is around 350/s. By tracing session-level events instead of packets, the overhead is reduced by around a hundred fold, becoming negligible.

The BCC version currently works by tracing the tcp_v4_connect() and tcp_v6_connect() kernel functions. A future version should switch to using the sock:inet_sock_set_state tracepoint if available.

BCC

Command line usage:

```
tcpconnect [options]
```

Options include:

- **-t:** Include a timestamp column
- **-p PID:** Trace this process only
- **-P PORT[,PORT,...]:** Trace these destination ports only

bpftrace

The following is the code for tcpconnect-tp(8), a bpftrace version of tcpconnect(8) that uses the sock:inet_sock_set_state tracepoint:

```
#!/usr/local/bin/bpftrace

#include <net/tcp_states.h>
#include <linux/socket.h>

BEGIN
{
        printf("%-8s %-6s %-16s %-3s ", "TIME", "PID", "COMM", "IP");
        printf("%-15s %-15s %-5s\n", "SADDR", "DADDR", "DPORT");
}

tracepoint:sock:inet_sock_set_state
/args->oldstate == TCP_CLOSE && args->newstate == TCP_SYN_SENT/
{
        time("%H:%M:%S ");
        printf("%-6d %-16s %-3d ", pid, comm, args->family == AF_INET ? 4 : 6);
        printf("%-15s %-15s %-5d\n", ntop(args->family, args->saddr),
            ntop(args->family, args->daddr), args->dport)
}
```

This matches active opens by the transition from TCP_CLOSE to TCP_SYN_SENT.

The bpftrace repository has a tcpconnect(8)[25] version for older Linux kernels that lack the sock:inet_sock_set_state tracepoint and traces the tcp_connect() kernel function instead.

---

25 Origin: This was created by Dale Hamel on 23-Nov-2018, for which he also added the ntop() builtin to bpftrace.

10.3.12   tcpaccept

tcpaccept(8)[26] is a BCC and bpftrace tool to trace new TCP passive connections; it's the counterpart to tcpconnect(8). It is named after the socket system call accept(2). These are often termed *inbound* connections, although they may also come from localhost. As with tcpconnect(8), this tool is useful for workload characterization: determining who is connecting to the local system, and at what rate.

The following shows tcpaccept(8) from BCC, from a 48-CPU production instance, running with the -t option to print a timestamp column:

```
# tcpaccept -t
TIME(s)   PID    COMM       IP RADDR          RPORT LADDR         LPORT
0.000     4218   java       4  100.2.231.20   53422 100.1.101.18  6001
0.004     4218   java       4  100.2.236.45   36400 100.1.101.18  6001
0.013     4218   java       4  100.2.221.222  29836 100.1.101.18  6001
0.014     4218   java       4  100.2.194.78   40416 100.1.101.18  6001
0.016     4218   java       4  100.2.239.62   53422 100.1.101.18  6001
0.016     4218   java       4  100.2.199.236  28790 100.1.101.18  6001
0.021     4218   java       4  100.2.192.209  35840 100.1.101.18  6001
0.022     4218   java       4  100.2.215.219  21450 100.1.101.18  6001
0.026     4218   java       4  100.2.231.176  47024 100.1.101.18  6001
[...]
```

This output shows many new connections to local port 6001 from different remote addresses, which were accepted by a Java process with PID 4218. The columns are similar to those for tcpconnect(8), with these differences:

- **RADDR**: Remote address
- **RPORT**: Remote port
- **LADDR**: Local address
- **LPORT**: Local port

This tool works by tracing the inet_csk_accept() kernel function. This might sound like an unusual name compared with other high-level TCP functions, and you might wonder why I chose it. I chose it because it's the accept function from the tcp_prot struct (net/ipv4/tcp_ipv4.c):

```
struct proto tcp_prot = {
        .name               = "TCP",
        .owner              = THIS_MODULE,
```

---

26 Origin: I created a similar tcpaccept.d tool for the 2011 DTrace book [Gregg 11], and earlier versions in 2006 (tcpaccept1.d and tcpaccept2.d) which counted connections, that I created while I was developing the DTrace TCP provider [106]. I was up late finishing them to demo in my first-ever conference talk at CEC2006 in San Francisco [107] and then overslept and barely made it to the venue in time. I created the BCC version on 13-Oct-2015, and the tcpconnect-tp(8) version on 7-Apr-2019.

```
    .close                = tcp_close,
    .pre_connect          = tcp_v4_pre_connect,
    .connect              = tcp_v4_connect,
    .disconnect           = tcp_disconnect,
    .accept               = inet_csk_accept,
    .ioctl                = tcp_ioctl,
[...]
```

IPv6 addresses are also supported, although the output columns can get untidy due to their width. As an example from a different production server:

```
# tcpaccept -t
TIME(s)  PID   COMM       IP RADDR            LADDR            LPORT
0.000    7013  java       6  ::ffff:100.1.54.4 ::ffff:100.1.58.46 13562
0.103    7013  java       6  ::ffff:100.1.7.19 ::ffff:100.1.58.46 13562
0.202    7013  java       6  ::ffff:100.1.58.59 ::ffff:100.1.58.46 13562
[...]
```

These addresses are IPv4 mapped over IPv6.

BCC

Command line usage:

```
tcpaccept [options]
```

tcpaccept(8) has similar options to tcpconnect(8), including:

- **-t**: Include a timestamp column
- **-p PID**: Trace this process only
- **-P PORT[,PORT,...]**: Trace these local ports only

bpftrace

The following is the code for tcpaccept-tp(8), a bpftrace version of tcpaccept(8) developed for this book that uses the sock:inet_sock_set_state tracepoint:

```
#!/usr/local/bin/bpftrace

#include <net/tcp_states.h>
#include <linux/socket.h>

BEGIN
{
        printf("%-8s %-3s %-14s %-5s %-14s %-5s\n", "TIME", "IP",
            "RADDR", "RPORT", "LADDR", "LPORT");
```

```
}


tracepoint:sock:inet_sock_set_state
/args->oldstate == TCP_SYN_RECV && args->newstate == TCP_ESTABLISHED/
{
        time("%H:%M:%S ");
        printf("%-3d %-14s %-5d %-14s %-5d\n", args->family == AF_INET ? 4 : 6,
            ntop(args->family, args->daddr), args->dport,
            ntop(args->family, args->saddr), args->sport);
}
```

Since the process ID is not expected to be on-CPU at the time of this TCP state transition, the pid and comm builtins have been elided from this version. Sample output:

```
# tcpaccept-tp.bt
Attaching 2 probes...
TIME     IP RADDR         RPORT LADDR         LPORT
07:06:46 4  127.0.0.1     63998 127.0.0.1     28527
07:06:47 4  127.0.0.1     64002 127.0.0.1     28527
07:06:48 4  127.0.0.1     64004 127.0.0.1     28527
[...]
```

The bpftrace repository has a version of tcpaccept(8)[27] that uses kernel dynamic tracing of the inet_csk_accept() function, as used by the BCC version. This function is expected to be application-process synchronous, so the PID and process name are printed using the pid and comm built-ins. An excerpt:

```
[...]
kretprobe:inet_csk_accept
{
        $sk = (struct sock *)retval;
        $inet_family = $sk->__sk_common.skc_family;

        if ($inet_family == AF_INET || $inet_family == AF_INET6) {
                $daddr = ntop(0);
                $saddr = ntop(0);
                if ($inet_family == AF_INET) {
                        $daddr = ntop($sk->__sk_common.skc_daddr);
                        $saddr = ntop($sk->__sk_common.skc_rcv_saddr);
                } else {
                        $daddr = ntop(
                            $sk->__sk_common.skc_v6_daddr.in6_u.u6_addr8);
```

27 Origin: This was created by Dale Hamel on 23-Nov-2018.

```
                    $saddr = ntop(
                        $sk->__sk_common.skc_v6_rcv_saddr.in6_u.u6_addr8);
                }
                $lport = $sk->__sk_common.skc_num;
                $dport = $sk->__sk_common.skc_dport;
                $qlen  = $sk->sk_ack_backlog;
                $qmax  = $sk->sk_max_ack_backlog;
[...]
```

The program fetches the protocol details from the sock struct. It also fetches tcp listen backlog details, and is an example of extending these tools to provide additional insights. This listen backlog was added to diagnose a Shopify production issue where Redis was degrading under peak load: it was found to be TCP listen drops.[28] Adding a column to tcpaccept.bt made it possible to see the current length of the listen backlog, useful for characterization and capacity planning.

A future change to bpftrace's variable scoping may cause variables initialized in if-statement clauses to be scoped to the clause only, which would cause a problem for this program because $daddr and $saddr are then used outside of the clause. To avoid this future constraint, this program initializes these variables beforehand to ntop(0) (ntop(0) returns type inet, which is printed as a string.) This initialization is unnecessary in the current version of bpftrace (0.9.1), but has been included to make this program future-proof.

10.3.13 tcplife

tcplife(8)[29] is a BCC and bpftrace tool to trace the lifespan of TCP sessions: showing their duration, address details, throughput, and when possible, the responsible process ID and name.

The following shows tcplife(8) from BCC, from a 48-CPU production instance:

```
# tcplife
PID   COMM   LADDR           LPORT RADDR          RPORT TX_KB RX_KB  MS
4169  java   100.1.111.231   32648 100.2.0.48     6001      0     0  3.99
4169  java   100.1.111.231   32650 100.2.0.48     6001      0     0  4.10
4169  java   100.1.111.231   32644 100.2.0.48     6001      0     0  8.41
4169  java   100.1.111.231   40158 100.2.116.192  6001      7    33  3590.91
4169  java   100.1.111.231   56940 100.5.177.31   6101      0     0  2.48
4169  java   100.1.111.231   6001  100.2.176.45   49482     0     0  17.94
4169  java   100.1.111.231   18926 100.5.102.250  6101      0     0  0.90
4169  java   100.1.111.231   44530 100.2.31.140   6001      0     0  2.64
```

---

28 Production example provided by Dale Hamel.

29 Origin: This began as a tweet from Julia Evans: "i really wish i had a command line tool that would give me stats on TCP connection lengths on a given port" [108]. In response I created tcplife(8) as a BCC tool on 18-Oct-2016, and I created the bpftrace version on 17-Apr-2019 after merging a needed bpftrace capability from Matheus Marchini that morning. This is one of the most popular tools I've developed. It forms the basis of several higher-level GUIs, as it provides efficient network flow stats that can be visualized as directed graphs.

```
4169   java       100.1.111.231   44406 100.2.8.109     6001    11   28 3982.11
34781  sshd       100.1.111.231   22    100.2.17.121    41566    5    7 2317.30
4169   java       100.1.111.231   49726 100.2.9.217     6001    11   28 3938.47
4169   java       100.1.111.231   58858 100.2.173.248   6001     9   30 2820.51
[...]
```

This output shows a series of connections that were either short-lived (less than 20 milliseconds) or long-lived (over three seconds), as shown in the duration column "MS" for milliseconds). This is an application server pool that listens on port 6001. Most of the sessions in this screenshot show connections to port 6001 on remote application servers, with only one connection to the local port 6001. An ssh session was also seen, owned by sshd and local port 22—an inbound session.

This works by tracing TCP socket state change events, and prints the summary details when the state changes to TCP_CLOSE. These state-change events are much less frequent than packets, making this approach much less costly in overhead than per-packet sniffers. This has made tcplife(8) acceptable to run continuously as a TCP flow logger on Netflix production servers.

The original tcplife(8) traced the tcp_set_state() kernel function using kprobes. Since Linux 4.16, a tracepoint has been added for this purpose: sock:inet_sock_set_state. The tcplife(8) tool uses that tracepoint if available; otherwise, it defaults to the kprobe. There is a subtle difference between these events, which can be seen in the following one-liner. This counts the TCP state number for each event:

```
# bpftrace -e 'k:tcp_set_state { @kprobe[arg1] = count(); }
    t:sock:inet_sock_set_state { @tracepoint[args->newstate] = count(); }'
Attaching 2 probes...
^C

@kprobe[4]: 12
@kprobe[5]: 12
@kprobe[9]: 13
@kprobe[2]: 13
@kprobe[8]: 13
@kprobe[1]: 25
@kprobe[7]: 25

@tracepoint[3]: 12
@tracepoint[4]: 12
@tracepoint[5]: 12
@tracepoint[2]: 13
@tracepoint[9]: 13
@tracepoint[8]: 13
@tracepoint[7]: 25
@tracepoint[1]: 25
```

See it? The tcp_set_state() kprobe never sees state 3, which is TCP_SYN_RECV. This is because the kprobe is exposing the kernel implementation, and the kernel never calls tcp_set_state() with TCP_SYN_RECV: it doesn't need to. This is an implementation detail that is normally hidden from end users. But with the addition of a tracepoint to expose these state changes, it was found to be confusing to leave out this state transition, so the tracepoint has been called to show all transitions.

BCC

Command line usage:

```
tcplife [options]
```

Options include:

- **-t**: Include time column (HH:MM:SS)
- **-w**: Wider columns (to better fit IPv6 addresses)
- **-p PID**: Trace this process only
- **-L PORT[,PORT[,...]]**: Trace only sessions with these local ports
- **-D PORT[,PORT[,...]]**: Trace only sessions with these remote ports

bpftrace

The following is the code for the bpftrace version, developed for this book, and which summarizes its core functionality. This version uses a kprobe of tcp_set_state() so that it runs on older kernels, and does not support options.

```
#!/usr/local/bin/bpftrace

#include <net/tcp_states.h>
#include <net/sock.h>
#include <linux/socket.h>
#include <linux/tcp.h>

BEGIN
{
        printf("%-5s %-10s %-15s %-5s %-15s %-5s ", "PID", "COMM",
            "LADDR", "LPORT", "RADDR", "RPORT");
        printf("%5s %5s %s\n", "TX_KB", "RX_KB", "MS");
}

kprobe:tcp_set_state
{
        $sk = (struct sock *)arg0;
        $newstate = arg1;
```

```
/*
 * This tool includes PID and comm context. From TCP this is best
 * effort, and may be wrong in some situations. It does this:
 * - record timestamp on any state < TCP_FIN_WAIT1
 *     note some state transitions may not be present via this kprobe
 * - cache task context on:
 *     TCP_SYN_SENT: tracing from client
 *     TCP_LAST_ACK: client-closed from server
 * - do output on TCP_CLOSE:
 *     fetch task context if cached, or use current task
 */

// record first timestamp seen for this socket
if ($newstate < TCP_FIN_WAIT1 && @birth[$sk] == 0) {
        @birth[$sk] = nsecs;
}


// record PID & comm on SYN_SENT
if ($newstate == TCP_SYN_SENT || $newstate == TCP_LAST_ACK) {
        @skpid[$sk] = pid;
        @skcomm[$sk] = comm;
}


// session ended: calculate lifespan and print
if ($newstate == TCP_CLOSE && @birth[$sk]) {
        $delta_ms = (nsecs - @birth[$sk]) / 1000000;
        $lport = $sk->__sk_common.skc_num;
        $dport = $sk->__sk_common.skc_dport;
        $dport = ($dport >> 8) | (($dport << 8) & 0xff00);
        $tp = (struct tcp_sock *)$sk;
        $pid = @skpid[$sk];
        $comm = @skcomm[$sk];
        if ($comm == "") {
                // not cached, use current task
                $pid = pid;
                $comm = comm;
        }

        $family = $sk->__sk_common.skc_family;
        $saddr = ntop(0);
        $daddr = ntop(0);
        if ($family == AF_INET) {
                $saddr = ntop(AF_INET, $sk->__sk_common.skc_rcv_saddr);
```

```
                        $daddr = ntop(AF_INET, $sk->__sk_common.skc_daddr);
                } else {
                        // AF_INET6
                        $saddr = ntop(AF_INET6,
                            $sk->__sk_common.skc_v6_rcv_saddr.in6_u.u6_addr8);
                        $daddr = ntop(AF_INET6,
                            $sk->__sk_common.skc_v6_daddr.in6_u.u6_addr8);
                }
                printf("%-5d %-10.10s %-15s %-5d %-15s %-6d ", $pid,
                    $comm, $saddr, $lport, $daddr, $dport);
                printf("%5d %5d %d\n", $tp->bytes_acked / 1024,
                    $tp->bytes_received / 1024, $delta_ms);

                delete(@birth[$sk]);
                delete(@skpid[$sk]);
                delete(@skcomm[$sk]);
        }
}


END
{
        clear(@birth); clear(@skpid); clear(@skcomm);
}
```

The logic in this tool is somewhat complex, and I added block comments to explain it in both the BCC and bpftrace versions. What it does is:

- Measure the time from the first state transition seen for the socket, to TCP_CLOSE. This is printed as the duration.

- Fetch throughput statistics from the struct tcp_sock in the kernel. This avoids tracing each packet and summing throughput from their sizes. These throughput counters are relatively recent, added since 2015 [109].

- Cache the process context on either TCP_SYN_SENT or TCP_LAST_ACK, or (if not cached by those) on TCP_CLOSE. This works reasonably well but relies on these events happening in process context, which is a kernel implementation detail. Future kernels could change their logic to make this approach much less reliable, at which point this tool would need to be updated to cache task context from socket events instead (see the earlier tools).

The BCC version of this tool has been extended by the Netflix network engineering team to record other useful fields from the sock and tcp_sock structs.

This bpftrace tool can be updated to use the sock:inet_sock_set_state tracepoint, which needs an additional check for args->protocol == IPPROTO_TCP as that tracepoint fires for more than just TCP. Using this tracepoint improves stability, but there will still be unstable parts: for example, transferred bytes still need to be fetched from the tcp_sock struct.

10.3.14 tcptop

tcptop(8)[30] is a BCC tool that shows top processes using TCP. For example, from a 36-CPU production Hadoop instance:

```
# tcptop
09:01:13 loadavg: 33.32 36.11 38.63 26/4021 123015

PID    COMM   LADDR                 RADDR                 RX_KB  TX_KB
118119 java   100.1.58.46:36246     100.2.52.79:50010     16840      0
122833 java   100.1.58.46:52426     100.2.6.98:50010          0   3112
122833 java   100.1.58.46:50010     100.2.50.176:55396    3112       0
120711 java   100.1.58.46:50010     100.2.7.75:23358      2922       0
121635 java   100.1.58.46:50010     100.2.5.101:56426     2922       0
121219 java   100.1.58.46:50010     100.2.62.83:40570     2858       0
121219 java   100.1.58.46:42324     100.2.4.58:50010          0   2858
122927 java   100.1.58.46:50010     100.2.2.191:29338     2351       0
[...]
```

This output shows one connection at the top receiving over 16 Mbytes during this interval. By default, the screen is updated every second.

This works by tracing the TCP send and receive code path, and summarizing data in a BPF map efficiency. Even so, these events can be frequent, and on high network throughput systems the overhead may become measurable.

The actual functions traced are tcp_sendmsg() and tcp_cleanup_rbuf(). I chose tcp_cleanup_rbuf() as it provides both the sock struct and size as entry arguments. To get the same details from tcp_recvmsg() requires two kprobes and thus more overhead: a kprobe on entry for the sock struct, and a kretprobe for the returned bytes.

Note that tcptop(8) does not currently trace TCP traffic that was sent via the sendfile(2) syscall, as it may not call tcp_sendmsg(). If your workload makes use of sendfile(2), check for an updated tcptop(8) version or enhance it.

Command line usage:

```
tcptop [options] [interval [count]]
```

Options include:

- **-C:** Don't clear the screen
- **-p PID:** Measure this process only

A future addition should be an option to truncate the number of rows shown.

---

30 Origin: I created tcptop using DTrace on 5-Jul-2005, inspired by William LeFebvre's top(1) tool. I created the BCC version on 2-Sep-2016.

10.3.15 tcpsnoop

tcpsnoop(8) was a popular Solaris DTrace tool of mine that I would have introduced at this point in this chapter if it existed for Linux BPF, but I have chosen not to port it; the version shown below is the Solaris one. I'm sharing it here because it taught me some important lessons the hard way.

tcpsnoop(8) printed a line for each packet, with addresses, packet size, process ID, and user ID. For example:

```
solaris# tcpsnoop.d
  UID    PID LADDR            LPORT DR RADDR        RPORT  SIZE CMD
    0    242 192.168.1.5         23 <- 192.168.1.1  54224    54 inetd
    0    242 192.168.1.5         23 -> 192.168.1.1  54224    54 inetd
    0    242 192.168.1.5         23 <- 192.168.1.1  54224    54 inetd
    0    242 192.168.1.5         23 <- 192.168.1.1  54224    78 inetd
    0    242 192.168.1.5         23 -> 192.168.1.1  54224    54 inetd
    0  20893 192.168.1.5         23 -> 192.168.1.1  54224    57 in.telnetd
    0  20893 192.168.1.5         23 <- 192.168.1.1  54224    54 in.telnetd
[...]
```

When I wrote this in 2004, network event analysis was the domain of packet sniffers: snoop(1M) for Solaris and tcpdump(8) for Linux. One blind spot of these tools is that they don't show the process ID. I wanted a tool to show which process was creating network traffic, and this seemed like the obvious solution: create a version of snoop(1M) with a PID column. To test my solution, I ran it alongside snoop(1M) to ensure that they both saw the same packet events.

This turned out to be quite challenging: I needed to cache the PID during socket-level events, and fetch the packet size from the other end of the stack after MTU fragmentation. I needed to trace the data transfer code, the TCP handshake code, and other code for handling packets to closed ports and other events. I succeeded, but my tool traced eleven different points in the kernel, and walked various kernel structures, which made it very brittle as it relied on many unstable kernel details. The tool itself was over 500 lines of code.

Over a six-year span, the Solaris kernel was updated over a dozen times, and tcpsnoop(8) stopped working on seven of those updates. Fixing it became a nightmare: I could fix it for one kernel version, but I then had to test across all prior versions to see if the fix introduced a regression. It became impractical, and I began releasing separate tcpsnoop(8) versions for specific kernels.

There are two lessons here. First: kernel code is subject to change, and the more kprobes and struct usage you have, the more likely it is that your tool will break. The tools in this book purposely use the fewest possible kprobes, making maintenance easier when they do break. Where possible, use tracepoints instead.

Second: the entire premise of the tool was a mistake. If my aim was to identify which processes were causing network traffic, I did not need to do this on a per-packet basis. I could have written a tool to summarize data transfers only, bearing in mind that it would miss other packets including TCP handshakes—but it would have been close enough to solve most problems. By way of example, socketio(8) or tcptop(8), covered earlier, each use only two kprobes, and tcplife(8) uses one tracepoint plus some struct walking.

10.3.16   tcpretrans

tcpretrans(8)[31] is a BCC and bpftrace tool to trace TCP retransmits, showing IP address and port details and the TCP state. The following shows tcpretrans(8) from BCC, on a production instance:

```
# tcpretrans
Tracing retransmits ... Hit Ctrl-C to end
TIME      PID     IP LADDR:LPORT          T> RADDR:RPORT         STATE
00:20:11 72475   4  100.1.58.46:35908    R> 100.2.0.167:50010   ESTABLISHED
00:20:11 72475   4  100.1.58.46:35908    R> 100.2.0.167:50010   ESTABLISHED
00:20:11 72475   4  100.1.58.46:35908    R> 100.2.0.167:50010   ESTABLISHED
00:20:12 60695   4  100.1.58.46:52346    R> 100.2.6.189:50010   ESTABLISHED
00:20:12 60695   4  100.1.58.46:52346    R> 100.2.6.189:50010   ESTABLISHED
00:20:12 60695   4  100.1.58.46:52346    R> 100.2.6.189:50010   ESTABLISHED
00:20:12 60695   4  100.1.58.46:52346    R> 100.2.6.189:50010   ESTABLISHED
00:20:13 60695   6  ::ffff:100.1.58.46:13562 R> ::ffff:100.2.51.209:47356 FIN_WAIT1
00:20:13 60695   6  ::ffff:100.1.58.46:13562 R> ::ffff:100.2.51.209:47356 FIN_WAIT1
[...]
```

This output shows a low rate of retransmits, a few per second (TIME column), which were mostly for sessions in the ESTABLISHED state. A high rate in the ESTABLISHED state can point to an external network problem. A high rate in the SYN_SENT state can point to an overloaded server application which is not consuming its SYN backlog fast enough.

This works by tracing TCP retransmit events in the kernel. Since these should occur infrequently, the overhead should be negligible. Compare this to how retransmits are historically analyzed using a packet sniffer to capture all packets, and then post-processing to find retransmits—both steps can cost significant CPU overhead. Packet-capture can also only see details that are on the wire, whereas tcpretrans(8) prints the TCP state directly from the kernel, and can be enhanced to print more kernel state if needed.

At Netflix, this tool was used to help diagnose a production issue caused by network traffic exceeding external network limits, causing dropped packets and retransmits. It was helpful to watch retransmits across different production instances, and be able to immediately see source, destination, and TCP state details without the overhead of processing per-packet dumps.

Shopify has also used this to debug a production network issue, where the workload was causing tcpdump(8) to drop so many packets that its output was not reliable, and the overhead was too painful. Both tcpretrans(8) and tcpdrop(8) (mentioned later) were used instead to gather enough information to point towards an external issue: in this case, it was a firewall configuration that became inundated under load and would drop packets.

---

31 Origin: I created a number of similar TCP retransmit tracing tools using DTrace in 2011 [110]. I created an Ftrace-based tcpretrans(8) on 28-Jul-2014 [111], then the BCC tcpretrans(8) on 14-Feb-2016. Matthias Tafelmeier added the counting mode. Dale Hamel created the bpftrace version on 23-Nov-2018.

BCC

Command line usage:

```
tcpretrans [options]
```

Options include:

- **-l**: Include tail loss probe attempts (adds a kprobe for tcp_send_loss_probe())
- **-c**: Counts retransmits per flow

The -c option changes the behavior of tcpretrans(8), causing it to print a summary of counts rather than per-event details.

bpftrace

The following is the code for the bpftrace version, which summarizes its core functionality. This version does not support options.

```
#!/usr/local/bin/bpftrace

#include <linux/socket.h>
#include <net/sock.h>

BEGIN
{
        printf("Tracing TCP retransmits. Hit Ctrl-C to end.\n");
        printf("%-8s %-8s %20s %21s %6s\n", "TIME", "PID", "LADDR:LPORT",
            "RADDR:RPORT", "STATE");

        // See include/net/tcp_states.h:
        @tcp_states[1] = "ESTABLISHED";
        @tcp_states[2] = "SYN_SENT";
        @tcp_states[3] = "SYN_RECV";
        @tcp_states[4] = "FIN_WAIT1";
        @tcp_states[5] = "FIN_WAIT2";
        @tcp_states[6] = "TIME_WAIT";
        @tcp_states[7] = "CLOSE";
        @tcp_states[8] = "CLOSE_WAIT";
        @tcp_states[9] = "LAST_ACK";
        @tcp_states[10] = "LISTEN";
        @tcp_states[11] = "CLOSING";
        @tcp_states[12] = "NEW_SYN_RECV";
}

kprobe:tcp_retransmit_skb
```

```
{
        $sk = (struct sock *)arg0;
        $inet_family = $sk->__sk_common.skc_family;

        if ($inet_family == AF_INET || $inet_family == AF_INET6) {
                $daddr = ntop(0);
                $saddr = ntop(0);
                if ($inet_family == AF_INET) {
                        $daddr = ntop($sk->__sk_common.skc_daddr);
                        $saddr = ntop($sk->__sk_common.skc_rcv_saddr);
                } else {
                        $daddr = ntop(
                            $sk->__sk_common.skc_v6_daddr.in6_u.u6_addr8);
                        $saddr = ntop(
                            $sk->__sk_common.skc_v6_rcv_saddr.in6_u.u6_addr8);
                }
                $lport = $sk->__sk_common.skc_num;
                $dport = $sk->__sk_common.skc_dport;

                // Destination port is big endian, it must be flipped
                $dport = ($dport >> 8) | (($dport << 8) & 0x00FF00);

                $state = $sk->__sk_common.skc_state;
                $statestr = @tcp_states[$state];

                time("%H:%M:%S ");
                printf("%-8d %14s:%-6d %14s:%-6d %6s\n", pid, $saddr, $lport,
                    $daddr, $dport, $statestr);
        }
}


END
{
        clear(@tcp_states);
}
```

This version traces the tcp_retransmit_skb() kernel function. On Linux 4.15,
tcp:tcp_retransmit_skb and tcp:tcp_retransmit_synack tracepoints were added, and this tool can
be updated to use them.

10.3.17 tcpsynbl

tcpsynbl(8)[32] traces the TCP SYN backlog limit and size, showing a histogram of the size measured each time the backlog is checked. For example, on a 48-CPU production edge server:

```
# tcpsynbl.bt
Attaching 4 probes...
Tracing SYN backlog size. Ctrl-C to end.
^C
@backlog[backlog limit]: histogram of backlog size

@backlog[128]:
[0]                    2 |@@@@@@@@@@@@@@@@@@@@@@@@@@@@@@@@@@@@@@@@@@@@@@@@@@@@|

@backlog[500]:
[0]                 2783 |@@@@@@@@@@@@@@@@@@@@@@@@@@@@@@@@@@@@@@@@@@@@@@@@@@@@|
[1]                    9 |                                                  |
[2, 4)                 4 |                                                  |
[4, 8)                 1 |                                                  |
```

The first histogram shows that a backlog of limit 128 had two connections arrive, where the backlog length was 0. The second histogram shows that a backlog limit of 500 had over two thousand connections arrive, and the length was usually zero, but sometimes reached the four to eight range. If the backlog exceeds the limit, this tool prints a line to say that a SYN has been dropped, which causes latency on the client host as it must retransmit.

This backlog size is tunable, and is an argument to the listen(2) syscall:

```
int listen(int sockfd, int backlog);
```

It is also truncated by a system limit set in /proc/sys/net/core/somaxconn.

This tool works by tracing new connection events, and checking the limit and size of the backlog. The overhead should be negligible, as these are usually infrequent compared to other events.

The source to tcpsynbl(8) is[33]:

```
#!/usr/local/bin/bpftrace

#include <net/sock.h>

BEGIN
{
```

---

32 Origin: I created a number of similar TCP SYN backlog tools using DTrace in 2012 [110]. I created this bpftrace version on 19-Apr-2019.

33 This tool contains a workaround for an int casting problem: & 0xffffffff. This should become unnecessary in a later version of bpftrace.

```
        printf("Tracing SYN backlog size. Ctrl-C to end.\n");
}


kprobe:tcp_v4_syn_recv_sock,
kprobe:tcp_v6_syn_recv_sock
{
        $sock = (struct sock *)arg0;
        @backlog[$sock->sk_max_ack_backlog & 0xffffffff] =
            hist($sock->sk_ack_backlog);
        if ($sock->sk_ack_backlog > $sock->sk_max_ack_backlog) {
                time("%H:%M:%S dropping a SYN.\n");
        }
}


END
{
        printf("\n@backlog[backlog limit]: histogram of backlog size\n");
}
```

If the backlog exceeds the limit, the time() builtin is used to print a line of output containing the time, and a message that a SYN was dropped. This was not seen in the previous production output as the limit was not exceeded.

10.3.18   tcpwin

tcpwin(8)[34] traces the TCP send congestion window size and other kernel parameters, so that the performance of congestion control can be studied. This tool produces comma-separated value output for importing into graphing software. For example, running tcpwin.bt and saving the output to a text file:

```
# tcpwin.bt > out.tcpwin01.txt

^C
# more out.tcpwin01.txt
Attaching 2 probes...
event,sock,time_us,snd_cwnd,snd_ssthresh,sk_sndbuf,sk_wmem_queued
rcv,0xffff9212377a9800,409985,2,2,87040,2304
rcv,0xffff9216fe306e80,534689,10,2147483647,87040,0
rcv,0xffff92180f84c000,632704,7,7,87040,2304
rcv,0xffff92180b04f800,674795,10,2147483647,87040,2304
[...]
```

---

34 Origin: I created this on 20-Apr-2019, inspired by the tcp_probe module and the many times I've seen it used for graphing congestion window size over time.

The second line of output is a header line, and the following are event details. The second field is the sock struct address, which can be used to uniquely identify connections. The awk(1) utility can be used to frequency count these sock addresses:

```
# awk -F, '$1 == "rcv" { a[$2]++ } END { for (s in a) { print s, a[s] } }'
out.tcpwin01.txt
[...]
0xffff92166fede000 1
0xffff92150a03c800 4564
0xffff9213db2d6600 2
[...]
```

This shows that the socket with the most TCP receive events while tracing had the address 0xffff92150a03c800. Events for this address only, and the header line, can also be extracted by awk to a new file, out.csv:

```
# awk -F, '$2 == "0xffff92150a03c800" || NR == 2' out.tcpwin01.txt > out.csv
```

This CSV file was imported into the R statistics software and plotted (see Figure 10-5).

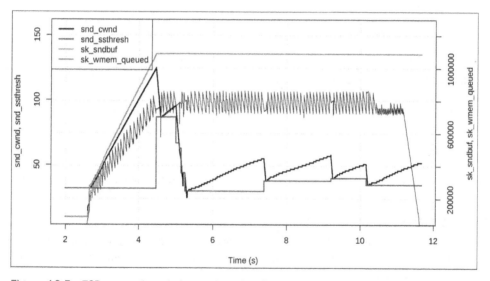

Figure 10-5   TCP congestion window and send buffer over time

This system is using the cubic TCP congestion control algorithm, showing an increase in send congestion window size and then a sharp drop when congestion is encountered (packet loss). This occurs several times, creating a sawtooth pattern, until an optimal window size is found.

The source to tcpwin(8) is:

```
#!/usr/local/bin/bpftrace

#include <net/sock.h>
#include <linux/tcp.h>

BEGIN
{
        printf("event,sock,time_us,snd_cwnd,snd_ssthresh,sk_sndbuf,");
        printf("sk_wmem_queued\n");
}

kprobe:tcp_rcv_established
{
        $sock = (struct sock *)arg0;
        $tcps = (struct tcp_sock *)arg0; // see tcp_sk()
        printf("rcv,0x%llx,%lld,%d,%d,%d,%d\n", arg0, elapsed / 1000,
            $tcps->snd_cwnd, $tcps->snd_ssthresh, $sock->sk_sndbuf,
            $sock->sk_wmem_queued);
}
```

This can be extended. The first field is the event type, but only "rcv" is used by this tool. You can add more kprobes or tracepoints, each with its own event string to identify it. For example, an event type "new" could be added when sockets are established, with fields to identify the IP addresses and TCP ports.

A kernel module was used for this type of congestion control analysis, tcp_probe, which recently has become a tracepoint: tcp:tcp_probe, in Linux 4.16. The tcpwin(8) tool can be rewritten to be based on this tracepoint, although not all socket details are visible from the tracepoint arguments.

10.3.19   tcpnagle

tcpnagle(8)[35] traces the usage of TCP nagle on the TCP transmit codepath, and measures the duration of transmit delays as a histogram: these delays are caused by nagle and other events. For example, on a production edge server:

```
# tcpnagle.bt
Attaching 4 probes...
Tracing TCP nagle and xmit delays. Hit Ctrl-C to end.
^C
```

---

35 Origin: I created it for this book on 23-Apr-2019.

```
@blocked_us:
[2, 4)                 3 |@@@@@@@@@@@@@@@@@@@@@@@@@@@@@@@@@@@@@@@@@@@@@@@@@@@@|
[4, 8)                 2 |@@@@@@@@@@@@@@@@@@@@@@@@@@@@@@@@@@@@@              |

@nagle[CORK]: 2
@nagle[OFF|PUSH]: 5
@nagle[ON]: 32
@nagle[PUSH]: 11418
@nagle[OFF]: 226697
```

During tracing, this showed that nagle was often off (perhaps because the application has called a setsockopt(2) with TCP_NODELAY) or set to push (perhaps because the application is using TCP_CORK). Only five times were transmit packets delayed, for at most the four to eight microsecond bucket.

This works by tracing the entry and exit of a TCP transmit function. This can be a frequent function, so the overhead may become noticeable on high network throughput systems.

The source to tcpnagle(8) is:

```
#!/usr/local/bin/bpftrace

BEGIN
{
        printf("Tracing TCP nagle and xmit delays. Hit Ctrl-C to end.\n");
        // from include/net/tcp.h; add more combinations if needed:
        @flags[0x0] = "ON";
        @flags[0x1] = "OFF";
        @flags[0x2] = "CORK";
        @flags[0x3] = "OFF|CORK";
        @flags[0x4] = "PUSH";
        @flags[0x5] = "OFF|PUSH";
}

kprobe:tcp_write_xmit
{
        @nagle[@flags[arg2]] = count();
        @sk[tid] = arg0;
}

kretprobe:tcp_write_xmit
/@sk[tid]/
{
        $inflight = retval & 0xff;
        $sk = @sk[tid];
```

```
        if ($inflight && !@start[$sk]) {
                @start[$sk] = nsecs;
        }
        if (!$inflight && @start[$sk]) {
                @blocked_us = hist((nsecs - @start[$sk]) / 1000);
                delete(@start[$sk]);
        }
        delete(@sk[tid]);
}


END
{
        clear(@flags); clear(@start); clear(@sk);
}
```

On the entry to tcp_write_xmit(), the nonagle flags (arg2) are converted to a readable string via the @flags lookup map. A sock struct point is also saved, as it is used in the kretprobe for saving timestamps with a connection for measuring the duration of transmit delays. The duration is measured from the first time tcp_write_xmit() returns non-zero (which shows that for some reason it did not send the packets; the reason may include nagle), to when tcp_write_xmit() next successfully sent packets for that socket.

10.3.20   udpconnect

udpconnect(8)[36] traces new UDP connections initiated from the local host that use connect(2) (this does not trace unconnected UDP). For example:

```
# udpconnect.bt
Attaching 3 probes...
TIME     PID    COMM              IP RADDR             RPORT
20:58:38 6039   DNS Res~er #540   4  10.45.128.25      53
20:58:38 2621   TaskSchedulerFo   4  127.0.0.53        53
20:58:39 3876   Chrome_IOThread   6  2001:4860:4860::8888 53
[...]
```

This shows two connections, both to remote port 53, one from a DNS resolver, and the other from Chrome_IOThread.

This works by tracing the UDP connection functions in the kernel. Their frequency should be low, making the overhead negligible.

---

36 Origin: I created it for this book on 20-Apr-2019.

The source to udpconnect(8) is:

```
#!/usr/local/bin/bpftrace

#include <net/sock.h>

BEGIN
{
        printf("%-8s %-6s %-16s %-2s %-16s %-5s\n", "TIME", "PID", "COMM",
            "IP", "RADDR", "RPORT");
}

kprobe:ip4_datagram_connect,
kprobe:ip6_datagram_connect
{
        $sa = (struct sockaddr *)arg1;
        if ($sa->sa_family == AF_INET || $sa->sa_family == AF_INET6) {
                time("%H:%M:%S ");
                if ($sa->sa_family == AF_INET) {
                        $s = (struct sockaddr_in *)arg1;
                        $port = ($s->sin_port >> 8) |
                            (($s->sin_port << 8) & 0xff00);
                        printf("%-6d %-16s 4  %-16s %-5d\n", pid, comm,
                            ntop(AF_INET, $s->sin_addr.s_addr), $port);
                } else {
                        $s6 = (struct sockaddr_in6 *)arg1;
                        $port = ($s6->sin6_port >> 8) |
                            (($s6->sin6_port << 8) & 0xff00);
                        printf("%-6d %-16s 6  %-16s %-5d\n", pid, comm,
                            ntop(AF_INET6, $s6->sin6_addr.in6_u.u6_addr8),
                            $port);
                }
        }
}
```

The ip4_datagram_connect() and ip6_datagram_connect() functions are the connect members of the udp_prot and udpv6_prot structs, which define the functions that handle the UDP protocol. Details are printed similarly to earlier tools.

Also see socketio(8) for a tool that shows UDP sends and receives by process. A UDP-specific one can be coded by tracing udp_sendmsg() and udp_recvmsg(), which would have the benefit of isolating the overhead to just the UDP functions rather than all the socket functions.

10.3.21   gethostlatency

gethostlatency(8)[37] is a BCC and bpftrace tool to trace host resolution calls (DNS) via the resolver library calls, getaddrinfo(3), gethostbyname(3), etc. For example:

```
# gethostlatency
TIME       PID    COMM                LATms HOST
13:52:39   25511  ping                 9.65 www.netflix.com
13:52:42   25519  ping                 2.64 www.netflix.com
13:52:49   24989  DNS Res~er #712     43.09 docs.google.com
13:52:52   25527  ping                99.26 www.cilium.io
13:52:53   19025  DNS Res~er #709      2.58 drive.google.com
13:53:05   21903  ping               279.09 www.kubernetes.io
13:53:06   25459  TaskSchedulerFo     23.87 www.informit.com
[...]
```

This output shows the latencies of various resolutions system-wide. The first was the ping(1) command resolving www.netflix.com, which took 9.65 milliseconds. A subsequent lookup took 2.64 milliseconds (likely thanks to caching). Other threads and lookups can be seen in the output, with the slowest a 279 ms resolution of www.kubernetes.io.[38]

This works by using user-level dynamic instrumentation on the library functions. During a uprobe the host name and a timestamp is recorded, and during a uretprobe the duration is calculated and printed with the saved name. Since these are typically low-frequency events, the overhead of this tool should be negligible.

DNS is a common source of production latency. At Shopify, the bpftrace version of this tool was executed on a Kubernetes cluster to characterize a DNS latency issue in production. The data did not point to an issue with a certain server or target of the lookup, but rather latency when many lookups were in flight. The issue was further debugged and found to be a cloud limit on the number of UDP sessions that could be open on each host. Increasing the limit resolved the issue.

BCC

Command line usage:

```
gethostlatency [options]
```

The only option currently supported is -p PID, to trace one process ID only.

---

37 Origin: I created a similar tool called getaddrinfo.d for the 2011 DTrace book [Gregg 11]. I created the BCC version on 28-Jan-2016 and the bpftrace version on 8-Sep-2018.

38 Slow DNS times for the .io domain from the United States is a known problem, believed to be due to the hosting location of the .io name servers [112].

bpftrace

The following is the code for the bpftrace version, which does not support options:

```
#!/usr/local/bin/bpftrace

BEGIN
{
        printf("Tracing getaddr/gethost calls... Hit Ctrl-C to end.\n");
        printf("%-9s %-6s %-16s %6s %s\n", "TIME", "PID", "COMM", "LATms",
            "HOST");
}

uprobe:/lib/x86_64-linux-gnu/libc.so.6:getaddrinfo,
uprobe:/lib/x86_64-linux-gnu/libc.so.6:gethostbyname,
uprobe:/lib/x86_64-linux-gnu/libc.so.6:gethostbyname2
{
        @start[tid] = nsecs;
        @name[tid] = arg0;
}

uretprobe:/lib/x86_64-linux-gnu/libc.so.6:getaddrinfo,
uretprobe:/lib/x86_64-linux-gnu/libc.so.6:gethostbyname,
uretprobe:/lib/x86_64-linux-gnu/libc.so.6:gethostbyname2
/@start[tid]/
{
        $latms = (nsecs - @start[tid]) / 1000000;
        time("%H:%M:%S  ");
        printf("%-6d %-16s %6d %s\n", pid, comm, $latms, str(@name[tid]));
        delete(@start[tid]);
        delete(@name[tid]);
}
```

The different possible resolver calls are traced from libc via its /lib/x86_64-linux-gnu/libc.so.6 location. If a different resolver library is used, or if the functions are implemented by the application, or statically included (static build), then this tool will need to be modified to trace those other locations.

10.3.22 ipecn

ipecn(8)[39] traces IPv4 inbound explicit congestion notification (ECN) events, and is a proof of concept tool. For example:

```
# ipecn.bt
Attaching 3 probes...
Tracing inbound IPv4 ECN Congestion Encountered. Hit Ctrl-C to end.
```

---

39 Origin: I created it for this book on 28-May-2019, based on a suggestion from Sargun Dhillon.

```
10:11:02 ECN CE from: 100.65.76.247
10:11:02 ECN CE from: 100.65.76.247
10:11:03 ECN CE from: 100.65.76.247
10:11:21 ECN CE from: 100.65.76.247
[...]
```

This shows congestion encountered (CE) events from 100.65.76.247. CE can be set by switches and routers in the network to notify endpoints of congestion. It can also be set by kernels based on a qdisc policy, although that is usually for testing and simulation purposes (with the netem qdisc). The DataCenter TCP (DCTCP) congestion control algorithm also makes use of ECN [Alizadeh 10] [113].

ipecn(8) works by tracing the kernel ip_rcv() function and reading the congestion encountered state from the IP header. Since this adds overhead to every received packet, this method is not ideal, and I'd rather call this a proof of concept. Much better would be to trace the kernel functions that handle CE events only, as these would fire less frequently. However, they are inlined and unavailable to trace directly (on my kernels). Best of all would be to have a tracepoint for ECN congestion encountered events.

The source to ipecn(8) is:

```
#!/usr/local/bin/bpftrace

#include <linux/skbuff.h>
#include <linux/ip.h>

BEGIN
{
        printf("Tracing inbound IPv4 ECN Congestion Encountered. ");
        printf("Hit Ctrl-C to end.\n");
}

kprobe:ip_rcv
{
        $skb = (struct sk_buff *)arg0;
        // get IPv4 header; see skb_network_header():
        $iph = (struct iphdr *)($skb->head + $skb->network_header);
        // see INET_ECN_MASK:
        if (($iph->tos & 3) == 3) {
                time("%H:%M:%S ");
                printf("ECN CE from: %s\n", ntop($iph->saddr));
        }
}
```

This is also an example of parsing the IPv4 header from a struct sk_buff. It uses similar logic to the kernel's skb_network_header() function, and will need updates to match any changes to that function (another reason that more-stable tracepoints would be preferred). This tool can also be extended to trace the outbound path, and IPv6 (see Section 10.5).

10.3.23 superping

superping(8)[40] measures the ICMP echo request to response latency from the kernel network stack, as a way to verify the round trip times reported by ping(8). Older versions of ping(8) measure the round trip time from user space, which can include CPU scheduling latency on busy systems, inflating the measured times. This older method is also used by ping(8) for kernels without socket timestamp support (SIOCGSTAMP or SO_TIMESTAMP).

Since I have a newer version of ping(8) and newer kernel, to demonstrate the older behavior I've run it with the -U option, which measures the original user-to-user latency. For example, in one terminal session:

```
terminal1# ping -U 10.0.0.1
PING 10.0.0.1 (10.0.0.1) 56(84) bytes of data.
64 bytes from 10.0.0.1: icmp_seq=1 ttl=64 time=6.44 ms
64 bytes from 10.0.0.1: icmp_seq=2 ttl=64 time=6.60 ms
64 bytes from 10.0.0.1: icmp_seq=3 ttl=64 time=5.93 ms
64 bytes from 10.0.0.1: icmp_seq=4 ttl=64 time=7.40 ms
64 bytes from 10.0.0.1: icmp_seq=5 ttl=64 time=5.87 ms
[...]
```

While in another terminal session I had already run superping(8):

```
terminal2# superping.bt
Attaching 6 probes...
Tracing ICMP echo request latency. Hit Ctrl-C to end.
IPv4 ping, ID 28121 seq 1: 6392 us
IPv4 ping, ID 28121 seq 2: 6474 us
IPv4 ping, ID 28121 seq 3: 5811 us
IPv4 ping, ID 28121 seq 4: 7270 us
IPv4 ping, ID 28121 seq 5: 5741 us
[...]
```

The output can be compared: it shows that the times reported by ping(8) can be inflated by over 0.10 ms, for this current system and workload. Without -U, so that ping(8) uses socket time-stamps, the time difference is often within 0.01 ms.

This works by instrumenting the send and receive of ICMP packets, saving a timestamp in a BPF map for each ICMP echo request, and compares the ICMP header details to match the echo

---

40 Origin: I first created this for the 2011 DTrace book [Gregg 11] and wrote this version for this book on 20-Apr-2019.

packets. The overhead should be negligible, since this is only instrumenting raw IP packets and not TCP packets.

The source to superping(8) is:

```
#!/usr/local/bin/bpftrace

#include <linux/skbuff.h>
#include <linux/icmp.h>
#include <linux/ip.h>
#include <linux/ipv6.h>
#include <linux/in.h>

BEGIN
{
        printf("Tracing ICMP ping latency. Hit Ctrl-C to end.\n");
}

/*
 * IPv4
 */
kprobe:ip_send_skb
{
        $skb = (struct sk_buff *)arg1;
        // get IPv4 header; see skb_network_header():
        $iph = (struct iphdr *)($skb->head + $skb->network_header);
        if ($iph->protocol == IPPROTO_ICMP) {
                // get ICMP header; see skb_transport_header():
                $icmph = (struct icmphdr *)($skb->head +
                    $skb->transport_header);
                if ($icmph->type == ICMP_ECHO) {
                        $id = $icmph->un.echo.id;
                        $seq = $icmph->un.echo.sequence;
                        @start[$id, $seq] = nsecs;
                }
        }
}

kprobe:icmp_rcv
{
        $skb = (struct sk_buff *)arg0;
        // get ICMP header; see skb_transport_header():
        $icmph = (struct icmphdr *)($skb->head + $skb->transport_header);
```

```
        if ($icmph->type == ICMP_ECHOREPLY) {
                $id = $icmph->un.echo.id;
                $seq = $icmph->un.echo.sequence;
                $start = @start[$id, $seq];
                if ($start > 0) {
                        $idhost = ($id >> 8) | (($id << 8) & 0xff00);
                        $seqhost = ($seq >> 8) | (($seq << 8) & 0xff00);
                        printf("IPv4 ping, ID %d seq %d: %d us\n",
                            $idhost, $seqhost, (nsecs - $start) / 1000);
                        delete(@start[$id, $seq]);
                }
        }
}

/*
 * IPv6
 */
kprobe:ip6_send_skb
{
        $skb = (struct sk_buff *)arg0;
        // get IPv6 header; see skb_network_header():
        $ip6h = (struct ipv6hdr *)($skb->head + $skb->network_header);
        if ($ip6h->nexthdr == IPPROTO_ICMPV6) {
                // get ICMP header; see skb_transport_header():
                $icmp6h = (struct icmp6hdr *)($skb->head +
                    $skb->transport_header);
                if ($icmp6h->icmp6_type == ICMPV6_ECHO_REQUEST) {
                        $id = $icmp6h->icmp6_dataun.u_echo.identifier;
                        $seq = $icmp6h->icmp6_dataun.u_echo.sequence;
                        @start[$id, $seq] = nsecs;
                }
        }
}

kprobe:icmpv6_rcv
{
        $skb = (struct sk_buff *)arg0;
        // get ICMPv6 header; see skb_transport_header():
        $icmp6h = (struct icmp6hdr *)($skb->head + $skb->transport_header);
        if ($icmp6h->icmp6_type == ICMPV6_ECHO_REPLY) {
                $id = $icmp6h->icmp6_dataun.u_echo.identifier;
                $seq = $icmp6h->icmp6_dataun.u_echo.sequence;
                $start = @start[$id, $seq];
```

```
            if ($start > 0) {
                    $idhost = ($id >> 8) | (($id << 8) & 0xff00);
                    $seqhost = ($seq >> 8) | (($seq << 8) & 0xff00);
                    printf("IPv6 ping, ID %d seq %d: %d us\n",
                        $idhost, $seqhost, (nsecs - $start) / 1000);
                    delete(@start[$id, $seq]);
            }
    }
}

END { clear(@start); }
```

Both IPv4 and IPv6 are handled by different kernel functions, and are traced separately. This code is another example of packet header analysis: the IPv4, IPv6, ICMP, and ICMPv6 packet headers are read by BPF. The method of finding these header structures from the struct sk_buff depends on the kernel source and its functions skb_network_header() and skb_transport_header(). As with kprobes, this is an unstable interface, and changes to how headers are found and processed by the network stack will require updates to this tool to match.

A minor note for this source: the ICMP identifier and sequence number are printed out after switching from network to host order (see $idhost = and $seqhost =). For the @start map that saves timestamps, I used the network order instead; this saved some instructions on the send kprobes.

10.3.24   qdisc-fq

qdisc-fq(8)[41] shows the time spent on the Fair Queue (FQ) qdisc. For example, from a busy production edge server:

```
# qdisc-fq.bt
Attaching 4 probes...
Tracing qdisc fq latency. Hit Ctrl-C to end.
^C

@us:
[0]                 6803 |@@@@@@@@@@@                                         |
[1]                20084 |@@@@@@@@@@@@@@@@@@@@@@@@@@@@@@@@@@@                  |
[2, 4)             29230 |@@@@@@@@@@@@@@@@@@@@@@@@@@@@@@@@@@@@@@@@@@@@@@@@@@@@@|
[4, 8)               755 |@                                                  |
[8, 16)              210 |                                                   |
[16, 32)              86 |                                                   |
[32, 64)              39 |                                                   |
[64, 128)             90 |                                                   |
[128, 256)            65 |                                                   |
[256, 512)            61 |                                                   |
```

---

41 Origin: I created it for this book on 21-Apr-2019.

```
[512, 1K)              26 |
[1K, 2K)                9 |
[2K, 4K)                2 |
```

This shows that packets usually spent less than four microseconds on this queue, with a very small percentage reaching up to the two to four-millisecond bucket. Should there be a problem with queue latency, it will show up as higher latencies in the histogram.

This works by tracing the enqueue and dequeue functions for this qdisc. For high network I/O systems, the overhead may become measurable as these can be frequent events.

The source to qdisc-fq(8) is:

```
#!/usr/local/bin/bpftrace

BEGIN
{
        printf("Tracing qdisc fq latency. Hit Ctrl-C to end.\n");
}

kprobe:fq_enqueue
{
        @start[arg0] = nsecs;
}

kretprobe:fq_dequeue
/@start[retval]/
{
        @us = hist((nsecs - @start[retval]) / 1000);
        delete(@start[retval]);
}

END
{
        clear(@start);
}
```

The argument to fq_enqueue(), and the return value of fq_dequeue(), is the struct sk_buff address, which is used as a unique key for storing the timestamp.

Note that this tool only works when the FQ qdisc scheduler is loaded. If it is not, this tool will error:

```
# qdisc-fq.bt
Attaching 4 probes...
cannot attach kprobe, Invalid argument
Error attaching probe: 'kretprobe:fq_dequeue'
```

This can be fixed by forcibly loading the FQ scheduler kernel module:

```
# modprobe sch_fq
# qdisc-fq.bt
Attaching 4 probes...
Tracing qdisc fq latency. Hit Ctrl-C to end.
^C
#
```

Although, if this qdisc is not in use, then there will be no queueing events to measure. Use tc(1) to add and administer qdisc schedulers.

10.3.25   qdisc-cbq, qdisc-cbs, qdisc-codel, qdisc-fq_codel, qdisc-red, and qdisc-tbf

There are many other qdisc schedulers, and the previous qdisc-fq(8) tool can usually be adapted to trace each. For example, here is a Class Based Queueing (CBQ) version:

```
# qdisc-cbq.bt
Attaching 4 probes...
Tracing qdisc cbq latency. Hit Ctrl-C to end.
^C

@us:
[0]                      152 |@@                                                 |
[1]                      766 |@@@@@@@@@@@@@@@                                    |
[2, 4)                  2033 |@@@@@@@@@@@@@@@@@@@@@@@@@@@@@@@@@@@@@@@@            |
[4, 8)                  2279 |@@@@@@@@@@@@@@@@@@@@@@@@@@@@@@@@@@@@@@@@@@@@        |
[8, 16)                 2663 |@@@@@@@@@@@@@@@@@@@@@@@@@@@@@@@@@@@@@@@@@@@@@@@@@@@@|
[16, 32)                 427 |@@@@@@@@                                           |
[32, 64)                  15 |                                                   |
[64, 128)                  1 |                                                   |
```

The enqueue and dequeue functions that are traced are from struct Qdisc_ops, which defines their arguments and return value (include/net/sch_generic.h):

```
struct Qdisc_ops {
        struct Qdisc_ops        *next;
        const struct Qdisc_class_ops    *cl_ops;
        char                    id[IFNAMSIZ];
        int                     priv_size;
        unsigned int            static_flags;
```

```
    int                     (*enqueue)(struct sk_buff *skb,
                                       struct Qdisc *sch,
                                       struct sk_buff **to_free);
    struct sk_buff *        (*dequeue)(struct Qdisc *);
[...]
```

This is why the skb_buff address was the first argument for the enqueue function, and the return value of the dequeue function.

This Qdisc_ops is declared for other schedulers. For the CBQ qdisc (net/sched/sch_cbq.c):

```
static struct Qdisc_ops cbq_qdisc_ops __read_mostly = {
    .next       =       NULL,
    .cl_ops     =       &cbq_class_ops,
    .id         =       "cbq",
    .priv_size  =       sizeof(struct cbq_sched_data),
    .enqueue    =       cbq_enqueue,
    .dequeue    =       cbq_dequeue,
[...]
```

A qdisc-cbq.bt tool can thus be written by changing qdisc-fq(8)'s fq_enqueue to cbq_enqueue, and fq_dequeue to cbq_dequeue. is Here is a table of substitutions for some of the qdiscs:

BPF Tool	Qdisc	Enqueue Function	Dequeue Function
qdisc-cbq.bt	Class Based Queueing	cbq_enqueue()	cbq_dequeue()
qdisc-cbs.bt	Credit Based Shaper	cbs_enqueue())	cbs_dequeue()
qdisc-codel.bt	Controlled-Delay Active Queue Management	codel_qdisc_enqueue()	codel_qdisc_dequeue()
qdisc-fq_codel.bt	Fair Queueing with Controlled Delay	fq_codel_enqueue()	fq_codel_dequeue()
qdisc-red	Random Early Detection	red_enqueue()	red_dequeue()
qdisc-tbf	Token Bucket Filter	tbf_enqueue()	tbf_dequeue()

It would be a straightforward exercise to create a shell script wrapper to bpftrace, called qdisclat, that accepted a qdisc name as an argument and then built and ran the bpftrace program to show its latency.

10.3.26   netsize

netsize(8)[42] shows the size of received and sent packets from the net device layer, both before and after software segmentation offload (GSO and GRO). This output can be used to investigate how packets become segmented before sending. For example, from a busy production server:

```
# netsize.bt
Attaching 5 probes...
Tracing net device send/receive. Hit Ctrl-C to end.
^C

@nic_recv_bytes:
[32, 64)              16291 |@@@@@@@@@@@@@@@@@@@@@@@@@@@@@@@@@@@@@@@@@@@@@@@@@@@@|
[64, 128)               668 |@@                                                |
[128, 256)               19 |                                                  |
[256, 512)               18 |                                                  |
[512, 1K)                24 |                                                  |
[1K, 2K)                157 |                                                  |


@nic_send_bytes:
[32, 64)                107 |                                                  |
[64, 128)               356 |                                                  |
[128, 256)              139 |                                                  |
[256, 512)               31 |                                                  |
[512, 1K)                15 |                                                  |
[1K, 2K)              45850 |@@@@@@@@@@@@@@@@@@@@@@@@@@@@@@@@@@@@@@@@@@@@@@@@@@@@|


@recv_bytes:
[32, 64)              16417 |@@@@@@@@@@@@@@@@@@@@@@@@@@@@@@@@@@@@@@@@@@@@@@@@@@@@|
[64, 128)               688 |@@                                                |
[128, 256)               20 |                                                  |
[256, 512)               33 |                                                  |
[512, 1K)                35 |                                                  |
[1K, 2K)                145 |                                                  |
[2K, 4K)                  1 |                                                  |
[4K, 8K)                  5 |                                                  |
[8K, 16K)                 3 |                                                  |
[16K, 32K)                2 |                                                  |
```

---

42 Origin: I created this for this book on 21-Apr-2019.

```
@send_bytes:
[32, 64)               107 |@@@                                                        |
[64, 128)              356 |@@@@@@@@@@                                                 |
[128, 256)             139 |@@@@                                                       |
[256, 512)              29 |                                                           |
[512, 1K)               14 |                                                           |
[1K, 2K)               131 |@@@@                                                       |
[2K, 4K)               151 |@@@@@                                                      |
[4K, 8K)               269 |@@@@@@@@                                                   |
[8K, 16K)              391 |@@@@@@@@@@@@                                               |
[16K, 32K)            1563 |@@@@@@@@@@@@@@@@@@@@@@@@@@@@@@@@@@@@@@@@@@@@@@@@@@@@@@@@@@@@@@|
[32K, 64K)             494 |@@@@@@@@@@@@@@@@                                           |
```

The output shows the packet sizes at the NIC (@nic_recv_bytes, @nic_send_bytes), and the packet sizes for the kernel network stack (@recv_bytes, @send_bytes). This shows that the server was receiving small packets, often smaller than 64 bytes, and mostly sending in the eight- to 64-Kbyte range (which becomes a one- to two-Kbyte range after segmentation for the NIC). These are likely 1500 MTU sends.

This interface does not support TCP segmentation offload (TSO), so the GSO was used to segment before delivery to the NIC. If TSO was supported and enabled, the @nic_send_bytes histogram would also show large sizes, as segmentation happens later in NIC hardware.

Switching to jumbo frames will increase the packet size and system throughput, although there can be issues with enabling jumbo frames in a datacenter, including consuming more switch memory and worsening TCP incast issues.

This output can be compared to the earlier output of socksize(8).

This works by tracing net device tracepoints and summarizing the length argument in BPF maps. The overhead may become measurable on high network I/O systems.

There is a Linux tool called iptraf-ng(8) that also shows histograms for network packet sizes. However, iptraf-ng(8) works by packet sniffing and processing packets in user space. This costs more CPU overhead than netsize(8), which summarizes in kernel space. For example, examining the CPU usage of each tool during a localhost iperf(1) benchmark:

```
# pidstat -p $(pgrep iptraf-ng) 1
Linux 4.15.0-47-generic (lgud-bgregg)      04/22/2019    _x86_64_     (8 CPU)

11:32:15 AM  UID    PID   %usr %system %guest   %wait    %CPU  CPU Command
11:32:16 AM    0  30825  18.00   74.00   0.00    0.00   92.00    2 iptraf-ng
11:32:17 AM    0  30825  21.00   70.00   0.00    0.00   91.00    1 iptraf-ng
11:32:18 AM    0  30825  21.00   71.00   0.00    1.00   92.00    6 iptraf-ng
[...]
```

```
# pidstat -p $(pgrep netsize) 1
Linux 4.15.0-47-generic (lgud-bgregg)      04/22/2019     _x86_64_       (8 CPU)

11:33:39 AM  UID    PID    %usr %system  %guest    %wait    %CPU  CPU Command
11:33:40 AM    0  30776    0.00    0.00    0.00     0.00    0.00    5 netsize.bt
11:33:41 AM    0  30776    0.00    0.00    0.00     0.00    0.00    7 netsize.bt
11:33:42 AM    0  30776    0.00    0.00    0.00     0.00    0.00    1 netsize.bt
[...]
```

iptraf-ng(8) consumes over 90% of one CPU to summarize packet sizes as histograms, whereas netsize(8) consumes 0%. This highlights a key difference between the approaches, although there are additional overheads not shown here for kernel processing.

The source to netsize(8) is:

```
#!/usr/local/bin/bpftrace

BEGIN
{
        printf("Tracing net device send/receive. Hit Ctrl-C to end.\n");
}

tracepoint:net:netif_receive_skb
{
        @recv_bytes = hist(args->len);
}

tracepoint:net:net_dev_queue
{
        @send_bytes = hist(args->len);
}

tracepoint:net:napi_gro_receive_entry
{
        @nic_recv_bytes = hist(args->len);
}

tracepoint:net:net_dev_xmit
{
        @nic_send_bytes = hist(args->len);
}
```

This uses the net tracepoints to watch the send path and receive paths.

10.3.27 nettxlat

nettxlat(8)[43] shows network device transmission latency: the time spent pushing the packet into the driver layer to enqueue it on a TX ring for the hardware to send out, until the hardware signals the kernel that packet transmission has completed (usually via NAPI) and the packet is freed. For example, from a busy production edge server:

```
# nettxlat.bt
Attaching 4 probes...
Tracing net device xmit queue latency. Hit Ctrl-C to end.
^C

@us:
[4, 8)               2230 |                                                    |
[8, 16)            150679 |@@@@@@@@@@@@@@@@@@@@@@@@@@@@                         |
[16, 32)           275351 |@@@@@@@@@@@@@@@@@@@@@@@@@@@@@@@@@@@@@@@@@@@@@@@@@@@@@@|
[32, 64)            59898 |@@@@@@@@@@@                                         |
[64, 128)           27597 |@@@@@                                               |
[128, 256)            276 |                                                    |
[256, 512)              9 |                                                    |
[512, 1K)               3 |                                                    |
```

This shows that device queued time was usually faster than 128 microseconds.

The source to nettxlat(8) is:

```
#!/usr/local/bin/bpftrace

BEGIN
{
        printf("Tracing net device xmit queue latency. Hit Ctrl-C to end.\n");
}

tracepoint:net:net_dev_start_xmit
{
        @start[args->skbaddr] = nsecs;
}

tracepoint:skb:consume_skb
/@start[args->skbaddr]/
{
        @us = hist((nsecs - @start[args->skbaddr]) / 1000);
        delete(@start[args->skbaddr]);
```

---

43 Origin: I created it for this book on 21-Apr-2019.

```
}

tracepoint:net:net_dev_queue
{
        // avoid timestamp reuse:
        delete(@start[args->skbaddr]);
}

END
{
        clear(@start);
}
```

This works by measuring the time from when a packet is issued to the device queue via the net:net_dev_start_xmit tracepoint, and then when that packet is freed via the skb:consume_skb tracepoint, which occurs when the device has completed sending it.

There are some edge cases where a packet may not pass through the usual skb:consume_skb path: this creates a problem as the saved timestamp may be reused by a later sk_buff, causing latency outliers to appear in the histogram. This has been avoided by deleting timestamps on net:net_dev_queue, to help eliminate their reuse.

As an example of breaking down by device name, the following lines were modified, turning nettxlat(8) into nettxlat-dev(8):

```
[...]
#include <linux/skbuff.h>
#include <linux/netdevice.h>
[...]
tracepoint:skb:consume_skb
/@start[args->skbaddr]/
{
        $skb = (struct sk_buff *)args->skbaddr;
        @us[$skb->dev->name] = hist((nsecs - @start[args->skbaddr]) / 1000);
[...]
```

The output then becomes:

```
# nettxlat-dev.bt
Attaching 4 probes...
Tracing net device xmit queue latency. Hit Ctrl-C to end.
^C
```

```
@us[eth0]:
[4, 8)                    65 |                                                    |
[8, 16)                 6438 |@@@@@@@@@@@@@@@@@@@@@@@@@@@@@@@                       |
[16, 32)               10899 |@@@@@@@@@@@@@@@@@@@@@@@@@@@@@@@@@@@@@@@@@@@@@@@@@@@@@@|
[32, 64)                2265 |@@@@@@@@@@                                           |
[64, 128)                977 |@@@@                                                 |
[...]
```

This server only has eth0, but if other interfaces were in use, there would be a separate histogram for each.

Note that this change reduces the stability of the tool, since it is now referring to unstable struct internals instead of just tracepoints and tracepoint arguments.

10.3.28 skbdrop

skbdrop(8)[44] traces unusual skb drop events, and shows their kernel stack traces along with network counters while tracing. For example, on a production server:

```
# bpftrace --unsafe skbdrop.bt
Attaching 3 probes...
Tracing unusual skb drop stacks. Hit Ctrl-C to end.
^C#kernel
IpInReceives                   28717           0.0
IpInDelivers                   28717           0.0
IpOutRequests                  32033           0.0
TcpActiveOpens                   173           0.0
TcpPassiveOpens                  278           0.0
[...]
TcpExtTCPSackMerged                1           0.0
TcpExtTCPSackShiftFallback         5           0.0
TcpExtTCPDeferAcceptDrop         278           0.0
TcpExtTCPRcvCoalesce            3276           0.0
TcpExtTCPAutoCorking             774           0.0
[...]

[...]
@[
    kfree_skb+118
    skb_release_data+171
    skb_release_all+36
```

---

44 Origin: I created this tool for this book on 21-Apr-2019.

```
    __kfree_skb+18
    tcp_recvmsg+1946
    inet_recvmsg+81
    sock_recvmsg+67
    SYSC_recvfrom+228
]: 50
@[
    kfree_skb+118
    sk_stream_kill_queues+77
    inet_csk_destroy_sock+89
    tcp_done+150
    tcp_time_wait+446
    tcp_fin+216
    tcp_data_queue+1401
    tcp_rcv_state_process+1501
]: 142
@[
    kfree_skb+118
    tcp_v4_rcv+361
    ip_local_deliver_finish+98
    ip_local_deliver+111
    ip_rcv_finish+297
    ip_rcv+655
    __netif_receive_skb_core+1074
    __netif_receive_skb+24
]: 276
```

This begins by showing network counter increments while tracing, and then stack traces for skb drops and counts for comparison. The above output shows that the most frequent drop path was via tcp_v4_rcv(), with 276 drops. The network counters show a similar count: 278 in TcpPassiveOpens and TcpExtTCPDeferAcceptDrop. (The slightly higher number can be explained: extra time is needed to fetch these counters.) This suggests that those events might be all related.

This works by instrumenting the skb:kfree_skb tracepoint, and automates running the nstat(8) tool for counting network statistics while tracing. nstat(8) must be installed for this tool to work: it is in the iproute2 package.

The skb:kfree_skb tracepoint is a counterpart of skb:consume_skb. The consume_skb tracepoint fires for the normal skb consumption code path, and kfree_skb fires for other unusual events that may be worth investigating.

The source to skbdrop(8) is:

```
#!/usr/local/bin/bpftrace

BEGIN
{
        printf("Tracing unusual skb drop stacks. Hit Ctrl-C to end.\n");
        system("nstat > /dev/null");
}


tracepoint:skb:kfree_skb
{
        @[kstack(8)] = count();
}


END
{
        system("nstat; nstat -rs > /dev/null");
}
```

This begins by setting the nstat(8) counters to zero in the BEGIN action, and then using nstat(8) again in the END action to print the interval counts, and then to reset nstat(8) back to its original state (-rs). This will interfere with other users of nstat(8) while tracing. Note that the bpftrace --unsafe option is necessary when executing this, due to the use of system().

10.3.29 skblife

skblife(8)[45] measures the lifespan of a sk_buff (skb), the object used to pass packets through the kernel. Measuring the lifespan can show if there is latency within the network stack, including packets waiting for locks. For example, on a busy production server:

```
# skblife.bt
Attaching 6 probes...
^C

@skb_residency_nsecs:
[1K, 2K)             163 |                                                    |
[2K, 4K)             792 |@@@                                                 |
[4K, 8K)            2591 |@@@@@@@@@@                                          |
[8K, 16K)           3022 |@@@@@@@@@@@@                                        |
[16K, 32K)         12695 |@@@@@@@@@@@@@@@@@@@@@@@@@@@@@@@@@@@@@@@@@@@@@@@@@@@@@@|
[32K, 64K)         11025 |@@@@@@@@@@@@@@@@@@@@@@@@@@@@@@@@@@@@@@@@@@@@@@@       |
```

---

45 Origin: I created it for this book on 4-Apr-2019.

```
[64K, 128K)         3277 |@@@@@@@@@@@@                              |
[128K, 256K)        2954 |@@@@@@@@@@@                               |
[256K, 512K)        1608 |@@@@@@                                    |
[512K, 1M)          1594 |@@@@@@                                    |
[1M, 2M)             583 |@@                                        |
[2M, 4M)             435 |@                                         |
[4M, 8M)             317 |@                                         |
[8M, 16M)            104 |                                          |
[16M, 32M)            10 |                                          |
[32M, 64M)            12 |                                          |
[64M, 128M)            1 |                                          |
[128M, 256M)           1 |                                          |
```

This shows that the lifespan of sk_buffs was often between 16 and 64 microseconds, however, there are outliers reaching as high as the 128 to 256 millisecond bucket. These can be further investigated with other tools, including the previously queue latency tools, to see if the latency is coming from those locations.

This works by tracing kernel slab cache allocations to find when sk_buffs are allocated and freed. Such allocations can be very frequent, and this tool may cause noticeable or significant overhead on very busy systems. It can be used for short-term analysis rather than long-term monitoring.

The source to skblife(8) is:

```
#!/usr/local/bin/bpftrace

kprobe:kmem_cache_alloc,
kprobe:kmem_cache_alloc_node
{
        $cache = arg0;
        if ($cache == *kaddr("skbuff_fclone_cache") ||
            $cache == *kaddr("skbuff_head_cache")) {
                @is_skb_alloc[tid] = 1;
        }
}

kretprobe:kmem_cache_alloc,
kretprobe:kmem_cache_alloc_node
/@is_skb_alloc[tid]/
{
        delete(@is_skb_alloc[tid]);
        @skb_birth[retval] = nsecs;
}
```

```
kprobe:kmem_cache_free
/@skb_birth[arg1]/
{
        @skb_residency_nsecs = hist(nsecs - @skb_birth[arg1]);
        delete(@skb_birth[arg1]);
}


END
{
        clear(@is_skb_alloc);
        clear(@skb_birth);
}
```

The kmem_cache_alloc() functions are instrumented, and the cache argument is matched to see if it is an sk_buff cache. If so, on the kretprobe a timestamp is associated with the sk_buff address, which is then retrieved on kmem_cache_free().

There are some caveats with this approach: sk_buffs can be segmented into other sk_buffs on GSO, or attached to others on GRO. TCP can also coalesce sk_buffs (tcp_try_coalesce()). This means that, while the lifespan of the sk_buffs can be measured, the lifespan of the full packet may be undercounted. This tool could be enhanced to take these code paths into account: copying an original birth timestamp to new sk_buffs as they are created.

Since this adds kprobe overhead to all kmem cache alloc and free calls (not just for sk_buffs), the overhead may become significant. In the future there may be a way to reduce this. The kernel already has skb:consume_skb and skb:free_skb tracepoints. If an alloc skb tracepoint was added, that could be used instead, and reduce this overhead to just the sk_buff allocations.

10.3.30 ieee80211scan

ieee80211scan(8)[46] traces IEEE 802.11 WiFi scanning. For example:

```
# ieee80211scan.bt
Attaching 5 probes...
Tracing ieee80211 SSID scans. Hit Ctrl-C to end.
13:55:07 scan started (on-CPU PID 1146, wpa_supplicant)
13:42:11 scanning channel 2GHZ freq 2412: beacon_found 0
13:42:11 scanning channel 2GHZ freq 2412: beacon_found 0
13:42:11 scanning channel 2GHZ freq 2412: beacon_found 0
[...]
13:42:13 scanning channel 5GHZ freq 5660: beacon_found 0
13:42:14 scanning channel 5GHZ freq 5785: beacon_found 1
```

---

46 Origin: I created this for this book on 23-Apr-2019. The first time I wrote a WiFi scanning tracer was out of necessity when I was in a hotel room in 2004 with a laptop that wouldn't connect to the WiFi, and no error messages to say why. I came up with a similar scanner tool using DTrace, although I don't think I published it.

```
13:42:14 scanning channel 5GHZ freq 5785: beacon_found 1
13:42:14 scanning channel 5GHZ freq 5785: beacon_found 1
13:42:14 scanning channel 5GHZ freq 5785: beacon_found 1
13:42:14 scanning channel 5GHZ freq 5785: beacon_found 1
13:42:14 scan completed: 3205 ms
```

This shows a scan likely initiated by a wpa_supplicant process, which steps through various channels and frequencies. The scan took 3205 ms. This provides insight that can be useful for debugging WiFi problems.

This works by instrumenting the ieee80211 scan routines. The overhead should be negligible as these routines should be infrequent.

The source to ieee80211scan(8) is:

```
#!/usr/local/bin/bpftrace

#include <net/mac80211.h>

BEGIN
{
        printf("Tracing ieee80211 SSID scans. Hit Ctrl-C to end.\n");
        // from include/uapi/linux/nl80211.h:
        @band[0] = "2GHZ";
        @band[1] = "5GHZ";
        @band[2] = "60GHZ";
}

kprobe:ieee80211_request_scan
{
        time("%H:%M:%S ");
        printf("scan started (on-CPU PID %d, %s)\n", pid, comm);
        @start = nsecs;
}

kretprobe:ieee80211_get_channel
/retval/
{
        $ch = (struct ieee80211_channel *)retval;
        $band = 0xff & *retval; // $ch->band; workaround for #776
        time("%H:%M:%S ");
        printf("scanning channel %s freq %d: beacon_found %d\n",
            @band[$band], $ch->center_freq, $ch->beacon_found);
}

kprobe:ieee80211_scan_completed
```

```
/@start/
{
        time("%H:%M:%S ");
        printf("scan compeleted: %d ms\n", (nsecs - @start) / 1000000);
        delete(@start);
}


END
{
        clear(@start); clear(@band);
}
```

More information can be added to show the different flags and settings used while scanning. Note that this tool currently assumes that only one scan will be active at a time, and has a global @start time-stamp. If scans may be active in parallel, this will need a key to associate a timestamp with each scan.

10.3.31 Other Tools

Other BPF tools worth mentioning:

- **solisten(8):** A BCC tool to print socket listen calls with details[47]
- **tcpstates(8):** A BCC tool that prints a line of output for each TCP session state change, with IP address and port details, and duration in each state
- **tcpdrop(8):** A BCC and bpftrace tool that prints IP address and TCP state details, and kernel stack traces, for packets dropped by the kernel tcp_drop() function
- **sofdsnoop(8):** A BCC tool to trace file descriptors passed through Unix sockets
- **profile(8):** Covered in Chapter 6, sampling of kernel stack traces can quantify time spent in network code paths
- **hardirqs(8) and softirqs(8):** Covered in Chapter 6, can be used to measure the time spent in networking hard and soft interrupts
- **filetype(8):** From Chapter 8, traces vfs_read() and vfs_write(), identifying which are socket reads and writes via the inode

Example output from tcpstates(8):

```
# tcpstates
SKADDR          C-PID C-COMM LADDR     LPORT  RADDR     RPORT OLDSTATE -> NEWSTATE    MS
ffff88864fd55a00 3294  record 127.0.0.1 0      127.0.0.1 28527 CLOSE    -> SYN_SENT    0.00
ffff88864fd55a00 3294  record 127.0.0.1 0      127.0.0.1 28527 SYN_SENT -> ESTABLISHED 0.08
ffff88864fd56300 3294  record 127.0.0.1 0      0.0.0.0   0     LISTEN   -> SYN_RECV    0.00
[...]
```

This uses the sock:inet_sock_set_state tracepoint.

---

47 solisten(8) was added by Jean-Tiare Le Bigot on 4-Mar-2016.

10.4   BPF One-Liners

These sections show BCC and bpftrace one-liners. Where possible, the same one-liner is implemented using both BCC and bpftrace.

10.4.1   BCC

Count failed socket connect(2)s by error code:

```
argdist -C 't:syscalls:sys_exit_connect():int:args->ret:args->ret<0'
```

Count socket connect(2)s by user stack trace:

```
stackcount -U t:syscalls:sys_enter_connect
```

TCP send bytes as a histogram:

```
argdist -H 'p::tcp_sendmsg(void *sk, void *msg, int size):int:size'
```

TCP receive bytes as a histogram:

```
argdist -H 'r::tcp_recvmsg():int:$retval:$retval>0'
```

Count all TCP functions (adds high overhead to TCP):

```
funccount 'tcp_*'
```

UDP send bytes as a histogram:

```
argdist -H 'p::udp_sendmsg(void *sk, void *msg, int size):int:size'
```

UDP receive bytes as a histogram:

```
argdist -H 'r::udp_recvmsg():int:$retval:$retval>0'
```

Count all UDP functions (adds high overhead to UDP):

```
funccount 'udp_*'
```

Count transmit stack traces:

```
stackcount t:net:net_dev_xmit
```

Count ieee80211 layer functions (adds high overhead to packets):

```
funccount 'ieee80211_*'
```

Count all ixgbevf device driver functions (adds high overhead to ixgbevf):

```
funccount 'ixgbevf_*'
```

10.4.2   bpftrace

Count socket accept(2)s by PID and process name:

```
bpftrace -e 't:syscalls:sys_enter_accept* { @[pid, comm] = count(); }'
```

Count socket connect(2)s by PID and process name:

```
bpftrace -e 't:syscalls:sys_enter_connect { @[pid, comm] = count(); }'
```

Count failed socket connect(2)s by process name and error code:

```
bpftrace -e 't:syscalls:sys_exit_connect /args->ret < 0/ { @[comm, - args->ret] =
    count(); }'
```

Count socket connect(2)s by user stack trace:

```
bpftrace -e 't:syscalls:sys_enter_connect { @[ustack] = count(); }'
```

Count socket send/receives by direction, on-CPU PID, and process name[48]:

```
bpftrace -e 'k:sock_sendmsg,k:sock_recvmsg { @[func, pid, comm] = count(); }'
```

Count socket send/receive bytes by on-CPU PID and process name:

```
bpftrace -e 'kr:sock_sendmsg,kr:sock_recvmsg /(int32)retval > 0/ { @[pid, comm] =
    sum((int32)retval); }'
```

Count TCP connects by on-CPU PID and process name:

```
bpftrace -e 'k:tcp_v*_connect { @[pid, comm] = count(); }'
```

Count TCP accepts by on-CPU PID and process name:

```
bpftrace -e 'k:inet_csk_accept { @[pid, comm] = count(); }'
```

Count TCP send/receives:

```
bpftrace -e 'k:tcp_sendmsg,k:tcp*recvmsg { @[func] = count(); }'
```

Count TCP send/receives by on-CPU PID and process name:

```
bpftrace -e 'k:tcp_sendmsg,k:tcp_recvmsg { @[func, pid, comm] = count(); }'
```

TCP send bytes as a histogram:

```
bpftrace -e 'k:tcp_sendmsg { @send_bytes = hist(arg2); }'
```

TCP receive bytes as a histogram:

```
bpftrace -e 'kr:tcp_recvmsg /retval >= 0/ { @recv_bytes = hist(retval); }'
```

Count TCP retransmits by type and remote host (assumes IPv4):

```
bpftrace -e 't:tcp:tcp_retransmit_* { @[probe, ntop(2, args->saddr)] = count(); }'
```

Count all TCP functions (adds high overhead to TCP):

```
bpftrace -e 'k:tcp_* { @[func] = count(); }'
```

---

48 The earlier socket syscalls are in process context, where PID and comm are reliable. These kprobes are deeper in
the kernel, and the process endpoint for these connections my not be currently on-CPU, meaning the pid and comm
shown by bpftrace could be unrelated. They usually work, but that may not always be the case.

Count UDP send/receives by on-CPU PID and process name:

```
bpftrace -e 'k:udp*_sendmsg,k:udp*_recvmsg { @[func, pid, comm] = count(); }'
```

UDP send bytes as a histogram:

```
bpftrace -e 'k:udp_sendmsg { @send_bytes = hist(arg2); }'
```

UDP receive bytes as a histogram:

```
bpftrace -e 'kr:udp_recvmsg /retval >= 0/ { @recv_bytes = hist(retval); }'
```

Count all UDP functions (adds high overhead to UDP):

```
bpftrace -e 'k:udp_* { @[func] = count(); }'
```

Count transmit kernel stack traces:

```
bpftrace -e 't:net:net_dev_xmit { @[kstack] = count(); }'
```

Show receive CPU histogram for each device:

```
bpftrace -e 't:net:netif_receive_skb { @[str(args->name)] = lhist(cpu, 0, 128, 1); }'
```

Count ieee80211 layer functions (adds high overhead to packets):

```
bpftrace -e 'k:ieee80211_* { @[func] = count()'
```

Count all ixgbevf device driver functions (adds high overhead to ixgbevf):

```
bpftrace -e 'k:ixgbevf_* { @[func] = count(); }'
```

Count all iwl device driver tracepoints (adds high overhead to iwl):

```
bpftrace -e 't:iwlwifi:*,t:iwlwifi_io:* { @[probe] = count(); }'
```

10.4.3 BPF One-Liners Examples

Including some sample output, as was done for each tool, is also useful for illustrating one-liners.

Counting Transmit Kernel Stack Traces

```
# bpftrace -e 't:net:net_dev_xmit { @[kstack] = count(); }'
Attaching 1 probe...
^C
[...]

@[
    dev_hard_start_xmit+945
    sch_direct_xmit+882
    __qdisc_run+1271
    __dev_queue_xmit+3351
    dev_queue_xmit+16
    ip_finish_output2+3035
    ip_finish_output+1724
```

```
    ip_output+444
    ip_local_out+117
    __ip_queue_xmit+2004
    ip_queue_xmit+69
    __tcp_transmit_skb+6570
    tcp_write_xmit+2123
    __tcp_push_pending_frames+145
    tcp_rcv_established+2573
    tcp_v4_do_rcv+671
    tcp_v4_rcv+10624
    ip_protocol_deliver_rcu+185
    ip_local_deliver_finish+386
    ip_local_deliver+435
    ip_rcv_finish+342
    ip_rcv+212
    __netif_receive_skb_one_core+308
    __netif_receive_skb+36
    netif_receive_skb_internal+168
    napi_gro_receive+953
    ena_io_poll+8375
    net_rx_action+1750
    __do_softirq+558
    irq_exit+348
    do_IRQ+232
    ret_from_intr+0
    native_safe_halt+6
    default_idle+146
    arch_cpu_idle+21
    default_idle_call+59
    do_idle+809
    cpu_startup_entry+29
    start_secondary+1228
    secondary_startup_64+164
]: 902
@[
    dev_hard_start_xmit+945
    sch_direct_xmit+882
    __qdisc_run+1271
    __dev_queue_xmit+3351
    dev_queue_xmit+16
    ip_finish_output2+3035
    ip_finish_output+1724
    ip_output+444
```

```
        ip_local_out+117
        __ip_queue_xmit+2004
        ip_queue_xmit+69
        __tcp_transmit_skb+6570
        tcp_write_xmit+2123
        __tcp_push_pending_frames+145
        tcp_push+1209
        tcp_sendmsg_locked+9315
        tcp_sendmsg+44
        inet_sendmsg+278
        sock_sendmsg+188
        sock_write_iter+740
        __vfs_write+1694
        vfs_write+341
        ksys_write+247
        __x64_sys_write+115
        do_syscall_64+339
        entry_SYSCALL_64_after_hwframe+68
]: 10933
```

This one-liner produced many pages of output; only the last two stack traces have been included here. The last shows a write(2) syscall passing through VFS, sockets, TCP, IP, net device, and then beginning the transmit to the driver. This illustrates the stack from the application to the device driver.

The first stack trace is even more interesting. It begins with the idle thread receiving an interrupt, running the net_rx_action() softirq, the ena driver ena_io_poll(), the NAPI (new API) network interface receive path, then IP, tcp_rcv_established(), and then...__tcp_push_pending_frames(). The real code path is tcp_rcv_established() -> tcp_data_snd_check() -> tcp_push_pending_ frames() -> tcp_push_pending_frames(). However, the middle two functions were tiny and inlined by the compiler, eliding them from that stack trace. What's happening is that TCP is checking for pending transmits during the receive codepath.

Counting All ixgbevf Device Driver Functions (Adding High Overhead to ixgbevf)

```
# bpftrace -e 'k:ixgbevf_* { @[func] = count(); }'
Attaching 116 probes...
^C

@[ixgbevf_get_link_ksettings]: 2
@[ixgbevf_get_stats]: 2
@[ixgbevf_obtain_mbx_lock_vf]: 2
@[ixgbevf_read_mbx_vf]: 2
@[ixgbevf_service_event_schedule]: 3
@[ixgbevf_service_task]: 3
@[ixgbevf_service_timer]: 3
```

```
@[ixgbevf_check_for_bit_vf]: 5
@[ixgbevf_check_for_rst_vf]: 5
@[ixgbevf_check_mac_link_vf]: 5
@[ixgbevf_update_stats]: 5
@[ixgbevf_read_reg]: 21
@[ixgbevf_alloc_rx_buffers]: 36843
@[ixgbevf_features_check]: 37842
@[ixgbevf_xmit_frame]: 37842
@[ixgbevf_msix_clean_rings]: 66417
@[ixgbevf_poll]: 67013
@[ixgbevf_maybe_stop_tx]: 75684
@[ixgbevf_update_itr.isra.39]: 132834
```

The internals of how network device drivers operate can be studied in detail using these kprobes. Don't forget to check whether the driver supports tracepoints as well, as shown in the next example.

Counting All iwl Device Driver Tracepoints (Adding High Overhead to iwl)

```
# bpftrace -e 't:iwlwifi:*,t:iwlwifi_io:* { @[probe] = count(); }'
Attaching 15 probes...
^C

@[tracepoint:iwlwifi:iwlwifi_dev_hcmd]: 39
@[tracepoint:iwlwifi_io:iwlwifi_dev_irq]: 3474
@[tracepoint:iwlwifi:iwlwifi_dev_tx]: 5125
@[tracepoint:iwlwifi_io:iwlwifi_dev_iowrite8]: 6654
@[tracepoint:iwlwifi_io:iwlwifi_dev_ict_read]: 7095
@[tracepoint:iwlwifi:iwlwifi_dev_rx]: 7493
@[tracepoint:iwlwifi_io:iwlwifi_dev_iowrite32]: 19525
```

This one-liner is showing only two of several groups of iwl tracepoints.

10.5 Optional Exercises

If not specified, these can be completed using either bpftrace or BCC:

1. Write an solife(8) tool to print per-session durations from connect(2) and accept(2) (and variants) to close(2) for that socket file descriptor. It can be similar to tcplife(8), although it does not necessarily need all the same fields (some are harder to fetch than others).

2. Write tcpbind(8): a tool for per-event tracing of TCP bind events.

3. Extend tcpwin.bt with a "retrans" event type, with the socket address and time as fields.

4. Extend tcpwin.bt with a "new" event type, that has socket address, time, IP addresses, and TCP ports as fields. This should be printed when the TCP session reaches the established state.

5. Modify tcplife(8) to emit connection details in DOT format, then plot using graphing software (e.g., GraphViz).

6. Develop udplife(8) to show the lifespan of UDP connections, similar to tcplife(8).

7. Extend ipecn.bt to instrument outbound CE events, as well as IPv6. CE events can be introduced at the qdisc layer using the netem qdisc. The following example command replaces the current qdisc on eth0 with one that causes 1% ECN CE events:

```
tc qdisc replace dev eth0 root netem loss 1% ecn
```

If you use this qdisc during development, be aware that it inserts CE events at a lower level than IP. If you traced, say, ip_output(), you may not see the CE events as they are added later.

8. (Advanced) Develop a tool to show TCP round-trip time by host. This could show either an average RTT by host, or a RTT histogram by host. The tool could time sent packets by sequence number and associate the timestamp on the ACK, or make use of struct tcp_sock->rtt_min, or another approach. If the first approach is used, the TCP header can be read, given a struct sk_buff * in $skb as (using bpftrace):

```
$tcph = (struct tcphdr *)($skb->head + $skb->transport_header);
```

9. (Advanced, unsolved) Develop a tool to show ARP or IPv6 neighbor discovery latency, either per-event or as a histogram.

10. (Advanced, unsolved) Develop a tool that shows the full sk_buff lifespan, dealing (when or if necessary) with GRO, GSO, tcp_try_coalesce(), skb_split(), skb_append(), skb_insert(), etc, and other events that modify an sk_buff during its lifespan. This tool will become much more complex than skblife(8).

11. (Advanced, unsolved) Develop a tool that breaks down the sk_buff lifespan (from (9)) into components or wait states.

12. (Advanced, unsolved) Develop a tool to show latency caused by TCP pacing.

13. (Advanced, unsolved) Develop a tool to show byte queue limit latency.

10.6 Summary

This chapter summarizes characteristics of the Linux network stack, and their analysis with traditional tools: netstat(8), sar(1), ss(8), and tcpdump(8). BPF tools were then used to provide extended observability of the socket layer, TCP, UDP, ICMP, qdiscs, net driver queues, and then a network device driver. This observability included showing new connections efficiently and their lifespans, connection and first byte latency, SYN backlog queue size, TCP retransmits, and various other events.

Chapter 11

Security

This chapter summarizes the security of BPF and BPF for security analysis, providing various tools that can be helpful for both security and performance observability. You can use these tools to detect intrusions, create whitelists of normal executable and privileged usage, and to enforce policies.

Learning Objectives:

- Understand use cases for BPF security
- Show new process execution to detect possible malicious software
- Show TCP connections and resets to detect possible suspicious activity
- Study Linux capability usage to aid the creation of whitelists
- Understand other forensic sources, such as shell and console logging

This chapter begins with background on security tasks and then summarizes BPF capabilities, configuring BPF security, strategy, and BPF tools.

11.1 Background

The term *security* covers a broad range of tasks, including:

- Security analysis
  - Sniffing activity for real-time forensics
  - Privilege debugging
  - Executable usage whitelists
  - Reverse engineering of malware
- Monitoring
  - Custom auditing
  - Host-based intrusion detection systems (HIDS)
  - Container-based intrusion detection systems (CIDS)
- Policy enforcement
  - Networking firewalls
  - Detecting malware and dynamically blocking packets and taking other preventive actions

Security engineering can be similar to performance engineering, as it can involve the analysis of a wide variety of software.

11.1.1 BPF Capabilities

BPF can help with these security tasks, including analysis, monitoring, and policy enforcement. For security analysis, the types of questions that BPF can answer include:

- Which processes are being executed?

- What network connections are being made? By which processes?

- Which system privileges are being requested by which processes?

- What permission denied errors are happening on the system?

- Is this kernel/user function being executed with these arguments (in checking for active exploits)?

Another way to summarize the analysis and monitoring capabilities of BPF tracing is by showing the targets that can be traced, as illustrated in Figure 11-1.[1]

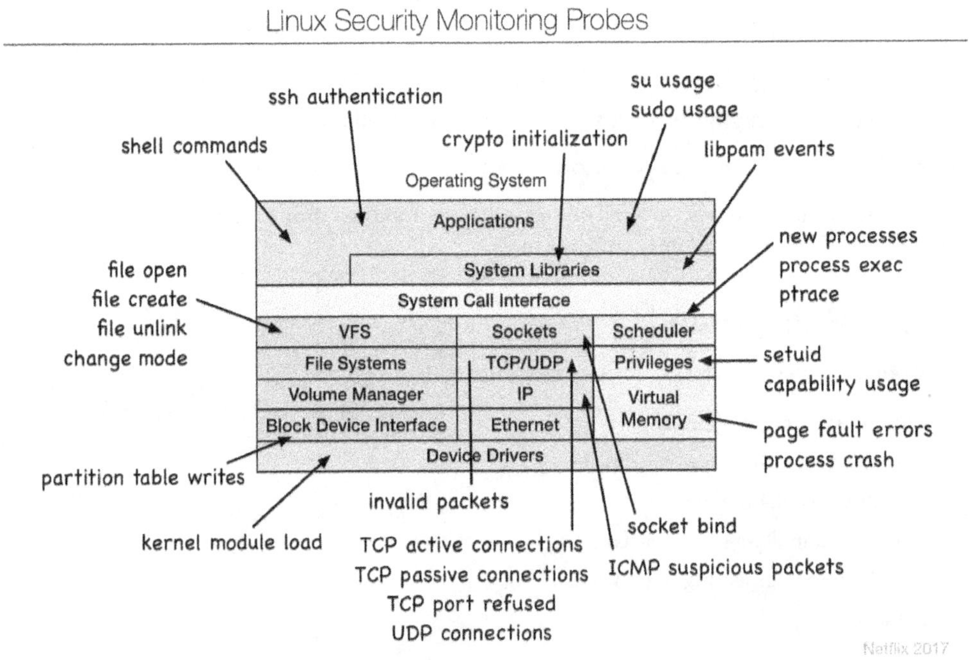

Figure 11-1 BPF security monitoring targets

---

1 Alex Maestretti and I presented this diagram in the talk "Linux Monitoring at Scale with eBPF" at the BSidesSF conference in 2017 [114].

While this figure illustrates many specific targets, it is also possible, using uprobes and kprobes, to instrument any user-level or kernel function—which is useful in zero-day vulnerability detection.

Zero-Day Vulnerability Detection

There is sometimes an urgent need to detect whether a new software vulnerability is in use; ideally, it can be detected on the first day that the vulnerability is disclosed (day zero). bpftrace is especially suited for this role, as its easy-to-program language allows custom tools to be created in minutes, and it can access not only tracepoints and USDT events, but also kprobes and uprobes, as well as their arguments.

As a real example, at the time of writing, a Docker vulnerability was disclosed that uses a symlink-race attack [115]. This involved calling the renameat2(2) syscall in a loop with the RENAME_EXCHANGE flag, while also using `docker cp`.

There are a number of ways this could have been detected. Since the renameat2(2) syscall with the RENAME_EXCHANGE flag is an uncommon activity on my production systems (I caught no natural cases of it being used), one way to detect this vulnerability in use is to trace that syscall and flag combination. For example, the following can be run on the host to trace all containers:

```
# bpftrace -e 't:syscalls:sys_enter_renameat2 /args->flags == 2/ { time();
    printf("%s RENAME_EXCHANGE %s <-> %s\n", comm, str(args->oldname),
    str(args->newname)); }'
Attaching 1 probe...
22:03:47
symlink_swap RENAME_EXCHANGE totally_safe_path <-> totally_safe_path-stashed
22:03:47
symlink_swap RENAME_EXCHANGE totally_safe_path <-> totally_safe_path-stashed
22:03:47
symlink_swap RENAME_EXCHANGE totally_safe_path <-> totally_safe_path-stashed
[...]
```

This one-liner normally emits no output, but in this case, a flood of output occurred as the vulnerability proof-of-concept code was running as a test. The output includes timestamps, the process name, and the filename arguments to renameat2(2). A different approach would be to trace the `docker cp` process as it operates on symlinks, from either syscalls or kernel function calls.

I can imagine a future where a vulnerability disclosure is accompanied by a bpftrace one-liner or tool for detecting its use in the wild. An intrusion detection system could be built to execute these tools across a company's infrastructure. This would not be dissimilar to how some network intrusion detection systems work, such as Snort [116], which shares rules for the detection of new worms.

Security Monitoring

BPF tracing programs can be used for security monitoring and intrusion detection. Current monitoring solutions often use loadable kernel modules to provide visibility of kernel and packet events. However, such modules introduce their own risk of kernel bugs and vulnerabilities. BPF programs are passed through a verifier and use existing kernel technologies, making them safer and more secure.

BPF tracing has also been optimized for efficiency. In a 2016 internal study, I compared the overhead of auditd logging to that of a similar BPF program; BPF introduced six times less overhead [117].

An important behavior of BPF monitoring is what happens under extreme load. BPF output buffers and maps have limits that can be exceeded, causing events to not be recorded. This may be exploited by an attacker as an attempt to evade proper logging or policy enforcement, by inundating the system with events. BPF is aware of when these limits are exceeded, and can report this to user space for appropriate action. Any security solution built using BPF tracing needs to record these overflow or dropped events, to satisfy non-repudiation requirements.

Another approach is to add a per-CPU map to count important events. Unlike the perf output buffer or maps involving keys, once BPF has created a per-CPU map of fixed counters, there is no risk of losing events. This could be used in conjunction with perf event output to provide more detail: the more detail may be lost, but the count of events will not be.

Policy Enforcement

A number of policy enforcement technologies already use BPF. While this topic is outside of the scope of this book, they are important developments in BPF and worth summarizing. They are:

- **seccomp:** The secure computing (seccomp) facility can execute BPF programs (currently classic BPF) to make policy decisions about allowing syscalls [118]. seccomp's programmable actions include killing the calling process (SECCOMP_RET_KILL_PROCESS) and returning an error (SECCOMP_RET_ERRNO). Complex decisions can also be offloaded by a BPF program to user-space programs (SECCOMP_RET_USER_NOTIF); this blocks the process while a user-space helper program is notified via a file descriptor. That program can read and process the event and then write a struct seccomp_notif_resp in response to the same file descriptor [119].

- **Cilium:** Cilium provides and transparently secures network connectivity and load balancing for workloads such as application containers or processes. It makes use of a combination of BPF programs at various layers such as XDP, cgroup and tc (traffic control) based hooks. The main networking data path in the tc layer, for example, employs a sch_clsact qdisc coupled with a BPF program through cls_bpf in order to mangle, forward, or drop packets [24] [120] [121].

- **bpfilter:** bpfilter is a proof-of-concept for replacing the iptables firewall with BPF entirely. To help with a transition from iptables, an iptables ruleset sent to the kernel can be redirected to a user-mode helper that converts it to BPF [122] [123].

- **Landlock:** Landlock is a BPF-based security module that provides fine-grained access control to kernel resources using BPF [124]. One example use case is to restrict access to subsets of a file system based on a BPF inode map, which can be updated from user space.

- **KRSI:** Kernel Runtime Security Instrumentation is a new LSM from Google for extensible auditing and enforcement. It uses a new BPF program type, BPF_PROG_TYPE_KRSI [186].

A new BPF helper, bpf_send_signal(), should be included in the upcoming Linux 5.3 release [125]. This will allow a new type of enforcement program that can send SIGKILL and other signals to processes from BPF programs alone, without needing seccomp. Taking the previous vulnerability detection example further, imagine a bpftrace program that not only detects a vulnerability, but immediately kills the process using it. For example:

```
bpftrace --unsafe -e 't:syscalls:sys_enter_renameat2 /args->flags == 2/ {
    time(); printf("killing PID %d %s\n", pid, comm); signal(9); }'
```

Such tools could be used as a temporary workaround until software can be properly patched.[2] Care must be taken when using signal(): this particular example kills *all* users of renameat2(2) who are using RENAME_EXCHANGE, and it can't tell whether the process was good or evil.

Other signals, such as SIGABRT, could be used to core dump the process to allow forensic analysis of the malicious software.

Until bpf_send_signal() is available, processes can be terminated by the user-space tracer, based on reading events from the perf buffer. For example, using bpftrace's system():

```
bpftrace --unsafe -e 't:syscalls:sys_enter_renameat2 /args->flags == 2/ {
    time(); printf("killing PID %d %s\n", pid, comm);
    system("kill -9 %d", pid); }'
```

system() is an asynchronous action (see Chapter 5) issued to bpftrace via the perf output buffer, and then executed by bpftrace some time after the event. This introduces a lag between detection and enforcement, which in some environments may be unacceptable. bpf_send_signal() solves this by sending the signal immediately, in kernel context, during the BPF program.

11.1.2   Unprivileged BPF Users

For unprivileged users, specifically those without the CAP_SYS_ADMIN capability, BPF can currently only be used for socket filters, as of Linux 5.2. The test is in the bpf(2) syscall source in kernel/bpf/syscall.c:

```
    if (type != BPF_PROG_TYPE_SOCKET_FILTER &&
        type != BPF_PROG_TYPE_CGROUP_SKB &&
        !capable(CAP_SYS_ADMIN))
            return -EPERM;
```

This code also allows cgroup skb programs for inspection and dropping of cgroup packets. However, these programs require CAP_NET_ADMIN in order to attach to BPF_CGROUP_INET_INGRESS and BPF_CGROUP_INET_EGRESS.

For users without CAP_SYS_ADMIN, the bpf(2) syscall will fail with EPERM, and BCC tools will report "Need super-user privileges to run". bpftrace programs currently check for UID 0, and if the user is not 0, will report "bpftrace currently only supports running as the root user". This is why all the BPF tools in this book are in section 8 of the man pages: they are superuser tools.

One day BPF should support unprivileged users for more than just socket filters.[3] One particular use case is container environments, where access to the host is limited, and it is desirable to be able to run BPF tools from the containers themselves. (This use case is mentioned in Chapter 15.)

---

2 In the past, Red Hat has published similar SystemTap tracing tools for vulnerability mitigation, such as Bugzilla [126].

3 Proposals were discussed at LSFMM 2019 in Puerto Rico [128]. One involved using a /dev/bpf device that when opened sets a task_struct flag to allow access, and which was also close-on-exec.

11.1.3   Configuring BPF Security

There are a number of system controls (tunables) for configuring BPF security. These can be configured using the sysctl(8) command or files in /proc/sys. They are:

```
# sysctl -a | grep bpf
kernel.unprivileged_bpf_disabled = 1
net.core.bpf_jit_enable = 1
net.core.bpf_jit_harden = 0
net.core.bpf_jit_kallsyms = 0
net.core.bpf_jit_limit = 264241152
```

kernel.unprivileged_bpf_disabled can disable unprivileged access using either of these commands:

```
# sysctl -w kernel.unprivileged_bpf_disabled=1
# echo 1 > /proc/sys/kernel/unprivileged_bpf_disabled
```

This is a one-time shot: setting this tunable back to zero will be rejected. The following sysctls can also be set using similar commands.

net.core.bpf_jit_enable enables the just-in-time BPF compiler. This improves both performance and security. As a mitigation for the Spectre v2 vulnerability, a CONFIG_BPF_JIT_ALWAYS_ON option was added to the kernel to permanently enable the JIT compiler, and to compile-out the BPF interpreter. Possible settings (in Linux 5.2) [127]:

- **0:** Disable JIT (default)
- **1:** Enable JIT
- **2:** Enable JIT and write compiler debug traces to the kernel log (this setting should be used for debugging only, not in production)

This has been enabled by default at companies including Netflix and Facebook. Note that the JIT is processor-architecture dependent. The Linux kernel comes with BPF JIT compilers for the vast majority of supported architectures, including x86_64, arm64, ppc64, s390x, sparc64, and even mips64 and riscv. While the x86_64 and arm64 compilers are feature-complete and battle tested in production, others might not be as yet.

net.core.bpf_jit_harden can be set to one to enable additional protections, including mitigation against JIT spraying attacks, at the cost of performance [129]. Possible settings (in Linux 5.2) [127]:

- **0:** Disable JIT hardening (default)
- **1:** Enable JIT hardening for unprivileged users only
- **2:** Enable JIT hardening for all users

net.core.bpf_jit_kallsyms exposes the compiled BPF JIT images via /proc/kallsyms for privileged users, providing symbols to aid debugging [130]. If bpf_jit_harden is enabled, this is disabled.

net.core.bpf_jit_limit sets a limit in bytes for module memory that can be consumed. Once the limit is reached, unprivileged user requests are blocked and redirected to the interpreter, if compiled in.

For more on BPF hardening, see the Cilium BPF reference guide section on hardening, written by BPF maintainer Daniel Borkmann [131].

11.1.4 Strategy

Here is a suggested strategy for the security analysis of system activity not already covered by other BPF tools:

1. Check whether there are tracepoints or USDT probes available to instrument the activity.

2. Check whether LSM kernel hooks can be traced: these begin with "security_".

3. Use kprobes/uprobes as appropriate to instrument the raw code.

11.2 BPF Tools

This section covers key BPF tools you can use for security analysis. They are shown in Figure 11-2.

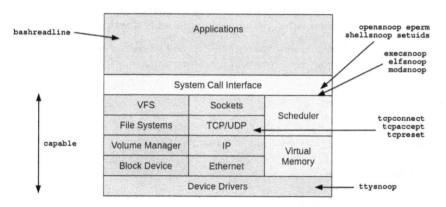

Figure 11-2   BPF tools for security analysis

These tools are either from the BCC and bpftrace repositories covered in Chapters 4 and 5, or were created for this book. Table 11-1 lists the origins of these tools (BT is short for bpftrace).

496   Chapter 11   Security

Table 11-1   **Security-Related Tools**

Tool	Source	Target	Description
execsnoop	BCC/BT	Syscalls	List new process execution
elfsnoop	Book	Kernel	Show ELF file loads
modsnoop	Book	Kernel	Show kernel module loads
bashreadline	BCC/BT	bash	List entered bash shell commands
shellsnoop	Book	shells	Mirror shell output
ttysnoop	BCC/book	TTY	Mirror tty output
opensnoop	BCC/BT	Syscalls	List files opened
eperm	Book	Syscalls	Count failed EPERM and EACCES syscalls
tcpconnect	BCC/BT	TCP	Trace outbound TCP connections (active)
tcpaccept	BCC/BT	TCP	Trace inbound TCP connections (passive)
tcpreset	Book	TCP	Show TCP send resets: port scan detection
capable	BCC/BT	Security	Trace kernel security capability checks
setuids	Book	Syscalls	Trace the setuid syscalls: privilege escalation

For the tools from BCC and bpftrace, see their repositories for full and updated lists of tool options and capabilities. Some of the following tools were introduced in earlier chapters and are recapped here.

Also refer to other chapters for more observability into any subsystem, especially network connections in Chapter 10, file usage in Chapter 8, and software execution in Chapter 6.

11.2.1   execsnoop

execsnoop(8) was introduced in Chapter 6; it is a BCC and bpftrace tool to trace new processes, and can be used to identify suspicious process execution. Example output:

```
# execsnoop
PCOMM         PID    PPID   RET ARGS
ls            7777   21086    0 /bin/ls -F
a.out         7778   21086    0 /tmp/a.out
[...]
```

This shows a process executing from /tmp named a.out.

execsnoop(8) works by tracing the execve(2) syscall. This is a typical step in the creation of new processes, which begins by calling fork(2) or clone(2) to create a new process and calls execve(2) to execute a different program. Note that this is not the only way new software can execute: a buffer overflow attack can add new instructions to an existing process, and execute malicious software without needing to call execve(2).

See Chapter 6 for more about execsnoop(8).

11.2.2 elfsnoop

elfsnoop(8)[4] is a bpftrace tool to trace the execution of binary files of the executable and linking format (ELF) commonly used on Linux. This traces execution from deep in the kernel, from a function where all ELF execution must pass. For example:

```
# elfsnoop.bt
Attaching 3 probes...
Tracing ELF loads. Ctrl-C to end
TIME      PID    INTERPRETER       FILE            MOUNT       INODE      RET
11:18:43 9022   /bin/ls           /bin/ls         /           29098068   0
11:18:45 9023   /tmp/ls           /tmp/ls         /           23462045   0
11:18:49 9029   /usr/bin/python   ./opensnoop.py  /           20190728   0
[...]
```

This shows the executed file with various details. Columns are:

- **TIME:** Timestamp as HH:MM:SS.
- **PID:** Process ID.
- **INTERPRETER:** For scripts, the interpreter that was executed.
- **FILE:** Executed file.
- **MOUNT:** Mount point for the executed file.
- **INODE:** Index node number for the executed file: with the mount point, this forms a unique identifier.
- **RET:** Return value from the attempted execution. 0 is success.

The mount point and inode number are printed out for further verification of the executed binary. An attacker may create their own version of system binaries with the same name (and perhaps use control characters so that when displayed it appears to have the same path as well), but these attacks will be unable to spoof the mount point and inode combination.

This tool works by tracing the load_elf_binary() kernel function, which is responsible for loading new ELF programs for execution. The overhead of this tool should be negligible, as the rate of this function should be low.

The source to elfsnoop(8) is:

```
#!/usr/local/bin/bpftrace

#include <linux/binfmts.h>
#include <linux/fs.h>
#include <linux/mount.h>
```

---

4 Origin: I created it for this book on 25-Feb-2019.

```
BEGIN
{
        printf("Tracing ELF loads. Ctrl-C to end\n");
        printf("%-8s %-6s %-18s %-18s %-10s %-10s RET\n",
            "TIME", "PID", "INTERPRETER", "FILE", "MOUNT", "INODE");
}


kprobe:load_elf_binary
{
        @arg0[tid] = arg0;
}


kretprobe:load_elf_binary
/@arg0[tid]/
{
        $bin = (struct linux_binprm *)@arg0[tid];
        time("%H:%M:%S ");
        printf("%-6d %-18s %-18s %-10s %-10d %3d\n", pid,
            str($bin->interp), str($bin->filename),
            str($bin->file->f_path.mnt->mnt_root->d_name.name),
            $bin->file->f_inode->i_ino, retval);
        delete(@arg0[tid]);
}
```

This tool can be enhanced to print extra details about the file that is executed, including the full path. Note that bpftrace currently has a seven-element limit to printf(), so multiple printf()s will be necessary to print extra fields.

11.2.3   modsnoop

modsnoop(8)[5] is a bpftrace tool to show kernel module loads. For example:

```
# modsnoop.bt
Attaching 2 probes...
Tracing kernel module loads. Hit Ctrl-C to end.
12:51:38 module init: msr, by modprobe (PID 32574, user root, UID 0)
[...]
```

This shows that at 10:50:26 the "msr" module was loaded by the modprobe(8) tool, with UID 0. Loading modules is another way for the system to execute code, and is one way that various rootkits work, making it a target for security tracing.

---

5 Origin: I created it for this book on 14-Mar-2019.

The source to modsnoop(8) is:

```
#!/usr/local/bin/bpftrace

#include <linux/module.h>

BEGIN
{
        printf("Tracing kernel module loads. Hit Ctrl-C to end.\n");
}


kprobe:do_init_module
{
        $mod = (struct module *)arg0;
        time("%H:%M:%S ");
        printf("module init: %s, by %s (PID %d, user %s, UID %d)\n",
            $mod->name, comm, pid, username, uid);
}
```

This works by tracing the do_init_module() kernel function, which can access details from the module struct.

There is also a module:module_load tracepoint, used by later one-liners.

11.2.4 bashreadline

bashreadline(8)[6] is a BCC and bpftrace tool to trace interactively entered commands in the bash shell, system-wide. For example, running the BCC version:

```
# bashreadline
bashreadline
TIME      PID    COMMAND
11:43:51  21086  ls
11:44:07  21086  echo hello book readers
11:44:22  21086  eccho hi
11:44:33  21086  /tmp/ls
[...]
```

This output shows commands that were entered while tracing, including shell built-ins (echo) and commands that failed (eccho). This works by tracing the readline() function from the bash

---

6 Origin: I wrote the first version for BCC on 28-Jan-2016 and for bpftrace on 6-Sep-2018. These were created as easy-to-demonstrate example programs of uprobes with BPF. Since then it's caught the eye of security professionals, especially for logging activity in locked-down environments where only one shell (bash) can be used.

shell, so any entered command will be shown. Note that while this can trace commands across all shells running on the system, it cánnot trace commands by other shell programs, and an attacker may install their own shell (e.g., a nanoshell) that is not traced.

bpftrace

The following is the code for the bpftrace version.

```
#!/usr/local/bin/bpftrace

BEGIN
{
        printf("Tracing bash commands... Hit Ctrl-C to end.\n");
        printf("%-9s %-6s %s\n", "TIME", "PID", "COMMAND");
}

uretprobe:/bin/bash:readline
{
        time("%H:%M:%S  ");
        printf("%-6d %s\n", pid, str(retval));
}
```

This traces the readline() function in /bin/bash using a uretprobe. Some Linux distributions build bash differently such that readline() is used from the libreadline library instead; see Section 12.2.3 in Chapter 12 for more about this and tracing readline().

11.2.5   shellsnoop

shellsnoop(8)[7] is a BCC and bpftrace tool that mirrors the output from another shell session. For example:

```
# shellsnoop 7866
bgregg:~/Build/bpftrace/tools> date
Fri May 31 18:11:02 PDT 2019
bgregg:~/Build/bpftrace/tools> echo Hello BPF
Hello BPF
bgregg:~/Build/bpftrace/tools> typo

Command 'typo' not found, did you mean:

  command 'typop' from deb terminology

Try: apt install <deb name>
```

---

7 Origin: I wrote the BCC version on 15-Oct-2016 and the bpftrace version on 31-May-2019. These were based on my earlier shellsnoop tool from 24-Mar-2004, inspired by ttywatcher. My earlier shellsnoop was mentioned in a 2005 Phrack ezine by Boris Loza as a security forensics tool [132].

This shows the commands and output from a shell session with PID 7866. It works by tracing writes by that process to STDOUT or STDERR, including children of that process. Tracing children is necessary to catch the output of their commands, such as the output of date(1) seen in this output.

shellsnoop(8) also has an option to emit a replay shell script. For example:

```
# shellsnoop -r 7866
echo -e 'd\c'
sleep 0.10
echo -e 'a\c'
sleep 0.06
echo -e 't\c'
sleep 0.07
echo -e 'e\c'
sleep 0.25
echo -e '
\c'
sleep 0.00
echo -e 'Fri May 31 18:50:35 PDT 2019
\c'
```

This can be saved to a file and executed using the bash(1) shell: it then replays the shell session output with the original timing. It's a little spooky.

BCC

Command line usage:

```
shellsnoop [options] PID
```

Options include:

- **s**: Shell only output (no subcommands)
- **-r**: Replay shell script

bpftrace

This bpftrace version shows the core functionality[8]:

```
#!/usr/local/bin/bpftrace

BEGIN
/$1 == 0/
{
```

---

8 This currently truncates each output to BPFTRACE_STRLEN (64) bytes. We are working to greatly increase this limit in the future by switching from BPF stack storage to map storage for strings.

```
        printf("USAGE: shellsnoop.bt PID\n");
        exit();
}

tracepoint:sched:sched_process_fork
/args->parent_pid == $1 || @descendent[args->parent_pid]/
{
        @descendent[args->child_pid] = 1;
}

tracepoint:syscalls:sys_enter_write
/(pid == $1 || @descendent[pid]) && (args->fd == 1 || args->fd == 2)/
{
        printf("%s", str(args->buf, args->count));
}
```

11.2.6   ttysnoop

ttysnoop(8)[9] is a BCC and bpftrace tool to mirror output from a tty or pts device. This can be used to watch a suspicious login session in real time. For example, watching /dev/pts/16:

```
# ttysnoop 16
$ uname -a
Linux lgud-bgregg 4.15.0-43-generic #46-Ubuntu SMP Thu Dec 6 14:45:28 UTC 2018 x86_64
x86_64 x86_64 GNU/Linux
$ gcc -o a.out crack.c
$ ./a.out
Segmentation fault
[...]
```

The output duplicates what the user on /dev/pts/16 is seeing. This works by tracing the tty_write() kernel function, and printing what is being written.

BCC

Command line usage:

```
ttysnoop [options] device
```

Options include:

- **-C**: Don't clear the screen

---

9 Origin: I wrote the BCC tool on 15-Oct-2016, inspired by an older Unix tool called ttywatcher, and my earlier cuckoo.d tool from 2011. As a sysadmin, I used ttywatcher to watch a non-root intruder in real time on a production system as they downloaded various privilege escalation exploits, compiled them, and ran them without success. Most annoying of all: watching them use the pico text editor instead of my favorite, vi. For a more exciting story of TTY snooping, see [Stoll 89], which was the inspiration for cuckoo.d. I wrote the bpftrace version for this book on 26-Feb-2019.

The device is either a full path to a pseudo terminal, e.g., /dev/pts/2, or just the number 2, or another tty device path: e.g., /dev/tty0. Running ttysnoop(8) on /dev/console shows what is printed on the system console.

bpftrace

The following is the code for the bpftrace version:

```
#!/usr/local/bin/bpftrace

#include <linux/fs.h>

BEGIN
{
        if ($1 == 0) {
                printf("USAGE: ttysnoop.bt pts_device    # eg, pts14\n");
                exit();
        }
        printf("Tracing tty writes. Ctrl-C to end.\n");
}

kprobe:tty_write
{
        $file = (struct file *)arg0;
        // +3 skips "pts":
        if (str($file->f_path.dentry->d_name.name) == str($1 + 3)) {
                printf("%s", str(arg1, arg2));
        }
}
```

This is an example of a bpftrace program that takes a required argument. If the device name is not specified, a USAGE message is printed, and bpftrace exits. This exit is necessary because tracing all devices will mix the output together and create a feedback loop with the tool itself.

11.2.7   opensnoop

opensnoop(8) was covered in Chapter 8 and shown in earlier chapters; it is a BCC and bpftrace tool to trace file opens, which can be used for a number of security tasks, such as understanding malware behavior and monitoring file usage. Example output from the BCC version:

```
# opensnoop
PID     COMM            FD ERR PATH
12748   opensnoop       -1   2 /usr/lib/python2.7/encodings/ascii.x86_64-linux-gnu.so
12748   opensnoop       -1   2 /usr/lib/python2.7/encodings/ascii.so
12748   opensnoop       -1   2 /usr/lib/python2.7/encodings/asciimodule.so
```

```
12748  opensnoop      18    0 /usr/lib/python2.7/encodings/ascii.py
12748  opensnoop      19    0 /usr/lib/python2.7/encodings/ascii.pyc
1222   polkitd        11    0 /etc/passwd
1222   polkitd        11    0 /proc/11881/status
1222   polkitd        11    0 /proc/11881/stat
1222   polkitd        11    0 /etc/passwd
1222   polkitd        11    0 /proc/11881/status
1222   polkitd        11    0 /proc/11881/stat
1222   polkitd        11    0 /proc/11881/cgroup
1222   polkitd        11    0 /proc/1/cgroup
1222   polkitd        11    0 /run/systemd/sessions/2
[...]
```

This output shows opensnoop(8) searching for and then loading an ascii python module: the first three opens were unsuccessful. Then polkitd(8) (PolicyKit daemon) is caught opening the passwd file and checking process statuses. opensnoop(8) works by tracing the open(2) variety of syscalls.

See Chapter 8 for more about opensnoop(8).

11.2.8   eperm

eperm(8)[10] is a bpftrace tool to count syscalls that failed with either EPERM "operation not permitted" or EACCES "permission denied" errors, both of which may be interesting for security analysis. For example:

```
# eperm.bt
Attaching 3 probes...
Tracing EACCESS and EPERM syscall errors. Ctrl-C to end.
^C

@EACCESS[systemd-logind, sys_setsockopt]: 1

@EPERM[cat, sys_openat]: 1
@EPERM[gmain, sys_inotify_add_watch]: 6
```

This shows the process name and the syscall that failed, grouped by failure. For example, this output shows there was one EPERM failure by cat(1) for the openat(2) syscall. These failures can be further investigated using other tools, such as opensnoop(8) for open failures.

This works by tracing the raw_syscalls:sys_exit tracepoint, which fires for all syscalls. The overhead may begin to be noticeable on systems with high I/O rates; you should test in a lab environment.

---

10 Origin: I created it for this book on 25-Feb-2019.

The source to eperm(8) is:

```
#!/usr/local/bin/bpftrace

BEGIN
{
        printf("Tracing EACCESS and EPERM syscall errors. Ctrl-C to end.\n");
}

tracepoint:raw_syscalls:sys_exit
/args->ret == -1/
{
        @EACCESS[comm, ksym(*(kaddr("sys_call_table") + args->id * 8))] =
            count();
}

tracepoint:raw_syscalls:sys_exit
/args->ret == -13/
{
        @EPERM[comm, ksym(*(kaddr("sys_call_table") + args->id * 8))] =
            count();
}
```

The raw_syscalls:sys_exit tracepoint provides only an identification number for the syscall. To convert this to a name, a lookup table of syscalls can be used, which is how the BCC syscount(8) tool does it. eperm(8) uses a different technique: the kernel system call table (sys_call_table) is read, finding the function that handles the syscall, and then it converts that function address to the kernel symbol name.

11.2.9 tcpconnect and tcpaccept

tcpconnect(8) and tcpaccept(8) were introduced in Chapter 10: they are BCC and bpftrace tools to trace new TCP connections, and can be used to identify suspicious network activity. Many types of attacks involve connecting to a system at least once. Example output from BCC tcpconnect(8):

```
# tcpconnect
PID    COMM       IP SADDR          DADDR           DPORT
22411  a.out       4  10.43.1.178    10.0.0.1        8080
[...]
```

The tcpconnect(8) output shows an a.out process making a connection to 10.0.0.1 port 8080, which sounds suspicious. (a.out is a default filename from some compilers and is not normally used by any installed software.)

Example output from BCC tcpaccept(8), also using the -t option to print timestamps:

```
# tcpaccept -t
TIME(s)   PID   COMM        IP RADDR          LADDR            LPORT
0.000     1440  sshd         4  10.10.1.201    10.43.1.178      22
0.201     1440  sshd         4  10.10.1.201    10.43.1.178      22
0.408     1440  sshd         4  10.10.1.201    10.43.1.178      22
0.612     1440  sshd         4  10.10.1.201    10.43.1.178      22
[...]
```

This output shows multiple connections from 10.10.1.201 to port 22, served by sshd(8). These are happening about every 200 milliseconds (from the "TIME(s)" column), which could be a brute-force attack.

A key feature of these tools is that, for efficiency, they instrument only TCP session events. Other tools trace every network packet, which can incur high overhead on busy systems.

See Chapter 10 for more about tcpconnect(8) and tcpaccept(8).

11.2.10   tcpreset

tcpreset(8)[11] is a bpftrace tool to trace when TCP sends reset (RST) packets. This can be used for the detection of TCP port scanning, which sends packets to a range of ports, including closed ones, triggering RSTs in response. For example:

```
# tcpreset.bt
Attaching 2 probes...
Tracing TCP resets. Hit Ctrl-C to end.
TIME      LADDR          LPORT  RADDR          RPORT
20:50:24  100.66.115.238 80     100.65.2.196   45195
20:50:24  100.66.115.238 443    100.65.2.196   45195
20:50:24  100.66.115.238 995    100.65.2.196   45451
20:50:24  100.66.115.238 5900   100.65.2.196   45451
20:50:24  100.66.115.238 443    100.65.2.196   45451
20:50:24  100.66.115.238 110    100.65.2.196   45451
20:50:24  100.66.115.238 135    100.65.2.196   45451
20:50:24  100.66.115.238 256    100.65.2.196   45451
20:50:24  100.66.115.238 21     100.65.2.196   45451
20:50:24  100.66.115.238 993    100.65.2.196   45451
20:50:24  100.66.115.238 3306   100.65.2.196   45451
20:50:24  100.66.115.238 25     100.65.2.196   45451
20:50:24  100.66.115.238 113    100.65.2.196   45451
20:50:24  100.66.115.238 1025   100.65.2.196   45451
```

---

11 Origin: I created it for this book on 26-Feb-2019.

```
20:50:24 100.66.115.238 18581   100.65.2.196    45451
20:50:24 100.66.115.238 199     100.65.2.196    45451
20:50:24 100.66.115.238 56666   100.65.2.196    45451
20:50:24 100.66.115.238 8080    100.65.2.196    45451
20:50:24 100.66.115.238 53      100.65.2.196    45451
20:50:24 100.66.115.238 587     100.65.2.196    45451
[...]
```

This shows many TCP RSTs were sent for different local ports within the same second: this looks like a port scan. It works by tracing the kernel function that sends resets, and the overhead should therefore be negligible, as this occurs infrequently in normal operation.

Note that there are different types of TCP port scans, and TCP/IP stacks can respond to them differently. I tested a Linux 4.15 kernel using the nmap(1) port scanner, and it responded with RSTs to SYN, FIN, NULL, and Xmas scans, making them all visible using tcpreset(8).

The columns are:

- **TIME:** Time in HH:MM:SS format
- **LADDR:** Local address
- **LPORT:** Local TCP port
- **RADDR:** Remote IP address
- **RPORT:** Remote TCP port

The source to tcpreset(8) is:

```
#!/usr/local/bin/bpftrace

#include <net/sock.h>
#include <uapi/linux/tcp.h>
#include <uapi/linux/ip.h>

BEGIN
{
        printf("Tracing TCP resets. Hit Ctrl-C to end.\n");
        printf("%-8s %-14s %-6s %-14s %-6s\n", "TIME",
            "LADDR", "LPORT", "RADDR", "RPORT");
}

kprobe:tcp_v4_send_reset
{
        $skb = (struct sk_buff *)arg1;
        $tcp = (struct tcphdr *)($skb->head + $skb->transport_header);
        $ip = (struct iphdr *)($skb->head + $skb->network_header);
```

```
        $dport = ($tcp->dest >> 8) | (($tcp->dest << 8) & 0xff00);
        $sport = ($tcp->source >> 8) | (($tcp->source << 8) & 0xff00);

        time("%H:%M:%S ");
        printf("%-14s %-6d %-14s %-6d\n", ntop(AF_INET, $ip->daddr), $dport,
            ntop(AF_INET, $ip->saddr), $sport);
}
```

This traces the tcp_v4_send_reset() kernel function, which only traces IPv4 traffic. The tool can be enhanced to trace IPv6 as well if desired.

This tool is also an example of reading IP and TCP headers from a socket buffer: the lines that set $tcp and $ip. This logic is based on the kernel's ip_hdr() and tcp_hdr() functions, and will need updates if the kernel changes this logic.

11.2.11 capable

capable(8)[12] is a BCC and bpftrace tool to show security capability usage. This may be useful for constructing whitelists of required capabilities by applications, with the intent of blocking others to improve security.

```
# capable
TIME       UID    PID    COMM        CAP   NAME              AUDIT
22:52:11   0      20007  capable     21    CAP_SYS_ADMIN     1
22:52:11   0      20007  capable     21    CAP_SYS_ADMIN     1
22:52:11   0      20007  capable     21    CAP_SYS_ADMIN     1
22:52:11   0      20007  capable     21    CAP_SYS_ADMIN     1
22:52:11   0      20007  capable     21    CAP_SYS_ADMIN     1
22:52:11   0      20007  capable     21    CAP_SYS_ADMIN     1
22:52:12   1000   20108  ssh         7     CAP_SETUID        1
22:52:12   0      20109  sshd        6     CAP_SETGID        1
22:52:12   0      20109  sshd        6     CAP_SETGID        1
22:52:12   0      20110  sshd        18    CAP_SYS_CHROOT    1
22:52:12   0      20110  sshd        6     CAP_SETGID        1
22:52:12   0      20110  sshd        6     CAP_SETGID        1
22:52:12   0      20110  sshd        7     CAP_SETUID        1
22:52:12   122    20110  sshd        6     CAP_SETGID        1
22:52:12   122    20110  sshd        6     CAP_SETGID        1
22:52:12   122    20110  sshd        7     CAP_SETUID        1
[...]
```

---

12 Origin: I wrote the first version using BCC on 13-Sep-2016 and ported it to bpftrace on 8-Sep-2018. I created it after a discussion with Michael Wardrop from the Netflix platform security team, who wanted this kind of visibility.

This output shows the capable(8) tool checking for the CAP_SYS_ADMIN capability (super user), and then ssh(1) checking CAP_SETUID, and then sshd(8) checking various capabilities. Documentation for these capabilities can be found in the capabilities(7) man page.

Columns include:

- **CAP:** Capability number
- **NAME:** Code name for the capability (see capabilities(7))
- **AUDIT:** Whether this capability check writes to the audit log

This works by tracing the kernel cap_capable() function, which determines whether the current task has a given capability. The frequency of this is typically so low that the overhead should be negligible.

There are options to show user- and kernel-stack traces. For example, including both:

```
# capable -KU
[...]
TIME      UID    PID    COMM          CAP   NAME                AUDIT
12:00:37  0      26069  bash          2     CAP_DAC_READ_SEARCH 1
        cap_capable+0x1 [kernel]
        ns_capable_common+0x68 [kernel]
        capable_wrt_inode_uidgid+0x33 [kernel]
        generic_permission+0xfe [kernel]
        __inode_permission+0x36 [kernel]
        inode_permission+0x14 [kernel]
        may_open+0x5a [kernel]
        path_openat+0x4b5 [kernel]
        do_filp_open+0x9b [kernel]
        do_sys_open+0x1bb [kernel]
        sys_openat+0x14 [kernel]
        do_syscall_64+0x73 [kernel]
        entry_SYSCALL_64_after_hwframe+0x3d [kernel]
        open+0x4e [libc-2.27.so]
        read_history+0x22 [bash]
        load_history+0x8c [bash]
        main+0x955 [bash]
        __libc_start_main+0xe7 [libc-2.27.so]
        [unknown]
[...]
```

This includes the kernel stack showing the openat(2) syscall and the user stack showing the bash process calling read_history().

BCC

Command line usage:

```
capable [options]
```

Options include:

- **-v**: Include non-audit checks (verbose)
- **-p PID**: Measure this process only
- **-K**: Include kernel stack traces
- **-U**: Include user-level stack traces

Some checks are considered "non-audit" and don't write a message to the audit log. These are excluded by default unless -v is used.

bpftrace

The following is the code for the bpftrace version, which summarizes its core functionality. This version does not support options and traces all capability checks, included non-audit.

```
#!/usr/local/bin/bpftrace

BEGIN
{
        printf("Tracing cap_capable syscalls... Hit Ctrl-C to end.\n");
        printf("%-9s %-6s %-6s %-16s %-4s %-20s AUDIT\n", "TIME", "UID", "PID",
            "COMM", "CAP", "NAME");
        @cap[0] = "CAP_CHOWN";
        @cap[1] = "CAP_DAC_OVERRIDE";
        @cap[2] = "CAP_DAC_READ_SEARCH";
        @cap[3] = "CAP_FOWNER";
        @cap[4] = "CAP_FSETID";
        @cap[5] = "CAP_KILL";
        @cap[6] = "CAP_SETGID";
        @cap[7] = "CAP_SETUID";
        @cap[8] = "CAP_SETPCAP";
        @cap[9] = "CAP_LINUX_IMMUTABLE";
        @cap[10] = "CAP_NET_BIND_SERVICE";
        @cap[11] = "CAP_NET_BROADCAST";
        @cap[12] = "CAP_NET_ADMIN";
        @cap[13] = "CAP_NET_RAW";
        @cap[14] = "CAP_IPC_LOCK";
        @cap[15] = "CAP_IPC_OWNER";
```

```
        @cap[16] = "CAP_SYS_MODULE";
        @cap[17] = "CAP_SYS_RAWIO";
        @cap[18] = "CAP_SYS_CHROOT";
        @cap[19] = "CAP_SYS_PTRACE";
        @cap[20] = "CAP_SYS_PACCT";
        @cap[21] = "CAP_SYS_ADMIN";
        @cap[22] = "CAP_SYS_BOOT";
        @cap[23] = "CAP_SYS_NICE";
        @cap[24] = "CAP_SYS_RESOURCE";
        @cap[25] = "CAP_SYS_TIME";
        @cap[26] = "CAP_SYS_TTY_CONFIG";
        @cap[27] = "CAP_MKNOD";
        @cap[28] = "CAP_LEASE";
        @cap[29] = "CAP_AUDIT_WRITE";
        @cap[30] = "CAP_AUDIT_CONTROL";
        @cap[31] = "CAP_SETFCAP";
        @cap[32] = "CAP_MAC_OVERRIDE";
        @cap[33] = "CAP_MAC_ADMIN";
        @cap[34] = "CAP_SYSLOG";
        @cap[35] = "CAP_WAKE_ALARM";
        @cap[36] = "CAP_BLOCK_SUSPEND";
        @cap[37] = "CAP_AUDIT_READ";
}


kprobe:cap_capable
{
        $cap = arg2;
        $audit = arg3;
        time("%H:%M:%S  ");
        printf("%-6d %-6d %-16s %-4d %-20s %d\n", uid, pid, comm, $cap,
            @cap[$cap], $audit);
}


END
{
        clear(@cap);
}
```

The program declares a hash for capability number to name lookups. This will need to be updated to match additions to the kernel.

11.2.12   setuids

setuids(8)[13] is a bpftrace tool to trace privilege escalation syscalls: setuid(2), setresuid(2), and setfsuid(2). For example:

```
# setuids.bt
Attaching 7 probes...
Tracing setuid(2) family syscalls. Hit Ctrl-C to end.
TIME     PID   COMM              UID    SYSCALL   ARGS (RET)
23:39:18 23436 sudo              1000   setresuid ruid=-1 euid=1000 suid=-1 (0)
23:39:18 23436 sudo              1000   setresuid ruid=-1 euid=0 suid=-1 (0)
23:39:18 23436 sudo              1000   setresuid ruid=-1 euid=0 suid=-1 (0)
23:39:18 23436 sudo              1000   setresuid ruid=0 euid=-1 suid=-1 (0)
23:39:18 23436 sudo              0      setresuid ruid=1000 euid=-1 suid=-1 (0)
23:39:18 23436 sudo              1000   setresuid ruid=-1 euid=-1 suid=-1 (0)
23:39:18 23436 sudo              1000   setuid    uid=0 (0)
23:39:18 23437 sudo              0      setresuid ruid=0 euid=0 suid=0 (0)
[...]
```

This shows a sudo(8) command that was changing a UID from 1000 to 0 and the various syscalls it used to do this. Logins via sshd(8) can also be seen via setuids(8), as they also change the UID.

The columns include:

- **UID:** The user ID before the setuid call.
- **SYSCALL:** The syscall name.
- **ARGS:** Arguments to the syscall.
- **(RET):** Return value. For setuid(2) and setresuid(2), this shows whether the call was successful. For setfsuid(2), it shows the previous UID.

This works by instrumenting the tracepoints for these syscalls. Since the rate of these syscalls should be low, the overhead of this tool should be negligible.

The source to setuids(8) is:

```
#!/usr/local/bin/bpftrace

BEGIN
{
        printf("Tracing setuid(2) family syscalls. Hit Ctrl-C to end.\n");
        printf("%-8s %-6s %-16s %-6s %-9s %s\n", "TIME",
            "PID", "COMM", "UID", "SYSCALL", "ARGS (RET)");
```

---

13 Origin: I created the first version as setuids.d on 9-May-2004, finding it useful as a way to trace logins as it caught them setting the uid: login, su, and sshd. I developed this bpftrace version on 26-Feb-2019 for this book.

```
}


tracepoint:syscalls:sys_enter_setuid,
tracepoint:syscalls:sys_enter_setfsuid
{
        @uid[tid] = uid;
        @setuid[tid] = args->uid;
        @seen[tid] = 1;
}


tracepoint:syscalls:sys_enter_setresuid
{
        @uid[tid] = uid;
        @ruid[tid] = args->ruid;
        @euid[tid] = args->euid;
        @suid[tid] = args->suid;
        @seen[tid] = 1;
}


tracepoint:syscalls:sys_exit_setuid
/@seen[tid]/
{
        time("%H:%M:%S ");
        printf("%-6d %-16s %-6d setuid    uid=%d (%d)\n", pid, comm,
            @uid[tid], @setuid[tid], args->ret);
        delete(@seen[tid]); delete(@uid[tid]); delete(@setuid[tid]);
}


tracepoint:syscalls:sys_exit_setfsuid
/@seen[tid]/
{
        time("%H:%M:%S ");
        printf("%-6d %-16s %-6d setfsuid  uid=%d (prevuid=%d)\n", pid, comm,
            @uid[tid], @setuid[tid], args->ret);
        delete(@seen[tid]); delete(@uid[tid]); delete(@setuid[tid]);
}


tracepoint:syscalls:sys_exit_setresuid
/@seen[tid]/
{
        time("%H:%M:%S ");
        printf("%-6d %-16s %-6d setresuid ", pid, comm, @uid[tid]);
        printf("ruid=%d euid=%d suid=%d (%d)\n", @ruid[tid], @euid[tid],
```

```
            @suid[tid], args->ret);
        delete(@seen[tid]); delete(@uid[tid]); delete(@ruid[tid]);
        delete(@euid[tid]); delete(@suid[tid]);
}
```

This traces the three syscall entry and exit tracepoints, stashing entry details into maps that can be fetched and printed on exit.

11.3   BPF One-Liners

These sections show BCC and bpftrace one-liners. Where possible, the same one-liner is implemented using both BCC and bpftrace.

11.3.1   BCC

Count security audit events for PID 1234:

```
funccount -p 1234 'security_*'
```

Trace pluggable authentication module (PAM) session starts:

```
trace 'pam:pam_start "%s: %s", arg1, arg2'
```

Trace kernel module loads:

```
trace 't:module:module_load "load: %s", args->name'
```

11.3.2   bpftrace

Count security audit events for PID 1234:

```
bpftrace -e 'k:security_* /pid == 1234 { @[func] = count(); }'
```

Trace pluggable authentication module (PAM) session starts:

```
bpftrace -e 'u:/lib/x86_64-linux-gnu/libpam.so.0:pam_start { printf("%s: %s\n",
    str(arg0), str(arg1)); }'
```

Trace kernel module loads:

```
bpftrace -e 't:module:module_load { printf("load: %s\n", str(args->name)); }'
```

11.3.3   BPF One-Liners Examples

Including some sample output, as was done for each tool, is also useful for illustrating one-liners. Here are some selected one-liners with example output.

Counting Security Audit Events

```
# funccount -p 21086 'security_*'
Tracing 263 functions for "security_*"... Hit Ctrl-C to end.
^C
FUNC                                COUNT
security_task_setpgid                   1
security_task_alloc                     1
security_inode_alloc                    1
security_d_instantiate                  1
security_prepare_creds                  1
security_file_alloc                     2
security_file_permission               13
security_vm_enough_memory_mm           27
security_file_ioctl                    34
Detaching...
```

This counts occurrences to the Linux Security Module (LSM) hooks for handling and auditing security events. Each of these hook functions can be traced for more information.

Tracing PAM Session Starts

```
# trace 'pam:pam_start "%s: %s", arg1, arg2'
PID     TID     COMM        FUNC                -
25568   25568   sshd        pam_start       sshd: bgregg
25641   25641   sudo        pam_start       sudo: bgregg
25646   25646   sudo        pam_start       sudo: bgregg
[...]
```

This shows sshd(8) and sudo(8) beginning a pluggable authentication module (PAM) session for the bgregg user. Other PAM functions can also be traced to see the final authentication request.

11.4 Summary

BPF can be used for various security uses, including sniffing activity for real-time forensics, privilege debugging, usage whitelists, and more. This chapter introduces these capabilities and demonstrates them with some BPF tools.

Chapter 12

Languages

There are many programming languages, as well as compilers and runtimes to execute them, and the way each language is executed affects how it can be traced. This chapter explains such differences and will help you find ways to trace any given language.

Learning Objectives:

- Understand compiled language instrumentation (e.g.: C)
- Understand JIT compiled language instrumentation (e.g.: Java, Node.js)
- Understand interpreted language instrumentation (e.g.: bash shell)
- Trace function calls, arguments, return value, and latency when possible
- Trace the user-level stack trace in a given language

This chapter begins by summarizing programming language implementations, then uses a few languages as examples: C for compiled languages, Java for a JIT-compiled language, and bash shell scripting for a fully interpreted language. For each, I cover how to find function names (symbols), function arguments, and how to investigate and trace stack traces. I have included notes for tracing other languages at the end of this chapter: JavaScript (Node.js), C++, and Golang.

Whatever your language of interest, this chapter should give you a head start in instrumenting it and understanding the challenges and solutions that have worked for other languages.

12.1 Background

To understand how to instrument a given language, you need to examine how it is converted into machine code for execution. This isn't usually an attribute of the language, but rather an attribute of how the language is implemented. Java, for example, is not a JIT-compiled language: Java is just a language. The commonly used JVM runtime from OracleJDK or OpenJDK executes Java methods with a pipeline that moves from interpretation to JIT compilation, but that is an attribute of the JVM. The JVM itself is also compiled C++ code, which runs functions such as class loading and garbage collection. In a fully instrumented Java application, you may encounter code that is compiled (C++ JVM functions), interpreted (Java methods), and JIT compiled (Java methods)—and there are differences in how each should be instrumented. Other languages have separate implementations of compilers and interpreters, and you need to know which is being used to understand how to trace it.

Put simply: if your task is to trace language X, your first question should be, what is the thing we are currently using to run X, and how does it work? Is it a compiler, JIT compiler, interpreter, animal, vegetable, or mineral?

This section provides general advice for tracing any language with BPF, by classifying language implementations by how they generate machine code: compiled, JIT compiled, or interpreted. Some implementations (e.g., the JVM) support multiple techniques.

12.1.1   Compiled

Examples of languages that are commonly compiled include C, C++, Golang, Rust, Pascal, Fortran, and COBOL.

For compiled languages, functions are compiled into machine code and stored in an executable binary, typically the ELF format, with the following attributes:

- For user-level software, symbol tables are included in the ELF binary file for mapping addresses to function and object names. These addresses do not move during execution, so the symbol table can be read at any time for correct mappings. Kernel-level software differs as it has its own dynamic symbol table in /proc/kallsyms, which can grow as modules are loaded.

- Function arguments and their return values are stored in registers and stack offsets. Their location usually follows a standard calling convention for each processor type; however, some compiled languages (e.g., Golang) use different conventions, and some (e.g., V8 built-ins) use no convention at all.

- The frame pointer register (RBP on x86_64) can be walked to reveal the stack trace, if the compiler initializes it in function prologues. Compilers often instead reuse it as a general purpose register (a performance optimization for register-limited processors). A side effect is that it breaks frame pointer–based stack walking.

Compiled languages are usually easy to trace, using uprobes for user-level software and kprobes for kernel-level software. There are numerous examples throughout this book.

When approaching compiled software, check whether the symbol tables are present (e.g., using nm(1), objdump(1), or readelf(1)). If they are not, check whether a debuginfo package is available for the software, which can provide the missing symbols. If that, too, is a dead end, check the compiler and build software to see why the symbols are missing in the first place: they may be stripped using strip(1). One fix is to recompile the software without calling strip(1).

Also check whether frame pointer-based stack walking is working. This is the current default for walking user-space stacks via BPF, and if it is not working, the software may need to be recompiled with a compiler flag to honor the frame pointer (e.g., gcc -fno-omit-frame-pointer). If this is infeasible, other stack-walking techniques can be explored, such as last branch record (LBR),[1] DWARF, user-level ORC, and BTF. There is still BPF tooling work needed to make use of these, discussed in Chapter 2.

---

1 There is not currently support for LBR in BPF or its front ends, but we intend to add it. perf(1) currently supports it with --call-graph lbr.

12.1.2 JIT Compiled

Examples of languages that are commonly JIT compiled include Java, JavaScript, Julia, .Net., and Smalltalk.

JIT compiled languages compile into bytecode, which is then compiled into machine code at runtime, often with feedback from runtime operation to direct compiler optimization. They have the following attributes (discussing user level only):

- Because functions are compiled on the fly, there is no pre-built symbol table. The mappings are usually stored in memory of the JIT runtime, and used for purposes such as printing exception stacks. These mappings may also change, as the runtime may recompile and move functions around.

- Function arguments and return values may or may not follow a standard calling convention.

- The JIT runtime may or may not honor the frame pointer register, so frame pointer–based stack walking may work, or it may be broken (in which case you would see the stack trace ending abruptly with a bogus address). The runtime usually has a way to walk its own stack for an exception handler to print the stack trace during errors.

Tracing JIT-compiled languages is difficult. There is no symbol table on the binary since it is dynamic and in memory. Some applications provide supplemental symbol files for the JIT mappings (/tmp/perf-PID.map); however, these cannot be used with uprobes for two reasons:

1. The compiler may move uprobe-instrumented functions in memory without informing the kernel. When the instrumentation is no longer needed, the kernel reverts the instructions back to normal, but it is now writing to the wrong location and will corrupt user-space memory.[2]

2. uprobes are inode based and require a file location to work, whereas the JIT functions may be stored in anonymous private mappings.[3]

Tracing compiled functions may be possible if the runtime provides USDT probes for each function, although this technique usually incurs high overhead, whether it is enabled or not. A more efficient approach is to instrument selected points with dynamic USDT. (USDT and dynamic USDT were introduced in Chapter 2.) USDT probes also provide a solution for instrumenting function arguments and return values as arguments to those probes.

If stack traces from BPF already work, supplemental symbol files can be used to translate them into the function names. For a runtime that doesn't support USDT, this provides one path for visibility into running JIT functions: stack traces can be collected on syscalls, kernel events, and via timed profiling, revealing the JIT functions that are running. This may be the easiest way you can get JIT function visibility to work, and can help solve many problem types.

If stack traces do not work, check whether the runtime supports frame pointers with an option or whether LBR can be used. If these are dead ends, there are a number of other ways to fix stack traces, although these may require significant engineering work. One way is to modify the runtime compiler to preserve the frame pointer. Another is to add USDT probes that use

---

2 I've asked the JVM team for a way to pause the c2 compiler so that functions stop moving during uprobe tracing.

3 Along with others, I have been looking into how to remove this limitation from the kernel.

the language's own means of getting the call stack, and providing this as a string argument. Yet another way is to signal the process from BPF and have a user-space helper write a stack trace to memory that BPF can read, as Facebook has implemented for hhvm [133].

Java is discussed later in this chapter as an example of how these techniques work in practice.

12.1.3 Interpreted

Examples of languages that are commonly interpreted include the bash shell, Perl, Python, and Ruby. There are also languages that commonly use interpretation as a stage before JIT compilation—for example, Java and JavaScript. The analysis of those staged languages during their interpretation stage is similar to analysis of languages that use only interpretation.

Interpreted language runtimes do not compile the program functions to machine code but instead parse and execute the program using their own built-in routines. They have the following attributes:

- The binary symbol table shows interpreter internals but no functions from the user-supplied program. The functions are likely stored in a memory table that is specific to the interpreter implementation and maps to interpreter objects.

- Function arguments and return values are processed by the interpreter. They are likely passed around by interpreter function calls and may be bundled as interpreter objects and rather than simple ints and strings.

- If the interpreter itself is compiled to honor the frame pointer, frame pointer stack walking will work, but it will show only the interpreter internals with no function name context from the user-supplied program that is running. The program stack is likely known by the interpreter and printed for exception stacks but stored in a custom data structure.

USDT probes may exist to show the start and end of function calls, with the function name and arguments as arguments to the USDT probe. For example, the Ruby runtime has built-in USDT probes in the interpreter. While this provides a way to trace function calls, it can come with high overhead: it usually means instrumenting all function calls, and then filtering on the name for the functions of interest. If there is a dynamic USDT library for the language runtime, it can be used to insert custom USDT probes only in the functions of interest, rather than tracing all functions and then filtering. (See Chapter 2 for an introduction to dynamic USDT.) For example, the ruby-static-tracing package provides this for Ruby.

If the runtime does not have built-in USDT probes, and no package provides runtime USDT support (such as libstapsdt/libusdt), its interpreter functions can be traced using uprobes and details such as function names and arguments can be fetched. They may be stored as interpreter objects and require some struct navigation to parse.

Stack traces may be very difficult to tease out of the interpreter's memory. One approach, albeit one with high overhead, is to trace all function calls and returns in BPF and construct a synthetic stack for each thread in BPF memory that can be read when needed. As with JIT-compiled languages, there may be other ways to add stack trace support, including via custom USDT probes and the runtime's own method for fetching a stack (as with ruby's "caller" built-in, or an exception method), or with a BPF signal to a user-space helper.

12.1.4 BPF Capabilities

The target capabilities for tracing a language with BPF are to answer these questions:

- What functions are called?

- What are the arguments to a function?

- What is the return value of a function? Did it error?

- What is code path (stack trace) that led to any event?

- What is the duration of a function? As a histogram?

How many of these questions can be answered with BPF depends on the language implementation. Many language implementations come with custom debuggers that can answer the first four of these questions easily, so you might wonder why we even need BPF for this. A primary reason is to trace multiple layers of the software stack in one tool. Instead of examining disk I/O or page faults with kernel context alone, you can trace them along with the user-level code path responsible, and with application context: which user requests led to how much disk I/O or page faults, etc. In many cases, kernel events can identify and quantify an issue, but it's the user-level code that shows how to fix it.

For some languages (e.g., Java), showing which stack trace led to an event is easier to get working than tracing its function/method calls. Combined with the numerous other kernel events that BPF can instrument, stack traces can accomplish much. You can see which application code paths led to disk I/O, page faults, and other resource usage; you can see which code paths led to the thread blocking and leaving the CPU; and you can use timed sampling to profile CPU usage and build CPU flame graphs.

12.1.5 Strategy

Here is a suggested overall strategy you can follow for the analysis of a language:

1. Determine how the language is executed. For the software that runs it, is it using compilation to binaries, JIT compilation on the fly, interpretation, or a mix of these? This directs your approach as discussed in this chapter.

2. Browse the tools and one-liners in this chapter to understand the kinds of things that are possible for each language type.

3. Do an internet search for "[e]BPF *language*", "BCC *language*", and "bpftrace *language*" to see if there are already tools and know-how for analyzing the language with BPF.

4. Check if the language software has USDT probes and if they are enabled in the distributed binaries (or if you need to recompile to enable them). These are a stable interface and preferable to use. If the language software does not have USDT probes, consider adding them. Most language software is open source.

5. Write a sample program to instrument. Call a function with a known name a known number of times, and with known latency (explicit sleep). This can be used to check if your analysis tools are working, by checking that they identify all these knowns correctly.

6. For user-level software, use uprobes to inspect the language execution at the native level. For kernel-level software, use kprobes.

The sections that follow are longer discussions on three example languages: C for compiled, Java for JIT compiled, and the bash shell for interpreted languages.

12.1.6 BPF Tools

The BPF tools covered in this chapter are pictured in Figure 12-1.

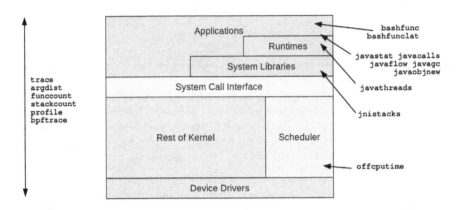

Figure 12-1   BPF tools for language analysis

These tools cover C, Java, and bash.

12.2   C

C is the easiest of the languages to trace.

For kernel-level C, the kernel has its own symbol table, and most distributions honor the frame pointer for their kernel builds (CONFIG_FRAME_POINTER=y). This makes tracing kernel functions with kprobes straightforward: the functions can be seen and traced, arguments follow the processor ABI, and stack traces can be fetched. At least, *most* functions can be seen and traced: exceptions include inlined functions, and those marked on a tracing blacklist by the kernel as unsafe to instrument.

For user-level C, if a compiled binary does not strip its symbol tables, and does not omit the frame pointer, then tracing is straightforward with uprobes: functions can be seen and traced, arguments follow the processor ABI, and stack traces can be fetched. Unfortunately, many binaries do strip their symbol tables and compilers do omit the frame pointer, meaning you need to recompile them or find other ways to read symbols and stacks.

USDT probes can be used in C programs for static instrumentation. Some C libraries, including libc, provide USDT probes by default.

This section discusses C function symbols, C stack traces, C function tracing, C function offset tracing, C USDT, and C one-liners. Table 12-1 lists tools for instrumenting custom C code that have already been covered in other chapters.

C++ tracing is similar to C and is summarized in Section 12.5.

Table 12-1 **C-Related Tools**

Tool	Source	Target	Description	Chapter
funccount	BCC	Functions	Count function calls	4
stackcount	BCC	Stacks	Count native stacks to events	4
trace	BCC	Functions	Print function calls and returns with details	4
argdist	BCC	Functions	Summarize function arguments or return value	4
bpftrace	BT	All	Custom function and stack instrumentation	5

12.2.1 C Function Symbols

Function symbols can be read from the ELF symbol tables. readelf(1) can be used to check if these are present. For example, here are symbols in a microbenchmark program:

```
$ readelf -s bench1

Symbol table '.dynsym' contains 10 entries:
   Num:    Value          Size Type    Bind   Vis      Ndx Name
     0: 0000000000000000     0 NOTYPE  LOCAL  DEFAULT  UND
     1: 0000000000000000     0 NOTYPE  WEAK   DEFAULT  UND _ITM_deregisterTMCloneTab
     2: 0000000000000000     0 FUNC    GLOBAL DEFAULT  UND puts@GLIBC_2.2.5 (2)
     3: 0000000000000000     0 FUNC    GLOBAL DEFAULT  UND __libc_start_main@GLIBC...
     4: 0000000000000000     0 NOTYPE  WEAK   DEFAULT  UND __gmon_start__
     5: 0000000000000000     0 FUNC    GLOBAL DEFAULT  UND malloc@GLIBC_2.2.5 (2)
     6: 0000000000000000     0 FUNC    GLOBAL DEFAULT  UND atoi@GLIBC_2.2.5 (2)
     7: 0000000000000000     0 FUNC    GLOBAL DEFAULT  UND exit@GLIBC_2.2.5 (2)
     8: 0000000000000000     0 NOTYPE  WEAK   DEFAULT  UND _ITM_registerTMCloneTable
     9: 0000000000000000     0 FUNC    WEAK   DEFAULT  UND __cxa_finalize@GLIBC_2.2.5 (2)

Symbol table '.symtab' contains 66 entries:
   Num:    Value          Size Type    Bind   Vis      Ndx Name
     0: 0000000000000000     0 NOTYPE  LOCAL  DEFAULT  UND
     1: 0000000000000238     0 SECTION LOCAL  DEFAULT    1
     2: 0000000000000254     0 SECTION LOCAL  DEFAULT    2
     3: 0000000000000274     0 SECTION LOCAL  DEFAULT    3
     4: 0000000000000298     0 SECTION LOCAL  DEFAULT    4
   [...]
    61: 0000000000000000     0 FUNC    GLOBAL DEFAULT  UND exit@@GLIBC_2.2.5
    62: 0000000000201010     0 OBJECT  GLOBAL HIDDEN     23 __TMC_END__
    63: 0000000000000000     0 NOTYPE  WEAK   DEFAULT  UND _ITM_registerTMCloneTable
    64: 0000000000000000     0 FUNC    WEAK   DEFAULT  UND __cxa_finalize@@GLIBC_2.2
    65: 0000000000000590     0 FUNC    GLOBAL DEFAULT   11 _init
```

The symbol table, ".symtab", has dozens of entries (truncated here). There is an additional symbol table used for dynamic linking, ".dynsym", which has six function symbols.

Now consider these symbol tables after the binary has been run through strip(1), which is often the case for many packaged binaries:

```
$ readelf -s bench1

Symbol table '.dynsym' contains 10 entries:
   Num:    Value          Size Type    Bind   Vis      Ndx Name
     0: 0000000000000000     0 NOTYPE  LOCAL  DEFAULT  UND
     1: 0000000000000000     0 NOTYPE  WEAK   DEFAULT  UND _ITM_deregisterTMCloneTab
     2: 0000000000000000     0 FUNC    GLOBAL DEFAULT  UND puts@GLIBC_2.2.5 (2)
     3: 0000000000000000     0 FUNC    GLOBAL DEFAULT  UND __libc_start_main@GLIBC...
     4: 0000000000000000     0 NOTYPE  WEAK   DEFAULT  UND __gmon_start__
     5: 0000000000000000     0 FUNC    GLOBAL DEFAULT  UND malloc@GLIBC_2.2.5 (2)
     6: 0000000000000000     0 FUNC    GLOBAL DEFAULT  UND atoi@GLIBC_2.2.5 (2)
     7: 0000000000000000     0 FUNC    GLOBAL DEFAULT  UND exit@GLIBC_2.2.5 (2)
     8: 0000000000000000     0 NOTYPE  WEAK   DEFAULT  UND _ITM_registerTMCloneTable
     9: 0000000000000000     0 FUNC    WEAK   DEFAULT  UND __cxa_finalize@GLIBC_2....
```

strip(1) removes the .symtab symbol table but leaves the .dynsym table. .dynsym contains external global symbols that are called, and .symtab contains the same plus local symbols from the application. Without .symtab, there are still some symbols in the binary for library calls, but it may be missing the most interesting ones.

Statically compiled applications that are stripped may lose all symbols, since they had all been placed in the .symtab that is removed.

There are at least two ways to fix this:

- Remove strip(1) from the software build process and recompile the software.

- Use a different source of symbols: DWARF debuginfo or BTF.

Debuginfo for software packages is sometimes available as a software package with a -dbg, -dbgsym, or -debuginfo extension. It is supported by the perf(1) command, BCC, and bpftrace.

Debuginfo

Debuginfo files may have the same name as the binary with a ".debuginfo" extension, or use a build ID unique checksum for the filename and reside under /usr/lib/debug/.build-id or a user version of this. For the latter, the build ID is stored in the binary ELF notes section, and can be seen using readelf -n.

As an example, this system has openjdk-11-jre and openjdk-11-dbg packages installed, providing both libjvm.so and libjvm.debuginfo files. Here are the symbol counts for each:

```
$ readelf -s /usr/lib/jvm/.../libjvm.so | wc -l
456
$ readelf -s /usr/lib/jvm/.../libjvm.debuginfo | wc -l
52299
```

The stripped version has 456 symbols, and the debuginfo version has 52,299.

Lightweight Debuginfo

While it might seem worthwhile to always install the debuginfo file, it comes at a file size cost: the debuginfo file is 222 Mbytes, compared to 17 Mbytes for libjvm.so. Much of this size is not symbol information but other debuginfo sections. The size of the symbol information can be checked using readelf(1):

```
$ readelf -S libjvm.debuginfo
There are 39 section headers, starting at offset 0xdd40468:

Section Headers:
  [Nr] Name              Type             Address           Offset
       Size              EntSize          Flags  Link  Info  Align
[...]
  [36] .symtab           SYMTAB           0000000000000000  0da07530
       00000000001326c0  0000000000000018           37    51845     8
[...]
```

This shows the size of .symtab is only 1.2 Mbytes. For comparison, the openjdk package that provided libjvm.so is 175 Mbytes.

If the full debuginfo size is a problem, you could explore stripping down the debuginfo file. The following commands use objcopy(1) to strip out the other debuginfo sections (which begin with ".debug_") to create a lightweight debuginfo file. This can be used as a debuginfo replacement that contains symbols, or it can also be reattached to the binary using eu-unstrip(1). Example commands:

```
$ objcopy -R.debug_\* libjvm.debuginfo libjvm.symtab
$ eu-unstrip -o libjvm.new.so libjvm.so libjvm.symtab
$ ls -lh libjvm.orig.so libjvm.debuginfo libjvm.symtab libjvm.new.so
-rwxr-xr-x 1 root root 222M Nov 13 04:53 libjvm.debuginfo*
-rwxr-xr-x 1 root root  20M Feb 16 19:02 libjvm.new.so*
-rw-r--r-- 1 root root  17M Nov 13 04:53 libjvm.so
-rwxr-xr-x 1 root root 3.3M Feb 16 19:00 libjvm.symtab*
$ readelf -s libjvm.new.so | wc -l
52748
```

The new libjvm.new.so is only 20 Mbytes and contains all the symbols. Note that this is a proof of concept technique I developed for this book, and has not yet had production testing.

BTF

In the future, the BPF Type Format (BTF) may provide another lightweight source of debuginfo, and one that was designed for use by BPF. So far BTF is kernel only: work has not yet began on a user-level version. See Chapter 2 for BTF.

Using bpftrace

Apart from using readelf(1), bpftrace can also list symbols from a binary by matching which uprobes are available to instrument[4]:

```
# bpftrace -l 'uprobe:/bin/bash'
uprobe:/bin/bash:rl_old_menu_complete
uprobe:/bin/bash:maybe_make_export_env
uprobe:/bin/bash:initialize_shell_builtins
uprobe:/bin/bash:extglob_pattern_p
uprobe:/bin/bash:dispose_cond_node
[...]
```

Wildcards can also be used:

```
# bpftrace -l 'uprobe:/bin/bash:read*'
uprobe:/bin/bash:reader_loop
uprobe:/bin/bash:read_octal
uprobe:/bin/bash:readline_internal_char
uprobe:/bin/bash:readonly_builtin
uprobe:/bin/bash:read_tty_modified
[...]
```

Section 12.2.3 instruments one of these as an example.

12.2.2   C Stack Traces

BPF currently supports frame pointer–based stack walking. For this to work, the software must be compiled to use the frame pointer register. For the gcc compiler, this is the -fno-omit-frame-pointer option. In the future, BPF may support other types of stack walking as well.

Since BPF is programmable, I was able to code a frame pointer stack walker in pure BPF before real support was added [134]. Alexei Starovoitov added official support with a new map type, BPF_MAP_TYPE_STACK_TRACE, and a helper, bpf_get_stackid(). The helper returns a unique ID

---

4 Matheus Marchini developed this feature after reviewing a draft of this chapter and realizing it was needed.

for the stack, and the map stores the contents of the stack. This minimizes storage for stack traces, since duplicates reuse the same ID and storage.

From bpftrace, stacks are available via the ustack and kstack built-ins, for user-level and kernel stacks. Here is an example of tracing the bash shell, which is a large C program, and printing the stack trace that led to a read of file descriptor 0 (STDIN):

```
# bpftrace -e 't:syscalls:sys_enter_read /comm == "bash" &&
    args->fd == 0/ { @[ustack] = count(); }'
Attaching 1 probe...
^C

@[
    read+16
    0x6c63004344006d
]: 7
```

This stack is actually broken: after the read() function is a hexadecimal number that does not look like an address. (pmap(1) can be used to check the address space mappings for a PID to see if it is in a range or not; in this case, it isn't.)

Now a bash shell that's been recompiled with -fno-omit-frame-pointer:

```
# bpftrace -e 't:syscalls:sys_enter_read /comm == "bash" &&
    args->fd == 0/ { @[ustack] = count(); }'
Attaching 1 probe...
^C

@[
    read+16
    rl_read_key+307
    readline_internal_char+155
    readline_internal_charloop+22
    readline_internal+23
    readline+91
    yy_readline_get+142
    yy_readline_get+412
    yy_getc+13
    shell_getc+464
    read_token+250
    yylex+184
    yyparse+776
    parse_command+122
    read_command+203
    reader_loop+377
```

```
    main+2355
    __libc_start_main+240
    0xa9de258d4c544155
]: 30
```

The stack trace is now visible. It is printed top-down from leaf to root. Put differently, top-down is also child to parent to grandparent and so on.

This example shows the shell reading from STDIN via readline() functions, in a read_command() code path. It is the bash shell reading input.

The bottom of the stack is another bogus address after __libc_start_main. The problem is that the stack has now walked into a system library, libc, and that has been compiled without the frame pointer.

See Section 2.4 in Chapter 2 for more about how BPF walks stacks and future work.

12.2.3 C Function Tracing

Functions can be traced using kprobes and kretprobes for kernel functions, and uprobes and uret-probes for user-level functions. These technologies were introduced in Chapter 2, and Chapter 5 covered how to use them from bpftrace. There are many examples of their use in this book.

As one example for this section: the following traces the readline() function, which is usually included in the bash shell. Since this is user-level software, it can be traced with uprobes. Here is the function signature:

```
char * readline(char *prompt)
```

It takes a string argument, the prompt, and also returns a string. Using a uprobe to trace the prompt argument, which is available as the arg0 built-in:

```
# bpftrace -e 'uprobe:/bin/bash:readline { printf("readline: %s\n", str(arg0)); }'
Attaching 1 probe...
readline: bgregg:~/Build/bpftrace/tools>
readline: bgregg:~/Build/bpftrace/tools>
```

This showed the prompt ($PS1) printed by a shell in another window.

Now tracing the return value and showing it as a string, using a uretprobe:

```
# bpftrace -e 'uretprobe:/bin/bash:readline { printf("readline: %s\n",
    str(retval)); }'
Attaching 1 probe...
readline: date
readline: echo hello reader
```

This showed the input I was typing in another window.

Apart from the main binary, shared libraries can also be traced by replacing the "/bin/bash" path in the probe with the path to the library. Some Linux distributions[5] build bash so that readline is called via libreadline, and the above one-liners will fail as the readline() symbol is not in /bin/bash. They may be traced using the path to libreadline, for example:

```
# bpftrace -e 'uretprobe:/usr/lib/libreadline.so.8:readline {
    printf("readline: %s\n", str(retval)); }'
```

12.2.4   C Function Offset Tracing

There may be times when you would like to trace an arbitrary offset within a function rather than just its start and return points. Apart from greater visibility to a function's code flow, by inspecting registers you could also determine the contents of local variables.

uprobes and kprobes support tracing at arbitrary offsets, as does BCC's attach_uprobe() and attach_kprobe() from its Python API. However, this capability is not yet exposed via BCC tools such as trace(8) and funccount(8), nor is it available yet in bpftrace. It should be straightforward to add to these tools. The difficulty will be adding it safely. uprobes does not check for instruction alignment, so tracing the wrong address (e.g., midway through a multi-byte instruction) will corrupt the instructions in the target program, causing it to fail in unpredictable ways. Other tracers, such as perf(1), use debuginfo to check for instruction alignment.

12.2.5   C USDT

USDT probes can be added to C programs to provide static instrumentation: a reliable API for tracing tools to use. Some programs and libraries already provide USDT probes, for example, listing libc USDT probes using bpftrace:

```
# bpftrace -l 'usdt:/lib/x86_64-linux-gnu/libc-2.27.so'
usdt:/lib/x86_64-linux-gnu/libc-2.27.so:libc:setjmp
usdt:/lib/x86_64-linux-gnu/libc-2.27.so:libc:longjmp
usdt:/lib/x86_64-linux-gnu/libc-2.27.so:libc:longjmp_target
usdt:/lib/x86_64-linux-gnu/libc-2.27.so:libc:memory_mallopt_arena_max
usdt:/lib/x86_64-linux-gnu/libc-2.27.so:libc:memory_mallopt_arena_test
usdt:/lib/x86_64-linux-gnu/libc-2.27.so:libc:memory_tunable_tcache_max_bytes
[...]
```

There are different libraries that provide USDT instrumentation, including systemtap-sdt-dev and Facebook's Folly. For an example of adding USDT probes to a C program, see Chapter 2.

---

5 For example, Arch Linux.

12.2.6   C One-Liners

These sections show BCC and bpftrace one-liners. Where possible, the same one-liner is implemented using both BCC and bpftrace.

BCC

Count kernel function calls starting with "attach":

```
funccount 'attach*'
```

Count function calls starting with "a" from a binary (e.g., /bin/bash):

```
funccount '/bin/bash:a*'
```

Count function calls starting with "a" from a library (e.g., libc.so.6):

```
funccount '/lib/x86_64-linux-gnu/libc.so.6:a*'
```

Trace a function and its argument (e.g., bash readline()):

```
trace '/bin/bash:readline "%s", arg1'
```

Trace a function and its return value (e.g., bash readline()):

```
trace 'r:/bin/bash:readline "%s", retval'
```

Trace a library function and its argument (e.g., libc fopen()):

```
trace '/lib/x86_64-linux-gnu/libc.so.6:fopen "%s", arg1'
```

Count a library function return value (e.g., libc fopen()):

```
argdist -C 'r:/lib/x86_64-linux-gnu/libc.so.6:fopen():int:$retval'
```

Count a user-level stack trace on a function (e.g., bash readline()):

```
stackcount -U '/bin/bash:readline'
```

Sample user stacks at 49 Hertz:

```
profile -U -F 49
```

bpftrace

Count kernel function calls starting with "attach":

```
bpftrace -e 'kprobe:attach* { @[probe] = count(); }'
```

Count function calls starting with "a" from a binary (e.g., /bin/bash):

```
bpftrace -e 'uprobe:/bin/bash:a* { @[probe] = count(); }'
```

Count function calls starting with "a" from a library (e.g., libc.so.6):

```
bpftrace -e 'u:/lib/x86_64-linux-gnu/libc.so.6:a* { @[probe] = count(); }'
```

Trace a function and its argument (e.g., bash readline()):

```
bpftrace -e 'u:/bin/bash:readline { printf("prompt: %s\n", str(arg0)); }'
```

Trace a function and its return value (e.g., bash readline()):

```
bpftrace -e 'ur:/bin/bash:readline { printf("read: %s\n", str(retval)); }'
```

Trace a library function and its argument (e.g., libc fopen()):

```
bpftrace -e 'u:/lib/x86_64-linux-gnu/libc.so.6:fopen { printf("opening: %s\n",
    str(arg0)); }'
```

Count a library function return value (e.g., libc fopen()):

```
bpftrace -e 'ur:/lib/x86_64-linux-gnu/libc.so.6:fopen { @[retval] = count(); }'
```

Count a user-level stack trace on a function (e.g., bash readline()):

```
bpftrace -e 'u:/bin/bash:readline { @[ustack] = count(); }'
```

Sample user stacks at 49 Hertz:

```
bpftrace -e 'profile:hz:49 { @[ustack] = count(); }'
```

12.3   Java

Java is a complex target to trace. The Java virtual machine (JVM) executes Java methods by compiling them to bytecode and then running them in an interpreter. Then, when they have exceeded an execution threshold (-XX:CompileThreshold), they are JIT compiled into native instructions. The JVM will also profile method execution and recompile methods to further improve their performance, changing their memory location on the fly. The JVM includes libraries written in C++ for compilation, thread management, and garbage collection. The most commonly used JVM is called HotSpot, originally developed by Sun Microsystems.

The C++ components of the JVM (libjvm) can be instrumented as with compiled languages, covered in the previous section. The JVM comes with many USDT probes to make tracing JVM internals easier. These USDT probes can also instrument Java methods, but they come with challenges that will be discussed in this section.

This section begins with a brief look at libjvm C++ tracing and then discusses Java thread names, Java method symbols, Java stack traces, Java USDT probes, and Java one-liners. The Java-related tools listed in Table 12-2 are also covered.

Table 12-2   **Java-Related Tools**

Tool	Source	Target	Description
jnistacks	Book	libjvm	Show JNI consumers by object stack trace
profile	BCC	CPUs	Timed sampling of stack traces, including Java methods
offcputime	BCC	Sched	Off-CPU time with stack traces, including Java methods
stackcount	BCC	Events	Show stacks traces for any given event
javastat	BCC	USDT	High-level language operation statistics
javathreads	Book	USDT	Trace thread start and stop events
javacalls	BCC/book	USDT	Count Java method calls

Tool	Source	Target	Description
javaflow	BCC	USDT	Show Java method code flow
javagc	BCC	USDT	Trace Java garbage collections
javaobjnew	BCC	USDT	Count Java new object allocations

Some of these tools show Java methods, and to show their output on Netflix production servers would require redacting internal code, making the examples difficult to follow. Instead, I will demonstrate these on an open source Java game: freecol. The software for this game is complex and performance sensitive, making it a similar target to Netflix production code.[6] The freecol website is: http://www.freecol.org.

12.3.1 libjvm Tracing

The JVM main library, libjvm, contains thousands of functions for running Java threads, loading classes, compiling methods, allocating memory, garbage collection, and more. These are mostly written in C++, and can be traced to provide different views of the running Java program.

As an example, I'll trace all the Java native interface (JNI) functions using BCC's funccount(8) (bpftrace can also be used):

```
# funccount '/usr/lib/jvm/java-11-openjdk-amd64/lib/server/libjvm.so:jni_*'
Tracing 235 functions
for "/usr/lib/jvm/java-11-openjdk-amd64/lib/server/libjvm.
so:jni_*"... Hit Ctrl-C to end.
^C
FUNC                                      COUNT
jni_GetObjectClass                            1
jni_SetLongArrayRegion                        2
jni_GetEnv                                   15
jni_SetLongField                             42
jni_NewWeakGlobalRef                         84
jni_FindClass                               168
jni_GetMethodID                             168
jni_NewObject                               168
jni_GetObjectField                          168
jni_ExceptionOccurred                       719
jni_CallStaticVoidMethod                   1144
jni_ExceptionCheck                         1186
jni_ReleasePrimitiveArrayCritical          3787
jni_GetPrimitiveArrayCritical              3787
Detaching...
```

---

6 At the SCaLE 2019 conference, I performed live BPF analysis of another complex Java game: Minecraft. While it has a similar analysis complexity to freecol and Netflix production applications, it is less suitable to analyze here as it is not open source.

This traced functions in libjvm.so matching "jni_*", and found that the most frequent was jni_ GetPrimitiveArrayCritical(), called 3552 while tracing. The libjvm.so path was truncated in the output to prevent line wrapping.

libjvm Symbols

The libjvm.so that is usually packaged with the JDK has been stripped, which means that the local symbol table is not available and these JNI functions cannot be traced without extra steps. The status can be checked using file(1):

```
$ file /usr/lib/jvm/java-11-openjdk-amd64/lib/server/libjvm.orig.so
/usr/lib/jvm/java-11-openjdk-amd64/lib/server/libjvm.orig.so: ELF 64-bit LSB shared
object, x86-64, version 1 (GNU/Linux), dynamically linked,
BuildID[sha1]=f304ff36e44ce8a68a377cb07ed045f97aee4c2f, stripped
```

Possible solutions:

- Build your own libjvm from source and do not use strip(1).

- Install the JDK debuginfo package, if available, which BCC and bpftrace support.

- Install the JDK debuginfo package and use elfutils unstrip(1) to add the symbol table back to libjvm.so (see the earlier "Debuginfo" section, under Section 12.2.1).

- Use BTF, when available (covered in Chapter 2).

For this example, I used the second option.

12.3.2 jnistacks

As an example libjvm tool, jnistacks(8)[7] counts stacks that led to the jni_NewObject() call seen in the previous output, and others starting with "jni_NewObject". This will reveal which Java code paths, including Java methods, led to new JNI objects. Some example output:

```
# bpftrace --unsafe jnistacks.bt
Tracing jni_NewObject* calls... Ctrl-C to end.
^C
Running /usr/local/bin/jmaps to create Java symbol files in /tmp...
Fetching maps for all java processes...
Mapping PID 25522 (user bgregg):
wc(1):    8350   26012 518729 /tmp/perf-25522.map

[...]
@[
    jni_NewObject+0
    Lsun/awt/X11GraphicsConfig;::pGetBounds+171
```

---

7 Origin: I created it for this book on 8-Feb-2019.

```
Ljava/awt/MouseInfo;::getPointerInfo+2048
Lnet/sf/freecol/client/gui/plaf/FreeColButtonUI;::paint+1648
Ljavax/swing/plaf/metal/MetalButtonUI;::update+232
Ljavax/swing/JComponent;::paintComponent+672
Ljavax/swing/JComponent;::paint+2208
Ljavax/swing/JComponent;::paintChildren+1196
Ljavax/swing/JComponent;::paint+2256
Ljavax/swing/JComponent;::paintChildren+1196
Ljavax/swing/JComponent;::paint+2256
Ljavax/swing/JLayeredPane;::paint+2356
Ljavax/swing/JComponent;::paintChildren+1196
Ljavax/swing/JComponent;::paint+2256
Ljavax/swing/JComponent;::paintToOffscreen+836
Ljavax/swing/BufferStrategyPaintManager;::paint+3244
Ljavax/swing/RepaintManager;::paint+1260
Interpreter+5955
Ljavax/swing/JComponent;::paintImmediately+3564
Ljavax/swing/RepaintManager$4;::run+1684
Ljavax/swing/RepaintManager$4;::run+132
call_stub+138
JavaCalls::call_helper(JavaValue*, methodHandle const&, JavaCallArguments*, Th...
JVM_DoPrivileged+1600
Ljava/security/AccessController;::doPrivileged+216
Ljavax/swing/RepaintManager;::paintDirtyRegions+4572
Ljavax/swing/RepaintManager;::paintDirtyRegions+660
Ljavax/swing/RepaintManager;::prePaintDirtyRegions+1556
Ljavax/swing/RepaintManager$ProcessingRunnable;::run+572
Ljava/awt/EventQueue$4;::run+1100
call_stub+138
JavaCalls::call_helper(JavaValue*, methodHandle const&, JavaCallArguments*, Th...
]: 232
```

For brevity, only the last stack has been included here. It can be inspected from bottom to top
to show the path to that call, or top-down to inspect ancestry. It looks like it begins with
an event from a queue (EventQueue), then moves through paint methods, and finally calls
sun.awt.X11GraphicsConfig::pGetBounds(), which is making the JNI call—I would guess because
it needs to call an X11 graphics library.

Some Interpreter() frames are seen: this is Java executing methods using its interpreter, before
they cross CompileThreshold and become natively compiled methods.

It is a little hard to read this stack since the Java symbols are class signatures. bpftrace does not yet support demangling them. The c++filt(1) tool does not currently support this version of Java class signatures either.[8] To show how these should be demangled, this symbol:

```
Ljavax/swing/RepaintManager;::prePaintDirtyRegions+1556
```

should be:

```
javax.swing.RepaintManager::prePaintDirtyRegions()+1556
```

The source code to jnistacks(8) is:

```
#!/usr/local/bin/bpftrace

BEGIN
{
        printf("Tracing jni_NewObject* calls... Ctrl-C to end.\n");
}

uprobe:/usr/lib/jvm/java-11-openjdk-amd64/lib/server/libjvm.so:jni_NewObject*
{
        @[ustack] = count();
}

END
{
        $jmaps = "/usr/local/bin/jmaps";
        printf("\nRunning %s to create Java symbol files in /tmp...\n", $jmaps);
        system("%s", $jmaps);
}
```

The uprobe traces all calls from libjvm.so that begin with "jni_NewObject*", and frequency counts the user stack trace.

The END clause runs an external program, jmaps, which sets up a supplemental Java method symbol file in /tmp. This uses the system() function, which requires the --unsafe command line argument, since the commands that system() runs cannot be verified by the BPF safety verifier.

The output from jmaps was included in the bpftrace output earlier. It is explained in Section 12.3.4. jmaps can be run externally and does not need to be in this bpftrace program (you can delete the END clause); however, the greater the time between its execution and when the symbol dump is used, the greater the chance for stale and mistranslated symbols. By including it in the bpftrace END clause, it is executed immediately before the stacks are printed out, minimizing the time between its collection and use.

---

8 Please feel free to fix bpftrace and c++filt(1).

12.3.3 Java Thread Names

The JVM allows custom names for each thread. If you try to match "java" as a process name, you may find no events since the threads are named something else. For example, using bpftrace:

```
# bpftrace -e 'profile:hz:99 /comm == "java"/ { @ = count(); }'
Attaching 1 probe...
^C
#
```

Now matching on the Java process ID and showing thread IDs and the comm built-in:

```
# bpftrace -e 'profile:hz:99 /pid == 16914/ { @[tid, comm] = count(); }'
Attaching 1 probe...
^C

@[16936, VM Periodic Tas]: 1
[...]
@[16931, Sweeper thread]: 4
@[16989, FreeColClient:b]: 4
@[21751, FreeColServer:A]: 7
@[21779, FreeColClient:b]: 18
@[21780, C2 CompilerThre]: 20
@[16944, AWT-XAWT]: 22
@[16930, C1 CompilerThre]: 24
@[16946, AWT-EventQueue-]: 51
@[16929, C2 CompilerThre]: 241
```

The comm built-in returns the thread (task) name, not the parent process name. This has the advantage of providing more context for the thread: the above profile shows that the C2 ComplierThread (name truncated) was consuming the most CPU while sampling. But this can also be confusing, since other tools including top(1) show the parent process name: "java".[9]

These thread names can be seen in /proc/PID/task/TID/comm. For example, using grep(1) to print them with filenames:

```
# grep . /proc/16914/task/*/comm
/proc/16914/task/16914/comm:java
[...]
/proc/16914/task/16959/comm:GC Thread#7
/proc/16914/task/16963/comm:G1 Conc#1
/proc/16914/task/16964/comm:FreeColClient:W
```

---

9 In the future, we may add a bpf_get_current_pcomm() to the kernel to return the process name, which could be used in addition to the thread name. In bpftrace, this may be exposed as "pcomm."

```
/proc/16914/task/16981/comm:FreeColClient:S
/proc/16914/task/16982/comm:TimerQueue
/proc/16914/task/16983/comm:Java Sound Even
/proc/16914/task/16985/comm:FreeColServer:S
/proc/16914/task/16989/comm:FreeColClient:b
/proc/16914/task/16990/comm:FreeColServer:-
```

The examples in the following sections match on the Java PID rather than the name "java", and now you know why. There is an additional reason: USDT probes that use a semaphore require a PID so that bpftrace knows to set the semaphore for that PID. See Section 2.10.1 in Chapter 2 for more details on these semaphore probes.

12.3.4   Java Method Symbols

The open source perf-map-agent can be used to create supplemental symbol files containing the addresses of the complied Java methods [135]. This is necessary any time you are printing stack traces or addresses containing Java methods; otherwise, the addresses will be unknown. perf-map-agent uses the convention created by Linux perf(1) of writing a text file in /tmp/perf-PID. map with the following format [136]:

```
START SIZE symbolname
```

Here are some example symbols from a production Java application, where the symbol contains "sun" (just as an example):

```
$ grep sun /tmp/perf-3752.map
[...]
7f9ce1a04f60 80 Lsun/misc/FormattedFloatingDecimal;::getMantissa
7f9ce1a06d60 7e0 Lsun/reflect/GeneratedMethodAccessor579;::invoke
7f9ce1a08de0 80 Lsun/misc/FloatingDecimal$BinaryToASCIIBuffer;::isExceptional
7f9ce1a23fc0 140 Lsun/security/util/Cache;::newSoftMemoryCache
7f9ce1a243c0 120 Lsun/security/util/Cache;::<init>
7f9ce1a2a040 1e80 Lsun/security/util/DerInputBuffer;::getBigInteger
7f9ce1a2ccc0 980 Lsun/security/util/DisabledAlgorithmConstraints;::permits
7f9ce1a36c20 200 Lcom/sun/jersey/core/reflection/ReflectionHelper;::findMethodOnCl...
7f9ce1a3a360 6e0 Lsun/security/util/MemoryCache;::<init>
7f9ce1a523c0 760 Lcom/sun/jersey/core/reflection/AnnotatedMethod;::hasMethodAnnota...
7f9ce1a60b60 860 Lsun/reflect/GeneratedMethodAccessor682;::invoke
7f9ce1a68f20 320 Lsun/nio/ch/EPollSelectorImpl;::wakeup
[...]
```

perf-map-agent can be run on-demand, and attaches to a live Java process and dumps the symbol table. Note that this procedure that can generate some performance overhead during the symbol dump, and for large Java applications it can take more than one second of CPU time.

Since this is a snapshot of the symbol table, it will quickly become out of date as the Java compiler recompiles methods, which it may continue to do after the workload seems to have reached a steady state. The more time between the symbol snapshot and the BPF tool translating method symbols, the more chances for symbols to be stale and mistranslated. For busy production workloads with high rates of compilation, I do not trust Java symbol dumps that are more than 60 seconds old.

Section 12.3.5 provides an example of a stack trace without the perf-map-agent symbol table, then with it after jmaps was run.

Automation

You can automate these symbol dumps to minimize the time between their creation and use by a BPF tool. The perf-map-agent project contains software to automate this, and I've published my own program called jmaps [137]. jmaps finds all java processes (based on their process name) and dumps their symbol tables. An example of running jmaps on a 48-CPU production server:

```
# time ./jmaps
Fetching maps for all java processes...
Mapping PID 3495 (user www):
wc(1):  116736  351865 9829226 /tmp/perf-3495.map


real    0m10.495s
user    0m0.397s
sys     0m0.134s
```

This output includes various statistics: jmaps runs wc(1) on the final symbol dump, which shows it is 116,000 lines (symbols) and 9.4 Mbytes (9829226 bytes). I also ran it through time(1) to show how long it took: this is a busy Java application with 174 Gbytes of main memory, and it took 10.5 seconds to run. (Much of the CPU time involved is not seen by the user and sys statistics, as it was in the running JVM.)

For use with BCC, jmaps can be run immediately before the tool. For example:

```
./jmaps; trace -U '...'
```

This would invoke the trace(8) command immediately after jmaps completed, minimizing the time for symbols to become stale. For tools that collect a summary of stack traces (e.g., stackcount(8)), the tool itself could be modified to call jmaps immediately before printing the summary.

With bpftrace, jmaps can be run in a BEGIN clause for tools that use printf(), and an END clause for those that print map summaries. The previous jnistacks(8) tool was an example of the latter.

Other Techniques and Future Work

With these techniques reducing symbol churn, the perf-map-agent approach has served many environments well. However, other approaches may better solve the stale symbol table problem, and may be supported by BCC in the future. In summary:

- **Timestamped symbol logging:** perf(1) supports this, and the software is in the Linux source.[10] It currently involves always-on logging, which incurs some performance overhead. Ideally, it would not require always-on logging but instead could be enabled on demand at the start of a trace, and then when disabled it could take a full symbol table snapshot. This would allow the symbol state over time to be reconstructed from the time-trace + snapshot data, without the performance overhead of always-on logging.[11]

- **Making the stale symbols visible:** It should be possible to dump a before and after symbol table, find locations that have changed, and then construct a new symbol table with these locations flagged as unreliable.

- **async-profile:** This marries perf_events stack traces with those fetched using Java's AsyncGetCallTrace interface. This approach does not require frame pointers to be enabled.

- **Kernel support:** This has been discussed in the BPF community. One day we may add kernel support to improve such stack trace collection with in-kernel symbol translation. This was mentioned in Chapter 2.

- **JVM built-in support for symbol dumps:** perf-map-agent is a single-threaded module that is bounded by the JVMTI interface. If the JVM were to support a way to write /tmp/perf-PID. map supplemental symbol files directly—say, when it received a signal or another JVMTI call—it is likely that such a built-in JVM version could be much more efficient.

This is an evolving space.

12.3.5 Java Stack Traces

By default, Java does not honor the frame pointer register, and that method of stack walking does not work. For example, using bpftrace to take timed stack samples of the Java process:

```
# bpftrace -e 'profile:hz:99 /pid == 3671/ { @[ustack] = count(); }'
Attaching 1 probe...
^C

@[
    0x7efcff88a7bd
    0x12f023020020fd4
]: 1
```

---

10 In the Linux source, see tools/perf/jvmti.

11 I have spoken about this to Stephane Eranian, who added the jvmti support to Linux perf(1),but I don't think he or I have had the time to code it.

```
@[
    0x7efcff88a736
    0x12f023020020fd4
]: 1
@[
    IndexSet::alloc_block_containing(unsigned int)+75
    PhaseChaitin::interfere_with_live(unsigned int, IndexSet*)+628
    PhaseChaitin::build_ifg_physical(ResourceArea*)+1812
    PhaseChaitin::Register_Allocate()+1834
    Compile::Code_Gen()+628
    Compile::Compile(ciEnv*, C2Compiler*, ciMethod*, int, bool, bool, bool, Direct...
    C2Compiler::compile_method(ciEnv*, ciMethod*, int, DirectiveSet*)+177
    CompileBroker::invoke_compiler_on_method(CompileTask*)+931
    CompileBroker::compiler_thread_loop()+1224
    JavaThread::thread_main_inner()+259
    thread_native_entry(Thread*)+240
    start_thread+219
]: 1
@[
    0x7efcff72fc9e
    0x620000cc4
]: 1
@[
    0x7efcff969ba8
]: 1
[...]
```

This output includes broken stacks, seen as just one or two hex addresses. The Java compiler has used the frame pointer register for local variables, as a compiler optimization. This makes Java slightly faster (on register-limited processors), at the expense of breaking this method of stack walking as used by debuggers and tracers. Attempting to walk the stack trace usually either fails after the first address. The above output includes such failures, and also a working stack that is entirely C++: since the code path didn't enter any Java methods, the frame pointer was intact.

PreserveFramePointer

Since Java 8 update 60, the JVM has provided the -XX:+PreserveFramePointer option to enable the frame pointer,[12] which fixes frame pointer–based stack traces. Now the same bpftrace one-liner, but with Java running with this option (this involved adding the -XX:+PreserveFramePointer option to the start script, /usr/games/freecol, in the run_java line):

---

12 I developed this capability and sent it as a patch to the hotspot-compiler-devs mailing list, with a CPU flame graph to explain its value. Zoltán Majó from Oracle rewrote it to be parameterized (PreserveFramePointer) and integrated it in the official JDK.

```
# bpftrace -e 'profile:hz:99 /pid == 3671/ { @[ustack] = count(); }'
Attaching 1 probe...
^C
[...]
@[
    0x7fdbdf74ba04
    0x7fdbd8be8814
    0x7fdbd8bed0a4
    0x7fdbd8beb874
    0x7fdbd8ca336c
    0x7fdbdf96306c
    0x7fdbdf962504
    0x7fdbdf62fef8
    0x7fdbd8cd85b4
    0x7fdbd8c8e7c4
    0x7fdbdf9e9688
    0x7fdbd8c83114
    0x7fdbd8817184
    0x7fdbdf9e96b8
    0x7fdbd8ce57a4
    0x7fdbd8cbecac
    0x7fdbd8cb232c
    0x7fdbd8cc715c
    0x7fdbd8c846ec
    0x7fdbd8cbb154
    0x7fdbd8c7fdc4
    0x7fdbd7b25849
    JavaCalls::call_helper(JavaValue*, methodHandle const&, JavaCallArguments*, Th...
    JVM_DoPrivileged+1600
    0x7fdbdf77fe18
    0x7fdbd8ccd37c
    0x7fdbd8cd1674
    0x7fdbd8cd0c74
    0x7fdbd8c8783c
    0x7fdbd8bd8fac
    0x7fdbd8b8a7b4
    0x7fdbd8b8c514
]: 1
[...]
```

These stack traces are now complete, except for the symbol translation.

Stacks and Symbols

As covered in Section 12.3.4, a supplemental symbol file can be created with the perf-map-agent software, automated by jmaps. After taking this step in an END clause:

```
# bpftrace --unsafe -e 'profile:hz:99 /pid == 4663/ { @[ustack] = count(); }
    END { system("jmaps"); }'
Attaching 2 probes...
^CFetching maps for all java processes...
Mapping PID 4663 (user bgregg):
wc(1):    6555  20559 388964 /tmp/perf-4663.map
@[
    Lsun/awt/X11/XlibWrapper;::RootWindow+31
    Lsun/awt/X11/XDecoratedPeer;::getLocationOnScreen+3764
    Ljava/awt/Component;::getLocationOnScreen_NoTreeLock+2260
    Ljavax/swing/SwingUtilities;::convertPointFromScreen+1820
    Lnet/sf/freecol/client/gui/plaf/FreeColButtonUI;::paint+1068
    Ljavax/swing/plaf/ComponentUI;::update+1804
    Ljavax/swing/plaf/metal/MetalButtonUI;::update+4276
    Ljavax/swing/JComponent;::paintComponent+612
    Ljavax/swing/JComponent;::paint+2120
    Ljavax/swing/JComponent;::paintChildren+13924
    Ljavax/swing/JComponent;::paint+2168
    Ljavax/swing/JLayeredPane;::paint+2356
    Ljavax/swing/JComponent;::paintChildren+13924
    Ljavax/swing/JComponent;::paint+2168
    Ljavax/swing/JComponent;::paintToOffscreen+836
    Ljavax/swing/BufferStrategyPaintManager;::paint+3244
    Ljavax/swing/RepaintManager;::paint+1260
    Ljavax/swing/JComponent;::_paintImmediately+12636
    Ljavax/swing/JComponent;::paintImmediately+3564
    Ljavax/swing/RepaintManager$4;::run+1684
    Ljavax/swing/RepaintManager$4;::run+132
    call_stub+138
    JavaCalls::call_helper(JavaValue*, methodHandle const&, JavaCallArguments*, Th...
    JVM_DoPrivileged+1600
    Ljava/security/AccessController;::doPrivileged+216
    Ljavax/swing/RepaintManager;::paintDirtyRegions+4572
    Ljavax/swing/RepaintManager;::paintDirtyRegions+660
    Ljavax/swing/RepaintManager;::prePaintDirtyRegions+1556
    Ljavax/swing/RepaintManager$ProcessingRunnable;::run+572
    Ljava/awt/event/InvocationEvent;::dispatch+524
    Ljava/awt/EventQueue;::dispatchEventImpl+6260
    Ljava/awt/EventQueue$4;::run+372
]: 1
```

The stack is now complete, and fully translated. This stack looks like it was painting a button in the UI (FreeColButtonUI::paint()).

Library Stacks

One last example, this time tracing stack traces from the read(2) syscall:

```
# bpftrace -e 't:syscalls:sys_enter_read /pid == 4663/ { @[ustack] = count(); }'
Attaching 1 probe...
^C

@[
    read+68
    0xc528280f383da96d
]: 11
@[
    read+68
]: 25
```

These stacks are still broken, even though Java is running with -XX:+PreserveFramePointer. The problem is that this syscall has walked into the libc library's read() function, and that library has not been compiled with the frame pointer. The fix is to recompile the library, or use a different stack walker once BPF tools support it (e.g., DWARF or LBR).

Fixing stack traces can be a lot of work. But it is worth it: it enables profiling including CPU flame graphs and stack trace context from any event.

12.3.6 Java USDT Probes

USDT probes, introduced in Chapter 2, have the advantage of providing a stable interface for instrumenting events. There are USDT probes in the JVM for various events, including:

- Virtual machine life cycle
- Thread life cycle
- Class loading
- Garbage collection
- Method compilation
- Monitor
- Application tracking
- Method calls
- Object allocation
- Monitor events

These are only available if the JDK has been compiled with the `--enable-dtrace` option, which, unfortunately, is not yet commonly enabled for Linux distributions of the JDK. To use these USDT probes, you will need to compile the JDK from source with `--enable-dtrace`, or ask the package maintainers to enable this option.

The probes are documented in the "DTrace Probes in HotSpot VM" section of the *Java Virtual Machine Guide* [138], which describes the purpose of each probe and its arguments. Table 12-3 lists some selected probes.

Table 12-3 **USDT Probes**

USDT Group	USDT Probe	Arguments
hotspot	thread__start, thread__stop	char *thread_name, u64 thread_name_len, u64 thread_id, u64 os_thread_id, bool is_daemon
hotspot	class__loaded	char *class_name, u64 class_name_len, u64 loader_id, bool is_shared
hotspot	gc__begin	bool is_full_gc
hotspot	gc__end	—
hotspot	object__alloc	int thread_id, char *class_name, u64 class_name_len, u64 size
hotspot	method__entry, method__return	int thread_id, char *class_name, int class_name_len, char *method_name, int method_name_len, char *signature, int signature_len
hotspot_jni	AllocObject__entry	void *env, void *clazz

See the *Java Virtual Machine Guide* for the full list.

Java USDT Implementation

As an example of how the USDT probes have been inserted into the JDK, the following shows the code behind a hotspot:gc__begin probe. For most people, it is not necessary to learn these details; they have been provided just to give some insight into how the probes work.

The probe is defined in src/hotspot/os/posix/dtrace/hotspot.d, a definitions file for the USDT probes:

```
provider hotspot {
[...]
  probe gc__begin(uintptr_t);
```

From this definition, the probe will be called hotspot:gc__begin. At build time this file is compiled to a hotspot.h header file, containing a HOTSPOT_GC_BEGIN macro:

```
#define HOTSPOT_GC_BEGIN(arg1) \
DTRACE_PROBE1 (hotspot, gc__begin, arg1)
```

This macro is then inserted where needed in the JVM code. It has been put in a notify_gc_begin() function, so that that function can be called for executing the probe. From src/hotspot/share/gc /shared/gcVMOperations.cpp:

```
void VM_GC_Operation::notify_gc_begin(bool full) {
  HOTSPOT_GC_BEGIN(
                   full);
  HS_DTRACE_WORKAROUND_TAIL_CALL_BUG();
}
```

This function happens to have a DTrace bug workaround macro, which is declared in a dtrace. hpp header file with the comment "// Work around dtrace tail call bug 6672627 until it is fixed in solaris 10".

If the JDK was built without --enable-dtrace, then a dtrace_disabled.hpp header file is used instead that returns nothing for these macros.

There is also a HOTSPOT_GC_BEGIN_ENABLED macro used for this probe: this returns true when the probe is under live instrumentation by a tracer, and is used by the code to know whether to calculate expensive probe arguments if the probe is enabled, or whether those can be skipped if no one is currently using the probe.

Listing Java USDT Probes

The tplist(8) tool from BCC can be used to list USDT probes from a file or a running process. On the JVM, it lists more than 500 probes. The output has been truncated here to show some interesting probes, and the full path to libjvm.so was elided ("..."):

```
# tplist -p 6820
/.../libjvm.so hotspot:class__loaded
/.../libjvm.so hotspot:class__unloaded
/.../libjvm.so hs_private:cms__initmark__begin
/.../libjvm.so hs_private:cms__initmark__end
/.../libjvm.so hs_private:cms__remark__begin
/.../libjvm.so hs_private:cms__remark__end
/.../libjvm.so hotspot:method__compile__begin
/.../libjvm.so hotspot:method__compile__end
/.../libjvm.so hotspot:gc__begin
/.../libjvm.so hotspot:gc__end
[...]
/.../libjvm.so hotspot_jni:NewObjectArray__entry
/.../libjvm.so hotspot_jni:NewObjectArray__return
/.../libjvm.so hotspot_jni:NewDirectByteBuffer__entry
/.../libjvm.so hotspot_jni:NewDirectByteBuffer__return
[...]
```

```
/.../libjvm.so hs_private:safepoint__begin
/.../libjvm.so hs_private:safepoint__end
/.../libjvm.so hotspot:object__alloc
/.../libjvm.so hotspot:method__entry
/.../libjvm.so hotspot:method__return
/.../libjvm.so hotspot:monitor__waited
/.../libjvm.so hotspot:monitor__wait
/.../libjvm.so hotspot:thread__stop
/.../libjvm.so hotspot:thread__start
/.../libjvm.so hotspot:vm__init__begin
/.../libjvm.so hotspot:vm__init__end
[...]
```

The probes are grouped into hotspot and hotspot_jni libraries. This output includes probes for class loading, garbage collection, safepoints, object allocation, methods, threads, and more. The use of double underscores was to create probe names that DTrace could refer to using a single dash, without the problem of putting minus signs in the code.

This example ran tplist(8) on a process; it can also be run on libjvm.so. So can readelf(1) to see the USDT probes in the ELF binary notes section (-n):

```
# readelf -n /.../jdk/lib/server/libjvm.so

Displaying notes found in: .note.gnu.build-id
  Owner                 Data size   Description
  GNU                   0x00000014  NT_GNU_BUILD_ID (unique build ID bitstring)
    Build ID: 264bc78da04c17524718c76066c6b535dcc380f2

Displaying notes found in: .note.stapsdt
  Owner                 Data size   Description
  stapsdt               0x00000050  NT_STAPSDT (SystemTap probe descriptors)
    Provider: hotspot
    Name: class__loaded
    Location: 0x00000000005d18a1, Base: 0x00000000010bdf68, Semaphore:
0x0000000000000000
    Arguments: 8@%rdx -4@%eax 8@152(%rdi) 1@%sil
  stapsdt               0x00000050  NT_STAPSDT (SystemTap probe descriptors)
    Provider: hotspot
    Name: class__unloaded
    Location: 0x00000000005d1cba, Base: 0x00000000010bdf68, Semaphore:
0x0000000000000000
    Arguments: 8@%rdx -4@%eax 8@152(%r12) 1@$0
[...]
```

Using Java USDT Probes

These probes can be used in both BCC and bpftrace. Their role and arguments are documented in the *Java Virtual Machine Guide* [138]. For example, using BCC trace(8) to instrument the gc-begin probe, and the first arguments which is a boolean to show whether this was a full garbage collection (1) or partial (0):

```
# trace -T -p $(pidof java) 'u:/.../libjvm.so:gc__begin "%d", arg1'
TIME      PID     TID    COMM        FUNC          -
09:30:34 11889   11900  VM Thread   gc__begin     0
09:30:34 11889   11900  VM Thread   gc__begin     0
09:30:34 11889   11900  VM Thread   gc__begin     0
09:30:38 11889   11900  VM Thread   gc__begin     1
```

This show partial GCs at 9:30:34 and a full GC at 9:30:38. Note that the JVM Guide documents this argument as args[0], however trace(8) numbers them beginning from 1, so it is arg1.

Here is an example with string arguments: the method__compile__begin probe has the compiler name, class name, and method name as the first, third, and fifth arguments. This shows the method name using trace(8):

```
# trace -p $(pidof java) 'u:/.../libjvm.so:method__compile__begin "%s", arg5'
PID     TID    COMM        FUNC          -
12600   12617  C1 CompilerThre method__compile__begin getLocationOnScreen
12600   12617  C1 CompilerThre method__compile__begin getAbsoluteX
12600   12617  C1 CompilerThre method__compile__begin getAbsoluteY
12600   12617  C1 CompilerThre method__compile__begin currentSegmentD
12600   12617  C1 CompilerThre method__compile__begin next
12600   12617  C1 CompilerThre method__compile__begin drawJoin
12600   12616  C2 CompilerThre method__compile__begin needsSyncData
12600   12617  C1 CompilerThre method__compile__begin getMouseInfoPeer
12600   12617  C1 CompilerThre method__compile__begin fillPointWithCoords
12600   12616  C2 CompilerThre method__compile__begin isHeldExclusively
12600   12617  C1 CompilerThre method__compile__begin updateChildGraphicsData
Traceback (most recent call last):
  File "_ctypes/callbacks.c", line 315, in 'calling callback function'
  File "/usr/local/lib/python2.7/dist-packages/bcc/table", line 572, in raw_cb_
    callback(cpu, data, size)
  File "/home/bgregg/Build/bcc/tools/trace", line 567, in print_event
    self._display_function(), msg))
UnicodeDecodeError: 'ascii' codec can't decode byte 0xff in position 10: ordinal not
in range(128)
12600   12616  C2 CompilerThre method__compile__begin getShowingSubPanel%
[...]
```

The first 11 lines show the method name as the last column, followed by a Python error about decoding a byte as ASCII. The problem is explained in the *Java Virtual Machine Guide* for these probes: the strings are not NULL terminated, and separate lengths are provided as additional arguments. To avoid errors like this, your BPF program needs to use the string length from the probe.

Switching to bpftrace, which can use the length argument in its str() built-in:

```
# bpftrace -p $(pgrep -n java) -e 'U:/.../libjvm.so:method__compile__begin
{ printf("compiling: %s\n", str(arg4, arg5)); }'
Attaching 1 probe...
compiling: getDisplayedMnemonicIndex
compiling: getMinimumSize
compiling: getBaseline
compiling: fillParallelogram
compiling: preConcatenate
compiling: last
compiling: nextTile
compiling: next
[...]
```

There are no more errors in the output, which is now printing the strings with their correct lengths. Any BCC or bpftrace program that uses these probes needs to use the length argument in this way.

As another example that leads to the next section, the following frequency counts all USDT probes beginning with "method":

```
# funccount -p $(pidof java) 'u:/.../libjvm.so:method*'
Tracing 4 functions for "u:/.../libjvm.so:method*"... Hit Ctrl-C to end.
^C
FUNC                              COUNT
method__compile__begin             2056
method__compile__end               2056
Detaching...
```

While tracing, the method_compile_begin and method_compile_end probes fired 2056 times. However, the method_entry and method_return probes were not traced. The reason is that they are part of the extended USDT probe set, covered next.

Extended Java USDT Probes

Some JVM USDT probes are not used by default: method entry and return, object-alloc, and Java monitor probes. This is because they are very high-frequency events, and their not-enabled overhead incurs a high performance penalty—likely exceeding 10%. This is just the overhead of making them available, and when they are not in use! When they are enabled and used, the overhead will slow down Java much more, possibly making Java run 10 times slower (10x) or more.

So that Java users do not pay a penalty for something they never use, these probes are not available unless Java is run with an option: -XX:+ExtendedDTraceProbes.

The following shows the Java game freecol with ExtendedDTraceProbes enabled, and frequency counting USDT probes beginning with "method" as before:

```
# funccount -p $(pidof java) 'u:/.../libjvm.so:method*'
Tracing 4 functions for "u:/.../libjvm.so:method*"... Hit Ctrl-C to end.
^C
FUNC                              COUNT
method__compile__begin              357
method__compile__end                357
method__return                 26762077
method__entry                  26762245
Detaching...
```

While tracing, there were 26 million calls to method__entry and method__return. The game also suffered extreme lag, taking around three seconds for any input to be processed. As a measure of before and after, the freecol start to splash screen time was 2 seconds by default, and 22 seconds when instrumenting these method probes: a slowdown of over 10x.

These high-frequency probes may be more useful for troubleshooting software issues in a lab environment than for the analysis of production workloads.

The sections that follow show different BPF tools for Java observability, now that I have covered the necessary background: libjvm, Java symbols, Java stack traces, and Java USDT probes.

12.3.7   profile

The BCC profile(8) tool was covered in Chapter 6. There are many profilers for Java. The advantage of BCC profile(8) is that it is efficient, frequency counting stacks in kernel context, and complete, showing user- and kernel-mode CPU consumers. Time spent in native libraries (e.g., libc), libjvm, Java methods, and the kernel can all be seen via profile(8).

Java Prerequisites

For profile(8) to see the full stack, Java must be running with -XX:+PreserveFramePointer, and a supplemental symbol file must be created using perf-map-agent, which profile(8) will make use of (see Section 12.3.4). To translate frames in libjvm.so, symbol tables are needed. These requirements were discussed in earlier sections.

CPU Flame Graph

This is an example of using profile(8) with Java to generate a mixed-mode CPU flame graph.

This Java program, freecol, is running with -XX:+PreserveFramePointer, and with an ELF symbol table for its libjvm functions. The jmaps utility, introduced earlier, is run immediately before the profile(8) tool to minimize symbol churn. This profiles at the default rate (99 Hertz), with kernel annotations on symbol names (-a), folded format for flame graphs (-f), for PID 16914 (-p) and for 10 seconds:

```
# jmaps; profile -afp 16914 10 > out.profile01.txt
Fetching maps for all java processes...
Mapping PID 16914 (user bgregg):
```

```
wc(1):     9078  28222  572219  /tmp/perf-16914.map
# wc out.profile01.txt
    215    3347 153742 out.profile01.txt
# cat out.profile01.txt
AWT-EventQueue-;start_thread;thread_native_entry(Thread*);Thread::call... 1
[...]
```

The wc(1) utility is used by jmaps to show the size of the symbol file, which is 9078 lines long, and therefore contains 9078 symbols. I've also used wc(1) to show the size of the profile file. The output of profile(8) in folded mode is one line per stack, semicolon-delimited frames, and a count for the number of times the stack was seen. wc(1) reported 215 lines in the profile output, so there were 215 unique stack traces collected.

This profile output can be converted into a flame graph using my open source FlameGraph software [37] and the command:

```
flamegraph.pl --color=java --hash < out.profile01.txt > out.profile02.svg
```

The --color=java option uses a palette that colors code types with different hues: java is green, C++ is yellow, user-level native is red, and kernel-level native is orange. The --hash option uses consistent coloring based on the function names rather than random saturation levels.

The resulting flame graph SVG file can be opened in a web browser. Figure 12-2 shows a screenshot.

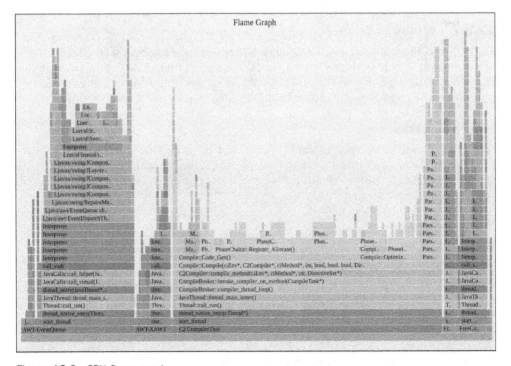

Figure 12-2   CPU flame graph

A mouse-over of each frame provides additional details, such as the percentage it was present in the profile. These showed that 55% of CPU time was in the C2 compiler, shown by the large wide tower (vertical column of rectangles) in the middle of C++ frames. Only 29% of time was spent in the Java freecol game, shown by the towers containing Java frames.

By clicking on the Java tower on the left, the Java frames can be zoomed in, as shown in Figure 12-3.

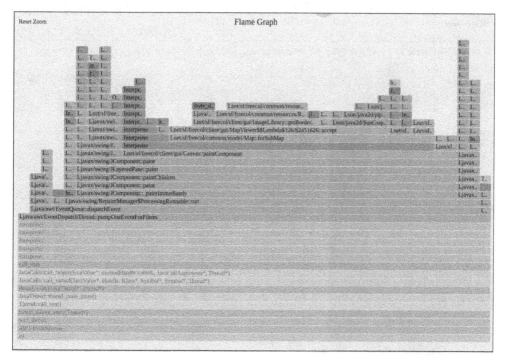

Figure 12-3 CPU flame graph zoomed

Now details of the Java freecol game and its methods can be read. Most of this time is in paint methods, and where exactly the CPU cycles were spent can be seen as the top edge in the flame graph.

If you were interested in improving the performance of freecol, this CPU flame graph has already provided two targets from an initial glance. You could look through the JVM tunables to see what options would cause the C2 compiler to consume less CPU time.[13] The paint methods can also be inspected in detail, with the freecol source, to look for more efficient techniques.

For long profiles (say, over two minutes), the time between the symbol table dump and when stack traces are collected can be so large that the C2 compiler has moved some methods in the meantime, so the symbol table is no longer accurate. This may be noticed by a code path that makes no sense at all, since some frames are mistranslated. A much more common issue with unexpected code paths is inlining.

---

13 Compiler tunables include -XX:CompileThreshold, -XX:MaxInlineSize, -XX:InlineSmallCode, and -XX:FreqInlineSize. Using -Xcomp to pre-compile methods may also be an illustrative experiment.

Inlining

Since this is visualizing the stack trace that is running on-CPU, it is showing Java methods after inlining. JVM inlining can be aggressive, inlining as much as two frames out of every three. This can make browsing the flame graph a little confusing, as methods appear to be directly calling other methods that they do not in the source code.

There is a solution to inlining: the perf-map-agent software supports dumping a symbol table that includes all inlined symbols. jmaps will use this capability with -u:

```
# jmaps -u; profile -afp 16914 10 > out.profile03.txt
Fetching maps for all java processes...
Mapping PID 16914 (user bgregg):
wc(1):     75467   227393 11443144 /tmp/perf-16914.map
```

The number of symbols has greatly increased, from the 9078 seen earlier to over 75,000. (I ran jmaps again, with -u, and it was still around 9000.)

Figure 12-4 shows a flame graph generated with the uninlined frame information.

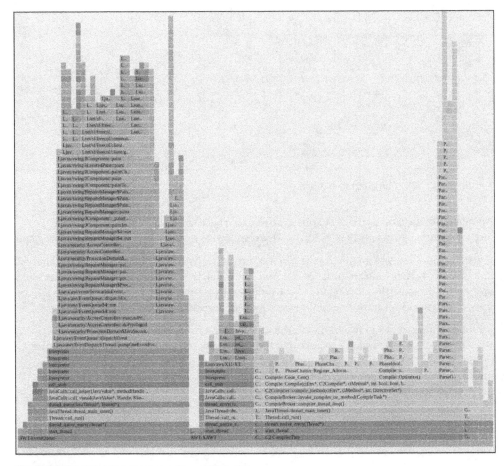

Figure 12-4   CPU flame graph with uninlining

The tower in the freecol stack is now much higher, as it includes uninlined frames (colored aqua).

Including inlined frames slows down the jmaps step as it must dump many more symbols, as well as the flame graph generation to parse and include them. In practice, this is sometimes necessary. Often, a flame graph without inlined frames is sufficient to solve issues because it still shows the overall code flow, while bearing in mind that some methods are not visible.

bpftrace

The profile(8) functionality can also be implemented in bpftrace, which has an advantage: the jmaps tool can be run in an END clause using the system() function. For example, the following one-liner was shown in an earlier section:

```
bpftrace --unsafe -e 'profile:hz:99 /pid == 4663/ { @[ustack] = count(); } END
{ system("jmaps"); }'
```

This samples user-level stack traces for PID 4663 at 99 Hertz across all CPUs that PID is running on. It can be adjusted to include the kernel stack and the process name by making the map `@[kstack, ustack, comm]`.

12.3.8 offcputime

The BCC offcputime(8) tool was covered in Chapter 6. It collects stacks on CPU blocking events (scheduler context switches), and sums the time spent blocked by stack trace. For offcputime(8) to work with Java, see Section 12.3.7.

For example, using offcputime(8) on the Java freecol game:

```
# jmaps; offcputime -p 16914 10
Fetching maps for all java processes...
Mapping PID 16914 (user bgregg):
wc(1):    9863   30589 623898 /tmp/perf-16914.map

Tracing off-CPU time (us) of PID 16914 by user + kernel stack for 10 secs.
^C

[...]

    finish_task_switch
    schedule
    futex_wait_queue_me
    futex_wait
    do_futex
    SyS_futex
    do_syscall_64
    entry_SYSCALL_64_after_hwframe
    __lll_lock_wait
```

```
SafepointSynchronize::block(JavaThread*, bool)
SafepointMechanism::block_if_requested_slow(JavaThread*)
JavaThread::check_safepoint_and_suspend_for_native_trans(JavaThread*)
JavaThread::check_special_condition_for_native_trans(JavaThread*)
Lsun/awt/X11/XlibWrapper;::XEventsQueued
Lsun/awt/X11/XToolkit;::run
Interpreter
Interpreter
call_stub
JavaCalls::call_helper(JavaValue*, methodHandle const&, JavaCallArguments*, Th...
JavaCalls::call_virtual(JavaValue*, Handle, Klass*, Symbol*, Symbol*, Thread*)
thread_entry(JavaThread*, Thread*)
JavaThread::thread_main_inner()
Thread::call_run()
thread_native_entry(Thread*)
start_thread
-               AWT-XAWT (16944)
    5171
```

[...]

```
finish_task_switch
schedule
io_schedule
bit_wait_io
__wait_on_bit
out_of_line_wait_on_bit
__wait_on_buffer
ext4_find_entry
ext4_unlink
vfs_unlink
do_unlinkat
sys_unlink
do_syscall_64
entry_SYSCALL_64_after_hwframe
__GI_unlink
Ljava/io/UnixFileSystem;::delete0
Ljava/io/File;::delete
Interpreter
Interpreter
Interpreter
Lnet/sf/freecol/client/control/InGameInputHandler;::handle
Interpreter
```

```
Lnet/sf/freecol/client/control/InGameInputHandler;::handle
Lnet/sf/freecol/common/networking/Connection;::handle
Interpreter
call_stub
JavaCalls::call_helper(JavaValue*, methodHandle const&, JavaCallArguments*, Th...
JavaCalls::call_virtual(JavaValue*, Handle, Klass*, Symbol*, Symbol*, Thread*)
thread_entry(JavaThread*, Thread*)
JavaThread::thread_main_inner()
Thread::call_run()
thread_native_entry(Thread*)
start_thread
-                     FreeColClient:b (8168)
    7679
```

[...]

```
finish_task_switch
schedule
futex_wait_queue_me
futex_wait
do_futex
SyS_futex
do_syscall_64
entry_SYSCALL_64_after_hwframe
pthread_cond_timedwait@@GLIBC_2.3.2
__pthread_cond_timedwait
os::PlatformEvent::park(long) [clone .part.12]
Monitor::IWait(Thread*, long)
Monitor::wait(bool, long, bool)
WatcherThread::sleep() const
WatcherThread::run()
thread_native_entry(Thread*)
start_thread
__clone
-                     VM Periodic Tas (22029)
    9970501
```

The output has been truncated as it was many pages long. A few interesting stacks have been included here to discuss.

The first shows Java blocking for 5.1 milliseconds (5717 us) in total on a safepoint, which was handled using a futex lock in the kernel. These times are totals, so this 5.1 ms may include multiple blocking events.

The last stack shows Java blocking in pthread_cond_timedwait() for almost the same 10-second duration of the trace: it is a WatcherThread waiting for work, with the thread name "VM Periodic Tas" (truncated to appear without the "k"). For some application types that use many threads that wait for work, the output of offcputime(8) can be dominated by these waiting stacks, and you need to read past them to find the stacks that matter: the wait events during application requests.

The second stack surprised me: it shows Java blocked on an unlink(2) syscall, to delete a file, which ended up blocking on disk I/O (io_schedule() etc). What files is freecol deleting during gameplay? A bpftrace one-liner to show unlink(2) with the pathname deleted reveals:

```
# bpftrace -e 't:syscalls:sys_enter_unlink /pid == 16914/ { printf("%s\n",
    str(args->pathname)); }'
Attaching 1 probe...
/home/bgregg/.local/share/freecol/save/autosave/Autosave-before
/home/bgregg/.local/share/freecol/save/autosave/Autosave-before
[...]
```

freecol is deleting auto savegames.

libpthread Stacks

Since this may be a commonly seen issue, here is how the final stack looked with a default install of libpthread:

```
    finish_task_switch
    schedule
    futex_wait_queue_me
    futex_wait
    do_futex
    SyS_futex
    do_syscall_64
    entry_SYSCALL_64_after_hwframe
    pthread_cond_timedwait
    -                VM Periodic Tas (16936)
        9934452
```

The stack ends at pthread_cond_timedwait(). The current default libpthread that is shipped with many Linux distributions has been compiled with -fomit-frame-pointer, a compiler optimization that breaks frame pointer–based stack walking. My earlier example used my own compiled version of libpthread with -fno-omit-frame-pointer. See Section 2.4 in Chapter 2 for more about this.

Off-CPU Time Flame Graphs

The output of offcputime(8) was hundreds of pages long. To navigate it more quickly, it can be used to generate off-CPU time flame graphs. Here is an example using the FlameGraph software [37]:

```
# jmaps; offcputime -fp 16914 10 > out.offcpu01.txt
Fetching maps for all java processes...
Mapping PID 16914 (user bgregg):
```

```
wc(1):    12015   37080 768710 /tmp/perf-16914.map
# flamegraph.pl --color=java --bgcolor=blue --hash --countname=us --width=800 \
    --title="Off-CPU Time Flame Graph" < out.offcpu01.txt > out.offcpu01.svg
```

This generated the graph shown in Figure 12-5.

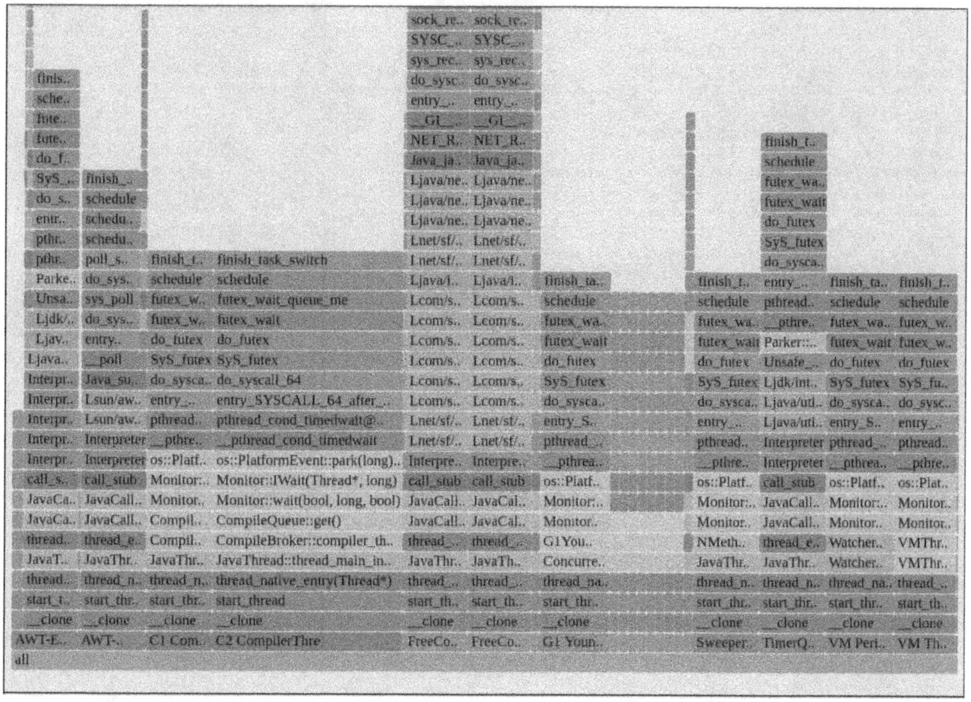

Figure 12-5   Off-CPU time flame graph

The top of this flame graph has been truncated. The width of each frame is relative to the
blocked off-CPU time. Since offcputime(8) is showing stack traces with their total blocking time
in microseconds, the `--countname=us` option to flamegraph.pl is used to match this, which
changes the information shown for mouse-overs. The background color was also changed to
blue, as a visual reminder that this is showing blocking stacks. (CPU flame graphs use a yellow
background.)

This flame graph is dominated by threads waiting for events. Since the thread name is included as
the first frame in the stack, it groups threads with the same name together as a tower. Each tower
in this flame graph shows waiting threads.

But I am not interested in threads waiting for events: I am interested in threads waiting during
an application request. This application was freecol, and using the flame graph search feature for
"freecol" highlighted those frames in magenta (see Figure 12-6).

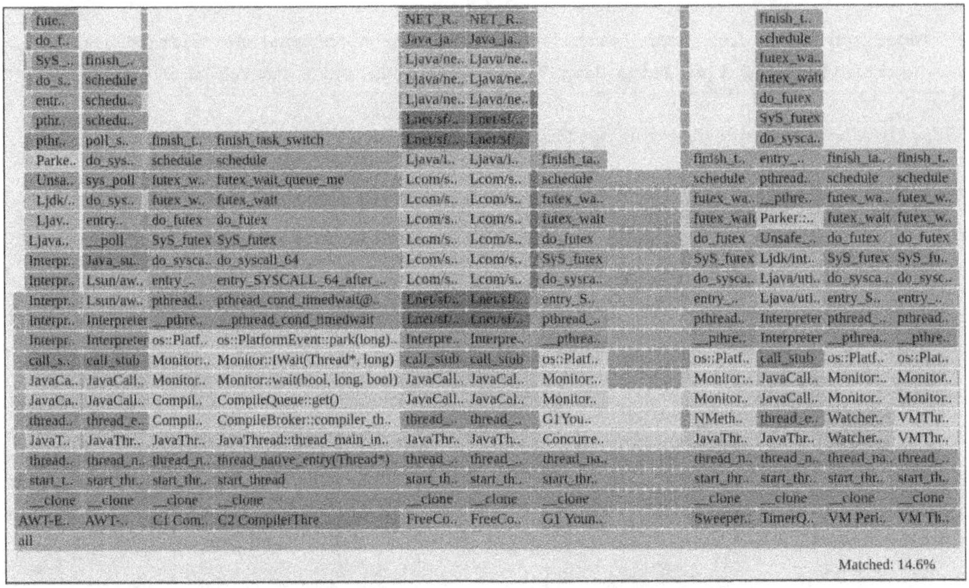

Figure 12-6   Off-CPU time flame graph, searching for application code

Using click-to-zoom on the narrow third tower showed code during the game (see Figure 12-7).

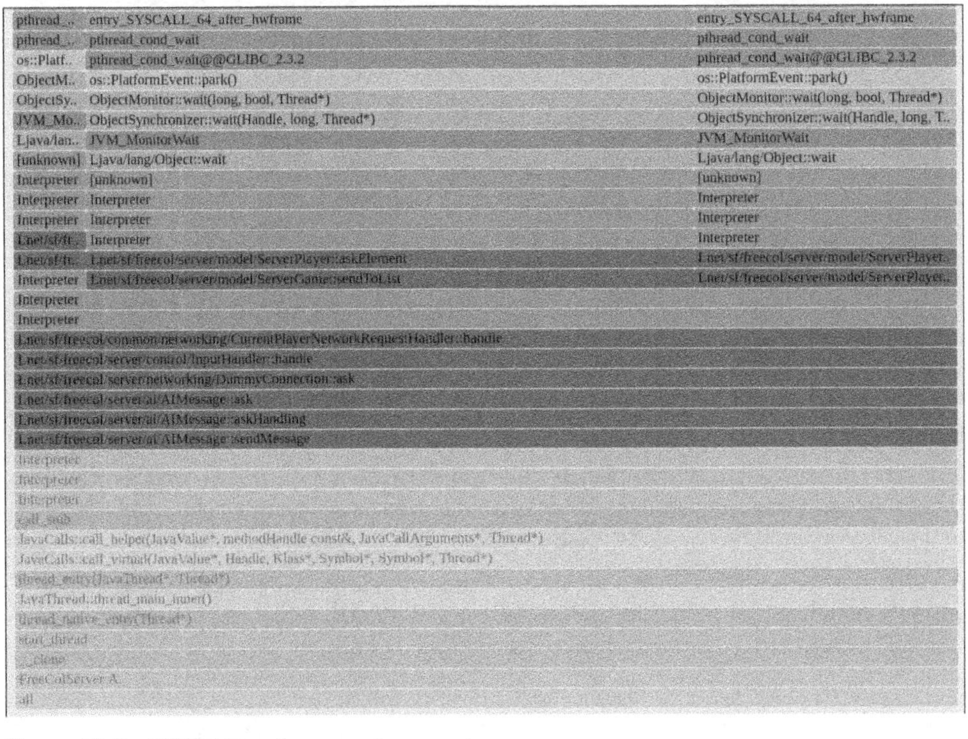

Figure 12-7   Off-CPU time flame graph zoomed

The graph shown in Figure 12-7 shows the blocking paths in freecol, providing targets to begin optimizing. Many of these frames were still "Interpreter", as the JVM had not executed that method enough times to hit the CompileThreshold.

Sometimes the application code paths can be so narrow due to other waiting threads that they are elided from the flame graph. One approach to solve this is to use grep(1) at the command line to include only the stacks of interest. For example, matching those containing the application name "freecol":

```
# grep freecol out.offcpu01.txt | flamegraph.pl ... > out.offcpu01.svg
```

It is one of the benefits of the folded-file format for stack traces: it can be easily manipulated as needed before generation as a flame graph.

12.3.9   stackcount

The BCC stackcount(8) tool, covered in Chapter 4, can collect stacks on any event, which can show the libjvm and Java method code paths that led to the event. For stackcount(8) to work with Java, see Section 12.3.7.

For example, using stackcount(8) to show user-level page faults, which is a measure of main memory growth:

```
# stackcount -p 16914 t:exceptions:page_fault_user
Tracing 1 functions for "t:exceptions:page_fault_user"... Hit Ctrl-C to end.
^C

[...]

  do_page_fault
  page_fault
  Interpreter
  Lnet/sf/freecol/server/control/ChangeSet$MoveChange;::consequences
  [unknown]
  [unknown]
  Lnet/sf/freecol/server/control/InGameController;::move
  Lnet/sf/freecol/common/networking/MoveMessage;::handle
  Lnet/sf/freecol/server/control/InGameInputHandler$37;::handle
  Lnet/sf/freecol/common/networking/CurrentPlayerNetworkRequestHandler;::handle
  [unknown]
  Lnet/sf/freecol/server/ai/AIMessage;::ask
  Lnet/sf/freecol/server/ai/AIMessage;::askHandling
  Lnet/sf/freecol/server/ai/AIUnit;::move
  Lnet/sf/freecol/server/ai/mission/Mission;::moveRandomly
  Lnet/sf/freecol/server/ai/mission/UnitWanderHostileMission;::doMission
  Ljava/awt/Container;::isParentOf
```

```
[unknown]
Lcom/sun/org/apache/xerces/internal/impl/XMLEntityScanner;::reset
call_stub
JavaCalls::call_helper(JavaValue*, methodHandle const&, JavaCallArguments*, Thre...
JavaCalls::call_virtual(JavaValue*, Handle, Klass*, Symbol*, Symbol*, Thread*)
thread_entry(JavaThread*, Thread*)
JavaThread::thread_main_inner()
Thread::call_run()
thread_native_entry(Thread*)
start_thread
  4


[...]


do_page_fault
page_fault
__memset_avx2_erms
PhaseChaitin::Register_Allocate()
Compile::Code_Gen()
Compile::Compile(ciEnv*, C2Compiler*, ciMethod*, int, bool, bool, bool, Directiv...
C2Compiler::compile_method(ciEnv*, ciMethod*, int, DirectiveSet*)
CompileBroker::invoke_compiler_on_method(CompileTask*)
CompileBroker::compiler_thread_loop()
JavaThread::thread_main_inner()
Thread::call_run()
thread_native_entry(Thread*)
start_thread
  414
```

Although many stacks were shown, only two have been included here. The first shows a page fault through freecol ai code; the second is from the JVM C2 compiler generating code.

Page Fault Flame Graph

A flame graph can be generated from the stack count output to aid browsing. For example, using the FlameGraph software [37]:

```
# jmaps; stackcount -p 16914 t:exceptions:page_fault_user > out.faults01.txt
Fetching maps for all java processes...
Mapping PID 16914 (user bgregg):
wc(1):  12015  37080 768710 /tmp/perf-16914.map
# stackcollapse.pl < out.faults01.txt | flamegraph.pl --width=800 \
    --color=java --bgcolor=green --title="Page Fault Flame Graph" \
    --countname=pages > out.faults01.svg
```

This generated the truncated graph shown in Figure 12-8.

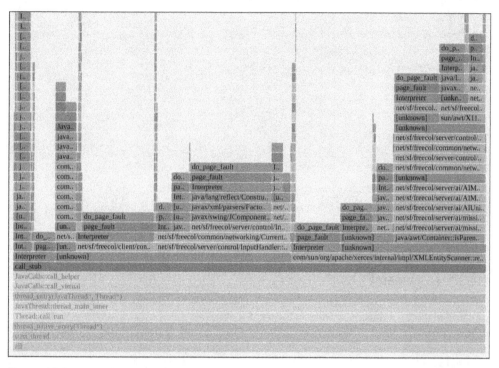

Figure 12-8 Page fault flame graph

A green background color was used as a visual reminder that this is a memory-related flame graph. In this screenshot I have zoomed to inspect the freecol code paths. This provides one view of memory growth by the application, and each path can be quantified (by its width) and studied from the flame graph.

bpftrace

The stackcount(8) functionality can be implemented as a bpftrace one-liner, for example:

```
# bpftrace --unsafe -e 't:exceptions:page_fault_user /pid == 16914/ {
    @[kstack, ustack, comm] = count(); } END { system("jmaps"); }'
Attaching 1 probe...
^C
[...]

@[
    do_page_fault+204
    page_fault+69
,
```

```
      0x7fa369bbef2d
      PhaseChaitin::Register_Allocate()+930
      Compile::Code_Gen()+650
      Compile::Compile(ciEnv*, C2Compiler*, ciMethod*, int, bool, bool, bool, Direct...
      C2Compiler::compile_method(ciEnv*, ciMethod*, int, DirectiveSet*)+188
      CompileBroker::invoke_compiler_on_method(CompileTask*)+1016
      CompileBroker::compiler_thread_loop()+1352
      JavaThread::thread_main_inner()+446
      Thread::call_run()+376
      thread_native_entry(Thread*)+238
      start_thread+219
, C2 CompilerThre]: 3


[...]
```

The execution of the jmaps for Java method symbols has been moved to the END clause, so it is run immediately before the stacks are printed out.

12.3.10   javastat

javastat(8)[14] is a BCC tool that provides high-level Java and JVM statistics. It refreshes the screen similarly to top(1), unless the -C option is used. For example, running javastat(8) for the Java freecol game:

```
# javastat -C
Tracing... Output every 1 secs. Hit Ctrl-C to end

14:16:56 loadavg: 0.57 3.66 3.93 2/3152 32738

PID     CMDLINE              METHOD/s   GC/s   OBJNEW/s   CLOAD/s   EXC/s   THR/s
32447   /home/bgregg/Build/o 0          0      0          0         169     0

14:16:58 loadavg: 0.57 3.66 3.93 8/3157 32744

PID     CMDLINE              METHOD/s   GC/s   OBJNEW/s   CLOAD/s   EXC/s   THR/s
32447   /home/bgregg/Build/o 0          1      0          730       522     6

14:16:59 loadavg: 0.69 3.64 3.92 2/3155 32747

PID     CMDLINE              METHOD/s   GC/s   OBJNEW/s   CLOAD/s   EXC/s   THR/s
32447   /home/bgregg/Build/o 0          2      0          8         484     1
[...]
```

---

14 Origin: This was created by Sasha Goldshtein as a wrapper to his ustat(8) tool from 26-Oct-2016. I created a similar tool for DTrace called j_stat.d on 9-Sep-2007 to demonstrate these new probes in the DTraceToolkit.

The columns show:

- **PID:** Process ID.

- **CMDLINE:** Process command line. This example has truncated the path to my custom JDK build.

- **METHOD/s:** Method calls per second.

- **GC/s:** Garbage collection events per second.

- **OBJNEW/s:** New objects per second.

- **CLOAD/s:** Class loads per second.

- **EXC/s:** Exceptions per second.

- **THR/s:** Threads created per second.

This works by using Java USDT probes. The METHOD/s and OBJNEW/s columns will be zero unless the -XX:+ExtendedDTraceProbes option is used, which activates those probes, however, with a high overhead cost. As described earlier, an application may run 10 times slower with these probes enabled and instrumented.

Command line usage:

```
javastat [options] [interval [count]]
```

Options include:

- **-C:** Don't clear the screen

javastat(8) is really a wrapper to a ustat(8) tool in BCC's tools/lib directory, which handles multiple languages.

12.3.11 javathreads

javathreads(8)[15] is a bpftrace tool to show thread start and stop events. Example output for when freecol was started:

```
# javathreads.bt
Attaching 3 probes...
TIME                 PID/TID   -- THREAD
14:15:00    3892/3904  => Reference Handler
14:15:00    3892/3905  => Finalizer
14:15:00    3892/3906  => Signal Dispatcher
14:15:00    3892/3907  => C2 CompilerThread0
14:15:00    3892/3908  => C1 CompilerThread0
14:15:00    3892/3909  => Sweeper thread
14:15:00    3892/3910  => Common-Cleaner
```

15 Origin: I created this for this book on 19-Feb-2019.

```
14:15:01   3892/3911   => C2 CompilerThread1
14:15:01   3892/3912   => Service Thread
14:15:01   3892/3911   <= C2 CompilerThread1
14:15:01   3892/3917   => Java2D Disposer
14:15:01   3892/3918   => AWT-XAWT
14:15:02   3892/3925   => AWT-Shutdown
14:15:02   3892/3926   => AWT-EventQueue-0
14:15:02   3892/3934   => C2 CompilerThread1
14:15:02   3892/3935   => FreeColClient:-Resource loader
14:15:02   3892/3937   => FreeColClient:Worker
14:15:02   3892/3935   <= FreeColClient:-Resource loader
14:15:02   3892/3938   => FreeColClient:-Resource loader
14:15:02   3892/3939   => Image Fetcher 0
14:15:03   3892/3952   => FreeColClient:-Resource loader
[...]
```

This shows the creation and execution of threads and also some that were short-lived and finished during tracing ("<=").

This tool uses the Java USDT probes. Since the rate of thread creation is low, the overhead of this tool should be negligible. Source code:

```
#!/usr/local/bin/bpftrace

BEGIN
{
        printf("%-20s  %6s/%-5s -- %s\n", "TIME", "PID", "TID", "THREAD");
}

usdt:/.../libjvm.so:hotspot:thread__start
{
        time("%H:%M:%S ");
        printf("%6d/%-5d => %s\n", pid, tid, str(arg0, arg1));
}

usdt:/.../libjvm.so:hotspot:thread__stop
{
        time("%H:%M:%S ");
        printf("%6d/%-5d <= %s\n", pid, tid, str(arg0, arg1));
}
```

The path to the library has been truncated in this source ("...") but needs to be replaced with your libjvm.so library path. In the future bpftrace should also support specifying the library name without the path, so that this can simply be written as "libjvm.so".

12.3.12 javacalls

javacalls(8)[16] is a BCC and bpftrace tool that counts Java method calls. For example:

```
# javacalls 16914
Tracing calls in process 16914 (language: java)... Ctrl-C to quit.
If you do not see any results, make sure you ran java with option -XX:
+ExtendedDTraceProbes
^C
METHOD                                                  # CALLS
net/sf/freecol/client/control/InGameInputHandler$$Lambda$443.get$Lambda        1
sun/awt/X11/XWindowPeer.getLocalHostname                 1
net/sf/freecol/common/model/UnitType.getSpace           1
[...]
java/awt/image/Raster.getHeight                     129668
java/lang/Math.min                                  177085
jdk/internal/misc/Unsafe.getByte                    201047
java/lang/AbstractStringBuilder.putStringAt         252367
java/lang/AbstractStringBuilder.getCoder            252367
java/lang/String.getBytes                           253184
java/lang/AbstractStringBuilder.append              258491
java/lang/Object.<init>                             258601
java/lang/AbstractStringBuilder.ensureCapacityInternal   258611
java/lang/String.isLatin1                           265540
java/lang/StringBuilder.append                      286637
jdk/internal/misc/Unsafe.putInt                     361628
java/lang/System.arraycopy                          399118
java/lang/String.length                             427242
jdk/internal/misc/Unsafe.getInt                     700137
java/lang/String.coder                             1268791
```

The most frequent method while tracing was java/lang/String.code(), which was called 1,268,791 times.

This works by using Java USDT probes with -XX:+ExtendedDTraceProbes, which comes with a high performance cost. As described earlier, an application may run 10 times slower with this enabled and instrumented.

BCC

Command line usage:

```
javacalls [options] pid [interval]
```

---

16 Origin: this was created by Sasha Goldshtein as a wrapper to his ucalls(8) tool from 19-Oct-2016, and I wrote the bpftrace version for this book on 11-Mar-2019. I created a similar tool for DTrace called j_calls.d on 9-Sep-2007.

Options include:

- **-L**: Show method latency instead of call counts
- **-m**: Report method latency as milliseconds

javacalls(8) is really a wrapper to a ucalls(8) tool in BCC's tools/lib directory, which handles multiple languages.

bpftrace

Here is the source for the bpftrace version:

```
#!/usr/local/bin/bpftrace

BEGIN
{
        printf("Tracing Java method calls. Ctrl-C to end.\n");
}

usdt:/.../libjvm.so:hotspot:method__entry
{
        @[str(arg1, arg2), str(arg3, arg4)] = count();
}
```

The key to the map is two strings: the class and then the method name. As with the BCC version, this tool will only work with -XX:+ExtendedDTraceProbes, and an expected high performance cost. Also note that the full path to libjvm.so has been truncated, and will need to be replaced by your libjvm.so path.

12.3.13 javaflow

javaflow(8)[17] is a BCC tool that shows the flow of Java method calls. For example:

```
# javaflow 16914
Tracing method calls in java process 16914... Ctrl-C to quit.
CPU PID   TID  TIME(us) METHOD
5   622   652  0.135      -> sun/awt/SunToolkit-.awtUnlock
5   622   652  0.135        -> java/util/concurrent/locks/ReentrantLock.unlock
5   622   652  0.135          -> java/util/concurrent/locks/AbstractQueuedSynchronize...
5   622   652  0.135            -> java/util/concurrent/locks/ReentrantLock$Sync.tryR...
```

---

17 Origin: This was created by Sasha Goldshtein as a wrapper to his uflow(8) tool from 27-Oct-2016. I created a similar tool for DTrace called j_flowtime.d on 9-Sep-2007.

```
5   622   652   0.135                  -> java/util/concurrent/locks/AbstractQueuedSynchro...
5   622   652   0.135                  <- java/util/concurrent/locks/AbstractQueuedSynchro...
5   622   652   0.135                  -> java/lang/Thread.currentThread
5   622   652   0.135                  <- java/lang/Thread.currentThread
5   622   652   0.135                   -> java/util/concurrent/locks/AbstractOwnableSynchr...
5   622   652   0.135                   <- java/util/concurrent/locks/AbstractOwnableSynchr...
5   622   652   0.135                   -> java/util/concurrent/locks/AbstractQueuedSynchro...
5   622   652   0.135                   <- java/util/concurrent/locks/AbstractQueuedSynchro...
5   622   652   0.135            <- java/util/concurrent/locks/ReentrantLock$Sync.tryR...
5   622   652   0.135          <- java/util/concurrent/locks/AbstractQueuedSynchronize...
5   622   652   0.135        <- java/util/concurrent/locks/ReentrantLock.unlock
5   622   652   0.135      <- sun/awt/SunToolkit-.awtUnlock
5   622   652   0.135    <- sun/awt/X11/XToolkit.getNextTaskTime
5   622   652   0.135    -> sun/awt/X11/XToolkit.waitForEvents
5   622   652   0.135     -> sun/awt/SunToolkit-.awtUnlock
[...]
1   622   654   4.159                             <- sun/java2d/SunGraphics2D.drawI...
Possibly lost 9 samples
1   622   654   4.159                             <- net/sf/freecol/common/model/Ti...
Possibly lost 9 samples
1   622   654   4.159                                <- java/util/AbstractList.<init>
[...]
```

This shows the code flow: which method calls which other method and so on. Each child method call increases the indentation in the METHOD column.

This works by using Java USDT probes with `-XX:+ExtendedDTraceProbes`, which comes with a high performance cost. As described earlier, an application may run 10 times slower with this enabled and instrumented. This example also shows "Possibly lost 9 samples" messages: BPF tooling cannot keep up with the events, and as a safety valve is letting events be missed rather than blocking the application, while informing the user that this happened.

Command line usage:

`javaflow [options] pid`

Options include:

- **-M METHOD**: Only trace calls to methods with this prefix

javaflow(8) is really a wrapper to a uflow(8) tool in BCC's tools/lib directory, which handles multiple languages.

12.3.14   javagc

javagc(8)[18] is a BCC tool that shows JVM garbage collection events. For example:

```
# javagc 16914
Tracing garbage collections in java process 16914... Ctrl-C to quit.
START    TIME(us) DESCRIPTION
5.586    1330.00  None
5.586    1339.00  None
5.586    1340.00  None
5.586    1342.00  None
5.586    1344.00  None
[...]
```

This shows when the GC event occurred as an offset from when javagc(8) began running (the START column, which is in seconds), and then the duration of the GC event (TIME column, in microseconds).

This works by using the standard Java USDT probes.

Command line usage:

```
javagc [options] pid
```

Options include:

- **-m:** Report times in milliseconds

javagc(8) is really a wrapper to a ugc(8) tool in BCC's tools/lib directory, which handles multiple languages.

12.3.15   javaobjnew

javaobjnew(8)[19] is a BCC tool that counts Java object allocations. For example, running it with -C 10 to show the top 10 allocations by count:

```
# javaobjnew 25102
Tracing allocations in process 25102 (language: java)... Ctrl-C to quit.
^C
NAME/TYPE                      # ALLOCS      # BYTES
java/util/ArrayList             429837            0
[Ljava/lang/Object;             434980            0
java/util/ArrayList$Itr         458430            0
java/util/HashMap$KeySet        545194            0
```

---

18 Origin: This was created by Sasha Goldshtein as a wrapper to his ugc(8) tool from 19-Oct-2016.

19 Origin: This was created by Sasha Goldshtein as a wrapper to his uobjnew(8) tool from 25-Oct-2016. I created a similar tool for DTrace called j_objnew.d on 9-Sep-2007.

[B	550624	0	
java/util/HashMap$Node	572089	0	
net/sf/freecol/common/model/Map$Position	663721		0
java/util/HashSet	696829	0	
java/util/HashMap	714633	0	
java/util/HashMap$KeyIterator	904244	0	

The most frequent new object while tracing was java/util/HashMap$KeyIterator, which was created 904,244 times. The BYTES column is zero as it is not supported for this language type.

This works by using Java USDT probes with `-XX:+ExtendedDTraceProbes`, which comes with a high performance cost. As described earlier, an application may run 10 times slower with this enabled and instrumented.

Command line usage:

```
javaobjnew [options] pid [interval]
```

Options include:

- **-C** **TOP_COUNT**: Show this many objects by count
- **-S** **TOP_SIZE**: Show this many objects by size

javaobjnew(8) is really a wrapper to a uobjnew(8) tool in BCC's tools/lib directory, which handles multiple languages (some of which do support the BYTES column).

12.3.16 Java One-Liners

These sections show BCC and bpftrace one-liners. Where possible, the same one-liner is implemented using both BCC and bpftrace.

BCC

Count JNI events beginning with "jni_Call":

```
funccount '/.../libjvm.so:jni_Call*'
```

Count Java method events:

```
funccount -p $(pidof java) 'u:/.../libjvm.so:method*'
```

Profile Java stack traces and thread names at 49 Hertz:

```
profile -p $(pidof java) -UF 49
```

bpftrace

Count JNI events beginning with "jni_Call":

```
bpftrace -e 'u:/.../libjvm.so:jni_Call* { @[probe] = count(); }'
```

Count Java method events:

```
bpftrace -e 'usdt:/.../libjvm.so:method* { @[probe] = count(); }'
```

Profile Java stack traces and thread names at 49 Hertz:

```
bpftrace -e 'profile:hz:49 /execname == "java"/ { @[ustack, comm] = count(); }'
```

Trace method compilation:

```
bpftrace -p $(pgrep -n java) -e 'U:/.../libjvm.so:method__compile__begin {
    printf("compiling: %s\n", str(arg4, arg5)); }'
```

Trace class loads:

```
bpftrace -p $(pgrep -n java) -e 'U:/.../libjvm.so:class__loaded {
    printf("loaded: %s\n", str(arg0, arg1)); }'
```

Count object allocation (needs ExtendedDTraceProbes):

```
bpftrace -p $(pgrep -n java) -e 'U:/.../libjvm.so:object__alloc {
    @[str(arg1, arg2)] = count(); }'
```

12.4   Bash Shell

The final language example is an interpreted language: the bash shell. Interpreted languages are typically much slower than compiled languages, due to the way they run their own functions to execute each step of the target program. This makes them an uncommon target for performance analysis, since other languages are usually chosen for performance sensitive workloads. BPF tracing may be performed, but the need may be for troubleshooting program errors, rather than finding performance wins.

How interpreted languages are traced is different for each language, reflecting the internals of the software that runs them. This section will show how I approach an unknown interpreted language and determine out how to trace it for the first time: an approach that you can follow for other languages.

The bash readline() function was traced earlier in this chapter, but I have not traced bash in depth beyond that. For this chapter I will determine out how to trace bash function and built-in calls, and develop some tools to automate this. See Table 12-4.

Table 12-4   **Bash Shell–Related Tools**

Tool	Source	Target	Description
bashfunc	Book	bash	Trace bash function calls
bashfunclat	Book	bash	Trace bash function call latency

As mentioned earlier, how bash is built affects the location of symbols. Here is bash on Ubuntu, showing its dynamic library usage with the ldd(1) tool:

```
$ ldd /bin/bash
        linux-vdso.so.1 (0x00007ffe7197b000)
        libtinfo.so.5 => /lib/x86_64-linux-gnu/libtinfo.so.5 (0x00007f08aeb86000)
        libdl.so.2 => /lib/x86_64-linux-gnu/libdl.so.2 (0x00007f08ae982000)
        libc.so.6 => /lib/x86_64-linux-gnu/libc.so.6 (0x00007f08ae591000)
        /lib64/ld-linux-x86-64.so.2 (0x00007f08af0ca000)
```

The targets to trace are /bin/bash and the shared libraries listed above. As an example of how this can cause differences: on many distributions, bash uses a readline() function from /bin/bash, but some distributions link to libreadline and call it from there.

Preparation

In preparation, I have built the bash software with these steps:

```
CFLAGS=-fno-omit-frame-pointer ./configure
make
```

This honors the frame pointer register so that I can use frame pointer–based stack walking during my analysis. It also provides a bash binary with local symbol tables, unlike /bin/bash which has been stripped.

Sample Program

The following is a sample bash program I wrote for analysis, welcome.sh:

```
#!/home/bgregg/Build/bash-4.4.18/bash

function welcome {
        echo "Hello, World!"
        echo "Hello, World!"
        echo "Hello, World!"
}

welcome
welcome
welcome
welcome
welcome
welcome
welcome
sleep 60
```

This begins with the path to my bash build. The program makes seven calls to the "welcome" function, where each function call makes three calls to echo(1) (which I expect is a bash built-in) for a total of 21 echo(1) calls. I choose these numbers hoping they stand out more from other activity while tracing.[20]

12.4.1 Function Counts

Using funccount(8) from BCC, I will guess that the function call is executed by an internal bash function containing the string "func":

```
# funccount 'p:/home/bgregg/Build/bash-4.4.18/bash:*func*'
Tracing 55 functions for "p:/home/bgregg/Build/bash-4.4.18/bash:*func*"... Hit Ctrl-C
to end.
^C
FUNC                                      COUNT
copy_function_def                           1
sv_funcnest                                 1
dispose_function_def                        1
bind_function                               1
make_function_def                           1
execute_intern_function                     1
init_funcname_var                           1
bind_function_def                           2
dispose_function_def_contents               2
map_over_funcs                              2
copy_function_def_contents                  2
make_func_export_array                      2
restore_funcarray_state                     7
execute_function                            7
find_function_def                           9
make_funcname_visible                      14
execute_builtin_or_function                28
get_funcname                               29
find_function                              31
Detaching...
```

While tracing, I ran the welcome.sh program, which calls the welcome function seven times. It looks like my guess was good: there were seven calls to restore_funcarray_state() and execute_function(), and the latter sounds most promising, just based on its name.

The name execute_function() gives me an idea: what other calls begin with "execute_"? Checking using funccount(8):

---

20 It would make this example too long, but I often use 23, a prime number.

```
# funccount 'p:/home/bgregg/Build/bash-4.4.18/bash:execute_*'
Tracing 29 functions for "p:/home/bgregg/Build/bash-4.4.18/bash:execute_*"... Hit
Ctrl-C to end.
^C
FUNC                             COUNT
execute_env_file                     1
execute_intern_function              1
execute_disk_command                 1
execute_function                     7
execute_connection                  14
execute_builtin                     21
execute_command                     23
execute_builtin_or_function         28
execute_simple_command              29
execute_command_internal            51
Detaching...
```

Some more numbers stand out: this has execute_builtin() 21 times, which equals the calls to echo(1). If I want to trace echo(1) and other built-ins, I can start by tracing execute_builtin(). There was also execute_command() called 23 times, which may be the echo(1) calls plus the function declaration plus the sleep(1) call. It sounds like another promising function to trace for understanding bash.

12.4.2   Function Argument Tracing (bashfunc.bt)

Now to trace execute_function() call. I want to know which function, hoping it will show that it is executing the "welcome" function. Hopefully this can be found from one of the arguments. The bash source has (execute_cmd.c):

```
static int
execute_function (var, words, flags, fds_to_close, async, subshell)
     SHELL_VAR *var;
     WORD_LIST *words;
     int flags;
     struct fd_bitmap *fds_to_close;
     int async, subshell;
{
  int return_val, result;
[...]
  if (subshell == 0)
    {
      begin_unwind_frame ("function_calling");
      push_context (var->name, subshell, temporary_env);
[...]
```

Browsing this source suggests that var, the first argument, is the executed function. It is of type SHELL_VAR, which is struct variable, from variables.h:

```
typedef struct variable {
  char *name;                   /* Symbol that the user types. */
  char *value;                  /* Value that is returned. */
  char *exportstr;              /* String for the environment. */
  sh_var_value_func_t *dynamic_value;   /* Function called to return a 'dynamic'
                                  value for a variable, like $SECONDS
                                  or $RANDOM. */
  sh_var_assign_func_t *assign_func; /* Function called when this 'special
                                  variable' is assigned a value in
                                  bind_variable. */
  int attributes;               /* export, readonly, array, invisible... */
  int context;                  /* Which context this variable belongs to. */
} SHELL_VAR;
```

char *'s are straightforward to trace. Let's look at the name member using bpftrace. I can either #include this header or declare the struct directly in bpftrace. I'll show both, starting with the header include. Here is bashfunc.bt[21]:

```
#!/usr/local/bin/bpftrace

#include "/home/bgregg/Build/bash-4.4.18/variables.h"

uprobe:/home/bgregg/Build/bash-4.4.18/bash:execute_function
{
        $var = (struct variable *)arg0;
        printf("function: %s\n", str($var->name));
}
```

Running this:

```
# ./bashfunc.bt
/home/bgregg/Build/bash-4.4.18/variables.h:24:10: fatal error: 'stdc.h' file not found
Attaching 1 probe...
function: welcome
function: welcome
function: welcome
function: welcome
```

---

21 Origin: I created this for this book on 9-Feb-2019.

```
function: welcome
function: welcome
function: welcome
^C
```

It worked! I can now trace bash function calls.

It also printed a warning about another missing header file. I'll show the second approach, where the struct is declared directly. In fact, since I only need the first member, I'll only declare that member and call it a "partial" struct.

```
#!/usr/local/bin/bpftrace

struct variable_partial {
        char *name;
};

uprobe:/home/bgregg/Build/bash-4.4.18/bash:execute_function
{
        $var = (struct variable_partial *)arg0;
        printf("function: %s\n", str($var->name));
}
```

Using this version of bashfunc.bt:

```
# ./bashfunc.bt
Attaching 1 probe...
function: welcome
function: welcome
function: welcome
function: welcome
function: welcome
function: welcome
function: welcome
^C
```

This works, without the error or the requirement for the bash source.

Note that uprobes are an unstable interface, so this program may stop working if bash changes its function names and arguments.

12.4.3   Function Latency (bashfunclat.bt)

Now that I can trace function calls, let's look at function latency: the duration of the function.

To start with, I modified welcome.sh so that the function was:

```
function welcome {
        echo "Hello, World!"
        sleep 0.3
}
```

This provides a known latency for the function call: 0.3 seconds.

Now I'll check whether execute_function() waits for the shell function to complete by measuring its latency using funclatency(8) from BCC:

```
# funclatency -m /home/bgregg/Build/bash-4.4.18/bash:execute_function
Tracing 1 functions for "/home/bgregg/Build/bash-4.4.18/bash:execute_function"... Hit
Ctrl-C to end.
^C

Function = execute_function [7083]
     msecs               : count     distribution
        0 -> 1           : 0         |                                        |
        2 -> 3           : 0         |                                        |
        4 -> 7           : 0         |                                        |
        8 -> 15          : 0         |                                        |
       16 -> 31          : 0         |                                        |
       32 -> 63          : 0         |                                        |
       64 -> 127         : 0         |                                        |
      128 -> 255         : 0         |                                        |
      256 -> 511         : 7         |****************************************|
Detaching...
```

Its latency was in the 256 to 511 millisecond bucket, which matches our known latency. It looks like I can simply time this function for the latency of the shell function.

Turning this into a tool so that shell function latency can be printed as a histogram by shell function name, bashfunclat.bt[22]:

```
#!/usr/local/bin/bpftrace

struct variable_partial {
        char *name;
};
```

```
BEGIN
{
        printf("Tracing bash function latency, Ctrl-C to end.\n");
}


uprobe:/home/bgregg/Build/bash-4.4.18/bash:execute_function
{
        $var = (struct variable_partial *)arg0;
        @name[tid] = $var->name;
        @start[tid] = nsecs;
}


uretprobe:/home/bgregg/Build/bash-4.4.18/bash:execute_function
/@start[tid]/
{
        @ms[str(@name[tid])] = hist((nsecs - @start[tid]) / 1000000);
        delete(@name[tid]);
        delete(@start[tid]);
}
```

This saves a pointer to a function name, and the timestamp, on the uprobe. On the uretprobe, it fetches the name and starting timestamp for creating the histogram.

Output:

```
# ./bashfunclat.bt
Attaching 3 probes...
Tracing bash function latency, Ctrl-C to end.
^C

@ms[welcome]:
[256, 512)              7 |@@@@@@@@@@@@@@@@@@@@@@@@@@@@@@@@@@@@@@@@@@@@@@@@@@@@|
```

This works. This latency could be presented in different ways if desired: per event or as a linear histogram.

12.4.4   /bin/bash

Up until now, tracing bash has been so straightforward that I started worrying it wasn't represen-tative of the gritty debugging adventures one normally encounters when tracing interpreters. But I needed to look no further than the default /bin/bash to share such an adventure. These earlier tools have instrumented my own build of bash, which includes the local symbol table and the frame pointer. I modified them and the welcome.sh program to use /bin/bash instead, and found that the BPF tools I wrote no longer worked.

Back to square one. Here's counting function calls containing "func" in /bin/bash:

```
# funccount 'p:/bin/bash:*func*'
Tracing 36 functions for "p:/bin/bash:*func*"... Hit Ctrl-C to end.
^C
FUNC                                COUNT
copy_function_def                       1
sv_funcnest                             1
dispose_function_def                    1
bind_function                           1
make_function_def                       1
bind_function_def                       2
dispose_function_def_contents           2
map_over_funcs                          2
copy_function_def_contents              2
restore_funcarray_state                 7
find_function_def                       9
make_funcname_visible                  14
find_function                          32
Detaching...
```

The execute_function() symbol is no longer available. Here's readelf(1) and file(1) highlighting our problem:

```
$ readelf --syms --dyn-syms /home/bgregg/Build/bash-4.4.18/bash
[...]
  2324: 000000000004cc49   195 FUNC    GLOBAL DEFAULT   14 restore_funcarray_state
[...]
   298: 000000000004cd0c  2326 FUNC    LOCAL  DEFAULT   14 execute_function
[...]
$ file /bin/bash /home/bgregg/Build/bash-4.4.18/bash
/bin/bash:                          ELF 64-bit LSB ..., stripped
/home/bgregg/Build/bash-4.4.18/bash: ELF 64-bit LSB ..., not stripped
```

execute_function() is a local symbol, and those have been stripped from /bin/bash to reduce the file size.

Fortunately, I still have a lead: the funccount(8) output showed that restore_funcarray_state() was called seven times, equal to our known workload. To check if it is related to function calls, I'll use stackcount(8) from BCC to show its stack trace:

```
# stackcount -P /bin/bash:restore_funcarray_state
Tracing 1 functions for "/bin/bash:restore_funcarray_state"... Hit Ctrl-C to end.
^C
  [unknown]
  [unknown]
    welcome0.sh [8514]
    7

Detaching...
```

The stack is broken: I wanted to include this to show what /bin/bash stacks look like by default. It's one of the reasons I compiled my own bash with frame pointers. Switching to that to investigate this function:

```
# stackcount -P /home/bgregg/Build/bash-4.4.18/bash:restore_funcarray_state
Tracing 1 functions for
"/home/bgregg/Build/bash-4.4.18/bash:restore_funcarray_state"... Hit Ctrl-C to end.
^C
  restore_funcarray_state
  without_interrupts
  run_unwind_frame
  execute_function
  execute_builtin_or_function
  execute_simple_command
  execute_command_internal
  execute_command
  reader_loop
  main
  __libc_start_main
  [unknown]
    welcome.sh [8542]
    7

Detaching...
```

This shows that restore_funcarray_state() is called as a child of execute_function(), so it is indeed related to the shell function calls.

The function is in execute_cmd.c:

```
void
restore_funcarray_state (fa)
     struct func_array_state *fa;
{
```

The struct func_array_state is, from execute_cmd.h:

```
struct func_array_state
  {
    ARRAY *funcname_a;
    SHELL_VAR *funcname_v;
    ARRAY *source_a;
    SHELL_VAR *source_v;
    ARRAY *lineno_a;
    SHELL_VAR *lineno_v;
  };
```

This seems to be used for creating local contexts while running functions. I guessed that funcname_a or funcname_v might contain what I am after: the name of the called function, so I declared structs and printed strings in a similar fashion to my earlier bashfunc.bt to find it. But I was unable to find the function name.

There are many paths forward, and given that I am using an unstable interface (uprobes), there isn't necessarily a right way to do this (the right way is USDT). Example next steps:

- funccount(8) also showed a few other interesting sounding functions: find_function(), make_funcname_visible(), and find_function_def(), all called more times than our known function. Perhaps the function name is in their arguments or return value, and I can cache it for later lookup in restore_funcarray_state().

- stackcount(8) showed higher level functions: Are any of these symbols still present in /bin/bash, and may they provide another path to tracing the function?

Here's a look at that second approach, by checking what "execute" functions are visible in /bin/bash:

```
# funccount '/bin/bash:execute_*'
Tracing 4 functions for "/bin/bash:execute_*"... Hit Ctrl-C to end.
^C
FUNC                            COUNT
execute_command                    24
execute_command_internal           52
Detaching...
```

The source code shows that execute_command() runs many things, including functions, and they can be identified by a type number from the first argument. This would be one path forward: filter for just function calls, and explore the other arguments to find the function name.

I found the first approach worked immediately: find_function() has the name as its argument, which I could cache for later lookup. An updated bashfunc.bt:

```
#!/usr/local/bin/bpftrace

uprobe:/bin/bash:find_function_def
{
        @currfunc[tid] = arg0;
}

uprobe:/bin/bash:restore_funcarray_state
{
        printf("function: %s\n", str(@currfunc[tid]));
        delete(@currfunc[tid]);
}
```

Output:

```
# bashfunc.bt
Attaching 2 probes...
function: welcome
function: welcome
function: welcome
function: welcome
function: welcome
function: welcome
function: welcome
```

While this works, this is tied to this version of bash and its implementation.

12.4.5   /bin/bash USDT

For tracing bash not to run into issues as bash internals change, USDT probes can be added to the code. For example, imagine USDT probes with the following format:

```
bash:execute__function__entry(char *name, char **args, char *file, int linenum)
bash:execute__function__return(char *name, int retval, char *file, int linenum)
```

Then printing the function name, as well as showing the arguments, return value, latency, source file, and line number, would all be straightforward.

As an example of instrumenting the shell, USDT probes were added to the Bourne shell for Solaris systems [139], with the following probe definitions:

```
provider sh {
    probe function-entry(file, function, lineno);
    probe function-return(file, function, rval);
    probe builtin-entry(file, function, lineno);
    probe builtin-return(file, function, rval);
    probe command-entry(file, function, lineno);
    probe command-return(file, function, rval);
    probe script-start(file);
    probe script-done(file, rval);
    probe subshell-entry(file, childpid);
    probe subshell-return(file, rval);
    probe line(file, lineno);
    probe variable-set(file, variable, value);
    probe variable-unset(file, variable);
};
```

This should also provide ideas for future bash shell USDT probes.

12.4.6 bash One-Liners

These sections show BCC and bpftrace one-liners for bash shell analysis.

BCC

Count execution types (requires symbols):

```
funccount '/bin/bash:execute_*'
```

Trace interactive command input:

```
trace 'r:/bin/bash:readline "%s", retval'
```

bpftrace

Count execution types (requires symbols):

```
bpftrace -e 'uprobe:/bin/bash:execute_* { @[probe] = count(); }'
```

Trace interactive command input:

```
bpftrace -e 'ur:/bin/bash:readline { printf("read: %s\n", str(retval)); }'
```

12.5 Other Languages

There are many more programming languages and runtimes, and more will be created. To instrument them, first identify how they are implemented: are they compiled into binaries, JIT compiled, interpreted, or some combination of these? Studying the relevant previous section on C (for compiled), Java (for JIT compiled), and the bash shell (for interpreted), will give you a head start on the approach and challenges involved.

On this book's website [140] I will link to articles about using BPF to instrument other languages as they are written. The following are tips for other languages that I have previously traced using BPF: JavaScript (Node.js), C++, and GoLang.

12.5.1 JavaScript (Node.js)

BPF tracing is similar to Java. The current runtime used by Node.js is v8, developed by Google for the Chrome web browser. v8 can run Java functions interpreted, or JIT compile them for native execution. The runtime also manages memory, and has a garbage collection routine.

The following summarizes Node.js USDT probes, stack walking, symbols, and function tracing.

USDT Probes

There are built-in USDT probes and a node-usdt library for adding dynamic USDT probes to the JavaScript code [141]. The Linux distribution currently does not ship with the USDT probes enabled: to use them, you must recompile Node.js from source with the `--with-dtrace` option. Example steps:

```
$ wget https://nodejs.org/dist/v12.4.0/node-v12.4.0.tar.gz
$ tar xf node-v12.4.0.tar.gz
$ cd node-v12.4.0
$ ./configure --with-dtrace
$ make
```

Listing USDT probes using bpftrace:

```
# bpftrace -l 'usdt:/usr/local/bin/node'
usdt:/usr/local/bin/node:node:gc__start
usdt:/usr/local/bin/node:node:gc__done
usdt:/usr/local/bin/node:node:http__server__response
usdt:/usr/local/bin/node:node:net__stream__end
usdt:/usr/local/bin/node:node:net__server__connection
usdt:/usr/local/bin/node:node:http__client__response
usdt:/usr/local/bin/node:node:http__client__request
usdt:/usr/local/bin/node:node:http__server__request
[...]
```

These show USDT probes for garbage collection, HTTP requests, and network events. For more on Node.js USDT, see my blog post "Linux bcc/BPF Node.js USDT Tracing" [142].

Stack Walking

Stack walking should work (frame pointer based), although translation of JITed JavaScript functions into symbols requires an extra step (explained next).

Symbols

As with Java, supplemental symbol files in /tmp are required to translate JITted function addresses to function names. If you are using Node.js v10.x or above, there are two ways to create these symbol files:

1. Using the v8 flags `--perf_basic_prof` or `--perf_basic_prof_only_functions`. These will create a rolling symbol logs that are continually updated, unlike Java which dumps snapshots of the symbol state. Since these rolling logs cannot be disabled while the process is running, over time it can lead to extremely large map files (Gbytes) containing mostly stale symbols.

2. The linux-perf module [143], which is a combination of how the flags work and how Java's perf-map-agent work: it will capture all functions on the heap and write to the map file, and then it will continue to write to the file while new functions are compiled. It's possible to start capturing new functions at any time. This method is recommended.

Using both approaches, I've needed to post-process the supplemental symbol files to remove stale entries.[23]

Another recommended flag is `--interpreted-frames-native-stack` (also available for Node.js v10.x and above). With this flag, Linux perf and BPF tools will be able to translate interpreted JavaScript functions into their actual names (instead of showing "Interpreter" frames on the stack).

A common use case that requires external Node.js symbols is CPU profiling and CPU flame graphs [144]. These can be generated using perf(1) or BPF tools.

Function Tracing

There are not currently USDT probes for tracing JavaScript functions, and due to V8's architecture, it would be challenging to add them. Even if someone adds it, as I discussed with Java, the overhead can be extreme: slowing applications by 10x while in use.

The JavaScript functions are visible in user-level stack traces, which can be collected on kernel events such as timed sampling, disk I/O, TCP events, and context switches. This provides many insights into Node.js performance, including with function context, without the penalty of tracing functions directly.

---

23 You might assume that tools like perf(1) would read the symbol file backwards and use the most recent mappings for a given address. I've found that not to be the case, and an older mapping is used when there is a newer mapping in the log. This is why I've needed to post process these logs: only retaining the newest mappings for addresses.

12.5.2   C++

C++ can be traced much the same as C, with uprobes for function entry, uprobes for function returns, and frame pointer–based stacks if the compiler has honored the frame pointer. There are a couple of differences:

- Symbol names are C++ signatures. Instead of ClassLoader::initialize(), that symbol may be traced as _ZN11ClassLoader10initializeEv. The BCC and bpftrace tools use demangling when printing symbols.

- Function arguments may not accommodate the processor ABI for support of objects and the self object.

Counting function calls, measuring function latency, and showing stack traces should all be straightforward. It may help to use wildcards to match function names from their signatures when possible (e.g., uprobe:/path:*ClassLoader*initialize*).

Inspecting arguments will require more work. Sometimes they are simply offset by one to accommodate a self object as the first argument. Strings are often not native C strings, but C++ objects, and can't simply be dereferenced. Objects need structs to be declared in the BPF program so that BPF can dereference members.

This may all become much easier with BTF, introduced in Chapter 2, which may provide the locations of arguments and object members.

12.5.3   Golang

Golang compiles to binaries, and tracing them is similar to tracing C binaries, but there are some important differences with its function calling conventions, goroutines, and dynamic stack management. Due to the latter, uretprobes are currently unsafe to use on Golang as they can crash the target program. There are also differences between the compiler used: by default Go gc emits statically linked binaries, whereas gccgo emits dynamically linked binaries. These topics are discussed in the following sections.

Note that there are already other ways to debug and trace Go programs that you should be aware of, including gdb's Go runtime support, the go execution tracer [145], and GODEBUG with gctrace and schedtrace.

Stack Walking and Symbols

Both Go gc and gccgo honor the frame pointer by default (Go since version 1.7) and include symbols in the resulting binaries. This means that stack traces that include Go functions can always be collected, from either user- or kernel-level events, and profiling via timed sampling will also work immediately.

Function Entry Tracing

The entry to functions can be traced with uprobes. For example, using bpftrace to count function calls that begin with "fmt" in a "Hello, World!" Golang program named "hello", which was compiled using Go gc:

```
# bpftrace -e 'uprobe:/home/bgregg/hello:fmt* { @[probe] = count(); }'
Attaching 42 probes...
^C

@[uprobe:/home/bgregg/hello:fmt.(*fmt).fmt_s]: 1
@[uprobe:/home/bgregg/hello:fmt.newPrinter]: 1
@[uprobe:/home/bgregg/hello:fmt.Fprintln]: 1
@[uprobe:/home/bgregg/hello:fmt.(*pp).fmtString]: 1
@[uprobe:/home/bgregg/hello:fmt.glob..func1]: 1
@[uprobe:/home/bgregg/hello:fmt.(*pp).printArg]: 1
@[uprobe:/home/bgregg/hello:fmt.(*pp).free]: 1
@[uprobe:/home/bgregg/hello:fmt.Println]: 1
@[uprobe:/home/bgregg/hello:fmt.init]: 1
@[uprobe:/home/bgregg/hello:fmt.(*pp).doPrintln]: 1
@[uprobe:/home/bgregg/hello:fmt.(*fmt).padString]: 1
@[uprobe:/home/bgregg/hello:fmt.(*fmt).truncate]: 1
```

While tracing I ran the hello program once. The output shows that various fmt functions were called once, including fmt.Println(), which I suspect is printing "Hello, World!".

Now counting the same functions from a gccgo binary. In this case, those functions are in the libgo library, and that location must be traced:

```
# bpftrace -e 'uprobe:/usr/lib/x86_64-linux-gnu/libgo.so.13:fmt* { @[probe] =
count(); }'
Attaching 143 probes...
^C

@[uprobe:/usr/lib/x86_64-linux-gnu/libgo.so.13:fmt.fmt.clearflags]: 1
@[uprobe:/usr/lib/x86_64-linux-gnu/libgo.so.13:fmt.fmt.truncate]: 1
@[uprobe:/usr/lib/x86_64-linux-gnu/libgo.so.13:fmt.Println]: 1
@[uprobe:/usr/lib/x86_64-linux-gnu/libgo.so.13:fmt.newPrinter]: 1
@[uprobe:/usr/lib/x86_64-linux-gnu/libgo.so.13:fmt.buffer.WriteByte]: 1
@[uprobe:/usr/lib/x86_64-linux-gnu/libgo.so.13:fmt.pp.printArg]: 1
@[uprobe:/usr/lib/x86_64-linux-gnu/libgo.so.13:fmt.pp.fmtString]: 1
@[uprobe:/usr/lib/x86_64-linux-gnu/libgo.so.13:fmt.fmt.fmt_s]: 1
@[uprobe:/usr/lib/x86_64-linux-gnu/libgo.so.13:fmt.pp.free]: 1
@[uprobe:/usr/lib/x86_64-linux-gnu/libgo.so.13:fmt.fmt.init]: 1
@[uprobe:/usr/lib/x86_64-linux-gnu/libgo.so.13:fmt.buffer.WriteString]: 1
```

```
@[uprobe:/usr/lib/x86_64-linux-gnu/libgo.so.13:fmt.pp.doPrintln]: 1
@[uprobe:/usr/lib/x86_64-linux-gnu/libgo.so.13:fmt.fmt.padString]: 1
@[uprobe:/usr/lib/x86_64-linux-gnu/libgo.so.13:fmt.Fprintln]: 1
@[uprobe:/usr/lib/x86_64-linux-gnu/libgo.so.13:fmt..import]: 1
@[uprobe:/usr/lib/x86_64-linux-gnu/libgo.so.13:fmt..go..func1]: 1
```

The naming convention for the functions is a little different. The output includes fmt.Println(), as seen earlier.

These functions can also be counted using the funccount(8) tool from BCC. The commands for the Go gc version and then the gccgo version are:

```
funccount '/home/bgregg/hello:fmt.*'
funccount 'go:fmt.*'
```

Function Entry Arguments

Go's gc compiler and gccgo use different function-calling conventions: gccgo uses the standard AMD64 ABI, whereas Go's gc compiler uses Plan 9's stack-passing approach. This means that fetching function arguments differs: with gccgo, the usual approach (e.g., via bpftrace arg0... argN) will work, but it will not with Go gc: custom code will need to be used to get it from the stack (see [146][147]).

For example, consider the add(x int, y int) function from the Golang tutorial [148], which is called with the arguments 42 and 13. To instrument its arguments on a gccgo binary:

```
# bpftrace -e 'uprobe:/home/bgregg/func:main*add { printf("%d %d\n", arg0, arg1); }'
Attaching 1 probe...
42 13
```

The arg0 and arg1 built-ins work. Note that I needed to compile using gccgo -O0 so that the add() function wasn't inlined by the compiler.

Now instrumenting its arguments on a Go gc binary:

```
# bpftrace -e 'uprobe:/home/bgregg/Lang/go/func:main*add { printf("%d %d\n",
    *(reg("sp") + 8), *(reg("sp") + 16)); }'
Attaching 1 probe...
42 13
```

This time the arguments needed to be read from their offsets the stack, accessed via reg("sp"). A future version of bpftrace may support these as aliases, such as sarg0, sarg1 [149], short for "stack argument". Note that I needed to compile this using go build -gcflags '-N -l' ... so that the add() function wasn't inlined by the compiler.

Function Returns

Unfortunately, uretprobe tracing is not safe with the current implementation of uretprobes. The Go compiler can modify the stack at any time, unaware that the kernel has added a uretprobe trampoline handler to the stack.[24] This can cause memory corruption: once the uretprobe is deactivated, the kernel will return those bytes to normal, however, those bytes may now contain other Golang program data, and will be corrupted by the kernel. This can cause Golang to crash (if you are lucky) or continue running with corrupt data (if you are unlucky).

Gianluca Borello has experimented with a solution that involves using uprobes on the return locations of functions rather than uretprobes. This involves disassembling a function to find the return points, and then placing a uretprobe on them (see [150]).

Another problem is goroutines: these can be scheduled between different OS threads as they are running, so the usual method of timing function latency by using a timestamp keyed on thread ID (e.g., with bpftrace: @start[tid] = nsecs) is no longer reliable.

USDT

The Salp library provides dynamic USDT probes via libstapsdt [151]. This allows static probe points to be placed in your Go code.

12.6 Summary

Whether your programming language of interest is compiled, JIT compiled, or interpreted, there is likely a way to analyze it with BPF. In this chapter I discussed these three types and then showed how to trace an example from each: C, Java, and the bash shell. With tracing it should be possible to examine their function or method calls, examining their arguments and return value, function or method latency, and also show stack traces from other events. Tips for other languages were also included for JavaScript, C++, and Golang.

---

24 Thanks Suresh Kumar for helping explain this problem; see his comment in [146].

Chapter 13

Applications

The applications running on a system can be studied directly using static and dynamic instrumentation, which provides important application context for understanding other events. Previous chapters studied applications via the resources they used: CPUs, memory, disks, and networking. This resource-based approach can solve many issues, but it may miss clues from the application, such as details about the requests it is currently servicing. To complete your observation of an application, you need both resource analysis and application-level analysis. With BPF tracing, this allows you to study the flow from the application and its code and context, through libraries and syscalls, kernel services, and device drivers.

I will use the MySQL database as a case study in this chapter. MySQL database queries are an example of application context. Imagine taking the various ways disk I/O was instrumented in Chapter 9 and adding query string as another dimension for breakdowns. Now you can see which queries are causing the most disk I/O, and their latencies and patterns, and so on.

Learning Objectives:

- Discover issues of excessive process and thread creation
- Solve CPU usage issues using profiling
- Solve off-CPU blocking issues using scheduler tracing
- Solve excessive I/O issues by showing I/O stack traces
- Trace application context using USDT probes and uprobes
- Investigate code paths responsible for lock contention
- Identify explicit application sleeps

This chapter is supplemental to the prior resource-oriented chapters; for full visibility of the software stack also see:

- Chapter 6, "CPUs"
- Chapter 7, "Memory"
- Chapter 8, "File Systems"
- Chapter 9, "Disk I/O"
- Chapter 10, "Networking"

Application behavior not covered in those other chapters is covered here: fetching application context, thread management, signals, locks, and sleeps.

13.1   Background

An application may be a service that responds to network requests, a program that responds to direct user input, or a program that runs on data from a database or a filesystem, or something else. Applications are typically implemented as user-mode software, visible as processes, and access resources via the syscall interface (or memory mappings).

13.1.1   Application Fundamentals

Thread Management

For multi-CPU systems, the operating system construct called threads allows applications to efficiently execute work across multiple CPUs in parallel, while sharing the same process address space. Applications can make use of threads in different ways, including:

- **Service thread pool:** A pool of threads services network requests, where each thread services one client connection and request at a time. If the request needs to block on a resource, including synchronization locks with other threads in the pool, the thread sleeps. The application may have a fixed number of threads in the pool, or it may increase and decrease them based on client demand. An example is the MySQL database server.

- **CPU thread pool:** The application creates one thread per CPU for executing work across them. This is commonly used for batch processing applications, which process one or more queued requests, continuously and without further input, whether that takes minutes, hours, or days. An example is video encoding.

- **Event worker thread:** Either one or multiple threads are event workers, processing a queue of client work until the queue is empty and the thread sleeps. Each thread services multiple clients concurrently, piecemeal: executing a part of a client request until it blocks on a later event, then switching to the next client event in the queue to process. Applications that use a single event worker thread may avoid the need for synchronization locks, but they risk becoming single-threaded bound under load. Node.js uses a single event worker thread and benefits from it in this way.

- **Staged Event-Driven Architecture (SEDA):** SEDA decomposes application requests into stages, which may be processed by pools of one or more threads [Welsh 01].

Locks

Locks are synchronization primitives for multi-threaded applications; they police access to memory from threads running in parallel, similarly to the way traffic lights regulate access to an intersection. And, like traffic lights, they can halt the flow of traffic, causing wait time (latency). On Linux, applications commonly use locks via the libpthread library, which provides different lock types, including mutual exclusive (mutex), reader-writer, and spin locks.

While locks protect memory, they can become a source of performance issues. Lock contention occurs when where multiple threads are competing to use one lock, and blocking while waiting their turn.

Sleeps

Applications can deliberately sleep for a period of time. Such sleeps may make sense (depending on the reason), or may not—and may therefore be opportunities for optimization. If you have ever developed applications there may be a time where you've thought: "I'll just add a sleep one second here so that the events I'm waiting for have completed; we can delete this sleep later and make it event-based." However, that later never comes, and now end users are wondering why some requests take at least one second.

13.1.2 Application Example: MySQL Server

As an example application to analyze in this chapter, I'll look at the MySQL database server. This service responds to network requests using a service thread pool. Depending on the size of the data frequently accessed, it is expected that MySQL will either be disk bound for large working sets or CPU bound for small working sets where queries return from its memory cache.

MySQL server is written in C++ and has embedded USDT probes for queries, commands, filesort, inserts, updates, network I/O, and other events. Table 13-1 provides some examples.

Table 13-1 MySQL Probe Examples

USDT Probe	Arguments
connection__start	unsigned long connection_id, char *user, char *host
connection__done	int status, unsigned long connection_id
command__start	unsigned long connection_id, int command, char *user, char *host
command__done	int status
query__start	char *query, unsigned long connection_id, char *db_name, char *user, char *host
query__done	int status
filesort__start	char *db_name, char *table
filesort__done	int status, unsigned long rows
net__write__start	unsigned long bytes
net__write__done	int status

See "mysqld DTrace Probe Reference" in the MySQL Reference Manual for the full list of probes [152]. These MySQL USDT probes are only available when MySQL is compiled with -DENABLE_DTRACE=1 as a parameter to cmake(1) during the build process. The current mysql-server package for Linux does not do this, so you will need to build your own MySQL server software to use USDT probes or ask the package maintainers to include this setting.

Since there are many scenarios where USDT probes may not be available for your application, this chapter includes MySQL tools that instrument the server using uprobes instead.

13.1.3   BPF Capabilities

BPF tracing tools can provide additional insight beyond application-provided metrics, with custom workload and latency metrics, latency histograms, and visibility of resource usage from within the kernel. These capabilities can answer:

- What are the application requests? What is their latency?
- Where is the time spent during application requests?
- Why is the application on CPU?
- Why does the application block and switch off CPU?
- What I/O is the application performing, and why (code path)?
- What locks is the application blocking on, and for how long?
- What other kernel resources is the application using, and why?

These can be answered by instrumenting the application using USDT and probes for request context, kernel resources and blocking events via tracepoints (including syscalls) and kprobes, and via timed sampling of on-CPU stack traces.

Overhead

The overhead application tracing depends on the rate of traced events. Typically, tracing the requests themselves costs negligible overhead, whereas tracing lock contention, off-CPU events, and syscalls can cost noticeable overhead for busy workloads.

13.1.4   Strategy

Here is a suggested overall strategy you can follow for application analysis. The next sections explain these tools in more detail.

1. Learn what the application does: what is its unit of work? It may already expose its unit of work in application metrics and logs. Also determine what would it mean to improve its performance: higher throughput, lower latency, or lower resource usage (or some combination)?

2. See if any documentation exists to describe application internals: major components such as libraries and caches, its API, and how it services requests: thread pools, event worker threads, or something else.

3. Apart from the application's main unit of work, find out if it uses any background periodic tasks that could impact performance (e.g., a disk flush event that happens every 30 seconds).

4. Check whether USDT probes are available for the application or its programming language.

5. Perform on-CPU analysis to understand CPU consumption and look for inefficiencies (e.g., using BCC profile(8)).

6. Perform off-CPU analysis to understand why the application is blocking and look for areas to optimize (e.g., BCC offcputime(8), wakeuptime(8), offwaketime(8)). Focus on blocking time during application requests.

7. Profile syscalls to understand an application's use of resources (e.g., BCC syscount(8)).

8. Browse and execute the BPF tools listed in Chapters 6–10.

9. Use uprobes to explore application internals: the previous on-CPU and off-CPU analysis stack traces should have identified many functions to begin tracing.

10. For distributed computing, consider tracing both server side and client side. For example, with MySQL it may be possible to trace the server as well as clients making requests by tracing the MySQL client library.

It may already be known whether the application is CPU bound, disk bound, or network bound, based on the resource it spends most of its time waiting for. After confirming that this assumption is true, the limiting resource can be investigated from the appropriate resource chapter in this book.

If you wish to write BPF programs to trace application requests, you need to take into account how requests are processed. Because service thread pools process a request entirely from the same thread, the thread ID (task ID) can be used to associate events from different sources, provided they are asynchronous. For example, when a database begins processing a query, the query string can be stored in a BPF map keyed on the thread ID. This query string could later be read when disk I/O is first initialized, so that disk I/O can be associated with the query that caused it. Other application architectures such as event worker threads require a different approach, since one thread processes different requests concurrently, and the thread ID is not unique to one request.

13.2 BPF Tools

This section covers the BPF tools you can use for application performance analysis and troubleshooting. These are shown in Figure 13-1.

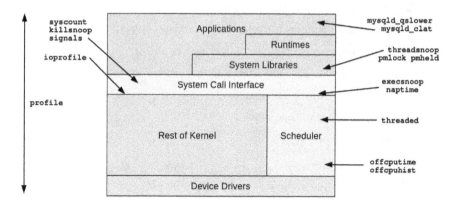

Figure 13-1 BPF tools for application analysis

These tools are either from the BCC and bpftrace repositories covered in Chapters 4 and 5 or were created for this book. Some tools appear in both BCC and bpftrace. Table 13-2 lists the origins of the tools covered in this section (BT is short for bpftrace).

Table 13-2 **Application-Related Tools**

Tool	Source	Target	Description
execsnoop	BCC/BT	Sched	List new process execution
threadsnoop	Book	pthread	List new thread creation
profile	BCC	CPUs	Sample on-CPU stack traces
threaded	Book	CPUs	Sample on-CPU threads
offcputime	BCC	Sched	Show off-CPU time with stack traces
offcpuhist	Book	Sched	Show off-CPU stacks with time histograms
syscount	BCC	Syscalls	Count syscalls by type
ioprofile	Book	I/O	Count stacks on I/O
mysqld_qslower	BCC/book	MySQL server	Show MySQL queries slower than a threshold
mysqld_clat	Book	MySQL server	Show MySQL command latency as a histogram
signals	Book	Signals	Summarize sent signals by target process
killsnoop	BCC/BT	Syscalls	Show kill(2) syscalls with sender details
pmlock	Book	Locks	Show pthread mutex lock times and user stacks
pmheld	Book	Locks	Show pthread mutex held times and user stacks
naptime	Book	Syscalls	Show voluntary sleep calls

For the tools from BCC and bpftrace, see their repositories for full and updated lists of tool options and capabilities. A selection of the most important capabilities are summarized here.

These tools can be grouped into the following topics:

- **CPU-analysis:** profile(8), threaded(8), and syscount(8)
- **Off-CPU analysis:** offcputime(8), offcpuhist(8), and ioprofile(8)
- **Application context:** mysqld_slower(8) and mysqld_clat(8)
- **Thread execution:** execsnoop(8), threadsnoop(8), and threaded(8)
- **Lock analysis:** rmlock(8) and pmheld(8)
- **Signals:** signals(8) and killsnoop(8)
- **Sleep analysis:** naptime(8)

There are also one-liners at the end of this chapter. The following tool sections also include a section on libc frame pointers, as a follow-on from ioprofile(8).

13.2.1 execsnoop

execsnoop(8), introduced in Chapter 6, is a BCC and bpftrace tool to trace new processes, and can identify if applications are using short-lived processes. Example output from an idle server:

```
# execsnoop
PCOMM        PID    PPID   RET ARGS
sh           17788  17787    0 /bin/sh -c /usr/lib/sysstat/sa1 1 1 -S ALL
sa1          17789  17788    0 /usr/lib/sysstat/sa1 1 1 -S ALL
sadc         17789  17788    0 /usr/lib/sysstat/sadc -F -L -S DISK 1 1 -S ALL /var/
log/sysstat
[...]
```

This shows that the server was not so idle: it has caught an invocation of the system activity recorder. execsnoop(8) is useful for catching unexpected process usage by applications. Sometimes applications call shell scripts for functionality, maybe as a temporary workaround until it can be coded properly within the application, causing inefficiencies.

See Chapter 6 for more about execsnoop(8).

13.2.2 threadsnoop

threadsnoop(8)[1] traces thread creation via the pthread_create() library call. For example, during MySQL server startup:

```
# threadsnoop.bt
Attaching 3 probes...
TIME(ms)  PID    COMM      FUNC
2049      14456  mysqld    timer_notify_thread_func
2234      14460  mysqld    pfs_spawn_thread
2243      14460  mysqld    io_handler_thread
2243      14460  mysqld    io_handler_thread
2243      14460  mysqld    io_handler_thread
2243      14460  mysqld    io_handler_thread
2243      14460  mysqld    io_handler_thread
2243      14460  mysqld    io_handler_thread
2243      14460  mysqld    io_handler_thread
2243      14460  mysqld    io_handler_thread
2243      14460  mysqld    io_handler_thread
2243      14460  mysqld    io_handler_thread
2243      14460  mysqld    buf_flush_page_cleaner_coordinator
2274      14460  mysqld    trx_rollback_or_clean_all_recovered
2296      14460  mysqld    lock_wait_timeout_thread
```

---

1 Origin: I created it for this book on 15-Feb-2019, inspired by my own execsnoop.

```
2296      14460   mysqld              srv_error_monitor_thread
2296      14460   mysqld              srv_monitor_thread
2296      14460   mysqld              srv_master_thread
2296      14460   mysqld              srv_purge_coordinator_thread
2297      14460   mysqld              srv_worker_thread
2297      14460   mysqld              srv_worker_thread
2297      14460   mysqld              srv_worker_thread
2298      14460   mysqld              buf_dump_thread
2298      14460   mysqld              dict_stats_thread
2298      14460   mysqld              _Z19fts_optimize_threadPv
2298      14460   mysqld              buf_resize_thread
2381      14460   mysqld              pfs_spawn_thread
2381      14460   mysqld              pfs_spawn_thread
```

This shows the rate of thread creation by examining the TIME(ms) column, as well as who is creating the thread (PID, COMM), and the starting function for the thread (FUNC). This output shows MySQL creating its pools of server worker threads (srv_worker_thread()), I/O handler threads (io_handler_thread()), and other threads for running the database.

This works by tracing the pthread_create() library call, which is expected to be relatively infrequent, such that the overhead of this tool should be negligible.

The source to threadsnoop(8) is:

```
#!/usr/local/bin/bpftrace

BEGIN
{
        printf("%-10s %-6s %-16s %s\n", "TIME(ms)", "PID", "COMM", "FUNC");
}

uprobe:/lib/x86_64-linux-gnu/libpthread.so.0:pthread_create
{
        printf("%-10u %-6d %-16s %s\n", elapsed / 1000000, pid, comm,
            usym(arg2));
}
```

The path to your libpthread library may need adjusting in this source.

The output line can also be adjusted. For example, to include the user-level stack trace:

```
        printf("%-10u %-6d %-16s %s%s\n", elapsed / 1000000, pid, comm,
            usym(arg2), ustack);
```

This produces:

```
# ./threadsnoop-ustack.bt
Attaching 3 probes...
TIME(ms)   PID    COMM            FUNC
1555       14976  mysqld          timer_notify_thread_func
        0x7fb5ced4b9b0
        0x55f6255756b7
        0x55f625577145
        0x7fb5ce035b97
        0x2246258d4c544155

1729       14981  mysqld          pfs_spawn_thread
        __pthread_create_2_1+0
        my_timer_initialize+156
        init_server_components()+87
        mysqld_main(int, char**)+1941
        __libc_start_main+231
        0x2246258d4c544155

1739       14981  mysqld          io_handler_thread
        __pthread_create_2_1+0
        innobase_start_or_create_for_mysql()+6648
        innobase_init(void*)+3044
        ha_initialize_handlerton(st_plugin_int*)+79
        plugin_initialize(st_plugin_int*)+101
        plugin_register_builtin_and_init_core_se(int*, char**)+485
        init_server_components()+960
        mysqld_main(int, char**)+1941
        __libc_start_main+231
        0x2246258d4c544155
[...]
```

This shows the code path that led to the thread's creation. For MySQL, the role of the threads was already apparent from the starting functions, but this won't always be the case with all applications, and the stack trace may be needed to identify what the new threads are for.

13.2.3   profile

profile(8), introduced in Chapter 6, is a BCC tool that does timed sampling of on-CPU stack traces and is a cheap and coarse way to show which code paths are consuming CPU resources. It was introduced in Chapter 6. For example, using profile(8) to profile a MySQL server:

```
# profile -d -p $(pgrep mysqld)
Sampling at 49 Hertz of PID 9908 by user + kernel stack... Hit Ctrl-C to end.

[...]

    my_hash_sort_simple
    hp_rec_hashnr
    hp_write_key
    heap_write
    ha_heap::write_row(unsigned char*)
    handler::ha_write_row(unsigned char*)
    end_write(JOIN*, QEP_TAB*, bool)
    evaluate_join_record(JOIN*, QEP_TAB*)
    sub_select(JOIN*, QEP_TAB*, bool)
    JOIN::exec()
    handle_query(THD*, LEX*, Query_result*, unsigned long long, unsigned long long)
    execute_sqlcom_select(THD*, TABLE_LIST*)
    mysql_execute_command(THD*, bool)
    Prepared_statement::execute(String*, bool)
    Prepared_statement::execute_loop(String*, bool, unsigned char*, unsigned char*)
    mysqld_stmt_execute(THD*, unsigned long, unsigned long, unsigned char*, unsign...
    dispatch_command(THD*, COM_DATA const*, enum_server_command)
    do_command(THD*)
    handle_connection
    pfs_spawn_thread
    start_thread
    -               mysqld (9908)
        14

[...]

    ut_delay(unsigned long)
    srv_worker_thread
    start_thread
    -               mysqld (9908)
        16
```

```
_raw_spin_unlock_irqrestore
_raw_spin_unlock_irqrestore
__wake_up_common_lock
__wake_up_sync_key
sock_def_readable
unix_stream_sendmsg
sock_sendmsg
SYSC_sendto
SyS_sendto
do_syscall_64
entry_SYSCALL_64_after_hwframe
--
__send
vio_write
net_write_packet
net_flush
net_send_ok(THD*, unsigned int, unsigned int, unsigned long long, unsigned lon...
Protocol_classic::send_ok(unsigned int, unsigned int, unsigned long long, unsi...
THD::send_statement_status()
dispatch_command(THD*, COM_DATA const*, enum_server_command)
do_command(THD*)
handle_connection
pfs_spawn_thread
start_thread
__clone
-                         mysqld (9908)
        17
```

The output was hundreds of stack traces and their frequency counts. Only three have been included here. The first stack shows MySQL statement becoming a join and finally a my_hash_sort_simple() on CPU. The last stack shows a socket send in the kernel: this stack has a delimiter between the kernel and user stacks ("-"), which was included due to the profile(8) -d option.

Since the output was hundreds of stack traces, it can be helpful to visualize it as a flame graph. profile(8) can generate folded format output (-f) for input by the flame graph software. For example, with a 30-second profile:

```
# profile -p $(pgrep mysqld) -f 30 > out.profile01.txt
# flamegraph.pl --width=800 --title="CPU Flame Graph" < out.profile01.txt \
    > out.profile01.svg
```

Figure 13-2 shows the same workload as a flame graph.

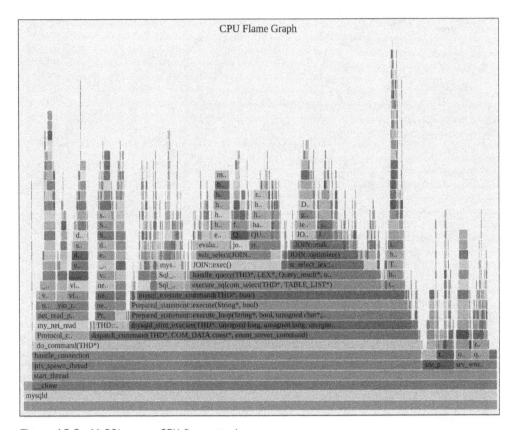

Figure 13-2   MySQL server CPU flame graph

The flame graph shows where the bulk of the CPU time is spent by the widest frames: in the middle, dispatch_command() was present in 69% of samples, and JOIN::exec() was present in 19%. These numbers are shown with a mouse-over of each frame, and frames can be clicked to zoom in on more details.

Apart from explaining CPU consumption, CPU flame graphs also show which functions are executing, which can become possible targets for BPF tracing. This flame graph showed functions such as do_command(), mysqld_stmt_execute(), JOIN::exec(), and JOIN::optimize(): these can all be instrumented directly using uprobes, and their arguments and latency studied.

This is only working because I'm profiling a MySQL server that has been compiled with frame pointers, with libc and libpthread versions that also have frame pointers. Without this, BPF would be unable to walk the stacks properly. This is discussed in Section 13.2.9.

See Chapter 6 for more about profile(8) and CPU flame graphs.

13.2.4 threaded

threaded(8)[2] samples on-CPU threads for a given process and shows how often they were on-CPU, for verifying how well they are multi-threaded. For example, for MySQL server:

```
# threaded.bt $(pgrep mysqld)
Attaching 3 probes...
Sampling PID 2274 threads at 99 Hertz. Ctrl-C to end.
23:47:13
@[mysqld, 2317]: 1
@[mysqld, 2319]: 2
@[mysqld, 2318]: 3
@[mysqld, 2316]: 4
@[mysqld, 2534]: 55

23:47:14
@[mysqld, 2319]: 2
@[mysqld, 2316]: 4
@[mysqld, 2317]: 5
@[mysqld, 2534]: 51

[...]
```

This tool prints per-second output, and for this MySQL server workload, it shows that only one thread (thread ID 2534) was significantly on CPU.

This is intended to characterize how well multi-threaded applications are spreading work across their threads. Since it uses timed sampling, it may miss short wakeups by threads that occur between the samples.

Some applications change the thread names. For example, using threaded(8) on the freecol Java application from the previous chapter:

```
# threaded.bt $(pgrep java)
Attaching 3 probes...
Sampling PID 32584 threads at 99 Hertz. Ctrl-C to end.
23:52:12
@[GC Thread#0, 32591]: 1
@[VM Thread, 32611]: 1
@[FreeColClient:b, 32657]: 6
@[AWT-EventQueue-, 32629]: 6
@[FreeColServer:-, 974]: 8
```

---

2 Origin: I created the first version as threaded.d on 25-Jul-2005 and used it during my performance classes where I wrote two sample applications with pools of worker threads, one that included a lock contention issue, and used threaded.d to show how other threads were unable to run with the issue. I also developed this version for this book.

```
@[FreeColServer:A,  977]: 11
@[FreeColServer:A,  975]: 26
@[C1 CompilerThre, 32618]: 29
@[C2 CompilerThre, 32617]: 44
@[C2 CompilerThre, 32616]: 44
@[C2 CompilerThre, 32615]: 48

[...]
```

This makes it clear that the CPU time consumed by this application is mostly spent in the compiler threads.

threaded(8) works by using timed sampling. The overhead should be negligible at this low frequency.

The source to threaded(8) is:

```
#!/usr/local/bin/bpftrace

BEGIN
{
        if ($1 == 0) {
                printf("USAGE: threaded.bt PID\n");
                exit();
        }
        printf("Sampling PID %d threads at 99 Hertz. Ctrl-C to end.\n", $1);
}

profile:hz:99
/pid == $1/
{
        @[comm, tid] = count();
}

interval:s:1
{
        time();
        print(@);
        clear(@);
}
```

This tool requires a PID as an argument, and exits if none was provided ($1 defaults to zero).

13.2.5 offcputime

offcputime(8), introduced in Chapter 6, is a BCC tool that traces when threads block and leave the CPUs, and records the duration they were off-CPU with the stack trace. Example output for MySQL server:

```
# offcputime -d -p $(pgrep mysqld)
Tracing off-CPU time (us) of PID 9908 by user + kernel stack... Hit Ctrl-C to end.

[...]

    finish_task_switch
    schedule
    jbd2_log_wait_commit
    jbd2_complete_transaction
    ext4_sync_file
    vfs_fsync_range
    do_fsync
    sys_fsync
    do_syscall_64
    entry_SYSCALL_64_after_hwframe
    --
    fsync
    fil_flush(unsigned long)
    log_write_up_to(unsigned long, bool) [clone .part.56]
    trx_commit_complete_for_mysql(trx_t*)
    innobase_commit(handlerton*, THD*, bool)
    ha_commit_low(THD*, bool, bool)
    TC_LOG_DUMMY::commit(THD*, bool)
    ha_commit_trans(THD*, bool, bool)
    trans_commit(THD*)
    mysql_execute_command(THD*, bool)
    Prepared_statement::execute(String*, bool)
    Prepared_statement::execute_loop(String*, bool, unsigned char*, unsigned char*)
    mysqld_stmt_execute(THD*, unsigned long, unsigned long, unsigned char*, unsign...
    dispatch_command(THD*, COM_DATA const*, enum_server_command)
    do_command(THD*)
    handle_connection
    pfs_spawn_thread
    start_thread
    -                 mysqld (9962)
        2458362
```

[...]

```
    finish_task_switch
    schedule
    futex_wait_queue_me
    futex_wait
    do_futex
    SyS_futex
    do_syscall_64
    entry_SYSCALL_64_after_hwframe
    --
    pthread_cond_timedwait@@GLIBC_2.3.2
    __pthread_cond_timedwait
    os_event::timed_wait(timespec const*)
    os_event_wait_time_low(os_event*, unsigned long, long)
    lock_wait_timeout_thread
    start_thread
    __clone
    -                mysqld (2311)
        10000904

    finish_task_switch
    schedule
    do_nanosleep
    hrtimer_nanosleep
    sys_nanosleep
    do_syscall_64
    entry_SYSCALL_64_after_hwframe
    --
    __nanosleep
    os_thread_sleep(unsigned long)
    srv_master_thread
    start_thread
    __clone
    -                mysqld (2315)
        10001003
```

The output was hundreds of stacks; only a few have been selected for this example. The first shows a MySQL statement becoming a commit, a log write, and then an fsync(). Then the code path crosses into the kernel ("--") with ext4 handling the fsync, and the thread finally blocks on a jbd2_log_wait_commit() function. The duration mysqld was blocked in this stack while tracing was 2458362 microseconds (2.45 seconds): this is the total across all threads.

The last two stacks show a lock_wait_timeout_thread() waiting for events via pthread_cond_timewait(), and the srv_master_thread() sleeping. The output of offcputime(8) can often be dominated by such waiting and sleeping threads, which are usually normal behavior and not a performance issue. Your task is to find the stacks that are blocking during application requests, which are the issue.

Off-CPU Time Flame Graph

Creating an off-CPU time flame graph provides a way to quickly focus on the blocked stacks of interest. The following commands capture 10 seconds of off-CPU stacks and then use my flame graph software to generate the flame graph:

```
# offcputime -f -p $(pgrep mysqld) 10 > out.offcputime01.txt
# flamegraph.pl --width=800 --color=io --title="Off-CPU Time Flame Graph" \
    --countname=us < out.offcputime01.txt > out.offcputime01.svg
```

This produced the flame graph shown in Figure 13-3, where I have used the search feature to highlight frames containing "do_command" in magenta: these are the code paths for MySQL requests and are what the clients are blocking on.

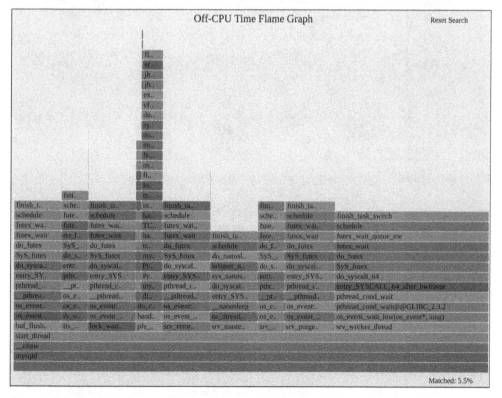

Figure 13-3   Off-CPU time flame graph for MySQL server, highlighting do_command

Most of the flame graph in Figure 13-3 is dominated by thread pools waiting for work. The time blocked in server commands is shown by the narrow tower that includes the do_command() frame, highlighted in magenta. Fortunately, flame graphs are interactive, and this tower can be clicked for zoom. This is shown in Figure 13-4.

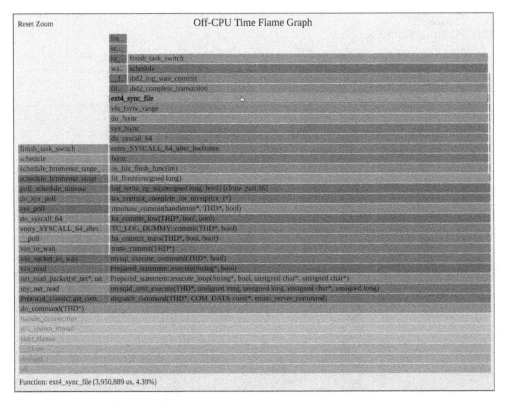

Figure 13-4   Off-CPU time flame graph zoomed to show server commands

The mouse pointer is over ext4_sync_file() to show the time spent in this path at the bottom: 3.95 seconds in total. This is the bulk of the blocking time in do_command(), and shows the target to optimize to improve server performance.

bpftrace

I wrote a bpftrace version of offcputime(8); see the next section on offcpuhist(8) for the source code.

Final Notes

This off-CPU analysis capability is the companion to CPU analysis by profile(8), and between them, these tools can shed light on a wide range of performance issues.

The performance overhead of offcputime(8) can be significant, exceeding 5%, depending on the rate of context switches. This is at least manageable: it could be run for short periods in production as needed. Prior to BPF, performing off-CPU analysis involved dumping all stacks to user-space for post processing, and the overhead was usually prohibitive for production use.

As with profile(8), this is only producing full stacks for all code because I've recompiled MySQL server and system libraries with frame pointers. See Section 13.2.9 for more about this.

See Chapter 6 for more about offcputime(8). Chapter 14 covers additional tools for off-CPU analysis: wakeuptime(8) and offwaketime(8).

13.2.6   offcpuhist

offcpuhist(8)[3] is similar to offcputime(8). It traces scheduler events to record off-CPU time with stack traces, but it shows the time as histograms instead of sums. Some example output from MySQL server:

```
# offcpuhist.bt $(pgrep mysqld)
Attaching 3 probes...
Tracing nanosecond time in off-CPU stacks. Ctrl-C to end.

[...]

@[
    finish_task_switch+1
    schedule+44
    futex_wait_queue_me+196
    futex_wait+266
    do_futex+805
    SyS_futex+315
    do_syscall_64+115
    entry_SYSCALL_64_after_hwframe+61
,
    __pthread_cond_wait+432
    pthread_cond_wait@@GLIBC_2.3.2+36
    os_event_wait_low(os_event*, long)+64
    srv_worker_thread+503
    start_thread+208
    __clone+63
, mysqld]:
[2K, 4K)            134 |@@@@@@@                                              |
[4K, 8K)            293 |@@@@@@@@@@@@@@@@@                                    |
[8K, 16K)           886 |@@@@@@@@@@@@@@@@@@@@@@@@@@@@@@@@@@@@@@@@@@@@@@@@@@@@@@|
[16K, 32K)          493 |@@@@@@@@@@@@@@@@@@@@@@@@@@@@@                         |
```

---

3 Origin: I created it for this book on 16-Feb-2019, inspired by my uoffcpu.d tool from the 2011 DTrace book [Gregg 11] that displayed user off-CPU stack traces with histograms. This is the first off-CPU analysis tool written for bpftrace.

```
[32K, 64K)              447 |@@@@@@@@@@@@@@@@@@@@@@@@@@      |
[64K, 128K)             263 |@@@@@@@@@@@@@@              |
[128K, 256K)             85 |@@@@                        |
[256K, 512K)              7 |                            |
[512K, 1M)                0 |                            |
[1M, 2M)                  0 |                            |
[2M, 4M)                  0 |                            |
[4M, 8M)                306 |@@@@@@@@@@@@@@@@            |
[8M, 16M)               747 |@@@@@@@@@@@@@@@@@@@@@@@@@@@@@@@@@@@@@@@@@@|

@[
    finish_task_switch+1
    schedule+44
    schedule_hrtimeout_range_clock+185
    schedule_hrtimeout_range+19
    poll_schedule_timeout+69
    do_sys_poll+960
    sys_poll+155
    do_syscall_64+115
    entry_SYSCALL_64_after_hwframe+61
,
    __GI___poll+110
    vio_io_wait+141
    vio_socket_io_wait+24
    vio_read+226
    net_read_packet(st_net*, unsigned long*)+141
    my_net_read+412
    Protocol_classic::get_command(COM_DATA*, enum_server_command*)+60
    do_command(THD*)+192
    handle_connection+680
    pfs_spawn_thread+337
    start_thread+208
    __clone+63
, mysqld]:
[2K, 4K)                753 |@@@@@@                      |
[4K, 8K)               2081 |@@@@@@@@@@@@@@@@            |
[8K, 16K)              5759 |@@@@@@@@@@@@@@@@@@@@@@@@@@@@@@@@@@@@@@@@@@@@@@|
[16K, 32K)             3595 |@@@@@@@@@@@@@@@@@@@@@@@@@@@   |
[32K, 64K)             4045 |@@@@@@@@@@@@@@@@@@@@@@@@@@@@@ |
[64K, 128K)            3830 |@@@@@@@@@@@@@@@@@@@@@@@@@@@   |
[128K, 256K)            751 |@@@@@@                      |
[256K, 512K)             48 |                            |
```

```
[512K, 1M)            16 |                                              |
[1M, 2M)               0 |                                              |
[2M, 4M)               7 |                                              |
```

The output has been truncated to show just the last two stack traces. The first shows a bi-modal latency distribution as the srv_worker_thread() threads wait for work: the output ranges are in nanoseconds, and show one mode around 16 microseconds and another between 8 and 16 milliseconds (labeled "[8M, 16M)"). The second stack shows many shorter waits in a net_read_packet() code path, usually taking less than 128 microseconds.

This works by tracing scheduler events using kprobes. The overhead, like with offcputime(8), can be significant, and it is only intended to be run for short durations.

The source to offcpuhist(8) is:

```
#!/usr/local/bin/bpftrace

#include <linux/sched.h>

BEGIN
{
        printf("Tracing nanosecond time in off-CPU stacks. Ctrl-C to end.\n");
}

kprobe:finish_task_switch
{
        // record previous thread sleep time
        $prev = (struct task_struct *)arg0;
        if ($1 == 0 || $prev->tgid == $1) {
                @start[$prev->pid] = nsecs;
        }

        // get the current thread start time
        $last = @start[tid];
        if ($last != 0) {
                @[kstack, ustack, comm, tid] = hist(nsecs - $last);
                delete(@start[tid]);
        }
}

END
{
        clear(@start);
}
```

This records a timestamp for the thread that is leaving the CPU and also records a histogram for the thread that is starting on the CPU, in the one finish_task_switch() kprobe.

13.2.7   syscount

syscount(8)[4] is a BCC tool for counting syscalls, which provides a view of resource usage by applications. It can be run system wide, or on individual processes. For example, on MySQL server, with per-second output (-i 1):

```
# syscount -i 1 -p $(pgrep mysqld)
Tracing syscalls, printing top 10... Ctrl+C to quit.
[11:49:25]
SYSCALL                 COUNT
sched_yield             10848
recvfrom                 6576
futex                    3977
sendto                   2193
poll                     2187
pwrite                    128
fsync                     115
nanosleep                   1

[11:49:26]
SYSCALL                 COUNT
sched_yield             10918
recvfrom                 6957
futex                    4165
sendto                   2314
poll                     2309
pwrite                    131
fsync                     118
setsockopt                  2
close                       2
accept                      1

[...]
```

This shows that the sched_yield() syscall was most frequent, called over 10,000 times per second. The most frequent syscalls can be explored with tracepoints for the syscall and using this and other tools. For example, BCC stackcount(8) can show the stack traces that led to it, and BCC

---

4 Origin: This was created by Sasha Goldshtein on 15-Feb-2017. I developed the first syscount tool using perf(1) on 7-Jul-2014, intended as a cheaper version of strace -c and with modes to count by process. It is loosely inspired by my procsystime tool from 22-Sep-2005.

argdist(8) can summarize its arguments. There should also be a man page for each syscall, to explain its purpose, arguments, and return value.

syscount(8) also can show the total time in syscalls with the -L option, For example, tracing for 10 seconds (-d 10) and summarizing in milliseconds (-m):

```
# syscount -mL -d 10 -p $(pgrep mysqld)
Tracing syscalls, printing top 10... Ctrl+C to quit.
[11:51:40]
SYSCALL                 COUNT        TIME (ms)
futex                   42158   108139.607626
nanosleep                   9     9000.992135
fsync                    1176     4393.483111
poll                    22700     1237.244061
sendto                  22795      276.383209
recvfrom                68311      275.933806
sched_yield             79759      141.347616
pwrite                   1352       53.346773
shutdown                    1        0.015088
openat                      1        0.013794

Detaching...
```

While tracing, the time in futex(2) was over 108 seconds in total for this 10-second trace: this is possible due to multiple threads calling it in parallel. The arguments and code paths will need to be inspected to understand the function of futex(2): it is likely called so often as a mechanism to wait for work, as was found with the prior offcputime(8) tool.

From top down, the most interesting syscall in this output is fsync(2), with 4393 milliseconds in total. This suggests one target for optimization: the file system and storage devices.

See Chapter 6 for more about syscount(8).

13.2.8   ioprofile

ioprofile(8)[5] traces I/O-related syscalls—reads, writes, sends, and receives—and shows their counts with calling user-level stack traces. For example, on MySQL server:

```
# ioprofile.bt $(pgrep mysqld)
Attaching 24 probes...
Tracing I/O syscall user stacks. Ctrl-C to end.
^C
```

---

5 Origin: I created it for this book on 15-Feb-2019, intending to use it as a new flame graph type in the Vector software at my employer. More than any other tool, it exposed how painful it was to not have frame pointers in libc and libpthread, and this may inspire a change in the Netflix BaseAMI libraries.

```
[...]

@[tracepoint:syscalls:sys_enter_pwrite64,
    pwrite64+114
    os_file_io(IORequest const&, int, void*, unsigned long, unsigned long, dberr_t...
    os_file_write_page(IORequest&, char const*, int, unsigned char const*, unsigne...
    fil_io(IORequest const&, bool, page_id_t const&, page_size_t const&, unsigned ...
    log_write_up_to(unsigned long, bool) [clone .part.56]+2426
    trx_commit_complete_for_mysql(trx_t*)+108
    innobase_commit(handlerton*, THD*, bool)+727
    ha_commit_low(THD*, bool, bool)+372
    TC_LOG_DUMMY::commit(THD*, bool)+20
    ha_commit_trans(THD*, bool, bool)+703
    trans_commit(THD*)+57
    mysql_execute_command(THD*, bool)+6651
    Prepared_statement::execute(String*, bool)+1410
    Prepared_statement::execute_loop(String*, bool, unsigned char*, unsigned char*...
    mysqld_stmt_execute(THD*, unsigned long, unsigned long, unsigned char*, unsign...
    dispatch_command(THD*, COM_DATA const*, enum_server_command)+5582
    do_command(THD*)+544
    handle_connection+680
    pfs_spawn_thread+337
    start_thread+208
    __clone+63
, mysqld]: 636

[...]

@[tracepoint:syscalls:sys_enter_recvfrom,
    __GI___recv+152
    vio_read+167
    net_read_packet(st_net*, unsigned long*)+141
    my_net_read+412
    Protocol_classic::get_command(COM_DATA*, enum_server_command*)+60
    do_command(THD*)+192
    handle_connection+680
    pfs_spawn_thread+337
    start_thread+208
    __clone+63
, mysqld]: 24255
```

The output was hundreds of stacks long, and only a couple have been included here. The first stack shows mysqld calling pwrite64(2) from a transaction write and file write code path. The second stack shows mysqld reading a packet via recvfrom(2).

An application performing too many I/O or unnecessary I/O is a commonly found performance issue. This may be due to log writes that can be disabled, small I/O sizes that should be increased, and so on. This tool can help identify these types of issues.

This works by tracing the tracepoints for the syscalls. The overhead may be noticeable as these syscalls can be frequent.

The source to ioprofile(8) is:

```
#!/usr/local/bin/bpftrace

BEGIN
{
        printf("Tracing I/O syscall user stacks. Ctrl-C to end.\n");
}

tracepoint:syscalls:sys_enter_*read*,
tracepoint:syscalls:sys_enter_*write*,
tracepoint:syscalls:sys_enter_*send*,
tracepoint:syscalls:sys_enter_*recv*
/$1 == 0 || pid == $1/
{
        @[probe, ustack, comm] = count();
}
```

An optional PID argument can be provided. Without it, the tool traces the entire system.

13.2.9 libc Frame Pointers

As an important aside, the ioprofile(8) tool output only contains full stacks because this MySQL server is running with a libc that has been compiled with frame pointers. Applications often make I/O via libc calls, and libc is often compiled without frame pointers. This means stack walking from the kernel back to the application often stops at libc. While this problem is present with other tools, it is most noticeable with ioprofile(8), and also brkstack(8) from Chapter 7.

Here is how the problem looks: this MySQL server has frame pointers, but is using the standard packaged libc:

```
# ioprofile.bt $(pgrep mysqld)
[...]
@[tracepoint:syscalls:sys_enter_pwrite64,
    __pwrite+79
```

```
    0x2ffffffdc020000
, mysqld]: 5
[...]
@[tracepoint:syscalls:sys_enter_recvfrom,
    __libc_recv+94
, mysqld]: 22526
```

The stack traces are incomplete, stopping after one or two frames. Ways to fix this include:

- Recompiling libc with -fno-omit-frame-pointer.

- Tracing libc interface functions before the frame pointer register has been reused.

- Tracing the MySQL server functions such as os_file_io(). This is an application-specific approach.

- Using a different stack walker. See Section 2.4 in Chapter 2 for a summary of other approaches.

libc is in the glibc package [153], which also provides libpthread and other libraries. It has been previously suggested that Debian provide an alternate libc package with frame pointers [154].

For more discussion on broken stacks, see Section 2.4 in Chapter 2 and Section 18.8 in Chapter18.

13.2.10   mysqld_qslower

mysqld_qslower(8)[6] is a BCC and bpftrace tool to trace MySQL queries on the server that were slower than a threshold. This is also an example of a tool that shows application context: the query string. Example output from the BCC version:

```
# mysqld_qslower $(pgrep mysqld)
Tracing MySQL server queries for PID 9908 slower than 1 ms...
TIME(s)     PID       MS QUERY
0.000000    9962  169.032 SELECT * FROM words WHERE word REGEXP '^bre.*n$'
1.962227    9962  205.787 SELECT * FROM words WHERE word REGEXP '^bpf.tools$'
9.043242    9962   95.276 SELECT COUNT(*) FROM words
23.723025   9962  186.680 SELECT count(*) AS count FROM words WHERE word REGEXP
'^bre.*n$'
30.343233   9962  181.494 SELECT * FROM words WHERE word REGEXP '^bre.*n$' ORDER BY
word
[...]
```

This output shows a time offset for the query, the MySQL server PID, the duration of the query in milliseconds, and the query string. Similar functionality is already available from MySQL's slow

---

6 Origin: I created it for this book on 15-Feb-2019, based on my earlier mysqld_qslower.d tool from the 2011 DTrace book [Gregg 11].

query log; with BPF, this tool can be customized to include details not present in that query log, such as disk I/O and other resource usage by the query.

This works by using the MySQL USDT probes: mysql:query__start and mysql:query__done. The overhead of this tool is expected to be small to negligible, due to the relative low rate of server queries.

BCC

Command line usage:

```
mysqld_qslower PID [min_ms]
```

A minimum millisecond threshold can be provided; otherwise, a default of one millisecond is used. If zero is provided, all queries are printed.

bpftrace

The following is the code for the bpftrace version, developed for this book:

```
#!/usr/local/bin/bpftrace

BEGIN
{
        printf("Tracing mysqld queries slower than %d ms. Ctrl-C to end.\n",
            $1);
        printf("%-10s %-6s %6s %s\n", "TIME(ms)", "PID", "MS", "QUERY");
}

usdt:/usr/sbin/mysqld:mysql:query__start
{
        @query[tid] = str(arg0);
        @start[tid] = nsecs;
}

usdt:/usr/sbin/mysqld:mysql:query__done
/@start[tid]/
{
        $dur = (nsecs - @start[tid]) / 1000000;
        if ($dur > $1) {
                printf("%-10u %-6d %6d %s\n", elapsed / 1000000,
                    pid, $dur, @query[tid]);
        }
        delete(@query[tid]);
        delete(@start[tid]);
}
```

This program uses a positional parameter, $1, for the millisecond latency threshold. If it is not provided, the tool defaults to zero, so all queries are printed.

Since MySQL server uses a service thread pool, and the same thread will process the entire request, so I can use the thread ID as a unique ID for the request. This is used with the @query and @start maps, so that I can save the query string pointer and start timestamp for each request, and then fetch them when the request completes.

Some example output:

```
# mysqld_qslower.bt -p $(pgrep mysqld)
Attaching 4 probes...
Tracing mysqld queries slower than 0 ms. Ctrl-C to end.
TIME(ms)    PID        MS QUERY
984         9908       87 select * from words where word like 'perf%'
[...]
```

A -p must be used during execution to enable the USDT probes, just as a PID was required with the BCC version. This makes the command line usage:

```
mysqld_qslower.bt -p PID [min_ms]
```

bpftrace: uprobes

If your mysqld does not have USDT probes compiled in, it is possible to implement a similar tool using uprobes of internal functions. The stack traces seen by previous commands show several possible functions to instrument; for example, from the earlier profile(8) output:

```
handle_query(THD*, LEX*, Query_result*, unsigned long long, unsigned long long)
execute_sqlcom_select(THD*, TABLE_LIST*)
mysql_execute_command(THD*, bool)
Prepared_statement::execute(String*, bool)
Prepared_statement::execute_loop(String*, bool, unsigned char*, unsigned char*)
mysqld_stmt_execute(THD*, unsigned long, unsigned long, unsigned char*, unsign...
dispatch_command(THD*, COM_DATA const*, enum_server_command)
do_command(THD*)
```

The following tool, mysqld_qslower-uprobes.bt, has traced dispatch_command():

```
#!/usr/local/bin/bpftrace

BEGIN
{
        printf("Tracing mysqld queries slower than %d ms. Ctrl-C to end.\n",
            $1);
        printf("%-10s %-6s %6s %s\n", "TIME(ms)", "PID", "MS", "QUERY");
```

```
}

uprobe:/usr/sbin/mysqld:*dispatch_command*
{
        $COM_QUERY = 3;                      // see include/my_command.h
        if (arg2 == $COM_QUERY) {
                @query[tid] = str(*arg1);
                @start[tid] = nsecs;
        }
}

uretprobe:/usr/sbin/mysqld:*dispatch_command*
/@start[tid]/
{
        $dur = (nsecs - @start[tid]) / 1000000;
        if ($dur > $1) {
                printf("%-10u %-6d %6d %s\n", elapsed / 1000000,
                    pid, $dur, @query[tid]);
        }
        delete(@query[tid]);
        delete(@start[tid]);
}
```

Since dispatch_command() traces more than just queries, this tool ensures that the command type is COM_QUERY. The query string is fetched from the COM_DATA argument, where the string is the first struct member for queries.

As is the case with uprobes, the traced function names, the arguments, and the logic, are all dependent on the version of MySQL (this is tracing 5.7), and this tool may not work on other versions if any of these details change. This is why USDT probes are preferred.

13.2.11   mysqld_clat

mysqld_clat(8)[7] is a bpftrace tool I developed for this book. It traces MySQL command latency and shows histograms for each command type. For example:

```
# mysqld_clat.bt
Attaching 4 probes...
Tracing mysqld command latencies. Ctrl-C to end.
^C
```

---

7 Origin: I created it for this book on 15-Feb-2019. It's similar to my mysqld_command.d that I wrote on 25-Jun-2013, although this tool is improved: it uses system-wide summaries and command names.

```
@us[COM_QUIT]:
[4, 8)                  1 |@@@@@@@@@@@@@@@@@@@@@@@@@@@@@@@@@@@@@@@@@@@@@@@@@@@@|

@us[COM_STMT_CLOSE]:
[4, 8)                  1 |@@@@@@                                            |
[8, 16)                 8 |@@@@@@@@@@@@@@@@@@@@@@@@@@@@@@@@@@@@@@@@@@@@@@@@@@@@|
[16, 32)                1 |@@@@@@                                            |

@us[COM_STMT_PREPARE]:
[32, 64)                6 |@@@@@@@@@@@@@@@@@@@@@@@@                           |
[64, 128)              13 |@@@@@@@@@@@@@@@@@@@@@@@@@@@@@@@@@@@@@@@@@@@@@@@@@@@@|
[128, 256)              3 |@@@@@@@@@@@                                       |

@us[COM_QUERY]:
[8, 16)                33 |@                                                 |
[16, 32)              185 |@@@@@@@@                                          |
[32, 64)             1128 |@@@@@@@@@@@@@@@@@@@@@@@@@@@@@@@@@@@@@@@@@@@@@@@@@@@@|
[64, 128)             300 |@@@@@@@@@@@@@                                     |
[128, 256)              2 |                                                  |

@us[COM_STMT_EXECUTE]:
[16, 32)             1410 |@@@@@@                                            |
[32, 64)             1654 |@@@@@@@                                           |
[64, 128)           11212 |@@@@@@@@@@@@@@@@@@@@@@@@@@@@@@@@@@@@@@@@@@@@@@@@@@@@|
[128, 256)           8899 |@@@@@@@@@@@@@@@@@@@@@@@@@@@@@@@@@@@@@@@@@           |
[256, 512)           5000 |@@@@@@@@@@@@@@@@@@@@@@@                            |
[512, 1K)            1478 |@@@@@@                                            |
[1K, 2K)                5 |                                                  |
[2K, 4K)             1504 |@@@@@@                                            |
[4K, 8K)              141 |                                                  |
[8K, 16K)               7 |                                                  |
[16K, 32K)              1 |                                                  |
```

This shows that queries took between 8 and 256 microseconds and that statement execution was bimodal, with modes of different latencies.

This works by instrumenting time (latency) between the USDT probes mysql:command__start and mysql:command__done, and reading the command type from the start probe. The overhead should be negligible, as the rate of commands is typically low (less than a thousand per second).

The source to mysqld_clat(8) is:

```
#!/usr/local/bin/bpftrace


BEGIN
{
        printf("Tracing mysqld command latencies. Ctrl-C to end.\n");

        // from include/my_command.h:
        @com[0] = "COM_SLEEP";
        @com[1] = "COM_QUIT";
        @com[2] = "COM_INIT_DB";
        @com[3] = "COM_QUERY";
        @com[4] = "COM_FIELD_LIST";
        @com[5] = "COM_CREATE_DB";
        @com[6] = "COM_DROP_DB";
        @com[7] = "COM_REFRESH";
        @com[8] = "COM_SHUTDOWN";
        @com[9] = "COM_STATISTICS";
        @com[10] = "COM_PROCESS_INFO";
        @com[11] = "COM_CONNECT";
        @com[12] = "COM_PROCESS_KILL";
        @com[13] = "COM_DEBUG";
        @com[14] = "COM_PING";
        @com[15] = "COM_TIME";
        @com[16] = "COM_DELAYED_INSERT";
        @com[17] = "COM_CHANGE_USER";
        @com[18] = "COM_BINLOG_DUMP";
        @com[19] = "COM_TABLE_DUMP";
        @com[20] = "COM_CONNECT_OUT";
        @com[21] = "COM_REGISTER_SLAVE";
        @com[22] = "COM_STMT_PREPARE";
        @com[23] = "COM_STMT_EXECUTE";
        @com[24] = "COM_STMT_SEND_LONG_DATA";
        @com[25] = "COM_STMT_CLOSE";
        @com[26] = "COM_STMT_RESET";
        @com[27] = "COM_SET_OPTION";
        @com[28] = "COM_STMT_FETCH";
        @com[29] = "COM_DAEMON";
        @com[30] = "COM_BINLOG_DUMP_GTID";
        @com[31] = "COM_RESET_CONNECTION";
}
```

```
usdt:/usr/sbin/mysqld:mysql:command__start
{
        @command[tid] = arg1;
        @start[tid] = nsecs;
}

usdt:/usr/sbin/mysqld:mysql:command__done
/@start[tid]/
{
        $dur = (nsecs - @start[tid]) / 1000;
        @us[@com[@command[tid]]] = hist($dur);
        delete(@command[tid]);
        delete(@start[tid]);
}

END
{
        clear(@com);
}
```

This includes a lookup table to convert from a command ID integer to a human-readable string: the command name. These names are from the MySQL server source in include/my_command.h and are also documented in the USDT probe reference [155].

If USDT probes are not available, this tool can be rewritten to use uprobes of the dispatch_command() function. Instead of reproducing the entire tool, here is a diff that highlights the required changes:

```
$ diff mysqld_clat.bt mysqld_clat_uprobes.bt
42c42
< usdt:/usr/sbin/mysqld:mysql:command__start
---
> uprobe:/usr/sbin/mysqld:*dispatch_command*
44c44
<        @command[tid] = arg1;
---
>        @command[tid] = arg2;
48c48
< usdt:/usr/sbin/mysqld:mysql:command__done
---
> uretprobe:/usr/sbin/mysqld:*dispatch_command*
```

The command is fetched from a different argument and uprobes are used instead, but the rest of the tool is the same.

13.2.12 signals

signals(8)[8] traces process signals and shows a summary distribution of the signal and target process. This is a useful troubleshooting tool for investigating why applications may be terminating unexpectedly, which may be because they were sent a signal. Example output:

```
# signals.bt
Attaching 3 probes...
Counting signals. Hit Ctrl-C to end.
^C
@[SIGNAL, PID, COMM] = COUNT

@[SIGKILL, 3022, sleep]: 1
@[SIGINT, 2997, signals.bt]: 1
@[SIGCHLD, 21086, bash]: 1
@[SIGSYS, 3014, ServiceWorker t]: 4
@[SIGALRM, 2903, mpstat]: 6
@[SIGALRM, 1882, Xorg]: 87
```

This output showed that a SIGKILL was sent to the sleep process with PID 3022 once (it only needs to be sent once), while SIGALRM was sent to Xorg PID 1882 a total of 87 times while tracing.

It works by tracing the signal:signal_generate tracepoint. Since these are infrequent, the overhead is expected to be negligible.

The source to signals(8) is:

```
#!/usr/local/bin/bpftrace

BEGIN
{
        printf("Counting signals. Hit Ctrl-C to end.\n");

        // from /usr/include/asm-generic/signal.h:
        @sig[0] = "0";
        @sig[1] = "SIGHUP";
        @sig[2] = "SIGINT";
        @sig[3] = "SIGQUIT";
        @sig[4] = "SIGILL";
        @sig[5] = "SIGTRAP";
        @sig[6] = "SIGABRT";
```

---

8 Origin: I created this for this book on 16-Feb-2019, plus earlier versions for other tracers. These were inspired by sig.d from the *Dynamic Tracing Guide*, Jan 2005 [Sun 05].

```
        @sig[7] = "SIGBUS";
        @sig[8] = "SIGFPE";
        @sig[9] = "SIGKILL";
        @sig[10] = "SIGUSR1";
        @sig[11] = "SIGSEGV";
        @sig[12] = "SIGUSR2";
        @sig[13] = "SIGPIPE";
        @sig[14] = "SIGALRM";
        @sig[15] = "SIGTERM";
        @sig[16] = "SIGSTKFLT";
        @sig[17] = "SIGCHLD";
        @sig[18] = "SIGCONT";
        @sig[19] = "SIGSTOP";
        @sig[20] = "SIGTSTP";
        @sig[21] = "SIGTTIN";
        @sig[22] = "SIGTTOU";
        @sig[23] = "SIGURG";
        @sig[24] = "SIGXCPU";
        @sig[25] = "SIGXFSZ";
        @sig[26] = "SIGVTALRM";
        @sig[27] = "SIGPROF";
        @sig[28] = "SIGWINCH";
        @sig[29] = "SIGIO";
        @sig[30] = "SIGPWR";
        @sig[31] = "SIGSYS";
}


tracepoint:signal:signal_generate
{
        @[@sig[args->sig], args->pid, args->comm] = count();
}

END
{
        printf("\n@[SIGNAL, PID, COMM] = COUNT");
        clear(@sig);
}
```

This uses a lookup table to convert the signal number to a readable code. In the kernel source, there is no name for signal number zero; however, it is used for health checks to determine if the target PID is still running.

13.2.13   killsnoop

killsnoop(8)[9] is a BCC and bpftrace tool to trace signals sent via the kill(2) syscall. This can show who is sending signals but, unlike signals(8), does not trace all signals sent on the system, only those sent via kill(2). Example output:

```
# killsnoop
TIME       PID    COMM            SIG  TPID   RESULT
00:28:00   21086  bash            9    3593   0
[...]
```

This output shows the bash shell sent a signal 9 (KILL) to PID 3593.

This works by tracing the syscalls:sys_enter_kill and syscalls:sys_exit_kill tracepoints. The overhead should be negligible.

BCC

Command line usage:

```
killsnoop [options]
```

Options include:

- **-x**: Only show failed kill syscalls
- **-p PID**: Measure this process only

bpftrace

The following is the code for the bpftrace version, which summarizes its core functionality. This version does not support options.

```
#!/usr/local/bin/bpftrace

BEGIN
{
        printf("Tracing kill() signals... Hit Ctrl-C to end.\n");
        printf("%-9s %-6s %-16s %-4s %-6s %s\n", "TIME", "PID", "COMM", "SIG",
            "TPID", "RESULT");
}

tracepoint:syscalls:sys_enter_kill
{
        @tpid[tid] = args->pid;
```

---

9 Origin: I created the first version as kill.d on 9-May-2004 to debug a case of mysterious application terminations. I also wrote the BCC version on 20-Sep-2015 and the bpftrace version on 7-Sep-2018.

```
        @tsig[tid] = args->sig;
}


tracepoint:syscalls:sys_exit_kill
/@tpid[tid]/
{
        time("%H:%M:%S  ");
        printf("%-6d %-16s %-4d %-6d %d\n", pid, comm, @tsig[tid], @tpid[tid],
            args->ret);
        delete(@tpid[tid]);
        delete(@tsig[tid]);
}
```

The program stores the target PID and signal on the entry to the syscall, so they can be referenced and printed on the exit. This could be enhanced like signals(8) to include a lookup table of signal names.

13.2.14   pmlock and pmheld

The pmlock(8)[10] and pmheld(8) bpftrace tools record libpthread mutex lock latency and held times as histograms, with user-level stacks. pmlock(8) can be used to identify an issue of lock contention, and then pmheld(8) can show the cause: which code path is responsible. Starting with pmlock(8) on MySQL server:

```
# pmlock.bt $(pgrep mysqld)
Attaching 4 probes...
Tracing libpthread mutex lock latency, Ctrl-C to end.
^C
[...]


@lock_latency_ns[0x7f3728001a50,
    pthread_mutex_lock+36
    THD::Query_plan::set_query_plan(enum_sql_command, LEX*, bool)+121
    mysql_execute_command(THD*, bool)+15991
    Prepared_statement::execute(String*, bool)+1410
    Prepared_statement::execute_loop(String*, bool, unsigned char*, unsigned char*...
, mysqld]:
[1K, 2K)             123 |                                                          |
[2K, 4K)            1203 |@@@@@@@@@                                                 |
[4K, 8K)            6576 |@@@@@@@@@@@@@@@@@@@@@@@@@@@@@@@@@@@@@@@@@@@@@@@@@@@@@@@@@@@@@|
[8K, 16K)           2077 |@@@@@@@@@@@@@@@@                                          |
```

---

10 Origin: I created these tools for this book on 17-Feb-2019, inspired by the Solaris lockstat(1M) tool, which also showed various lock times with latency histograms and partial stack traces.

```
@lock_latency_ns[0x7f37280019f0,
    pthread_mutex_lock+36
    THD::set_query(st_mysql_const_lex_string const&)+94
    Prepared_statement::execute(String*, bool)+336
    Prepared_statement::execute_loop(String*, bool, unsigned char*, unsigned char*...
    mysqld_stmt_execute(THD*, unsigned long, unsigned long, unsigned char*, unsign...
, mysqld]:
[1K, 2K)              47 |                                                             |
[2K, 4K)             945 |@@@@@@@@                                                      |
[4K, 8K)            3290 |@@@@@@@@@@@@@@@@@@@@@@@@@@@@@                                  |
[8K, 16K)           5702 |@@@@@@@@@@@@@@@@@@@@@@@@@@@@@@@@@@@@@@@@@@@@@@@@@@@@@@@@@@@@@@@@@|

@lock_latency_ns[0x7f37280019f0,
    pthread_mutex_lock+36
    THD::set_query(st_mysql_const_lex_string const&)+94
    dispatch_command(THD*, COM_DATA const*, enum_server_command)+1045
    do_command(THD*)+544
    handle_connection+680
, mysqld]:
[1K, 2K)              65 |                                                             |
[2K, 4K)            1198 |@@@@@@@@@@@                                                   |
[4K, 8K)            5283 |@@@@@@@@@@@@@@@@@@@@@@@@@@@@@@@@@@@@@@@@@@@@@@@@@@@@@@@@@@@@@@@@@|
[8K, 16K)           3966 |@@@@@@@@@@@@@@@@@@@@@@@@@@@@@@@@@@@@@@@@@@@@@@@@@              |
```

The last two stacks show latency on lock address 0x7f37280019f0, from code paths involving THD::set_query(), and with times usually in the 4 to 16-microsecond range.

Now running pmheld(8):

```
# pmheld.bt $(pgrep mysqld)
Attaching 5 probes...
Tracing libpthread mutex held times, Ctrl-C to end.
^C
[...]

@held_time_ns[0x7f37280019c0,
    __pthread_mutex_unlock+0
    close_thread_table(THD*, TABLE**)+169
    close_thread_tables(THD*)+923
    mysql_execute_command(THD*, bool)+887
    Prepared_statement::execute(String*, bool)+1410
, mysqld]:
[2K, 4K)            3311 |@@@@@@@@@@@@@@@@@@@@@@@@@@@@@@@@@@@@@@@@@@@             |
[4K, 8K)            4523 |@@@@@@@@@@@@@@@@@@@@@@@@@@@@@@@@@@@@@@@@@@@@@@@@@@@@@@@@|
```

```
@held_time_ns[0x7f37280019f0,
    __pthread_mutex_unlock+0
    THD::set_query(st_mysql_const_lex_string const&)+147
    dispatch_command(THD*, COM_DATA const*, enum_server_command)+1045
    do_command(THD*)+544
    handle_connection+680
, mysqld]:
[2K, 4K)          3848 |@@@@@@@@@@@@@@@@@@@@@@@@@@@@@@@@@@@@@@@@@          |
[4K, 8K)          5038 |@@@@@@@@@@@@@@@@@@@@@@@@@@@@@@@@@@@@@@@@@@@@@@@@@@@|
[8K, 16K)            0 |                                                 |
[16K, 32K)           0 |                                                 |
[32K, 64K)           1 |                                                 |

@held_time_ns[0x7f37280019c0,
    __pthread_mutex_unlock+0
    Prepared_statement::execute(String*, bool)+321
    Prepared_statement::execute_loop(String*, bool, unsigned char*, unsigned char*...
    mysqld_stmt_execute(THD*, unsigned long, unsigned long, unsigned char*, unsign...
    dispatch_command(THD*, COM_DATA const*, enum_server_command)+5582
, mysqld]:
[1K, 2K)          2204 |@@@@@@@@@@@@@@@@@@@@@@@                           |
[2K, 4K)          4803 |@@@@@@@@@@@@@@@@@@@@@@@@@@@@@@@@@@@@@@@@@@@@@@@@@@@|
[4K, 8K)          2845 |@@@@@@@@@@@@@@@@@@@@@@@@@@@@@@                    |
[8K, 16K)            0 |                                                 |
[16K, 32K)          11 |                                                 |
```

This shows paths that were holding the same lock and the duration it was held, as a histogram.

There are various courses of action given all this data: the size of thread pools could be tuned to reduce lock contention, and a developer could look at the holding code paths to optimize them to hold the lock for shorter durations.

It is recommended to output these tools to files for later analysis. For example:

```
# pmlock.bt PID > out.pmlock01.txt
# pmheld.bt PID > out.pmheld01.txt
```

An optional PID can be provided to only trace that process ID, which is also recommended to reduce the overhead on the system. Without it, all pthread lock events system-wide are recorded.

These tools work by instrumenting libpthread functions using uprobes and uretprobes: pthread_mutex_lock() and pthread_mutex_unlock(). The overhead can be significant, as these lock events can be very extremely frequent. For example, timing them using BCC funccount for one second:

```
# funccount -d 1 '/lib/x86_64-linux-gnu/libpthread.so.0:pthread_mutex_*lock'
Tracing 4 functions for
"/lib/x86_64-linux-gnu/libpthread.so.0:pthread_mutex_*lock"... Hit Ctrl-C to end.

FUNC                              COUNT
pthread_mutex_trylock              4525
pthread_mutex_lock                44726
pthread_mutex_unlock              49132
```

At such rates, adding a tiny amount of overhead to each call will add up.

pmlock

The source to pmlock(8) is:

```
#!/usr/local/bin/bpftrace

BEGIN
{
        printf("Tracing libpthread mutex lock latency, Ctrl-C to end.\n");
}

uprobe:/lib/x86_64-linux-gnu/libpthread.so.0:pthread_mutex_lock
/$1 == 0 || pid == $1/
{
        @lock_start[tid] = nsecs;
        @lock_addr[tid] = arg0;
}

uretprobe:/lib/x86_64-linux-gnu/libpthread.so.0:pthread_mutex_lock
/($1 == 0 || pid == $1) && @lock_start[tid]/
{
        @lock_latency_ns[usym(@lock_addr[tid]), ustack(5), comm] =
            hist(nsecs - @lock_start[tid]);
        delete(@lock_start[tid]);
        delete(@lock_addr[tid]);
}

END
{
        clear(@lock_start);
        clear(@lock_addr);
}
```

This records a timestamp and the lock address when pthread_mutex_lock() begins, then fetches these when it ends to calculate the latency and save it with the lock address and stack trace. The ustack(5) can be adjusted to record as many frames as you wish.

The path to /lib/x86_64-linux-gnu/libpthread.so.0 may need to be adjusted to match your system. Stack traces may not work without frame pointers in the calling software, and libpthread as well. (It may work without libpthread frame pointers since it's tracing the entry point to the library, and the frame pointer register may not have been reused yet.)

The latency to pthread_mutex_trylock() is not traced as it is assumed to be fast, as is the purpose of the try-lock call. (This can be verified with BCC funclatency(8).)

pmheld

The source code to pmheld(8) is:

```
#!/usr/local/bin/bpftrace

BEGIN
{
        printf("Tracing libpthread mutex held times, Ctrl-C to end.\n");
}

uprobe:/lib/x86_64-linux-gnu/libpthread.so.0:pthread_mutex_lock,
uprobe:/lib/x86_64-linux-gnu/libpthread.so.0:pthread_mutex_trylock
/$1 == 0 || pid == $1/
{
        @lock_addr[tid] = arg0;
}

uretprobe:/lib/x86_64-linux-gnu/libpthread.so.0:pthread_mutex_lock
/($1 == 0 || pid == $1) && @lock_addr[tid]/
{
        @held_start[pid, @lock_addr[tid]] = nsecs;
        delete(@lock_addr[tid]);
}

uretprobe:/lib/x86_64-linux-gnu/libpthread.so.0:pthread_mutex_trylock
/retval == 0 && ($1 == 0 || pid == $1) && @lock_addr[tid]/
{
        @held_start[pid, @lock_addr[tid]] = nsecs;
        delete(@lock_addr[tid]);
}
```

```
uprobe:/lib/x86_64-linux-gnu/libpthread.so.0:pthread_mutex_unlock
/($1 == 0 || pid == $1) && @held_start[pid, arg0]/
{
        @held_time_ns[usym(arg0), ustack(5), comm] =
            hist(nsecs - @held_start[pid, arg0]);
        delete(@held_start[pid, arg0]);
}


END
{
        clear(@lock_addr);
        clear(@held_start);
}
```

The time is now measured from when the pthread_mutex_lock() or pthread_mutex_trylock() function returns—and hence the caller holds the lock—to when it calls unlock().

These tools used uprobes, but libpthread has USDT probes as well, so these tools could be rewritten to use them.

13.2.15   naptime

naptime(8)[11] traces the nanosleep(2) syscall and shows who is calling it and for what sleep duration. I wrote this tool to debug a slow internal build process that would take minutes without seemingly doing anything, and I suspected it included voluntary sleeps. The output:

```
# naptime.bt
Attaching 2 probes...
Tracing sleeps. Hit Ctrl-C to end.
TIME       PPID  PCOMM        PID    COMM         SECONDS
19:09:19 1       systemd      1975   iscsid       1.000
19:09:20 1       systemd      2274   mysqld       1.000
19:09:20 1       systemd      1975   iscsid       1.000
19:09:21 2998    build-init   25137  sleep        30.000
19:09:21 1       systemd      2274   mysqld       1.000
19:09:21 1       systemd      1975   iscsid       1.000
19:09:22 1       systemd      2421   irqbalance   9.999
[...]
```

This has caught a sleep for 30 seconds by build-init. I was able to track down that program and "tune" this sleep, making my build 10 times faster. This output also shows mysqld and iscsid

---

11 Origin: I created it for this book on 16-Feb-2019, inspired by Sasha Goldsthein's SyS_nanosleep() example from trace(8), and to debug the slow build described here. The build was of an internal nflx-bpftrace package I was developing.

threads sleeping for one second every second. (We've seen that mysqld sleep in earlier tool outputs.) Sometimes applications can call sleep as a workaround for other issues, and the workaround can stay in the code for years, causing performance problems. This tool can help detect this issue.

This works by tracing the syscalls:sys_enter_nanosleep tracepoint, and the overhead is expected to be negligible.

The source to naptime(8) is:

```
#!/usr/local/bin/bpftrace

#include <linux/time.h>
#include <linux/sched.h>

BEGIN
{
        printf("Tracing sleeps. Hit Ctrl-C to end.\n");
        printf("%-8s %-6s %-16s %-6s %-16s %s\n", "TIME", "PPID", "PCOMM",
            "PID", "COMM", "SECONDS");
}

tracepoint:syscalls:sys_enter_nanosleep
/args->rqtp->tv_sec + args->rqtp->tv_nsec/
{
        $task = (struct task_struct *)curtask;
        time("%H:%M:%S ");
        printf("%-6d %-16s %-6d %-16s %d.%03d\n", $task->real_parent->pid,
            $task->real_parent->comm, pid, comm,
            args->rqtp->tv_sec, args->rqtp->tv_nsec / 1000000);
}
```

Parent process details are fetched from the task_struct, but this method is unstable and may require updates if that task_struct changes.

This tool can be enhanced: the user-level stack trace could be printed out as well to show the code path that led to the sleep (provided that the code path was compiled with frame pointers so that the stack can be walked by BPF).

13.2.16   Other Tools

Another BPF tool is **deadlock(8)**,[12] from BCC, which detects potential deadlocks with mutex usage of the form of lock order inversions. It builds a directed graph representing the mutex usage for detecting deadlocks. While the overhead of this tool can be high, it helps debug a difficult issue.

---

12 deadlock(8) was developed by Kenny Yu on 01-Feb-2017.

13.3 BPF One-Liners

These sections show BCC and bpftrace one-liners. Where possible, the same one-liner is implemented using both BCC and bpftrace.

13.3.1 BCC

New processes with arguments:

```
execsnoop
```

Syscall count by process:

```
syscount -P
```

Syscall count by syscall name:

```
syscount
```

Sample user-level stacks at 49 Hertz, for PID 189:

```
profile -U -F 49 -p 189
```

Count off-CPU user stack traces:

```
stackcount -U t:sched:sched_switch
```

Sample all stack traces and process names:

```
profile
```

Count libpthread mutex lock functions for one second:

```
funccount -d 1 '/lib/x86_64-linux-gnu/libpthread.so.0:pthread_mutex_*lock'
```

Count libpthread conditional variable functions for one second:

```
funccount -d 1 '/lib/x86_64-linux-gnu/libpthread.so.0:pthread_cond_*'
```

13.3.2 bpftrace

New processes with arguments:

```
bpftrace -e 'tracepoint:syscalls:sys_enter_execve { join(args->argv); }'
```

Syscall count by process:

```
bpftrace -e 'tracepoint:raw_syscalls:sys_enter { @[pid, comm] = count(); }'
```

Syscall count by syscall name:

```
bpftrace -e 'tracepoint:syscalls:sys_enter_* { @[probe] = count(); }'
```

Sample user-level stacks at 49 Hertz, for PID 189:

```
bpftrace -e 'profile:hz:49 /pid == 189/ { @[ustack] = count(); }'
```

Sample user-level stacks at 49 Hertz, for processes named "mysqld":

```
bpftrace -e 'profile:hz:49 /comm == "mysqld"/ { @[ustack] = count(); }'
```

Count off-CPU user stack traces:

```
bpftrace -e 'tracepoint:sched:sched_switch { @[ustack] = count(); }'
```

Sample all stack traces and process names:

```
bpftrace -e 'profile:hz:49 { @[ustack, stack, comm] = count(); }'
```

Sum malloc() requested bytes by user stack trace (high overhead):

```
bpftrace -e 'u:/lib/x86_64-linux-gnu/libc-2.27.so:malloc { @[ustack(5)] =
    sum(arg0); }'
```

Trace kill() signals showing sender process name, target PID, and signal number:

```
bpftrace -e 't:syscalls:sys_enter_kill { printf("%s -> PID %d SIG %d\n", comm,
    args->pid, args->sig); }'
```

Count libpthread mutex lock functions for one second:

```
bpftrace -e 'u:/lib/x86_64-linux-gnu/libpthread.so.0:pthread_mutex_*lock {
    @[probe] = count(); } interval:s:1 { exit(); }'
```

Count libpthread conditional variable functions for one second:

```
bpftrace -e 'u:/lib/x86_64-linux-gnu/libpthread.so.0:pthread_cond_* {
    @[probe] = count(); } interval:s:1 { exit(); }'
```

Count LLC misses by process name:

```
bpftrace -e 'hardware:cache-misses: { @[comm] = count(); }'
```

13.4 BPF One-Liners Examples

Including some sample output, as was done for each tool, is also useful for illustrating one-liners. Here is a selected one-liner with example output.

13.4.1 Counting libpthread Conditional Variable Functions for One Second

```
# bpftrace -e 'u:/lib/x86_64-linux-gnu/libpthread.so.0:pthread_cond_* {
    @[probe] = count(); } interval:s:1 { exit(); }'
Attaching 19 probes...
@[uprobe:/lib/x86_64-linux-gnu/libpthread.so.0:pthread_cond_wait@@GLIBC_2.3.2]: 70
@[uprobe:/lib/x86_64-linux-gnu/libpthread.so.0:pthread_cond_wait]: 70
@[uprobe:/lib/x86_64-linux-gnu/libpthread.so.0:pthread_cond_init@@GLIBC_2.3.2]: 573
@[uprobe:/lib/x86_64-linux-gnu/libpthread.so.0:pthread_cond_timedwait@@GLIBC_2.3.2]: 673
```

```
@[uprobe:/lib/x86_64-linux-gnu/libpthread.so.0:pthread_cond_destroy@@GLIBC_2.3.2]: 939
@[uprobe:/lib/x86_64-linux-gnu/libpthread.so.0:pthread_cond_broadcast@@GLIBC_2.3.2]: 1796
@[uprobe:/lib/x86_64-linux-gnu/libpthread.so.0:pthread_cond_broadcast]: 1796
@[uprobe:/lib/x86_64-linux-gnu/libpthread.so.0:pthread_cond_signal]: 4600
@[uprobe:/lib/x86_64-linux-gnu/libpthread.so.0:pthread_cond_signal@@GLIBC_2.3.2]: 4602
```

These pthread functions can be frequently called, so to minimize performance overhead only one second is traced. These counts show how conditional variables (CVs) are in use: there are timed waits for threads waiting on a CV and other threads sending signals or broadcasts to wake them up.

This one-liner can be modified to analyze these further: including the process name, stack traces, timed wait durations, and other details.

13.5   Summary

In this chapter I showed additional BPF tools beyond the prior resource-oriented chapters for application analysis, covering application context, thread usage, signals, locks, and sleeps. I used MySQL server as an example target application, and read its query context from BPF using both USDT probes and uprobes. On-CPU and off-CPU analysis using BPF tools was covered again for this example application due to its importance.

Chapter 14

Kernel

The kernel is the heart of the system; it is also a complex body of software. The Linux kernel employs many different strategies for improving CPU scheduling, memory placement, disk I/O performance, and TCP performance. As with any software, sometimes things go wrong. Previous chapters instrumented the kernel to help understand application behavior. This chapter uses kernel instrumentation to understand kernel software, and will be of use for kernel troubleshooting and to aid in kernel development.

Learning Objectives:

- Continue off-CPU analysis by tracing wakeups
- Identify kernel memory consumers
- Analyze kernel mutex lock contention
- Show activity of work queue events

If you are working on a particular subsystem, you should first browse the tools in the relevant previous chapters. By Linux subsystem name, these are:

- **sched:** Chapter 6
- **mm:** Chapter 7
- **fs:** Chapter 8
- **block:** Chapter 9
- **net:** Chapter 10

Chapter 2 also covers tracing technologies, including BPF, tracepoints, and kprobes. This chapter focuses on studying the kernel rather than the resources, and includes additional kernel topics beyond the previous chapters. I begin with background discussion, then BPF capabilities, kernel analysis strategy, traditional tools including Ftrace, and BPF tools for additional analysis: wakeups, kernel memory allocation, kernel locks, tasklets, and work queues.

14.1   Background

The kernel manages access to resources and schedules processes on the CPUs. Previous chapters have already introduced many kernel topics. In particular, see:

- Section 6.1.1 for the CPU Modes and the CPU Scheduler sections
- Section 7.1.1 for the Memory Allocators, Memory Pages and Swapping, Page-Out Daemon, and File System Caching and Buffering sections
- Section 8.1.1 for the I/O Stack and File System Caches sections
- Section 9.1.1 for the Block I/O Stack and I/O Schedulers sections
- Section 10.1.1 for the Network Stack, Scaling, and TCP sections

Additional topics for kernel analysis are explored in this chapter.

14.1.1   Kernel Fundamentals

Wakeups

When threads block and go off CPU to wait for an event, they usually return to the CPU when triggered by a wakeup event. An example is disk I/O: a thread may block on a file system read that issues a disk I/O and is later woken up by a worker thread that processes the completion interrupt.

In some cases, there is a dependency chain of wakeups: one thread wakes up another, and that thread wakes up another, until it wakes up the blocked application.

Figure 14-1 shows how an application thread can block and go off CPU for a syscall, to be later woken up by a resource thread with possible dependency threads.

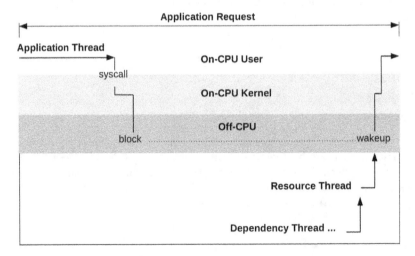

Figure 14-1   Off-CPU and wakeups

Tracing the wakeups can reveal more information about the duration of the off-CPU event.

Kernel Memory Allocation

Two main allocators in the kernel are the:

- **slab allocator:** A general-purpose memory allocator for objects of fixed sizes, which supports caching allocations and recycling them for efficiency. In Linux this is now the slub allocator: it is based on the slab allocator paper [Bonwick 94], but with reduced complexity.

- **page allocator:** For allocating memory pages. It uses a buddy algorithm, which refers to finding neighboring pages of free memory so that they can be allocated together. This is also NUMA aware.

These allocators were mentioned in Chapter 7 as background for application memory usage analysis. This chapter focuses on kernel memory usage analysis.

The API calls for kernel memory allocation include kmalloc(), kzalloc(), and kmem_cache_alloc() (slab allocation) for small chunks, vmalloc() and vzalloc() for large areas, and alloc_pages() for pages [156].

Kernel Locks

User-level locks were covered in Chapter 13. The kernel supports locks of different types: spin locks, mutex locks, and reader-writer locks. Since locks block threads, they are a source of performance issues.

Linux kernel mutex locks are a hybrid with three acquisition paths, tried in the following order [157]:

1. **fastpath:** Using a compare-and-swap instruction (cmpxchg)

2. **midpath:** Optimistically spinning first if the lock holder is running in case it is about to be released

3. **slowpath:** Blocking until the lock is available

There is also the read-copy-update (RCU) synchronization mechanism that allows multiple reads to occur concurrently with updates, improving performance and scalability for data that is mostly read.

Tasklets and Work Queues

For Linux, device drivers are modeled as two halves, with the top half handling the interrupt quickly and scheduling work to a bottom half to be processed later [Corbet 05]. Handling the interrupt quickly is important because the top half runs in interrupt-disabled mode to postpone the delivery of new interrupts, which can cause latency problems if it runs for too long. The bottom half can be either tasklets or work queues; the latter are threads that can be scheduled by the kernel and can sleep when necessary. This is pictured in Figure 14-2.

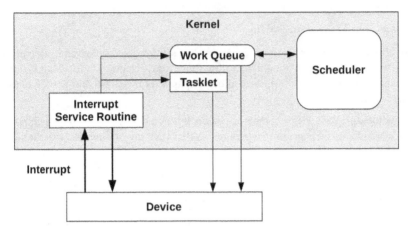

Figure 14-2   Tasklets and work queues

14.1.2   BPF Capabilities

BPF tracing tools can provide additional insight beyond kernel metrics, including answering such questions as:

- Why are threads leaving the CPU, and how long are they off CPU?
- What events did off-CPU threads wait for?
- Who is currently using the kernel slab allocator?
- Is the kernel moving pages to balance NUMA?
- What work queue events are occurring? With what latencies?
- For kernel developers: which of my functions are called? With what arguments and return value? With what latency?

These can be answered by instrumenting tracepoints and kernel functions to measure their latency, arguments, and stack traces. Timed sampling of stack traces can also be used to provide a view of on-CPU code paths, which usually works because the kernel is typically compiled with stack support (either frame pointers or ORC).

Event Sources

Kernel event types are listed in Table 14-1, along with instrumentation sources.

Table 14-1   **Kernel Event Types and Instrumentation Sources**

Event Type	Event Source
Kernel function execution	kprobes
Scheduler events	sched tracepoints
System calls	syscalls and raw_syscalls tracepoints

Event Type	Event Source
Kernel memory allocation	kmem tracepoints
Page out daemon scanning	vmscan tracepoints
Interrupts	irq and irq_vectors tracepoints
Workqueue execution	workqueue tracepoints
Timers	timer tracepoints
IRQ and preemption disabled	preemptirq traceponts[1]

Check your kernel version to see what other tracepoints exist, such as by using bpftrace:

```
bpftrace -l 'tracepoint:*'
```

Or using perf(1):

```
perf list tracepoint
```

Prior chapters covered resource events, including block and network I/O.

14.2 Strategy

If you are new to kernel performance analysis, here is a suggested overall strategy that you can follow. The next sections explain the tools involved in more detail.

1. If possible, create a workload that triggers the events of interest, ideally a known number of times. This might involve writing a short C program.

2. Check for the existence of tracepoints that instrument the event or existing tools (including those in this chapter).

3. If the event can be called frequently so that it consumes significant CPU resources (>5%), CPU profiling can be a quick way to show the kernel functions involved. If not, a longer profile may be used to capture enough samples for study (e.g., using perf(1) or BCC profile(8), with CPU flame graphs). CPU profiling will also reveal the use of spin locks, and mutex locks during optimistic spin.

4. As another way to find related kernel functions, count function calls that likely match the event. For example, if analyzing ext4 file system events, you could try counting all calls that matched "ext4_*" (using BCC funccount(8)).

5. Count stack traces from kernel functions to understand the code path (using BCC stackcount(8)). These code paths should already be known if profiling was used.

6. Trace function call flow through its child events (using perf-tools Ftrace-based funcgraph(8)).

7. Inspect function arguments (using BCC trace(8) and argdist(8), or bpftrace).

8. Measure function latency (using BCC funclatency(8) or bpftrace).

9. Write a custom tool to instrument the events and print or summarize them.

---

1 Requires CONFIG_PREEMPTIRQ_EVENTS.

The following section shows some of these steps using traditional tools, which you can try before turning to BPF tools.

14.3   Traditional Tools

Many traditional tools were covered in prior chapters. Some additional tools that can be used for kernel analysis are included here and listed in Table 14-2.

Table 14-2   **Traditional Tools**

Tool	Type	Description
Ftrace	Tracing	Linux built-in tracer
perf sched	Tracing	Linux official profiler: scheduler analysis subcommand
slabtop	Kernel statistics	Kernel slab cache usage

14.3.1   Ftrace

Ftrace[2] was created by Steven Rostedt and added to Linux 2.6.27 in 2008. Like perf(1), Ftrace is a multi-tool with many capabilities. There are at least four ways to use Ftrace:

A. Via the /sys/kernel/debug/tracing files, controlled using cat(1) and echo(1) or a higher-level language. This usage is documented in the kernel source under Documentation/trace/ftrace.rst [158].

B. Via the trace-cmd front-end by Steven Rostedt [159][160].

C. Via the KernelShark GUI by Steven Rostedt and others [161].

D. Via the tools in the perf-tools collection by myself [78]. These are shell wrappers to the /sys/kernel/debug/tracing files.

I will demonstrate Ftrace capabilities using perf-tools, but any of these methods can be used.

Function Counting

Let's say I wanted to analyze file system read-ahead in the kernel. I can begin by counting all functions containing "readahead" using funccount(8) (from perf-tools) while generating a workload that is expected to trigger it:

```
# funccount '*readahead*'
Tracing "*readahead*"... Ctrl-C to end.
^C
FUNC                          COUNT
page_cache_async_readahead       12
```

---

2 It is often written as "ftrace"; however, Steven would like to standardize on "Ftrace." (I asked for this book.)

```
__breadahead                      33
page_cache_sync_readahead         69
ondemand_readahead                81
__do_page_cache_readahead         83


Ending tracing...
```

This shows five functions that were called, with their frequency.

Stack Traces

The next step is to learn more about these functions. Ftrace can collect stack traces on events, which show why the function was called—their parent functions. Analyzing the first one from the previous output using kprobe(8):

```
# kprobe -Hs 'p:page_cache_async_readahead'
Tracing kprobe page_cache_async_readahead. Ctrl-C to end.
# tracer: nop
#
#                                 _-----=> irqs-off
#                                / _----=> need-resched
#                               | / _---=> hardirq/softirq
#                               || / _--=> preempt-depth
#                               ||| /     delay
#            TASK-PID    CPU#   ||||    TIMESTAMP  FUNCTION
#               | |        |    ||||       |          |
            cksum-32372 [006] .... 1952191.125801: page_cache_async_readahead:
(page_cache_async_readahead+0x0/0x80)
            cksum-32372 [006] .... 1952191.125822: <stack trace>
 => page_cache_async_readahead
 => ext4_file_read_iter
 => new_sync_read
 => __vfs_read
 => vfs_read
 => SyS_read
 => do_syscall_64
 => entry_SYSCALL_64_after_hwframe
            cksum-32372 [006] .... 1952191.126704: page_cache_async_readahead:
(page_cache_async_readahead+0x0/0x80)
            cksum-32372 [006] .... 1952191.126722: <stack trace>
 => page_cache_async_readahead
 => ext4_file_read_iter
[...]
```

This prints a stack trace per event, showing that it was triggered during a read() syscall. kprobe(8) also allows function arguments and the return value to be inspected.

For efficiency, these stack traces can be frequency counted in kernel context rather than printed one by one. This requires a newer Ftrace feature, hist triggers, short for histogram triggers. Example:

```
# cd /sys/kernel/debug/tracing/
# echo 'p:kprobes/myprobe page_cache_async_readahead' > kprobe_events
# echo 'hist:key=stacktrace' > events/kprobes/myprobe/trigger
# cat events/kprobes/myprobe/hist
# event histogram
#
# trigger info: hist:keys=stacktrace:vals=hitcount:sort=hitcount:size=2048 [active]
#

{ stacktrace:
         ftrace_ops_assist_func+0x61/0xf0
         0xffffffffc0e1b0d5
         page_cache_async_readahead+0x5/0x80
         generic_file_read_iter+0x784/0xbf0
         ext4_file_read_iter+0x56/0x100
         new_sync_read+0xe4/0x130
         __vfs_read+0x29/0x40
         vfs_read+0x8e/0x130
         SyS_read+0x55/0xc0
         do_syscall_64+0x73/0x130
         entry_SYSCALL_64_after_hwframe+0x3d/0xa2
} hitcount:         235

Totals:
    Hits: 235
    Entries: 1
    Dropped: 0
[...steps to undo the tracing state...]
```

This output shows that this stack trace path was taken 235 times during tracing.

Function Graphing

Finally, funcgraph(8) can show the child functions called:

```
# funcgraph page_cache_async_readahead
Tracing "page_cache_async_readahead"... Ctrl-C to end.
 3)               |  page_cache_async_readahead() {
 3)               |    inode_congested() {
 3)               |      dm_any_congested() {
 3)   0.582 us    |        dm_request_based();
 3)               |        dm_table_any_congested() {
 3)               |          dm_any_congested() {
 3)   0.267 us    |            dm_request_based();
 3)   1.824 us    |            dm_table_any_congested();
 3)   4.604 us    |          }
 3)   7.589 us    |        }
 3) + 11.634 us   |      }
 3) + 13.127 us   |    }
 3)               |    ondemand_readahead() {
 3)               |      __do_page_cache_readahead() {
 3)               |        __page_cache_alloc() {
 3)               |          alloc_pages_current() {
 3)   0.234 us    |            get_task_policy.part.30();
 3)   0.124 us    |            policy_nodemask();
[...]
```

This reveals not just the code path taken but, as with stack traces, these functions can also be traced for more information arguments and return values.

14.3.2 perf sched

The perf(1) command is another multi-tool, and Chapter 6 summarized its use with PMCs, profiling, and tracing. It also has a `sched` subcommand for scheduler analysis. For example:

```
# perf sched record
# perf sched timehist


Samples do not have callchains.
           time   cpu  task name          wait time  sch delay   run time
                        [tid/pid]           (msec)     (msec)     (msec)
--------------- ------ ------------------ --------- --------- ---------
 991962.879971 [0005]  perf[16984]           0.000     0.000     0.000
 991962.880070 [0007]  :17008[17008]         0.000     0.000     0.000
 991962.880070 [0002]  cc1[16880]            0.000     0.000     0.000
 991962.880078 [0000]  cc1[16881]            0.000     0.000     0.000
 991962.880081 [0003]  cc1[16945]            0.000     0.000     0.000
 991962.880093 [0003]  ksoftirqd/3[28]       0.000     0.007     0.012
 991962.880108 [0000]  ksoftirqd/0[6]        0.000     0.007     0.030
[...]
```

This output shows per-scheduling event metrics of the time spent blocked and waiting for a wakeup ("wait time"), the scheduler delay (aka run queue latency, "sch delay"), and the on-CPU run time ("run time").

14.3.3   slabtop

The slabtop(1) tool shows the current sizes of the kernel slab allocation caches. For example, from a large production system, sorting by cache size (-s c):

```
# slabtop -s c
Active / Total Objects (% used)    : 1232426 / 1290213 (95.5%)
Active / Total Slabs (% used)      : 29225 / 29225 (100.0%)
Active / Total Caches (% used)     : 85 / 135 (63.0%)
Active / Total Size (% used)       : 288336.64K / 306847.48K (94.0%)
Minimum / Average / Maximum Object : 0.01K / 0.24K / 16.00K

  OBJS ACTIVE   USE OBJ SIZE  SLABS OBJ/SLAB CACHE SIZE NAME
 76412  69196    0%   0.57K   2729       28     43664K radix_tree_node
313599 313599  100%   0.10K   8041       39     32164K buffer_head
  3732   3717    0%   7.44K    933        4     29856K task_struct
 11776   8795    0%   2.00K    736       16     23552K TCP
 33168  32277    0%   0.66K    691       48     22112K proc_inode_cache
 86100  79990    0%   0.19K   2050       42     16400K dentry
 25864  24679    0%   0.59K    488       53     15616K inode_cache
[...]
```

This output shows around 43 Mbytes in the radix_tree_node cache and around 23 Mbytes in the TCP cache. For a system with a total of 180 Gbytes of main memory, these kernel caches are relatively tiny.

This is a useful tool for troubleshooting memory pressure problems, to check whether some kernel component is unexpectedly consuming significant memory.

14.3.4   Other Tools

/proc/lock_stat shows various statistics on kernel locks but is only available if CONFIG_LOCK_STAT is set.

/proc/sched_debug provides many metrics to aid scheduler development.

14.4   BPF Tools

This section covers additional BPF tools you can use for kernel analysis and troubleshooting. They are shown in Figure 14-3.

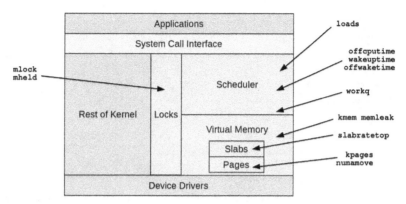

Figure 14-3   Additional BPF tools for kernel analysis

These tools are either from the BCC and bpftrace repositories covered in Chapters 4 and 5 or were created for this book. Some tools appear in both BCC and bpftrace. Table 14-3 lists the tool origins (BT is short for bpftrace).

Table 14-3   **Kernel-Related Tools**

Tool	Source	Target	Description
loads	BT	CPUs	Show load averages
offcputime	BCC/book	Sched	Summarize off-CPU stack traces and times
wakeuptime	BCC	Sched	Summarize waker stack traces and blocked times
offwaketime	BCC	Sched	Summarize waker with off-CPU stack traces
mlock	Book	Mutexes	Show mutex lock times and kernel stacks
mheld	Book	Mutexes	Show mutex held times and kernel stacks
kmem	Book	Memory	Summarize kernel memory allocations
kpages	Book	Pages	Summarize kernel page allocations
memleak	BCC	Memory	Show possible memory leak code paths
slabratetop	BCC/book	Slab	Show kernel slab allocation rates by cache
numamove	Book	NUMA	Show NUMA page migration statistics
workq	Book	Work queues	Show work queue function execution times

For the tools from BCC and bpftrace, see their repositories for full and updated lists of tool options and capabilities.

See the previous chapters for more tools for kernel analysis, including for system calls, networking, and block I/O.

The following tool summaries include a discussion on instrumenting spin locks and tasklets.

14.4.1   loads

loads(8)[3] is a bpftrace tool to print the system load averages every second:

```
# loads.bt
Attaching 2 probes...
Reading load averages... Hit Ctrl-C to end.
18:49:16 load averages: 1.983 1.151 0.931
18:49:17 load averages: 1.824 1.132 0.926
18:49:18 load averages: 1.824 1.132 0.926
[...]
```

As discussed in Chapter 6, these load averages are not very useful, and you should quickly move on to deeper metrics. The loads(8) tool may be more useful as an example of fetching and printing a kernel variable, in this case avenrun:

```
#!/usr/local/bin/bpftrace

BEGIN
{
        printf("Reading load averages... Hit Ctrl-C to end.\n");
}

interval:s:1
{
        /*
         * See fs/proc/loadavg.c and include/linux/sched/loadavg.h for the
         * following calculations.
         */
        $avenrun = kaddr("avenrun");
        $load1 = *$avenrun;
        $load5 = *($avenrun + 8);
        $load15 = *($avenrun + 16);
        time("%H:%M:%S ");
        printf("load averages: %d.%03d %d.%03d %d.%03d\n",
            ($load1 >> 11), (($load1 & ((1 << 11) - 1)) * 1000) >> 11,
            ($load5 >> 11), (($load5 & ((1 << 11) - 1)) * 1000) >> 11,
            ($load15 >> 11), (($load15 & ((1 << 11) - 1)) * 1000) >> 11
        );
}
```

---

3 Origin: I created this as loads.d for DTrace on 10-Jun-2005 and the bpftrace version on 10-Sep-2018.

The kaddr() built-in is used to fetch the address of the avenrun kernel symbol, which is then dereferenced. Other kernel variables can be fetched in the same way.

14.4.2   offcputime

offcputime(8) was introduced in Chapter 6. In this section, I will look at its ability to examine a task state, and also problems that led to the creation of additional tools included in this chapter.

Non-interruptible I/O

Matching on the TASK_UNINTERRUPTIBLE thread state can shed light on time that applications were blocked waiting for a resource. This helps exclude time that applications spend sleeping in between work, which can otherwise drown out the real performance issues in an offcputime(8) profile. This TASK_UNINTERRUPTIBLE time is also included in the system load averages on Linux, leading to much confusion when people expect them to reflect only CPU time.

Measuring this thread state (2) for user-level process and kernel stacks only:

```
# offcputime -uK --state 2
Tracing off-CPU time (us) of user threads by kernel stack... Hit Ctrl-C to end.
[...]

    finish_task_switch
    __schedule
    schedule
    io_schedule
    generic_file_read_iter
    xfs_file_buffered_aio_read
    xfs_file_read_iter
    __vfs_read
    vfs_read
    ksys_read
    do_syscall_64
    entry_SYSCALL_64_after_hwframe
    -               tar (7034)
        1088682
```

Only the last stack has been included, which shows a tar(1) process waiting on storage I/O via the XFS file system. This command has filtered out other thread states, including:

- **TASK_RUNNING (0)**: Threads can block in this state due to involuntary context switches, as the CPUs are running at saturation. In such a case, the stack trace that was interrupted is not very interesting, as it does not show why the thread moved off-CPU.

- **TASK_INTERRUPTIBLE (1)**: This normally pollutes the output with many off-CPU stacks in sleeping and waiting for work code paths.

Filtering these out helps focus the output to show the stacks that are blocking during application requests, which have more impact on performance.

Inconclusive Stacks

Many stack traces printed by offcputime(8) are inconclusive, showing a blocking path but not its cause. Here is an example that traces off-CPU kernel stacks for five seconds for a gzip(1) process:

```
# offcputime -Kp $(pgrep -n gzip) 5
Tracing off-CPU time (us) of PID 5028 by kernel stack for 5 secs.

    finish_task_switch
    __schedule
    schedule
    exit_to_usermode_loop
    prepare_exit_to_usermode
    swapgs_restore_regs_and_return_to_usermode
    -               gzip (5028)
        21

    finish_task_switch
    __schedule
    schedule
    pipe_wait
    pipe_read
    __vfs_read
    vfs_read
    ksys_read
    do_syscall_64
    entry_SYSCALL_64_after_hwframe
    -               gzip (5028)
        4404219
```

The output shows that 4.4 seconds out of five were in pipe_read(), but you can't tell from the output what was on the other end of the pipe that gzip was waiting for or why it took so long. The stack just tells us that it is waiting on someone else.

Such inconclusive off-CPU stack traces are common—not just with pipes but also with I/O and lock contention. You may see threads blocked waiting for a lock, but you can't see why the lock was unavailable (e.g., who was the holder and what they were doing).

Examining wakeup stacks using wakeuptime(8) can often reveal what is on the other side of the wait.

See Chapter 6 for more about offcputime(8).

14.4.3 wakeuptime

wakeuptime(8)[4] is a BCC tool that shows the stack traces from threads performing scheduler wakeups and the time that the target was blocked. This can be used to further explore off-CPU time. Continuing the previous example:

```
# wakeuptime -p $(pgrep -n gzip) 5
Tracing blocked time (us) by kernel stack for 5 secs.


    target:          gzip
    ffffffff94000088 entry_SYSCALL_64_after_hwframe
    ffffffff93604175 do_syscall_64
    ffffffff93874d72 ksys_write
    ffffffff93874af3 vfs_write
    ffffffff938748c2 __vfs_write
    ffffffff9387d50e pipe_write
    ffffffff936cb11c __wake_up_common_lock
    ffffffff936caffc __wake_up_common
    ffffffff936cb65e autoremove_wake_function
    waker:           tar
        4551336


Detaching...
```

This output shows that the gzip(1) process was blocked on the tar(1) process doing a vfs_write(). Now I'll reveal the command that caused this workload:

```
tar cf - /mnt/data | gzip - > /mnt/backup.tar.gz
```

From this one-liner, it may be obvious that gzip(1) spends much of its time waiting for data from tar(1). tar(1) in turn spends much of its time waiting for data from disk, which can be shown by offcputime(8):

```
# offcputime -Kp $(pgrep -n tar) 5
Tracing off-CPU time (us) of PID 5570 by kernel stack for 5 secs.
[...]


    finish_task_switch
    __schedule
    schedule
```

---

4 Origin: I developed wakeuptime tracing using DTrace and visualized it with flame graphs on 7-Nov-2013. This started out as part of a 45-minute talk on flame graphs that I had to develop at the last minute for the USENIX LISA conference [Gregg 13a] when the talk I had originally planned suddenly became impossible to do. Then I was asked to also fill in for another speaker who had become ill, so I ended up giving this as part two of a 90-minute plenary on flame graphs. I created the BCC tool on 14-Jan-2016.

```
io_schedule
generic_file_read_iter
xfs_file_buffered_aio_read
xfs_file_read_iter
__vfs_read
vfs_read
ksys_read
do_syscall_64
entry_SYSCALL_64_after_hwframe
-                 tar (5570)
    4204994
```

This stack shows tar(1) blocked on io_schedule(): block device I/O. Given the output of both offcputime(8) and wakeuptime(8), you can see why an application was blocked (offcputime(8) output) and then the reason the application was woken up (wakeuptime(8) output). Sometimes the wakeup reason better identifies the source of issues than the blocked reason.

To keep these examples short, I'm using -p to match on a PID. You can trace system-wide instead by not specifying -p.

This tool works by tracing scheduler functions schedule() and try_to_wake_up(). These can be very frequent on busy systems, so the overhead may be significant.

Command line usage:

```
wakeuptime [options] [duration]
```

Options include:

- **-f**: Output in folded format, for generating a wakeup time flame graph
- **-p PID**: This process only

As with offcputime(8), if it is run without -p, it will trace system-wide—and likely produce hundreds of pages of output. A flame graph will help you navigate this output quickly.

14.4.4   offwaketime

offwaketime(8)[5] is a BCC tool that combines offcputime(8) and wakeuptime(8). Continuing the previous example:

```
# offwaketime -Kp $(pgrep -n gzip) 5
Tracing blocked time (us) by kernel off-CPU and waker stack for 5 secs.
```

---

5 Origin: I developed this initially as chain graphs for the USENIX LISA 2013 conference on 7-Nov-2013 [Gregg 13a], where I walked multiple wakeups and showed the output as a flame graph. That version used DTrace, and since DTrace can't save and retrieve stacks I needed to dump all events and post-process, which was too expensive for real production use. BPF allows saving and retrieving stack traces (which I used when creating this BCC tool on 13-Jan-2016), as well as limiting it to one wakeup level. Alexei Starovoitov added a version to the kernel source, under samples/bpf/offwaketime_*.c.

```
[...]

    waker:              tar 5852
    entry_SYSCALL_64_after_hwframe
    do_syscall_64
    ksys_write
    vfs_write
    __vfs_write
    pipe_write
    __wake_up_common_lock
    __wake_up_common
    autoremove_wake_function
    --                  --
    finish_task_switch
    __schedule
    schedule
    pipe_wait
    pipe_read
    __vfs_read
    vfs_read
    ksys_read
    do_syscall_64
    entry_SYSCALL_64_after_hwframe
    target:             gzip 5851
        4490207
```

This output shows tar(1) waking up gzip(1), which was blocked in this path for 4.49 seconds. Both stack traces are shown, delimited by "--", and the top waker stack has been inverted. This way, the stack traces meet in the middle at the point where the waker stack (top) is waking the blocked stack (bottom).

This tool works by tracing scheduler functions schedule() and try_to_wake_up(), and saves the waker stack trace in a BPF stack map for later lookup by the blocked thread so that they can be summarized together in kernel context. These can be very frequent on busy systems, so the overhead may be significant.

Command line usage:

```
offwaketime [options] [duration]
```

Options include:

- **-f**: Output in folded format, for generating an off-wake time flame graph
- **-p PID**: This process only
- **-K**: Only kernel stack traces
- **-U**: Only user-level stack traces

Without -p, it will trace system-wide, likely producing hundreds of pages of output. The use of options such as -p, -K, and -U will help reduce overhead.

Off-Wake Time Flame Graphs

The folded output (using -f) can be visualized as a flame graph using the same orientation: waker stack on the top, inverted, and blocked stack on the bottom. An example is shown in Figure 14-4.

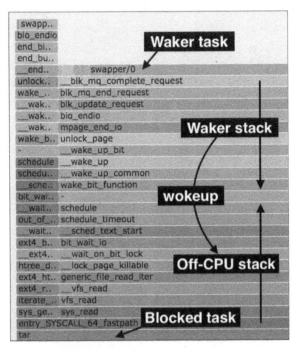

Figure 14-4   Off-wake time flame graph

14.4.5   mlock and mheld

The mlock(8)[6] and mheld(8) tools trace the kernel mutex lock latency and held times as histograms, with kernel-level stacks. mlock(8) can be used to identify issues of lock contention, and then mheld(8) can show the cause: which code path is responsible for hogging the lock. Starting with mlock(8):

```
# mlock.bt
Attaching 6 probes...
Tracing mutex_lock() latency, Ctrl-C to end.
```

---

6 Origin: I created these tools for this book on 14-Mar-2019. This approach is inspired by the Solaris lockstat(1M) tool by Jeff Bonwick, which also showed partial stacks with latency histograms for lock and held times.

```
^C
[...]

@lock_latency_ns[0xffff9d015738c6e0,
    kretprobe_trampoline+0
    unix_stream_recvmsg+81
    sock_recvmsg+67
    ___sys_recvmsg+245
    __sys_recvmsg+81
, chrome]:
[512, 1K)          5859 |@@@@@@@@@@@@@@@@@@@@@@@@@@@@@@@@@@@@@@                  |
[1K, 2K)           8303 |@@@@@@@@@@@@@@@@@@@@@@@@@@@@@@@@@@@@@@@@@@@@@@@@@@@@@@@@|
[2K, 4K)           1689 |@@@@@@@@@@                                            |
[4K, 8K)            476 |@@                                                    |
[8K, 16K)           101 |                                                      |
```

The output included many stack traces and locks, only one of which has been included here. It shows the address of the lock (0xffff9d015738c6e0), the stack trace to mutex_lock(), the process name ("chrome"), and the latency of mutex_lock(). This lock was acquired thousands of times while tracing, although it was usually fast: for example, the histogram shows that 8303 times it took between 1024 and 2048 nanoseconds (roughly one to two microseconds).

Now running mheld(8):

```
# mheld.bt
Attaching 9 probes...
Tracing mutex_lock() held times, Ctrl-C to end.
^C
[...]

@held_time_ns[0xffff9d015738c6e0,
    mutex_unlock+1
    unix_stream_recvmsg+81
    sock_recvmsg+67
    ___sys_recvmsg+245
    __sys_recvmsg+81
, chrome]:
[512, 1K)         16459 |@@@@@@@@@@@@@@@@@@@@@@@@@@@@@@@@@@@@@@@@@@@@@@@@@@@@@@@|
[1K, 2K)           7427 |@@@@@@@@@@@@@@@@@@@@@@@@                               |
```

This shows that the same process and stack trace was the holder for this lock.

These tools work by tracing the mutex_lock(), mutex_lock_interruptible(), and mutex_trylock() kernel functions because mutex tracepoints do not yet exist. Since these can be frequent, the overhead while tracing may become significant for busy workloads.

mlock

The source to mlock(8) is:

```
#!/usr/local/bin/bpftrace

BEGIN
{
        printf("Tracing mutex_lock() latency, Ctrl-C to end.\n");
}

kprobe:mutex_lock,
kprobe:mutex_lock_interruptible
/$1 == 0 || pid == $1/
{
        @lock_start[tid] = nsecs;
        @lock_addr[tid] = arg0;
}

kretprobe:mutex_lock
/($1 == 0 || pid == $1) && @lock_start[tid]/
{
        @lock_latency_ns[ksym(@lock_addr[tid]), kstack(5), comm] =
            hist(nsecs - @lock_start[tid]);
        delete(@lock_start[tid]);
        delete(@lock_addr[tid]);
}

kretprobe:mutex_lock_interruptible
/retval == 0 && ($1 == 0 || pid == $1) && @lock_start[tid]/
{
        @lock_latency_ns[ksym(@lock_addr[tid]), kstack(5), comm] =
            hist(nsecs - @lock_start[tid]);
        delete(@lock_start[tid]);
        delete(@lock_addr[tid]);
}

END
{
        clear(@lock_start);
        clear(@lock_addr);
}
```

This times the duration of mutex_lock(), and also mutex_lock_interruptible() only if it returned successfully. mutex_trylock() is not traced, as it is assumed to have no latency. An optional argument to mlock(8) can be provided to specify the process ID to trace; without it, the entire system is traced.

mheld

The source to mheld(8) is:

```
#!/usr/local/bin/bpftrace

BEGIN
{
        printf("Tracing mutex_lock() held times, Ctrl-C to end.\n");
}

kprobe:mutex_lock,
kprobe:mutex_trylock,
kprobe:mutex_lock_interruptible
/$1 == 0 || pid == $1/
{
        @lock_addr[tid] = arg0;
}

kretprobe:mutex_lock
/($1 == 0 || pid == $1) && @lock_addr[tid]/
{
        @held_start[@lock_addr[tid]] = nsecs;
        delete(@lock_addr[tid]);
}

kretprobe:mutex_trylock,
kretprobe:mutex_lock_interruptible
/retval == 0 && ($1 == 0 || pid == $1) && @lock_addr[tid]/
{
        @held_start[@lock_addr[tid]] = nsecs;
        delete(@lock_addr[tid]);
}

kprobe:mutex_unlock
/($1 == 0 || pid == $1) && @held_start[arg0]/
{
        @held_time_ns[ksym(arg0), kstack(5), comm] =
            hist(nsecs - @held_start[arg0]);
        delete(@held_start[arg0]);
}
```

```
END
{
        clear(@lock_addr);
        clear(@held_start);
}
```

This traces the held duration from the different mutex functions. As with mlock(8), an optional process ID argument can be provided.

14.4.6 Spin Locks

As with mutex locks traced previously, there are not yet tracepoints for tracing spin locks. Note that there are several types of spin locks, including spin_lock_bh(), spin_lock(), spin_lock_irq(), and spin_lock_irqsave() [162]. They are defined as follows in include/linux/spinlock.h:

```
#define spin_lock_irqsave(lock, flags)                          \
do {                                                            \
        raw_spin_lock_irqsave(spinlock_check(lock), flags);     \
} while (0)
[...]
#define raw_spin_lock_irqsave(lock, flags)                      \
        do {                                            \
                typecheck(unsigned long, flags);        \
                flags = _raw_spin_lock_irqsave(lock);   \
        } while (0)
```

You can see them using funccount(8):

```
# funccount '*spin_lock*'
Tracing 16 functions for "*spin_lock*"... Hit Ctrl-C to end.
^C
FUNC                                    COUNT
_raw_spin_lock_bh                        7092
native_queued_spin_lock_slowpath         7227
_raw_spin_lock_irq                     261538
_raw_spin_lock                        1215218
_raw_spin_lock_irqsave                1582755
Detaching...
```

funccount(8) is instrumenting the entry of these functions using kprobes. The return of these functions cannot be traced using kretprobes,[7] so it's not possible to time their duration directly from these functions. Look higher in the stack for functions that can be traced, e.g., by using stackcount(8) on the kprobe to see the call stack.

I usually debug spin lock performance issues using CPU profiling and flame graphs, since they appear as CPU-consuming functions.

14.4.7 kmem

kmem(8)[8] is a bpftrace tool to trace kernel memory allocations by stack trace and prints statistics on the number of allocations, the average allocation size, and the total bytes allocated. For example:

```
# kmem.bt
Attaching 3 probes...
Tracing kmem allocation stacks (kmalloc, kmem_cache_alloc). Hit Ctrl-C to end.
^C
[...]
@bytes[
    kmem_cache_alloc+288
    getname_flags+79
    getname+18
    do_sys_open+285
    SyS_openat+20
, Xorg]: count 44, average 4096, total 180224
@bytes[
    __kmalloc_track_caller+368
    kmemdup+27
    intel_crtc_duplicate_state+37
    drm_atomic_get_crtc_state+119
    page_flip_common+51
, Xorg]: count 120, average 2048, total 245760
```

This output has been truncated to show only the last two stacks. The first one shows an open(2) syscall that led to a slab allocation (kmem_cache_alloc()) during getname_flags() by the Xorg process. That allocation occurred 44 times while tracing, allocating an average of 4096 bytes, for a total of 180,224 bytes.

---

7 It was found that instrumenting these using kretprobes could deadlock the system [163], so BCC has added a section for banned kretprobes. There are other functions that are banned in the kernel using NOKPROBE_SYMBOL; I hope these are not included, as it may break kprobes for these functions as well, and kprobes have many uses even without the kretprobes.

8 Origin: I created it for this book on 15-Mar-2019.

This works by tracing kmem tracepoints. Since allocations can be frequent, the overhead may become measurable on busy systems.

The source to kmem(8) is:

```
#!/usr/local/bin/bpftrace

BEGIN
{
        printf("Tracing kmem allocation stacks (kmalloc, kmem_cache_alloc). ");
        printf("Hit Ctrl-C to end.\n");
}

tracepoint:kmem:kmalloc,
tracepoint:kmem:kmem_cache_alloc
{
        @bytes[kstack(5), comm] = stats(args->bytes_alloc);
}
```

This uses the stats() built-in to print the triplet: count of allocations, average bytes, and total bytes. This can be switched to hist() for printing histograms if desired.

14.4.8   kpages

kpages(8)[9] is a bpftrace tool that traces the other type of kernel memory allocation, alloc_pages(), via the kmem:mm_page_alloc tracepoint. Example output:

```
# kpages.bt
Attaching 2 probes...
Tracing page allocation stacks. Hit Ctrl-C to end.
^C
[...]
@pages[
    __alloc_pages_nodemask+521
    alloc_pages_vma+136
    handle_pte_fault+959
    __handle_mm_fault+1144
    handle_mm_fault+177
, chrome]: 11733
```

The output has been truncated to show only one stack; this one shows Chrome processes allocating 11,733 pages while tracing during page faults. This tool works by tracing kmem tracepoints. Since allocations can be frequent, the overhead may become measurable on busy systems.

---

9 Origin: I created it on 15-Mar-2019 for this book.

The source to kpages(8) is:

```
#!/usr/local/bin/bpftrace

BEGIN
{
        printf("Tracing page allocation stacks. Hit Ctrl-C to end.\n");
}

tracepoint:kmem:mm_page_alloc
{
        @pages[kstack(5), comm] = count();
}
```

This can be implemented as a one-liner, but, to ensure that it isn't overlooked, I've created it as the kpages(8) tool.

14.4.9 memleak

memleak(8) was introduced in Chapter 7: it is a BCC tool that shows allocations that were not freed while tracing, which can identify memory growth or leaks. By default it traces kernel allocations, for example:

```
# memleak
Attaching to kernel allocators, Ctrl+C to quit.

[13:46:02] Top 10 stacks with outstanding allocations:
[...]
        6922240 bytes in 1690 allocations from stack
                __alloc_pages_nodemask+0x209 [kernel]
                alloc_pages_current+0x6a [kernel]
                __page_cache_alloc+0x81 [kernel]
                pagecache_get_page+0x9b [kernel]
                grab_cache_page_write_begin+0x26 [kernel]
                ext4_da_write_begin+0xcb [kernel]
                generic_perform_write+0xb3 [kernel]
                __generic_file_write_iter+0x1aa [kernel]
                ext4_file_write_iter+0x203 [kernel]
                new_sync_write+0xe7 [kernel]
                __vfs_write+0x29 [kernel]
                vfs_write+0xb1 [kernel]
                sys_pwrite64+0x95 [kernel]
                do_syscall_64+0x73 [kernel]
                entry_SYSCALL_64_after_hwframe+0x3d [kernel]
```

Just one stack has been included here, showing allocations via ext4 writes. See Chapter 7 for more about memleak(8).

14.4.10   slabratetop

slabratetop(8)[10] is a BCC and bpftrace tool that shows the rate of kernel slab allocations by slab cache name, by tracing kmem_cache_alloc() directly. This is a companion to slabtop(1), which shows the volume of the slab caches (via /proc/slabinfo). For example, from a 48-CPU production instance:

```
# slabratetop

09:48:29 loadavg: 6.30 5.45 5.46 4/3377 29884

CACHE                     ALLOCS      BYTES
kmalloc-4096                 654    2678784
kmalloc-256                 2637     674816
filp                         392     100352
sock_inode_cache              94      66176
TCP                           31      63488
kmalloc-1024                  58      59392
proc_inode_cache              69      46920
eventpoll_epi                354      45312
sigqueue                     227      36320
dentry                       165      31680
[...]
```

This output shows that the kmalloc-4096 cache had the most bytes allocated in that output interval. As with slabtop(1), this tool can be used when troubleshooting unexpected memory pressure.

This works by using kprobes to trace the kmem_cache_alloc() kernel function. Since this function can be called somewhat frequently, the overhead of this tool might become noticeable on very busy systems.

BCC

Command line usage:

```
slabratetop [options] [interval [count]]
```

Options:

- ■ -C: Don't clear the screen

---

10 Origin: I created it on 15-Oct-2016 for BCC, and I wrote the bpftrace version for this book on 26-Jan-2019.

bpftrace

This version only counts allocations by cache name, printing output each second with a timestamp:

```
#!/usr/local/bin/bpftrace

#include <linux/mm.h>
#include <linux/slab.h>
#ifdef CONFIG_SLUB
#include <linux/slub_def.h>
#else
#include <linux/slab_def.h>
#endif

kprobe:kmem_cache_alloc
{
        $cachep = (struct kmem_cache *)arg0;
        @[str($cachep->name)] = count();
}

interval:s:1
{
        time();
        print(@);
        clear(@);
}
```

A check for the kernel compile option CONFIG_SLUB is needed so that the correct version of the slab allocator header files are included.

14.4.11 numamove

numamove(8)[11] traces page migrations of type "NUMA misplaced." These pages are moved to different NUMA nodes to improve memory locality and overall system performance. I've encountered production issues where up to 40% of CPU time was spent doing such NUMA page migrations; this performance loss outweighed the benefits of NUMA page balancing. This tool helps me keep an eye on NUMA page migrations in case the problem returns. Example output:

```
# numamove.bt
Attaching 4 probes...
TIME            NUMA_migrations NUMA_migrations_ms
22:48:45                      0                  0
```

11 Origin: I created it for this book on 26-Jan-2019 and to use to check for recurrence of an issue.

22:48:46	0	0
22:48:47	308	29
22:48:48	2	0
22:48:49	0	0
22:48:50	1	0
22:48:51	1	0
[...]		

This output caught a burst of NUMA page migrations at 22:48:47: 208 migrations, taking 29 milliseconds in total. The columns show the per-second rate of migrations and the time spent doing migrations in milliseconds. Note that NUMA balancing must be enabled (sysctl kernel. numa_balancing=1) for this activity to occur.

The source to numamove(8) is:

```
#!/usr/local/bin/bpftrace

kprobe:migrate_misplaced_page { @start[tid] = nsecs; }

kretprobe:migrate_misplaced_page /@start[tid]/
{
        $dur = nsecs - @start[tid];
        @ns += $dur;
        @num++;
        delete(@start[tid]);
}


BEGIN
{
        printf("%-10s %18s %18s\n", "TIME",
            "NUMA_migrations", "NUMA_migrations_ms");
}


interval:s:1
{
        time("%H:%M:%S");
        printf("   %18d %18d\n", @num, @ns / 1000000);
        delete(@num);
        delete(@ns);
}
```

This uses a kprobe and kretprobe to trace the start and end of the kernel function migrate_misplaced_page(), and an interval probe to print out the statistics.

14.4.12 workq

workq(8)[12] traces workqueue requests and times their latency. For example:

```
# workq.bt
Attaching 4 probes...
Tracing workqueue request latencies. Ctrl-C to end.
^C
[...]

@us[intel_atomic_commit_work]:
[1K, 2K)               7 |                                                    |
[2K, 4K)               9 |                                                    |
[4K, 8K)             132 |@@@@                                                |
[8K, 16K)           1524 |@@@@@@@@@@@@@@@@@@@@@@@@@@@@@@@@@@@@@@@@@@@@@@@@@@@@@@|
[16K, 32K)          1019 |@@@@@@@@@@@@@@@@@@@@@@@@@@@@@@@@@@@@                  |
[32K, 64K)             2 |                                                    |

@us[kcryptd_crypt]:
[2, 4)                 2 |                                                    |
[4, 8)              4864 |@@@@@@@@@@@@@@@@@@@@@@@                              |
[8, 16)            10746 |@@@@@@@@@@@@@@@@@@@@@@@@@@@@@@@@@@@@@@@@@@@@@@@@@@@@@@|
[16, 32)            2887 |@@@@@@@@@@@@@@                                      |
[32, 64)             456 |@@                                                  |
[64, 128)            250 |@                                                   |
[128, 256)           190 |                                                    |
[256, 512)            29 |                                                    |
[512, 1K)             14 |                                                    |
[1K, 2K)               2 |                                                    |
```

This output shows that the kcryptd_crypt() workqueue function was called frequently, usually taking between four and 32 microseconds.

This works by tracing the workqueue:workqueue_execute_start and workqueue:workqueue_execute_end tracepoints.

The source to workq(8) is:

```
#!/usr/local/bin/bpftrace

BEGIN
{
        printf("Tracing workqueue request latencies. Ctrl-C to end.\n");
}
```

12 Origin: I created it for this book on 14-Mar-2019.

```
tracepoint:workqueue:workqueue_execute_start
{
        @start[tid] = nsecs;
        @wqfunc[tid] = args->function;
}

tracepoint:workqueue:workqueue_execute_end
/@start[tid]/
{
        $dur = (nsecs - @start[tid]) / 1000;
        @us[ksym(@wqfunc[tid])] = hist($dur);
        delete(@start[tid]);
        delete(@wqfunc[tid]);
}

END
{
        clear(@start);
        clear(@wqfunc);
}
```

This measures the time from execute start to end and saves it as a histogram keyed on the function name.

14.4.13 Tasklets

In 2009, a patch to add tasklet tracepoints was proposed by Anton Blanchard, but these are not in the kernel as of today [164]. The tasklet functions, initialized in tasklet_init(), can be traced using kprobes. For example, in net/ipv4/tcp_output.c:

```
[...]
                tasklet_init(&tsq->tasklet,
                        tcp_tasklet_func,
                        (unsigned long)tsq);
[...]
```

This creates a tasklet to call the tcp_tasklet_func() function. Tracing its latency using BCC funclatency(8):

```
# funclatency -u tcp_tasklet_func
Tracing 1 functions for "tcp_tasklet_func"... Hit Ctrl-C to end.
^C
     usecs               : count    distribution
         0 -> 1          : 0        |                                        |
         2 -> 3          : 0        |                                        |
         4 -> 7          : 3        |*                                       |
         8 -> 15         : 10       |****                                    |
        16 -> 31         : 22       |********                                |
        32 -> 63         : 100      |****************************************|
        64 -> 127        : 61       |************************                |
Detaching...
```

Custom tools can be created using bpftrace and kprobes for tasklet functions as desired.

14.4.14   Other Tools

Other tools worth mentioning for kernel analysis:

- **runqlat(8):** Summarizes CPU run queue latency (Chapter 6).
- **syscount(8):** Summarizes system calls by type and process (Chapter 6).
- **hardirq(8):** Summarizes hard interrupt time (Chapter 6).
- **softirq(8):** Summarizes soft interrupt time (Chapter 6).
- **xcalls(8):** Times CPU cross calls (Chapter 6).
- **vmscan(8):** Measures VM scanner shrink and reclaim times (Chapter 7).
- **vfsstat(8):** Counts common VFS operation statistics (Chapter 8).
- **cachestat(8):** Shows page cache statistics (Chapter 8).
- **biostacks(8):** Shows block I/O initialization stacks with latency (Chapter 9).
- **skblife(8):** Measures sk_buff lifespans (Chapter 10).
- **inject(8):** Uses bpf_override_return() to modify kernel functions to return errors, for testing error paths. A BCC tool.
- **criticalstat(8)**[13]: Measures atomic critical sections in the kernel, showing durations and stack traces. By default, it shows IRQ-disabled paths that lasted longer than 100 microseconds. This is a BCC tool that can help you locate a source of latency in the kernel. It requires CONFIG_DEBUG_PREEMPT and CONFIG_PREEMPTIRQ_EVENTS.

Kernel analysis often involves custom instrumentation beyond the tools, and one-liners are a way to begin developing custom programs.

---

13 Origin: It was developed by Joel Fernandes on 18-Jun-2018.

14.5 BPF One-Liners

These sections show BCC and bpftrace one-liners. Where possible, the same one-liner is implemented using both BCC and bpftrace.

14.5.1 BCC

Count system calls by process:

```
syscount -P
```

Count system calls by syscall name:

```
syscount
```

Count kernel function calls starting with "attach":

```
funccount 'attach*'
```

Time the kernel function vfs_read() and summarize as a histogram:

```
funclatency vfs_read
```

Frequency count the first integer argument to kernel function "func1":

```
argdist -C 'p::func1(int a):int:a'
```

Frequency count the return value from kernel function "func1":

```
argdist -C 'r::func1():int:$retval'
```

Cast the first argument as a sk_buff and frequency count the len member:

```
argdist -C 'p::func1(struct sk_buff *skb):unsigned int:skb->len'
```

Sample kernel-level stacks at 99 Hertz:

```
profile -K -F99
```

Count context switch stack traces:

```
stackcount -p 123 t:sched:sched_switch
```

14.5.2 bpftrace

Count system calls by process:

```
bpftrace -e 'tracepoint:raw_syscalls:sys_enter { @[pid, comm] = count(); }'
```

Count system calls by syscall probe name:

```
bpftrace -e 'tracepoint:syscalls:sys_enter_* { @[probe] = count(); }'
```

Count system calls by syscall function:

```
bpftrace -e 'tracepoint:raw_syscalls:sys_enter {
    @[ksym(*(kaddr("sys_call_table") + args->id * 8))] = count(); }'
```

Count kernel function calls starting with "attach":

```
bpftrace -e 'kprobe:attach* { @[probe] = count(); }'
```

Time the kernel function vfs_read() and summarize as a histogram:

```
bpftrace -e 'k:vfs_read { @ts[tid] = nsecs; } kr:vfs_read /@ts[tid]/ {
    @ = hist(nsecs - @ts[tid]); delete(@ts[tid]); }'
```

Frequency count the first integer argument to kernel function "func1":

```
bpftrace -e 'kprobe:func1 { @[arg0] = count(); }'
```

Frequency count the return value from kernel function "func1":

```
bpftrace -e 'kretprobe:func1 { @[retval] = count(); }'
```

Sample kernel-level stacks at 99 Hertz, excluding idle:

```
bpftrace -e 'profile:hz:99 /pid/ { @[kstack] = count(); }'
```

Sample on-CPU kernel function at 99 Hertz:

```
bpftrace -e 'profile:hz:99 { @[kstack(1)] = count(); }'
```

Count context switch stack traces:

```
bpftrace -e 't:sched:sched_switch { @[kstack, ustack, comm] = count(); }'
```

Count workqueue requests by kernel function:

```
bpftrace -e 't:workqueue:workqueue_execute_start { @[ksym(args->function)] =
    count() }'
```

Count hrtimer starts by kernel function:

```
bpftrace -e 't:timer:hrtimer_start { @[ksym(args->function)] = count(); }'
```

14.6   BPF One-Liners Examples

Including some sample output, as was done for each tool, is also useful for illustrating one-liners.

14.6.1   Counting System Calls by Syscall Function

```
# bpftrace -e 'tracepoint:raw_syscalls:sys_enter {
    @[ksym(*(kaddr("sys_call_table") + args->id * 8))] = count(); }'
Attaching 1 probe...
^C
[...]
@[sys_writev]: 5214
@[sys_sendto]: 5515
@[SyS_read]: 6047
@[sys_epoll_wait]: 13232
@[sys_poll]: 15275
```

```
@[SyS_ioctl]: 19010
@[sys_futex]: 20383
@[SyS_write]: 26907
@[sys_gettid]: 27254
@[sys_recvmsg]: 51683
```

This output shows that the sys_recvmsg() function, likely for the recvmsg(2) syscall, was called the most while tracing: 51,683 times.

This one-liner uses the single raw_syscalls:sys_enter tracepoint, rather than matching all the syscalls:sys_enter_* tracepoints, making it much faster to initialize and terminate. However, the raw_syscall tracepoint only provides an ID number for the syscall; this one-liner translates it into the syscall function by looking up its entry in the kernel sys_call_table.

14.6.2 Counting hrtimer Starts by Kernel Function

```
# bpftrace -e 't:timer:hrtimer_start { @[ksym(args->function)] = count(); }'
Attaching 1 probe...
^C

@[timerfd_tmrproc]: 2
@[sched_rt_period_timer]: 2
@[watchdog_timer_fn]: 8
@[intel_uncore_fw_release_timer]: 63
@[it_real_fn]: 78
@[perf_swevent_hrtimer]: 3521
@[hrtimer_wakeup]: 6156
@[tick_sched_timer]: 13514
```

This shows the timer functions in use; the output caught perf_swevent_hrtimer() as perf(1) was doing a software-based CPU profile. I wrote this one-liner to check which CPU profile mode was in use (cpu-clock versus cycles events), since the software version uses timers.

14.7 Challenges

Some challenges when tracing kernel functions:

- Some kernel functions are inlined by the compiler. This can make them invisible to BPF tracing. One workaround is to trace a parent or child function that isn't inlined to accomplish the same task (perhaps requiring a filter). Another is to use kprobe instruction offset tracing.

- Some kernel functions are unsafe to trace as they run in special modes, such as interrupts disabled, or are part of the tracing framework itself. These are blacklisted by the kernel to make them unavailable to trace.

- Any kprobe-based tool will need maintenance to match changes to the kernel. Several BCC tools have already broken and required fixes to span newer kernels. The long-term solution is to use tracepoints instead where possible.

14.8 Summary

This chapter focused on kernel analysis, as supplemental material beyond the prior resource-oriented chapters. Traditional tools including Ftrace were summarized, then off-CPU analysis was explored in more detail with BPF, as well as kernel memory allocation, wakeups, and work queue requests.

Chapter 15

Containers

Containers have become a commonly used method for deploying services on Linux, providing security isolation, application startup times, resource controls, and ease of deployment. This chapter covers how to use BPF tools in container environments and covers some differences in tools and methods for analysis that are specific to containers.

Learning Objectives:

- Understand the makeup of containers and their targets for tracing
- Understand challenges with privileges, container IDs, and FaaS
- Quantify CPU sharing between containers
- Measure blk cgroup I/O throttling
- Measure the performance of overlay FS

This chapter begins with the necessary background for container analysis, then describes BPF capabilities. Various BPF tools and one-liners are then introduced.

The knowledge and tools you need to analyze the performance of applications in containers is mostly covered in prior chapters: with containers, CPUs are still CPUs, file systems are still file systems, and disks are still disks. This chapter focuses on the container-specific differences, such as namespaces and cgroups.

15.1 Background

Containers allow multiple instances of an operating system to execute on a single host. There are two main ways containers can be implemented:

- **OS virtualization:** This involves partitioning the system using namespaces on Linux and is usually combined with cgroups for resource controls. A single kernel is running, shared between all containers. This is the approach used by Docker, Kubernetes, and other container environments.

- **Hardware (HW) virtualization:** This involves running lightweight virtual machines, each with its own kernel. This approach is used by Intel Clear Containers (now Kata Containers [165]) and Firecracker from AWS [166].

Chapter 16 provides some insights for the analysis of HW-virtualized containers. This chapter covers OS-virtualized containers.

A typical Linux container implementation is pictured in Figure 15-1.

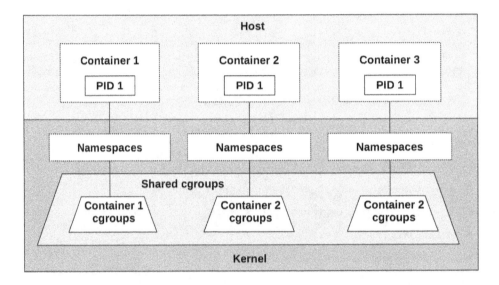

Figure 15-1   Linux OS-virtualized containers

A namespace restricts the view of the system. Namespaces include cgroup, ipc, mnt, net, pid, user, and uts. A pid namespace restricts the container's processes view of /proc to see only the container's own processes; an mnt namespace restricts the file system mounts that can be seen; the uts[1] namespace isolates details returned from the uname(2) syscall, and so on.

The control group (cgroup) restricts usage of resources. There are two versions of cgroups in the Linux kernel, v1 and v2; many projects such as Kubernetes are still using v1. cgroups for v1 include blkio, cpu, cpuacct, cpuset, devices, hugetlb, memory, net_cls, net_prio, pids, and rmda. These can be configured to limit resource contention between containers, for example by putting a hard limit on CPU and memory usage, or softer limits (share-based) for CPU and disk usage. There can also be a hierarchy of cgroups, including system cgroups that are shared between the containers, as pictured in Figure 15-1.[2]

---

1 Named after the utsname structure from the uname(2) syscall, which itself is named after UNIX Time-sharing System [167].

2 I also used parallelograms for cgroups, to imply a range of usage between soft and hard limits, rather than the ridged

cgroups v2 solves various shortcomings of v1, and it is expected that container technologies will migrate to v2 in the coming years, with v1 eventually being deprecated.

A common concern for container performance analysis is the possible presence of "noisy neighbors": container tenants that are aggressively consuming resources and causing access contention for others. Since these container processes are all under one kernel and can be analyzed simultaneously from the host, this is not dissimilar to traditional performance analysis of multiple applications running on one time-sharing system. The main difference is that cgroups may impose additional software limits for resources that are encountered before the hardware limits. Monitoring tools that have not been updated to support containers may be blind to these soft limits and the performance issues they cause.

15.1.1 BPF Capabilities

Container analysis tools are typically metrics based, showing which containers, cgroups, and namespaces exist, their settings, and their sizes. BPF tracing tools can provide many more details, answering:

- What is the run-queue latency per container?
- Is the scheduler switching between containers on the same CPU?
- Are CPU or disk soft limits encountered?

These questions can be answered with BPF by instrumenting tracepoints for scheduler events and kprobes for kernel functions. As has been discussed in prior chapters, some of these events (such as scheduling) can be very frequent and are more suited to ad hoc analysis than continuous monitoring.

There are tracepoints for cgroup events, including cgroup:cgroup_setup_root, cgroup:cgroup_attach_task, and others. These are high-level events that can help debug container startup.

Network packet programs can also be attached to cgroup ingress and egress using the BPF_PROG_TYPE_CGROUP_SKB program type (not shown in this chapter).

15.1.2 Challenges

Some challenges when using BPF tracing with containers are covered in the following topics.

BPF Privileges

BPF tracing currently requires root privileges, which for most container environments means that BPF tracing tools can only be executed from the host, not from within containers. This should change; non-privileged BPF access is currently being discussed specifically to solve the container problem.[3] This was also summarized in Section 11.1.2 in Chapter 11.

---

rectangles of namespaces.

3 I'm writing this from the BPF track at the LSFMM summit 2019, where the discussions are happening in real-time.

Container IDs

Container IDs used by technologies such as Kubernetes and Docker are managed by user-space software. For example (highlighted in bold):

```
# kubectl get pod
NAME                            READY    STATUS              RESTARTS    AGE
kubernetes-b94cb9bff-kqvml      0/1      ContainerCreating   0           3m
[...]
# docker ps
CONTAINER ID   IMAGE    COMMAND    CREATED      STATUS       PORTS    NAMES
6280172ea7b9   ubuntu   "bash"     4 weeks ago  Up 4 weeks            eager_bhaskara
[...]
```

In the kernel, a container is a set of cgroups and namespaces, but there is no kernel-space identifier tying these together. Adding a container ID to the kernel has been suggested [168], but so far it has not happened.

This can be a problem for when you run BPF tracing tools from the host (as they are normally executed: see the subsection "BPF Privileges" under Section 15.1.2). From the host, BPF tracing tools capture events from all containers, and you may want to be able to filter for just one container or break down events per container. But there is no container ID available in the kernel to use for filters or breakdowns.

Fortunately, there are a number of workarounds, although each depends on the specific configuration of the containers under investigation. Containers use some combination of namespaces; their details can be read from the nsproxy struct in the kernel. From linux/nsproxy.h:

```
struct nsproxy {
        atomic_t count;
        struct uts_namespace *uts_ns;
        struct ipc_namespace *ipc_ns;
        struct mnt_namespace *mnt_ns;
        struct pid_namespace *pid_ns_for_children;
        struct net           *net_ns;
        struct cgroup_namespace *cgroup_ns;
};
```

A container almost certainly uses a PID namespace, so you can at least use that to differentiate them. As an example of accessing this for the current task using bpftrace:

```
#include <linux/sched.h>
[...]
        $task = (struct task_struct *)curtask;
        $pidns = $task->nsproxy->pid_ns_for_children->ns.inum;
```

This sets $pidns to be the PID namespace ID (integer), which can be printed or filtered. It will match the PID namespace seen in the /proc/PID/ns/pid_for_children symlink.

If the container runtime uses a UTS namespace and sets the nodename to be the container name (as is often the case with Kubernetes and Docker), then the nodename can also be fetched from a BPF program to identify containers on output. For example, using bpftrace syntax:

```
#include <linux/sched.h>
        [...]
        $task = (struct task_struct *)curtask;
        $nodename = $task->nsproxy->uts_ns->name.nodename;
```

The pidnss(8) tool (covered in Section 15.3.2) does this.

The network namespace can be a useful identifier for the analysis of Kubernetes pods since containers in the pod will likely share the same network namespace.

You can add these namespace identifiers to the tools covered in prior chapters to make them container-aware, including the PID namespace ID or UTS nodename string, along with the PID. Note that this only works if the instrumentation is in process context, so that curtask is valid.

Orchestration

Running BPF tools across multiple container hosts presents a similar problem to a cloud deployment across many VMs. Your company may already have orchestration software to manage this that can run a given command across multiple hosts and collect the output. There are also tailored solutions, including kubectl-trace.

kubectl-trace is a Kubernetes scheduler for running bpftrace programs across a Kubernetes cluster. It also provides a $container_pid variable for use in bpftrace programs that refers to the pid of the root process. For example, this command:

```
kubectl trace run -e 'k:vfs* /pid == $container_pid/ { @[probe] = count() }' mypod -a
```

counts kernel vfs*() calls for the mypod container application until you press Ctrl-C. Programs can be specified as one-liners, as in this example, or read from files using -f [169]. kubectl-trace is covered further in Chapter 17.

Function as a Service (FaaS)

A new model for computing involves defining application functions that a service provider runs, likely in containers. The end user defines only functions and may not have SSH access to the system that runs the functions. Such an environment is not expected to support end users running BPF tracing tools. (It cannot run other tools, either.) When non-privileged BPF tracing is supported by the kernel, it might be possible for an application function to make BPF kernel calls directly, but this presents many challenges. FaaS analysis with BPF will likely only be possible from the host, performed by users or interfaces that have access to the host.

15.1.3 Strategy

If you are new to container analysis, it can be difficult to know where to start—which target to begin analyzing and with which tool. Here is an overall suggested strategy that you can follow. The next sections explain the tools involved in more detail.

1. Examine the system for hardware resource bottlenecks and other issues covered in previous chapters (Chapter 6, Chapter 7, etc.). In particular, create CPU flame graphs for the running applications.

2. Check whether cgroup software limits have been encountered.

3. Browse and execute the BPF tools listed in Chapters 6 to 14.

Most container issues that I've encountered were caused by application or hardware problems, not the container configuration. CPU flame graphs would often show an application-level issue that had nothing to do with running within containers. Do check for such issues, as well as investigating the container limits.

15.2   Traditional Tools

Containers can be analyzed using the numerous performance tools covered by earlier chapters. Analysis of container specifics from the host and within containers using traditional tools is summarized here.[4]

15.2.1 From the Host

For the analysis of container-specific behavior, especially the usage of cgroups, there are some tools and metrics that can be used from the host, shown in Table 15-1.

Table 15-1   **Traditional Host Tools for Container Analysis**

Tool	Type	Description
systemd-cgtop	Kernel statistics	Top for cgroups
kubectl top	Kernel statistics	Top for Kubernetes resources
docker stats	Kernel statistics	Resource usage by Docker container
/sys/fs/cgroups	Kernel statistics	Raw cgroup statistics
perf	Statistics and tracing	Multitool tracer that supports cgroup filters

These tools are summarized in the sections that follow.

---

4 For more details on this topic, see my "Linux Container Performance Analysis" talk video and slides from USENIX LISA 2017 [Gregg 17].

15.2.2   From the Container

Traditional tools can also be used within the containers themselves, bearing in mind that some metrics exposed will refer to the entire host and not just the container. Table 15-2 lists the state of commonly-used tools, as they are for a Linux 4.8 kernel.

Table 15-2   **Traditional Tools When Run from The Container**

Tool	Description
top(1)	Process table shows container processes; summary heading shows the host
ps(1)	Shows container processes
uptime(1)	Shows host statistics, including host load averages
mpstat(1)	Shows host CPUs, and host CPU usage
vmstat(8)	Shows host CPUs, memory, and other statistics
iostat(1)	Shows host disks
free(1)	Shows host memory

The term *container-aware* is used to described tools that, when run from the container, will show only the container processes and resources. None of the tools in this table are fully container-aware. This may change over time as the kernel and these tools are updated. For now, this is a known gotcha for performance analysis within containers.

15.2.3   systemd-cgtop

The systemd-cgtop(1) command shows the top resource-consuming cgroups. For example, from a production container host:

```
# systemd-cgtop
Control Group                              Tasks   %CPU   Memory  Input/s Output/s
/                                              -  798.2   45.9G        -        -
/docker                                     1082  790.1   42.1G        -        -
/docker/dcf3a...9d28fc4a1c72bbaff4a24834     200  610.5   24.0G        -        -
/docker/370a3...e64ca01198f1e843ade7ce21     170  174.0    3.0G        -        -
/system.slice                                748    5.3    4.1G        -        -
/system.slice/daemontools.service            422    4.0    2.8G        -        -
/docker/dc277...42ab0603bbda2ac8af67996b     160    2.5    2.3G        -        -
/user.slice                                    5    2.0   34.5M        -        -
/user.slice/user-0.slice                       5    2.0   15.7M        -        -
/user.slice/u....slice/session-c26.scope       3    2.0   13.3M        -        -
/docker/ab452...c946f8447f2a4184f3ccff2a     174    1.0    6.3G        -        -
/docker/e18bd...26ffdd7368b870aa3d1deb7a     156    0.8    2.9G        -        -
[...]
```

This output shows that a cgroup named "/docker/dcf3a..." is consuming 610.5% total CPU for this update interval (across many CPUs) and 24 Gbytes of main memory, with 200 running tasks. The output also shows a number of cgroups created by systemd for system services (/system.slice) and user sessions (/user.slice).

15.2.4   kubectl top

The Kubernetes container orchestration system provides a way to check basic resource usage using kubectl top. Checking hosts ("nodes"):

```
# kubectl top nodes
NAME                       CPU(cores)   CPU%   MEMORY(bytes)   MEMORY%
bgregg-i-03cb3a7e46298b38e 1781m        10%    2880Mi          9%
```

The "CPU(cores)" time shows cumulative milliseconds of CPU time, and "CPU%" shows the current usage of the node. Checking containers ("pods"):

```
# kubectl top pods
NAME                       CPU(cores)   MEMORY(bytes)
kubernetes-b94cb9bff-p7jsp 73m          9Mi
```

This shows the cumulative CPU time and current memory size.

These commands require a metrics server to be running, which may be added by default depending on how you initialized Kubernetes [170]. Other monitoring tools can also display these metrics in a GUI, including cAdvisor, Sysdig, and Google Cloud Monitoring [171].

15.2.5   docker stats

The Docker container technology provides some docker(1) analysis subcommands, including stats. For example, from a production host:

```
# docker stats
CONTAINER      CPU %     MEM USAGE / LIMIT     MEM %    NET I/O      BLOCK I/O          PIDS
353426a09db1   526.81%   4.061 GiB / 8.5 GiB   47.78%   0 B / 0 B    2.818 MB / 0 B     247
6bf166a66e08   303.82%   3.448 GiB / 8.5 GiB   40.57%   0 B / 0 B    2.032 MB / 0 B     267
58dcf8aed0a7   41.01%    1.322 GiB / 2.5 GiB   52.89%   0 B / 0 B    0 B / 0 B          229
61061566ffe5   85.92%    220.9 MiB / 3.023 GiB 7.14%    0 B / 0 B    43.4 MB / 0 B      61
bdc721460293   2.69%     1.204 GiB / 3.906 GiB 30.82%   0 B / 0 B    4.35 MB / 0 B      66
[...]
```

This shows that a container with UUID "353426a09db1" was consuming a total of 527% CPU for this update interval and was using four Gbytes of main memory versus an 8.5 Gbyte limit. For this interval there was no network I/O, and only a small volume (Mbytes) of disk I/O.

15.2.6 /sys/fs/cgroups

This directory contains virtual files of cgroup statistics. These are read and graphed by various container monitoring products. For example:

```
# cd /sys/fs/cgroup/cpu,cpuacct/docker/02a7cf65f82e3f3e75283944caa4462e82f...
# cat cpuacct.usage
1615816262506
# cat cpu.stat
nr_periods 507
nr_throttled 74
throttled_time 3816445175
```

The cpuacct.usage file shows the CPU usage of this cgroup in total nanoseconds. The cpu.stat file shows the number of times this cgroup was CPU throttled (nr_throttled), as well as the total throttled time in nanoseconds. This example shows that this cgroup was CPU throttled 74 times out of 507 time periods, for a total of 3.8 throttled seconds.

There is also a cpuacct.usage_percpu, this time showing a Kubernetes cgroup:

```
# cd /sys/fs/cgroup/cpu,cpuacct/kubepods/burstable/pod82e745...
# cat cpuacct.usage_percpu
37944772821 35729154566 35996200949 36443793055 36517861942 36156377488 36176348313
35874604278 37378190414 35464528409 35291309575 35829280628 36105557113 36538524246
36077297144 35976388595
```

The output includes 16 fields for this 16-CPU system, with total CPU time in nanoseconds.

These cgroupv1 metrics are documented in the kernel source under Documentation/cgroup-v1/cpuacct.txt [172].

15.2.7 perf

The perf(1) tool, introduced in Chapter 6, can be run from the host and can filter on cgroups using --cgroup (-G). This can be used for CPU profiling, for example, with the perf record subcommand:

```
perf record -F 99 -e cpu-clock --cgroup=docker/1d567... -a -- sleep 30
```

The event can be anything that occurs in process context, including syscalls.

This switch is also available with the perf stat subcommand, so that counts of events can be collected instead of writing events to the perf.data file. For example, counting the read family of syscalls and showing a different format of cgroup specification (with identifiers elided):

```
perf stat -e syscalls:sys_enter_read* --cgroup /containers.slice/5aad.../...
```

Multiple cgroups can be specified.

perf(1) can trace the same events that BPF can, although without the programmatic capabilities that BCC and bpftrace provide. perf(1) does have its own BPF interface: an example is in Appendix D. For other uses of perf that can be adapted to container inspection, see my perf examples page [73].

15.3   BPF Tools

This section covers the BPF tools you can use for container performance analysis and troubleshooting. These are either from BCC or were created for this book. Table 15-3 lists the tool origins.

Table 15-3   **Container-Specific Tools**

Tool	Source	Target	Description
runqlat	BCC	Sched	Summarize CPU run queue latency by PID namespace
pidnss	Book	Sched	Count PID namespace switches: containers sharing a CPU
blkthrot	Book	Block I/O	Count block I/O throttles by blk cgroup
overlayfs	Book	Overlay FS	Show overlay FS read and write latency

For container analysis, these should be used in conjunction with the many tools from the prior chapters.

15.3.1   runqlat

runqlat(8) was introduced in Chapter 6: it shows run queue latency as a histogram, helping to identify CPU saturation issues. It supports a --pidnss option to show the PID namespace. For example, on a production container system:

```
host# runqlat --pidnss -m
Tracing run queue latency... Hit Ctrl-C to end.
^C
pidns = 4026532382
     msecs               : count    distribution
        0 -> 1           : 646      |****************************************|
        2 -> 3           : 18       |*                                       |
        4 -> 7           : 48       |**                                      |
        8 -> 15          : 17       |*                                       |
       16 -> 31          : 150      |*********                               |
       32 -> 63          : 134      |*******                                 |

[...]
pidns = 4026532870
     msecs               : count    distribution
        0 -> 1           : 264      |****************************************|
        2 -> 3           : 0        |                                        |
[...]
```

This shows that one PID namespace (4026532382) is suffering much higher run queue latency than the other.

This tool does not print the container name, since the mapping of a namespace to a container is specific to the container technology used. At the very least, the ls(1) command can be used as the root user to determine the namespace for a given PID. For example:

```
# ls -lh /proc/181/ns/pid
lrwxrwxrwx 1 root root 0 May  6 13:50 /proc/181/ns/pid -> 'pid:[4026531836]'
```

This shows that PID 181 is running in PID namespace 4026531836.

15.3.2 pidnss

pidnss(8)[5] counts when a CPU switches between running one container and another, by detecting a PID namespace switch during a scheduler context switch. This tool can be used to confirm or exonerate issues of multiple containers contending for a single CPU. For example:

```
# pidnss.bt
Attaching 3 probes...
Tracing PID namespace switches. Ctrl-C to end
^C
Victim PID namespace switch counts [PIDNS, nodename]:


@[0, ]: 2
@[4026532981, 6280172ea7b9]: 27
@[4026531836, bgregg-i-03cb3a7e46298b38e]: 28
```

The output shows two fields and then a switch count. The fields are the PID namespace ID and the nodename (if present). This output shows a PID namespace with the nodename "bgregg-i-03cb3a7e46298b38e" (the host) switched to another namespace 28 times while tracing, and another with nodename "6280172ea7b9" (a Docker container) switched 27 times. These details can be confirmed from the host:

```
# uname -n
bgregg-i-03cb3a7e46298b38e
# docker ps
CONTAINER ID  IMAGE   COMMAND   CREATED      STATUS       PORTS  NAMES
6280172ea7b9  ubuntu  "bash"    4 weeks ago  Up 4 weeks          eager_bhaskara
[...]
```

---

5 Origin: I created this for this book on 6-May-2019, based on a suggestion from my colleague Sargun Dhillon.

This works by tracing the kernel context switch path using kprobes. The overhead is expected to become significant for busy I/O workloads.

Here is another example, this time during the setup of a Kubernetes cluster:

```
# pidnss.bt
Attaching 3 probes...
Tracing PID namespace switches. Ctrl-C to end
^C
Victim PID namespace switch counts [PIDNS, nodename]:


@[-268434577, cilium-operator-95ddbb5fc-gkspv]: 33
@[-268434291, cilium-etcd-g9wgxqsnjv]: 35
@[-268434650, coredns-fb8b8dccf-w7khw]: 35
@[-268434505, default-mem-demo]: 36
@[-268434723, coredns-fb8b8dccf-crrn9]: 36
@[-268434509, etcd-operator-797978964-7c2mc]: 38
@[-268434513, kubernetes-b94cb9bff-p7jsp]: 39
@[-268434810, bgregg-i-03cb3a7e46298b38e]: 203
[...]
@[-268434222, cilium-etcd-g9wgxqsnjv]: 597
@[-268434295, etcd-operator-797978964-7c2mc]: 1301
@[-268434808, bgregg-i-03cb3a7e46298b38e]: 1582
@[-268434297, cilium-operator-95ddbb5fc-gkspv]: 3961
@[0, ]: 8130
@[-268434836, bgregg-i-03cb3a7e46298b38e]: 8897
@[-268434846, bgregg-i-03cb3a7e46298b38e]: 15813
@[-268434581, coredns-fb8b8dccf-w7khw]: 39656
@[-268434654, coredns-fb8b8dccf-crrn9]: 40312
[...]
```

The source to pidnss(8) is:

```
#!/usr/local/bin/bpftrace

#include <linux/sched.h>
#include <linux/nsproxy.h>
#include <linux/utsname.h>
#include <linux/pid_namespace.h>

BEGIN
{
        printf("Tracing PID namespace switches. Ctrl-C to end\n");
}
```

```
kprobe:finish_task_switch
{
        $prev = (struct task_struct *)arg0;
        $curr = (struct task_struct *)curtask;
        $prev_pidns = $prev->nsproxy->pid_ns_for_children->ns.inum;
        $curr_pidns = $curr->nsproxy->pid_ns_for_children->ns.inum;
        if ($prev_pidns != $curr_pidns) {
                @[$prev_pidns, $prev->nsproxy->uts_ns->name.nodename] = count();
        }
}


END
{
        printf("\nVictim PID namespace switch counts [PIDNS, nodename]:\n");
}
```

This is also an example of pulling out namespace identifiers. The identifiers from other namespaces can be fetched similarly.

Should more container-specific details be needed beyond the kernel namespace and cgroup info, this tool could be ported to BCC so that it can include code that fetches details directly from Kubernetes, Docker, etc.

15.3.3 blkthrot

blkthrot(8)[6] counts when the cgroup blk controller throttles I/O based on a hard limit. For example:

```
# blkthrot.bt
Attaching 3 probes...
Tracing block I/O throttles by cgroup. Ctrl-C to end
^C

@notthrottled[1]: 506

@throttled[1]: 31
```

While tracing this, I saw that blk cgroup with ID 1 was throttled 31 times and not throttled 506 times.

This works by tracing the kernel blk_throtl_bio() function. The overhead should be minimal as block I/O is typically a relatively low-frequency event.

---

6 Origin: I created this for this book on 6-May-2019.

The source to blkthrot(8) is:

```
#!/usr/local/bin/bpftrace

#include <linux/cgroup-defs.h>
#include <linux/blk-cgroup.h>

BEGIN
{
        printf("Tracing block I/O throttles by cgroup. Ctrl-C to end\n");
}

kprobe:blk_throtl_bio
{
        @blkg[tid] = arg1;
}

kretprobe:blk_throtl_bio
/@blkg[tid]/
{
        $blkg = (struct blkcg_gq *)@blkg[tid];
        if (retval) {
                @throttled[$blkg->blkcg->css.id] = count();
        } else {
                @notthrottled[$blkg->blkcg->css.id] = count();
        }
        delete(@blkg[tid]);
}
```

This is also an example of pulling out a cgroup ID, which is in the cgroup_subsys_state struct, in this case as css in the blkcg.

If desired, a different approach could be used: checking for the presence of the BIO_THROTTLED flag on the struct bio, upon block completions.

15.3.4   overlayfs

overlayfs(8)[7] traces the latency of overlay file system reads and writes. The overlay FS is commonly used for containers, so this tool provides a view of container file system performance. For example:

---

7 Origin: My colleague Jason Koch created this on 18-Mar-2019 while working on container performance.

```
# overlayfs.bt 4026532311
Attaching 7 probes...


21:21:06 --------------------
@write_latency_us:
[128, 256)             1 |                                                    |
[256, 512)           238 |@@@@@@@@@@@@@@@@@@@@@@@@@@@@@@@@@@@@@@@@@@@@@@@@@@@@@@|

@read_latency_us:
[1]                    3 |@                                                   |
[2, 4)                 1 |                                                    |
[4, 8)                 3 |@                                                   |
[8, 16)                0 |                                                    |
[16, 32)             115 |@@@@@@@@@@@@@@@@@@@@@@@@@@@@@@@@@@@@@@@@@@@@@@@@@     |
[32, 64)             123 |@@@@@@@@@@@@@@@@@@@@@@@@@@@@@@@@@@@@@@@@@@@@@@@@@@@@@@|
[64, 128)              0 |                                                    |
[128, 256)             1 |                                                    |


21:21:07 --------------------
[...]
```

This shows the latency distribution of reads and writes, with the reads usually taking between
16 and 64 microseconds during the 21:21:06 interval.

This works by tracing the overlayfs file_operations_t kernel functions for read and write. The overhead is relative to the rate of these functions, and should be negligible for many workloads.

The source to overlayfs(8) is:

```
#!/usr/local/bin/bpftrace

#include <linux/nsproxy.h>
#include <linux/pid_namespace.h>

kprobe:ovl_read_iter
/((struct task_struct *)curtask)->nsproxy->pid_ns_for_children->ns.inum == $1/
{
        @read_start[tid] = nsecs;
}


kretprobe:ovl_read_iter
/((struct task_struct *)curtask)->nsproxy->pid_ns_for_children->ns.inum == $1/
{
        $duration_us = (nsecs - @read_start[tid]) / 1000;
        @read_latency_us = hist($duration_us);
        delete(@read_start[tid]);
}
```

```
kprobe:ovl_write_iter
/((struct task_struct *)curtask)->nsproxy->pid_ns_for_children->ns.inum == $1/
{
        @write_start[tid] = nsecs;
}

kretprobe:ovl_write_iter
/((struct task_struct *)curtask)->nsproxy->pid_ns_for_children->ns.inum == $1/
{
        $duration_us = (nsecs - @write_start[tid]) / 1000;
        @write_latency_us = hist($duration_us);
        delete(@write_start[tid]);
}

interval:ms:1000
{
        time("\n%H:%M:%S --------------------\n");
        print(@write_latency_us);
        print(@read_latency_us);
        clear(@write_latency_us);
        clear(@read_latency_us);
}

END
{
        clear(@write_start);
        clear(@read_start);
}
```

The ovl_read_iter() and ovl_write_iter() functions were added in Linux 4.19. This tool accepts
the PID namespace ID as an argument: it was developed for Docker, to be run with the following
wrapper (overlayfs.sh) that accepted the Docker container ID as the argument.

```
#!/bin/bash

PID=$(docker inspect -f='{{.State.Pid}}' $1)
NSID=$(stat /proc/$PID/ns/pid -c "%N" | cut -d[ -f2 | cut -d] -f1)

bpftrace ./overlayfs.bt $NSID
```

You can adjust this to match the container technology you use. That this step is necessary is discussed in Section 15.1.2: there is no in-kernel container ID; it is a construct of user space. This is a user space wrapper to convert the container ID into a PID namespace that the kernel can match on.

15.4 BPF One-Liners

This section shows bpftrace one-liners.

Count cgroup ID at 99 Hertz:

```
bpftrace -e 'profile:hz:99 { @[cgroup] = count(); }'
```

Trace open filenames for cgroup v2 named "container1":

```
bpftrace -e 't:syscalls:sys_enter_openat
    /cgroup == cgroupid("/sys/fs/cgroup/unified/container1")/ {
    printf("%s\n", str(args->filename)); }'
```

15.5 Optional Exercises

If not specified, these can be completed using either bpftrace or BCC:

1. Modify runqlat(8) from Chapter 6 to include the UTS namespace nodename (see pidnss(8)).

2. Modify opensnoop(8) from Chapter 8 to include the UTS namespace nodename.

3. Develop a tool to show which containers are swapping out due to the mem cgroup (see the mem_cgroup_swapout() kernel function).

15.6 Summary

This chapter summarized Linux containers and showed how BPF tracing can expose container CPU contention and cgroup throttling durations, as well as overlay FS latency.

Chapter 16

Hypervisors

This chapter discusses the use of BPF tools with virtual machine hypervisors for hardware virtualization, of which Xen and KVM are popular examples. BPF tools with OS-level virtualization—containers—was discussed in the previous chapter.

Learning Objectives:

- Understand hypervisor configurations and BPF tracing capabilities
- Trace guest hypercalls and exits, where possible
- Summarize stolen CPU time

This chapter begins with the necessary background for hardware virtualization analysis, describes BPF capabilities and strategies for the different hypervisor situations, and includes some example BPF tools.

16.1   Background

Hardware virtualization creates a virtual machine (VM) that can run an entire operating system, including its own kernel. Two common configurations of hypervisors are shown in Figure 16-1.

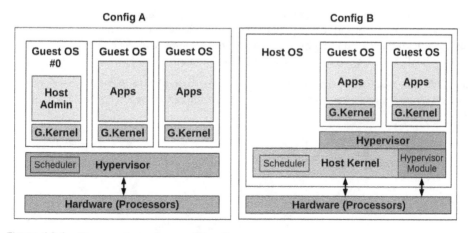

Figure 16-1   Common hypervisor configurations

A common classification of hypervisors identifies them as type 1 or 2 [Goldberg 73]. However, with advancements in these technologies these types are no longer a practical distinction [173] as type 2 has become type 1-ish by using kernel modules. The following instead describes two common configurations shown in Figure 16-1:

- **Config A:** This configuration is called a native hypervisor or a bare-metal hypervisor. The hypervisor software runs directly on the processors, which creates domains for running guest virtual machines and schedules virtual guest CPUs onto the real CPUs. A privileged domain (number 0 in Figure 16-1) can administer the others. A popular example is the Xen hypervisor.

- **Config B:** The hypervisor software is executed by a host OS kernel and may be composed of kernel-level modules and user-level processes. The host OS has privileges to administer the hypervisor, and its kernel schedules the VM CPUs along with other processes on the host. By use of kernel modules, this configuration also provides direct access to hardware. A popular example is the KVM hypervisor.

Both configurations may involve running an I/O proxy (e.g., the QEMU software) in domain 0 (Xen) or the host OS (KVM) for serving guest I/O. This adds overhead to I/O, and over the years has been optimized by adding shared memory transports and other techniques.

The original hardware hypervisor, pioneered by VMware in 1998, used binary translations to perform full hardware virtualization [VMware 07]. This has since been improved by:

- **Processor virtualization support:** The AMD-V and Intel VT-x extensions were introduced in 2005–2006 to provide faster hardware support for VM operations by the processor.

- **Paravirtualization (paravirt or PV):** Instead of running an unmodified OS, with paravirtualization, an OS can be made aware that it is running on a hardware virtual machine and make special calls (hypercalls) to the hypervisor for more efficient processing of some operations. For efficiency, Xen batches these hypercalls into a multicall.

- **Device hardware support:** To further optimize VM performance, hardware devices other than processors have been adding virtual machine support. This includes SR-IOV for network and storage devices and special drivers to use them: ixgbe, ena, and nvme.

Over the years, Xen has evolved and improved its performance. Modern Xen VMs often boot in hardware VM mode (HVM) and then use PV drivers with HVM support to achieve the best of both worlds: a configuration called PVHVM. This can further be improved by depending entirely on hardware virtualization for some drivers, such as SR-IOV for network and storage devices.

In 2017, AWS launched the Nitro hypervisor, with parts based on KVM, and hardware support for all main resources: processors, network, storage, interrupts, and timers [174]. No QEMU proxy is used.

16.1.1 BPF Capabilities

Because hardware VMs run their own kernel, they can use BPF tools from the guest. Questions that BPF can help answer from the guest include:

- What is the performance of the virtualized hardware resources? This can be answered using tools described in previous chapters.

- If paravirtualization is in use, then what is hypercall latency, as a measure of hypervisor performance?

- What are the frequency and duration of stolen CPU time?

- Are hypervisor interrupt callbacks interfering with an application?

If run from the host, BPF can help answer more questions (host access is available to cloud computing providers but not to their end users):

- If QEMU is in use, what workload is applied by the guest? What is the resulting performance?

- For config B hypervisors, for what reasons are guests exiting to the hypervisor?

Hardware hypervisor analysis with BPF is another area that may have future developments, adding more capabilities and possibilities. Some future work is mentioned in the later tools sections.

AWS EC2 Guests

As hypervisors optimize performance by moving from emulation to paravirtualization to hardware support, there are fewer targets to trace from the guest because events have moved to hardware. This has been apparent with the evolution of AWS EC2 instances and the types of hypervisor targets that can be traced, listed below:

- **PV:** Hypercalls (multicalls), hypervisor call backs, driver calls, stolen time

- **PVHVM:** Hypervisor callbacks, driver calls, stolen time

- **PVHVM+SR-IOV drivers:** Hypervisor callbacks, stolen time

- **KVM (Nitro):** Stolen time

The most recent hypervisor, Nitro, has little code running in the guest that is special to hypervisors. This is by design: it improves performance by moving hypervisor functionality to hardware.

16.1.2 Suggested Strategies

Start by determining what configuration of hardware hypervisor is in use. Are hypercalls being used, or special device drivers?

For guests:

1. Instrument hypercalls (if in use) to check for excessive operations.

2. Check for CPU stolen time.

3. Use tools from prior chapters for resource analysis, bearing in mind that these are virtual resources. Their performance may be capped by resource controls imposed by the hypervisor or external hardware, and they may also suffer contention with access from other guests.

For hosts:

1. Instrument VM exits to check for excessive operations.

2. If an I/O proxy is in use (QEMU), instrument its workload and latency.

3. Use tools from prior chapters for resource analysis.

As hypervisors move functionality to hardware, as is the case with Nitro, more analysis will need to be conducted using tools from prior chapters, rather than specialized tools for hypervisors.

16.2 Traditional Tools

There are not many tools for hypervisor performance analysis and troubleshooting. From the guest, in some situations there are tracepoints for hypercalls, as shown in Section 16.3.1.

From the host, Xen provides its own tools, including x1 top and xentrace, for inspecting guest resource usage. For KVM, the Linux perf(1) utility has a kvm subcommand. Example output:

```
# perf kvm stat live
11:12:07.687968


Analyze events for all VMs, all VCPUs:


             VM-EXIT Samples Samples%   Time%  Min Time     Max Time      Avg time

           MSR_WRITE  1668   68.90%    0.28%   0.67us      31.74us     3.25us ( +-   2.20% )
                 HLT   466   19.25%   99.63%   2.61us  100512.98us  4160.68us ( +-  14.77% )
     PREEMPTION_TIMER  112    4.63%    0.03%   2.53us      10.42us     4.71us ( +-   2.68% )
    PENDING_INTERRUPT   82    3.39%    0.01%   0.92us      18.95us     3.44us ( +-   6.23% )
   EXTERNAL_INTERRUPT   53    2.19%    0.01%   0.82us       7.46us     3.22us ( +-   6.57% )
      IO_INSTRUCTION    37    1.53%    0.04%   5.36us      84.88us    19.97us ( +-  11.87% )
            MSR_READ     2    0.08%    0.00%   3.33us       4.80us     4.07us ( +-  18.05% )
        EPT_MISCONFIG     1    0.04%    0.00%  19.94us      19.94us    19.94us ( +-   0.00% )


Total Samples:2421, Total events handled time:1946040.48us.
```

This shows the reasons for virtual machine exit and statistics for each reason. The longest-duration exits in this example output were for HLT (halt), as virtual CPUs enter the idle state.

There are tracepoints for KVM events, including exits, which can be used with BPF to create more detailed tools.

16.3   Guest BPF Tools

This section covers the BPF tools you can use for guest VM performance analysis and trouble-shooting. These are either from the BCC and bpftrace repositories covered in Chapters 4 and 5 or were created for this book.

16.3.1   Xen Hypercalls

If the guest uses paravirt and makes hypercalls, they can be instrumented using existing tools: funccount(8), trace(8), argdist(8), and stackcount(8). There are even Xen tracepoints you can use. Measuring hypercall latency requires custom tooling.

Xen PV

For example, this system has booted into paravirtualization (PV):

```
# dmesg | grep Hypervisor
[    0.000000] Hypervisor detected: Xen PV
```

Using BCC funccount(8) to count the available Xen tracepoints:

```
# funccount 't:xen:*'
Tracing 30 functions for "t:xen:*"... Hit Ctrl-C to end.
^C
FUNC                                 COUNT
xen:xen_mmu_flush_tlb_one_user          70
xen:xen_mmu_set_pte                     84
xen:xen_mmu_set_pte_at                  95
xen:xen_mc_callback                     97
xen:xen_mc_extend_args                 194
xen:xen_mmu_write_cr3                  194
xen:xen_mc_entry_alloc                 904
xen:xen_mc_entry                       924
xen:xen_mc_flush                      1175
xen:xen_mc_issue                      1378
xen:xen_mc_batch                      1392
Detaching...
```

The xen_mc tracepoints are for multicalls: batched hypercalls. These begin with a xen:xen_mc_batch call, then xen:xen_mc_entry calls for each hypercall, and finish with a xen:xen_mc_issue. The real hypercall only happens in a flush operation, traced by xen:xen_mc_flush. As a performance optimization, there are two "lazy" paravirt modes where the issue will be ignored, allowing multicalls to buffer and be flushed later: one for MMU updates, and one for context switching.

Various kernel code paths are bracketed by xen_mc_batch and xen_mc_issue, to group possible xen_mc_calls. But if no xen_mc_calls are made, the issue and flush are for zero hypercalls.

The xenhyper(8) tool in the next section is an example of using one of these tracepoints. With so many tracepoints available, more such tools could be written, but unfortunately Xen PV guests are becoming less frequently used, giving way to HVM guests (PVHVM). I've only included one tool as a demonstration, and the following one-liners.

Xen PV: Counting Hypercalls

The number of issued hypercalls can be counted via the xen:xen_mc_flush tracepoint, along with its mcidx argument, which shows how many hypercalls were made. For example, using BCC argdist(8):

```
# argdist -C 't:xen:xen_mc_flush():int:args->mcidx'
[17:41:34]
t:xen:xen_mc_flush():int:args->mcidx
        COUNT      EVENT
        44         args->mcidx = 0
        136        args->mcidx = 1
[17:41:35]
t:xen:xen_mc_flush():int:args->mcidx
        COUNT      EVENT
        37         args->mcidx = 0
        133        args->mcidx = 1
[...]
```

This frequency counts how many hypercalls were issued on each flush. If the count is zero, no hypercall was made. The above output shows about 130 hypercalls per second and no cases of batching beyond a single hypercall per batch while tracing.

Xen PV: Hypercall Stacks

Each of the Xen tracepoints can be traced using stackcount(8) to reveal the code path that triggered them. For example, tracing when a multicall was issued:

```
# stackcount 't:xen:xen_mc_issue'
Tracing 1 functions for "t:xen:xen_mc_issue"... Hit Ctrl-C to end.
^C
[...]

  xen_load_sp0
  __switch_to
  __schedule
  schedule
  schedule_preempt_disabled
  cpu_startup_entry
  cpu_bringup_and_idle
    6629
```

```
xen_load_tls
  16448

xen_flush_tlb_single
flush_tlb_page
ptep_clear_flush
wp_page_copy
do_wp_page
handle_mm_fault
__do_page_fault
do_page_fault
page_fault
  46604

xen_set_pte_at
copy_page_range
copy_process.part.33
_do_fork
sys_clone
do_syscall_64
return_from_SYSCALL_64
  565901


Detaching...
```

Excessive multicalls (hypercalls) can be a performance issue, and this output helps reveal the reason for them. The overhead of hypercall tracing depends on their rate, which for busy systems may be frequent, costing noticeable overhead.

Xen PV: Hypercall Latency

The real hypercall only happens during the flush operation, and there are no tracepoints for when this begins and ends. You can switch to kprobes to trace the xen_mc_flush() kernel function, which includes the real hypercall. Using BCC funclatency(8):

```
# funclatency xen_mc_flush
Tracing 1 functions for "xen_mc_flush"... Hit Ctrl-C to end.
^C
     nsecs               : count     distribution
         0 -> 1          : 0         |                                        |
         2 -> 3          : 0         |                                        |
         4 -> 7          : 0         |                                        |
         8 -> 15         : 0         |                                        |
        16 -> 31         : 0         |                                        |
```

```
      32 -> 63        : 0        |                                          |
      64 -> 127       : 0        |                                          |
     128 -> 255       : 0        |                                          |
     256 -> 511       : 32508    |****************                          |
     512 -> 1023      : 80586    |******************************************|
    1024 -> 2047      : 21022    |**********                                |
    2048 -> 4095      : 3519     |*                                         |
    4096 -> 8191      : 12825    |******                                    |
    8192 -> 16383     : 7141     |***                                       |
   16384 -> 32767     : 158      |                                          |
   32768 -> 65535     : 51       |                                          |
   65536 -> 131071    : 845      |                                          |
  131072 -> 262143    : 2        |                                          |
```

This can be an important measure of hypervisor performance from the guest. A BCC tool can be written to remember which hypercalls were batched so that this hypercall latency can be broken down by hypercall operation type.

Another way to determine issues of hypercall latency is to try CPU profiling, covered in Chapter 6, and look for CPU time spent in hypercalls, either in the hypercall_page() function (which is really a table of hypercall functions) or in the xen_hypercall*() functions. An example is shown in Figure 16-2.

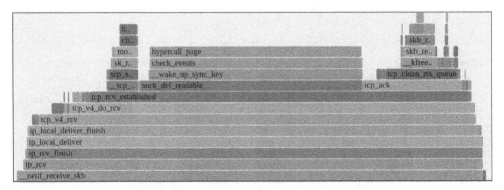

Figure 16-2   CPU Flame graph excerpt showing Xen PV hypercall

This shows a TCP receive codepath ending in hypercall_page(). Note that this CPU profiling approach may be misleading as it may not be possible to sample some hypercall code paths from the guest. This is because PV guests usually do not have access to PMC-based profiling, and instead will default to software-based profiling, which cannot sample during IRQ-disabled code paths, which can include hypercalls. This issue was described in Section 6.2.4 in Chapter 6.

Xen HVM

For an HVM guest, the xen tracepoints usually do not fire:

```
# dmesg | grep Hypervisor
[    0.000000] Hypervisor detected: Xen HVM
# funccount 't:xen:xen*'
Tracing 27 functions for "t:xen:xen*"... Hit Ctrl-C to end.
^C
FUNC                            COUNT
Detaching...
```

This is because those code paths no longer hypercall but instead make native calls that are trapped and handled by the HVM hypervisor. This makes inspection of hypervisor performance more difficult: it must be inspected using the normal resource-oriented tools covered in earlier chapters, bearing in mind that these resources are accessed via a hypervisor, and therefore observed latencies are due to the resource plus hypervisor latency.

16.3.2   xenhyper

xenhyper(8)[1] is a bpftrace tool to count hypercalls via the xen:xen_mc_entry tracepoint and prints a count of the hypercall names. This is only useful for Xen guests booting into paravirt mode and using hypercalls. Example output:

```
# xenhyper.bt
Attaching 1 probe...
^C

@[mmu_update]: 44
@[update_va_mapping]: 78
@[mmuext_op]: 6473
@[stack_switch]: 23445
```

The source to xenhyper(8) is:

```
#!/usr/local/bin/bpftrace

BEGIN
{
        printf("Counting Xen hypercalls (xen_mc_entry). Ctrl-C to end.\n");

        // needs updating to match your kernel version: xen-hypercalls.h
        @name[0] = "set_trap_table";
        @name[1] = "mmu_update";
```

---

1 Origin: I developed it for this book on 22-Feb-2019.

```
        @name[2] = "set_gdt";
        @name[3] = "stack_switch";
        @name[4] = "set_callbacks";
        @name[5] = "fpu_taskswitch";
        @name[6] = "sched_op_compat";
        @name[7] = "dom0_op";
        @name[8] = "set_debugreg";
        @name[9] = "get_debugreg";
        @name[10] = "update_descriptor";
        @name[11] = "memory_op";
        @name[12] = "multicall";
        @name[13] = "update_va_mapping";
        @name[14] = "set_timer_op";
        @name[15] = "event_channel_op_compat";
        @name[16] = "xen_version";
        @name[17] = "console_io";
        @name[18] = "physdev_op_compat";
        @name[19] = "grant_table_op";
        @name[20] = "vm_assist";
        @name[21] = "update_va_mapping_otherdomain";
        @name[22] = "iret";
        @name[23] = "vcpu_op";
        @name[24] = "set_segment_base";
        @name[25] = "mmuext_op";
        @name[26] = "acm_op";
        @name[27] = "nmi_op";
        @name[28] = "sched_op";
        @name[29] = "callback_op";
        @name[30] = "xenoprof_op";
        @name[31] = "event_channel_op";
        @name[32] = "physdev_op";
        @name[33] = "hvm_op";
}


tracepoint:xen:xen_mc_entry
{
        @[@name[args->op]] = count();
}


END
{
        clear(@name);
}
```

This uses a translation table based on mappings from the kernel source to convert between the hypercall operation number and a name. This will need to be updated to match your kernel version, as these mappings change over time.

xenhyper(8) can be customized to include such details as the process name or user stack trace that led to the hypercall, by modifying the @ map keys.

16.3.3 Xen Callbacks

Rather than the guest making a hypercall to the hypervisor, these occur when Xen calls the guest, such as for IRQ notifications. There are per-CPU counts for these calls in /proc/interrupts:

```
# grep HYP /proc/interrupts
HYP:    12156816    9976239    10156992    9041115    7936087    9903434    9713902
8778612    Hypervisor callback interrupts
```

Each number is the count for one CPU (this is an eight-CPU system). These can also be traced using BPF, via a kprobe of the kernel function xen_evtchn_do_upcall(). For example, counting which process is interrupted using bpftrace:

```
# bpftrace -e 'kprobe:xen_evtchn_do_upcall { @[comm] = count(); }'
Attaching 1 probe...
^C

@[ps]: 9
@[bash]: 15
@[java]: 71
@[swapper/7]: 100
@[swapper/3]: 110
@[swapper/2]: 130
@[swapper/4]: 131
@[swapper/0]: 164
@[swapper/1]: 192
@[swapper/6]: 207
@[swapper/5]: 248
```

The output is showing that most of the time CPU idle threads ("swapper/*") were interrupted by the Xen callbacks.

The latency of these can also be measured, for example, using BCC funclatency(8):

```
# funclatency xen_evtchn_do_upcall
Tracing 1 functions for "xen_evtchn_do_upcall"... Hit Ctrl-C to end.
^C
     nsecs           : count     distribution
        0 -> 1        : 0         |                                        |
        2 -> 3        : 0         |                                        |
```

```
        4 -> 7          : 0     |                                              |
        8 -> 15         : 0     |                                              |
       16 -> 31         : 0     |                                              |
       32 -> 63         : 0     |                                              |
       64 -> 127        : 0     |                                              |
      128 -> 255        : 0     |                                              |
      256 -> 511        : 1     |                                              |
      512 -> 1023       : 6     |                                              |
     1024 -> 2047       : 131   |********                                      |
     2048 -> 4095       : 351   |**********************                        |
     4096 -> 8191       : 365   |***********************                       |
     8192 -> 16383      : 602   |**********************************************|
    16384 -> 32767      : 89    |*****                                         |
    32768 -> 65535      : 13    |                                              |
    65536 -> 131071     : 1     |                                              |
```

This shows that, most of the time, processing took between one and 32 microseconds.

More information about the interrupt type can be traced from the child functions of xen_evtchn_do_upcall().

16.3.4 cpustolen

cpustolen(8)[2] is a bpftrace tool to show the distribution of stolen CPU time, showing whether time is stolen in short or long runs. This is CPU time unavailable to the guest as it was used by other guests (which, in some hypervisor configurations, can include CPU time consumed by an I/O proxy in another domain on behalf of the guest itself, so the term "stolen" is misleading[3]). Example output:

```
# cpustolen.bt
Attaching 4 probes...
Tracing stolen CPU time. Ctrl-C to end.
^C


@stolen_us:
[0]                  30384 |@@@@@@@@@@@@@@@@@@@@@@@@@@@@@@@@@@@@@@@@@@@@@@@@@@@@|
[1]                      0 |                                                  |
[2, 4)                   0 |                                                  |
[4, 8)                  28 |                                                  |
[8, 16)                  4 |                                                  |
```

---

2 Origin: I developed it for this book on 22-Feb-2019.

3 Because of the way it is measured, stolen can also include time in the VMM on behalf of the guest [Yamamoto 16].

This output showed that, most of the time, there was no stolen CPU time (the "[0]" bucket), though on four occasions time the stolen time was in the eight- to 16-microsecond range. The "[0]" bucket has been included in the output so that the ratio of stolen time vs total time can be calculated: in this case it was 0.1% (32 / 30416).

This works by tracing the stolen_clock paravirt ops call using kprobes of the Xen and KVM versions: xen_stolen_clock() and kvm_stolen_clock(). This is called on many frequent events, such as context switches and interrupts, so the overhead of this tool may be noticeable depending on your workload.

The source to cpustolen(8) is:

```
#!/usr/local/bin/bpftrace

BEGIN
{
        printf("Tracing stolen CPU time. Ctrl-C to end.\n");
}

kretprobe:xen_steal_clock,
kretprobe:kvm_steal_clock
{
        if (@last[cpu] > 0) {
                @stolen_us = hist((retval - @last[cpu]) / 1000);
        }
        @last[cpu] = retval;
}

END
{
        clear(@last);
}
```

This will need to be updated for hypervisors other than Xen and KVM. Other hypervisors will likely have a similar steal_clock function to satisfy a table of paravirt ops (pv_ops). Note that there is a higher-level function, paravirt_steal_clock(), which sounds more suitable to trace as it isn't tied to one hypervisor type. However, it is not available for tracing (likely inlined).

16.3.5   HVM Exit Tracing

With the move from PV to HVM guests, we lose the ability to instrument explicit hypercalls, but the guest is still making exits to the hypervisor for access to resources, and we'd like to trace those. The current approach is to analyze resource latency using all the existing tools in the prior chapters, while bearing in mind that some component of that latency may be hypervisor related, and we will not be able to measure that directly. We may be able to infer it by comparing latency measurements from a bare-metal machine.

An interesting research prototype that could shed light on exit visibility by guests is a research technology called hyperupcalls [Amit 18]. These provide a safe way for a guest to request the hypervisor to run a mini program; its example use cases include hypervisor tracing from the guest. They are implemented using an extended BPF VM in the hypervisor, which the guest compiles BPF bytecode to run. This is not currently made available by any cloud providers (and may never be) but is another interesting project that uses BPF.

16.4   Host BPF Tools

This section covers the BPF tools you can use for from-the-host VM performance analysis and troubleshooting. These are either from the BCC and bpftrace repositories covered in Chapters 4 and 5, or were created for this book.

16.4.1   kvmexits

kvmexits(8)[4] is a bpftrace tool to show the distribution of guest exit time by reason. This will reveal hypervisor-related performance issues and direct further analysis. Example output:

```
# kvmexits.bt
Attaching 4 probes...
Tracing KVM exits. Ctrl-C to end
^C
[...]

@exit_ns[30, IO_INSTRUCTION]:
[1K, 2K)             1 |                                                    |
[2K, 4K)            12 |@@@                                                 |
[4K, 8K)            71 |@@@@@@@@@@@@@@@@@@                                  |
[8K, 16K)         198 |@@@@@@@@@@@@@@@@@@@@@@@@@@@@@@@@@@@@@@@@@@@@@@@@@@@@@@|
[16K, 32K)        129 |@@@@@@@@@@@@@@@@@@@@@@@@@@@@@@@@@@                   |
[32K, 64K)         94 |@@@@@@@@@@@@@@@@@@@@@@@@@                            |
[64K, 128K)        37 |@@@@@@@@@                                          |
[128K, 256K)       12 |@@@                                                |
[256K, 512K)       23 |@@@@@@                                             |
[512K, 1M)          2 |                                                   |
[1M, 2M)            0 |                                                   |
[2M, 4M)            1 |                                                   |
[4M, 8M)            2 |                                                   |
```

---

4 Origin: I first developed this tool as kvmexitlatency.d using DTrace, published in the 2013 *Systems Performance* book [Gregg 13b]. I developed it using bpftrace for this book on 25-Feb-2019.

```
@exit_ns[1, EXTERNAL_INTERRUPT]:
[256, 512)           28 |@@@                                             |
[512, 1K)           460 |@@@@@@@@@@@@@@@@@@@@@@@@@@@@@@@@@@@@@@@@@@@@@@@   |
[1K, 2K)            463 |@@@@@@@@@@@@@@@@@@@@@@@@@@@@@@@@@@@@@@@@@@@@@@@@@@|
[2K, 4K)            150 |@@@@@@@@@@@@@@@                                  |
[4K, 8K)            116 |@@@@@@@@@@@@                                     |
[8K, 16K)            31 |@@@                                             |
[16K, 32K)           12 |@                                               |
[32K, 64K)            7 |                                                |
[64K, 128K)           2 |                                                |
[128K, 256K)          1 |                                                |

@exit_ns[32, MSR_WRITE]:
[512, 1K)          5690 |@@@@@@@@@@@@@@@@@@@@@@@@@@@@@@@@@@@@@@@@@@@@@@@@@@|
[1K, 2K)           2978 |@@@@@@@@@@@@@@@@@@@@@@@@@@@                       |
[2K, 4K)           2080 |@@@@@@@@@@@@@@@@@@                               |
[4K, 8K)            854 |@@@@@@@                                          |
[8K, 16K)           826 |@@@@@@@                                          |
[16K, 32K)          110 |@                                               |
[32K, 64K)            3 |                                                |

@exit_ns[12, HLT]:
[512, 1K)            13 |                                                |
[1K, 2K)            23 |                                                |
[2K, 4K)            10 |                                                |
[4K, 8K)            76 |                                                |
[8K, 16K)          234 |@@                                              |
[16K, 32K)         4167 |@@@@@@@@@@@@@@@@@@@@@@@@@@@@@@@@@@@@@@@@@@@@@@@   |
[32K, 64K)         3920 |@@@@@@@@@@@@@@@@@@@@@@@@@@@@@@@@@@@@@@@@@@@@@     |
[64K, 128K)        4467 |@@@@@@@@@@@@@@@@@@@@@@@@@@@@@@@@@@@@@@@@@@@@@@@@@@|
[128K, 256K)       3483 |@@@@@@@@@@@@@@@@@@@@@@@@@@@@@@@@@@@@@@@@          |
[256K, 512K)       1764 |@@@@@@@@@@@@@@@@@@@                              |
[512K, 1M)          922 |@@@@@@@@@@                                      |
[1M, 2M)            113 |@                                               |
[2M, 4M)            128 |@                                               |
[4M, 8M)             35 |                                                |
[8M, 16M)            40 |                                                |
[16M, 32M)           42 |                                                |
[32M, 64M)           97 |@                                               |
[64M, 128M)          95 |@                                               |
[128M, 256M)         58 |                                                |
[256M, 512M)         24 |                                                |
[512M, 1G)            1 |                                                |
```

```
@exit_ns[48, EPT_VIOLATION]:
[512, 1K)          6160 |@@@@@@@@@@@@@@@@@@@@@@@@@@@@@@@@@@@@@@@@@         |
[1K, 2K)           6885 |@@@@@@@@@@@@@@@@@@@@@@@@@@@@@@@@@@@@@@@@@@@        |
[2K, 4K)           7686 |@@@@@@@@@@@@@@@@@@@@@@@@@@@@@@@@@@@@@@@@@@@@@@@@@@@|
[4K, 8K)           2220 |@@@@@@@@@@@@@@                                   |
[8K, 16K)           582 |@@@                                             |
[16K, 32K)          244 |@                                               |
[32K, 64K)           47 |                                                |
[64K, 128K)           3 |                                                |
```

This output shows the distribution of exits by type, including the exit code number and exit
reason string, if known. The longest exits, reaching one second, were for HLT (halt), which is
normal behavior: this is the CPU idle thread. The output also showed IO_INSTRUCTIONS taking
up to eight milliseconds.

This works by tracing the kvm:kvm_exit and kvm:kvm_entry tracepoints, which are only used
when the kernel KVM module is in use to accelerate performance.

The source to kvmexit(8) is:

```
#!/usr/local/bin/bpftrace

BEGIN
{
        printf("Tracing KVM exits. Ctrl-C to end\n");

        // from arch/x86/include/uapi/asm/vmx.h:
        @exitreason[0] = "EXCEPTION_NMI";
        @exitreason[1] = "EXTERNAL_INTERRUPT";
        @exitreason[2] = "TRIPLE_FAULT";
        @exitreason[7] = "PENDING_INTERRUPT";
        @exitreason[8] = "NMI_WINDOW";
        @exitreason[9] = "TASK_SWITCH";
        @exitreason[10] = "CPUID";
        @exitreason[12] = "HLT";
        @exitreason[13] = "INVD";
        @exitreason[14] = "INVLPG";
        @exitreason[15] = "RDPMC";
        @exitreason[16] = "RDTSC";
        @exitreason[18] = "VMCALL";
        @exitreason[19] = "VMCLEAR";
        @exitreason[20] = "VMLAUNCH";
        @exitreason[21] = "VMPTRLD";
        @exitreason[22] = "VMPTRST";
        @exitreason[23] = "VMREAD";
```

```
        @exitreason[24] = "VMRESUME";
        @exitreason[25] = "VMWRITE";
        @exitreason[26] = "VMOFF";
        @exitreason[27] = "VMON";
        @exitreason[28] = "CR_ACCESS";
        @exitreason[29] = "DR_ACCESS";
        @exitreason[30] = "IO_INSTRUCTION";
        @exitreason[31] = "MSR_READ";
        @exitreason[32] = "MSR_WRITE";
        @exitreason[33] = "INVALID_STATE";
        @exitreason[34] = "MSR_LOAD_FAIL";
        @exitreason[36] = "MWAIT_INSTRUCTION";
        @exitreason[37] = "MONITOR_TRAP_FLAG";
        @exitreason[39] = "MONITOR_INSTRUCTION";
        @exitreason[40] = "PAUSE_INSTRUCTION";
        @exitreason[41] = "MCE_DURING_VMENTRY";
        @exitreason[43] = "TPR_BELOW_THRESHOLD";
        @exitreason[44] = "APIC_ACCESS";
        @exitreason[45] = "EOI_INDUCED";
        @exitreason[46] = "GDTR_IDTR";
        @exitreason[47] = "LDTR_TR";
        @exitreason[48] = "EPT_VIOLATION";
        @exitreason[49] = "EPT_MISCONFIG";
        @exitreason[50] = "INVEPT";
        @exitreason[51] = "RDTSCP";
        @exitreason[52] = "PREEMPTION_TIMER";
        @exitreason[53] = "INVVPID";
        @exitreason[54] = "WBINVD";
        @exitreason[55] = "XSETBV";
        @exitreason[56] = "APIC_WRITE";
        @exitreason[57] = "RDRAND";
        @exitreason[58] = "INVPCID";
}

tracepoint:kvm:kvm_exit
{
        @start[tid] = nsecs;
        @reason[tid] = args->exit_reason;
}

tracepoint:kvm:kvm_entry
/@start[tid]/
```

```
{
        $num = @reason[tid];
        @exit_ns[$num, @exitreason[$num]] = hist(nsecs - @start[tid]);
        delete(@start[tid]);
        delete(@reason[tid]);
}


END
{
        clear(@exitreason);
        clear(@start);
        clear(@reason);
}
```

Some KVM configurations do not use the kernel KVM module, so the needed tracepoints will not fire, and this tool will be unable to measure the guest exists. In that case, the qemu process can be instrumented directly using uprobes to read the exit reason. (The addition of USDT probes would be preferred.)

16.4.2   Future Work

With KVM and similar hypervisors, the guest CPUs can be seen running as processes, and these processes show up in tools including top(1). This leads me to wonder whether the following questions can be answered:

- What is the guest doing on CPU? Can functions or stack traces be read?
- Why is the guest calling I/O?

Hosts can sample the on-CPU instruction pointer and can also read it when I/O is performed based on its exit to the hypervisor. For example, using bpftrace to show the IP on I/O instructions:

```
# bpftrace -e 't:kvm:kvm_exit /args->exit_reason == 30/ {
    printf("guest exit instruction pointer: %llx\n", args->guest_rip); }'
Attaching 1 probe...
guest exit instruction pointer: ffffffff81c9edc9
guest exit instruction pointer: ffffffff81c9ee8b
guest exit instruction pointer: ffffffff81c9edc9
guest exit instruction pointer: ffffffff81c9edc9
guest exit instruction pointer: ffffffff81c9ee8b
guest exit instruction pointer: ffffffff81c9ee8b
[...]
```

However, the host lacks a symbol table to convert these instruction pointers to function names, or process context to know which address space to use or even which process is running. Possible solutions to this have been discussed for years, including in my last book [Gregg 13b]. These include reading the CR3 register for the root of the current page table, to try to figure out which process is running, and using guest-supplied symbol tables.

These questions can currently be answered by instrumentation from the guest, but not the host.

16.5 Summary

This chapter summarized hardware hypervisors and showed how BPF tracing can expose details from the guest and the host, including hypercalls, stolen CPU time, and guest exits.

Chapter 17

Other BPF Performance Tools

This chapter tours other observability tools built upon BPF. These are all open source and freely available online. (Thanks to my colleague Jason Koch on the Netflix performance engineering team for developing much of this chapter.)

While this book contains dozens of command-line BPF tools, it is expected that most people will end up using BPF tracing via GUIs. This is especially the case for cloud computing environments composed of thousands or even hundreds of thousands of instances; these are, of necessity, usually administered via GUIs. Studying the BPF tools covered in previous chapters should help you use and understand these BPF-based GUIs, which are created as front ends to the same tools.

The GUIs and tools discussed in this chapter:

- **Vector and Performance Co-Pilot (PCP):** For remote BPF monitoring
- **Grafana with PCP:** For remote BPF monitoring
- **eBPF Exporter:** For BPF integration with Prometheus and Grafana
- **kubectl-trace:** For tracing Kubernetes pods and nodes

The role of this chapter is to show you some possibilities of BPF-based GUIs and automation tools, using these as examples. This chapter has sections for each tool, summarizing what the tools does, its internals and usage, and further references. Note that these tools are under heavy development at the time of writing, and it is likely that their capabilities will grow.

17.1 Vector and Performance Co-Pilot (PCP)

Netflix Vector is an open source host-level performance monitoring tool that visualizes high-resolution system and application metrics, in near real-time. It is implemented as a web application, and leverages the battle-tested open source system monitoring framework Performance Co-Pilot (PCP), layering on top a flexible and user-friendly UI. The UI polls metrics every second or longer, rendering the data in completely configurable dashboards that simplify cross-metric correlation and analysis.

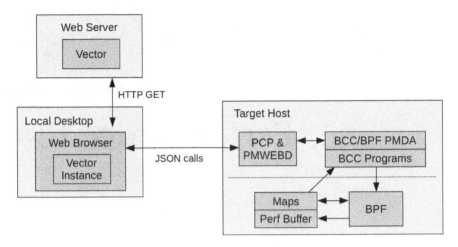

Figure 17-1 Vector monitors BCC program outputs remotely with the help of PCP

Figure 17-1 shows how Vector running in a local web browser fetches its application code from a web server and then connects directly to a target host and PCP to execute BPF programs. Note that the internal PCP components may change in future versions.

Features of Vector include:

- High-level dashboards are provided to show utilization across a number of resources (CPU, disk, network, memory) for a running instance.

- More than 2000 metrics are available for deeper analysis. You can add or remove metrics by modifying the configuration of performance metrics domain agents (PMDAs).

- Visualize the data over time, down to a one-second granularity.

- Compare metric data between different metrics and different hosts at the same time, including comparing metrics from the container vs the host. For example, it is possible to compare resource utilization at the container and the host level at the same time, to see how the two correlate.

Vector now supports BPF-based metrics in addition to the other sources it uses. This was made possible by the addition of a PCP agent for accessing the BCC front end of BPF. BCC is covered in Chapter 4.

17.1.1 Visualizations

Vector can present data to the user in multiple formats. Time series data can be visualized using line charts, as shown in Figure 17-2.

Vector also supports other graph types that better suit visualizing the data produced by per-second BPF histograms and per-event logs: specifically, heat maps and tabular data.

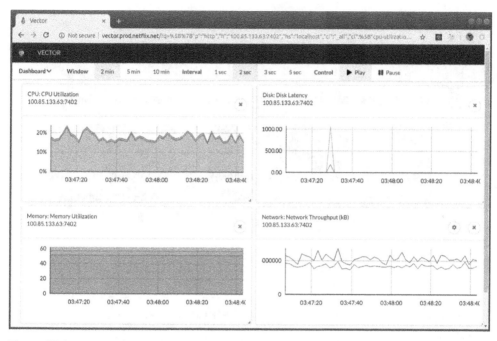

Figure 17-2   Example Vector line charts of system metrics

17.1.2   Visualization: Heat Maps

Heat maps can be used to show a histogram over time and are well suited for visualizing per-second BPF latency histogram summaries. A latency heat map has time on both axes, and is composed of buckets that show a count for a particular time and latency range [Gregg 10]. The axes are:

- **x-axis:** Is the passage of time, where each column is one second (or one interval)
- **y-axis:** Is latency
- **z-axis (color saturation):** Shows the number of I/O that fell into that time and latency range

It is possible to use a scatter plot for visualizing time and latency; however, with thousands or millions of I/O, the number of points drawn bleed into each other and details are lost. The heat map solves this by scaling its color range as needed.

In Vector, heat maps are generally available for the relevant BCC tools. At the time of writing this includes biolatency(8) for block I/O latency, runqlat(8) for CPU run queue latency, and the ext4-, xfs-, and zfs-dist tools for monitoring file system latency. By configuring the BCC PMDA (explained in Section 17.1.5) and launching an appropriate BCC chart in Vector, you can see the outputs represented visually over time. Figure 17-3 shows block I/O latency collected on a host with two-second samples running some simple fio(1) jobs.

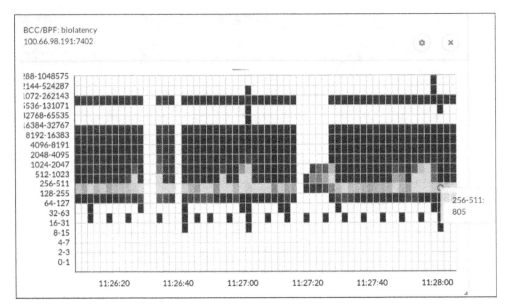

Figure 17-3   Vector latency heat map showing BCC/BPF biolatency(8)

You can see that the most common block latencies are in the 256- to 511-microsecond range, and at the cursor point a tooltip shows there were 805 samples in that bucket.

For comparison, the following is the result from the command line biolatency(8) capturing a similar time period:

```
# biolatency
Tracing block device I/O... Hit Ctrl-C to end.
^C
     usecs              : count     distribution
        0 -> 1          : 0         |                                        |
        2 -> 3          : 0         |                                        |
        4 -> 7          : 0         |                                        |
        8 -> 15         : 0         |                                        |
       16 -> 31         : 5         |                                        |
       32 -> 63         : 19        |                                        |
       64 -> 127        : 1         |                                        |
      128 -> 255        : 2758      |********                                |
      256 -> 511        : 12989     |****************************************|
      512 -> 1023       : 11425     |***********************************      |
     1024 -> 2047       : 2406      |*******                                 |
     2048 -> 4095       : 1034      |***                                     |
     4096 -> 8191       : 374       |*                                       |
     8192 -> 16383      : 189       |                                        |
    16384 -> 32767      : 343       |*                                       |
    32768 -> 65535      : 0         |                                        |
    65536 -> 131071     : 0         |                                        |
   131072 -> 262143     : 42        |                                        |
```

The same latencies are visible in the aggregate; however, it is much easier to see the variation over time with the heat map. It is also much more apparent that the I/O in the 128- to 256-millisecond range is consistent over time and not the result of a short burst.

There are many BPF tools that produce such histograms, not just of latency but also byte sizes, run queue lengths, and other metrics: these can all be visualized using Vector heat maps.

17.1.3   Visualization: Tabular Data

In addition to visualizing the data, it can be helpful to see the raw data in a table. This can be especially useful for some of the BCC tools as tables can provide additional context, or help to make sense as a list of values.

For example, you can monitor execsnoop(8) output to show a list of processes that were recently started. Shown in Figure 17-4, a Tomcat (catalina) process is starting on the monitored host. A table suits visualizing these event details.

BCC/BPF: execsnoop
100.66.98.191:7402

COMM	PID	PPID	RET	ARGS
dirname	19709	19682	0	/usr/bin/dirname /apps/tomcat/bin/catalina.sh
catalina.sh	19682	4680	0	/apps/tomcat/bin/catalina.sh start
setuidgid	19682	4680	0	/usr/local/bin/setuidgid www-data /apps/tomcat/bin/catalina.sh start
ldconfig.real	19708	19707	0	/sbin/ldconfig.real -p

Figure 17-4   Vector displaying per-event output from BCC/BPF execsnoop(8)

Or, for example, you can monitor TCP sockets with tcplife(8), showing host address and port details, transferred bytes, and session duration. This is shown in Figure 17-5. (tcplife(8) was introduced in Chapter 10.)

BCC/BPF: tcplife
100.66.98.191:7402

PID	COMM	LADDR	LPORT	DADDR	DPORT	TX_KB	RX_KB	MS
3745	amazon-ssm-agen	100.66.98.191	29104	52.94.209.3	443	4	6	20037
17336	wget	100.66.98.191	30424	128.112.18.21	80	0	2050272	41595
3745	amazon-ssm-agen	100.66.98.191	25798	52.94.210.188	443	4	6	20025
3745	amazon-ssm-agen	100.66.98.191	45840	52.119.164.173	443	2	6	75016

Figure 17-5   Vector listing TCP sessions via BCC/BPF tcplife(8)

In this case, you can see amazon-ssm-agent, which appears to be long-polling for 20 seconds, and a wget(1) command was executed that received two Gbytes of data in 41.595 seconds.

17.1.4   BCC Provided Metrics

The majority of the tools available in the bcc-tools package are currently available with the PCP PMDA.

Vector has pre-configured charts for the following BCC tools:

- biolatency(8) and biotop(8)
- ext4dist(8), xfsdist(8), and zfsdist(8)
- tcplife(8), tcptop(8), and tcpretrans(8)
- runqlat(8)
- execsnoop(8)

Many of these tools support configuration options that can be provided on the host. Additional BCC tools can also be added to Vector, with custom charts, tables, or heat maps to visualize the data.

Vector also supports adding custom event metrics for tracepoints, uprobe, and USDT events.

17.1.5   Internals

Vector itself is a web application that runs completely inside the user's browser. It was built with React and leverages D3.js for charting. The metrics are collected and made available from the Performance Co-Pilot [175], a toolkit for collecting, archiving, and processing performance metrics from multiple operating systems. A typical Linux PCP installation offers more than 1000 metrics by default and is in turn extensible with its own plugins, or PMDAs.

To understand how Vector visualizes BPF metrics, it is important to understand how PCP collects these metrics (see Figure 17-6):

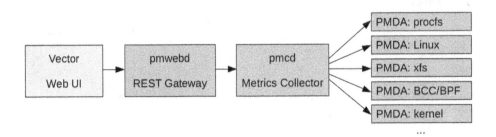

Figure 17-6   Vector metric source internals

- PMCD (performance metrics collector daemon) is the central component of PCP. It typically runs on the target host and coordinates collection of metrics from numerous agents.

- PMDA (performance metrics domain agent) is the term given to an agent hosted by PCP. Many PMDAs are available and can each expose different metrics. For example, there are agents to collect kernel data, agents for different filesystems, agents for NVIDIA GPUs, and many more. To use BCC metrics with PCP, the BCC PMDA must be installed.

- Vector is a single-page web app that can be deployed to a server or executed locally and allows connection to a target pmwebd instance.

- pmwebd acts as a REST gateway to the pmcd instance on the target host. Vector connects to the exposed REST port and uses this to interact with pmcd.

PCP's stateless model makes it lightweight and robust. Its overhead on hosts is negligible, as clients are responsible for keeping track of state, sampling rate, and computation. Additionally, metrics are not aggregated across hosts or persisted outside of the user's browser session, keeping the framework light.

17.1.6 Installing PCP and Vector

To try out PCP and Vector, you can run them both on a single host for local monitoring. In a real production deployment, you likely would run Vector on a different host than the PCP agent and PMDAs. Refer to the latest project documentation for details.

The steps to install Vector are documented and updated online [176][177]. They currently involve installing pcp and pcp-webapi packages and running the Vector UI from a Docker container. Follow these additional instructions to ensure that the BCC PMDA is enabled:

```
$ cd /var/lib/pcp/pmdas/bcc/
$ ./Install
[Wed Apr  3 20:54:06] pmdabcc(18942) Info: Initializing, currently in 'notready'
state.
[Wed Apr  3 20:54:06] pmdabcc(18942) Info: Enabled modules:
[Wed Apr  3 20:54:06] pmdabcc(18942) Info: ['biolatency', 'sysfork', 'tcpperpid',
'runqlat']
```

When Vector and PCP are running on the system with a configured BCC PMDA, you can connect and view system metrics.

17.1.7 Connecting and Viewing Data

Browse to http://localhost/ (if testing on your local machine) or the appropriate address where Vector is installed. Enter the hostname of the target system in the dialog shown in Figure 17-7.

Add connection

Hostname

localhost

Port

44323

Hostspec

localhost

Container

All

Add

Figure 17-7   Vector target system selection

The connection area will show a new connection. As shown in Figure 17-8, the icon should shortly show green (1), and the large buttons will become available. This example will use a specific chart instead of a prepared dashboard, so flip across to the Custom tab (2), and choose runqlat (3). Any modules not available on the server will be dimmed and not available. Click on the enabled module and click the Dashboard ^ (4) arrow to close the dashboard.

Figure 17-8   Vector selection of BCC/BPF tool

In the connection dialog, by switching to the Custom tab and looking at the BCC/BPF options, you can see the available BCC/BPF metrics. In this case, many of these BPF programs appear grayed out as they are not enabled in the PMDA. When you select runqlat and close the Dashboard panel, a run queue latency heat map is shown that is updated live each second, as shown in Figure 17-9. This sources the runqlat(8) BCC tool.

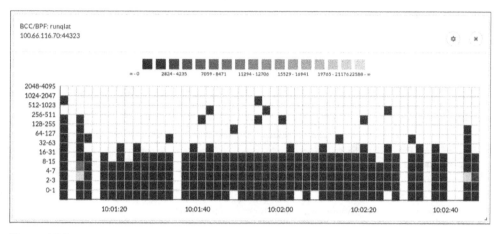

Figure 17-9   Vector run queue latency heat map

Be sure to explore the configuration widget for other available BCC metrics.

17.1.8   Configuring the BCC PMDA

As noted previously, much of the BCC PMDA functionality is not available unless it is specifically configured. The BCC PMDA man page (pmdabcc(1)) describes the configuration file format in detail. The following show steps for configuring the tcpretrans BCC module to make it available in Vector, so that you can see TCP session statistics.

```
$ cd /var/lib/pcp/pmdas/bcc
$ sudo vi bcc.conf
[pmda]
# List of enabled modules
modules = biolatency,sysfork,tcpperpid,runqlat,tcplife
```

In the full file you will see additional configuration options for the tcplife module and many others. This file is important for configuration of the BCC PMDA.

```
# This module summarizes TCP sessions
#
# Configuration options:
# Name              - type    - default
#
# process           - string - unset : list of names/pids or regex of processes to
monitor
```

```
# dport            - int    - unset : list of remote ports to monitor
# lport            - int    - unset : list of local ports to monitor
# session_count    - int    - 20    : number of closed TCP sessions to keep in cache
# buffer_page_count - int   - 64    : number of pages for the perf ring buffer,
power of two
[tcplife]
module = tcplife
cluster = 3
#process = java
#lport = 8443
#dport = 80,443
```

Any time the PMDA configuration changes, you should recompile and restart the PMDA:

```
$ cd /var/lib/pcp/pmdas/bcc
$ sudo ./Install
...
```

You can now refresh your browser and select the tcpretrans chart.

17.1.9   Future Work

More work is still required between Vector and PCP to improve integration with the full suite of BCC tools. Vector has served Netflix well for many years as a detailed on-host metrics solution. Netflix is currently investigating whether Grafana can also provide this capability, which would allow more development focus to be on the host and metrics. Grafana is covered in Section 17.2.

17.1.10   Further Reading

For more information on Vector and PCP, see:

- https://getvector.io/
- https://pcp.io/

17.2   Grafana and Performance Co-Pilot (PCP)

Grafana is a popular open source charting and visualization tool with support for connecting to and displaying data stored in many back-end data sources. By using Performance Co-Pilot (PCP) as a data source, you can visualize any of the metrics exposed in PCP. PCP is covered in more detail in Section 17.1.

There are two approaches for configuring PCP to support the presentation of metrics in Grafana. It is possible to present historic data, and it is possible to present live metric data. Each has a slightly different use case and configuration.

17.2.1 Installation and Configuration

The two options for presenting PCP data in Grafana are:

- **Grafana PCP live data source:** For this you use the grafana-pcp-live plugin. This plugin polls a PCP instance for the latest metric data and keeps a short history (a few minutes' worth) of results in the browser. There is no long-term persistence of the data. The advantage is that there is no load on the system being monitored while you are not watching, which makes it great for deep dive viewing of a wide range of live metrics on a host.

- **Grafana PCP archived data source:** For this you use the grafana-pcp-redis plugin. This plugin fetches data from the source using the PCP pmseries data storage and collates the data into a Redis instance. This relies on a configured pmseries instance and means PCP will poll and store the data. This makes it more suitable for collecting larger time series data that will be looked at across multiple hosts.

It is assumed that you have performed the PCP configuration steps previously described in Section 17.1.

For both options, the projects are undergoing changes, so the best approach for installation is to see the links in Section 17.2.4 and look at the installation instructions for each plugin.

17.2.2 Connecting and Viewing Data

The grafana-pcp-live plugin is under heavy development. At the time of writing, the approach to connecting to a back end relies on the setup of variables required for the PCP client. Since it does not have any storage, this allows the dashboard to be dynamically reconfigured to connect to multiple different hosts. These variables are _proto, _host, and _port.

Create a new dashboard, enter the dashboard settings, create variables for the dashboard, and set them up with the required configuration settings. You can see the result in Figure 17-10 (where you fill in the host field with an appropriate host):

Variable	Definition
$_proto	http
$_host	
$_port	7402

Figure 17-10   Setting up dashboard variables in grafana-pcp-live

Once the dashboard is configured, you can add a new chart. Select a PCP metric; the available metric bcc.runq.latency is a good one to start with (see Figure 17-11).

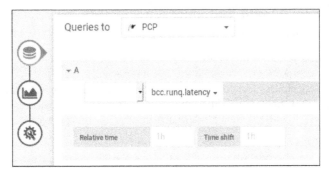

Figure 17-11   Choosing the query in Grafana

You also need to configure an appropriate visualization(see Figure 17-12). In this case, choose the Heatmap visualization and set the format to "Time series buckets," with Unit set to "microseconds (μs)." The Bucket bound should be set to "Upper" (see Figure 17-13).

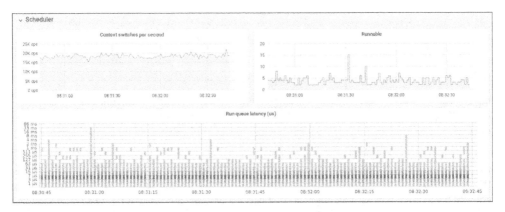

Figure 17-12   Grafana PCP, showing standard PCP metrics (context switches, runnable count) as well as run queue latency (runqlat) BCC metrics

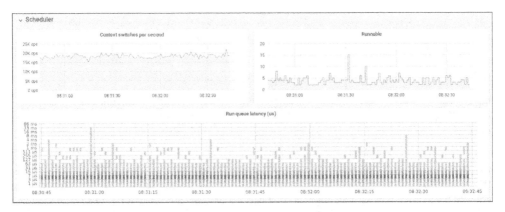

Figure 17-13   Setting up the visualization in Grafana

17.2.3   Future Work

More work is still needed between Grafana and PCP to improve integration with the full suite of packaged bcc-tools. Support for visualizing custom bpftrace programs will hopefully be available in a future update. In addition, the grafana-pcp-live plugin needs some significant additional work before it should be considered battle-hardened.

17.2.4   Further Reading

The following links are quite likely to change as the projects mature:

- grafana-pcp-live data source:

  https://github.com/Netflix-Skunkworks/grafana-pcp-live/

- grafana-pcp-redis data source:

  https://github.com/performancecopilot/grafana-pcp-redis/

17.3   Cloudflare eBPF Prometheus Exporter (with Grafana)

The Cloudflare eBPF exporter is an open source tool that plugs into the well-defined Prometheus monitoring format. Prometheus has become especially popular for metric collection, storage, and querying because it provides a simple, well-known protocol. This makes it easy to integrate from any language, and a number of simple language bindings are available. Prometheus also provides alerting functionality and integrates well with dynamic environments such as Kubernetes. Although Prometheus only provides a basic UI, a number of graphing tools—including Grafana— are also built on top of it to provide a coherent dashboard experience.

Prometheus also integrates into existing application operations tools. Within Prometheus, the tool that collects and exposes metrics is known as an *exporter*. There are official and third-party exporters available to collect Linux host statistics, JMX exporters for Java applications, and many more for applications such as web servers, storage layers, hardware, and database services. Cloudflare has open sourced an exporter for BPF metrics that allows exposure and visualization of these metrics through Prometheus and thence to Grafana.

17.3.1   Build and Run the ebpf Exporter

Note that the build uses Docker:

```
$ git clone https://github.com/cloudflare/ebpf_exporter.git
$ cd ebpf_exporter
$ make
...
$ sudo ./release/ebpf_exporter-*/ebpf_exporter --config.file=./examples/runqlat.yaml
2019/04/10 17:42:19 Starting with 1 programs found in the config
2019/04/10 17:42:19 Listening on :9435
```

17.3.2 Configure Prometheus to Monitor the ebpf_exporter Instance

This depends on your approach for monitoring targets in your environment. Assuming the instance is running the ebpf_exporter on port 9435, you can find a sample target configuration as follows:

```
$ kubectl edit configmap -n monitoring prometheus-core
  - job_name: 'kubernetes-nodes-ebpf-exporter'
    scheme: http
    kubernetes_sd_configs:
      - role: node
    relabel_configs:
      - source_labels: [__address__]
        regex: '(.*):10250'
        replacement: '${1}:9435'
        target_label: __address__
```

17.3.3 Set Up a Query in Grafana

As soon as the ebpf_exporter is running, it will produce metrics. You can graph these metrics using the following query and additional format (see Figure 17-14):

```
query : rate(ebpf_exporter_run_queue_latency_seconds_bucket[20s])
legend format : {{le}}
axis unit : seconds
```

(For more information on the query format and graph configuration, refer to the Grafana and Prometheus documentation.)

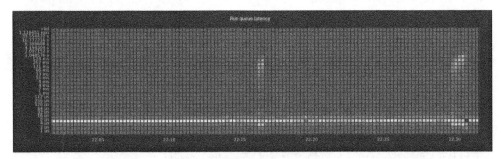

Figure 17-14 Grafana run queue latency heat map, showing latency spikes when schbench is executed with more threads than cores

17.3.4 Further Reading

For more information on Grafana and Prometheus, see:

- https://grafana.com/
- https://github.com/prometheus/prometheus

For more information on the Cloudflare eBPF exporter, see:

- https://github.com/cloudflare/ebpf_exporter
- https://blog.cloudflare.com/introducing-ebpf_exporter/

17.4 kubectl-trace

Kubectl-trace is a Kubernetes command line front end for running bpftrace across nodes in a Kubernetes cluster. It was created by Lorenzo Fontana and is hosted at the IO Visor project (see https://github.com/iovisor/kubectl-trace).

To follow the examples here, you will need to download and install kubectl-trace. You also need an installation of Kubernetes (which is beyond the scope of this book):

```
$ git clone https://github.com/iovisor/kubectl-trace.git
$ cd kubectl-trace
$ make
$ sudo cp ./_output/bin/kubectl-trace /usr/local/bin
```

17.4.1 Tracing Nodes

Kubectl is the Kubernetes command line front end. Kubectl-trace supports running bpftrace commands across a cluster node. Tracing whole nodes is the simplest option available, but pay attention to the overhead of your BPF instrumentation: a bpftrace invocation that consumes high overhead will affect the entire cluster node.

For example, using vfsstat.bt to capture bpftrace output for a Kubernetes node in the cluster:

```
$ kubectl trace run node/ip-1-2-3-4 -f /usr/share/bpftrace/tools/vfsstat.bt
trace 8fc22ddb-5c84-11e9-9ad2-02d0df09784a created
$ kubectl trace get
NAMESPACE NODE      NAME                                                       STATUS  AGE
default   ip-1-2-34 kubectl-trace-8fc22ddb-5c84-11e9-9ad2-02d0df09784a Running 3s
$ kubectl trace logs -f kubectl-trace-8fc22ddb-5c84-11e9-9ad2-02d0df09784a
00:02:54
@[vfs_open]: 940
@[vfs_write]: 7015
@[vfs_read]: 7797
```

```
00:02:55
@[vfs_write]: 252
@[vfs_open]: 289
@[vfs_read]: 924


^C
```

```
$ kubectl trace delete kubectl-trace-8fc22ddb-5c84-11e9-9ad2-02d0df09784a
trace job kubectl-trace-8fc22ddb-5c84-11e9-9ad2-02d0df09784a deleted
trace configuration kubectl-trace-8fc22ddb-5c84-11e9-9ad2-02d0df09784a deleted
```

This output shows all vfs statistics in the entire node, not just the pod. Because bpftrace is executed from the host, kubectl-trace also runs in the context of the host. Therefore, it is tracing all applications running on that node. This may be helpful in some cases for system administrators, but for many use cases, it will be important to focus on the processes running inside the container.

17.4.2   Tracing Pods and Containers

bpftrace—and therefore kubectl-trace—has indirect support for containers by matching tracing through kernel data structures. kubectl-trace provides help for pods in two ways. First, when you specify the pod name, kubectl-trace will locate and deploy the bpftrace program on the correct node automatically. Second, kubectl-trace introduces an extra variable into your script: $container_pid. The $container_pid variable is set to the PID of the container root process, using the host PID namespace. This allows you to perform filtering or other actions targeting only the pod you prefer.

For this example, we will ensure that the PID is the only PID running inside the container we're looking at. For more complex scenarios, such as when you are running an init process or have a forking server, you will need to build on top of this tooling to map PIDs to their parent PIDs.

Create a new deployment using the following specification. Note that the command specifies the Docker entry point to ensure that the node process is the only process inside the container, and the vfsstat-pod.bt includes an additional filter on the PID:

```
$ cat <<EOF | kubectl apply -f -
apiVersion: apps/v1
kind: Deployment
metadata:
  name: node-hello
spec:
  selector:
    matchLabels:
      app: node-hello
  replicas: 1
  template:
    metadata:
      labels:
        app: node-hello
```

```
      spec:
        containers:
        - name: node-hello
          image: duluca/minimal-node-web-server
          command: ['node', 'index']
          ports:
          - containerPort: 3000
EOF
deployment.apps/node-hello created
$ kubectl get pods
NAME                          READY    STATUS    RESTARTS    AGE
node-hello-56b8dbc757-th2k2   1/1      Running   0           4s
```

Create a copy of vfsstat.bt called vfsstat-pod.bt, as shown below, and then start a tracer implementation (these steps show how to start a trace and review tracing output):

```
$ cat vfsstat-pod.bt
...
kprobe:vfs_read,
kprobe:vfs_write,
kprobe:vfs_fsync,
kprobe:vfs_open,
kprobe:vfs_create
/pid == $container_pid/
{
...
$ kubectl trace run pod/node-hello-56b8dbc757-th2k2 -f vfsstat-pod.bt
trace 552a2492-5c83-11e9-a598-02d0df09784a created
$ kubectl trace logs -f 552a2492-5c83-11e9-a598-02d0df09784a
if your program has maps to print, send a SIGINT using Ctrl-C, if you want to
interrupt the execution send SIGINT two times
Attaching 8 probes...
Tracing key VFS calls... Hit Ctrl-C to end.
[...]
17:58:34
@[vfs_open]: 1
@[vfs_read]: 3
@[vfs_write]: 4

17:58:35

17:58:36
@[vfs_read]: 3
@[vfs_write]: 4
[...]
```

You will notice that there are significantly fewer vfs operations at the pod level than at the node level, which is to be expected for a mostly idle web server.

17.4.3   Further Reading

- https://github.com/iovisor/kubectl-trace

17.5   Other Tools

Some other BPF-based tools include:

- **Cilium:** Applies network and application security policies in containerized environments using BPF.

- **Sysdig:** Uses BPF to extend container observability.

- **Android eBPF:** Monitors and manages device network usage on Android devices.

- **osquery eBPF:** Exposes operating system information for analytics and monitoring. It now supports monitoring of kprobes with BPF.

- **ply:** A BPF-based CLI tracer similar to bpftrace but with minimal dependencies, making it well suited for environments including embedded targets [5]. ply was created by Tobias Waldekranz.

As BPF usage is growing, there will likely be many more BPF-based GUI tools developed in the future.

17.6   Summary

The BPF tool space is rapidly growing, and more tools and features will be developed. This chapter presented four currently available tools that build upon BPF. Vector/PCP, Grafana, and Cloudflare's eBPF exporter are graphical tools that provide the ability to present visually large amounts of complex data including time series BPF outputs. The final tool, kubectl-trace, allows for straightforward execution of bpftrace scripts against a Kubernetes cluster. In addition, a short list of other BPF tools was provided.

Chapter 18

Tips, Tricks, and Common Problems

This chapter shares tips and tricks for successful BPF tracing, along with common problems that you might encounter and how to fix them.

Tips and Tricks:

Common Problems:

18.1 Typical Event Frequency and Overhead

Three main factors determine the CPU overhead of a tracing program:

- The frequency of the event that is traced.
- The action performed while tracing.
- The number of CPUs on the system.

An application will suffer this overhead on a per-CPU basis using the relationship:

Overhead = (Frequency × Action performed) / CPUs

Tracing one million events per second on a single-CPU system may bring an application to a crawl, whereas a 128-CPU system may be barely affected. The CPU count must be considered.

The number of CPUs and the overhead of the work performed can both vary by a single order of magnitude. Event frequency, however, can vary by several orders of magnitude, making it the biggest wildcard in trying to estimate overhead.

18.1.1 Frequency

It helps to have some intuitive understanding of typical event rates, so I have created Table 18-1.[1] This includes a column where the maximum rate has been scaled to human-understandable terms: once per second becomes once per year. Imagine that you are subscribed to a mailing list that sends you email at this scaled rate.

Table 18-1   **Typical Event Frequencies**

Event	Typical Frequency[2]	Maximum Scaled	Max Estimated Tracing Overhead[3]
Thread sleeps	1 per second	Yearly	Negligible
Process execution	10 per second	Monthly	Negligible
File opens	10–50 per second	Weekly	Negligible
Profiling at 100 Hz	100 per second	Twice a week	Negligible
New TCP sessions	10–500 per second	Daily	Negligible
Disk I/O	10–1000 per second	Every eight hours	Negligible
VFS calls	1000–10,000 /s	Hourly	Measurable
Syscalls	1000–50,000 /s	Every ten minutes	Significant
Network packets	1000–100,000 /s	Every five minutes	Significant
Memory allocations	10,000–1,000,000 /s	Every thirty seconds	Expensive

---

1 This was inspired by the scaled latency table from Chapter 2 of *Systems Performance* [Gregg 13b], which became popular and has been shared many times. While I created this scaled frequency table, I did not come up with the idea of a scaled latency table: I first saw that when I was a university student.

2 It is hard to pick something "typical" as workloads vary. Databases often have higher disk I/O rates, and web and proxy servers often have higher packet rates.

3 This is the estimated CPU overhead of tracing the event at its maximum rate (see below). CPU instructions and cycles cannot be traced individually and directly, although in theory their software execution by CPU simulators could be traced.

Event	Typical Frequency[2]	Maximum Scaled	Max Estimated Tracing Overhead[3]
Locking events	50,000–5,000,000 /s	Every five seconds	Expensive
Function calls	Up to 100,000,000 /s	Three times per second	Extreme
CPU instructions	Up to 1,000,000,000+ per second	Thirty times per second: As a beat, C contra-octave on the piano scale: the limit of human hearing	Extreme (CPU simulators)
CPU cycles	Up to 3,000,000,000+ per second	Ninety times per second: G on the piano scale	Extreme (CPU simulators)

Throughout this book I have described the overhead for BPF tools, sometimes with measurements but often with the words *negligible, measurable, significant*, and *expensive*. I chose these terms to be both deliberately vague and sufficiently descriptive. Using hard numbers would be misleading as the specific metrics depend on the workload and system. With that caveat in mind, here is a rough guide to those terms:

- Negligible: <0.1%
- Measurable: ~1%
- Significant: >5%
- Expensive: >30%
- Extreme: >300%

In Table 18-1, I extrapolated from event frequency to these overhead descriptions assuming the minimum tracing action: an in-kernel count and for typical system sizes of today. The next section shows how different actions can cost more.

18.1.1.2 Action Performed

The following measurements describe BPF overhead as the absolute per-event cost, illustrating how different actions can cost more. They were calculated by instrumenting reads for a dd(1) workload performing over one million reads per second: the previous section on frequency should already have suggested that BPF tracing will add expensive overhead at this high rate.

The workload is:

```
dd if=/dev/zero of=/dev/null bs=1 count=10000k
```

This is executed with different bpftrace one-liners, such as:

```
bpftrace -e 'kprobe:vfs_read { @ = count(); }'
```

Based on the runtime difference and known event counts, the per-event CPU cost can be calculated (ignoring dd(1) process startup and termination costs). This is shown in Table 18-2.

Table 18-2   bpftrace Per-Event Costs

bpftrace	Test Purpose	dd Runtime (secs)	BPF per-event cost (nsecs)
<none>	Control	5.97243	—
k:vfs_read { 1 }	Kprobe	6.75364	76
kr:vfs_read { 1 }	Kretprobe	8.13894	212
t:syscalls:sys_enter_read { 1 }	Tracepoint	6.95894	96
t:syscalls:sys_exit_read { 1 }	Tracepoint	6.9244	93
u:libc:__read { 1 }	Uprobe	19.1466	1287
ur:libc:__read { 1 }	Uretprobe	25.7436	1931
k:vfs_read /arg2 > 0/ { 1 }	Filter	7.24849	124
k:vfs_read { @ = count() }	Map	7.91737	190
k:vfs_read { @[pid] = count() }	Single key	8.09561	207
k:vfs_read { @[comm] = count() }	String key	8.27808	225
k:vfs_read { @[pid, comm] = count() }	Two key	8.3167	229
k:vfs_read { @[kstack] = count() }	Kernel stack	9.41422	336
k:vfs_read { @[ustack] = count() }	User stack	12.648	652
k:vfs_read { @ = hist(arg2) }	Histogram	8.35566	233
k:vfs_read { @s[tid] = nsecs } kr:vfs_read /@s[tid]/ { @ = hist(nsecs - @s[tid]); delete(@s[tid]); }	Timing	12.4816	636 / 2 [4]
k:vfs_read { @[kstack, ustack] = hist(arg2) }	Multiple	14.5306	836
k:vfs_read { printf("%d bytes\n", arg2) } > out.txt	Per event	14.6719	850

This shows that kprobes (on this system) are fast, adding only 76 nanoseconds per call, increasing to around 200 nanoseconds when a map with a key is used. Kretprobes are much slower, as would be expected due to instrumenting the function entry and inserting a trampoline handler for the return (see Chapter 2 for details). Uprobes and uretprobes add the most overhead, over one microsecond per event: this is a known problem that we would like to improve in a future version of Linux.

These are all short BPF programs. It is possible to write lengthy BPF programs that cost much more, measured in microseconds.

---

4 This added 636 nanoseconds per read, but two probes were used—a kprobe and a kretprobe—so this is really 636 nanoseconds for two BPF events.

These were measured on Linux 4.15 with BPF JIT enabled, Intel(R) Core(TM) i7-8650U CPU @ 1.90GHz CPUs, using taskset(1) to bind to one CPU only for consistency, and taking the fastest of 10 runs (principle of least perturbations) while checking the standard deviation for consistency. Bear in mind that these numbers can all change based on the speed and architecture of the system, the running workload, and future changes to BPF.

18.1.3   Test Yourself

If you can accurately measure an application's performance, you can do so with and without a BPF tracing tool running and measure the difference. If a system is running at CPU saturation (100%), then BPF will take CPU cycles away from the application, and the difference may be measurable as a drop in request rate. If the system is running with CPU idle, then the difference may be seen as a drop in available CPU idle.

18.2   Sample at 49 or 99 Hertz

The point of sampling at these seemingly odd rates is to avoid lockstep sampling.

We take timed samples to paint a coarse picture of the target software. A rate of 100 samples per second (100 Hertz), or 50 per second, is usually sufficient to provide details for solving both big and small performance wins.

Consider 100 Hertz. This takes a sample every 10 milliseconds. Now consider an application thread that wakes up every 10 milliseconds to do 2 milliseconds of work. It's consuming 20% of one CPU. If we sample at 100 Hertz, and by coincidence run our profiling tool at just the right time, every sample will coincide with the two-millisecond window of work, so our profile will show it on-CPU 100% of the time. Or, if we hit Enter at a different time, every sample will miss and show that application thread 0% of the time. Both results are deeply misleading and are examples of aliasing errors.

By using 99 Hertz instead of 100, the time offsets where we take samples will no longer always coincide with the application's work. Over enough seconds, it will show that the application is on-CPU 20% of the time. It's also close enough to 100 Hertz that we can reason about it as though it were 100. Eight-CPU system for one second? Roughly 800 samples. I frequently make such calculations when sanity-checking my results.

If instead we picked, say, 73, that would also avoid lockstep sampling, but we wouldn't be able to make such quick calculations in our heads. 73 Hertz on four CPUs for eight seconds? Give me a calculator!

The 99 Hertz strategy only works because application programmers usually pick round numbers for their timed activity: every 1 second, 10 times per second, every 20 milliseconds, etc. If application developers began picking 99 times per second for their timed activities, we'd have the lockstep problem again.

Let's call 99 the "profiler number." Don't use it for anything other than profiling!

18.3   Yellow Pigs and Gray Rats

In mathematics, the number 17 is special and has been nicknamed the "yellow pig" number; there is even a yellow pig day, July 17 [178]. It is also a useful number for tracing analysis, although I prefer 23.

You will often be faced with an unknown system to analyze, not knowing which events to start tracing. If you are able to inject a known workload, then frequency counting events may reveal which are related to your workload.

To show how this works, let's say you wanted to understand how the ext4 file system performed write I/O, but you didn't know which events to trace. We will create a known workload using dd(1) to perform 23 writes, or even better, 230,000 writes so that they stand out from other activity:

```
# dd if=/dev/zero of=test bs=1 count=230000
230000+0 records in
230000+0 records out
230000 bytes (230 kB, 225 KiB) copied, 0.732254 s, 314 kB/s
```

While this ran, all functions beginning with "ext4_" were traced for 10 seconds:

```
# funccount -d 10 'ext4_*'
Tracing 509 functions for "ext4_*"... Hit Ctrl-C to end.
^C
FUNC                            COUNT
ext4_rename2                        1
ext4_get_group_number               1
[...]
ext4_bio_write_page                89
ext4_es_lookup_extent             142
ext4_es_can_be_merged             217
ext4_getattr                     5125
ext4_file_getattr                6143
ext4_write_checks              230117
ext4_file_write_iter           230117
ext4_da_write_end              230185
ext4_nonda_switch              230191
ext4_block_write_begin         230200
ext4_da_write_begin            230216
ext4_dirty_inode               230299
ext4_mark_inode_dirty          230329
ext4_get_group_desc            230355
ext4_inode_csum.isra.56        230356
ext4_inode_csum_set            230356
ext4_reserve_inode_write       230357
ext4_mark_iloc_dirty           230357
```

```
ext4_do_update_inode                    230360
ext4_inode_table                        230446
ext4_journal_check_start                460551
Detaching...
```

Notice that 15 of these functions were called a little over 230,000 times: these are very likely related to our known workload. Out of the 509 ext4 functions traced, using this trick we've narrowed them down to 15 candidates. I like using 23 (or 230, 2300, etc.) as it is unlikely to coincide with other unrelated event counts. What else would also happen 230,000 times during 10 seconds of tracing?

23 and 17 are prime numbers, which tend to occur less naturally in computing than other numbers, such as powers of 2 or 10. I prefer 23 because it has distance from other power-of-two and 10 numbers, unlike 17. I'd call 23 the "gray rat" number.[5]

See Section 12.4 in Chapter 12, which also used this trick to discover functions.

18.4   Write Target Software

It can save you time and headaches to write load generation software first, then write the tracing tool to measure it.

Let's say you wanted to trace DNS requests and show latency and request details. Where do you start, and how do you know if your program is working? If you begin by writing a simple DNS request generator, you'll learn which functions to trace, how the request details are stored in structs, and the return values of the request functions. You'll likely learn this quickly, as there is usually an abundance of documentation for programmers that can be found with Internet searches, including code snippets.

In this case, the man page for the getaddrinfo(3) resolver function contains entire programs that you can use:

```
$ man getaddrinfo
[...]
        memset(&hints, 0, sizeof(struct addrinfo));
        hints.ai_family = AF_UNSPEC;    /* Allow IPv4 or IPv6 */
        hints.ai_socktype = SOCK_DGRAM; /* Datagram socket */
        hints.ai_flags = 0;
        hints.ai_protocol = 0;          /* Any protocol */

        s = getaddrinfo(argv[1], argv[2], &hints, &result);
        if (s != 0) {
            fprintf(stderr, "getaddrinfo: %s\n", gai_strerror(s));
            exit(EXIT_FAILURE);
        }
[...]
```

5 It counts how many whiskers there are on a gray rat. I also own many gray rat stuffed toys from Ikea—maybe 23.

By starting here, you'll end up with a tool to generate known requests. You can even modify it to make 23 requests (or 2300) to help you find other related functions in the stack (see Section 18.3).

18.5   Learn Syscalls

System calls are rich targets for tracing.

They are documented in man pages, they have tracepoints, and they provide useful insight for resource usage by applications. For example, you use the BCC syscount(8) tool and discover a high rate of setitimer(2). What is that?

```
$ man setitimer
GETITIMER(2)                  Linux Programmer's Manual                  GETITIMER(2)


NAME
       getitimer, setitimer - get or set value of an interval timer

SYNOPSIS
       #include <sys/time.h>

       int getitimer(int which, struct itimerval *curr_value);
       int setitimer(int which, const struct itimerval *new_value,
                     struct itimerval *old_value);


DESCRIPTION
       These  system  calls provide access to interval timers, that is, timers
       that initially expire at some point in the future, and (optionally)  at
       regular intervals after that.  When a timer expires, a signal is gener
       ated for the calling process, and the timer is reset to  the  specified
       interval (if the interval is nonzero).

[...]

   setitimer()
       The function setitimer() arms or disarms the timer specified by  which,
       by setting the timer to the value specified by new_value.  If old_value
       is non-NULL, the buffer it points to is used  to  return  the  previous
       value  of  the  timer  (i.e.,  the same information that is returned by
       getitimer()).

[...]

RETURN VALUE
       On  success,  zero is returned.  On error, -1 is returned, and errno is
       set appropriately.
```

The man page explains what setitimer(2) does, along with its entry arguments and return value. These can all be inspected by the tracepoints syscalls:sys_enter_setitimer and syscalls:sys_exit_setitimer.

18.6 Keep It Simple

Avoid writing long and complex tracing programs.

BPF tracing is a superpower that can trace everything, and it can be easy to get carried away and add more and more events to a tracing program and lose sight of the original problem you wanted to solve. This has the following drawbacks:

- **Unnecessary overhead:** The original problem might have been solved by tracing only a few events, but the tool now traces many more, adding little insight to the common use case but costing overhead for everyone who uses it.

- **Maintenance burden:** This is especially the case with kprobes and uprobes, as they are an unstable interface that can change between software versions. We've already had a number of kernel changes during the Linux 4.x series that have broken BCC tools. The fix was to include code for each kernel version (often selected by checking for the existence of functions, as kernel version numbers are an unreliable indicator due to backports), or to simply duplicate the tools, keeping copies for older kernels in the tools/old directory. Best case: tracepoints were added so that such breakage stops happening (e.g., with sock:inet_sock_set_state for the tcp tools).

Fixing the BCC tools has not been arduous, as each one typically traces only a few events or event types (as I designed them to do). Were they to trace dozens of events each, breakage would be more frequent, and fixing them would be more complicated. Also, the tests required would be magnified: testing all event types across all kernel versions that the tool has specific code for.

I learned this the hard way when I developed a tool called tcpsnoop(1m) 15 years ago. My goal was to show which processes were causing TCP I/O, but I solved this by writing a tool to trace all packet types with the PID (TCP handshake, port refused packets, UDP, ICMP, etc.) so that it matched the output of a network sniffer. This involved tracing many unstable kernel details, and the tool broke several times due to kernel updates. I'd lost sight of the original problem and developed something that became impractical to maintain. (For more details on this lesson, see tcpsnoop in Chapter 10.)

The bpftrace tools I developed and included in this book are the result of 15 years of experience: I'm deliberately restricting them to trace the fewest events required, solving the specific problem and no more. Where possible, I recommend that you do the same.

18.7 Missing Events

This is a common problem: an event can be instrumented successfully, but it doesn't seem to fire, or a tool produces no output. (If the event can't be instrumented at all, see Section 18.10.) Instrumenting the events using the Linux perf(1) utility can help determine whether the issue is with BPF tracing or with the event itself.

The following demonstrates using perf(1) to check if the block:block_rq_insert and block:block_rq_requeue tracepoints are occurring:

```
# perf stat -e block:block_rq_insert,block:block_rq_requeue -a
^C
 Performance counter stats for 'system wide':

                41        block:block_rq_insert
                 0        block:block_rq_requeue


      2.545953756 seconds time elapsed
```

In this example, the block:block_rq_insert tracepoint fired 41 times, and the block:block_rq_requeue tracepoint fired zero times. If a BPF tool was tracing block:block_rq_insert at the same time, and it did not see any events, then it would suggest a problem with the BPF tool. If both a BPF tool and perf(1) showed zero events, then it would suggest there is a problem with the event: it is not occurring.

Now an example of checking if the vfs_read() kernel function is called, using kprobes:

```
# perf probe vfs_read
Added new event:
  probe:vfs_read       (on vfs_read)

You can now use it in all perf tools, such as:

        perf record -e probe:vfs_read -aR sleep 1

# perf stat -e probe:vfs_read -a
^C
 Performance counter stats for 'system wide':

            3,029        probe:vfs_read


      1.950980658 seconds time elapsed
# perf probe --del probe:vfs_read
Removed event: probe:vfs_read
```

The perf(1) interface required separate commands to create and delete the kprobe, and it is similar with uprobes. This example showed that vfs_read() was called 3029 times while tracing.

Missing events sometimes happen after a software change where previously instrumented events are no longer called.

One common occurrence is where a library function is traced from its shared library location, but the target application is statically compiled, and that function is called from the application binary instead.

18.8 Missing Stacks Traces

This is where printed stack traces look incomplete or are completely missing. It may also involve missing symbols (covered Section 18.9) so that frames appear as "[unknown]".

Here is some example output, using BCC trace(8) to print user-level stack traces for the execve() tracepoint (new process execution):

```
# trace -U t:syscalls:sys_enter_execve
PID     TID     COMM        FUNC
26853   26853   bash        sys_enter_execve
        [unknown]
        [unknown]

26854   26854   bash        sys_enter_execve
        [unknown]
        [unknown]
[...]
```

This is another opportunity to use perf(1) for cross-checks before digging deeper into BCC/BPF debugging. Reproducing this task using perf(1):

```
# perf record -e syscalls:sys_enter_execve -a -g
^C[ perf record: Woken up 1 times to write data ]
[ perf record: Captured and wrote 3.246 MB perf.data (2 samples) ]

# perf script
bash 26967 [007] 2209173.697359: syscalls:sys_enter_execve: filename: 0x56172df05030,
argv: 0x56172df3b680, envp: 0x56172df2df00
                    e4e37 __GI___execve (/lib/x86_64-linux-gnu/libc-2.27.so)
            56172df05010 [unknown] ([unknown])

bash 26968 [001] 2209174.059399: syscalls:sys_enter_execve: filename: 0x56172df05090,
argv: 0x56172df04440, envp: 0x56172df2df00
                    e4e37 __GI___execve (/lib/x86_64-linux-gnu/libc-2.27.so)
            56172df05070 [unknown] ([unknown])
```

This shows similar broken stacks. There are three problems:

- **Stacks are incomplete.** They are tracing the bash(1) shell calling a new program: I know from prior experience that it is several frames deep, yet only two frames (lines) are shown above. If your stack traces are one or two lines long and don't end with an initial frame (e.g., "main" or "start_thread"), it's reasonable to assume that they may be incomplete as well.

- **The last line is [unknown].** Even perf(1) could not resolve the symbol. There may be a problem with symbols in bash(1), or libc's __GI___execve() may have trampled the frame pointer, breaking further walking.

- **The libc __GI___exceve() call was seen by perf(1) but is not in BCC's output.** This points to another problem with BCC's trace(8) that should be fixed.[6]

18.8.1   How to Fix Broken Stack Traces

Incomplete stack traces are unfortunately common and are usually caused by a confluence of two factors: (1) the observability tool using a frame pointer-based approach for reading the stack trace and (2) the target binary not reserving a register (RBP on x86_64) for the frame pointer, instead reusing it as a general-purpose register, as a compiler performance optimization. The observability tool reads this register expecting it to be a frame pointer, but in fact it now could contain anything: numbers, object address, pointers to strings. The observability tool tries to resolve this number in the symbol table and, if it is lucky, it doesn't find it and can print "[unknown]". If it is unlucky, that random number resolves to an unrelated symbol, and now the printed stack trace has a function name that is wrong, confusing the end user.

The easiest fix is usually to fix the frame pointer register:

- **For C/C++ software and other software compiled with gcc or LLVM**: Recompile the software with `-fno-omit-frame-pointer`.

- **For Java**: Run java(1) with `-XX:+PreserveFramePointer`.

This may come with a performance cost, but it has often been measured at less than 1%; the benefits of being able to use stack trace to find performance wins usually far outweigh this cost. These are also discussed in Chapter 12.

The other approach is to switch to a stack walking technique that is not frame pointer based. perf(1) supports DWARF-based stack walking, ORC, and last branch record (LBR). At the time of writing, DWARF-based and LBR stack walking are not available from BPF, and ORC is not yet available for user-level software. For more on this topic, see Section 2.4 in Chapter 2.

18.9   Missing Symbols (Function Names) When Printing

This is where symbols are not printed correctly in stack traces or via symbol lookup functions: instead of function names, they are shown as hexadecimal numbers or the string "[unknown]". One culprit is broken stacks, explained in the previous section. Another is short-lived processes that exit before the BPF tool can read its address space and look up symbol tables. A third is that the symbol table information is not available. How to fix this differs between JIT runtimes and ELF binaries.

---

6 I would guess that perf(1) may have used debuginfo to get that frame. See a similar investigation in bpftrace #646 [179].

18.9.1   How to Fix Missing Symbols: JIT Runtimes (Java, Node.js, ...)

Missing symbols commonly occur for just-in-time (JIT) compiler runtimes like Java and Node.js. In those cases, the JIT compiler has its own symbol table that is changing at runtime and is not part of the pre-compiled symbol tables in the binary. The common fix is to use supplemental symbol tables generated by the runtime, which are placed in /tmp/perf-<PID>.map files read by both perf(1) and BCC. This approach, some caveats, and future work are discussed in Section 12.3 of Chapter 12.

18.9.2   How to Fix Missing Symbols: ELF binaries (C, C++, ...)

Symbols may be missing from compiled binaries, especially those that are packaged and distributed, as they have been processed using strip(1) to reduce their file size. One fix is to adjust the build process to avoid stripping symbols; another is to use a different source of symbol information, such as debuginfo or BTF. BCC and bpftrace support debuginfo symbols. These approaches, caveats, and future work are discussed in Section 12.2 of Chapter 12.

18.10   Missing Functions When Tracing

This is where a known function cannot be traced with uprobes, uretprobes, kprobes, or kretprobes: it appears to be missing or doesn't fire. The problem may be missing symbols (covered earlier). It may also be due to compiler optimizations, or other reasons:

- **Inlining:** With inlining, the function instructions have been included in the calling function. This can happen for functions with few instructions, to save making call, ret, and function prologue instructions. The function symbol may be gone completely, or it may be present but not fire for that code path.

- **Tail-call optimization:** When the code flow is A()->B()->C(), and C() is called last in B(), then the compiler may have C() return directly to A() as an optimization. This means the uretprobe or kretprobe for the function does not fire.

- **Static and dynamic linking:** This is where a uprobe defines a function to be in a library, but the target software has switched from dynamic to static linking, and the function location has changed: it is now in the binary. The same is possible in reverse, where a uprobe defines a function to be in a binary, but it has since moved to a shared library.

Dealing with this may mean tracing a different event: the parent function, a child function, or a neighboring function. kprobes and uprobes also support instruction offset tracing (bpftrace should support this in the future), so the location of an inlined function can be instrumented if you know its offset.

18.11   Feedback Loops

If you trace yourself tracing, you can create a feedback loop.

Examples of things to avoid:

```
# bpftrace -e 't:syscalls:sys_write_enter { printf(...) }'
remote_host# bpftrace -e 'k:tcp_sendmsg { printf(...) }'
# bpftrace -e 'k:ext4_file_write_iter{ printf(...) }' > /ext4fs/out.file
```

The first two will accidentally trace the bpftrace printf() event by creating another printf() event, which is traced and creates another. The event rate will explode, creating a performance issue until you can kill bpftrace.

The third does the same as bpftrace triggers ext4 writes to save the output, which causes more output to be generated and saved, and so on.

You can avoid this by using filters to exclude tracing your own BPF tool or just trace the target process of interest.

18.12   Dropped Events

Be aware of dropped events rendering the tool output incomplete.

BPF tools can emit output so quickly that it overflows the perf output buffer, or can try to save too many stack IDs and overflow the BPF stack map, etc.

For example:

```
# profile
[...]
WARNING: 5 stack traces could not be displayed.
```

The tools should tell you when events have been dropped, as the output above shows. These drops can often be fixed by tuning. profile(8), for example, has the -stack-storage-size option to increase the size of the stack map, which by default can store 16,384 unique stack traces. If tuning becomes commonplace, the tool defaults should be updated so that users do not need to change them.

Appendix A

bpftrace One-Liners

This is a selection of one-liners used throughout this book.

Chapter 6 CPUs

New processes with arguments:

```
bpftrace -e 'tracepoint:syscalls:sys_enter_execve { join(args->argv); }'
```

Syscall count by process:

```
bpftrace -e 'tracepoint:raw_syscalls:sys_enter { @[pid, comm] = count(); }'
```

Sample running process name at 99 Hertz:

```
bpftrace -e 'profile:hz:99 { @[comm] = count(); }'
```

Sample user-level stacks at 49 Hertz, for PID 189:

```
bpftrace -e 'profile:hz:49 /pid == 189/ { @[ustack] = count(); }'
```

Trace new threads via pthread_create():

```
bpftrace -e 'u:/lib/x86_64-linux-gnu/libpthread-2.27.so:pthread_create {
    printf("%s by %s (%d)\n", probe, comm, pid); }'
```

Chapter 7 Memory

Count process heap expansion (brk()) by code path:

```
bpftrace -e tracepoint:syscalls:sys_enter_brk { @[ustack, comm] = count(); }
```

Count page faults by process:

```
bpftrace -e 'software:page-fault:1 { @[comm, pid] = count(); }'
```

Count user page faults by user-level stack trace:

```
bpftrace -e 'tracepoint:exceptions:page_fault_user { @[ustack, comm] =
    count(); }'
```

Count vmscan operations by tracepoint:

```
bpftrace -e 'tracepoint:vmscan:* { @[probe]++; }'
```

Chapter 8 File Systems

Trace files opened via open(2) with process name:

```
bpftrace -e 't:syscalls:sys_enter_open { printf("%s %s\n", comm,
   str(args->filename)); }'
```

Show the distribution of read() syscall request sizes:

```
bpftrace -e 'tracepoint:syscalls:sys_enter_read { @ = hist(args->count); }'
```

Show the distribution of read() syscall read bytes (and errors):

```
bpftrace -e 'tracepoint:syscalls:sys_exit_read { @ = hist(args->ret); }'
```

Count VFS calls:

```
bpftrace -e 'kprobe:vfs_* { @[probe] = count(); }'
```

Count ext4 tracepoints:

```
bpftrace -e 'tracepoint:ext4:* { @[probe] = count(); }'
```

Chapter 9 Disk I/O

Count block I/O tracepoints:

```
bpftrace -e 'tracepoint:block:* { @[probe] = count(); }'
```

Summarize block I/O size as a histogram:

```
bpftrace -e 't:block:block_rq_issue { @bytes = hist(args->bytes); }'
```

Count block I/O request user stack traces:

```
bpftrace -e 't:block:block_rq_issue { @[ustack] = count(); }'
```

Count block I/O type flags:

```
bpftrace -e 't:block:block_rq_issue { @[args->rwbs] = count(); }'
```

Trace block I/O errors with device and I/O type:

```
bpftrace -e 't:block:block_rq_complete /args->error/ {
   printf("dev %d type %s error %d\n", args->dev, args->rwbs, args->error); }'
```

Count SCSI opcodes:

```
bpftrace -e 't:scsi:scsi_dispatch_cmd_start { @opcode[args->opcode] =
   count(); }'
```

Count SCSI result codes:

```
bpftrace -e 't:scsi:scsi_dispatch_cmd_done { @result[args->result] = count(); }'
```

Count scsi driver funcitons:

```
bpftrace -e 'kprobe:scsi* { @[func] = count(); }'
```

Chapter 10 Networking

Count socket accept(2)s by PID and process name:

```
bpftrace -e 't:syscalls:sys_enter_accept* { @[pid, comm] = count(); }'
```

Count socket connect(2)s by PID and process name:

```
bpftrace -e 't:syscalls:sys_enter_connect { @[pid, comm] = count(); }'
```

Count socket send/receive bytes by on-CPU PID and process name:

```
bpftrace -e 'kr:sock_sendmsg,kr:sock_recvmsg /retval > 0/ {
    @[pid, comm, retval] = sum(retval); }'
```

Count TCP send/receives:

```
bpftrace -e 'k:tcp_sendmsg,k:tcp*recvmsg { @[func] = count(); }'
```

TCP send bytes as a histogram:

```
bpftrace -e 'k:tcp_sendmsg { @send_bytes = hist(arg2); }'
```

TCP receive bytes as a histogram:

```
bpftrace -e 'kr:tcp_recvmsg /retval >= 0/ { @recv_bytes = hist(retval); }'
```

Count TCP retransmits by type and remote host (assumes IPv4):

```
bpftrace -e 't:tcp:tcp_retransmit_* { @[probe, ntop(2, args->saddr)] =
    count(); }'
```

UDP send bytes as a histogram:

```
bpftrace -e 'k:udp_sendmsg { @send_bytes = hist(arg2); }'
```

Count transmit kernel stack traces:

```
bpftrace -e 't:net:net_dev_xmit { @[kstack] = count(); }'
```

Chapter 11 Security

Count security audit events for PID 1234:

```
bpftrace -e 'k:security_* /pid == 1234 { @[func] = count(); }'
```

Trace pluggable authentication module (PAM) session starts:

```
bpftrace -e 'u:/lib/x86_64-linux-gnu/libpam.so.0:pam_start {
    printf("%s: %s\n", str(arg0), str(arg1)); }'
```

Trace kernel module loads:

```
bpftrace -e 't:module:module_load { printf("load: %s\n", str(args->name)); }'
```

Chapter 13 Applications

Sum malloc() requested bytes by user stack trace (high overhead):

```
bpftrace -e 'u:/lib/x86_64-linux-gnu/libc-2.27.so:malloc { @[ustack(5)] =
    sum(arg0); }'
```

Trace kill() signals showing sender process name, target PID, and signal number:

```
bpftrace -e 't:syscalls:sys_enter_kill { printf("%s -> PID %d SIG %d\n",
    comm, args->pid, args->sig); }'
```

Count libpthread mutex lock functions for one second:

```
bpftrace -e 'u:/lib/x86_64-linux-gnu/libpthread.so.0:pthread_mutex_*lock {
    @[probe] = count(); } interval:s:1 { exit(); }'
```

Count libpthread conditional variable functions for one second:

```
bpftrace -e 'u:/lib/x86_64-linux-gnu/libpthread.so.0:pthread_cond_* {
    @[probe] = count(); } interval:s:1 { exit(); }'
```

Chapter 14 Kernel

Count system calls by syscall function:

```
bpftrace -e 'tracepoint:raw_syscalls:sys_enter {
    @[ksym(*(kaddr("sys_call_table") + args->id * 8))] = count(); }'
```

Count kernel function calls starting with "attach":

```
bpftrace -e 'kprobe:attach* { @[probe] = count(); }'
```

Time the kernel function vfs_read() and summarize as a histogram:

```
bpftrace -e 'k:vfs_read { @ts[tid] = nsecs; } kr:vfs_read /@ts[tid]/ {
    @ = hist(nsecs - @ts[tid]); delete(@ts[tid]); }'
```

Frequency count the first integer argument to kernel function "func1":

```
bpftrace -e 'kprobe:func1 { @[arg0] = count(); }'
```

Frequency count the return value from kernel function "func1":

```
bpftrace -e 'kretprobe:func1 { @[retval] = count(); }'
```

Sample kernel-level stacks at 99 Hertz, excluding idle:

```
bpftrace -e 'profile:hz:99 /pid/ { @[kstack] = count(); }'
```

Count context switch stack traces:

```
bpftrace -e 't:sched:sched_switch { @[kstack, ustack, comm] = count(); }'
```

Count work queue requests by kernel function:

```
bpftrace -e 't:workqueue:workqueue_execute_start { @[ksym(args->function)] =
    count() }'
```

Appendix B

bpftrace Cheat Sheet

Synopsis

```
bpftrace -e 'probe /filter/ { action; }'
```

Probes

BEGIN, END	Program start and end
tracepoint:syscalls:sys_enter_execve	execve(2) syscall
tracepoint:syscalls:sys_enter_open	open(2) syscall (also trace openat(2))
tracepoint:syscalls:sys_exit_read	trace read(2) syscall return (one variant)
tracepoint:raw_syscalls:sys_enter	All syscalls
block:block_rq_insert	Queue block I/O request
block:block_rq_issue	Issue block I/O request to storage device
block:block_rq_complete	Block I/O completion
sock:inet_sock_set_state	Socket state change
sched:sched_process_exec	Process execution
sched:sched_switch	Context switch
sched:sched_wakeup	Thread wakeup event
software:faults:1	Page faults
hardware:cache-misses:1000000	Once every 1,000,000 LLC cache miss
kprobe:vfs_read	Trace vfs_read() kernel function entry
kretprobe:vfs_read	Trace return of vfs_read() kernel function
uprobe:/bin/bash:readline	Trace readline() from /bin/bash
uretprobe:/bin/bash:readline	Trace return of readline() from /bin/bash
usdt:path:probe	Trace USDT probe from path
profile:hz:99	Sample on all CPUs at 99 Hertz
interval:s:1	Run on one CPU once per second

Probe Aliases

t	tracepoint	U	usdt	k	kprobe	kr	kretprobe	p	profile
s	software	h	hardware	u	uprobe	ur	uretprobe	i	interval

Vars

comm	On-CPU process name	username	Username string
pid, tid	On-CPU PID, Thread ID	uid	User ID
cpu	CPU ID	kstack	Kernel stack trace
nsecs	Time, nanoseconds	ustack	User stack trace
elapsed	Time since program start, nsecs	probe	Current full probe name
arg0..N	[uk]probe arguments	func	Current function name
args->	Tracepoint args	$1..$N	CLI args, int
retval	[uk]retprobe return value	str($1)...	CLI args, string
cgroup	Current cgroup ID	curtask	Pointer to current task struct

Actions

@map[key1, ...] = count()	Frequency count
@map[key1, ...] = sum(var)	Sum variable
@map[key1, ...] = hist(var)	Power of two histogram
@map[key1, ...] = lhist(var, min, max, step)	Linear histogram
@map[key1, ...] = stats(var)	Statistics: count, average, and total
min(var), max(var), avg(var)	Min, max, average
printf("format", var0..varN)	Print vars; use print() for aggregations
kstack(num), ustack(num)	Print num lines of kernel, user stack
ksym(ip), usym(ip)	Kernel/user symbol string from instruction pointer
kaddr("name"), uaddr("name")	Kernel/user address from symbol name
str(str[, len])	String from address
ntop([af], addr)	IP address to string

Asynchronous Actions

printf("format", var0..varN)	Print vars; use print() for aggregations
system("format", var0..varN)	Run at command line
time("format")	Print formatted time
clear(@map)	Clear a map: delete all keys
print(@map)	Print a map
exit()	Exit

Switches

-e	Trace this probe description
-l	List probes instead of tracing them
-p PID	Enable USDT probes on PID
-c 'command'	Invoke this command
-v, -d	Verbose and debug output

Appendix C

BCC Tool Development

This appendix summarizes BCC tool development using examples and is an extension of Chapter 4. This is optional content for those readers who are interested. Chapter 5 covers how to develop tools in bpftrace, a higher-level language that is expected to be sufficient and preferred in many cases. Also see Chapter 18 for a discussion on minimizing overhead, which is common to both BCC and bpftrace tool development.

Resources

I created three detailed documents for learning BCC tool development and made them available for free as part of the BCC repository where they are online and maintained by other contributors. They are:

- **BCC Python Developer Tutorial:** This contains more than 15 lessons for BCC tool development using the Python interface, where each lesson highlights a number of details to learn [180].

- **BCC Reference Guide:** This is a full reference for the BPF C API, and the BCC Python API. It covers all the capabilities of BCC, and includes short code examples for every capability. It is intended to be searched when needed [181].

- **Contributing BCC/eBPF scripts:** This provides a checklist for tool developers who wish to contribute their tools to the BCC repository. This summarizes years of lessons learned when developing and maintaining tracing tools [63].

In this appendix I provide an additional resource for learning BCC tool development: a crash course of learning by example. This includes four Python programs: hello_world.py as a basic example; sleepsnoop.py for per-event output; bitehist.py to introduce histogram maps, function signatures, and structs; and biolatency.py as an example of a real tool.

Five Tips

Here are five tips you should know before writing BCC tools:

1. BPF C is restricted: no loops or kernel function calls. You can only use the bpf_* kernel helper functions and some compiler built-ins.

2. All memory must be read through bpf_probe_read(), which does necessary checks. If you want to dereference a->b->c->d, then try doing it first, as BCC has a rewriter that may turn it into the necessary bpf_probe_read()s. If it doesn't work, add explicit bpf_probe_reads()s.

   - Memory can only be read to the BPF stack or BPF maps. The stack is limited in size; use BPF maps for storing large objects.

3. There are three ways to output data from kernel to user:

   - **BPF_PERF_OUTPUT():** A way to send per-event details to user space, via a custom struct you define.

   - **BPF_HISTOGRAM() or other BPF maps:** Maps are a key/value hash from which more advanced data structures can be built. They can be used for summary statistics or histograms, and read periodically from user space (efficient).

   - **bpf_trace_printk():** Debugging only, this writes to trace_pipe and can clash with other programs and tracers.

4. Use static instrumentation (tracepoints, USDT) instead of dynamic instrumentation (kprobes, uprobes) wherever possible. Dynamic instrumentation is an unstable API, so your tools will break if the code it is instrumenting changes.

5. Check for BCC developments for new features and capabilities, and bpftrace developments in case it becomes sufficient for your needs.

Tool Examples

The following example tools have been selected to teach you the essentials of BCC programming. They are hello_world.py and sleepsnoop.py as examples of per-event output, and bitehist.py and biolatency.py as examples of histogram output.

Tool 1: hello_world.py

This is a basic example to begin with. First, consider the output:

```
# hello_world.py
ModuleProcessTh-30136 [005] .... 2257559.959119: 0x00000001: Hello, World!
SendControllerT-30135 [002] .... 2257559.971135: 0x00000001: Hello, World!
SendControllerT-30142 [007] .... 2257559.974129: 0x00000001: Hello, World!
ModuleProcessTh-30153 [000] .... 2257559.977401: 0x00000001: Hello, World!
SendControllerT-30135 [003] .... 2257559.996311: 0x00000001: Hello, World!
[...]
```

It prints a line of output for some event, ending with the text "Hello, World!"

Now the source code, hello_world.py:

```
1  #!/usr/bin/python
2  from bcc import BPF
3  b = BPF(text="""
4  int kprobe__do_nanosleep()
5  {
6      bpf_trace_printk("Hello, World!\\n");
7      return 0;
8  }""");
9  b.trace_print()
```

Line 1 sets the interpreter to Python. Some environments prefer using "#!/usr/bin/env python" to use the first python found in the shell environment.

Line 4 imports the BPF library from BCC.

Lines 4 to 8, highlighted in bold, declare the kernel-level BPF program, written in C. This program is included in the parent Python program in quotation marks and passed as the text argument to a new BPF() object, b.

Line 4 uses a shortcut to instrument a kprobe. This shortcut is a function declaration that begins with "kprobe__". The rest of the string is treated as the function name to instrument, in this case, do_nanosleep(). This shortcut is not used by many tools yet, since those tools predate his capability. The tools often use a BPF.attach_kprobe() Python call instead.

Line 6 calls bpf_trace_printk() with the "Hello World!" string, followed by a newline (which is escaped with an extra "\" so that the "\n" is preserved for the final compilation step). bpf_trace_printk() prints a string to the shared trace buffer.

Line 9 calls a Python trace_print() function from the BPF object. This fetches the trace buffer messages from the kernel and prints them out.

To keep this example short, the bpf_trace_printk() interface was used. However, this is for debugging only as it utilizes a buffer that is shared with other tools (which can be read from user space via /sys/kernel/debug/tracing/trace_pipe.) Running this at the same time as other tracing tools may cause their outputs to clash. The recommended interface is demonstrated by the next tool, sleepsnoop.py.

Tool 2: sleepsnoop.py

This tool shows calls to do_nanosleep() with a timestamp and process ID. This is provided as an example of using the perf output buffer. Sample output:

```
# sleepsnoop.py
TIME(s)             PID    CALL
489488.676744000    5008   Hello, World!
489488.676740000    4942   Hello, World!
```

```
489488.676744000    32469   Hello, World!
489488.677674000    5006    Hello, World!
[...]
```

The source code is:

```
1   #!/usr/bin/python
2
3   from bcc import BPF
4
5   # BPF program
6   b = BPF(text="""
7   struct data_t {
8       u64 ts;
9       u32 pid;
10  };
11
12  BPF_PERF_OUTPUT(events);
13
14  int kprobe__do_nanosleep(void *ctx) {
15      struct data_t data = {};
16      data.pid = bpf_get_current_pid_tgid();
17      data.ts = bpf_ktime_get_ns() / 1000;
18      events.perf_submit(ctx, &data, sizeof(data));
19      return 0;
20  };
21  """)
22
23  # header
24  print("%-18s %-6s %s" % ("TIME(s)", "PID", "CALL"))
25
26  # process event
27  def print_event(cpu, data, size):
28      event = b["events"].event(data)
29      print("%-18.9f %-6d Hello, World!" % ((float(event.ts) / 1000000),
30          event.pid))
31
32  # loop with callback to print_event
33  b["events"].open_perf_buffer(print_event)
34  while 1:
35      try:
36          b.perf_buffer_poll()
37      except KeyboardInterrupt:
38          exit()
```

Lines 7 to 10 define the output struct, data_t. It contains two members, a u64 (unsigned 64-bit int) for a timestamp, and a u32 for a pid.

Line 12 declares the perf event output buffer, named "events".

Line 14 instruments do_nanosleep(), as did the earlier hello_world.py example.

Line 15 declares a data_t struct named data and initializes it to zero, which is required (the BPF verifier will reject access to uninitialized memory).

Lines 16 and 17 populate members of data using BPF helper functions.

Line 18 submits the data struct via the events perf buffer.

Line 27 to 30 declare a callback named print_event() that handles an event from the perf buffer. It reads the event data on line 28 as the object named event and accesses its members on lines 29 and 30. (Older versions of BCC required more manual steps to declare in Python the layout of the data struct; that is now automatic).

Line 33 registers the perf_event() callback with the perf event buffer named events.

Lines 34 to 38 poll open perf buffers. If there are events, their callbacks are executed. On a Ctrl-C, the program will exit.

If the events are frequent, the user-space Python program may wake up often to process them. As an optimization, some tools introduce a small sleep in the final `while` loop to allow several events to be buffered, reducing the number of times Python runs on CPU, and lowering overall overhead.

If events are frequent, you should consider whether summarizing them in kernel context can better answer your questions, as it should cost lower overhead. The next tool is an example of this, bitehist.py.

Tool 3: bitehist.py

This tool prints the size of disk I/O as a power-of-two histogram; a similar version is in the BCC examples/tracing directory. I'll begin with the output of this tool to show what it does before looking at the source code:

```
# bitehist.py
Tracing block I/O... Hit Ctrl-C to end.
^C
     kbytes              : count     distribution
        0 -> 1           : 3        |**                                        |
        2 -> 3           : 0        |                                          |
        4 -> 7           : 55       |******************************************|
        8 -> 15          : 26       |******************                        |
       16 -> 31          : 9        |******                                    |
       32 -> 63          : 4        |**                                        |
```

```
 64 -> 127        : 0          |                                              |
128 -> 255        : 1          |                                              |
256 -> 511        : 0          |                                              |
512 -> 1023       : 1          |                                              |
```

The full BCC program, with enumerated lines:

```python
 1  #!/usr/bin/python
 2  #[...]
 3  from __future__ import print_function
 4  from bcc import BPF
 5  from time import sleep
 6
 7  # load BPF program
 8  b = BPF(text="""
 9  #include <uapi/linux/ptrace.h>
10
11  BPF_HISTOGRAM(dist);
12
13  int kprobe__blk_account_io_completion(struct pt_regs *ctx,
14      void *req, unsigned int bytes)
15  {
16      dist.increment(bpf_log2l(bytes / 1024));
17      return 0;
18  }
19  """)
20
21  # header
22  print("Tracing block I/O... Hit Ctrl-C to end.")
23
24  # trace until Ctrl-C
25  try:
26      sleep(99999999)
27  except KeyboardInterrupt:
28      print()
29
30  # output
31  b["dist"].print_log2_hist("kbytes")
```

Lines 1–8 include details covered in the previous hello_world.py example.

Line 9 includes header information used by the BPF program (for struct pt_regs).

Line 11 declares a BPF map histogram, named "dist", used for storage and output.

Lines 13 and 14 declare the function signature for blk_account_io_completion(). The first argument, "struct pt_regs *ctx," refers to register state from the instrumentation, and is not from the target function. The remaining arguments are from the function, which is from the kernel in block/blk-core.c:

```
void blk_account_io_completion(struct request *req, unsigned int bytes)
```

I am interested in the bytes argument, but I must also declare the "struct request *req" argument so that the positions match, even though I am not using struct request *req in the BPF program. However, struct request is not known by default by BPF, so including it in the function signature would cause the BPF tool to fail to compile. There are two workarounds: (1) #include <linux/blkdev.h>, so that struct request is known, or (2) replace "struct request *req" with "void *req," since void is already known, and that I have lost the real type information is unimportant since the program does not dereference it. In this example I used workaround 2.

Line 16 takes the bytes argument and divides it by 1024, then passes this Kbyte value to bpf_log2l(), a function that generates a power-of-two index from the value. This index value is then saved in the dist histogram via dist.increment(): which increments the value at that index by one. To explain with an example:

1. Imagine the for the first event the bytes variable was 4096

2. 4096 / 1024 = 4

3. bpf_log2l(4) = 3

4. dist.increment(3) adds 1 to index 3, so the dist histogram now contains:

    index 1: value 0 (refers to 0 → 1 Kbytes)

    index 2: value 0 (refers to 2 → 3 Kbytes)

    index 3: value 1 (refers to 4 → 7 Kbytes)

    index 4: value 0 (refers to 8 → 15 Kbytes)

    ...

These indexes and values will be read by user space and printed as a histogram.

Line 22 prints a header. When using this tool, it can be useful to see when the header is printed: it tells you that the BCC compilation stages and attaching event instrumentation has completed, and is about to start tracing. The contents of this introductory message follow a convention that explains what the tool is doing and when it will finish:

- **Tracing:** This tells the user that the tool is doing per-event tracing. If it were sampling (profiling), it would say that instead.

- **block I/O:** This tells the user what events are instrumented.

- **Hit Ctrl-C to end.:** This tells the user when the program will end. Tools that generate interval output may include this as well—for example, "Output every 1 second, Ctrl-C to end."

Lines 25 to 28 cause the program to wait until Ctrl-C is pressed. When it is, a newline is printed to prepare the screen for output.

Line 31 prints the dist histogram as a power-of-2 histogram, with a label for the range column of "kbytes". This involves fetching the values for the indexes from the kernel. How does this Python BPF.print_log2_hist() call understand what ranges each index refers to? These ranges are not passed from the kernel to user space, only the values are. The ranges are known because the user-space and kernel log2 algorithms match.

There is another way to write the BPF code, which serves as an example of struct dereferencing:

```
#include <uapi/linux/ptrace.h>
#include <linux/blkdev.h>

BPF_HISTOGRAM(dist);

int kprobe__blk_account_io_completion(struct pt_regs *ctx, struct request *req)
{
        dist.increment(bpf_log2l(req->__data_len / 1024));
        return 0;
}
```

Now, the bytes value is fetched from struct request and its __data_len member. Since I'm now processing struct request, I have needed to include the linux/blkdev.h header that has its definition. Since I'm not using the second bytes argument to this function, I have not declared it in the function signature: trailing unused arguments can be elided, which still preserves the position of earlier arguments.

What's really happening is that the arguments (after struct pt_regs *ctx) defined in the BPF program are mapped to the function calling convention registers. On x86_64, this is %rdi, %rsi, %rdx, etc. If you write the wrong function signature, the BPF tool will compile successfully and apply that signature to the registers, leading to invalid data.

Shouldn't the kernel know what these function arguments are? Why am I redeclaring them in the BPF program? The answer is that the kernel does know, if kernel debuginfo is installed on your system. But that's rarely the case in practice, since the debuginfo files can be large.

Lightweight metadata has been in development that should solve this problem: BPF Type Format, which can be included in the kernel vmlinux binary, and one day may be available for user-level binaries as well. This should hopefully remove the need to include header files and redeclare function signatures. See Section 2.3.9 in Chapter 2.

Tool 4: biolatency

The following are all the lines from my original biolatency.py tool, enumerated and commented:

```
 1 #!/usr/bin/python
 2 # @lint-avoid-python-3-compatibility-imports
```

Line 1: We're Python.

Line 2 suppresses a lint warning (these were added for Facebook's build environment).

```
 3 #
 4 # biolatency    Summarize block device I/O latency as a histogram.
 5 #               For Linux, uses BCC, eBPF.
 6 #
 7 # USAGE: biolatency [-h] [-T] [-Q] [-m] [-D] [interval] [count]
 8 #
 9 # Copyright (c) 2015 Brendan Gregg.
10 # Licensed under the Apache License, Version 2.0 (the "License")
11 #
12 # 20-Sep-2015   Brendan Gregg   Created this.
```

I have a certain style to my header comments. Line 4 names the tool and has a single-sentence description. Line 5 adds any caveats: for Linux only, uses BCC/eBPF.[1] It then has a synopsis line, a copyright, and a history of major changes.

```
13
14 from __future__ import print_function
15 from bcc import BPF
16 from time import sleep, strftime
17 import argparse
```

Note that I import BPF, which I'll use to interact with BPF in the kernel.

```
18
19 # arguments
20 examples = """examples:
21     ./biolatency           # summarize block I/O latency as a histogram
22     ./biolatency 1 10      # print 1 second summaries, 10 times
23     ./biolatency -mT 1     # 1s summaries, milliseconds, and timestamps
24     ./biolatency -Q        # include OS queued time in I/O time
25     ./biolatency -D        # show each disk device separately
```

---

1 The "eBPF" dates back to when we were still calling it that. Today, we just call it BPF.

```
26 """
27 parser = argparse.ArgumentParser(
28     description="Summarize block device I/O latency as a histogram",
29     formatter_class=argparse.RawDescriptionHelpFormatter,
30     epilog=examples)
31 parser.add_argument("-T", "--timestamp", action="store_true",
32     help="include timestamp on output")
33 parser.add_argument("-Q", "--queued", action="store_true",
34     help="include OS queued time in I/O time")
35 parser.add_argument("-m", "--milliseconds", action="store_true",
36     help="millisecond histogram")
37 parser.add_argument("-D", "--disks", action="store_true",
38     help="print a histogram per disk device")
39 parser.add_argument("interval", nargs="?", default=99999999,
40     help="output interval, in seconds")
41 parser.add_argument("count", nargs="?", default=99999999,
42     help="number of outputs")
43 args = parser.parse_args()
44 countdown = int(args.count)
45 debug = 0
46
```

Lines 19 to 44 are argument processing. I'm using Python's argparse here.

My intent is to make this a Unix-like tool, something similar to vmstat(8) or iostat(1), to make it easy for others to recognize and learn—hence the style of options and arguments and also to do one thing and do it well (in this case, showing disk I/O latency as a histogram). I could have added a mode to dump per-event details but made that a separate tool, biosnoop.py.

You may be writing BCC/eBPF for other reasons, including agents to other monitoring software, and don't need to worry about the user interface.

```
47 # define BPF program
48 bpf_text = """
49 #include <uapi/linux/ptrace.h>>
50 #include <linux/blkdev.h>
51
52 typedef struct disk_key {
53     char disk[DISK_NAME_LEN];
54     u64 slot;
55 } disk_key_t;
56 BPF_HASH(start, struct request *);
57 STORAGE
58
```

```
59 // time block I/O
60 int trace_req_start(struct pt_regs *ctx, struct request *req)
61 {
62     u64 ts = bpf_ktime_get_ns();
63     start.update(&req, &ts);
64     return 0;
65 }
66
67 // output
68 int trace_req_completion(struct pt_regs *ctx, struct request *req)
69 {
70     u64 *tsp, delta;
71
72     // fetch timestamp and calculate delta
73     tsp = start.lookup(&req);
74     if (tsp == 0) {
75         return 0;    // missed issue
76     }
77     delta = bpf_ktime_get_ns() - *tsp;
78     FACTOR
79
80     // store as histogram
81     STORE
82
83     start.delete(&req);
84     return 0;
85 }
86 """
```

The BPF program is declared as an inline C assigned to the variable bpf_text.

Line 56 declares a hash array called "start", which uses a struct request pointer as the key. The trace_req_start() function fetches a timestamp using bpf_ktime_get_ns() and then stores it in this hash, keyed by *req. (I'm just using that pointer address as a UUID.) The trace_req_completion() function then does a lookup on the hash with its *req, to fetch the start time of the request, which is then used to calculate the delta time on line 77. Line 83 deletes the timestamp from the hash.

The prototypes to these functions begin with a struct pt_regs * for registers, and then as many of the probed function arguments as you want to include. I've included the first function argument in each, struct request *.

This program also declares storage for the output data and stores it, but there's a problem: biolatency has a -D option to emit per-disk histograms, instead of one histogram for everything, and this changes the storage code. So this BPF program contains the text STORAGE and

STORE (and FACTOR) which are merely strings that I'll search and replace with code next, depending on the options. I'd rather avoid code-that-writes-code if possible, since it makes it harder to debug.

```
87
88 # code substitutions
89 if args.milliseconds:
90     bpf_text = bpf_text.replace('FACTOR', 'delta /= 1000000;')
91     label = "msecs"
92 else:
93     bpf_text = bpf_text.replace('FACTOR', 'delta /= 1000;')
94     label = "usecs"
95 if args.disks:
96     bpf_text = bpf_text.replace('STORAGE',
97         'BPF_HISTOGRAM(dist, disk_key_t);')
98     bpf_text = bpf_text.replace('STORE',
99         'disk_key_t key = {.slot = bpf_log2l(delta)}; ' +
100        'bpf_probe_read(&key.disk, sizeof(key.disk), ' +
101        'req->rq_disk->disk_name); dist.increment(key);')
102 else:
103     bpf_text = bpf_text.replace('STORAGE', 'BPF_HISTOGRAM(dist);')
104     bpf_text = bpf_text.replace('STORE',
105        'dist.increment(bpf_log2l(delta));')
```

The FACTOR code just changes the units of the time I'm recording, depending on the –m option.

Line 95 checks if per-disk has been requested (–D), and if so, replaces the STORAGE and STORE strings with code to do per-disk histograms. It uses the disk_key struct declared on line 52, which is the disk name and the slot (bucket) in the power-of-two histogram. Line 99 takes the delta time and turns it into the power-of-two slot index using the bpf_log2l() helper function. Lines 100 and 101 fetch the disk name via bpf_probe_read(), which is how all data is copied onto BPF's stack for operation. Line 101 includes many dereferences: req->rq_disk, rq_disk->disk_name: BCC's rewriter has transparently turned these into bpf_probe_read()s as well.

Lines 103 to 105 deal with the single histogram case (not per disk). A histogram is declared named "dist" using the BPF_HISTOGRAM macro. The slot (bucket) is found using the bpf_log2l() helper function and then incremented in the histogram.

This example is a little gritty, which is both good (realistic) and bad (intimidating). See the tutorial I linked to earlier for more simple examples.

```
106 if debug:
107     print(bpf_text)
```

Since I have code that writes code, I need a way to debug the final output. If debug is set, print it out.

```
108
109 # load BPF program
110 b = BPF(text=bpf_text)
111 if args.queued:
112     b.attach_kprobe(event="blk_account_io_start", fn_name="trace_req_start")
113 else:
114     b.attach_kprobe(event="blk_start_request", fn_name="trace_req_start")
115     b.attach_kprobe(event="blk_mq_start_request", fn_name="trace_req_start")
116 b.attach_kprobe(event="blk_account_io_completion",
117     fn_name="trace_req_completion")
118
```

Line 110 loads the BPF program.

Since this program was written before BPF had tracepoint support, I wrote it to use kprobes (kernel dynamic tracing). It should be rewritten to use tracepoints, as they are a stable API, although that then also requires a later kernel version (Linux 4.7+).

biolatency.py has a -Q option to include time queued in the kernel. You can see how it's implemented in this code. If it is set, line 112 attaches the BPF trace_req_start() function with a kprobe on the blk_account_io_start() kernel function, which tracks the request when it's first queued in the kernel. If not set, lines 114 and 115 attach the BPF function to different kernel functions, which is when the disk I/O is issued (it can be either of these). This only works because the first argument to any of these kernels functions is the same: struct request *. If their arguments were different, I'd need separate BPF functions for each to handle that.

```
119 print("Tracing block device I/O... Hit Ctrl-C to end.")
120
121 # output
122 exiting = 0 if args.interval else 1
123 dist = b.get_table("dist")
```

Line 123 fetches the "dist" histogram that was declared and populated by the STORAGE/STORE code.

```
124 while (1):
125     try:
126         sleep(int(args.interval))
127     except KeyboardInterrupt:
128         exiting = 1
129
130     print()
```

```
131    if args.timestamp:
132        print("%-8s\n" % strftime("%H:%M:%S"), end="")
133
134    dist.print_log2_hist(label, "disk")
135    dist.clear()
136
137    countdown -= 1
138    if exiting or countdown == 0:
139        exit()
```

This has logic for printing every interval a certain number of times (countdown). Lines 131 and 132 print a timestamp if the -T option was used.

Line 134 prints the histogram, or per-disk histograms. The first argument is the label variable, which contains "usecs" or "msecs" and decorates the column of values in the output. The second argument labels the secondary key if dist has per-disk histograms. How print_log2_hist() can identify whether this is a single histogram or has a secondary key, I'll leave as an adventurous exercise in code spelunking of BCC and BPF internals.

Line 135 clears the histogram, ready for the next interval.

Here is some sample output, using -D for per-disk histograms:

```
# biolatency -D
Tracing block device I/O... Hit Ctrl-C to end.
^C
disk = 'xvdb'
    usecs              : count    distribution
        0 -> 1         : 0        |                                        |
        2 -> 3         : 0        |                                        |
        4 -> 7         : 0        |                                        |
        8 -> 15        : 0        |                                        |
       16 -> 31        : 0        |                                        |
       32 -> 63        : 0        |                                        |
       64 -> 127       : 18       |****                                    |
      128 -> 255       : 167      |****************************************|
      256 -> 511       : 90       |*********************                   |

disk = 'xvdc'
    usecs              : count    distribution
        0 -> 1         : 0        |                                        |
        2 -> 3         : 0        |                                        |
        4 -> 7         : 0        |                                        |
        8 -> 15        : 0        |                                        |
       16 -> 31        : 0        |                                        |
```

```
    32 -> 63        : 0       |                                          |
    64 -> 127       : 22      |****                                      |
   128 -> 255       : 179     |*****************************************|
   256 -> 511       : 88      |******************                        |
[...]
```

More Info

Refer to the section "Resources," at the beginning of this appendix, for more about BCC tool development, and see Chapter 4 for BCC in general.

Appendix D

C BPF

This appendix shows examples of BPF tools implemented in C, either as compiled C programs or executed via the perf(1) utility. This appendix is optional material for those readers who are interested in developing a deeper understanding of how BPF works, as well as other BPF interfaces that are supported by the Linux kernel.

Chapter 5 covers how to develop tools in bpftrace, a higher-level language that is expected to be sufficient and preferred in many cases, and Appendix C covers the BCC interface as another preferred option. This appendix is a follow-on from the BPF sections in Chapter 2.

This appendix begins with a discussion on C programming and five tips before you begin. The first program included is hello_world.c, for demonstrating BPF instruction-level programming, followed by two C tools, bigreads and bitehist, to demonstrate per-event output and histograms, respectively. The final tool included is a perf(1) version of bigreads, as an example of using C programming via perf(1).

Why Program in C?

Back in 2014, C was all we had. Then came the BCC project, which provided an improved C language[1] for the kernel BPF programs, and other languages for the front end. And now we have the bpftrace project, where the entire program is a high-level language.

Reasons for continuing to write tracing tools entirely in C include the following, along with counterpoints:

- **Lower startup overhead:** On my system, bpftrace costs around 40 ms of CPU time to start up, and BCC costs around 160 ms. These costs can be eliminated with a stand-alone C binary. But they can also be reduced by compiling a BPF kernel object file once and re-sending it to the kernel when needed: Cilium and Cloudflare have orchestration systems that do this with BPF object file templating, where certain data in the program (IP address, etc.) can be rewritten as needed. For your environment, consider how much this matters: how frequently will you be starting BPF programs? If frequently, then

---

1 BCC includes Clang-based memory dereference rewriters: so that a->b->c automatically expands into the necessary bpf_probe_read() calls. In C programs, you need to make these calls explicitly.

should they be left running ("pinned")? I also suspect that we can tune BCC down to bpftrace's startup cost,[2] plus the following point may reduce startup time further.

- **No bulky compiler dependencies:** BCC and bpftrace currently use LLVM and Clang to compile their programs, which can add over 80 Mbytes to the file system. On some environments, including embedded systems, this can be prohibitive. A C binary containing pre-compiled BPF does not need these dependencies. Another issue with LLVM and Clang is that there are frequent new versions with API changes (during bpftrace development, we've worked through LLVM versions 5.0, 6.0, 7, and 8), creating a maintenance burden. However, there are a number of projects in various stages of progress to change compilation. Some are to build a lightweight and sufficient BPF compiler as a replacement for LLVM and Clang, at the cost of losing LLVM optimizations. The SystemTap tracer with its BPF back end and the ply(1) tracer [5] already do this. Others are for pre-compiling BPF programs from BCC/bpftrace and just sending the BPF binary to the target system. These projects should also improve startup overhead.

- **Lower runtime overhead:** At first glance, this doesn't make sense, as any front end will ultimately run the same BPF bytecode in the kernel and pay the same kprobe and uprobe costs, etc. There are also many BCC and bpftrace tools that use in-kernel summaries, and while running, there is no user CPU time from those front ends. Rewriting them in C will accomplish nothing. A case where the front end can matter is if many events are frequently printed, such that the user-space front end is needing to read and process thousands of events per second (so much so that you can see the front end's CPU consumption in tools such as top(1)). In that case, a C rewrite may yield more efficiency. More efficiency can also be found by tuning BCC's ring-buffer polling code,[3] after which, the difference between C and Python may be negligible. An optimization not yet employed by BCC or bpftrace would be to create consumer threads bound to each CPU that read the per-CPU ring buffer for the CPU they are bound to.

- **BPF hacking:** If you have a use case that's outside the capabilities of BCC and bpftrace, writing in C will allow you to code anything that the BPF verifier accepts. Note that BCC already accepts arbitrary C code, so it's hard to imagine a case where this will be necessary.

- **For use with perf(1):** perf(1) supports BPF programs to enhance the capabilities of its `record` and `trace` subcommands. perf(1) has a number of uses beyond the other BPF tools: for example, if you needed a tool to record many events efficiently in a binary output file, perf(1) has already optimized this use case. See the section "perf C," later in this appendix.

Note that many BPF networking projects use C, including Cilium [182]. For tracing, it is expected that bpftrace and BCC will almost always be sufficient.

---

2 See https://github.com/iovisor/bcc/issues/2367.

3 See https://github.com/iovisor/bcc/issues/1033.

Five Tips

Here are tips you should know before writing C tools:

1. BPF C is restricted: no unbounded loops or kernel function calls are possible. You can only use the bpf_* kernel helper functions, BPF tail calls, BPF to BPF function calls, and some compiler built-ins.

2. All memory must be read through bpf_probe_read(), which does necessary checks. The destination is usually stack memory, but for large objects, you can use BPF map storage.

3. There are three ways to output data from kernel to user:

   - **bpf_perf_event_output() (BPF_FUNC_perf_event_output):** This is the preferred way to send per-event details to user space, via a custom struct you define.

   - **BPF_MAP_TYPE.* and map helpers (e.g., bpf_map_update_elem()):** A map is a key-value hash from which more advanced data structures can be built. Maps can be used for summary statistics or histograms, and read periodically from user space (efficient).

   - **bpf_trace_printk():** For debugging only, this writes to trace_pipe and can clash with other programs and tracers.

4. Use static instrumentation (tracepoints, USDT) instead of dynamic instrumentation (kprobes, uprobes) wherever possible, as static instrumentation provides a more stable interface.

5. If you get stuck, rewriting the tool in BCC or bpftrace and then examining its debug or verbose output may reveal steps that you missed. For example, BCC's DEBUG_PREPROCESSOR mode shows the C code after the preprocessor.

Some tools use the following macro wrapper to bpf_probe_read():

```
#define _(P) ({typeof(P) val; bpf_probe_read(&val, sizeof(val), &P); val;})
```

So "_(skb->dev)" will expand to the appropriate bpf_probe_read() for that member.

C Programs

When a new BPF feature is developed, a sample C program and/or a kernel self-test suite test case is often provided in the same patch set to demonstrate its use. The C programs are stored in the Linux source under samples/bpf, and the self-tests are under tools/testing/selftests/bpf.[4] These Linux samples and self-tests demonstrate two ways to specify BPF programs in C [Zannoni 16]:

---

4 These were written by many from the BPF kernel community. Developers with more than twenty commits to these locations include: Alexei Starovoitov, Daniel Borkmann, Yonghong Song, Stanislav Fomichev, Martin KaFai Lau, John Fastabend, Jesper Dangaard Brouer, Jakub Kicinski, and Andrey Ignatov. There is more development work happening on self-tests, and to keep everything in BPF working as it grows, new developers are encouraged to add to self-tests instead of samples.

- **BPF instructions:** As an array of BPF instructions embedded in a C program, passed to the bpf(2) syscall.

- **C program:** As a C program that can be compiled to BPF, which is later passed to the bpf(2) syscall. This method is preferred.

Compilers typically support cross-compiling, where different architectural targets can be specified. The LLVM compiler has a BPF target[5] so that C programs can be compiled to BPF in ELF files, just like they can to x86/ELF. The BPF instructions can be stored in an ELF section named after the BPF program type ("socket", "kprobe/...", etc.). Some object loaders will parse this type for use with the bpf(2) syscall;[6] for other loaders (including the ones in this appendix) the type is used as a label.

Note that other techniques to build BPF programs are also possible: for example, specifying the BPF program in LLVM intermediate representation format, which LLVM can compile to BPF bytecode.

The following sections cover API changes, compilation, and example tools for each type described earlier: an instruction-level example, hello_world.c; and C programming examples, bigread_kern.c and bitehist_kern.c.

WARNING: API Changes

Between December 2018 and August 2019, this appendix has been rewritten twice to match changes in the BPF C library APIs. In case of further changes, it is recommended to follow updates to the libraries as they occur. The libraries are libbpf in the Linux source (tools/lib/bpf) and libbcc from iovisor BCC [183].

The older API from the Linux 4.x series was a simple library of common functions defined in bpf_load.c and bpf_load.h in samples/bpf. It has been deprecated in favor of libbpf in the kernel, and at some point this older bpf_load API may be removed. Most of the networking samples have already been converted to use libbpf instead, which is developed in sync with the kernel features and is used by external projects (BCC, bpftrace). We recommend that you use libbpf and libbcc instead of either the bpf_load library or creating your own custom library, as they will lag features and fixes that are in libbpf and libbcc and hinder BPF adoption.

The tracing tools in this appendix use libbpf and libbcc. Thanks to Andrii Nakryiko for rewriting these to use the latest API, which should be present in Linux 5.4, and for his work on libbpf. Earlier versions of these tools were written for Linux 4.15 and can be found in the tool repository for this book (the URL can be found on http://www.brendangregg.com/bpf-performance-tools-book.html).

Compilation

Starting with an Ubuntu 18.04 (Bionic) server, here are example steps for fetching, compiling, and installing a newer kernel, and compiling the bpf samples. (WARNING: Try this on a test

---

5 A BPF target has been developed for gcc as well, although it has not yet been merged.

6 Including samples/bpf/bpf_load.*, although that library is deprecated.

system first, as mistakes such as missing necessary CONFIG options for virtualized environments may cause the system to fail to boot):

```
# apt-get update
# apt-get install bc libssl-dev llvm-9 clang libelf-dev
# ln -s llc-9 /usr/bin/llc
# cd /usr/src
# wget https://git.kernel.org/torvalds/t/linux-5.4.tar.gz
# cd linux-5.4
# make olddefconfig
# make $(getconf _NPROCESSORS_ONLN)
# make modules_install && make install && make headers_install
# reboot
[...]
# make samples/bpf/
```

llvm-9 or a newer LLVM version is required for BTF support. These steps are provided as an example: as your OS distribution, the kernel, LLVM, Clang, and the BPF samples are updated, these steps will need to be adjusted to match.

At times there have been problems with the packaged LLVM, and it has been necessary to build the latest LLVM and Clang from source. Some example steps:

```
# apt-get install -y cmake gcc g++
# git clone --depth 1 http://llvm.org/git/llvm.git
# cd llvm/tools
# git clone --depth 1 http://llvm.org/git/clang.git
# cd ..; mkdir build; cd build
# cmake -DLLVM_TARGETS_TO_BUILD="X86;BPF" -DLLVM_BUILD_LLVM_DYLIB=ON \
    -DLLVM_ENABLE_RTTI=ON -DCMAKE_BUILD_TYPE=Release ..
# make -j $(getconf _NPROCESSORS_ONLN)
# make install
```

Note how the build targets were restricted to X86 and BPF only in these steps.

Tool 1: Hello, World!

As an example of instruction programming, I have rewritten the hello_world.py program from Appendix C as a C program, hello_world.c. It can be compiled from samples/bpf/ as described earlier, after adding it to thesamples/bpf/Makefile. Some sample output:

```
# ./hello_world
        svscan-1991  [007] .... 2582253.708941: 0: Hello, World!
          cron-983   [008] .... 2582254.363956: 0: Hello, World!
        svscan-1991  [007] .... 2582258.709153: 0: Hello, World!
[...]
```

This shows the "Hello, World!" text, along with other default fields from the trace buffer (process name and ID, CPU ID, flags, and timestamp).

The hello_world.c file is:

```
 1  #include <stdio.h>
 2  #include <stdlib.h>
 3  #include <string.h>
 4  #include <errno.h>
 5  #include <unistd.h>
 6  #include <linux/version.h>
 7  #include <bpf/bpf.h>
 8  #include <bcc/libbpf.h>
 9
10  #define DEBUGFS "/sys/kernel/debug/tracing/"
11
12  char bpf_log_buf[BPF_LOG_BUF_SIZE];
13
14  int main(int argc, char *argv[])
15  {
16      int prog_fd, probe_fd;
17
18      struct bpf_insn prog[] = {
19              BPF_MOV64_IMM(BPF_REG_1, 0xa21), /* '!\n' */
20              BPF_STX_MEM(BPF_H, BPF_REG_10, BPF_REG_1, -4),
21              BPF_MOV64_IMM(BPF_REG_1, 0x646c726f), /* 'orld' */
22              BPF_STX_MEM(BPF_W, BPF_REG_10, BPF_REG_1, -8),
23              BPF_MOV64_IMM(BPF_REG_1, 0x57202c6f), /* 'o, W' */
24              BPF_STX_MEM(BPF_W, BPF_REG_10, BPF_REG_1, -12),
25              BPF_MOV64_IMM(BPF_REG_1, 0x6c6c6548), /* 'Hell' */
26              BPF_STX_MEM(BPF_W, BPF_REG_10, BPF_REG_1, -16),
27              BPF_MOV64_IMM(BPF_REG_1, 0),
28              BPF_STX_MEM(BPF_B, BPF_REG_10, BPF_REG_1, -2),
29              BPF_MOV64_REG(BPF_REG_1, BPF_REG_10),
30              BPF_ALU64_IMM(BPF_ADD, BPF_REG_1, -16),
31              BPF_MOV64_IMM(BPF_REG_2, 15),
32              BPF_RAW_INSN(BPF_JMP | BPF_CALL, 0, 0, 0,
33                              BPF_FUNC_trace_printk),
34              BPF_MOV64_IMM(BPF_REG_0, 0),
35              BPF_EXIT_INSN(),
36      };
37      size_t insns_cnt = sizeof(prog) / sizeof(struct bpf_insn);
38
```

```
39        prog_fd = bpf_load_program(BPF_PROG_TYPE_KPROBE, prog, insns_cnt,
40                             "GPL", LINUX_VERSION_CODE,
41                             bpf_log_buf, BPF_LOG_BUF_SIZE);
42        if (prog_fd < 0) {
43                printf("ERROR: failed to load prog '%s'\n", strerror(errno));
44                return 1;
45        }
46
47        probe_fd = bpf_attach_kprobe(prog_fd, BPF_PROBE_ENTRY, "hello_world",
48                             "do_nanosleep", 0, 0);
49        if (probe_fd < 0)
50                return 2;
51
52        system("cat " DEBUGFS "/trace_pipe");
53
54        close(probe_fd);
55        bpf_detach_kprobe("hello_world");
56        close(prog_fd);
57        return 0;
58  }
```

This example is about the "Hello, World!" BPF instruction program on lines 19 to 35. The remainder of this program uses the older file-descriptor based API and trace pipe output as shortcuts to keep this example small. The newer API and output methods are shown in the later bigreads and bitehist examples in this appendix, and as you will see, they make the program much longer.

The BPF program is declared as the prog array using BPF instruction helper macros. See Appendix E for a summary of these BPF macros and BPF instructions. This program also uses functions from libbpf and libbcc to load the program and attach it to a kprobe.

Lines 19 to 26 store "Hello, World!\n" on the BPF stack. For efficiency, instead of storing this character string one character at a time, groups of four characters are declared and stored as a 32-bit integer (type BPF_W for word). The final two bytes are stored as a 16-bit integer (type BPF_H for half-word).

Lines 27 to 33 prepare and call BPF_FUNC_trace_printk, which writes the string to the shared trace buffer.

Lines 39 to 41 call the bpf_load_program() function from libbpf (the library in the Linux source under tools/lib/bpf). It loads the BPF program and sets the type to kprobe, and returns a file descriptor for the program.

Lines 47 to 48 call the bpf_attach_kprobe() function from libbcc (the library from the iovisor BCC repository; it is defined in BCC's src/cc/libbpf.h), which attaches the program to a kprobe for the entry of the do_nanosleep() kernel function. The event name "hello_world" is used, which can be helpful for debugging (it appears in /sys/kernel/debug/tracing/kprobe_events). bpf_attach_kprobe() returns a file descriptor for the probe. This library function will also print an error message on failure, so I do not print an additional error message for the test on line 49.

Line 52 uses system() to call cat(1) on the shared trace pipe, printing out messages.[7]

Lines 54 to 56 close the probe file descriptor, detach the kprobe, and close the program file descriptor. If you miss these calls, earlier Linux kernels can be left with probes configured and enabled, costing overhead but with no user-level consumer. This can be checked using cat /sys/kernel/debug/tracing/kprobe_events or bpftool(8) prog show, and can be cleaned up using BCC's reset-trace(8) (which cancels all tracers). By Linux 5.2, the kernel has switched to file descriptor–based probes, which are automatically closed on process exit.

BPF_FUNC_trace_printk and system() were used to make this example as short as possible. They operate using the shared trace buffer (/sys/kernel/debug/tracing/trace_pipe), which can clash with other tracing or debugging programs, for which the kernel offers no protection. The recommended interface is via BPF_FUNC_perf_event_output: this is explained in the section "Tool 2: bigreads," later in this appendix.

To compile this program, hello_world was added to the Makefile. The following diff shows the extra three lines for Linux 5.3, highlighted in bold:

```
# diff -u Makefile.orig Makefile
--- ../orig/Makefile 2019-08-03 19:50:23.671498701 +0000
+++ Makefile 2019-08-03 21:23:04.440589362 +0000
@@ -10,6 +10,7 @@
 hostprogs-y += sockex1
 hostprogs-y += sockex2
 hostprogs-y += sockex3
+hostprogs-y += hello_world
 hostprogs-y += tracex1
 hostprogs-y += tracex2
 hostprogs-y += tracex3
@@ -64,6 +65,7 @@
 sockex1-objs := sockex1_user.o
 sockex2-objs := sockex2_user.o
 sockex3-objs := bpf_load.o sockex3_user.o
+hello_world-objs := hello_world.o
 tracex1-objs := bpf_load.o tracex1_user.o
 tracex2-objs := bpf_load.o tracex2_user.o
 tracex3-objs := bpf_load.o tracex3_user.o
@@ -180,6 +182,7 @@
 HOSTCFLAGS_bpf_load.o += -I$(objtree)/usr/include -Wno-unused-variable

 KBUILD_HOSTLDLIBS            += $(LIBBPF) -lelf
```

---

7 This trace pipe can also be read by bpftool prog tracelog.

```
+HOSTLDLIBS_hello_world     += -lbcc
 HOSTLDLIBS_tracex4         += -lrt
 HOSTLDLIBS_trace_output    += -lrt
 HOSTLDLIBS_map_perf_test   += -lrt
```

It can then be compiled and executed as described in the "Compilation" section, later in this appendix.

While instruction-level programming is possible, as shown by this tool, it is not recommended for tracing tools. The following two tools switch to developing the BPF code via C programming.

Tool 2: bigreads

bigreads traces the return of vfs_read() and prints a message for reads larger than one Mbyte. This time the BPF program is declared using C.[8] bigreads is equivalent to the following bpftrace one-liner:

```
# bpftrace -e 'kr:vfs_read /retval > 1024 * 1024/ {
    printf("READ: %d bytes\n", retval); }'
```

Some sample output from running the bigreads C program:

```
# ./bigreads
            dd-5145   [003] d... 2588681.534759: 0: READ: 2097152 bytes
            dd-5145   [003] d... 2588681.534942: 0: READ: 2097152 bytes
            dd-5145   [003] d... 2588681.535085: 0: READ: 2097152 bytes
[...]
```

This output shows that a dd(1) command was used to issue three reads, each with a size of two Mbytes. As with hello_world.c, extra fields are added to the output from the shared trace buffer.

bigreads is split into separate kernel and user-level C files. This allows the kernel component to be compiled separately to a file using BPF as the target architecture, and then the user component reads that file and sends the BPF instructions to the kernel.

The kernel component, bigreads_kern.c, is:

```
1   #include <uapi/linux/bpf.h>
2   #include <uapi/linux/ptrace.h>
3   #include <linux/version.h>
4   #include "bpf_helpers.h"
5
```

---

8 I first wrote this on 6-Jun-2014, when C was the highest-level language available. Andrii Nakryiko rewrote these C BPF tools to use the latest BPF interfaces on 1-Aug-2019.

```
 6   #define MIN_BYTES (1024 * 1024)
 7
 8   SEC("kretprobe/vfs_read")
 9   int bpf_myprog(struct pt_regs *ctx)
10   {
11       char fmt[] = "READ: %d bytes\n";
12       int bytes = PT_REGS_RC(ctx);
13       if (bytes >= MIN_BYTES) {
14               bpf_trace_printk(fmt, sizeof(fmt), bytes, 0, 0);
15       }
16
17       return 0;
18   }
19
20   char _license[] SEC("license") = "GPL";
21   u32 _version SEC("version") = LINUX_VERSION_CODE;
```

Line 6 defines the bytes threshold.

Line 8 declares an ELF section named "kretprobe/vfs_read", followed by a BPF program. This will be seen in the final ELF binary. Some user-level loaders will use these section headers to determine where to attach programs. The bitehist_user.c loader (covered in a moment) does not, although this section header may still be useful for debugging purposes.

Line 9 begins a function called for the kretprobe event. The struct pt_regs argument contains register state and BPF context. From the registers, function arguments and return values can be read. This struct pointer is also a required argument to a number of BPF helper functions (see include/uapi/linux/bpf.h).

Line 11 declares a format string for use with printf().

Line 12 fetches the return value from the pt_regs struct register using a macro (it will map long bytes = PT_REGS_RC(ctx) to ctx->rax on x86).

Line 13 performs the test.

Line 14 prints the output string using a debugging function: bpf_trace_printk(). This writes to the output to a shared trace buffer and is only used here to keep this example short. It has the same caveats as explained in Appendix C: it can clash with other concurrent users.

Lines 20 and 21 declare other necessary sections and values.

The user-level component, bigreads_user.c, is:

```
1   // SPDX-License-Identifier: GPL-2.0
2   #include <stdio.h>
3   #include <stdlib.h>
4   #include <unistd.h>
```

```c
 5   #include <string.h>
 6   #include <errno.h>
 7   #include <sys/resource.h>
 8   #include "bpf/libbpf.h"
 9
10   #define DEBUGFS "/sys/kernel/debug/tracing/"
11
12   int main(int ac, char *argv[])
13   {
14       struct bpf_object *obj;
15       struct bpf_program *prog;
16       struct bpf_link *link;
17       struct rlimit lim = {
18               .rlim_cur = RLIM_INFINITY,
19               .rlim_max = RLIM_INFINITY,
20       };
21       char filename[256];
22
23       snprintf(filename, sizeof(filename), "%s_kern.o", argv[0]);
24
25       setrlimit(RLIMIT_MEMLOCK, &lim);
26
27       obj = bpf_object__open(filename);
28       if (libbpf_get_error(obj)) {
29               printf("ERROR: failed to open prog: '%s'\n", strerror(errno));
30               return 1;
31       }
32
33       prog = bpf_object__find_program_by_title(obj, "kretprobe/vfs_read");
34       bpf_program__set_type(prog, BPF_PROG_TYPE_KPROBE);
35
36       if (bpf_object__load(obj)) {
37               printf("ERROR: failed to load prog: '%s'\n", strerror(errno));
38               return 1;
39       }
40
41       link = bpf_program__attach_kprobe(prog, true /*retprobe*/, "vfs_read");
42       if (libbpf_get_error(link))
43               return 2;
44
45       system("cat " DEBUGFS "/trace_pipe");
46
47       bpf_link__destroy(link);
```

```
48      bpf_object__close(obj);
49
50      return 0;
51  }
```

Lines 17 to 19 and 25 set RLIMIT_MEMLOCK to infinity, to avoid any BPF memory allocation issues.

Line 27 creates a struct bpf_object to refer to the BPF components in the _kern.o file. This bpf_object may contain multiple BPF programs and maps.

Line 28 checks that the bpf_object was initialized successfully.

Line 33 creates a struct bpf_program based on the BPF program that matches the section title "kretprobe/vfs_read", as set by SEC() in the kernel source.

Line 36 initializes and loads the BPF objects from the kernel file into the kernel, including all maps and programs.

Line 41 attaches the earlier selected program to a kprobe for vfs_read(), and returns a bpf_link object. This is later used on line 47 to detach the program.

Line 45 prints the shared trace buffer using system() to keep this tool short.

Line 48 unloads the BPF programs from the bpf_object from the kernel and frees all associated resources.

These files can be added to samples/bpf and compiled by adding a bigreads target to the samples/bpf/Makefile. The lines you need to add are (place each among similar lines in the Makefile):

```
# grep bigreads Makefile
hostprogs-y += bigreads
bigreads-objs := bigreads_user.o
always += bigreads_kern.o
```

Compiling and execution is the same as for the previous hello_world example. This time, there is a separate bigreads_kern.o file created containing the BPF program in a section that bigreads_user.o reads. You can inspect it using readelf(1) or objdump(1):

```
# objdump -h bigreads_kern.o

bigreads_kern.o:    file format elf64-little

Sections:
Idx Name          Size      VMA               LMA               File off  Algn
  0 .text         00000000  0000000000000000  0000000000000000  00000040  2**2
                  CONTENTS, ALLOC, LOAD, READONLY, CODE
```

```
1 kretprobe/vfs_read 000000a0  0000000000000000  0000000000000000  00000040  2**3
                  CONTENTS, ALLOC, LOAD, READONLY, CODE
2 .rodata.str1.1 0000000f  0000000000000000  0000000000000000  000000e0  2**0
                  CONTENTS, ALLOC, LOAD, READONLY, DATA
3 license        00000004  0000000000000000  0000000000000000  000000ef  2**0
                  CONTENTS, ALLOC, LOAD, DATA
4 version        00000004  0000000000000000  0000000000000000  000000f4  2**2
                  CONTENTS, ALLOC, LOAD, DATA
5 .llvm_addrsig 00000003  0000000000000000  0000000000000000  00000170  2**0
                  CONTENTS, READONLY, EXCLUDE
```

The "kretprobe/vfs_read" section is highlighted.

To turn this into a reliable tool, the bpf_trace_printk() must be replaced with print_bpf_output(), which emits records to user space via a BPF map that accesses perf per-CPU ring buffers. The kernel program will then include code such as the following (this uses the newer BTF-based deceleration)[9]:

```
struct {
        __uint(type, BPF_MAP_TYPE_PERF_EVENT_ARRAY)
        __uint(key_size, sizeof(int));
        __uint(value_size, sizeof(u32));
} my_map SEC(".maps");
[...]
bpf_perf_event_output(ctx, &my_map, 0, &bytes, sizeof(bytes));
```

Changes to the user-level program are more extensive: the system() call will be removed, and a function added to process the map output events. This function will then be registered using perf_event_poller(). An example of this is in the Linux source samples/bpf directory: trace_output_user.c.

Tool 3: bitehist

This tool is based on BCC bitehist.py from the Appendix C. It demonstrates output via BPF maps, which it uses for storing a histogram of block device I/O sizes. Example output:

```
# ./bitehist
Tracing block I/O... Hit Ctrl-C to end.
^C
```

---

9 This was declared differently on earlier kernels, which also included setting max_entries to __NR_CPUS__ so that there was a buffer per CPU. This max_entries setting has become the default for BPF_MAP_TYPE_PERF_EVENT_ARRAY.

```
kbytes         : count    distribution
   4 -> 7      : 11       |****************                        |
   8 -> 15     : 24       |**************************************** |
  16 -> 31     : 12       |******************                      |
  32 -> 63     : 10       |**************                          |
  64 -> 127    : 5        |******                                  |
 128 -> 255    : 4        |*****                                   |
Exiting and clearing kprobes...
```

As with bigreads, bitehist is composed of two C files: bitehist_kern.c and bitehist_user.c. The full source can be found at this book's website: http://www.brendangregg.com/bpf-performance-tools-book.html. The following are excerpts.

From bitehist_kern.c:

```
[...]
struct hist_key {
        u32 index;
};

struct {
        __uint(type, BPF_MAP_TYPE_HASH);
        __uint(max_entries, 1024);
        __type(key, struct hist_key);
        __type(value, long);
} hist_map SEC(".maps");
[...]
SEC("kprobe/blk_account_io_completion")
int bpf_prog1(struct pt_regs *ctx)
{
        long init_val = 1;
        long *value;
        struct hist_key key = {};

        key.index = log2l(PT_REGS_PARM2(ctx) / 1024);
        value = bpf_map_lookup_elem(&hist_map, &key);
        if (value)
                __sync_fetch_and_add(value, 1);
        else
                bpf_map_update_elem(&hist_map, &key, &init_val, BPF_ANY);
        return 0;
}
[...]
```

This declares a map of type BPF_MAP_TYPE_HASH called hist_map: this style of declaration will be propagated using BTF. The key is a struct hist_key that only contains a bucket index, and the value is a long: the count for the bucket.

The BPF program reads the size from the second argument of blk_account_io_completion using the PT_REGS_PARM2(ctx) macro. This is turned into a histogram bucket index using log2() C function (not included here).

A pointer to the value for that index is fetched using bpf_map_lookup_elem(). If a value is found, it is incremented using __sync_fetch_and_add(). If it is not found, it is initialized using bpf_map_update_elem().

From bitehist_user.c:

```c
struct bpf_object *obj;
struct bpf_link *kprobe_link;
struct bpf_map *map;

static void print_log2_hist(int fd, const char *type)
{
[...]
        while (bpf_map_get_next_key(fd, &key, &next_key) == 0) {
                bpf_map_lookup_elem(fd, &next_key, &value);
                ind = next_key.index;
// logic to print the histogram
[...]
}

static void int_exit(int sig)
{
        printf("\n");
        print_log2_hist(bpf_map__fd(map), "kbytes");
        bpf_link__destroy(kprobe_link);
        bpf_object__close(obj);
        exit(0);
}

int main(int argc, char *argv[])
{
        struct rlimit lim = {
                .rlim_cur = RLIM_INFINITY,
                .rlim_max = RLIM_INFINITY,
        };
        struct bpf_program *prog;
        char filename[256];
```

```
        snprintf(filename, sizeof(filename), "%s_kern.o", argv[0]);

        setrlimit(RLIMIT_MEMLOCK, &lim);

        obj = bpf_object__open(filename);
        if (libbpf_get_error(obj))
                return 1;

        prog = bpf_object__find_program_by_title(obj,
            "kprobe/blk_account_io_completion");
        if (prog == NULL)
                return 2;
        bpf_program__set_type(prog, BPF_PROG_TYPE_KPROBE);

        if (bpf_object__load(obj)) {
                printf("ERROR: failed to load prog: '%s'\n", strerror(errno));
                return 3;
        }

        kprobe_link = bpf_program__attach_kprobe(prog, false /*retprobe*/,
            "blk_account_io_completion");
        if (libbpf_get_error(kprobe_link))
                return 4;

        if ((map = bpf_object__find_map_by_name(obj, "hist_map")) == NULL)
                return 5;

        signal(SIGINT, int_exit);

        printf("Tracing block I/O... Hit Ctrl-C to end.\n");
        sleep(-1);

        return 0;
}
```

The main() program loads the BPF program using similar steps to bigreads.

A BPF map object is fetched using bpf_object__find_map_by_name(), and saved as the global map variable that is later printed during int_exit().

int_exit() is a signal handler attached to SIGINT (Ctrl-C). After initializing the signal handler, the main() program sleeps. When Ctrl-C is pressed, int_exit() is run, which calls the print_log2_hist() function.

print_log2_hist() iterates over the map using a bpf_get_next_key() loop calling bpf_lookup_elem() to read each value. The rest of the function, elided here, turns the keys and values into the printed histogram.

This tool can be compiled and run from the samples/bpf directory, using similar Makefile additions as bigreads.

perf C

The Linux perf(1) utility has the ability to run BPF programs on events[10] from one of two interfaces:

- **perf record:** For running programs on events that can apply custom filters and emit additional records to the perf.data file.
- **perf trace:** For "beautifying" trace output: using BPF programs to filter and enhance the output of perf trace events (e.g., showing a filename string on syscalls instead of just a filename pointer [84]).

perf(1)'s BPF capabilities are rapidly growing, and there is currently a lack of documentation on how to use them. The best source of documentation at the moment is a search of the Linux kernel mailing list archives for the keywords "perf" and "BPF."

The following section demonstrates perf and BPF.

Tool 1: bigreads

bigreads is based on the same tool shown earlier, in the section "C Programs," which traces the return of vfs_read() and shows reads larger than one Mbyte. Here is some sample output to show how it works:

```
# perf record -e bpf-output/no-inherit,name=evt/ \
    -e ./bigreads.c/map:channel.event=evt/ -a
^C[ perf record: Woken up 1 times to write data ]
[ perf record: Captured and wrote 0.255 MB perf.data (3 samples) ]
# perf script
            dd 31049 [009] 2652091.826549:          0                    evt:
ffffffffb5945e20 kretprobe_trampoline+0x0
(/lib/modules/5.0.0-rc1-virtual/build/vmlinux)
    BPF output: 0000: 00 00 20 00 00 00 00 00  .. .....
                0008: 00 00 00 00               ....

            dd 31049 [009] 2652091.826718:          0                    evt:
ffffffffb5945e20 kretprobe_trampoline+0x0
(/lib/modules/5.0.0-rc1-virtual/build/vmlinux)
```

---

10 perf(1) BPF support was first added by Wang Nan.

```
    BPF output: 0000: 00 00 20 00 00 00 00 00   .. .....
                0008: 00 00 00 00               ....


        dd 31049 [009] 2652091.826838:          0                    evt:
ffffffffb5945e20 kretprobe_trampoline+0x0
(/lib/modules/5.0.0-rc1-virtual/build/vmlinux)
    BPF output: 0000: 00 00 20 00 00 00 00 00   .. .....
                0008: 00 00 00 00               ....
```

The perf.data record file only contains entries for reads larger than one Mbyte, followed by BPF output events that contain the size of the read. While tracing, I issued three two Mbyte reads using dd(1), which can be seen in the BPF output: "00 00 20" is two Mbytes, 0x200000, in little-endian format (x86).

The bigreads.c source is:

```c
#include <uapi/linux/bpf.h>
#include <uapi/linux/ptrace.h>
#include <linux/types.h>

#define SEC(NAME) __attribute__((section(NAME), used))

struct bpf_map_def {
        unsigned int type;
        unsigned int key_size;
        unsigned int value_size;
        unsigned int max_entries;
};

static int (*perf_event_output)(void *, struct bpf_map_def *, int, void *,
    unsigned long) = (void *)BPF_FUNC_perf_event_output;

struct bpf_map_def SEC("maps") channel = {
        .type = BPF_MAP_TYPE_PERF_EVENT_ARRAY,
        .key_size = sizeof(int),
        .value_size = sizeof(__u32),
        .max_entries = __NR_CPUS__,
};

#define MIN_BYTES (1024 * 1024)

SEC("func=vfs_read")
int bpf_myprog(struct pt_regs *ctx)
```

```
{
        long bytes = ctx->rdx;
        if (bytes >= MIN_BYTES) {
                perf_event_output(ctx, &channel, BPF_F_CURRENT_CPU,
                    &bytes, sizeof(bytes));
        }

        return 0;
}

char _license[] SEC("license") = "GPL";
int _version SEC("version") = LINUX_VERSION_CODE;
```

This issues perf_event_output() via a "channel" map for reads larger than MIN_BYTES: these become the BPF output events in the perf.data file.

The perf(1) interface is gaining more capabilities, and it is becoming possible to run BPF programs with just "perf record -e program.c." Check for new developments and examples.

More Info

For more on BPF C programming, see:

- Documentation/networking/filter.txt in the Linux source [17].
- Cilium's "BPF and XDP Reference Guide" [19].

Appendix E
BPF Instructions

This appendix is a summary of selected BPF instructions, and is provided to aid in reading instruction listings from tracing tools and the source to the hello_world.c program in Appendix D. Developing BPF tracing programs from scratch directly using instructions is not recommended and not covered here.

The BPF instructions included in this appendix are only a selection. For a complete reference, see the following header files in the Linux source and the references at the end of this appendix:

- **Classic BPF:** include/uapi/linux/filter.h and include/uapi/linux/bpf_common.h
- **Extended BPF:** include/uapi/linux/bpf.h and include/uapi/linux/bpf_common.h

The bpf_common.h is shared between them as the encodings are mostly the same.

Helper Macros

The BPF instructions from the Appendix D hello_world.c example include:

```
        BPF_MOV64_IMM(BPF_REG_1, 0xa21), /* '!\n' */
        BPF_STX_MEM(BPF_H, BPF_REG_10, BPF_REG_1, -4),
        BPF_MOV64_IMM(BPF_REG_1, 0x646c726f), /* 'orld' */
        BPF_STX_MEM(BPF_W, BPF_REG_10, BPF_REG_1, -8),
[...]
        BPF_RAW_INSN(BPF_JMP | BPF_CALL, 0, 0, 0,
                    BPF_FUNC_trace_printk),
        BPF_MOV64_IMM(BPF_REG_0, 0),
        BPF_EXIT_INSN(),
```

These are actually higher-level helper macros. They are summarized in Table E-1.

Table E-1   **Selected BPF Instruction Helper Macros**[1]

BPF Instruction Macro	Description
BPF_ALU64_REG(OP, DST, SRC)	ALU 64-bit register operation
BPF_ALU32_REG(OP, DST, SRC)	ALU 32-bit register operation
BPF_ALU64_IMM(OP, DST, IMM)	ALU 64-bit immediate value operation
BPF_ALU32_IMM(OP, DST, IMM)	ALU 32-bit immediate value operation
BPF_MOV64_REG(DST, SRC)	Move 64-bit source register to destination
BPF_MOV32_REG(DST, SRC)	Move 32-bit source register to destination
BPF_MOV64_IMM(DST, IMM)	Move 64-bit immediate value to destination
BPF_MOV32_IMM(DST, IMM)	Move 32-bit immediate value to destination
BPF_LD_IMM64(DST, IMM)	Load 64-bit immediate value
BPF_LD_MAP_FD(DST, MAP_FD)	Load map FD into register
BPF_LDX_MEM(SIZE, DST, SRC, OFF)	Memory load from register
BPF_STX_MEM(SIZE, DST, SRC, OFF)	Memory store from register
BPF_STX_XADD(SIZE, DST, SRC, OFF)	Atomic memory add by register
BPF_ST_MEM(SIZE, DST, OFF, IMM)	Memory store from immediate value
BPF_JMP_REG(OP, DST, SRC, OFF)	Conditional jump against register
BPF_JMP_IMM(OP, DST, IMM, OFF)	Conditional jump against immediate value
BPF_JMP32_REG(OP, DST, SRC, OFF)	Compare registers as 32-bit
BPF_JMP32_IMM(OP, DST, IMM, OFF)	Compare register-to-immediate as 32-bit
BPF_JMP_A(OFF)	Unconditional jump
BPF_LD_MAP_VALUE(DST, MAP_FD, OFF)	Load map value pointer to register
BPF_CALL_REL(IMM)	Relative call (BPF-to-BPF)
BPF_EMIT_CALL(FUNC)	Helper function call
BPF_RAW_INSN(CODE, DST, SRC, OFF, IMM)	Raw BPF code
BPF_EXIT_INSN()	Exit

These macros and arguments use abbreviations that may or may not be obvious. In alphabetical order:

- **32:** 32-bit
- **64:** 64-bit
- **ALU:** Arithmetic Logic Unit

---

1 BPF_LD_ABS() and BPF_LD_IND() have been left out as they are deprecated and included for mostly historical reasons.

- **DST:** destination
- **FUNC:** function
- **IMM:** immediate value: a provided constant
- **INSN:** instruction
- **JMP:** jump
- **LD:** load
- **LDX:** load from register
- **MAP_FD:** map file descriptor
- **MEM:** memory
- **MOV:** move
- **OFF:** offset
- **OP:** operation
- **REG:** register
- **REL:** relative
- **ST:** store
- **SRC:** source
- **STX:** store from register

These BPF macros expand to BPF instructions, in some cases based on the operation specified.

Instructions

BPF instructions include those listed in Table E-2. (See the earlier header files for a complete list.)

Table E-2 **Selected BPF Instructions, Fields, and Registers**

Name	Type	Origin	Numeric	Description
BPF_LD	Instruction class	Classic	0x00	Load
BPF_LDX	Instruction class	Classic	0x01	Load into X
BPF_ST	Instruction class	Classic	0x02	Store
BPF_STX	Instruction class	Classic	0x03	Store from X
BPF_ALU	Instruction class	Classic	0x04	Arithmetic Logic Unit
BPF_JMP	Instruction class	Classic	0x05	Jump
BPF_RET	Instruction class	Classic	0x06	Return
BPF_ALU64	Instruction class	Extended	0x07	ALU 64-bit

Name	Type	Origin	Numeric	Description
BPF_W	Size	Classic	0x00	32-bit word
BPF_H	Size	Classic	0x08	16-bit half word
BPF_B	Size	Classic	0x10	8-bit byte
BPF_DW	Size	Extended	0x18	64-bit double word
BPF_XADD	Store modifier	Extended	0xc0	Exclusive add
BPF_ADD	ALU/Jump operation	Classic	0x00	Addition
BPF_SUB	ALU/Jump operation	Classic	0x10	Subtraction
BPF_K	ALU/Jump operand	Classic	0x00	Immediate value operand
BPF_X	ALU/Jump operand	Classic	0x08	Register operand
BPF_MOV	ALU/Jump operation	Extended	0xb0	Move register to register
BPF_JLT	Jump operation	Extended	0xa0	Unsigned jump less than
BPF_REG_0	Register number	Extended	0x00	Register 0
BPF_REG_1	Register number	Extended	0x01	Register 1
BPF_REG_10	Register number	Extended	0x0a	Register 10

Instructions are often composed of combinations of instruction classes and fields that are bitwise OR'd together.

Encoding

The extended BPF instruction format is (struct bpf_insn):

Table E-3 **Extended BPF Instruction Format**

Opcode	Dest Register	Source Register	Signed Offset	Signed Immediate Constant
8-bit	8-bit	8-bit	16-bit	32-bit

So, for the first instruction in the hello_world.c program:

```
BPF_MOV64_IMM(BPF_REG_1, 0xa21)
```

the opcode expands to:

```
BPF_ALU64 | BPF_MOV | BPF_K
```

Referring to Tables E-3 and E-2, this opcode becomes 0xb7. The arguments to the instruction set the destination register BPF_REG_1 (0x01) and the constant (operand) 0xa21. The resulting instruction bytes can be verified using bpftool(8):

```
# bpftool prog
[...]
907: kprobe  tag 9abf0e9561523153  gpl
        loaded_at 2019-01-08T23:22:00+0000  uid 0
        xlated 128B  jited 117B  memlock 4096B
# bpftool prog dump xlated id 907 opcodes
   0: (b7)  r1 = 2593
      b7 01 00 00 21 0a 00 00
   1: (6b)  *(u16 *)(r10 -4) = r1
      6b 1a fc ff 00 00 00 00
   2: (b7)  r1 = 1684828783
      b7 01 00 00 6f 72 6c 64
   3: (63)  *(u32 *)(r10 -8) = r1
      63 1a f8 ff 00 00 00 00
[...]
```

For tracing tools, much of the BPF instructions will be for loading data from structures and then calling BPF helper functions to store values in maps or emit perf records. See the "BPF Helper Functions" subsection under Section 2.3.6 in Chapter 2.

References

For more about BPF instruction-level programming, see the Linux source headers listed at the start of this appendix and:

- Documentation/networking/filter.txt [17]
- include/uapi/linux/bpf.h [184]
- Cilium's "BPF and XDP Reference Guide" [19]

Glossary

ALU Arithmetic logic unit: a subsystem of a CPU that processes arithmetic instructions.

API Application programming interface.

array A variable type that consists of a set of values, referenced by an integer index.

associative array A collection of values that are each assigned and retrieved using a unique key.

BCC BPF Compiler Collection: an open source software framework and toolkit for using BPF. See Chapter 4.

bpftrace An open source BPF-based tracer with a high-level programming language. See Chapter 5.

BPF Berkeley Packet Filter: a lightweight in-kernel technology from 1992 created for improving the performance of packet filtering and extended since 2014 to become a general-purpose execution environment (see *eBPF*).

BPF map An in-kernel BPF storage object that is used to store metrics, stack traces, and other data.

BTF BPF Type Format. See Chapter 2.

buffer A region of memory used to store data, often temporary I/O data.

byte A unit of digital data. This book follows the industry standard where one byte equals eight bits, and a bit is a zero or one.

C The C programming language.

command   A program executed at the shell.

core   An execution pipeline on a processor. Cores may be exposed on an OS as a single CPU or via hyperthreads as multiple CPUs.

CPU   Central processing unit. In this book, CPU refers to the virtual CPU managed by the OS, which may be a core or hyperthread.

CSV   Comma-separated values: a file type.

daemon   A system program that continually runs to provide a service.

DNS   Domain Name System.

drops   Trace events that are dropped (not recorded) because they arrive at a rate higher than can be stored in an output buffer.

DTrace   A dynamic tracing facility from Sun Microsystems, released for Solaris 10 in 2005.

DTraceToolkit   A collection of 230 DTrace tools, mostly written by myself and first released on April 20, 2005, as open source software with documentation. The DTraceToolkit is the origin of various tracing tools—execsnoop, iosnoop, iotop, etc.—that have since been ported to different languages and operating systems.

dynamic instrumentation   Also known as dynamic tracing after the tracing tools that use it. This is a technology that can instrument any software event, including function calls and returns, through live modification of instruction text and the insertion of temporary tracing instructions. Target software usually does not need special capabilities to support dynamic instrumentation. Since this can instrument any software function, it is not considered a stable API.

dynamic tracing   The software that implements dynamic instrumentation.

eBPF   Extended BPF (see *BPF*). The eBPF abbreviation originally described the extended BPF from 2014, which updated the register size and instruction set, added map storage, and limited kernel calls. By 2015, the e was dropped, and extended BPF was called just BPF.

ELF   Executable and Linkable Format: a common file format for executable programs.

enable   In tracing context, to activate a dormant instrumentation point so it can begin running tracing programs.

fault   A possible failure mode of hardware and software. Faults are usually expected failures, and a fault handler is used to deal with them appropriately.

fire   In tracing context, fire refers to when an instrumentation point runs a tracing program.

flame graph   A visualization for a set of stack traces. See Chapter 2.

Ftrace   A built-in Linux kernel technology that provides various tracing capabilities. It is currently separate from eBPF. See Chapter 14.

globbing   A set of wildcards commonly used for filename matching (*, ?, []).

GUI   Graphical user interface.

Hertz   Cycles per second.

HTTP   Hypertext Transfer Protocol.

hyperthreading   An Intel technology for scaling CPUs that allows the operating system to create multiple virtual CPUs for one core and schedule work on them, which the processor attempts to process in parallel.

ICMP   Internet Control Message Protocol: a protocol used by ping(1) (ICMP echo request/reply).

inline   A compiler optimization that places a function's instructions in its parent function.

instance   A virtual server. Cloud computing provides server instances.

IOPS   I/O per second.

IO Visor   A Linux Foundation project that hosts the BCC and bpftrace repositories on Github and facilitates collaboration between BPF developers at different companies.

iovisor   See *IO Visor*.

IP   Internet Protocol: a protocol whose main versions are IPv4 and IPv6. See Chapter 10.

IPC   Instructions per cycle.

Java   The Java programming language.

JavaScript   The JavaScript programming language.

Kbytes   Kilobytes.

kernel   The core program on a system that runs in privileged mode to manage resources and user-level processes.

kernel land   Kernel software.

kernel level   The processor privilege mode that kernel execution uses.

kernel space   The address space of the kernel.

kprobes   A Linux kernel technology for kernel-level dynamic instrumentation.

kretprobe   A kprobe for instrumenting the return of a kernel function.

latency   The time for an event to occur, such as the time for I/O to complete. Latency is important for performance analysis because it is often the most effective measure of a performance issue. Where exactly it is measured can be ambiguous without further qualifiers. For example, "disk latency" could mean time spent waiting on a disk driver queue only, or from an application, it could mean the entire time waiting for disk I/O to complete, including queued and service time.

LBR   Last branch record: a processor technology that can collect limited stack traces. See Chapter 2.

lockstep   Refers to sampling at the same rate as another timed event, which could over-represent the event in the collected sample data.

LRU   Least recently used.

malloc   Memory allocate. This usually refers to the function performing memory allocation.

map   See *BPF map*.

Mbytes   Megabytes.

memory   System memory, which is usually implemented as DRAM.

MMU   Memory management unit: a hardware component that is responsible for presenting memory to a CPU and for performing virtual-to-physical address translation.

ms   Milliseconds.

mutex   Mutual exclusion lock: a software lock that can become a source of performance bottlenecks and is often studied. See Chapters 13 and 14.

MySQL   An open source relational database management system.

native   In computing, refers to code and data that can be processed directly by processors, without additional interpretation or compilation.

observability   The practice and tools used to observe and analyze the state of computing systems. The tools in this book are observability tools.

off-CPU   Refers to a thread that is not currently running on a CPU and so is "off-CPU," due to either having blocked on I/O, a lock, a voluntary sleep, or another event.

on-CPU   Refers to a thread that is currently running on a CPU.

ORC   Oops Rewind Capability: a stack trace unwinding technology supported by the Linux kernel.

OS   Operating system: a collection of software including the kernel for managing resources and user-level processes.

page   A chunk of memory managed by the kernel and processor. All memory used by the system is broken up into pages for reference and management. Typical page sizes are 4 Kbytes and 2 Mbytes (depending on the processor).

pagefault   A system trap that occurs when a program references a memory location where the backing page is not currently mapped to virtual memory. Pagefaults are normal consequences of the Linux on-demand allocation memory model.

pagein/pageout   Functions performed by an operating system (kernel) to move chunks of memory (pages) to and from external storage devices.

PEBS   Precise event-based sampling: a processor technology for use with PMCs to provide more accurate recording of CPU state during events.

perf(1)   The standard Linux profiler and tracer, which is included in the Linux source tree. perf(1) began as a tool for PMC analysis and has been extended to include tracing capabilities as well.

perf_events   The Linux kernel framework that supports the perf(1) command and its instrumentation of events and that records event data into ring buffers. Other tracers, including BPF, make use of this framework for event instrumentation and event data buffering.

PID   Process identifier: an operating system unique numeric identifier for processes.

PMCs   Performance monitoring counters: special hardware registers on the processor that can be programmed to instrument low-level CPU events, such as cycles, stall cycles, instructions, memory loads/stores, etc.

POSIX   Portable Operating System Interface for Unix: a family of related standards by the IEEE to define a Unix API.

probe   An instrumentation point in software or hardware.

process   An operating system abstraction of an executing user-level program. Each process is identified by PID (see *PID*) and may have one or more running threads (see *thread*).

profiling   A technique that involves collecting data that characterizes the performance of a target. A common profiling technique is timed sampling (see *sampling*).

provider   The term DTrace uses for a library of related probes and arguments. The Linux terminology for provider varies depending on the tool: it may be referred to as a system, category, or probe type.

Python   The Python programming language.

reader/writer lock   A mutual exclusion primitive used by threaded software to protect shared data.

RCU Read-copy-update: a Linux synchronization mechanism.

RFC Request for Comments: a public document by the Internet Engineering Task Force (IETF). RFCs are used to define networking protocols; for example, RFC 793 defines TCP.

ring buffer A principal buffer policy that wraps when full, thereby keeping only recent events.

RSS Resident set size: a measure of main memory.

run queue A CPU scheduler queue of tasks waiting their turn to run on a CPU. In reality, the queue may be implemented as a tree structure, but the term run queue is still used.

sampling A technique involving understanding a target by taking a subset (or sample) of measurements. For tracing, this often refers to timed sampling, where an instruction pointer or stack trace is collected at a timed interval (e.g., 99 Hertz across all CPUs).

script In computing, an executable program that is usually short and in a high-level language. bpftrace may be considered a scripting language.

SCSI Small Computer System Interface: an interface standard for storage devices.

server A physical computer, typically a rack-mounted enterprise-grade computer that is housed in a datacenter. A server typically runs a kernel, an operating system, and applications.

Shell A command-line interpreter and scripting language.

SLA Service level agreement.

SLO Service level objective: a specific and measurable goal.

SNMP Simple Network Management Protocol.

socket A software abstraction that represents a network endpoint for communication.

Solaris A Unix operating system originally developed by Sun Microsystems that shipped with DTrace by default in 2005. Oracle Corporation acquired Sun, and Solaris is now called Oracle Solaris.

spin A software mechanism that involves executing in a tight loop while trying to acquire a resource, typically a spin lock or an adaptive mutual exclusion (mutex) lock.

SSH Secure Shell: an encrypted remote shell protocol.

stable Refers to a commitment level of a programming interface in which the interface is not expected to change.

stack Short for stack trace.

stack back trace See *stack trace*.

stack frame A data structure that contains function state information, including pointers to the function, return address, and function arguments.

stack trace A call stack composed of multiple stack frames, showing the ancestry of executing functions. Reading a stack trace from bottom to top shows which functions have called which other functions and, from this, the path through code. This is also called a *stack back trace*, since reading the stack from top down begins with the most recent function and works backward to the least recent.

static instrumentation/tracing   Refers to the inclusion of instrumentation points explicitly in code. Some software may support static instrumentation because the programmer inserted it, whereas some may have none. Static instrumentation often has the benefit of being a stable interface.

struct   A structured object, usually from the C programming language.

SVG   Scalable Vector Graphics: a file format.

syscall   See *system call*.

sysctl   A tool used to view and modify kernel parameters; often used to describe a parameter as well.

system call   The interface for processes to request privileged actions from the kernel.

task   A Linux term for a thread.

TCP   Transmission Control Protocol: a protocol originally defined in RFC 793. See Chapter 10.

thread   A software abstraction that represents a program that can be scheduled and executed.

TLB   Translation Lookaside Buffer: a cache for memory translation on virtual memory systems, used by the MMU (see *MMU*).

tracer   A tracing tool (see *tracing*).

tracepoints   A Linux kernel technology for providing static instrumentation.

tracing   Event-based recording. Tracing events may be static or dynamic instrumentation based, or they may be timer based. The tools in this book are tracing tools; they instrument events and run BPF programs to record data.

UDP   User Datagram Protocol: a protocol originally defined in RFC 768. See Chapter 10.

unstable   Refers to a commitment level of a programming interface in which there is no commitment and changes may occur over time across different software versions. Since kprobes and uprobes instrument software internals, the API they expose is considered an unstable interface.

uprobes   A Linux kernel technology for user-level dynamic instrumentation.

uretprobe   A type of uprobe for instrumenting the return of user-level functions.

µs   Microseconds.

USDT   User-land Statically Defined Tracing: a type of tracing that involves static instrumentation placed in application code by the programmer to provide useful probes.

user land   User-level software and files, including executable programs in /usr/bin, /lib, etc.

user level   The processor privilege mode that user-land execution uses. This is a lower privilege level than the kernel has; it denies direct access to resources, forcing user-level software to request access to those resources via the kernel.

user space   The address space of user-level processes.

variable   A named storage object used by programming languages.

VFS   Virtual File System: an abstraction used by the kernel for supporting different file system types.

workload   Requests for a system or resource.

ZFS   A combined file system and volume manager created by Sun Microsystems.

Bibliography

[Aho 78]   Aho, A. V., Kernighan, B. W., and Weinberger, P. J., "Awk: A Pattern Scanning and Processing Language (Second Edition)," *Unix 7th Edition man pages*, 1978, http://plan9.bell-labs.com/7thEdMan/index.html

[Alizadeh 10]   Alizadeh, M., Greenberg, A., Maltz, D., Padhye, J., Patel, P., Prabhakar, B., Sengupta, S., and Sridharan, M., "DCTCP: Efficient Packet Transport for the Commoditized Data Center," *MSR-TR-2010-68*, January 2010, https://www.microsoft .com/en-us/research/publication/dctcp-efficient-packet-transport-for-the-commoditized-data-center/

[AMD 10]   *AMD, BIOS and Kernel Developer's Guide (BKDG) for AMD Family 10h Processors*, April 2010, https://developer.amd.com/wordpress/media/2012/10/31116. pdf

[Amit 18]   Amit, N., and Wei, M., "The Design and Implementation of Hyperupcalls," *USENIX Annual Technical Conference*, 2018.

[Bezemer 15]   Bezemer, D.-P., Pouwelse, J., and Gregg, B., "Understanding Software Performance Regressions Using Differential Flame Graphs," *IEEE International Conference on Software Analysis, Evolution, and Reengineering (SANER)*, 2015.

[Bonwick 94]   Bonwick, J., "The Slab Allocator: An Object-Caching Kernel Memory Allocator," *USENIX Summer Conference*, 1994.

[Bostock 10]   Heer, J., Bostock, M., and Ogievetsky, V., "A Tour Through the Visualization Zoo," *acmqueue*, Volume 8, Issue 5, May 2010, http://queue.acm.org/ detail.cfm?id=1805128.

[Cheng 16]   Cheng, Y., and Cardwell, N., "Making Linux TCP Fast," *netdev 1.2*, Tokyo, 2016, https://netdevconf.org/1.2/papers/bbr-netdev-1.2.new.new.pdf

[Cockcroft 98]   Cockcroft, A., and Pettit, R., *Sun Performance and Tuning: Java and the Internet*. Prentice Hall, 1998.

[Corbet 05]   Corbet, J., Rubini, A., and Kroah-Hartman, G., *Linux Device Drivers*, 3rd edition, O'Reilly, 2005.

[Desnoyers 09a]   Desnoyers, M., *Low-Impact Operating System Tracing*, University of Montreal, December 2009, https://lttng.org/files/thesis/desnoyers-dissertation-2009-12-v27.pdf

[Desnoyers 09b]   Desnoyers, M., and Dagenais, M., *Adaptive Fault Probing*, École Polytechnique de Montréal, December 2009, http://dmct.dorsal.polymtl.ca/sites/ dmct.dorsal.polymtl.ca/files/SOTA2009-Desnoyers.pdf

[Elling 00]   Elling, R., *Static Performance Tuning*, Sun Blueprints, 2000.

[Goldberg 73]   Goldberg, R. P., *Architectural Principals for Virtual Computer Systems*, Harvard University, 1973.

[Gorman 04]   Gorman, M., *Understanding the Linux Virtual Memory Manager*. Prentice Hall, 2004.

[Graham 82]   Graham, S., Kessler, P., and McKusick, M., "gprof: A Call Graph Execution Profiler," *Proceedings of the SIGPLAN '82 Symposium on Compiler Construction, SIGPLAN Notices*, Volume 6, Issue 17, pp. 120–126, June 1982.

[Gregg 10]   Gregg, B. "Visualizing System Latency," *Communications of the ACM*, July 2010.

[Gregg 11]   Gregg, B., and Mauro, J., *DTrace: Dynamic Tracing in Oracle Solaris, Mac OS X and FreeBSD*, Prentice Hall, 2011.

[Gregg 13a]   Gregg, B., "Blazing Performance with Flame Graphs," *USENIX LISA '13 Conference*, November 2013, https://www.usenix.org/conference/lisa13/technical-sessions/plenary/gregg

[Gregg 13b]   Gregg, B., *Systems Performance: Enterprise and the Cloud*, Prentice Hall, 2013.

[Gregg 13c]   Gregg, B., "Thinking Methodically About Performance," *Communications of the ACM*, Volume 56 Issue 2, February 2013.

[Gregg 16]   Gregg, B., "The Flame Graph," *Communications of the ACM*, Volume 59, Issue 6, pp. 48–57, June 2016.

[Gregg 17]   Gregg, B., "Linux Container Performance Analysis," *USENIX LISA '17 Conference*, November 2017, https://www.usenix.org/conference/lisa17/conference-program/presentation/gregg

[Hiramatsu 14]   Hiramatsu, M., "Scalability Efforts for Kprobes or: How I Learned to Stop Worrying and Love a Massive Number of Kprobes," *LinuxCon Japan*, 2014, https://events.static.linuxfound.org/sites/events/files/slides/Handling%20the%20Massive%20Multiple%20Kprobes%20v2_1.pdf

[Hollingsworth 94]   Hollingsworth, J., Miller, B., and Cargille, J., "Dynamic Program Instrumentation for Scalable Performance Tools," *Scalable High-Performance Computing Conference (SHPCC)*, May 1994.

[Høiland-Jørgensen 18]   Høiland-Jørgensen, T., et al., "The eXpress Data Path: Fast Programmable Packet Processing in the Operating System Kernel," *Proceedings of the 14th International Conference on emerging Networking EXperiments and Technologies*, 2018.

[Hubicka 13]   Hubicka, J., Jaeger, A., Matz, M., and Mitchell, M., *System V Application Binary Interface AMD64 Architecture Processor Supplement (With LP64 and ILP32 Programming Models)*, July 2013, https://software.intel.com/sites/default/files/article/402129/mpx-linux64-abi.pdf

[Intel 16]   Intel, *Intel 64 and IA-32 Architectures Software Developer's Manual Volume 3B: System Programming Guide, Part 2*, September 2016, https://www.intel.com/content/www/us/en/architecture-and-technology/64-ia-32-architectures-software-developer-vol-3b-part-2-manual.html

[Jacobson 18]   Jacobson, V., "Evolving from AFAP: Teaching NICs About Time," *netdev 0x12*, July 2018, https://www.files.netdevconf.org/d/4ee0a09788fe49709855/files/?p=/Evolving%20from%20AFAP%20%E2%80%93%20Teaching%20NICs%20about%20time.pdf

[McCanne 92]   McCanne, S., and Jacobson, V., "The BSD Packet Filter: A New Architecture for User-Level Packet Capture," *USENIX Winter Conference*, 1993.

[Stoll 89]   Stoll, C., *The Cuckoo's Egg: Tracking a Spy Through the Maze of Computer Espionage*, The Bodley Head Ltd., 1989.

[Sun 05]   Sun, *Sun Microsystems Dynamic Tracing Guide* (Part No: 817–6223–11), January 2005.

[Tamches 99]   Tamches, A., and Miller, B., "Fine-Grained Dynamic Instrumentation of Commodity Operating System Kernels," *Proceedings of the 3rd Symposium on Operating Systems Design and Implementation*, February 1999.

[Tikhonovsky 13]   Tikhonovsky, I., "Web Inspector: Implement Flame Chart for CPU Profiler," *Webkit Bugzilla*, 2013, https://bugs.webkit.org/show_bug.cgi?id=111162

[Vance 04]   Vance, A., "Sun Delivers Unix Shocker with DTrace: It Slices, It Dices, It Spins, It Whirls," *The Register*, July 2004, https://www.theregister.co.uk/2004/07/08/dtrace_user_take/anc

[VMware 07]   VMware, *Understanding Full Virtualization, Paravirtualization, and Hardware Assist*, 2007, https://www.vmware.com/content/dam/digitalmarketing/vmware/en/pdf/techpaper/VMware_paravirtualization.pdf

[Welsh 01]   Welsh, M., Culler, D., and Brewer, E., "seda: An Architecture for Well-Conditioned, Scalable Internet Services," *ACM SIGOPS*, Volume 35, Issue 5, December 2001.

[Yamamoto 16]   Yamamoto, M., and Nakashima, K., "Execution Time Compensation for Cloud Applications by Subtracting Steal Time Based on Host-Level Sampling," *ICPE*, 2016, https://research.spec.org/icpe_proceedings/2016/companion/p69.pdf

[Zannoni 16]   Zannoni, E., "BPF and Linux Tracing Infrastructure," *LinuxCon Europe*, 2016, https://events.static.linuxfound.org/sites/events/files/slides/tracing-linux-ezannoni-berlin-2016-final.pdf

[1]   https://events.static.linuxfound.org/sites/events/files/slides/bpf_collabsummit_2015feb20.pdf

[2]   https://lkml.org/lkml/2013/9/30/627

[3]   https://lore.kernel.org/netdev/1395404418-25376-1-git-send-email-dborkman@redhat.com/T/

[4]   https://lore.kernel.org/lkml/1435328155-87115-1-git-send-email-wangnan0
      @huawei.com/T/

[5]   https://github.com/iovisor/ply

[6]   http://halobates.de/on-submitting-patches.pdf

[7]   https://www.usenix.org/legacy/publications/library/proceedings/sd93/

[8]   https://www.slideshare.net/vh21/meet-cutebetweenebpfandtracing

[9]   https://lwn.net/Articles/437981/

[10] https://lwn.net/Articles/475043/

[11] https://lwn.net/Articles/575444/

[12] https://patchwork.ozlabs.org/patch/334837/

[13] https://kernelnewbies.org/Linux_3.18

[14] http://vger.kernel.org/vger-lists.html#netdev

[15] http://www.brendangregg.com/blog/2015-05-15/ebpf-one-small-step.html

[16] http://www.brendangregg.com/blog/2014-07-10/perf-hacktogram.html

[17] https://www.kernel.org/doc/Documentation/networking/filter.txt

[18] https://llvm.org/doxygen/classllvm_1_1IRBuilderBase.html

[19] https://cilium.readthedocs.io/en/latest/bpf/

[20] https://graphviz.org/

[21] https://lore.kernel.org/lkml/CAHk-=wib9VSbwbS+N82ZPNtvt4vrvYyHyQduhFi
      mX8nyjCyZyA@mail.gmail.com/

[22] http://www.brendangregg.com/blog/2014-05-11/strace-wow-much-syscall.html

[23] https://patchwork.ozlabs.org/patch/1030266/

[24] https://github.com/cilium/cilium

[25] https://source.android.com/devices/architecture/kernel/bpf#files_available_in_
      sysfs

[26] https://www.kernel.org/doc/Documentation/bpf/btf.rst

[27] https://git.kernel.org/pub/scm/linux/kernel/git/bpf/bpf-next.git/commit/?id=
      c04c0d2b968ac45d6ef020316808ef6c82325a82

[28] https://git.kernel.org/pub/scm/linux/kernel/git/bpf/bpf-next.git/tree/
      Documentation/bpf/bpf_design_QA.rst#n90

[29] https://www.kernel.org/doc/Documentation/bpf/bpf_design_QA.txt

[30] http://www.man7.org/linux/man-pages/man2/bpf.2.html

[31] http://man7.org/linux/man-pages/man7/bpf-helpers.7.html

[32] https://lwn.net/Articles/599755/

[33] https://www.iovisor.org/blog/2015/10/15/bpf-internals-ii

[34] https://gcc.gnu.org/ml/gcc-patches/2004-08/msg01033.html

[35] https://blogs.oracle.com/eschrock/debugging-on-amd64-part-one

[36] https://github.com/sysstat/sysstat/pull/105

[37] http://www.brendangregg.com/flamegraphs.html

[38] https://github.com/spiermar/d3-flame-graph

[39] https://medium.com/netflix-techblog/netflix-flamescope-a57ca19d47bb

[40] https://lwn.net/Articles/132196/

[41] http://phrack.org/issues/67/6.html#article

[42] https://www.kernel.org/doc/Documentation/kprobes.txt

[43] https://www.ibm.com/developerworks/library/l-kprobes/index.html

[44] https://lwn.net/Articles/499190/

[45] https://events.static.linuxfound.org/images/stories/pdf/eeus2012_desnoyers.pdf

[46] https://www.kernel.org/doc/Documentation/trace/uprobetracer.txt

[47] https://www.kernel.org/doc/Documentation/trace/tracepoints.rst

[48] https://lkml.org/lkml/2018/2/28/1477

[49] http://www.brendangregg.com/blog/2015-07-03/hacking-linux-usdt-ftrace.html

[50] http://blogs.microsoft.co.il/sasha/2016/03/30/usdt-probe-support-in-bpfbcc/

[51] http://blog.srvthe.net/usdt-report-doc/

[52] https://github.com/sthima/libstapsdt

[53] https://medium.com/sthima-insights/we-just-got-a-new-super-power-runtime-usdt-comes-to-linux-814dc47e909f

[54] https://github.com/dalehamel/ruby-static-tracing

[55] https://xenbits.xen.org/docs/4.11-testing/misc/xen-command-line.html

[56] https://medium.com/netflix-techblog/linux-performance-analysis-in-60-000-milliseconds-accc10403c55

[57] http://www.brendangregg.com/blog/2016-10-27/dtrace-for-linux-2016.html

[58] https://github.com/iovisor/bcc/blob/master/INSTALL.md

[59] https://github.com/iovisor/bcc/blob/master/CONTRIBUTING-SCRIPTS.md

[60] https://github.com/iovisor/bcc#tools

[61] https://snapcraft.io/bpftrace

[62] https://packages.debian.org/sid/bpftrace

[63] https://github.com/iovisor/bpftrace/blob/master/INSTALL.md

[64]   https://github.com/iovisor/bcc/blob/master/docs/kernel-versions.md

[65]   https://github.com/iovisor/bpftrace/blob/master/docs/tutorial_one_liners.md

[66]   https://github.com/iovisor/bpftrace/blob/master/docs/reference_guide.md

[67]   https://github.com/iovisor/bpftrace/issues/26

[68]   https://github.com/iovisor/bpftrace/issues/305

[69]   https://github.com/iovisor/bpftrace/issues/614

[70]   https://lore.kernel.org/lkml/CAHk-=wib9VSbwbS+N82ZPNtvt4vrvYyHyQduhFi
        mX8nyjCyZyA@mail.gmail.com/

[71]   https://github.com/iovisor/bpftrace/pull/790

[72]   http://www.brendangregg.com/blog/2017-08-08/linux-load-averages.html

[73]   http://www.brendangregg.com/perf.html

[74]   https://github.com/brendangregg/pmc-cloud-tools

[75]   http://www.brendangregg.com/blog/2018-02-09/kpti-kaiser-meltdown-
        performance.html

[76]   https://github.com/Netflix/flamescope

[77]   https://medium.com/netflix-techblog/netflix-flamescope-a57ca19d47bb

[78]   https://github.com/brendangregg/perf-tools

[79]   https://github.com/pmem/vltrace

[80]   http://agentzh.org/misc/slides/off-cpu-flame-graphs.pdf

[81]   https://www.kernel.org/doc/Documentation/admin-guide/mm/concepts.rst

[82]   http://www.brendangregg.com/FlameGraphs/memoryflamegraphs.html#brk

[83]   https://docs.oracle.com/cd/E23824_01/html/821-1448/zfspools-4.
        html#gentextid-11970

[84]   http://vger.kernel.org/~acme/perf/linuxdev-br-2018-perf-trace-eBPF

[85]   https://www.spinics.net/lists/linux-fsdevel/msg139937.html

[86]   https://lwn.net/Articles/787473/

[87]   http://www.brendangregg.com/blog/2014-12-31/linux-page-cache-hit-ratio.
        html

[88]   https://www.kernel.org/doc/ols/2002/ols2002-pages-289-300.pdf

[89]   https://github.com/torvalds/linux/blob/16d72dd4891fecc1e1bf7ca193bb7d5b9
        804c038/kernel/bpf/verifier.c#L7851-L7855

[90]   https://lwn.net/Articles/552904/

[91]   https://oss.oracle.com/~mason/seekwatcher/

[92]   https://github.com/facebook/folly/tree/master/folly/tracing

[93]   https://cilium.io/

[94]   https://code.fb.com/open-source/open-sourcing-katran-a-scalable-network-load-balancer/

[95]   https://www.coverfire.com/articles/queueing-in-the-linux-network-stack/

[96]   https://www.kernel.org/doc/Documentation/networking/scaling.rst

[97]   https://patchwork.ozlabs.org/cover/910614/

[98]   https://lwn.net/Articles/659199/

[99]   https://patchwork.ozlabs.org/patch/610370/

[100]   https://www.kernel.org/doc/Documentation/networking/segmentation-offloads.rst

[101]   https://www.bufferbloat.net/

[102]   https://www.kernel.org/doc/Documentation/networking

[103]   https://flent.org/

[104]   https://www.wireshark.org/

[105]   https://blog.cloudflare.com/the-story-of-one-latency-spike/

[106]   http://www.brendangregg.com/DTrace/DTrace_Network_Providers.html

[107]   http://www.brendangregg.com/DTrace/CEC2006_demo.html

[108]   https://twitter.com/b0rk/status/765666624968003584

[109]   http://www.brendangregg.com/blog/2016-10-15/linux-bcc-tcptop.html

[110]   https://github.com/brendangregg/dtrace-cloud-tools/tree/master/net

[111]   http://www.brendangregg.com/blog/2014-09-06/linux-ftrace-tcp-retransmit-tracing.html

[112]   https://www.reddit.com/r/networking/comments/47jv98/dns_resolution_time_for_io_in_us/

[113]   https://git.kernel.org/pub/scm/linux/kernel/git/torvalds/linux.git/commit/?id=e3118e8359bb7c59555aca60c725106e6d78c5ce

[114]   https://www.slideshare.net/AlexMaestretti/security-monitoring-with-ebpf

[115]   https://seclists.org/oss-sec/2019/q2/131

[116]   https://www.snort.org/

[117]   https://www.slideshare.net/AlexMaestretti/security-monitoring-with-ebpf/17

[118]   https://www.kernel.org/doc/Documentation/userspace-api/seccomp_filter.rst

[119]   https://lwn.net/Articles/756233/

[120]   https://lore.kernel.org/netdev/cover.1425208501.git.daniel@iogearbox.net/T/

[121]   https://lore.kernel.org/netdev/61198814638d88ce3555dbecf8ef87552
        3b95743.1452197856.git.daniel@iogearbox.net/

[122]   https://lwn.net/Articles/747551/

[123]   https://lore.kernel.org/netdev/20180216134023.15536-1-daniel@iogearbox.net/

[124]   https://landlock.io/

[125]   https://git.kernel.org/pub/scm/linux/kernel/git/bpf/bpf-next.git/commit/?id=8b401f9ed2441ad9e219953927a842d24ed051fc

[126]   https://bugzilla.redhat.com/show_bug.cgi?id=1384344

[127]   https://www.kernel.org/doc/Documentation/sysctl/net.txt

[128]   http://vger.kernel.org/bpfconf.html

[129]   https://lore.kernel.org/netdev/2f24a9bbf761accb982715c761c0840a14c0b5cd.1463158442.git.daniel@iogearbox.net/

[130]   https://lore.kernel.org/netdev/36bb0882151c63dcf7c624f52bf92db8adbfb80a.1487279499.git.daniel@iogearbox.net/

[131]   https://cilium.readthedocs.io/en/stable/bpf/#hardening

[132]   http://phrack.org/issues/63/3.html

[133]   https://lore.kernel.org/netdev/8f751452-271f-6253-2f34-9e4cecb347b8@iogearbox.net/T/

[134]   http://www.brendangregg.com/blog/2016-01-18/ebpf-stack-trace-hack.html

[135]   https://github.com/jvm-profiling-tools/perf-map-agent

[136]   https://github.com/torvalds/linux/blob/master/tools/perf/Documentation/jit-interface.txt

[137]   https://github.com/brendangregg/FlameGraph/blob/master/jmaps

[138]   https://docs.oracle.com/en/java/javase/11/vm/dtrace-probes-hotspot-vm.html

[139]   http://www.brendangregg.com/blog/2007-08-10/dtrace-bourne-shell-sh-provider1.html

[140]   http://www.brendangregg.com/bpfperftools.html

[141]   https://github.com/sthima/node-usdt

[142]   http://www.brendangregg.com/blog/2016-10-12/linux-bcc-nodejs-usdt.html

[143]   https://github.com/mmarchini/node-linux-perf

[144]   http://www.brendangregg.com/blog/2014-09-17/node-flame-graphs-on-linux.html

[145]   https://golang.org/pkg/runtime/trace/

[146]   http://www.brendangregg.com/blog/2017-01-31/golang-bcc-bpf-function-tracing.html

[147]   https://github.com/iovisor/bcc/issues/934

[148]   https://tour.golang.org/basics/4

[149]   https://github.com/iovisor/bpftrace/issues/740

[150]   https://github.com/iovisor/bcc/issues/1320#issuecomment-407927542

[151]   https://github.com/mmcshane/salp

[152]   https://wiki.tcl-lang.org/page/DTrace

[153]   https://www.gnu.org/software/libc/

[154]   https://bugs.debian.org/cgi-bin/bugreport.cgi?bug=767756

[155]   https://dev.mysql.com/doc/refman/5.7/en/dba-dtrace-ref-command.html

[156]   https://www.kernel.org/doc/html/latest/core-api/memory-allocation.html

[157]   https://www.kernel.org/doc/Documentation/locking/mutex-design.txt

[158]   https://www.kernel.org/doc/Documentation/trace/ftrace.rst

[159]   https://github.com/rostedt/trace-cmd

[160]   https://git.kernel.org/pub/scm/linux/kernel/git/rostedt/trace-cmd.git

[161]   http://kernelshark.org/

[162]   https://www.kernel.org/doc/Documentation/kernel-hacking/locking.rst

[163]   https://github.com/iovisor/bpftrace/pull/534

[164]   https://lore.kernel.org/patchwork/patch/157488/

[165]   https://clearlinux.org/news-blogs/kata-containers-next-evolution-clear-containers

[166]   https://github.com/firecracker-microvm/firecracker/blob/master/docs/design.md

[167]   https://lwn.net/Articles/531114/

[168]   https://lwn.net/Articles/750313/

[169]   https://github.com/iovisor/kubectl-trace

[170]   https://github.com/kubernetes-incubator/metrics-server

[171]   https://kubernetes.io/docs/tasks/debug-application-cluster/resource-usage-monitoring/

[172]   https://www.kernel.org/doc/Documentation/cgroup-v1/cpuacct.txt

[173]   http://blog.codemonkey.ws/2007/10/myth-of-type-i-and-type-ii-hypervisors.html

[174]   http://www.brendangregg.com/blog/2017-11-29/aws-ec2-virtualization-2017.html

[175]   http://www.pcp.io/

[176]   http://getvector.io/

[177]   https://github.com/Netflix/vector

[178]   https://www.timeanddate.com/holidays/fun/yellow-pig-day

[179]   https://github.com/iovisor/bpftrace/issues/646

[180]   https://github.com/iovisor/bcc/blob/master/docs/tutorial_bcc_python_
developer.md

[181]   https://github.com/iovisor/bcc/blob/master/docs/tutorial_bcc_python_
developer.md

[182]   https://github.com/cilium/cilium/tree/master/bpf

[183]   https://github.com/iovisor/bcc

[184]   https://github.com/torvalds/linux/blob/master/include/uapi/linux/bpf.h

[185]   http://www.brendangregg.com/psio.html

[186]   https://static.sched.com/hosted_files/lssna19/8b/Kernel%20Runtime%20
Security%20Instrumentation.pdf

[187]   https://gihub.com/torvalds/linux/commits/master/drivers/nvme/host/trace.h

Index

C

Register Your Product at informit.com/register

Access additional benefits and **save 35%** on your next purchase

- Automatically receive a coupon for 35% off your next purchase, valid for 30 days. Look for your code in your InformIT cart or the Manage Codes section of your account page.
- Download available product updates.
- Access bonus material if available.*
- Check the box to hear from us and receive exclusive offers on new editions and related products.

Registration benefits vary by product. Benefits will be listed on your account page under Registered Products.

InformIT.com—The Trusted Technology Learning Source

InformIT is the online home of information technology brands at Pearson, the world's foremost education company. At InformIT.com, you can:

- Shop our books, eBooks, software, and video training
- Take advantage of our special offers and promotions (informit.com/promotions)
- Sign up for special offers and content newsletter (informit.com/newsletters)
- Access thousands of free chapters and video lessons

Connect with InformIT—Visit informit.com/community

the trusted technology learning source

Addison-Wesley • Adobe Press • Cisco Press • Microsoft Press • Pearson IT Certification • Prentice Hall • Que • Sams • Peachpit Press

Pearson